A Transatlantic Love Affair

— *A* —
TRANSATLANTIC
LOVE AFFAIR

SIMONE DE BEAUVOIR

Letters to Nelson Algren

The New Press New York

Compilation and annotation © 1997 by Sylvie Le Bon de Beauvoir.
Notes and English translations by Sylvie Le Bon de Beauvoir, Sara Holloway, Vanessa Kling,
Kate LeBlanc, and Ellen Gordon Reeves © 1998 by The New Press. All rights reserved.

We are grateful to reprint copyrighted material from the following sources:

After the War: Force of Circumstance, Vol. 1, 1944-1952, © 1963 Librairie Gallimard.
English translation by Richard Howard, © 1964, 1965 G.P. Putnam's Sons.
Used by permission of the publisher Marlowe & Company.

Simone de Beauvoir: A Biography by Deirdre Bair, Touchstone Books, 1991.

LIBRARY OF CONGRESS CATALOGING-IN-PUBLICATION DATA

Beauvoir, Simone de, 1908–

   A transatlantic love affair : letters to Nelson Algren / Simone de Beauvoir;
   compiled and annotated by Sylvie Le Bon de Beauvoir;
   translations from the French by Ellen Gordon Reeves;
   notes by Vanessa Kling, Sara Holloway, and Ellen Gordon Reeves.
     p. cm.
   Letters first published in French, but originally written in English.
   ISBN 1-56584-422-x
   1. Beauvoir, Simone de, 1908–   —Correspondence. 2. Algren, Nelson, 1909–
   —Correspondence. 3. Authors, French—20th century—Correspondence.
   I. Algren, Nelson, 1909–. II. Le Bon de Beauvoir, Sylvie.
   III. Reeves, Ellen Gordon. IV. Kling, Vanessa. V. Sara Holloway. VI. Title.

PQ2603.E362Z4828 1998
848'.91409—dc21
[b]   97-53085
                 CIP

Published in the United States by The New Press, New York
Distributed by W. W. Norton & Company, Inc., New York
Published in the United Kingdom by Victor Gollancz, London
Originally published in France by Gallimard in 1997

The New Press was established in 1990 as a not-for-profit alternative to the large,
commercial publishing houses currently dominating the book publishing industry.
The New Press operates in the public interest rather than for private gain,
and is committed to publishing, in innovative ways, works of educational, cultural,
and community value that might not be considered sufficiently profitable.
The New Press's editorial offices are located at the City University of New York.

Printed in the United States of America
Design and composition by BAD

9 8 7 6 5 4 3 2 1

EDITOR'S NOTE

Simone de Beauvoir learned English at school. She was an avid reader of anything she could find in English, from detective stories to more complex books of philosophy. While she gave all her talks and interviews in the United States in fluent English, she spoke with a thick French accent. She later credited her written fluency to her long correspondence with Algren.

The charm of reading the original manuscript with errors intact encouraged us to preserve de Beauvoir's original grammar and orthography, leaving what may look like a series of errors. As the correspondence progresses, de Beauvoir's spelling and vocabulary improve considerably. Tracing the evolution should prove worth the occasional distraction.

PREFACE

SYLVIE LE BON DE BEAUVOIR

Simone de Beauvoir's letters to Nelson Algren, written in English, were acquired by Ohio State University, at a public sale; she kept those Algren wrote to her. This chronicle of a "transatlantic love affair" is unique among the prolific correspondence that Simone de Beauvoir conducted throughout her life, for it involved, for once, someone from a wholly different orbit. Her other regular correspondents were always like minds, close even before becoming intimate, all springing from a "shared world." Their writings reveal differences, but within a chosen kinship. Her letters to Algren, however, reflect not an encounter with someone similar—as was the case with those to Jean-Paul Sartre, for example—but a meeting with someone totally "other." The explanation for this transcends the differences of nationality and the trite categorization of the two protagonists as "foreigners," as stereotypes of "the American male" and "the French woman"; rather, this difference in their nationalities serves as a simple and perceptible symbol of a more fundamental "alienness" that both separated and fascinated them.

The unanticipated arrival of this boor, this alien being, into her universe in 1947 forced Simone de Beauvoir to re-examine all that usually "went without saying": the obvious, the assumptions, the things taken for granted, the familiar realities of the world she shared with her old friends. Would she have felt the need to introduce these realities to Cocteau, Gide, Colette, as if they were Martians? Would she have introduced herself, filling out her background, her past, her life in Paris? No, this was completely part of her existence as a woman and a writer. There was no need to recount to them the Nazis' arrival at La Pouèze, Giacometti, the frenzied rehearsals before one of Sartre's opening nights, the uncontained joy when Paris was liberated, her literary likes and dislikes, Camus, Koestler, Dullin, her love of hiking, her horror of the emptiness of family, the "existentialist" clubs, Pierre Brasseur, the political meetings....But Midwesterner Nelson Algren may as well have come from another planet; he needed to be taught everything, to have everything explained, to be initiated. She could no longer fall back on unspoken understandings, shared

6

assumptions, anything tacit or implicit. They were trying to bridge light-years of distance. Of course, there were things that did bring them together, not least the fact that they were both writers. The deep bond that this created between them was as powerful and vital as the work they both lived for. But it also highlighted their dissimilarities; looking at their consciences, their experiences, their respective hopes as writers, what did they concretely have in common? The barriers seemed insurmountable, far wider than a mere difference in culture.

When things no longer go without saying, when the reassuring familiarity of the world has vanished, all that remains is the nakedness of pure presence. We are left with two individuals, a man and a woman who love, but do not know, one another. They imbibe the potion, then look at one another, only to ask: who is this standing before me? An entrancing, exhilarating, unsettling experience. What so enthralled Simone de Beauvoir when she began each letter to Algren must have been the stimulating distance he created between her and her self, the need to begin anew on virgin territory. A fresh start, totally exposed and without a safety net, as hazardous as a transatlantic flight between Paris and New York, back then. Their love lived and died by the airplane. Their affair was conducted, from beginning to end, to the drone of the engines of the "Comets" that flew the Atlantic, an exciting, perilous adventure in those far-off days. The fear of fatal crash, the anguished pangs of love—impossible to untangle one from the other.

It was Algren who brought this shared journey to an end. It was he who decided to re-establish the insurmountable distance between himself and Simone de Beauvoir, first in 1950, then, forever, in 1964. Why? Readers can only interpret, guess, speculate. The explanations and rationalizations lie somewhere beyond reason in the essential incompatibility of their substance, being fundamental choices, subjective make-up—little matter how it is expressed. Simone de Beauvoir with her "talent for happiness," Algren victim of a neurotic fear of failure. In the end, his loathsome twin, "the man in the starched detachable collar like Hoover's," the inflexible and deathly automaton riddled with resentment overpowered the "nice man," the "nice local youth," lively, gay, and warm. A terrible, pitiful, and tragic end.

The U.S. edition of *Force of Circumstance* was published in 1965. In it, Simone de Beauvoir briefly touched on her relationship with Algren, its meaning, and the painful dilemmas posed by its very nature. "I hope that you will not be unpleased by what I tell about you because it was written with all my heart," she wrote him. He responded angrily, with repeated bitter, hateful public comments. Followed by silence, unbroken until he died in 1951 under circumstances fraught with symbolism so heavy that even a novelist would have hesitated: the lonely death at home of a reclusive writer whom no one could be bothered to bury. "Algren's Body Unclaimed!" screamed the headline in one newspaper. Given his furious rejection of her, de Beauvoir was surprised to learn that Algren had kept all her letters.

She later agreed to their being published, provided that she were given the final say regarding form and translation. Until such time, she forbade any use of her letters or quotation from them. It is this project, which she did not have the time to pursue, that I took up and completed. I was motivated not only by the intrinsic interest of the letters themselves, but the difficulty of ensuring, from so far away, that her express wishes be respected: the unscrupulous plundering of her manuscripts, poorly protected in open archives, that began during her lifetime merely intensified after 1986. Self-proclaimed "authorized" biographers, journalists, researchers, and academics, relentlessly ferreting out any unpublished material in both the United States and France, have indulged in literary piracy and unauthorized use, perpetuating an endless stream of inaccuracy and distortion. What Simone de Beauvoir so feared came to pass: she was made to say just about anything. Problems with deciphering her difficult handwriting were worsened by misunderstandings, both deliberate and inevitable. The results of such incompetence, inexperience, or malice are amazing. When "beloved" is coldly transcribed as "blond," who only knows what else has been done to less innocent words and phrases? There was a crying need to establish a definitive authentic text once and for all, to offer an exact reading. The same could not be done for Algren's replies, which Simone de Beauvoir kept all her life and are now in my sole possession. Reading them proved invaluable to me; his letters provided a very necessary counterpoint, for hers would otherwise have suffered some diffuse distortion, no matter how benevolent the approach taken. Though I had originally hoped for the publication of the cross-correspondence, this project did not prove possible. When necessary, I have added whatever explanations—Algren's responses, descriptions of daily occurrences or important milestones—are needed to ensure continuity and intelligibility.

translated from the French by Kate LeBlanc

CHRONOLOGY

JANUARY 9, 1908: Simone de Beauvoir born
MARCH 28, 1909: Nelson Algren born

1947
JANUARY: de Beauvoir arrives in the United States
FEBRUARY: Algren and de Beauvoir meet for the first time in Chicago
APRIL: de Beauvoir spends three days in Chicago
MAY 1: Algren comes to New York with de Beauvoir
MAY 10: Algren gives de Beauvoir a silver ring
MAY 17: de Beauvoir leaves America
SEPTEMBER 11: de Beauvoir arrives in Chicago
SEPTEMBER 14: de Beauvoir returns to Paris

1948
MAY 8: de Beauvoir arrives in Chicago
MAY 14: de Beauvoir and Algren leave for a trip to Mexico
JULY 3: de Beauvoir returns to Paris
LATE OCTOBER: de Beauvoir moves to 11 rue de la Bucherie
America Day by Day published

1949
MAY 7: Algren arrives in Paris
MID-SEPTEMBER: Algren returns to Chicago
The Man with the Golden Arm published and
wins the National Book Award
The Second Sex published

1950
JULY 8: de Beauvoir leaves for America
SEPTEMBER 30: de Beauvoir returns to France

1951
OCTOBER 15: de Beauvoir flies to Chicago
OCTOBER 29: de Beauvoir returns to France

1952
de Beauvoir begins affair with Claude Lanzmann

1953
FEBRUARY 23: *The Second Sex* published in America
Algren remarries his ex-wife Amanda

1954
LATE OCTOBER: *The Mandarins* published in France
and wins the Prix Goncourt

1955
MID-AUGUST: de Beauvoir moves to 11a rue Schoelcher
Algren divorces Amanda

1956
The Mandarins published in America

1958
Memoirs of a Dutiful Daughter published

1959
de Beauvoir's relationship with Lanzmann ends

1960
The Prime of Life published
MARCH: Algren visits Paris
AUGUST: de Beauvoir leaves for Cuba
SEPTEMBER: Algren returns to America

1963
Force of Circumstance published

1964
Contact between de Beauvoir and Algren ends

1981
MAY 9: Algren dies

1986
APRIL 14: de Beauvoir dies;
she is buried wearing Algren's ring

1947

✻ *Invited to speak at a number of American universities, Simone de Beauvoir traveled across the United States from January through May 1947. In February, she arrived in Chicago, where she looked up the writer Nelson Algren at the suggestion of a friend. Algren showed de Beauvoir the underside of the city, taking her to Polish bars until she left by train for Los Angeles. De Beauvoir described the meeting in* Force of Circumstance:

"When you get to Chicago, go and see Algren for me," a young intellectual called Nelly Benson had told me when I was having dinner with her in New York. "He's an amazing man, and a great friend of mine." I have given a faithful account of my first meeting with him in *America Day by Day*, our evening in lower depths of the city and the following afternoon spent in the bars of the Polish district; but I did not mention the complicity that immediately sprang up between us, nor how disappointed we were not to be able to have dinner together: I was obliged to accept an invitation from two French officials. I called him before I left for the railroad station; they had to take the telephone away from me by force. On the train to Los Angeles I read one of his books and thought about him; he lived in a hovel, without a bathroom or a refrigerator, alongside an alley full of steaming trash cans and flapping newspapers; this poverty seemed refreshing, after the heavy odour of the dollars in the big hotels and the elegant restaurants, which I found hard to take. "I'll go back to Chicago," I said to myself; Algren had asked me to, and I wanted to; but if we found this parting painful already, wouldn't the next one hurt us even more? I asked that question in the letter I sent him. "Too bad for us if another separation is going to be difficult," he answered.

Dear Nelson Algren,

I'll try to write in English. So, excuse my grammar, and if I do not use the words in the right meaning, try to understand. My writing is so bad, too, and then I write in the train.

When leaving you, I went to the hotel, and I had the article finish, not too well I think, but it does not matter. Then I had a dinner with these French men and I hated them because they were hateful, and because they did not let me have a dinner with you. After phoning to you, they put me in the train, and lying on my berth I began reading your book[1] and I read it until I slept. Today, I sat near the window looking at the landscape and reading it. It was a very quiet day, and before going to sleep I have to tell you I really liked the book very much, and I have thought I liked you very much too. I think you felt it, though we spoke so little. I am not going to say thank you any more, because it does not mean much; but you have to know I was happy, being with you. I did not like to say good bye, perhaps not to see you again in my whole life. I should be pleased to come back to Chicago in April, and then I should speak about myself, and you would speak about yourself. But I don't know if I'll have enough time. And then, I ask to myself: if it was unpleasant for us to say good bye, yesterday, will not it be worse saying good bye when we shall have spent five or six days together and surely be quite good friends? I don't know.

Anyway, good bye or farewell. I'll sure not forget these two days in Chicago, I mean I'll not forget you.

S. de Beauvoir

✳ *February 23, 1947—By return mail, Algren expressed regret that de Beauvoir had checked out of her hotel without picking up the books he had left for her at the front desk. It was clear that he was immediately taken with her. He was amused at the contrast between their instant connection and his complete ignorance about who Simone de Beauvoir was and what her thinking and writing meant to the world; he knew nothing about her, in fact, beyond what he learned in a* New Yorker *article about existentialism.*

1) *The Neon Wilderness*, his collection of short stories.

Dear friend,

Coming back from a trip in California I just find your letter and the books. You know, I looked for these books in all the desks of the Palmer House, and I was very sad, not finding them, not only because I wished to read them, but because it was a gift from you and that made them very precious to me. So now I am very glad for the books and very pleased with the letter too.

I do not know yet if it will be possible to come to Chicago in April. I have many lectures to give all around New York. But anyways, I am pretty sure now to come back to America next year. My friends here in Los Angeles are selling the subject of my last novel to a producer.[1] I am very happy with it. I could come back for a long time and I'll manage to stay a while in Chicago. Are you really intending to come to Paris? I should like to show it to you. I should like first of all to get your own book, I mean, your novel.[2] Try to find it for me, please.

I had a very beautiful time in California. I saw San Francisco and wonderful landscapes and some nice people, and I met here my best girl-friend whom I did not see since a whole year,[3] when she left Paris to marry an American man. I could read a little, I read Thomas Wolfe's *You Can't Come Home Again*,[4] which I rather like. But I did not forget the Chicago Bowery, the little Polish bars, the cold wind; I'll never forget them.

Good bye. I am happy to have met you and I am sure we'll met again, this year or next year.

S. de Beauvoir

1) *All Men Are Mortal*, 1946. 2) *Never Come Morning.* 3) Nathalie Sorokine. See *The Prime of Life.* 4) 1940.

Dear friend,

I have come back to New York and given lectures in the surrounding colleges and universities, and now I have two weeks more to spend in New York. I am leaving America by airplane on the 10th of May; I should not like to leave without seeing you again. But it is really *very* difficult for me to go to Chicago; I have articles to write and discussions with people, and two lectures in New York. Would not it be possible for you to come between the 27th April and the 10th May? We could see much of each other and speak together quietly. If it would be possible, I could call you at any time you would suggest and discuss the exact day together. If it is impossible, I'll try to come for two days. Answer to me. And please try to get your novel for me. I saw one copy yesterday with a very bad picture which did not look like you at all. I was tempted to steal the book but I could not.

Good bye. I shall be very happy seeing you again.

S. de Beauvoir

✳ *April 24, 1947 — Back in New York, de Beauvoir called Algren. After some hesitation, and because the situation with Sartre necessitated prolonging her stay in the United States, she decided to see Algren again in Chicago.*

> Our first day together was very like the one Anne and Lewis spent together in *The Mandarins*; embarrassment, impatience, misunderstanding, fatigue, and finally the intoxication of understanding. I was staying in Chicago only three days; I had a great many things to settle in New York; I persuaded Algren to go there with me — it was the first time he'd been in an aeroplane. I went around arranging things, shopping, saying goodbye; at about five in the afternoon I came back to our room and we staying with each other until morning. People would often talk about him to me; they said he was unstable, moody, even neurotic; I liked being the only one who understood him. If he was sometimes blunt and rude, as people claimed, it was certainly only as a defense. For he possessed that rarest of all gifts, which I should call goodness if the word had not been abused; let me say that he really cared about people. (*Force of Circumstance*)

De Beauvoir returned to Paris on May 17.

K.L.M. Royal Dutch Airlines, Newfoundland
Saturday afternoon, 17 Mai 1947

My own nice, wonderful, and beloved local youth,[1] you made me cry once more, but these were sweet tears as everything which comes from you. I just sat in the airplane and began to read the book, and then I whished to

14

see your handwriting, and I came to the first page, regretting not to have asked you to write anything on it, and there it was, the tender, loving and lovely lines you had written for me.[2] So I put my forehead against the window and I cried, with the beautiful blue sea below me, and crying was sweet because it was love, your love and my love, our love. I love you. The taxi driver asked me: "Is he your husband?" "No," I said. "Ah! A friend?" And he added with a very sympathetic voice: "He looked so sad!" I could not help to say: "We are very sad to part. Paris is so far." And then he began to speak very nicely about Paris. I am glad you did not come with me. At Madison Avenue and La Guardia, there were people I know, with French voices and French faces, the worst French voices and faces, which can really be very bad. I was a little groggy, not even able to cry then, just groggy. Then the airplane went away. I love airplanes. I think, when you are at a high pitch of emotion, it is the only way of travelling which fits with your own heart. Airplane and love, the sky and the sadness and the hope were one only thing. I thought of you, remembering carefully everything, and I read the book which I like yet better than the other one, and we had whisky and a nice lunch: creamed chicken, chocolate ice cream. I thought you should have liked so much the landscape, the clouds and the sea, the coast, the woods and villages — we saw the ground very well and you would have smiled with your warm, beautiful and childish smile.

When we arrived above Newfoundland it was already the end of the afternoon, though only 3 P.M. in New York. The island is very beautiful, all dark pines and sad lakes, with a touch of snow here and there. You would like it, too. We landed and we are to stay here for two hours. Where are you, just now? Maybe in an airplane yourself. When you'll find our little home, I'll be there, hidden under the bed and everywhere. Now I'll always be with you. In the sad streets of Chicago, under the Elevated, in the lonely room, I'll be with you, my beloved one, as a loving wife with her beloved husband. We shall never have to wake up, because it was not a dream; it is a wonderful true story which is only beginning. I feel you with me, and where I shall pass you will pass, not the look only but all of you. I love you. There is no more to say. You take me in your arms and I cling to you and I kiss you as I kissed you.

Your Simone

1) Born in 1909, Algren was a year younger than Simone de Beauvoir. 2) I send this book with you/ That it may pass/Where you shall pass:/Down the murmurous evening light/Of storied streets/ In your own France/Simone, I send this poem there, too/That part of me may go with you.

My precious, beloved Chicago man,

I think of you in Paris, in Paris I miss you. The whole journey was marvellous. We had nearly no night since we went to the East. At Newfoundland the sun began to set, but five hours later it was rising in Shannon, above a sweet green Irish landscape. Everything was so beautiful and I had so much to think that I hardly slept. This morning at 10 (it was 6 by your time), I was in the heart of Paris. I hoped the beauty of Paris would help me to get over my sadness; but it did not. First, Paris is not beautiful today. It is grey and cloudy; it is Sunday, the streets are empty, and everything seems dull, dark, and dead. Maybe it is my heart which is dead to Paris. My heart is yet in New York, at the corner of Broadway where we said good bye; it is in my Chicago home, in my own warm place against your loving heart. I suppose in two or three days it will be a bit different. I must be concerned again by all the French intellectual and politic life, by my work and my friends. But today I don't even whish to get interested in all these things; I feel lazzy and tired, and I can enjoy only memories. My beloved one, I don't know why I waited so long before saying I loved you. I just wanted to be *sure* and not to say easy, empty words. But it seems to me now love was there since the beginning. Anyway, now it is here, it is love and my heart aches. I am happy to be so bitterly unhappy because I know you are unhappy, too, and it is sweet to have part of the same sadness. With you pleasure was love, and now pain is love too. We must know every kind of love. We'll know the joy of meeting again. I want it, I need it, and I'll get it. Wait for me. I wait for you. I love you more even than I said, more maybe than you know. I'll write very often. Write to me very often too. I am your wife forever.

Your Simone

I read the whole book and I like it *very* much. I'll have it translated, sure. Kisses and kisses and kisses. It was so sweet when you kissed me. I love you.

My beloved husband,

Paris was so sad and unpleasant that I went away this afternoon. I did not go very far, perhaps twenty miles or so,[1] but it seems very far, indeed; it is

16

really the country, with birds singing, green meadows and woods. It is hardly a village, just some little houses scattered among the trees. I shall stay here about two weeks in a nice little blue and yellow inn. Just now it is about seven o'clock, the sun is slowly setting, and I am sitting in a little garden in front of the house, with a very pleasant view all around me and a warm breeze blowing. I feel very happy here, and very close to you. I came here because I needed rest, sleep, and peace; I wish to begin to work again, to read and to have time for leisure, for thinking and remembering. I met some friends during these days, but nearly everybody seemed cold or at least very cool. I am afraid you have spoilt me, being so warm and generous and loving. Maybe *I* was cool and cold myself; it all seemed a rather tedious dream and I did not care much for anything nor anybody. Yesterday evening, nevertheless, my heart melted a little as I was sitting at a terrace on the boulevard Saint-Germain; the leafy trees, the evening light were very beautiful and I thought I should be so happy to show you the streets of Paris; I felt Paris was waiting for you and I began loving it again with and for you.

I have brought your book to Gallimard; they will read it during these two weeks and tell me if they intend to have it published. If not, I'll look for another publisher. Anyway we are going to print a piece of it in the *Temps modernes*.[2] I begin to wait with much impatience for a letter from you; from Paris they'll send it here. Maybe I'll get it within two or three days. You must write to me very often, my beloved friend and lover, my dearest husband; for we must not feel apart from each other. On the contrary, when we'll meet again in nine or ten months, we must be closer, more intimate yet than when we have parted. We must try to live these months together, in spite of Atlantic Ocean and the wide plains between us. I deeply regret your not being able to read French books. Why do not you try to learn? You could know me and my life much better. I'll send you my books if you hope you could do something with them.

Just now I am reading Kafka's *Diary*. I have read all his other books and I like them very much. Do you like them? I know you do not like the country very much. Nevertheless, I should like to have you here, in the little garden in front of the blue and yellow inn. I see you sitting near me, smiling to me. How much I love this smile! Did you think, two weeks ago, you should so nicely smile in a French little garden, in a French loving heart? Here you are, my beloved one, smiling to me and loving me while the cuckoo is singing nearby. And I smile to you and love you, in the French garden and in Chicago too; I am in our Chicago home as well as you are in France with me. We have not parted and we'll never part. I am your wife for ever.

Your Simone

Friday, 23 Mai 1947

Mon bien-aimé,

It is nice to write to you from this little room. It is 5 P.M., the sun shines very softly above the village and the green hills; my window is open and the table is against the window, so I am *in* the landscape, being in my own room. It is a very old French scenery. At one mile from this inn is Port-Royal-des-Champs, the famous monastery where Pascal lived a long time; Racine was educated there and you can see nearby a little path where he used to walk, hearing the birds singing—he even wrote a poem about it, a very bad poem which is printed on some square stones people have put all along the path. I have spent two very quiet days since I wrote to you from the garden. I went to bed at ten, and as there was no nice man to prevent me from sleeping, I slept until twelve the next morning. So today I am fed up with sleep. But I needed it badly. At twelve I have a lunch—very good and fresh food, with French red wine—then I walk a little in the country, and I come back to my room and I read or I try to write a little. At eight I have my dinner and then I sleep. You see, it happens very seldom to me to live this way but I just needed it. I have read a novel of Carson Mac Cullers; I was pleased to read an American book, but it was not good at all. I read Kafka, too, as I told you. I thought I really should like you to read all you can find of French modern literature: *The Stranger* of Camus, *The Flies* and *No Exit* by Sartre have been translated. And, too, some articles by Sartre and by myself in *Partisan Review* and other magazines. Mary Goldstein will be very much pleased to get them for you, I am sure. You must, my dearest husband, you must try to get something of my French life as I tried to live your Chicago life with you. Will you?

I write to you with the little red bright stylo you have given to me, and I have your ring at my finger. It is the first time I ever wore a ring and everybody in Paris was very amazed, but they found the ring beautiful. I wait eagerly for a letter. I miss you, you know. I miss your lips, your hands, your whole warm and strong body, and your face and your smiles, your voice. I miss you. But I like missing you so hard because it makes me feel strongly that you are not a dream, you are real, you are living, and I'll meet you again. A week ago we were yet together in the New York room. It seems long before meeting you again. I kiss your dear face, your sweet lips with the most loving kisses.

Your Simone

Here are little flowers of France I just gathered for you.

Saturday, 24 Mai 1947

Dearest N. Algren,*

I got your letters today, the little yellow letters, and I was very happy. The letters look like yourself, both sad and gay, and loving in a clumsy, awkward way, so genuine too. You say I feel what is genuine and what is not, and I am very proud of your saying so. I think I felt at once how genuine you were yourself, and it was the beginning of my liking you so much, and afterwards of my love for you. All is genuine in you, words and behaviours, love and hate, pleasure, pain; your whole life is genuine. And living with you I felt genuine myself; everything was all right because everything was true. I am happy if you felt I was still present in the little Chicago home; I'll never leave it until we'll go together to New Orleans. I think you too have got some of my letters now, the one I wrote from Newfoundland and the wire from Paris and perhaps one or two more.

Today I tried very hardly to work. I read all I had written six months ago about women. It does not look bad. But it is very difficult to begin to write again. Just now I do not see exactly why anybody should ever write again. Just now I do not see exactly why anybody should ever write anything. The world just as it is is so big; it exists and needs no words. I remember Chicago, I see the green French landscape. What else? But I'll begin again tomorrow; I hope I'll be more successful. I must be.

Write often, very often. Your yellow letters were such a joy. I like writing to you. I hope you can read what I write? I should write more nicely in French, but I think my English is good enough to make you feel how I love you, and it is the most important thing. I love you, my crazy, nice man.

Your Simone

19

Mon bien-aimé, I send this letter only today because Sunday and yesterday it was "Pentecôte" (how do you say it in English?) and the postman did not come. I begin to come to life again, I begin to be able to work, for instance. I feel a little as if I had been sick this whole week; I was so dreamy, everything seemed unreal around me. I don't know how many times I told me again and again our Chicago-New York story, from your first kiss in the airport to your last smile at the corner of the street. I know all of this story by heart, every smile and look and kiss and word, and I am never tired of brooding on it for hours and hours. My dearest one, if you felt how much I miss you, you would become so proud and conceited that you would not be nice any more.

I am going to Paris today to see some friends and, first of all, I'll go to the hotel,[1] hoping to find a letter. Write to me very often, please. I'll go on writing myself. I love you so warmly, so deeply that I am a little amazed at it. I did not think it could happen to me now. Well, it happened and I am glad of it, though it is pain too. Oh! I should like so much to be near you, to feel your shoulder against my cheek and your arms tightly enclosing me — and you should look at me, I should look at you, and we should know all there is to know and be so happy.

Your Simone

∗ N. Algren is the name of a Chicago local youth who happens to be my beloved friend and lover, my one-week and forever husband.

1) Hôtel de la Louisiane, Rue de Seine. See *Force of Circumstance.*

Thursday, 19 Mai 1947

Dearest,

As soon as I arrived in Paris, I jumped from the train into a taxi-cab, and from the taxi-cab I rushed upstairs to see if there was a letter from you — there was not and I was very sad, but I knew you were not guilty for it. The only thing is, Chicago is too far away, the airplanes fly too slowly. Nevertheless, my beloved one, it is sad not to know what happened to you since the other Sunday. I remember you were to see your sister, and maybe you went to the horse races with her, but what else? I think you have lost money at the horse race. I should like so much to know things about you, little things, day after day.

Paris was beautiful. You must come to Paris as soon as you have money for the airplane. I'll have money for living in Paris together. My beloved husband, don't frown and look concerned about taking my money. I'll take yours if it happens I need your money to see you. What is yours is mine and what is mine is yours as long as we love each other. Come, come to Paris; we'll be happy there as we were in New York. I should love to show Paris to you. These are not empty words, I don't say empty words, you must know. I should give much, much more than money to have you in Paris with me. Don't forget I love you, my beloved Chicago local youth.

So, Paris was beautiful. It was blue and warm, with leafy green trees, nice smells, fine women dressed in gay summer dresses, and lovers kissing each other in the streets, and people looking happy. I went with friends to the Place du Tertre in Montmartre. Do you know this place? It is wonderful. You may have your dinner in the open air, while people play nice bad music, you eat very good food with very good wine, feeling the sky above your head and the big city at your feet. We'll go there together. Then we went down the hill, walking and talking and we stopped in a very nice bar. There was a piano and scotch-and-sodas. It was open on the street, and full of people talking brightly to one another as they never do in America. A crazy woman came in, a very crazy one. She was rather old and very ugly but with much make up on her face, red and pink and blue and white, and a huge straw hat on her painted hair. She began to dance, pulling her shirt above her knees and exhibiting poor sad legs and naked thighs and she said sad, crazy obscenities. I stayed there until people told us to go away, it was time to close the bar, then we went down to Saint-Germain-des-Prés where I live, crossing Paris, walking while the dawn began to appear. It was beautiful, dawn arising above the Seine, it was dark blue, it looked like a country dawn and yet it was Paris. Then I went to bed and slept, and I thought of you, my beloved one, whishing to have parted with you this Paris night.

The next day I came back to my blue and yellow inn. I can write now and I work very much. Friends come and see me very often.[1] We talk and talk. I should like to speak to you about them, but it is difficult in letters and writing in English, and chiefly I whish to feel I am yet all alone with you for some while. I am afraid my writing and my English are worst than ever today, because it is late, I write from my bed and being very sleepy. I should like to dream of you but I don't do what I whish with my dreams.

I love you and I kiss you passionately.

Your Simone

1) Sartre and Bost. (Jacques Laurent Bost, close friend of de Beauvoir and Sartre. Brother of Pierre Bost, French novelist and screenwriter.)

Monday, *2 Juin 1947*

Mon bien-aimé,

This time the letter was there and I ran to my room and I read it, and my heart was beating fast because I could feel with my fingers this bit of paper which you had touched with your fingers. I was very happy, and yet there is a sadness in letters: in fact our fingers did not meet. I read the letter many times, but I could not have you (not even the Tiger)[1] suddenly appearing in the room. Thanks for the books. I have read *Sanctuary* and the Kouprine too.[2] You are really a nice man, but I like your letters better than any book. Tell me things about your life, how you swam in the morning, what kind of bones you have eaten. Everything is important for me.

I am in Paris for a whole week. There are people I must see, and I must take care of *Les Temps modernes*. Paris is very, very hot now during the day; the nights are warm too, but very sweet and beautiful; you may have dinner outside, in gardens or on little places, and afterwards take long walks in the streets which are full of people and very gay. In the morning, the street where I live is very gay, too; there is a market there and women buy fish and meat and cherries and vegetables, making much noise, speaking and arguing and laughing.[3] All is very expensive yet but there are things to buy nevertheless and it seems very gay when you think of the time the street was empty. I love to follow this noisy, lively street in the morning. Then I go to the Café des Deux Magots and I write. Now I write to you and afterwards I'll work for two or three hours. I begin to like it again, but not enough.

Yesterday morning I went to the first presentation of a very good French movie,[4] the best I have ever seen I think. It is a very simple story, but beautifully told and full of meaning: it is about two very young boy and girl loving each other during the 1914–1918 war. The boy is seventeen years old, the girl twenty and just married to a soldier she does not love. The war is a kind of holiday for the childish lovers, but then their love is crushed by grown-up people, they are too young to struggle, they have to part and the girl dies. Everybody had a lump in the throat when they gave the lights again. I hope you'll see it once. I think they do a very good job in the French movies just now. It is much more daring and human and true than Hollywood.

Life is very interesting here, but a bit difficult, a bit sophisticated, maybe, for many reasons. It is difficult to speak to you about it, because I had so little time in Chicago to explain things to you. Next year it will be different. We'll spend a long time together, and I'll not allow you to be

22

busy, busy, busy, always running to some zoo; I'll have you sitting near me for hours and hours as in New York and we'll talk and talk and talk. I wish so strongly to have a deep intimacy with you, I wish we shall know each other as well as we love each other. I need it. Yet love is the most important thing, and it is knowledge too. And I feel proud of you and me; we are really smart people because we did so much with the short time we had. I remember as you told me the first night in the cab: "We have no time to waste." And I had just the same words on my lips: "No time to waste." Well, we have wasted nothing. It does not seem to me we had just a week together. I feel I am tied to you by hundreds and hundreds of ties, and they will never be broken.

My dearest friend, my beloved lover, you gave much to me and you go on giving much even being far away. Thinking of you makes me peaceful and happy. I should like to tell you with kisses how dear you are to me. I love you.

Your Simone

1) Algren's cat. 2) Alexander Ivanovich Kuprin (1870–1938), Russian novelist and short story writer. One of the last Russian realists, author of *Yama*, 1909, which inspired the epigraph to Algren's novel *The Man with the Golden Arm*. 3) The Buci market, still in existence today. 4) *Devil in the Flesh*, 1947, directed by Claude Autant-Lara; screenplay by Pierre Bost, with Micheline Presle and Gerard Philipe.

Wednesday, 4 Juin 1947

My beloved husband,

I was so glad today when coming downstairs I found your letter—such a nice letter. Reading it, it seemed to me I heard your dear teasing voice and I saw your warm smile; you were near me and we spoke gaily together. It becomes really pleasant to write letters when you get answers quickly enough and a true conversation becomes possible. You don't seem far at all just now. I feel you love me just as well as if you were looking at me, and I feel you feel I love you. Dearest, I am happy, feeling it. You don't know yet, I did not know myself how much happiness you can give to me. The whole day was sunny, bright, wonderful because I received this sweet letter in my heart. I am even jealous at our writing such nice letters, it is not fair. I cannot say what I wish, writing in a foreign language. You can be witty and describe things and tell stories in the best way. And I can just write a broken childish English, yet I am not so stupid, you know. I am afraid you are going to feel yourself so much smarter and more clever and interesting than I am and to have some haughty contempt for my clumsiness.

Dearest, It is midnight—here in Paris it is midnight, but what time does it mean in Chicago? Dinner time, I guess. What are you doing just now? Eating a dish of bones? I am in my room; it is really a very lousy room; I should be ashamed to show it to you. The walls are pink—that is nice—as pink as a tooth-paste, but the ceiling is so dirty, the room so small, and nothing cosy or nice in it—it needs a good housekeeper-man to give it something womanly and appealing. Yet I like this lousy room where I lived during the whole war, cooking noodles and potatoes, and I cannot go away, which would be the only sensible thing to do.

I do not feel sensible at all this night, I feel unhappy. Let me cry a little. It would be so fine to cry in your arms. I cry because I do not cry in your arms; this is not sensible at all, because if I were in your arms I should not cry. It is stupid to write love letters, love is not something you can put in letters, but what is to be done when there is this dreadful Atlantic Ocean between you and the man you love? I should like to send you something, but what? Even flowers fade away when you send them, you cannot send kisses, nor tears. Only words, and then I cannot write in English. What a smart man you must be to have your girl crying for you through the whole Atlantic Ocean! You may be very proud, indeed!

I am too tired and I miss you too much. You know, it is very hard to *come back*. It is very difficult for me to go through this coming back. There is something so sad in France, yet I love this sadness. And then America was holidays. I did not ask anything from myself; here I have something to do, I do not know exactly what, neither if I am able to do it.

I had a strange evening and I drank very much, to help, and I feel strange yet now. I told you about a very ugly woman who was in love with me.[1] I remember: we were in the twin beds in New York, and we spoke about this woman and I could see your dear face, I was happy. I had dinner with her. Four days ago I met her. She was spying me (she told me herself), and then she came to the café where I sat and she was shaking in her bones while speaking to me, and I told her I should have a dinner with her. She gave me the manuscript of a book she is writing and it is a diary in which she tells everything about her love for me. It is a wonderful book. She is a very good writer; she feels things deeply and tells them with wonderful words. So it is very upsetting to read her diary, specially when it is about yourself. I have a kind of admiration for her, and much friendship; but I see her about once a month when I stay in Paris. I don't really care for her and she knows it. What is strange is she can talk very freely about her love for me and discuss it as if it were a disease. Nevertheless, you can guess that to spend an evening with her is not a very easy thing. She always takes me to one of the best restaurants in Paris and she orders champagne and the most expensive dishes and I speak much and much, telling stories and trying to be gay and casual. And she drinks very much, and after dinner we go to some bar and she becomes very pathetic and I feel awful and then I say good bye and she goes away, crying, I know, and hitting her head against the walls and thinking about killing herself. She does not accept to have one friend, except me. She lives alone from morning to morning and sees me six times a year. I hate leaving her in the streets, alone and hopeless and thinking of death. But what may I do? Too much kindness would be the worst of all. Anyhow, I could never kiss her and that is the question. What may I do?

This morning I went to the *Temps modernes* and I gathered a lot of manuscripts which I read during the day. One of them was a strange document: the life of a prostitute written by herself.[2] My God! To think this is the way the world appeared to her for her whole and one life and she will die without knowing anything else! It is terrific! She writes in such a genuine and crude way it is nearly impossible to print the story. But that is something one could cry about rather than about one's own petty worries. Yet it is very funny too in many ways.

My beloved one, I go to sleep now. It helped me much to write to you. It helps me much to know you are living and waiting for me and we'll be happy again, loving each other. You told me once that I was more important to you than you to me. But I do not think it is true any more. I miss you and love you and I am your wife as you are my husband. I'll go to sleep in your arms, my beloved one.

Your Simone

1) The French novelist Violette Leduc, who referred to herself this way. In 1945 she met Simone de Beauvoir, who encouraged her to publish her first novel, *L'Asphyxie*, in *Les Temps modernes*. The manuscript in question would become *L'Affamée*, published in 1948. 2) Published in *Les Temps modernes* (December 1947–January 1948).

Saturday, 6th June 1947

Dearest,

It is awfully raining this morning in Paris, and there is a strike in the railways so I don't know how I may come back to my little country home. I should like to come back and rest and work after these days in Paris. I had a kind of

25

depression Wednesday night when I wrote to you, but now it begins to be better. First, I can work again and it is much for me. I think I was wrong to try at once to write the book about women which I began before going to America—it is dead for me just now; I cannot begin again where I left just as if nothing had happened. I'll write it later on and now I want to write about my travel.[1] I should not like this travel to be lost; I must keep something of it, with words if nothing else is possible. I shall speak of America, but about myself, too; I should like to describe the whole experience of "myself-in-America" altogether; what means arrival and departure and passing by, and the attempt to look at things, to get something of them and so on. And at the same time I'll try to get the things themselves. Do you see what I mean? I am afraid I don't explain very well, but I am very interested by this purpose.

I had some pleasant time in Paris. Yesterday morning Sartre took me to the studio to see the projection of a feature whose script and dialogue he has written, and which Delannoy is shooting just now.[2] I think it will be a very good movie. I told you that the French movies are getting better and better because people try really to say something in movies, to express a peculiar view of life as we do in our books. What was very interesting there was to see the feature before it has been all put in the right order and cut off where it must be; the shooting is not yet over, so you can really see the work, the different ways of shooting a scene and all the problems arising when you have to make the last choice. Then I knew many of the actors and it is always very funny to see in their movie personnality such or such young man or woman you use to meet in the cafés of Saint-Germain-des-Prés.

Then in the afternoon I went to a cocktail party at Gallimard's, my publisher. He has won so much money now by exploiting the poor writers that he gives cocktails each week. It was the first time I went there; there were hundreds of people in the gardens and the big rooms and I met nearly all the friends I had not seen since my departure and they were very warm and gay, asking questions about America and telling funny things about life in Paris during these months. We took an appointment to meet again in the night. So about midnight I went to a very crazy but funny place where the young French so-called intellectual people dance and drink with very pretty pseudo-intellectual girls. It is a long cave under a little bar, a rather dark cave with reddish walls and ceiling, little tables and stools and hundreds of people dancing where there is place only for twenty of them. But it is nice because boys and girls were dressed in a very fancy way, with many colors, and they dance in a very fancy way too; some boys have brain and some girls very good faces. Music was nice too; they play better than most of white people in America and it means so much for them. I like chiefly the young man with the horn. He is an interesting guy, being by profession an engineer (so he wins his money), being a very good writer too and playing horn with passion, though he has a heart disease and may die by playing too much.[3] He has written a terrific book,[4] pretending that it was written by an American Negro and that he only translated it; he won a lot of money this way, because the book was very obscene in a sadistic way and people like it. Well, we drank a little and talked much and listened to the horn and looked at people dancing (I cannot dance myself, I never liked it). It was a nice evening, though I should not care to see these people again before a rather long time. I should not care to see them but I like to know they are living in France, in Paris, writing books and listening to jazz and looking at the same streets I look at, and seeing the same sky I see.

I think I'll live this way for a month, coming from the country to Paris once or twice a week and writing the book about America and writing to you, too. I wait for the letter number four, now. I hope I'll get it next Monday. I hoped a little I should get it this morning, but I was mistaken. Write to me and mail your letters rather twice a week than once, my beloved one. I spoke to many people about your book, and it seemed to me I was secretly pressing your hand and smiling at you. It is noon in Paris, eight o'clock in Chicago. Maybe you are swimming. Or you have put on the "peignoir" and you make yourself busy in the kitchen. Maybe you sleep. I should rather think you sleep and it is very easy to come near you and to kiss you awake. I kiss you and kiss you again.

Your Simone

1) This becomes *America Day by Day.* 2) *Les jeux sont faits* (*The Chips Are Down*) with Micheline Presle and Pagliero. 3) Boris Vian, novelist (*L'Ecume des jours*, 1947) playwright, poet, translator, jazz musician, composer, and literary critic; one of the most significant Saint-Germain-des-Prés figures of the postwar period. 4) *J'irai cracher sur vos tombes.*

Thursday, 12th June 1947

Mon bien-aimé,

No letter from you. More than a week without any letter from you. I could stand much more without suspecting you do not write to me. We told each other: "I shall not lose you; you shall not lose me." And I believe in you, knowing you believe in me. I know you do not forget me. Nevertheless, it is sad. When I arrive in Paris, first of all I rush to my hotel to find a letter from you; the little box was empty yesterday, it was empty this morning and remained so the whole day.

I spent three days in the country; I went by a taxi-cab, which was a bit expensive, but very nice. I saw nice French villages, little roads and woods and valleys; I liked it. Then I worked pretty well. I am interested by this book about America; it will be a long job, because I can never write quickly; and what I intend to do is rather difficult. I do not know yet if what I have done is good or bad, but I go on, and I feel pleased during it. So for three days I worked very much. And yesterday I came back to Paris.

This evening I am giving a party! I invited about twenty friends and we'll drink to my coming back from America. (Going away from America, dearest, but they think "coming back from.") I have found a nice little cave where people will dance if they choose. We'll have many fine jazz records, and a little orchestra. I bought a lot of bottles of whisky, cognac, gin, vodka, and I dressed as smartly as I could with the Mexican dress I bought in New York and which you liked, and the little glass-necklace you liked. I *look* elegant, though you told me I never could *be* elegant. Dearest, how gladly I should let the people away, and break the bottles, and tear off the Mexican dress if you just came in my tooth-paste pink room! Dearest, it will happen. We'll see each other's face again and I'll have your lips kissing my lips, and I'll hear your beloved voice. It will happen. But not to night, so I'll go to the party. I hope I'll enjoy it. I'll tell you in my next letter.

I have three publishers interested in your book. I am sure it will take some time before getting a sure answer. But I am sure, too, we'll get it. And maybe you'll have some French money this way.

Paris was nice today. On the little places around Saint-Germain-des-Prés, there were lots of painters sitting in the open air and painting trees, or churches, painting the little places. They were not good painters (I do not know why, but they never are) but they looked very happy and you felt happy yourself looking at them. How is Wabansia Avenue, dearest? Please write to me.

Speak to me, smile to me, kiss me. I love you.

Your Simone

Here are little photos from New York with Wright.

Dearest,

So yesterday morning, the letter was there, brightly red and blue and white as a French flag. It was a nice long letter and I was very pleased: you can read it four or five times without knowing it by heart. You really are a nice man. The party was a regular failure. But I enjoyed it because I always enjoy everything. The cave was really fine, big, and dark with a nice bar, and the records were good; we had plenty of gin, whisky, cognac and the guests were well chosen. Yet it was a failure. I guess people drank too much and they do not know how to drink. I drank much myself but I remained all right. While after two hours there were boys and girls sleeping, crying, and chiefly vomiting in every corner. I helped them to vomit, I gave them handkerchiefs to cry, I was very busy, but it was a pity. The musicians fell dead drunk since the beginning, so we had no guitar, no piano, no horn. About ten of us remained in good health and the party went on until five in the morning; but nobody was very lively except myself. At five, Paris was very fine, it was a pleasure to walk in the dawn.

I must say, when I saw people afterwards, they all told me they enjoyed the party very much too, even the sleeping, crying, vomiting ones said so. So, maybe it was not such a failure, after all. I had forgotten my bag in the cave. The next morning, I went to the hotel to which the cave belongs and I asked for my bag. The woman of the hotel gave it to me, then she asked, "Did you not find an *eye*?" It was very unpleasant to hear, I was very scared. I said "no!" And she said, "One of the young men came this morning and said he had forgotten his eye on the bar near the pot of flowers; we did not find it. He has a glass eye and he took it off in the night to show it to a friend, then he forgot it." So it was nothing very terrific, after all, but just a moment, the whole world had seemed very strange to me.

I was glad to hear about the phoney blonde[1] and the Tiger and Mademoiselle G. Glad to know you work to your novel. Make it good. I am not sure I like the titles you propose for your book,[2] anyway I think the second one would be better, though a bit Célinish indeed. Maybe you'll find something really good one of these days.

Since you are interested in existentialism, I'll tell you Camus, the one who wrote *The Stranger*, has just published a very interesting book. It is called *La peste*. It is in fact the story of the occupation of Paris by German soldiers, under the cover of the story of the plague in Oran. He describes the dreadful disease, the loneliness of the city where it happens and whose doors are closed by fear of contagion, the fear of some people, the courage of others. And through all that he tries to find the meaning of human life, the reasons and the way of accepting it. I do not agree with everything, but he writes the finest French language and some parts of the book are really moving and speak to the heart.

I am very proud because I received some letters of American people congratulating me for the article you read in the *Sunday Supplement*, and which the gendarme 3 despised so meanly. I am proud because they seemed to think I had understood something about America. You know, I am absolutely decided to come back to America for a long time next year. I know I can contrive it, it is something really sure. So even if you cannot come to France, God and the horses not helping you, 4 we'll have a fine time together. Maybe we'll buy a car to sell it back afterwards, or we'll go by planes and buses through the country. And we'll stay a good time in New Orleans. I feel very excited when I think of it. I should like so much to have a real travel with you. If you enjoy everything as you did in the plane and in New York, it must be a real fun. You are very funny, you know, and besides loving each other we'll be able to laugh a good deal together, which is a good thing to do. Loving each other and laughing, it would be a nice way of travelling.

Now it is Saturday evening, I am back to the country, it is raining and there is a loud wind, I like it. What about my English? Is it very weak? And do you like my writing? Well, sure my English is good enough to allow me to tell you I love you. And sure you can read it. Dearest, I kiss you with many long loving kisses.

Your Simone

1) A prostitute and drug addict friend of Algren's, married to a thief. 2) Algren had asked her advice on possible titles for his novel: "...*Descent to the Edge of the Night*? Too Célinian?" 3) Another strange acquaintance of Algren's. 4) Algren was given to gambling and losing at the races; playing poker was another passion.

Tuesday, 17th June 1947

Dearest,

I am working since more than two hours, so I decided to take a short holiday; I asked for a brandy (no scotch and soda, here, alas!) and I am writing to you. I write from the first floor of the "Café de Flore"—that is our existentialist café. There are many people in the big room opening on the street, and at the terrace, but nobody here, I am all alone. The windows are open, I see the trees of the boulevard Saint-Germain, it is very pleasant. I am very pleased because Sartre read the beginning of the American diary (I pretend it is a diary) and he thought it is good, so I enjoy writing it. The pity is I cannot speak about people quite freely, which would be very interesting; for instance I cannot say all what I think about Richard Wright, he would not be pleased though I like him very much. The same thing for other people. Yet such a book would be interesting only if it had a quality of truth. I try to make it true. And to speak about America is to speak about such and such American people. Sad. But I'll do my best with what I can say. Sad too to think you will not read it! I should like to think it is a long letter I am writing to you. I must make it so good that it will be translated in America. But cannot you learn French too? Let us see. Suppose you should write to me ten lines in French in each letter and I tell you your mistakes? Then you read a French book? You would know something when you come to Marseille. What about it?

I speak about my work because nothing else is very important just now. It goes on: the country, Paris, the country again. It is a nice way of living. I do not know why I never did it before. I feel so quiet in the country; and after three days reading and working, I feel so glad when I come to Paris, and drink in the cafés and see my friends. Yesterday I went to dinner in a very nice place: a restaurant in the open air in the middle of a fine garden called "le parc Montsouris," there are beautiful trees, a little lake. At ten o'clock, the garden is closed, everybody goes away, but the people of the restaurant stay and you are nearly alone in a deserted garden at night. It is a magic feeling. I felt very happy in a childish way. Then I tried to get some whisky in the bars of the Champs-Elysées; some of the bars are nice, but there was a strike in the ice department (there is always some kind of strike or other, just now in France) and there was no ice in the whisky. It was scotch, they said, but it did not taste like American scotch. I did not like it. Paris is all right in its way, but you must not look for America in Paris, no more than looking for Paris in Chicago.

Something funny happened to me just now. I was called at the telephone. Somebody I did not know spoke to me, he asked: "please, will you pronounce the words 'orange juice'?" I said, "What is the matter? Who are you?" He said, "I ask the questions, not you. How do you say 'orange juice'?" I said, "It makes no sense." He said, "I should like to know if you say 'orange juice' or 'orange joys.'" I said, "How do you know I say 'orange joys'?" "Oh!" he said, "there are newspapermen everywhere." "Even in the drugstores?" I said. "The Café de Flore is not a drugstore," he said. "Indeed!" I said, "and I am sad it is not." And then I hung down the phone. I was very amazed. In fact a friend told me in New York I pronounce it "orange joys." But who knows it? Then I understood. I have lost in a little bar near the Café de Flore a piece of my manuscript: just a leaf of paper, where I spoke about my bad accent and I gave this exemple. Some young men found it and made a joke. But I am unconfortable. There is nothing wrong in this bit of paper, but people are very wicked in France and they may do very bad jokes about anything. Maybe they'll do, you never know. I hate now people caring for me in any way in Paris, because it is rather in a bad way they care for you.

Now I propose a little version for you: you must send the translation to me in your next letter. I'll make it very easy. I'll tell you back if you understood rightly. Take care! It is the most interesting part of the letter:

> Mon bien-aimé est très loin. Mais je pense à lui tous les jours, tout le jour. Je penserai à lui jusqu'à ce que je le retrouve. Alors je a'aurai plus à penser. Il me prendra dans ses bras, nos lèvres se toucheront, nous serons heureux comme nous avons été heureux, et davantage encore parce que nous nous aimerons encore davantage. Il est très loin, mais personne n'est plus près de moi puisqu'il habite mon coeur. Il s'appelle Nelson Algren.

If you do not understand, I tell you it means: I love you, I kiss you. But it is nicer in the French version. Yet, even if you are a stupid man you must know I love you. I am waiting for the day of our meeting again.

Your Simone

Friday, 20th June 1947

Dearest,

You know? I live a bit in a crocodile peace myself,[1] and when I look at the big world around me, I am a bit amazed. Yesterday I left my green nest and I went to Paris, and in Paris I left my tooth-paste-pink room and I went to one of these smart caves in which smart people dance and drink nowadays in Paris. I spoke to you about two of these caves. This one was yet another one. It was just in the street where I live. One year ago it was a private club for colored people of the Antilles. Nowadays all Saint-Germain-des-Prés intellectuals meet there at night. So, at about eleven o'clock, we knocked at the door of a little café, in a rather mysterious way, and a dark-haired woman mysteriously opened the door. We went downstairs. It was a very elegant cave indeed, with carpets and deep red armchairs, a bar, a piano, some records. All kinds of people came there, all of them mysteriously knocking at the door, all of them intellectual people bearing fierce-flying banners, different banners. Micheline Presle came there, the beautiful French star who plays in *Le diable au corps* about which I wrote to you and who plays now in the Sartre's feature. Pagliero, the Italian actor of *Open City* who is her partner in the same feature came too, and two other movie people I knew. They held no banner. But the other ones were either existentialist (including myself) or communist or fascist. There was a very strange bad crazy and hateful man who should have been shot after the Libération and who danced with a drunk hateful girl: they had some other ex-collaborationist and pro-fascist boys with them. So the atmosphere was very tense. In the end of the evening, the fascist ones made some unpleasant reflexion about Jews: they said it in a loud voice and a communist boy asked what was the matter with Jews? So some existentialists came and said to the communists they must make a kind of union for just a while and fight the fascists with their fists. But the communists would not, and they began to argue harshly with the existentialists, each of them *wearing* the fierce-flying banners. Then the communists went away. The existentialists grumbled and one of them went to one of the fascists and walked on his toes. Then he said, "You have crushed my toes," and they began to fight with words. Then all the men parted in two groups (except three or four who were lying dead drunk in the red armchairs) and they went outside to fight with their fists. Women stayed there, waiting and yawning because it was four o'clock in the morning. Then the men came back, and nothing had happened. I was told this kind of thing happens every night in this smart intellectual cave.

I went to sleep at five, and slept well and went back to my yellow and blue inn. Here I am. Dearest, I gave to you a glimpse of the world with flying banners—if you were pleased of it, all right. But it was more precious, surely, to learn from you that there was such a happy world of roots and grubs and old bones. I felt safe in your ditch. I am happy to think there is such a ditch, with such a crocodile man lying in it, a man who'll let me lie near him in the mud and the sun when I'll ask him to let me do so. So, we'll go together sometimes in the bright green fierce world; and sometimes we'll stay still, hidden among the roots and in each other's arms. I know now there is something on earth such as peace and happiness, lying in your arms, dearest. If you were to come in, unannounced, without waking anyone, and quietly lie down beside me... dearest, you should wake me. And then? You know. Let us dream of it since it will happen. And I just feel as if I just opened my eyes and smiled to you, knowingly.

Your Simone

What about these dreadful airplanes accidents? I read the whole story in the *Times* and I am not sure we shall ever go in a plane again. To be burnt alive, would you like it? We were very lucky indeed. The director of the Sunday *New York Times* called me; I couldn't see him.

1) In her biography of Simone de Beauvoir, Dierdre Bair writes: "De Beauvoir chafed because she had to spend so many hours of her final day in Chicago away from Algren, giving a lecture and lunching with some of the French officials who sponsored her visit. They were all set to entertain her until dinner, when she was to dine with another group, but she told them she had to pay a call on a sick friend. She told them her friend's address—really Algren's—and they insisted that she could not take a taxi to such a dangerous place. They drove her there in a sleek new official car, the object of much subsequent curiosity in the neighborhood. She jumped out and pounded on the surprised Algren's door; she caught him quietly waiting for the phone call she had promised to make that night from the station. 'My impetuosity thrilled him,' she remembered, and they made love again. Later, as they drank whiskey together, Algren joked about her arrival in such a spectacular car, saying this "Crazy Frog" had given him just the sort of status he did not need among his neighbors, because they would now think him rich and ask to borrow money they could not repay. He was so visibly touched by her unexpected visit that she called him her "Crocodile" because of his "funny, toothy grin." Thus their pet names for each other were set for the rest of their affair. However, he "was a gentleman and did not ask about Sartre," and she never mentioned him, either."

Tuesday, 24th June 1947

Nelson, my love,

You know, I became very fond of your name, seeing it written with your handwriting at the bottom of your dear beloved letters, I decided to use this name. Indeed, it is a nice name for a nice man. It suits you. Well, it is your name, it is enough. I am not going to make any choice about you: I take everything.

So, my beloved Nelson, I have to tell you how beautiful the country was this morning. So peaceful, so silent, so warm. I cannot tell it with English words. In a way, it is very good for me to write in English, I cannot do any bad literature, I cannot do any kind of literature. Just say what I have to say in the most direct and simple way: the country was peaceful, silent and warm; and it was beautiful. After dinner I sat a long time in the garden and looked at the sky which was losing its blue and pink colors, and looked at the nice bit of glittering moon above the roof, and I felt happy to be a human being with two eyes and a heart. There are such fine roses blooming in the garden! I do not like flowers so much, except when *you* have bought them for me (then I eat them greedily), but these roses amaze me. It is very strange that such beautiful things may be given by *nobody*: it looks like a gift, without anybody making the gift to you. Some people would think of God about it but in fact, it is not at all the kind of gift any God could do. I like the cherry-trees too. All along the railway track, from Saint-Rémy to Paris there are cherry-trees all red with cherries; it is a very old picture you have seen since childhood, and yet it is so new — new in every new summer as my love for you is new every day.

So, after having spoken about flowers and cherries, a very moral and quiet and dignified topic, I'll speak about pansies and fairies. Yesterday evening I was in Paris and I went to a very funny night club, not in a cave but rather in a garret: the public was made of very quiet, ugly, stupid middle-class people; the orchestra was as bad as possible. But the show was stupendous: rather beautiful young men with girl dresses and make-up and long waving hair. You know this kind of thing, sure. Some of them really looked like women: very tall, big women but pretty and graceful. What was stupendous was the kind of plays they were playing: a strange mixture of obscenity and poetry. The poetry was not intended but it was there. They played for instance the story of Adam and Eve. One of the men was the tree of Evil and Good: it was exactly the tree of Charlot in *Charlot Soldier*,[1] if you remember it. And there was a long naked snake, with just a long black tail on him, and a very ugly Eve (because they loathe woman) and a ridiculous little Adam; and a lovely apple-man; and they danced amazing little ballets. There were other stories, afterwards, but this was the best one. I stayed until three o'clock in the morning with my friends, drinking bad bourbon and looking.

I go on writing the book about America. I write everything, just the way I felt it, and afterwards I'll make a choice. I have told the story of the three first weeks now and I am just coming to Chicago. It is very difficult. I do not know what I want to say about this first encounter. Indeed, I am not to speak of you and me, but what do I know about Chicago if not through you? Well, I have to find a way of saying the truth without saying it; that is exactly what is literature, after all: clever lies which secretly say the truth.

You know, I am planning to go to Sweden for a month, in August? Do you know something about Sweden, since you are half Swedish? Do you feel something for this country? They translated a book of mine there, that is why I got some money in this country. But you cannot read Swedish, neither, can you?

I am dead tired because I went to bed so late last night. Now I am in bed and I am going to sleep. Just one or two words more. I do not care for what I am writing; but I just like the fact of writing to you. It is like kissing you. It is something physical; I can feel my love for you in my fingers when I write; it is good to feel one's love with any living part of one's body, not only in one's head. Writing is not as pleasant as kissing; it is even a little dry, and lonely and sad, but it is better than nothing: I have no choice left. So just now I am writing anything, you see, stupid things, just not to say good bye. This morning I spent a whole hour with the American girl I met the other night. We sat at the terrace of the Café de Flore and spoke. She is good-looking but silly, in a bad way. Yet I was pleased to speak English. In the beginning I was very shy; afterwards I remembered some words. From my window here, from the garden, at every hour of the day I see airplanes coming slowly down to an airport in the neighbourhood or flying fiercely away towards the sky. Every time I see one of them, I think of you. And I think of you in many other circonstances too, and without any circonstances, chiefly. You live with me, night and day.

Now you are going to live with me sleeping. Good bye, good bye, I am too tired. If you do not wish to say good bye, you have to come into my dreams. I hope you'll do though you never do, which is not very kind of you. I kiss you on the paper, then I'll put off the lights and shut my eyes, and I'll try to remember with my lips the taste of your real kisses; I'll try to fancy I feel your arms around me and I hope I'll go to sleep in this way.

Your Simone

I like the title *High-yellow and the Dealer.* I think it sounds very nicely.

Wednesday

Beloved Nelson, here is a big yellow letter with the little pictures, how much I like them! I like very much the one with you and me, you have really a good local face. How could any letter from me make you feel badly, since there is always so much love in them? Dearest, whatever I do, working or drinking, alone or with people, I always keep you in my heart, you must know it. I begin to plan things too about America with you; anyway, we'll be happy. I want to mail this today so good bye! I love you, my crazy man.

I was a bit angry with you because you felt badly after receiving one of my letters, and it is too stupid even from a crazy man to feel bad about letters so full of the deepest love. Dearest Nelson, I cannot bear to have you feeling bad about me, yet if it happens, you must tell it to me, indeed, we must never lie to each other, we must even try to speak the truth. But you did not make me cry; I felt your own love, reading your letter.

1) Charlie Chaplin's *Shoulder Arms* (1918).

Saturday morning, 28 Juin 1947

Nelson, my love,

I stayed in Paris and it was dreadfully hot, it was never so hot in Paris since 1900. I thought of Chicago and how hard life must be when it is so hot on Wabansia Avenue. Here it was really a murder, as you say in America. It was very difficult to write or do anything. I had a dinner with the ugly woman. We went to a very nice old restaurant in the Palais Royal gardens and we drank champagne. I do not know why we always drink champagne when we have a dinner together. In the same restaurant there was Jean Cocteau, a very well known French poet and pederast; he is sixty years old and he had a dinner with three rather beautiful young homosexuals. He was very friendly and funny and we talked some time together; as the ugly woman is rather a lesbian if she is anything, I was the only heterosexual one in this meeting and I felt a little vicious, being so. The way these young homosexual behave always makes me laugh: the way they try to be very manly and tough and yet very womanly too. They are friends with the ugly woman and I think I rather do some good to her, helping her to write good books and to make friends through these books. She is not quite so unhappy as before. She is surely the most interesting woman I know and we spent a good evening.

In the afternoon there had been all kinds of literary festivities at Gallimard's, the publisher. First they gave a prize of 100,000 francs to a young writer and there was a big lunch about it. The prize was given to this other homosexual poet about whom I spoke to you,[1] who was a foundling, not knowing father nor mother, and who became a burglar and who writes beautiful obscene books. So today his picture is in all the newspapers, just when his boy-friend was put into jail for eighteen months for having stolen silver spoons in a big hotel. I think he is pleased because of the money, but not pleased with the pictures. Then at Gallimard's there was a cocktail and Steinbeck came as a guest. But I did not care to see him and chiefly among such a crowd and I did not go there. There are many American people now in Paris. Why not just you, my beloved one? I saw some very old friends too during these two days, friends I know since nearly twenty years: a charming old lady,[2] who fascinated me when I was a girl and she was forty years old; I thought it was wonderful and very impressing to be a forty years old woman: well, now it has come—it is not better nor worse than any other age. Now she is sixty and does not impress me any more but I like her very much. Then there were two married people who are younger friends of hers and mine too.[3] The young woman just recovered after swallowing a pin. She was in a car and put a pin in mouth, and there was some shake and she swallowed the pin, a rather big one! They took her to the hospital and she remained there for four days. With X rays they saw the pin first in her stomach, then coming down slowly in the intestine. Then it went away. I should have been very scared with a pin in my stomach, but she was not. This kind of things always happens to her and it is dreadful for her poor husband.

Well, now I am going to work. I must begin again to write the book about women because I promised a bit of it to a New York magazine. They already gave me 250 dollars and they'll give me 250 more when the article is published. I'll keep the money in New York and it'll help us to live in New Orleans, dearest. So, writing it, I begin to work for our travel together, for our happiness and love: it is very stimulating. Good bye, my beloved one. I hope there is no poison in this letter which can make you feel badly: plain paper and ink, and plain love. I don't think it could harm you, but I am a little afraid. Nelson, my love, I would never have you feeling badly about me. You can miss me and be sorry not to have me near you; so do I miss you, I am sorry, but that is not feeling bad. I should like my love would wrap you very softly, and warmly, and you would feel very comfortable in it. You know, dearest, I love you so much. I did not believe in Chicago I should love you so much in this French hot summer. I kiss you.

Your Simone

1) Jean Genet (1910-1986). Novelist and playwright; a leading figure in the Theater of the Absurd.
2) Madame Morel. See *The Prime of Life.* 3) The Guilles.

Nelson, my love,

It was such a good letter you wrote to me, I should cry with tenderness about this letter as I did about the white flower. I love you. I am happy you say it is a good love because I think it is surely a *good* love, and you must know it. I am glad first because the letter was so long, and when it is so long I can read it for a whole week before knowing it by heart, and at the end of the week there is another letter. Then, it came so quickly: from Saturday, I got it yesterday, it seemed very lively, very fresh; it was pleasant. Then you spoke to me very leisurely, in a very quiet and friendly way, and I could think we were sitting in the Wabansia nest, drinking Southern Confort, or lying in the New York twin beds, and talking, and feeling very near of each other. You know, in the beginning I was afraid we should go away, farther and farther from each other, and then your first letters were a bit restrained, you did not say much; it was the same way you were on the first day, being busy, not talking, always going away. I feel now, instead, we are getting nearer and nearer through these letters. Do you feel it, too? I am glad you spoke a little about yourself, it is so important for me. There are many things I should like to know. First; *why* did you always try to keep people *away* from you? It is very interesting, but a little puzzling. I should under-stand you better if I knew the reasons of it. Then, in which way did the c p [1] fail you? I am not in a hurry to get the answer, but if it happens you would like to explain something of this to me, I should like to know.

Dearest, I am so proud to think I can make you as proud about your nerves and brain as silken underwear would do! But *do* buy cigars if you like them.

Only one thing did not make me happy neither proud of you; it is our French lesson. The version was all wrong, and you did not do the half of it. And when you write in French, I just understand nothing. You are not a smart pupil at all. Yet tomorrow I'll send two of my books to you, and I hope you'll become able to read them.

Dearest, you say first you were not aware of me. Neither was I aware of you, that is the strangest thing in our whole story. I knew I was fond of you when leaving Chicago the first time, but I did not know *who* you were. I came to Chicago, being very tired of intellectual arguments, of all the kind of abstract life I had in New York and wishing to feel a woman in a good man's heart. I had felt I was a woman for you, and I liked it since I liked you.

But I did not know exactly what would happen. I did not know if I should be as fond of you as the first time; that is why I wanted a room of my own. And then all the day long I liked you more and more, and I was glad when you kissed me. and I was happy sleeping with you in the Wabansia nest. And on the following day I really became aware of you, and first I loved the way you loved me, and then I just loved you myself. Now it seems to me I know you since a very long time, it seems to me, though our love is so new that we have been friends all our life long. Dearest, night and day I feel wrapped in your love, it protects me against every unpleasant thing; when the weather is hot, it is cool, when the wind is cold, it is warm; it seems to me I'll never get old, I'll never die as long as you love me. When I think of your arms around me, I feel in my stomach the same shaking you speak about, which leaves all my body aching.

Thursday, 3 Juillet 1947

I led a very quiet life since my last letter: no cave, no party, no wit. There was a wonderful storm in the country, it was really beautiful. The whole day had been so hot, you really wanted to die, love or work or happiness did not mean anything more. And then came a huge black smoke in the sky, and strange phantasms went by in the dim light, and soon you could not see the sky nor the landscape any more, just a cherry tree beaten by the wind while the rain fell crazily, and thunder shaked the sky. Many trees were broken, flowers killed, the landscape was a battle field. I never saw such a storm, not even in Greece at Delphes where it sounded very religious and terrifying, not even in New Orleans where the sky and earth had became mad.

Afterwards, everything was strangely peaceful. Friends came and we had a dinner and a long evening: the woman who has swallowed a pin, her husband, the old lady I like so much, and Sartre. But I was not very quiet myself; the storm had gone on my nerves, and I drank much, and, dearest, when I drink much I am no longer sensible at all; when the other friends left I became a storm myself, and poor Sartre was very bored with me who spoke about life and death and everything in a rather mad way. When I am drunk everything seems very tragic and pathetic and terrifying to me—so dreadfully important, and yet without importance since death is at the end; I should knock my head against the walls. I did not knock my head but I spoke and raved late in the night on the peaceful little country roads, and I decided not to drink any more for some time.

You see, it has never been very easy for me to live, though I am always very happy — maybe because I want so much to be happy. I like so much to live and I hate the idea of dying one day. And then I am awfully greedy; I want everything from life, I want to be a woman and to be a man, to have many friends and to have loneliness, to work much and write good books, and to travel and enjoy myself, to be selfish and to be unselfish... You see, it is difficult to get all which I want. And then when I do not succeed I get mad with anger...

Well, after this storm I became quiet again and wrote the piece about women in order to get dollars to go with you to New Orleans. Then Tuesday I came to Paris. I saw the Jew girl whom I spoke to you about: she was a very bright student and then she married without real love an Aryan boy and she had to hide herself for four years, and now she is no more bright at all and very unhappy. She cares for me very much and I do not care so much for her. I have another Russian girlfriend who is ill,[2] she had tuberculosis in her lungs and she cares very much for me too. But that is sad: I never care very much for my girl friends. Either they are too young, or too crazy. I do not know, but the only woman I really like and respect is the old lady I spoke to you about. For the other ones I am something like a mother, an elder sister, but I do not feel they are my daughters. I do not wish any daughter. Well, I forgot: I have a kind of daughter whom I like very much, she is the other Russian girl, married at Los Angeles, and with whom I travelled this year.[3] This one is very important for me. Well, I'll speak to you another day about it. I cannot go on writing for hours because I am very busy.

As Sartre left Paris for a long week, I decided to go to some sea-side and swim and walk and have a good time of my own and I am going away, for a week too, to Corsica. I'll fly to Ajaccio tomorrow morning. I went once to Corsica ten years ago with the woman who swallowed the pin, her sister and her husband; we slept under tents and cooked in the open air. It is a beautiful country. I wished to go back there since a long time but until now it was difficult to have any reservation on boat or airplane. So I am glad to go. I hope I shall not be toasted myself; you'll know by the newspapers. Don't be surprised if, for a week, you don't receive my letters as quickly as before; from Corsica it must take more time. But I'll write the same way.

Dearest, I just sent the books an hour ago by airplane. Begin with *Le sang des autres*,[4] please. Dearest, I should like to give you as much happiness with my letters as you did with yours. I should like you to feel me near

41

you as I felt you near me. If we cannot see each other it is only because the lights are off, but I could touch you with my hand, I could kiss you with my lips, and so do I, my beloved nice man.

Your Simone

1) Communist Party. 2) Olga Kosakievitch. See *The Prime of Life.* 3) Natalie Sorokine. 4) *The Blood of Others.*

Tuesday, 8th July 1947

My own Nelson,

This is the first time I do not observe my schedule which is to mail letters to you twice a week. It seems so useless to mail a letter in Corsica! I am not sure this one will arrive before my next letter from Paris. Nevertheless I feel badly, not writing to you. All the day long I think of what I should like to tell you about what I do, what I see. So, I'll take a chance with the little Corsican buses, and the Ajaccio airplane.

This is a marvellous country, as beautiful as I remembered. It is very wild and lonely, with blue sea and high mountains and deep, rich colors; and most of all I like this smell of "maquis,"[1] a smell of dry plants the English name of which I do not know; when I wake up in the morning, I smell it, it is in my room, in all the houses as well as outside. When I came by boat twelve years ago, I smelt it from the middle of the sea and I smelt it Friday when going out the airplane. But it is very harsh to live here: nearly nothing to eat, nearly no buses, lonely paths where you lose yourself. I lost myself in the mountains, I'll tell you. And in three days I became so ugly that you would be very disappointed with me: the face all red with sun, the hair undone by sea-water, the legs scratched with briars and bushes, and wearing a very old dress and plain shoes.

So I'll tell you everything in the right order. I went to the Paris airplane station at seven in the morning and I was dreadfully angry because they forget to put my name on the passagers list, though I had reserved my place a week before. They told me to go to Le Bourget, which is the airport, and to see what would happen. At the airport they told me I could take a chance and go onto Lyon but they could not grant that I should go onto Marseille. So the beginning of the travel was spoilt by anger and anxiety. In fact I went to Marseille, and from Marseille to Ajaccio. I like to go above the sea, and the arrival on the Corsican airport, near the sea and surrounded by mountains, was very beautiful. It was two o'clock. I had a lunch in a very poor restaurant where I ate lobster: you always eat lobster in Corsica, but all the dishes are cooked with a dreadful kind of olive oil which tastes of mud, not a nice taste. So I ate a very muddy meal and I went and put my rucksack in another hotel, which is called "Grand Hôtel" and is supposed to have been a rather smart place but which is all rotten now. I like it this way. There is a big garden with palm trees and flowers but all of them very dusty, and the inside of the hotel is falling in pieces. From my window I had a large view on the sea and the coast, I loved it. I went and had a bath on a nice sandy shore. I nearly had the whole shore and blue sea for myself, there are no tourists now in this poor country. What is very sad for me is I cannot swim; I never went to the sea-side when I was a child and ten years ago I learnt a bit how to swim, but I just can stay on the water without moving. Nevertheless I enjoyed the bath very much. Then I went back to Ajaccio and walked in the narrow streets, on the little port. It is a very pleasant place, you would like it; it looks a little like Marseille but much smaller, it is rather a village than a town. Young men were playing "boules" in the streets, very skillfully, in the warm sunset; after dinner young men and girls walk leisurely on the place near the sea, to and fro, without going anywhere, and the voices make a very soft noise. It seemed so pleasant, so gay when I thought of the hard, dry streets of American towns with everybody going somewhere and being busy.

The next day, I had a bath in the morning. It was even better than the first time. On the afternoon I wanted to go to the mountains, at thirty miles from Ajaccio. I knew there was a little bus going there at about three o'clock, you cannot fancy what an expedition it is to take this bus. First there were twice as many people waiting as the bus could contain. So we waited and waited until four, and then they brought another bus and everybody rushed into it. Then they put the luggage in, and we went away at about five. Then, all along the road, the driver stopped to drink pastis and to chat with his friend. So it needed two hours to go to the village. Any average American man would have been dead with scandal by the way, only some crazy local youth could have enjoyed it, as I did. Then in the village I found a room and something to eat, a very pleasant village high in the mountains. I went to sleep early and I woke up at six because I wanted to take a long walk through the mountains. I had a map and a blue guide which describes the way, and I asked several peasants who explained to me which paths I must follow and said it was very easy to find one's way. So, I drank coffee and milk and ate a a bit of hard Corsican bread with some raw ham, and I went through woods and stones. For two hours, it was all right, and then I arrived at a little wooden bridge on a stream, and I did not find any path where I should have. Luckily I saw a house, and a man was cutting grass near it. He told me where was the path, and I came back to the bridge and looked for the path; and I found one, and followed it a long time, and I understood it was not the right one; and I tried another, which was not right neither. I became more and more tired, with an empty stomach, and when it was one o'clock I just lay on the ground and slept a little, not knowing what to do. I hated the idea of just coming back to the village, which would have ruined all which I planned for this little trip. So I came back to the house, climbing a very harsh hill, and I found nobody and was very distressed. At the last minute, I saw the man. He could not give me anything to eat, but he gave me something to drink and he was so kind as to come with me for half an hour in the woods and find the path for me: indeed, it was not at all a path in the beginning and it was impossible to find it if you did not know it already. He would not take any money from me; Corsican peasants are especially kind with people, though they are so poor or maybe because of that. So I walked on the path onto the top of a mountain; the landscape was really beautiful, but I did not find any path to go down on the other side, I walked through bushes and stones, in an adventurous way, and I was a little anxious. At the end I came to a path and followed it for two hours, and I found myself in a village which was not the one I intended to go, but by this time I did not care any more, I just wanted a roof on my head and something to eat. I got something to eat with nice wine, and a room and I felt very well; but I was too tired to write to you as I intended to do. You know, I walked from seven to seven, just with a two hours rest, and being anxious about losing my way, so my hands were shaking and my legs aching. Next day, it was yesterday, I did not wish to walk any more. I woke up at six once more and I took buses which brought me to Bonifacio, a beautiful trip. I am yet in Bonifacio just now. It is built on a huge rock above the sea, with very, very old half rotten houses, and Sardinia can be seen at some miles on the large sea. I drank pastis on the little place where the local youths meet to drink pastis. I ate lobster at lunch, and lobster at dinner, and other fishes yet. I woke up at ten, now it is nearly twelve o'clock, I go to another little port this afternoon. I'll come back to Ajaccio on Friday, and Saturday I'll fly back to Paris. I'll write to you these next days. Just now a letter from you must be waiting for me in my hotel.

Dearest, if you knew how I hate writing sometimes, chiefly when I am travelling, chiefly when walking much and being physically tire, you would know this letter is the most loving letter you got from me. I loathe writing just now. I do not like to stay in a dreary dining room instead of going outside in the sun and looking at the sea and loitering in the little streets. Yet I write and I stay in the dining room because I like speaking to you more than anything. Now I say good bye. Will you come to Corsica with me one day and lose yourself in the woods too? Good bye, my own Nelson, my beloved one. I think of you night and day, everywhere I go you go with me. We never part.

Your Simone

Next spring we must go from New Orleans to some place in Florida where we'll have bathes and you'll teach me to swim.

1) Corsican scrub.

Saturday, 12th July 1947

Nelson, my love,

I'll go on telling you what a fine country Corsica is and how much I enjoy it. I wrote to you from Bonifacio. I wanted to go to another little port called Porto Vecchio. But the buses always go away at four or five in the morning, it is really too early, so I hired a taxi. The taxi was due at two in the afternoon and after a lobster lunch I began to wait. Then I slept, then it was 4: no taxi. I went to phone about it and somebody heard me and said the driver must just be in Ajaccio, he had met him on the road in the morning; so I was rather angry, though you can never be really angry with Corsican people. But the man said he could himself take me to Porto Vecchio, and so did he. I had a fine evening in this fine little village. First when I went into the dirty little inn, I saw high-colored pictures on the walls: half-naked girls of all kinds with black or red hair, it seemed very strange in this place, but then I saw it had been painted by an American soldier, a Chicago local painter (he had written on the walls he was from Chicago). Then in my room I found a nice little tortoise walking on the bed and everywhere. Then after dinner I saw a little communist meeting in a room widely open on the street, decorated with a lot of red flags and by pictures of Stalin and Thorez[1] and, as the electric light was off in the whole village, lighted with candles. Young and old people listened in a very intense way to a young dark-haired communist girl who explained to them what is fascism. I do not like the CP, but I liked the people trying so hard to learn something about the big world surrounding their poor beautiful island. Next day, I went to the mountains, I walked on little winding roads, and I stopped a big truck which took me to a nice village. There was another very Corsican story there. On Tuesday morning I wanted to take a bus; I was told the bus departed at six, and I got up early and at six I was on the village place: no bus. I waited and waited and people came and told me the driver had been drinking very much in the night and he sure was still sleeping. At seven o'clock we went and looked at the windows of the driver, but it was all closed, we could do nothing. We waited yet another hour and then a local youth knocked hard at the door of the inn (the inn-keeper was dead drunk too) and he went up to the driver's room and woke him. The driver came down, only half-dressed and rushed into the bus, and the bus rushed along the narrow winding roads, everybody laughing and laughing and nobody caring for the lost time. I had a fine day walking in the mountains and talking with people in the villages about the German and Italian occupation and the Corsican maquis and so on. It is so pleasant to arrive at night in some poor dirty little inn where peasants are eating very bad oily soup, and to drink red wine and to speak with everybody. You learn much, and in this country people are not at all stupid, they are interested in everything, girls are very good-looking and they seem happy though they are so poor. Yesterday morning I took the bus for Ajaccio; in the middle of the road we met a lot of little partridges: the driver stopped the bus and men rushed out through the windows and they picked up little partridges and brought them back, everybody being crazy with excitement. On the evening in Ajaccio I heard the sound of a gun being fired and everybody became mad with excitement too and rushed in the streets; but they were very disappointed for nobody was killed. I like the way they enjoy life and make excitement about everything.

I can swim a little better than in the beginning but not much, I just move a little in the water. Yet I like it very much.

Sunday, 13 Juillet 1947

Dearest, There was your letter waiting for me and I read it with much love. It was strange to have a bathe in Ajaccio yesterday morning and to be in Paris for dinner. The airplane trip was marvellous and quick. Yes, I have read *Moby Dick*, it is even one of the books I like the best; I read too the Mark Twain[2] this year in America. I think you have fought in a very heroic way for existentialism and you should be rewarded with a decoration. Nelson, my beloved one, I need nothing from America but you, and if you cannot go into the mail box, just send letters to me as you do, I wish nothing more. I am pleased because the professional readers to whom I gave your book in order to have it published like it very much; I hope they will come to some decision. I just spend this day in Paris and tomorrow I leave for London where I'll spend four days: I go with Sartre to see the first performance of his play *Morts sans sépulture.*[3] I am all sunburnt and the skin of my nose and my forehead is going away, you cannot fancy how ugly it is, but I feel fine.

Nearly two months now since we have parted, I have forgotten nothing about you, and you never seemed nearer to me. Your ring goes everywhere with me, it takes soap when I wash myself in the morning, it took sand on the Corsican shores, tomorrow it will catch something of the London dust. So you are mixed with all my life.

I kiss you many long loving kisses before going.

Your Simone

1) Maurice Thorez, secretary-general of the French Communist Party from 1930 until his death in 1964. 2) *On the Mississippi.* 3) *Men Without Shadows*, Gallimard, 1946.

Tuesday, 15th July 1947

Nelson, my love,

I am pleased to have a long quiet hour to spend with you in this hot London afternoon. I went there once, for a fortnight, more than ten years ago, with Sartre. I am very glad to see it again. It is a little sad because so many houses have been destroyed by the bombs and V-1, they have very little to eat just now, very little to dress with; at eleven o'clock they begin to close all the bars and cafés, and you cannot get any drink. It seems they are yet in war, everybody is poor and serious, no glamour at all. But on the other hand it is not really sad; they are very courageous people and they accept the situation in a very fine way. The ruins themselves do not look sad now, they are all covered with flowers: purple, red, yellow wild flowers, it is magnificent. When you walk in London you see not only fine parks and squares full of big green trees, but too strange unexpected gardens full of flowers which are the places of mined houses. It looks very old, coming from America, much older than Paris, which begins to imitate America in many ways. London does not. The cars, the buses are the most antique things in the world, I feel in a kind of modern Middle Age, if you see what I mean. As the weather is warm, people loiter in the streets, they sit on the edge of the fountain in Piccadilly Circus: there are sailors, chiefly, and prostitutes. In the parks people lie in the grass, chiefly lovers kissing each other very passionately without any care for people around them — it is all very gay and nice. Then I like the streets, the little places, the Thames, the old pubs, the inns, the whole stone and earth body of London. I should like to come here with you once.

It happened I came here with Sartre and one of Sartre's publishers who chiefly acts as business-man for his theater. He is called N. and looks like a very ugly little frog. He is afraid of flying so we came Monday by the Golden Arrow which is a very luxurious train, with armchairs and little tables. N. is the man who thinks of publishing your book, so I spoke much about you; I did not say what a nice crazy man you were, but I pretended you were somebody really dignified and important and a great crack of young American literature. He was very much interested, but we must make sure he will pay all right. He had hired a whole suite in a big hotel: the point was we did not want to spend any time with him; he is not stupid but very garrulous with an ugly little soul of business man. So we had to be rather impolite with him, but he did not care too much because he steals much money from Sartre, so he likes him. He makes us laugh very often, indeed. Anyway we left him in the hotel. Today we walked the whole morning, and we went on the top of the big red buses — a good sight-seeing. We were a little hungry because they give you so little to eat in the restaurants and you can buy nothing without tickets. But we drank scotch and soda as much as we wanted.

Wednesday, 16 Juillet 1947

Good morning, dearest,

I did not finish this letter yesterday because I fell asleep. Then I went into London streets again. I had a very nice but very little dinner in a French restaurant of Soho, and afterwards walked and walked. I like London more and more, the only bad thing is I do not work at all since a long time, and yet I long to work and I must do it. I do not know the name of the magazine I am writing for, it does not exist yet, it will begin in October. It belongs to the group of *Time*, *Life*, and so on; so I am not very proud to write in it, I'll do it just once. Do you know? I received many letters from America about my article in the *N.Y. Times*. Some people seemed glad to read harsh criticism about their country, other ones were not so pleased. It is strange to hear English spoken around me, and yet to be so far from you, to hear your language and not to be in America. I looked often at the little pictures while writing to you, I told them many things: many tender, loving words. Did you hear them? You must hear them and feel my arms around you, I love you.

Your Simone

Saturday, 19th July 1947

My beloved one,

I was sad yesterday in the Golden Arrow because I thought I should not find any letter in the hotel pigeon-hole, and there they were, two of them! I do not know what you have made with your schedule, you mixed up everything, I am so happy of it. Two long loving letters which made me feel so near you. Just as you ask: "Do you feel we have got closer?" I wrote to you: "It seems to me we are nearer than ever." Yes. That is true. Something happened when we parted, that is, we began to understand what had happened, and it was love. Afterwards, I thought, I was amazed, I knew. And as sure as I have a heart, I know we shall not be disappointed in each other. Dearest, you will put your arm round my waist, and kiss me, and be my husband again.

So, I stayed in London one day more. We went on loitering in the streets and liking the old fashioned town very much. On Thursday evening it was the first performance of Sartre's plays in a little art theater of Hammersmith, that is one of the nicest boroughs of London. There was the beautiful Rita Hayworth, bright as an evening star. The first play *Men Without Shadows* was half killed, because the interesting point is Sartre showed French "miliciens" torturing and killing French "résistants": French young men on both side, all of them French and young and some of them having done a bad choice, and the others a right one. That was the very harsh and crude and non-conventional thing. But the English director was afraid and he cut nearly everything about the bad French "miliciens," and what he did not suppress he did not understand; so he left only an heroic story of good French "résistants" struggling against nobody. I was very angry with it though the actors acted very well. The second play was wonderfully acted; it is called *The Respectful Whore*. It is the story of a young prostitute whose conscience is all mixed up by 100 per cent American powerful well-speaking people of the South, and who is inducted to give a false testimony against a poor innocent Negro. It is very harsh about America—about the

South states of America. English people love and hate American people as twin brothers can do, so they were delighted with the satire; the mere fact of hearing American accents on the stage made them laugh to tears, they caught every point and it was a real triumph with Sartre being brought on the stage, very clumsy and shy and silent. Afterwards there was a party; you could think it would be rather bright with Sartre who has good brain and Rita Hayworth who has such good looks. But is was really funny (in a way). I never saw such a dull supper. We went to a little sad dining room and we sat at small tables; Sartre was alone in a corner, eating sadly some corned-beef, and I sat in front of Rita Hayworth, trying to speak with her, and looking at her beautiful shoulders and breasts which could have made so many men crazy but which were so useless for me. She was very bored, and Sartre very bored too, and everybody was bored. So we left as soon as we could. Yesterday, we rode the Golden Arrow and crossed the sea; Sartre and I and the little frog-looking man, so excited about women during the whole trip, he was really disgusting.

Darling, now it is midnight, I have worked very much today and seen some people and I am back in the little pink room and I just read your letter once more. It happens very often I just should have to copy your own letters to tell you what I feel: "I did not think I could miss anybody so hardly. If I were to hold you just now I should cry with pain and happiness." I am glad to suffer by you, I am glad to miss you so badly since you miss me too. I feel as if I were you and you were me. You'll believe in me as I'll believe in you, whatever happens, and we shall never feel apart anymore. There will never be anything but love between us. I wait for you, I long for you. Take me in your arms and kiss me and make me your wife once more.

Your own Simone

Wednesday, 23 Juillet 1947

My own beloved one,

No new letters from you, indeed, since I got two letters last week, so I just read the old ones again. You know, I do not disapprove so much of your gambling. If you really work during the day, why not? The only important thing is to work well when you work, and when you do not and look for some rest you can do what you like. I rather drink, but drinking is not better than gambling, nor worse. I think I drink a little too much just now because I miss you so much. I did not think it would happen this way. Nelson, darling, you are the nicest man in the world, it is so nice the way you say you wish to make everything right for my coming back, but just wish. If you are still living and still loving me, what else? There is nothing to do. Well, if you can buy a car for ten bucks, and if you know how to manage it, it will be very pleasant, but with buses and planes, with just buses without planes, with steak and corn in the little kitchen, even with just corn without steak, we shall be happy, shall we not? You know I am not smart, I can live on bread and potatoes, water and love. You have nothing to care about.

In a way I am a little afraid, it is true, This afternoon I saw Sartre's movie,[1] it is over now, rather good, but not as good as it could have been. No matter, it is not the question. The question is I was a little disturbed by the story. It is the story of a dead man and a dead woman meeting each other and loving each other: and as they are in love they are allowed to come back to earth: if they succeed in making this love a real living human one, they will live a whole human life once more; if not, they will die again. And indeed, they fail. It is very moving and I thought of you and me. We love each other through remembrances and hopes, through distance and letters: shall we succeed in making this love a happy living human love? We must. I believe we shall, but it will not be so easy. Nelson, I love you. But do I deserve your love if I do not give you my life? I tried to explain to you I cannot give my life to you.[2] Do you understand it? Are you not resentful about it? Will you never be? Will you always believe yet it is really love I am giving to you? Maybe I should not ask these questions, it hurts me to put them so harshly. But then I cannot escape, I ask these questions to myself. I am not to lie to you, to hide something from you. I think I am so disturbed since two months because the question is in my heart and my heart aches with it: Is it right to give something of oneself without being ready to give everything? May I love him and tell him I love him without intending to give my whole life if he asked for it? Will he never hate me? Nelson, my love, it would be easier for me not to speak about it. It would be easy since you never did, but you said so nicely we cannot ever lie or be silent with each other. I should hate any kind of bad feeling, of deception, resentment between us. Well, now it is written, so let it be. Do not answer if you do not like to do, we'll speak about it when we'll meet. You remember I told you once I respected you so much: that is why I wrote this last page. I do not mean you ask for my life, but just this: when we shall meet again, we do not know what will happen, I just know that whatever happens, I could never give everything to you, and I just feel bad about it. Oh, darling, it is the hell to be far away and unable to look at each other when you speak about such important things. Do you feel it is love to try to speak the truth yet, more than just saying "I love you"? Do you feel I want to deserve your love as much as I want your love? You must read this letter with a very loving heart, with my head on your shoulder. Maybe it will sound very childish to you because all what I say, you knew it already. I just could not help to write it this evening. Our love must be true, we must succeed when we'll meet. I hope in you as well as in me. Whatever you think, kiss me very hard.

Your Simone

1) *Les jeux sont faits* (*The Chips Are Down*). 2) Algren had just written that he hoped her next visit would be permanent.

✴ *July 23, 1947—Algren responded that he had planned to ask de Beauvoir to marry him when she returned. He would have preferred to wait until they were together to broach such a serious issue, but her letter of the 23rd made him come to his senses.*

For each of them, marriage would have meant giving up a substantial part of their worlds. How could they uproot themselves, from Paris or Chicago, without committing a sort of spiritual and creative suicide? He felt more married to her than he ever had to his real wife in the seven years of their marriage (1938–1945). Gratefully, he agreed to a less than conventional relationship: after a period of time together, she would leave; if he could, he would join her in France, and then he would go home. They agreed there would be no scenes, no melodrama.

Samedi, 28th Juillet 1947

Nelson, my love,

I write today on this bright blue paper because there is a bright blue hope in my heart: something very happy is going to happen to us. If there is nothing new, I am coming to Wabansia in the beginning of September, exactly from the 7th to the 20th—nearly two weeks to spend together in our goat-nest, in each other's arms. I'll take an airplane directly from Paris to Chicago on the 6th at night and I'll arrive on the 7th at eighteen o'clock of your time, at Chicago local time. You will not come to the airport because there are tedious formalities to do, it is very long and I should not like to feel you are nearby, not being able to see you, then the airport is not a nice place for a husband and wife meeting. Please, you'll wait for me in our house, you'll have got some nice whisky to drink and ham and jam to eat because I shall be very thirsty, and hungry and tired. You'll have much love to give too, whole cans and bottles of the best Chicago local love you can buy at your grocer's. Dearest, I do not even try to say how happy I am; well, it happened rather suddenly, I knew I could dispose of two weeks in September but Chicago seemed so far away. I was shy in thinking of coming as you were when I asked you to come to New York. Yet, I knew I could get the money at my publisher's if I really wanted to,[1] and I asked myself; what means the words "far away"? What is a twenty-four hours airplane trip if you really wish to see the man you love? As soon as asked, the question was answered, I understood I could go, and so it was decided I should go. I rushed to a travel agency and I learnt I could have a reservation for the 6th September, coming back the 20th. My visa is always all right, I have nothing to do but pay the ticket and go to the airplane. It is really not much. I shall have no money, only fifty dollars, but I think it does not matter even if you are poor at that time. You are not to reserve any room for me, are you? And we shall eat in the little kitchen, and we might stay there the whole days, speaking, and working a little, listening to records, and loving each other. I pay the return ticket, too, with French money. I cannot think of anything but these very mean, practical things. I cannot write about anything else; I am too much excited. Yesterday I found your dear letter, you told me, "Now you know you have to come back to me." And I said "Yes!" I know it so well that I am coming back, I could not help it. And it was pleasant and strange to think that you did not knew yet that indeed I was coming. At the same time I received the big book, the little paper about Chicago and poetry. Thank you, I liked it. Yes I know Dreiser's works, I read nearly all of them. The title "The Dead, the Drunk and the Dying" is not bad indeed, maybe it is even really good.

Nelson, my beloved husband, within six weeks I shall be in your arms.

Your Simone

---

1) Sartre encouraged her to go, even offering her the money for the trip.

My beloved one, my dearest husband,

I was awakened this morning by your wire and had a pang in the heart as if you had knocked yourself at my door. I think when I shall see you for good my legs and whole body will come limp, even just thinking of it I feel over-whelmed by something too strong for me. I am so happy, Nelson, now I know you know that I am coming, within five weeks I shall kiss you, it seems a dream. I have not much to say because I am too disturbed by this idea of seeing you, it kills the pleasure of writing, it is talking I want. It is dreadly hot in Paris since a week, the hottest summer ever seen in this town, everybody is melting in water. Just now writing to you I must stop at every other minute to wipe my face with my handkerchief, my whole body is per-spiring; all people are murdered by heat, I have bad dreams and drink too much and I hardly work, I am pleased to go away. The only bad point is I shall have no letter from you before a week. I take the airplane tomorrow at noon for Copenhagen with Sartre, I'll stay there four or five days, then I shall go to Swedish lakes and to Stockholm, to the northern mountains and back to Stockholm; then about 3 or 4th September airplane to Paris and 6th evening, airplane to Chicago. They will send me your letters at Stockholm, write there, "General Delivery," until the end of August; and I should love to get a letter in Paris when coming back, just before flying to you.

I had another dear letter from you. Yes I know Jack London, I read nearly all of his books when I was a young girl and afterwards — some of them, and chiefly Martin Eden, I was very fond of. Well, you insult me when you seem to think I am really a bit of a party-woman. In fact I never go to parties in Paris, I loathe it, and I am not altogether too well dressed; I never waste any time about dressing. When it happens that I have a nice coat or dress, I like it, but I do not care for it. I'll try to be very stylish when I shall come to Wabansia but it is only because Wabansia is such a smart place and I want you to be proud of your wife. When I looked at you from head to feet, I am sure I was not cool at all, but rather very interested and a little anxious, asking to myself: "Who is he?" So next time do not waste too much time trying to be smart.

Well, I'll say good bye, no leisure for a long letter today. I must pack every thing and do things I never do and hate to do; such as washing, mending stockings, putting order in my papers, and so on. So good bye, good bye my beloved one, my husband. I have no need to write today, knowing I'll see you so soon. I shall sleep in your arms; when I shall open my eyes at morning I shall see your face smiling at me. I love your smile so much, and your dear voice. Now all memories are promises. To remember is to hope, and I have so much to remember.

I love you; I'll be your Wabansia wife.

Your Simone

Nelson, my beloved husband,

In a month I shall be with you in the Wabansia home. I never was so happy since I went away. The idea of coming back makes everything around me still more pleasant than it is. I arrived in Copenhagen Friday evening and I like the town; I'll tell you everything in the right order.

Well, I had a very busy morning, Friday, looking for papers and money and doing all I had to do before leaving; then after a hasty lunch I went to the airport and took place in the nicest airplane I ever saw, all white and red inside, with little tables in front of each seat, it looked like a toy. I slept a great deal and I thought, "in a month the plane will bring me to Chicago, I shall be going to my beloved local youth." When landing, we had a very unpleasant shock: ten men were on the ground with Kodaks to shoot poor Sartre who thought that he was coming incognito. They shoot him and me too and took us to a little room where they kept us a quarter of an hour asking questions for an interview. Sartre had many plays acted here and Danish people like him very much, chiefly because he took something of is philosophy from Kierkegaard, and Kierkegaard is, with Andersen, the great man of Denmark. So they asked questions about Kierkegaard and Andersen. Then we went to the hotel and we were afraid people should be very boring, but they just published huge photos of Sartre in the newspapers with long articles in first page and nothing else happened. It is a very little quiet country, they have not much to do and the least thing is for them an important event. Did you ever read Andersen's tales when you were a boy? I read them passionately and I think he is more than a children's writer; I really like him. And I like him more being in Copenhagen because he really felt the town very well; it is exactly the human world of which he speaks in his tales: the soldiers in front of the king's palace, the ducks in the pools, the flowers on the market place look exactly like toys. There are strange green fountains, green statues and palaces in the town, decorated with monsters, dragons, sirens and swans. What is really nice is the port, with the white ships, the canals, the women in peasant clothes selling hard-smelling fish. It is a very quiet town, but there is a very funny unquiet place called Tivoli; it is a big garden with cafés, restaurants, scenic railways, little ponds, marvelous lights, waterfalls and so on; it is full of people, half smart, half popular and rather nice in a cheap way. At midnight, before closing, they have fireworks; just now, writing to you in my hotel room, I see the fireworks bursting in the sky with a big noise. The best thing in Copenhagen is the port, there are a lot of little cafés and dancings along the pier. Tonight I went in these dancings and drank schnaps. There are many kinds of people, sailors chiefly, but students too and rather pretty girls, all of them more or less drunk. I thought I should like so much to have much money, (or you would have), and we should go through old Europe together and see Anvers, Amsterdam, Copenhagen. I should like so much that you would see these places, you would like them.

Well, I had a fine life here. The idea was to work in the morning and at the end of the afternoon, and to look at the town for some hours in the day and in the evening. It happened that I often slept instead of working, I don't know why I am so sleepy all this time, maybe I am a little tired. Anyway, I work a little and I enjoy it. One pleasant thing here was to find fresh air; it is a rest after the dreadly heat in Paris.

Dearest, I hope I shall find letters from you in Stockholm. I long for letters and I long much more for you. You know how much I love you. Take my love and my kisses, and go on waiting for me as I wait for you.

Your Simone

Thursday, 7th to Sunday,
10th August 1947

My beloved Nelson,

I write to you from your ancestral land. It is a rocky Swedish island, very lonely and sad and beautiful, all surrounded by a grey sea: it looks like a moon landscape and you feel very near the North Pole. I spent the Monday in Copenhagen and I began to think it was a rather sad, mean town. I chiefly worked the whole day; in the evening I went to the Tivoli fairyland and saw a pantomime in the old Italian style; it was pleasant because it was acted in open air and many fair little children laughed at it (the hair of children is marvellous in these countries, so fair it is nearly white) but it was not too good. We went to the little sailor-dancings which I like: how these people drink! They really can drink! The next day I worked very nicely the whole morning, and in the afternoon we rode the train to Elsinore; we saw the castle, Hamlet's castle: it is a Renaissance castle, very fine with its green roof and grey stone, but nothing to do with Shakespeare. We got across the channel on a ferry-boat and landed in Sweden, at Hälsingborg. There, it became a difficult and very funny situation. Sartre was to receive money from a Swedish businessman at the Grand Hôtel: but it was not there, so we had not a penny, and we could not find any room in the whole town. He went to the French consul to borrow money, but he was not a real consul, just an old Swedish crook who knew nothing about Sartre and would not lend a penny. Yet, while we were phoning to Stockholm without success and becoming a bit anxious, the porter of the hotel told us he had rooms for us since Sartre is Sartre, and newspaper men came and shot us, and at dinner we had a French flag on the table yet not a penny in our pocket, and not knowing at all how to get money. Well, money came the next morning indeed, just as huge pictures of Sartre appeared in the newspapers and the consul phoned, apologizing and offering money. It was not very new for us; it happened often that we found ourselves without a cent in a very faraway foreign land, and always it had some issue.

Yesterday, we spent a working morning, and the whole afternoon we were in the train for Göteborg, all along the coast which is rocky, grey, sad, and lovely in its sad way. The earth was covered with golden corn and dark pines, that is a rather unusual mixture. I read a little, and looked very much, and dreamt much too. Then we arrived Göteborg, and though we never say where we go and try to be very secret, there was a man waiting for us at the station and newspaper men at the hotel. But they did not bore us a long time. Göteborg seemed very pleasant at night because it is a port and I always like to see water glittering in the dark, but in daylight it is very dull. So we went away by boat, it was wonderful journey, the sea was silver-grey, both glittering and sad, and the boat sailed among hundreds and hundreds of deserted rocky islands; I felt quite lost in this wide sea, far from earth, on a strange planet. The weather is so mild, too, there was a very reluctant sun hidden behind clouds. Then I arrived on this little island. you know, I have worked very well this whole week, the long chapter about women is done and I'll begin again to write about America. I am no more sleepy; I do not drink any more, so I am very relaxed, everything is fine for me and in a month I shall see you again. I'll have so many things to tell you! So much love to give to you.

I spent two fine days. I got up early enough and worked four hours before lunch, a nice lunch with much fish and akvavit, the Swedish "eau de vie." Today I am writing to you from another boat. It is 10 A.M. and the boat just started, a small one with nice tiny berths and not too many people on it; just now I am sitting in an armchair on the deck, and there is plenty of sun on my face and we glide slowly between green meadows and woods. Poor Sartre is having an interview with a newspaper woman who pursued him into the boat. In the lonely island too we found newspaper people and they shot us. I do not know why Sartre is so popular in Scandinavia. It is so more funny because in France on the contrary everybody is spitting at his face. But here his name is a kind of Sesame[1] and I am even afraid we'll be rather bored in Stockholm. From Stockholm we'll go to the north, to see the Lapps and the midnight sun on the icy mountains. Nobody speaks French here, so I always speak English and as they speak worse English than mine, it seems to me that English is my native language. I'll be very disappointed in Chicago when we shall not understand each other, and you'll pretend it is all my fault. Swedish people do not look a bit like you, no more than Jews do; you seem to be a very peculiar specimen. It is not very easy to write in the wind; I am afraid my writing is worse than ever. Let us plan something. First you must take care there will be no "fou," no "gendarme," nobody but the Tiger in the little house the first evening, neither on the following evenings indeed. Just you and me and the Tiger. And indeed nobody must know I am in Chicago, it is all a secret. Then I want to go to the stockyards once, everybody here reproaches me for not having gone. Then do you care for painting? Shall we go together to the Art Institute and look at the beautiful French paintings? Sure, we'll do, and maybe once we'll hear some jazz. But sight-seeing is not the important thing, you know, it is Nelson-seeing I want, seeing and kissing and loving. At night we'll stay in the little home and hear records and drink . . . will it be South Confort? I should rather like whisky if possible. And you'll tell me everything about yourself, and I'll tell you everything about myself, and I'll teach you French. Then if we have time left we shall work a little in the day: here are my plans. Which are yours? I hope we shall not be disappointed in each other, having expected so much. Indeed, I am sure I shall not be, I could not be, but maybe I shall be very tired by the 24 hours airplane trip and very disturbed by seeing you; so if you do not find me such as you had dreamed, if I am cool and aloof or more silly or less smart than you thought, wait until the next day. Dearest, tell me something very important: is it warm or cold in Chicago in September? Must I bring summer dresses or woolen clothes? Tell me too, if there something you should like from Paris, besides your own girl? Nelson, my love, I write all that in a bad way, but the fact is when I think of seeing you, of feeling you, I become all dizzy in my head; it seems my heart will burst. All day long I think of it, and often it is so strong I can hardly bear it, my throat becomes so tight and my mouth dry. It will come true, in less than a month it will come true. You know how it will be, Nelson, you know.

Your Simone

1) "Sesame" in French; "password" in English.

Wednesday, 13th August 1947

Nelson, my love,

I got your letters this afternoon at Stockholm, and I went in a little conditorei opposite to the central post and read them. I felt overwhelmed with love and the whole day I thought "I love you so much." Now it is midnight and I am dead tired but I must write to you to say "I love you so much." It is strange how quickly I understand you and you understand me, it is one of the most precious things in our love, this understanding. Yes, when I wrote the serious composed letter I meant exactly what you understood; and I am so glad to see that you admit that sometimes not to be able to give one's life does not mean you do not love much, because I know both things are true: in a way our lives are to stay apart and yet I love you so much. It is true what you say: we'll have much more, we'll love much more than many married people; we'll meet in love and leave in love and be happy together or miss each other always in love. And just now let us be happy and think of our meeting: three weeks. The cab will stop, I'll go up the stairs and open the door, and in a blink you'll be here and I'll feel your arms around me. My beloved unmarried husband, I want you as much as you want me.

Yes, I should be interested in visiting the country jail; yes, I should enjoy some bathing on a shore. I have a blue bathing suit, not very daring but convenient. We shall do all what you'll like since we are alone, just you and me, nobody else.

So I write from Stockholm, it is a fine town. I spent two more days on the nice little boat, gliding on the canals and the lakes very quietly, writing and reading and thinking of you. Every day we stopped for two hours in some nice old town, and every day there were some students or newspaper men to ask interviews and take pictures. It looked like a regular joke. And when we arrived in Stockholm, yesterday evening, there were twelve people at least with flowers and so on to wait for Sartre and me: they shot and shot and asked questions and invited us to dinners and parties which we refused as much as we could. In another country such things never happened. Swedish people have nothing to do, they yawn their whole life away, they are always bored so they like to bore other people and try to find some fun in them. I was mad with anger the whole evening though Stockholm was so fine in the night with the bright water and glittering lights. I must say the people who take care of us (they give us the money they owe to us and feel very generous and friendly doing so) had reserved rooms in the nicest hotel I ever saw.

Well, it is Thursday now because I fell asleep yesterday evening. There is a very old district in Stockholm, from the xviiith and even older, which is really fine and I walked there the whole morning. I had a lunch in an old restaurant with a cave: it looked like a play in a theater. I ate all kinds of caviar and wonderful fishes. In the afternoon I went to find your letters, and then to the Frisor to have my hair washed. At five o'clock our Swedish friends took us to a kind of park which is very interesting: it is a little rocky island in which people have brought or built all kinds of old houses and shops, farms, chemistry, hand-printing press, old grocery and so on. The old farms chiefly with the old furniture and embroidery and everything are wonderful. I enjoyed seeing these things, but then we had a dreadful dinner with French "important" people and Swedish, and French flags on the table, and newspaper men. I was as angry as you can be at a family dinner, and anger when it is so strong makes me nearly sick. I drank as much as I could of akvavit, and wine, and cognac, but it was not enough. Yet the sunset was very long and beautiful from the top of the hill—where the dinner took place; we saw the dark green water, and the lights of the town and a big sky, and the whole town with its green roofs. We went away as soon as we could and had a little quiet walk by ourselves afterwards.

Today I worked the whole morning and walked in the streets. What is interesting here is it is a very modern young town, except the nice old district, but the architecture is really good. It is the best modern town I ever saw. It is difficult to explain why but I'll try when we'll meet.

Yesterday at dinner the French people looked at my ring and said it was beautiful and asked from where it came. I was very proud about it — for a minute I was less angry with them.

Good bye Nelson, my love, good bye. I'll see you soon. I kiss you. I love you more than ever.

Your Simone

Castle Hotel, Stockholm
Monday, 18th August 1947

Dearest,

Within three weeks, it will just be 9 A.M. in Chicago. I'll open an eye and I'll see beside me the "nice man" I had just forgotten while sleeping. I'll wake up for the first time in the Wabansia home. I saw a book of yours, in a library where I was buying some American books: Thomas Wolfe, Fitzgerald, and mysteries for the journey on train. I should have liked to put a little flag on the book saying: "you must read this one, it is a good book, by the nicest man in the world." I like so much the way you are, so greedy about life and yet so quiet, your eager greediness and your patience, and your way of not asking much of life and yet taking much because you are so human and alive that you find much in everything. I thought about your humour and your tenderness, such as I found it in you and in our books, and I fell in love with you once more, my sweet crocodile-man.

I spent some quiet nice days in Stockholm, working much at the book about America. I am not really writing, but just remembering; I mean, I write everything I remember without trying to make it good, it is very pleasant for me. Friday I had a very smart evening. I was invited with Sartre to the castle of Prince Wilhelm, who is the second son of the King; he knows Sartre and was nice with him in former times, and we had to go. It was not unpleasant because he is very simple and not stupid; and then I enjoyed seeing a true aristocrat, which never happened to me. But the pity was he lives at 100km from Stockholm and one of our dreadful, stupid, boring friends (what a friend!) took us in his car at 11 in the morning in order not

61

be late for dinner at 6! I never saw any people as slow as the Swedish. I loathe them. So we had to leave work and rest, and to ride the car from 11. I must acknowledge that we went to a very beautiful old castle on the bank of a large blue lake and we visited it. But then we had to lunch with him, and I could not say a word, I was too angry. One of the tyres bursted, and neither Sartre neither the Swedish man could mend it; they had to wait for people who helped us. We arrived about 6, indeed, and were shot many times by newspaper men, but then we had nice scotch and soda, and local schnaps, and the best French dinner. The house was really beautiful, with a great view on the country, and many nice old Swedish things in it. There was only the Swedish friend, Sartre and myself, with the Prince and his wife, who is an old French lady. We drank coffee in the garden. Coming back to the car we saw the most marvellous thing: they call it nordish light, in French we say *aurore boréale*. Do you know what it is? The whole sky is lighted as by strange lighthouse of every color, greenish, reddish, white; it is a kind of phantom-light, a little frightful. It comes from the pole, they say. I thought of Edgar Poe. By the way, why do you American people not like Poe more than you do? But maybe you do? What about it?

I am in a hurry because I am going away by train to the north, it is a twenty-four hours journey and I enjoy the idea of it. First I'll go to the post-office to see if there is a new letter of the man I love. Dearest, write to Paris now. I'll be back the 3rd September, I have the tickets. And the 6th, away to Chicago. It is hard to believe you really are as nice as I think. Don't become different. Nelson, my dearest unmarried husband, how much I love you. Kisses and kisses.

Your Simone

Wednesday, 20th August 1947

My beloved nice man, my own Nelson,

I feel so happy writing to you from this beautiful place. Now it is a quarter past ten, a month ago there was the midnight sun, here. We are 1500km from Stockholm (about 1000 miles), we have passed the Arctic Circle, very far in the north, farther than Iceland. The nights are wonderful: the sun sleeps a little, two or three hours every night, but the sky remains white and you see no star. The hotel is the only house in the place with the little railway station; in front of the hotel is a big sad, beautiful lake surrounded with mountains, not very high mountains, but yet they have some snow on the top. The lake too is white all night in a strange glittering way. There is no village for hundreds of miles, not even a road coming here, just a railway with four or five trains moaning every day. When you look at the landscape you know there is nobody nowhere and you feel on the moon rather than on earth. Would you like to be on the moon with me, darling, or would you be afraid?

I was a little disappointed Monday because there was no letter from you at the General Delivery. Maybe you did not understand I was staying in Sweden so long? I miss your letters very much. I cannot go on reading always over the ones I got a week ago. Yet I am not too sad because I feel you are so near now; in little more than two weeks I'll touch you, see you, kiss you, speak to you. I don't intend to be "serious," but I intend to speak. Do you remember how pleasant it was to lie quietly in the twin beds in New York and to speak in a very relaxed confident way?

So, after having been a little disappointed I went to the train and was very glad to say good-bye to the Swedish man who took so much care of us in Stockholm; well, he is not wicked but so stubbornly stupid you should like better wicked. I waved my hand very heartily when the train went away, so that he must have felt something and we did not see him the last three days. We arrived at Abisko; the hotel is very nice, with huge windows everywhere so you do not feel shut in, and yet very warm. I took some walks but I chiefly enjoy staying in my room and writing my book about America, and from time to time looking at the strange, beautiful, always changing landscape. I read a little too, Fitzgerald's novel, *Tender is the Night*, but I like better *Great Gatsby*. I began *Of Time and the River* but it seems a hard job. Some mysteries, too, I enjoy them. And always thinking of you with love and happiness.

Darling, would you do something for me? Indeed you would. I should like to get a whole collection of some newspapers, like *New York Times*, or *Chicago Tribune*, or *Chicago Sun*, of the time I was in America, that is from 1st February to 18th May. Do you think it is possible? Any one of them would fit. Maybe I should like to have all the *Times* of the same period. Can you get them for me so that I find them when coming? But do not bother too much about it, I am not in a hurry anyway. Do it, please, just if it does not bother you. What could I do for you? Give me a nice idea. Tell me at least what I could bring to you from Paris, besides my heart. Now I'll go to sleep, I'll write a little more tomorrow.

I worked the whole morning, now it is half past one. I feel dreadfully hungry. I like the way you eat here: they put all the dishes on a large table and you go and take all you want and bring it to your own little table and eat it; it is very quickly done. I became crazy with the slowness in Stockholm. So, going to eat, I kiss you once more. Kisses and love, my dearest own Nelson.

Your Simone

Saturday, 23th August 1947

My own Nelson,

I do not like not to have letters from you. I should have said at Stockholm to send them here, but then I was not sure to like the place and to stay, and I did not want them to get lost. So I'll have another week to wait before hearing anything from you. I hope you still live in Wabansia, you are not ill, you have not decided not to love me anymore, and you wait for me on the 7th September.[1]

It is always very fine to be here. Yesterday I took a little trip in motor-boat, around the lake I have spoken to you of. We stopped on the other bank, and had a little walk in the steep forest, link-forests all littered with nice little red and blue berries. We saw some Lapp people who live in some huts, wooden and earthen huts, but rather confortable. They are dressed with bright gay clothes, but very ugly. Today I worked four hours and after lunch I went to the top of a mountain from which it was said the view was wonderful: it was indeed. I like very much climbing mountains, do you? Often I take a little rucksack and go away for one or two or three weeks, as I did in Corsica, and climb on mountains. This one was not very high, nor very steep, no more than two hours going up and one hour going down; yet, as this country is very wild, when you are 3000 feet high, you find yourself among sad rocks, on a black land where no plant grows and not far away from big patches of snow. It looked really weird and lonely and a little scaring, and yet you could see the sweet blue lake at your feet. I like the whole thing very much. I'll stay three more days here, then go for a trip in motor-boat (about four days) and be back in Stockholm next Sunday. The other Sunday will be Chicago.

My beloved one, since you like to plan things, you have only to plan what you would like to do with me, and I'll enjoy doing them. I enjoy doing things you like to do, even if it is going to the horse-races or base-ball game. And if you plan nothing, it will be all right too. Everything will be all right if you are near me and if you love me. For I come for nothing else than being near you and loving you. I'll wire to you from Paris on the 4th or 5th September to say exactly at what time I am due.

Feel how much I love you, please feel it just now, because just now I love you so much.

Your Simone

1) In fact, her flight was delayed two days.

✳ *On Tuesday, September 9, Simone de Beauvoir boarded a flight for Chicago. It was a turbulent trip, one she would never forget: twelve hours from Shannon to the Azores in an old plane whose engine failed, a 180-degree turn over the ocean to get back to Shannon, hours of fear, and a two-day delay for repairs. In the Azores, a tire blew out as they landed; another eighteen-hour wait. Finally, a bumpy crossing through several storms and a drop of 1500 meters.*

De Beauvoir left Chicago on September 23. During this trip, she explored the city in depth. She and Algren planned to travel together for several months in the spring.

Friday, 26th Septembre 1947

Nelson, my love,

Today I begin to miss you and wait for you, to wait for the blessed day when you hold me again in your strong loving arms. It hurts very much, Nelson, but I am glad it hurts so much because this hard pain is love and I know you love me too. You so near and so far away, so far and so near, my beloved one. So, the cab went away, and I passed Rago's funeral home, and the pizzeria where I was so happy, drinking Chianti and smiling to you, and many shops and streets which I did not know but which were Chicago. Then I arrived to the airport; it was too early, so I sat and closed my eyes. After some time a man came with a little box and said to me, "Miss de Beauvoir, you must have some friends here, this is for you." I looked at the beautiful white flowers, smelling so sweetly and put them on my heart. I did not cry then; I just went to the phone and called you. There was your beloved voice, so near, so far; and when I hung up, something broke up in my heart, something which will remain silent and cold, dead, until the blessed day when you kiss me again. It is difficult to write, because writing to you I cannot help crying madly. I love you so much.

Well, at eleven we went to the airplane, but they soon told us to go down: the starter did not start. We came back at midnight and went away. For hours and hours we flew between clouds and stars, then between sea and sky, while the flowers faded quietly on my heart. I was a little scared and could not sleep. I read some mysteries, and the plays, and the book about Philippines that you bought for me. From time to time I drank whisky from the bottle you bought for me. Doing so many things for me, so quietly and tenderly. Love was everywhere, in the smell of flowers, and the taste of whisky, in the color of the paperback books so precious, so sweet, and so painful.

It was only twenty-three hours to arrive to Paris, we landed at six, it was dawn. I was very tired after two nights without sleep. I drank coffee and took two little pills in order to keep myself awake through the long day. Paris was very beautiful, a little foggy, with a mild grey sky, and the smell of dying leaves. I was very glad to find I had much to do here, so much to do that I shall go to the country only next month. First the radio gives to the *Temps modernes* a full hour each week to speak about what we like in the way we like. You know what it means? The possibility of reaching thousands of people, and trying to make them think and feel in the way we believe right to think and feel. This must be managed with much care and we had a kind of conference this morning to speak about it. Then the Socialist Party whishes to confer with us, to try to make a connexion between policy and philosophy. People here seem to begin to believe ideas are something important. Then, there were letters of many kinds, and for the magazine itself much work to do. I was glad; I want to work, to work very much. Because the reason I do not stay in Chicago is just this need I always felt in me to work and give my life a meaning by working. You have the same need, and that is one of the reasons for which we understand each other so well. You want to write books, good books, and by writing them to help the world to be a little better, I want it too. I want to convey to people the way of thinking which is mine and which I believe true. I should give up travels and all kinds of entertainments. I should give up friends and the sweetness of Paris to be able to remain forever with you;

but I could not live just for happiness and love, I could not give up writing and working in the only place where my writing and work may have a meaning. It is very hard, because I told you our work here is not very hopeful, and love and happiness are something so true, so sure. But yet, it has to be done. Among the lies of communism and of anticommunism, against this lack of freedom which happens nearly everywhere in France, something has to be done by people who can try to do it, and who care for it. My love, this does not make any discrepancy between us; on the contrary, I feel very near you in this attempt to struggle for what I feel true and good, just as you do yourself. But, knowing it is all right, I cannot help nevertheless to cry madly this evening, because I was so happy with you, I loved you so much, and you are far away.

Saturday

I was so tired, I slept fourteen hours, I just woke up once in the middle of the night to think of you and cry a little more. I was so ugly this morning by crying so hard that, meeting Camus in the street, he asked me if I was not pregnant: he told me I had the mask! I saw a young English man who has just translated my play *Useless Mouths* and would like to have it acted in England. I'll send to you his translation. I was too tired still today to begin to work; I just walked in Paris, which was lovely, and spoke with friends, and thought of you. It is not thinking; I belong to you and I just feel you with body, heart, soul, all day long, just as I feel myself.

Nelson, you were so nice and tender, and loving, and everything. I should thank you for all, for the flowers and the whisky, for the rum-cake and the candies, for your smiles and your kisses, your words and your silences, for the days and the night, for the love you give to me and the love I give to you: for everything. But there is no words to say, thanks. What you gave is too much. I can just say; I love you. It was so sweet to cry on your warm shoulder while the records were playing, and you told me with the voice I love, " I too am crying a little inside." Nelson my love, now I know how precious you are to me. As long as you love and want me, I know I'll do everything to share with you all that I have to share. Now I wait for your letters; I wait for spring and our life together. I wait with faith and hope, and with pain which is happiness too. "Roll me in your arms, my love." I am your loving little frog.

Your own Simone

Nelson my love,

Having slept fourteen hours from Friday to Saturday, and twelve hours the last night, I begin to feel a little better, I mean I am no more in a crying mood, and I am overwhelmed by the sweetness and the warmth of our love, instead of being crashed by the bitterness of departure. Yea, as you said, we are very lucky since we love each other so much. I am very lucky to feel again in my chest such a young heart. I can be happy; I can suffer because of you as if I were fifteen years old: that is youth, the power of suffering and being happy, and that is what you gave to me among so many beautiful gifts.

I was very busy today. At noon, these socialist guys of whom I spoke to you came with a big car and took us to the country, Merleau-Ponty[1] (one of the leaders of *Temps modernes*), Sartre and myself. We had a lunch with some old men and some younger ones and we spoke about a possible connexion between existentialism and socialism. I don't hope much, because this Socialist Party is very corny, very old and weak, yet, it is the only chance between conservative MRP[2] and the Communist Party.[3] So we have to try something with them and we shall do it: meetings and things of this kind. I'll tell you how it goes.

Then, I wrote some pages of the book about America. I should like to have it done when I come back to you. Then it was late, I had some dinner and I took a walk with Sartre on the banks of the Seine which were lovely with the moon shining in a mild sky; we spoke about the Socialist Party, indeed, then we went to see the nice painter of whom I spoke to you, André Masson,[4] who could not eat at a time, because he felt he was eating colors. He told us many strange stories about haunted houses, believing very steadily in ghosts and things of this kind without being too much disturbed by them. He told funny stories too about surrealism, which was something very glamourous when it was young, but very old-fashioned, and rather cold and dead now. Then I came back to my pink room and I write to you. I have some scotch left in the bottle you bought for me, and the Turkish cigarettes, and the giant matches, and I feel you so near that it seems to me I am going to see you tomorrow or the day after. Well, time does not matter so much, I'll see you again, I'll hear your voice, I'll see your smile, it will happen.

I'll send to you tomorrow morning the translation of my play[5] which was acted in winter 1945. My Russian friend played the part of Clarice. I know it has many faults but I should like you to read something from me. Tell me quite frankly what you think of it, even if you think it stinks. Now it is 6 o'clock in Chicago, maybe you are sitting in front of the typewriter and typing a short story. I know what you see from the window, I know how you look. O my love, try not to get married before spring, I want so deeply, so passionately to spend a long time with you. Where you'll choose, the way you'll choose, I do not care. But sleeping in your arms night after night, and seeing your dear smiling face morning after morning...We must have it, Nelson, we must. I'll do anything for it. Good night, my beloved one, my friend, husband and lover. We were so happy, we shall be so happy. I love you so much, my local youth, my crocodile, my own, Nelson.

Tuesday

The mornings are so hard, my love, when I open my eyes and you are not there. Last year my life here was full and rich, now everything is empty.

Well, yesterday I worked in the Café des Deux Magots and Koestler[6] came to see me, you know *Darkness at Noon* and the *A Spanish Testament*, which I think very good. I do not remember what you think about him as a writer; I believe I told you what a strange night we spent with him, Sartre and Camus, everybody being drunk and crying about friendship and political discrepancies; it was very funny. I like him and he has a very pretty sweet wife; we went together to an exhibition of pictures: Monet, Manet, Renoir, Toulouse-Lautrec, the same painters whom we saw together in the Chicago Museum, and so my heart was aching once more. What I did not tell you is that I happened last year to sleep with Koestler one night; it was rather strange because we were attracted by each other, but in the same time there were "political discrepancies." He thought I was not anticommunist enough. I do not care for such differences, but he does and so he was very challenging, and I hate challenge, chiefly in sexual business; so it never happened any more. What I felt yesterday anyway is this: it is true what you said once, you have not to be faithful in the conventional way if you don't feel like it. But for myself, I just know I could not sleep with any man now until I meet you again. I just could not bear to feel another man's hands or lips when I long so bitterly for your beloved hands and kips. I'll be faithful as a dutiful and conventional wife just because I could not help it — that is the way it is.

Coming back to the Deux Magots I found Jean Genet, the pederast-burglar. He was very nice and funny but I could not work; and other people came afterwards and I wasted the morning, so I decided to stay in my room the morning and just now I have some tea and bread and jam and I am going to work at home, it is better.

Towards evening I met Sartre and the man of the radio. We'll have half an hour each week to speak about social and political business. We begin Saturday. I spoke of this piece you and Motley[7] have done about juvenile delinquency; they were enthousiastic. They said it was just the kind of thing we were to do about anti-Semitism and colonialism and so on. But it will be much work even if some young friends help us. Now not only socialists but the anarcho-syndicalists ask for us to help them with an ideology; it is much more interesting because they are young and daring and really working people. We shall meet them. But what is sad is that all these opportunities of doing something real and concrete just come when there is nothing to hope. Everybody here thinks it will be the war within two years. What do you think?

Paris is lovely now. We sat at the terrace of a café, on the Boulevard Montparnasse, and we spoke about Hegel whom we are studying together and who is a very difficult philosopher. I worked very nicely the whole day; that is the only thing which really helps me. I went to the *Temps modernes* to read letters and answer to them, and I wrote my book. I learnt that the issue of *Politics* in which there is one of my articles, and some by Sartre and Merleau-Ponty, is the issue of July-August. I should be glad if you read it. I have lots of things to tell you because I think much about you and me, nice things. I'll tell them tomorrow. Now I'll just say good-bye and mail this letter. There is so much love in this little letter that the airplane could break. I wait for our letter very feverishly.

Good night, honey. I love you so much, I have no words to say it.

Your own Simone

1) Maurice Merleau-Ponty (1908–1961). French philosopher and writer, co-editor of *Les Temps modernes* from 1945 to 1952. 2) *Mouvement Républicain Populaire* (Popular Republican Movement). The new party of the Catholic Left founded in France in 1944, at its peak during the postwar period. It disappeared with the decline of the Fourth Republic in 1958. 3) *Parti Communiste Francais* (PCF). Founded in 1920 by the left wing of the French Socialist party, the PCF played an important role in the French Resistance. 4) André Masson (1896–1987), French surrealist painter. 5) *Les Bouches inutiles*. 6) Arthur Koestler (1905–1983). Hungarian-born British novelist, journalist, and critic. 7) Algren's friend Willard Motley, black American author of *Knock on Any Door*.

Nelson, my love,

I got this morning a nice letter and I read it lovingly, but now I must wait for a week before getting another one, and once more I feel bitterly how far away you are. You asked me once if I were a child or a wise woman. I do not feel childish but I am sure I am not very wise. A wise woman would not miss you so painfully.

Something happened when we said good bye in New York, and it was the beginning of love. But something happened too when I found you again in the Wabansia home and I stood quivering in your arms, and it was the fulfillment of love. I am not wise but rather a bit coward, and until my coming back to Paris I was a little reluctant, a little afraid to admit love in all its deepness and strength. Loving you so much means I can suffer very much because of you, when I say good bye, when you are ill-tempered or chiefly if you would love me less. It means now my happiness is in your hands, and in a way I should rather have kept it in mine. But, well, it is done now; I cannot help it any more. I have to admit this dependence, and I do it willingly since I love you. Something has made me uneasy since a certain evening in Wabansia and I have to talk to you about it: when I spoke of my coming to America in spring, I do not know why I spoke rather casually of spending a long time with you. I spoke of it amoung other things: travelling, seeing people in New York, lecturing and so on. But that is not the truth and you have to know it. Besides my working-life in France, I care for nothing actually but you. There is one thing I really have to do in America, to see my Californian friend, who is a kind of daughter for me. But Canada, New York, trips, friends, I should throw everything else away to spend a longer time with you. I could have a room of my own so you could work quietly and be alone when you would wish. And I should be so nice: I'll wash the dishes and mop the floor, and go to buy eggs and rum-cake by myself; I shall not touch your hair or cheek or shoulder without being allowed to do so; I shall try not to be sad when you'll be ill-tempered because of the morning mail or for any other reason; I shall not interfere with your freedom...Well, you have not even to answer to that. March is still far away and nothing is quite sure and you'll have to see what you can do and want to do. But I feel better for having told you the truth: I, myself, wish with all my soul and heart and body to stay with you as long as possible. I hardly care for going here or there or staying in

Chicago; to live near you is the only thing I care for. That is how you trapped me; that is how I love you now. But do not be afraid in your turn. I belong to you, I am glad of it, I want it, but my love will never be a burden for you, I shall never be a Mary G.,[1] and do things you do not want me to do.

My own Nelson, my sweet crocodile, maybe you are smiling because you think I am so serious, maybe you think all that is just chattering like a garrulous little frog, and maybe you are right. That is why I am a little afraid of love, it makes me rather stupid. Anyway, I spoke in the way I felt. I shall say something more since I have it in my heart: Nelson, now I love you so much, do not begin to love me less.

I would give to you all the loveliness of Paris! Such a warm and blue and light morning, with a little breeze and old remembrances, and quivering hopes. But I cannot.

Yea, I know Henry James very well: I was crazy about him when I was young. I do not know why now I rather feel the way you do. Yet I think too *The Turn of the Screw* is one of his best. I am glad you go on writing the book; I like it. I should be pleased to know what will happen to high-yellow and the dealer. The idea about dope, at the radio, seems to me very good. I hope it will work all right.

I told you why I did not go to the country house: too much work to do here. The nice old lady has come to Paris and we work in her home in the afternoon; it is very quiet and confortable. She gives us tea and little things to eat, we talk a little with her and then we sit at our tables and write our books. The morning, I write in my room; the evening, I see people. On Tuesday, I saw Koestler and his wife; Sartre was there too. Koestler is a strange, interesting man; sometimes, when he is drunk, he is very conceited and he feels a kind of a martyr, and he takes himself so seriously it is awful. But last Tuesday he was very sincere, and simple and friendly. I think he tries to begin something again with me, but as I told you, I did not want it, for many reasons, and chiefly because of my love for you which kills in me curiosity and taste for little adventures. So nothing happened. Yesterday evening we had dinner and whisky with Camus, who was very friendly and nice too; he too is an interesting but difficult guy. When he was not pleased with the book he was writing, he was very arrogant; now, he has got a rather great success and he has become very modest and sincere; it is funny. I feel very accutely all the petty and twisted sides of these people, after living with you who are never petty nor twisted, but so generous and genuine. Did you ask for *Politics*, the July-August number? Did you read my play? Koestler and Camus told me I looked younger than before and "disgustingly happy." Youth and happiness were given by you. Yea, it is happiness even through so many tears. I'll never forget, until my death, this minute when I put the bags on the ground and I felt your arms around me.

Saturday

I worked nicely yesterday, and in the afternoon we went to the radio and spent four hours preparing a little talk between people of *Temps modernes* and then having it registred.[2] It will be every Tuesday. On the evening I went to the first presentation of a very good new French movie. It is called *Quai des orfèvres*,[3] just a silly mystery but the director did a marvellous job. Now I have to work a little more. I am not pleased with this letter, anyway it is hard to make love on paper when I remember Wabansia, Wabansia does not look dreamlike, it remains true, and Paris is often a sad dream. Good night, honey. I belong to you. Vous êtes mon amour.

Your Simone

1) Algren's friend, with whom he was involved at one point. 2) Recorded (French, *enregistré*). 3) Directed by Henri Georges Clouzot, with Louis Jouvet and Charles Dullin.

Tuesday, 7th October 1947

Nelson, my love,

It is so beautiful just now in Paris that it is impossible not to feel happy and to hope. To hope for seeing you and living with you for days and weeks and months, to hope for having you in this lovely town and showing to you all the little streets I love. Yesterday I spent the afternoon walking in Belleville and Ménilmontant, very poor and lively neighbourhoods on little hills in the north of Paris; there are lots and lots of little forgotten houses in little forgotten streets. You would like them so much. I go on being a very good girl, working and thinking of you. Not much happened. Sunday I went with Sartre, Camus and the old André Gide and some other writers to a meeting about African problems. You know Negroes are still worst used in French colonies than in America, and one of them asked White writers to help. But what was rather strange is this Negro is a Christian man, very pious and subdued, very conservative, while we all of us were on the left side. So he spoke of France and freedom in a very polite way and said he hoped Negroes could become happy without any revolution, without putting White people away, with the help of French people. We were all very angry, thinking he was a kind of collaborationist. We said that France acted very badly about colonies, and that all white people in the colonies were scoundrels. So the Black boy was not pleased. There was Richard Wright[1] there and he was not pleased neither when the other Negro said that in fact all American Negroes are African. You know I like Wright and as I am so sentimental that just hearing American language is a joy for me now, I was very pleased when he passed the terrace of Les Deux Magots where I was writing. He seems very happy to live en France, even though he finds it difficult to get food and coal and gazoline; he works much at his novel. But we think, and Sartre chiefly was of this opinion, that you are right when you say he takes everything a little too much seriously, even with a kind of "importance."

Yesterday evening I had a dinner and drank a glass with the ugly woman. She brought to me the last part of the diary she wrote about me: it is tremendously good. She writes a beautiful language and then living all alone as she does, being in heart a lesbian, she is much more daring than any woman I know; she is daring as to the things she says and the way she says them. Nearly all women-writers are a little shy, even in the artistic ground, a little too sweet and subtle, if you see what I mean. This one writes like a man with a very feminine sensitiveness. I am pleased because I really was useful for her: I had her books published, and I gave her faith in herself, and now there are many good critics and writers who begin to think much of her, an it is important for her, in her tragic lonely life. You know, she feels so ugly that she does not want to sleep with man or woman, and yet she says quite frankly she needs it and she waits eagerly for old age, when she'll be older. Maybe she will not care for sex any more and she will be quieter! I should not like to live in her skin. She spoke to me about love in a very moving and even beautiful way: she speaks and I listen as if it was not about me, and yet not hiding the fact it is about me; that makes very strange talks. She speaks about herself the whole time, and then she says in a distressed voice: "We always speak of me! Let us speak of you!" And of course it kills every wish of speaking about me. Anyway I should not, I hardly ever speak about me with anybody. What was very bad is when she spoke of love: of not seeing the person you love, of the strangeness of sudden presence after absence, and so on. I was thinking of you, of seeing or missing you, of being happy or unhappy about you, and it would have been so hard for her if she had known. She does not ask for any love from me, but when she begins to think I can love somebody else, it is the hell for her. In the end she was drunk, and when the

74

waiter said we had to go, the night-club was closing, when she understood she had to say goodbye, she nearly fainted. But do not tell me not to see her, because, in spite of all, it gives some meaning to her life to see me once a month and now I like her books. And I like her too, very much, but liking is not much when people need love. I'll be very sad when you'll just like me.

Wednesday

Love and love for my crocodile. Yesterday evening coming back from a little night-club, I found your letter; I just read it and fell asleep. I love you. A friend of mine had an exhibition of paintings. She is a nice and even beautiful woman[2] but a very poor painter. So it was sad, everybody knowing it was so poor, and looking at the paintings without saying anything, and she knew too that it was not good. So on the evening we tried to confort her, and went to eat couscous and then to drink whisky with her and her husband who is an American sculptor. The man looked very poetical for me because he takes the airplane for New York this morning. It was his last night in Paris; USA seemed so near when you thought he should be there on Thursday, and yet *you* remained as far as ever. They spoke of my going to Canada with them, in canoe on the big lakes, and I was secretly proud and happy to think in myself: "If it is convenient for my beloved crocodile, I should rather lie in his own little sun than to see the most beautiful lakes with the nicest people." The night-club where we went just opened yesterday, always in my own neighbourhood,[3] and the Spanish dancer was very bad and the singers too, but there was something friendly and gay in the place. In Paris we all go to the same places, and I spoke English the whole evening, which is always a great pleasure for me.

Now I must work. It is very bad never to come in my dreams in night, and then to come all day long, smiling to me, looking at me, speaking to me or kissing me in the most unconvenient circumstances. Good bye, it will be long before getting another letter, this one came so quickly. Yes, I like the stories about the Philippines.

Let me kiss you a very long kiss. Je vous aime, mon amour.

Your little frog and own Simone

It is not true at all I do all the speaking and you stay silent. You chatter as much as I do, and it is not fair you have such nice dreams.

1) Wright, a close friend of Algren's, had published *Native Son* in 1940 and *Black Boy* in 1945. 2) Jaqueline Breton, whose second husband was playwright David Hare. 3) The Catalan, Rue des Grands-Augustins.

My beloved crocodile,

It is nice to write from my bed, just before sleeping.

I had a very thrilling time, yesterday evening. Well, it was not so thrilling. I spoke to you about Koestler: yesterday we went with him and his wife to Camus' (and wife's) to spend the evening. Camus' wife had prepared a nice supper and we brought many bottles of wine and brandy and the evening began rather nicely. But Koestler is so dreadfully serious when he chooses to be—no humour at all. He wanted to speak about politics and science and he was angry because we all tried not to do it, since we disagree with him on all points. Then he had invited a very unpleasant American man, a good friend of *Partisan Review*, a tenant of Truman's policy; he works at the American embassy and is a kind of a spy. We all loathe him —he is a Jew but he is anti-Semitic and he hates Negroes and so on. We told to Koestler we did not like him, then the man came. We teased him in many ways, and when he went away Sartre said he disliked him. Koestler likes him because he is anticommunist, and I think it becomes as bad as being communist when you like everybody who is anticommunist. Koestler was a little drunk and he was so angry he quarrelled seriously with Sartre, and went away saying; "Now we are enemies." He was really stupid; he can be so unpleasant. I had no regrets about it. The whole evening was very dull, though Camus was very nice and gay. Koestler killed all the fun and all humour. So I drank really much, but I was all right nevertheless. I went to bed at three o'clock and slept the whole morning, but I have no remorse because I worked the whole afternoon. I wrote a little more about New York, but it is strange, Chicago killed all my remembrances of New York; I remember it too vividly, so New York faded away. I am annoyed about it because I wanted to write about N.Y. too.

Good night, honey. Sometimes closing my eyes in the dark, I do not know if it is Paris or Chicago and I think of you so tensely that I really feel you, with my hands and lips and whole body. You fade away very quickly. Maybe if I become a little more tense, you'll be there really: in India I heard fakirs do thing of this kind. I must try.

Sunday

I go on working nicely and I spent very quiet days. Koestler wrote a very funny letter (not willingly funny) to apologize and Sartre answered the same way, but we did not meet again.

I heard about the strange woman about whom I spoke to you at night once, who read Nietzsche in kind of brothels and drank so much and lives with Dullin.[1] I heard she is drunk from morning to night now, all red and swollen, and trembling and falling asleep under the table when there are guests. I was told she is going to die soon, her liver is so much swollen, it will burst. It seems rather sad, she was some woman.

We have a meeting about the next radio-emission. We shall talk about de Gaulle who did a very bad and unpleasant speech last Sunday. And with these socialist guys and others of different tendencies, we discussed about a kind of manifesto we are going to produce, saying fiercely that some French political and intellectual men do not accept to choose between America and Russia, still hope in peace and refuse the war, will try to contrive to a socialist Europe and so on. Nobody is doing anything about it here, though many people just think the way we do, so it could be of some importance, chiefly if the leaders of some labor unions support us as it seems to happen. Afterwards we'll try to get it published and signed by political and intellectual people of the whole world. And they hope then to have something to oppose to the Communist Party and to the pro-American capitalists. I'll have it translated for you. There were more than fifteen men and I was the only woman so I gave my jaw a good rest and did not say a word. Anyway it was an interesting discussion.

I began to rewrite my book; I could not go along any more and it is much more pleasant to try to write nicely what was already written, but roughly. Just now, writing to you, I am drinking a little of the scotch which remained in the bottle; it makes Wabansia very near. The bottle gives to me a pang in the heart; I see so vividly the shop where we bought it. I remember many and many things so vividly: the little porch at night when we talked about leprosy, the religious meeting when your hard heart melted and I became happy again, the coming back with the Chianti bottle in the night. It was very precious too just staying in the room and reading Stephen Crane and being near you. Yes, I am very lucky, my love. I am lucky for having given and received so much love. But it is sad now to have just words on the paper today. Nelson, my own Nelson, I love you.

Your Simone

1) Simone Jollivet. See *The Prime of Life*, in which she appears under the name Camille.

My beloved crocodile, my own Nelson,

The little gods seem to be more friendly now: true, you helped them by mailing your letter on Friday, but the fact is I had it yesterday, that is in three days the sheets of yellow paper came from Chicago to Paris — and such a long, nice letter. Indeed, I suspected you would not get married, but I am glad to be sure. It must be nice and warm and confortable for a little frog to lie leisurely in your crocodile stomach; you'll have no difficulty in having me for your dinner.

I understand very well what you say about the play. Even in French it is a little stiff. Some critics liked it very much and others disliked it as much, but nearly everybody agreed it was too stiff and didactic. I think you would find me better in the novels: I tried to put in them much more of myself, there is more humour anyway though they are rather tragic. But don't wonder if I always look at you with a laughing face and look at the world in an other way. You are much more nicer than the world; it is really pleasant to look at you. You know, the world is not altogether so good, don't you think so? In fact I think I take some things seriously, very seriously: for instance, love, hate, friendship, death, some good books and good paintings, the evil hearts of some men and the good ones of some others, and the wrong done to some people. Well, taking some things seriously makes the other things look really unimportant. Then my own life seems important to me, since I have no other change on this earth: yet I know I'll die and so it is not important in the way people think. But as long as I am living, I can be rather passionate, you know, and take a few things really at heart. It is the same for you? I thought so.

I need nothing from America, I told you, except your letters and your love. But if you really want to play the UNRA[1] by yourself, maybe, if it does not bother you, you could send some rice and condensed milk or preserved butter or some canned meat to my mother. I help her with some money but as she has no money at all by herself, she never has very much to eat. Her place is 8 bis rue Blomet, Paris, xve; thanks if you do it.

Koestler is an Hungarian Jew who belonged to the CP when he was a young newspaper man; he lived in Russia some time and was important and very official in Moscow. After the Spanish was (he was in Spain during the war) he left the CP and became strongly anticommunist. He went to live in England and wrote his books in English. I am sure you would like the first one, *A Spanish Testament*, he told the whole story very well. His great success in France was *Darkness at Noon*, about Moscow trials. It is not very accurate, maybe, but is is very clever and thrilling. What is rather wrong with him is that he hates communists so much he can be friend with the most conservative people and write in conservative papers and support a conservative policy, and like the people of *Partisan Review*. That is exactly what we try not to do at the *Temps modernes*. If you have a little time and we can get the books, try to read the ones I am speaking about. You are right about syndicalists: they are much more interesting than socialists. We saw an important leader of the oppositionnal section of CGT[2] and he explained to us in a very interesting way how communists are killing democratic spirit into the syndical life and what would be done to keep it.

The story of the radio turned a strange way. We learnt it was all contrived by the government, by Ramadier, because he wanted us to do some anticommunist and anti-Gaullist propaganda just before the elections. And we were going to be paid not by the radio (which depends upon the government but has and must have its autonomy) but by Ramadier himself. Then, we are anticommunist and anti-Gaullist, indeed, but we do not intend to support Ramadier's policy; chiefly what he did in Indochina disgusts us. So yesterday we had prepared something rather funny and striking about de Gaulle, but we decided to drop everything. Now something will happen for Ramadier thought the radio people (who being mostly communist do not want our participation) had purposely said to us we were governmental agents, which he himself had tried to hide, in order to get our demission.[3] He got very angry and told them to ask themselves for our regular participation or he would fire them. So now they are very annoyed. For us it seems a very French story and rather sad.

Wednesday

We said good bye to Koestler yesterday, he is coming back to England. After quarrelling and apologizing, after so much fretting, it all ended by him saying suddenly: "I am hundred per cent *Gaullist*." So we said nothing and everybody kissed everybody good bye very warmly, but Sartre and I knew all friendship is impossible with Koestler. Gaullism is hateful and there is nothing to do about it. So it seemed useless to have spent so much time with K. and given our jaws so much work, hoping to find some ground of understanding—and this sudden declaration: "I am a Gaullist."

Well, good bye to him. After this meeting I saw a very, very interesting movie; it has been done by a nice young woman I meet sometimes at Saint-Germain-des-Prés: about Paris and France from 1900 to 1914. She went to public and private collections, and she gathered lots and lots of old features of the time. She cut and chose, and put photographs together and she gave the most striking picture of French life during this period. Some old people cry when they see this feature because they feel it is so true. There are pictures of writers, painters, players, poets, politicians, and the streets of Paris, marriages, burials, music-halls, all the popular life, and too factories, strikes, and the rising of the war, the German Kaiser hunting deers in the German forests, soldiers, armies, and so you feel all this "nice time," "peaceful period" was just leading to bloody murder. Most of little things were very funny: the dresses and hats of women, old bicycles and cars and airplanes, men with big whiskers, twenty years old Maurice Chevalier and so on. And yet, you went away with a pang in the heart, the whole life looking useless, dismal, absurd. Then Paris was wonderful in the misty night, there was the metro and buses strike, so the streets were full of people on bicycles as in the days of German occupation, and all the old cars and cabs were out. It made thousands and thousands of yellow fires on the misty Champs Elysées and the feeling of something dreadful ready to burst. As we had an appointment and were late, we rode a cab: it was very nice, the old coach, with the old horse in this strange night, through the Champs Elysées gardens. Under the trees the lights of restaurants seemed very far away, everything was remote, unusual, and everybody felt it. So there was an oddly warm feeling between people: I think it reminded us of occupation and in a way we have a kind of longing for this time when you really knew your friends from your enemies.

Midnight

Well, the radio story ended the way I thought: the director, who hates us, came and prayed us, nearly at his knees, to go on with our programs. Everybody seems dirty in this business, all these people stinks. I spent the evening with Sartre at R. Wright's. He was really nice, when he wants he had humour. He made us laugh about his connexions with French P C. He always speaks of you with much regard. Good night, honey. I wish we were in the bottom of the Mississippi water and it were time for your dinner. You can eat all the bones. I love you.

Your own Simone

Friday, 17 Octobre 1947

Love to my crocodile,

I am sitting in a lonely little bar, hearing bad music with American bad songs, and drinking good scotch, and I feel very poetical. The strike is going on, many people on bicycles and on feet in Paris, and there are all old kinds of trucks and cars to take people from one place to another. It is not very disturbing for me, because I nearly always stay in my Saint-Germain-des-Prés neighbourhood. Always a lovely autumn, smelling of burnt leaves, with sun through grey clouds and strange yellow light about the Seine. I think of the moving shadow of the tree in the Wabansia kitchen; a few minutes ago I was just thinking how these ten days we spent together must be different for each of us. Of course you saw *me* when I saw you. In a way it is a difference, isn't it? But then *you* saw *me* loving *you*, and I, *you* loving *me*, so anyway we were both present to both of us—and it was *our* love. The difference is rather I came into your home, your town, your life; it was the same world with just a little frog it it. And I landed in a very faraway place, a wonderful, strange foreign place, your crocodile place. The little home cannot be as precious to you as it is to me: the porch, the tree, the whole street, the whole night coming into our bed, all that seems as remote and stupendous as fairy land and yet as true and sure as my love, as my heart and blood. Well, we were both happy, in our peculiar way, were we not? I do not cry any more: I feel very lucky and happy.

I'll tell you how I live day after day a really good girl's life: I get up between eight and nine, I arrive to Café des Deux Magots half an hour later and I have tea with little cakes. I write my book the whole morning after reading the newspapers. Often I have lunch with my Russian or Jewish girlfriends, or with other friends, or at my mother's. Then I meet Sartre and we talk together or see people (we have meetings for the radio or about politics), at the end of the day we work for two or three hours at the old lady's. Then we spend the evening together, alone or with nice friends, and at midnight I am asleep. The book grows rather quickly this way.

81

I saw in the *New York Herald* a very bad article about what they call Loyalty: how you cannot have work in the State Department if you shake hands with a communist or if you listen to Wallace at the radio. I think it becomes worse and worse every day in your country. It is not better here, in another way. Today is the day of municipal elections and everybody is feverish. The strike is going on: no subway, no buses to go to vote. The strike is not popular because it is very tiring for working people to go by feet all day long. Yet, sure these people of the subway don't earn enough money. Everybody is anxious to know what result it will have in regard to the elections.

My Californian friend wrote to me a very funny and distressed letter. She says her little girl who is eighteen months old, when she is meditating about an important point puts two fingers in her mouth and two fingers in her little sex; and sometimes she touches first her sex and then her mouth and seems very happy. So my friend asks; "What am I going to do?" Indeed, I don't think there is anything to do, the girl will change her ways by herself.

I like the beginning of the week because I begin to expect the yellow letter from Wabansia. Maybe I'll get it tomorrow or Tuesday, if the plane does not crash. Two days ago, a plane crashed on sea between Marseille and Oran, and I thought we'll go to Algiers by boat, when we'll go, and I'll come back to Wabansia by boat. I felt too vividly last time what is could be to crash on the sea and be drowned, bones and all. I want to live, more than ever, at least, as long as we love each other. Sometimes it seems strange to have spent so many years without you; I'll be very careful to have yet some long years to enjoy now that I know you. Life is so warm and good now: your warmth and goodness, my beloved one. Love and kisses from your loving frog-wife.

Your own Simone

Sunday night

A rather disturbing night. From bars to bars I heard the first results of elections, by radio. These elections mean nothing by themselves, but they mean much as to people want and think; so it was 50% RPF[1]—that is de Gaulle—and 40% communists. I think Communists chose to have this kind of results: no Socialist Party, no third way. Just de Gaulle or communism. Maybe it is the meaning of this strike which we do not exactly understand, but I am sure they did not expect this. Very bad. Two blocks in

France now, just as outside: USA or USSR, De Gaulle or Thorez, a kind of civil war. All no-Gaullist people will join Thorez, and both are so bad.

I came back in the pink room. I have drunk a little, a little too much maybe. I do not want to care for politics anymore. God let me live just some more years to love you and be loved by you. Why should I care for anything else? Well, I cannot, even being a little drunk, think exactly this way, even our love involves many other things. So, I shall say it in another way: just now, I do not care for anything but loving you and being loved by you; just now, in this minute, I choose not to think of anything but you coming into the pink room and taking me in your arms, as a husband his wife. Nelson, you cannot know, though you know much about me, what it means for me to have been given something so precious as our love. You began it, and even if I become the more loving one, I'll always be grateful to you for it; even if one day I really suffer because of it. It is something true, genuine, and deep; it is something worth living—so few things are.

Dearest, beloved one, this letter seems so poor, reading it again. I should have put in it all my love and heart and body, all the autumn in Paris, the yellow trees, the peaceful sky, the feverish people. And just words, dry words. But I hope you'll know how to read it; maybe you are smart enough to find in it all I wanted to put. Maybe you'll even find *me*. I wait for you, Nelson. I'll wait until you come to me.

Your Simone

1) *Rassemblement du people français*, the movement founded by General Charles de Gaulle in 1947.

Tuesday night, 21 Octobre 1947

Nelson, my love,

I went twice to the hotel, today, but the little gods did not help this week: no letter. I thought, coming from the hotel to the little café where I am writing, that this beautiful misty night looks like you; if you do not feel by yourself that you look like a beautiful misty night, I cannot explain it to you. Sad in happiness, laughing in sorrow as in Villon's poetry:

I am dying with thirst near a fountain
I cry laughing and laugh crying . . .

And much more mystery in the deep delicate leaves of the trees than in the bright afternoon. A very strange yellow half-moon in the sky too, a rich and full meaning just whispered in half-darkness. Well, I cannot describe, and chiefly in English, what is a beautiful misty evening in Paris. I love it more than anything in the world.

Much fretting and fuming about the radio feature. I am very pleased, it is "fun," as you say in your country. So we had the elections, and success for RPF and on the first moment I felt rather bad, as I wrote to you. Then in the morning it did not seem that bad. The people of the conservative parties just made a block, but in fact they did not win any voice; the communists did not win nor lose, and the SFIO[1] rather won a little. Then in the afternoon we went to the radio and spoke against de Gaulle, and I must say we spoke very harshly, very rudely; it was skilfull at the same time, I think, and true and funny, a good job. The radio responsible man was scared: "This will make much noise!" And yes, all the Gaullist newspapers had big articles against Sartre and insulted all of us; they were raving with anger. Gaullist leaders asked Sartre to go to the radio and discuss with them, and they quarrelled and quarrelled, in front of the mike too. They say, never at the radio anybody spoke so rudely about anybody else. I don't think we'll go on a long time; they will fire us, but it was pleasant to be able to say in so loud a voice what we thought. An hour ago I met a young American man who just arrived at Paris. He works at the Unesco for films, had written some articles and novels. Borneman is his name, do you know him? He is Canadian in fact, but mostly living in New York. He was a friend of Bernard Wolfe who was my best friend in NY and he seems rather nice. He spoke to me very severely about R. Wright: about Wright not writing the end of *Black Boy* and Wright having written in *Atlantic Monthly*. We spoke for an hour, and then I said good bye, and I felt ashamed because all American people were so nice for me, helping me, taking me to places, spending time with me, and this one feels lost in Paris and I do not help. I'll try to find some girlfriend and some interesting men for him to see, but myself I have no time; but then I feel full of remorse. I am always attracted when I can speak about America with some American people, but I am a little angry and sad too, because I think: why is *he* here and not the man I long to see, whom I should be so wildly happy to see in this misty night which looks like him? So in a secret corner of my heart I hated the poor innocent American boy who was not you. Nelson, my beloved own Nelson, I miss you so much. I want so much to share this lovely autumn with you.

I spoke to you, I remember, but not very much, of a man who spent three years at Buchenwald and wrote two very good books—the best ones —about it. *The Days of Our Death* is not yet translated, but I heard the

84

other one has just been translated with the title *The Other Kingdom*. His name is David Rousset. Please, ask for the book, you'll be very interested, and I am so pleased when we can be interested in the same things. We are working with Rousset in this political project. You should enjoy seeing him: he lost an eye and he had a black piece of material on it; he had lost nearly all his teeth, they are all broken; then he is very fat, strong, with a broad face. What I like is he is always laughing at the most dreadful things. When old men tell dreadful stories of blood and murder, he tells them in yet a more dreadful way, but laughing at it. He is very strong by mind and heart, and at the same time a bit crazy, you cannot help to be a little scared when you see him for the first time, but then you like him. He is going to Germany now to see what remains of Communist Party there, and so on.

My beloved crocodile, I am going to sleep. I spent the evening, until eleven, discussing with Sartre and Merleau-Ponty about radio and Gaullism; then I came to this little silent café on the place Saint-Germain-des-Prés and wrote to you. There is nobody, just me, and now they close. So I'll go through the misty night which reminds me of you. Sometimes it is so warm in my heart when I see your smile, your eyes, when I hear your voice, that tears come to my eyes. But that is not crying; it is just love. I have a good memory, I can unfold hour by hour these days we spent together, and all is as vivid as when it happened. And I have more time to brood on it. Some words you said, some of your looks are so precious that I scarcely allow me to remember them. They remain very fresh and unexpected and they give me nearly as much emotion as the first time.

Wednesday

I was loving you so much this morning while brushing my teeth and doing my hair, and then I found the letter at the bottom of the stairs, a particularly good letter, as they all are. The latest is always the best because it makes me feel anew you are living and loving me. I do not read anything just now; I have no time. I'll read much within a month when I'll go to the country house, so I do not read the books you speak of.

Please, please, don't take the phoney blonde in our nest. She would drink *my* whisky, eat *my* rum-cake, sleep in *my* bed and maybe with *my* husband. And then, as our Wabansia nest is the best place in the world, she would never leave it, so I should have to get away when I should come to see you, and I should have to take morphine myself. A very sad story. Please, struggle hard and keep *my* home for myself. I feel dreadfully selfish and stubborn about it. Well, indeed, I am kidding, darling. You'll do what you have to do; I shall not interfere with your freedom.

More and more fretting and fuming today about our radio-feature. All night people phoned to the man who is at the head of the radio, threatening to kill him and Sartre too. The newspapers this morning were full of long articles about it. Communist papers did not say anything for us because they hate Sartre as much as de Gaulle. All the conservative papers were dreadfully insulting. Just two or three non-communist progressive papers supported us. We had many pictures published, but mine were so ugly I do not sent them to you; but maybe you'll enjoy this cartoon about Sartre. The point is in France the radio belongs to the government; it is not a private business, and they were hurt in their sense of respect: no humour at all. As you say, it is the worse disease not to be capable of humour. All or friends are very pleased, and even people who are not friends but think the way we do were laughing at us in the streets this morning. The waiter in the restaurant shook hands with me very warmly. So we enjoyed very much this little incursion in political life.

Thursday

I saw Malaquais,[2] he waits for your answer and then he'll begin the translation. I learnt the barman to whom I gave your other books takes morphine too and does not make much good work, so I'll look for something else.

Good bye, my beloved one. This beautiful October morning looks like you, my heart finds you in everything I love. I kiss you as a loving wife has to do.

Your Simone

1) SFIO: *Section française de l'Internationale ouvrière* (French workers' movement). 2) A translator.

Thursday evening, 23 Octobre 1947

Good night, my love,

I was in a little Nordish bar of Montparnasse one hour ago and I drank scotch, and I suddenly heard "Lily Marlène" and then I was drinking scotch in Wabansia; you were in the peignoir doing things in the kitchen, some nice man's job. I felt I could not sleep before telling you I love you so much; it seemed very urging. I love you so much, Nelson, my own husband.

In this working temperate, mild life, it is wonderful, you know, to feel such a treasure of emotion, pain, happiness, of burning love in one's heart. And there is always a word coming to my lips: thanks. Thanks, darling, thanks, my husband and friend and lover, for all that you give to me from our Wabansia nest. You know, I really never wrote love letters in English. I feel it is very silly to give so much importance to one's own feelings when the world is so big and so many things happen: cholera in Egypt, de Gaulle in France, to say nothing about USA. It is silly, but it is a nice bed-story to tell to myself when going to sleep: faraway, on Wabansia Avenue, there is a man I love so much. Good night, my Nelson. When I'll shut my eyes, you'll come. Take me in your arms, give me your mouth...

Sunday

It smells of winter in the street. Well, winter has to come and pass so that spring comes too and I see you again.

Poor Sartre receives now *twenty* letters every day certifying him he ought to be beaten to death. Thursday, two dozens of young officers who were going away for Indochina the next day looked for him in all the night-clubs of Saint-Germain-des-Prés, wanting to give him a good beating. So we have to take care. Friday, Sartre stayed to sleep at some friends[1] with whom we had dinner, and I asked for a bed myself. I enjoyed to sleep in this place because it was the place where we had slept in the last month of German occupation, when we thought we had to hide from Gestapo, and also during the Liberation. From these windows, on the banks of the Seine, I saw young German soldiers being killed, as I told you. It is full of memories.

I did not believe de Gaulle was that much worshipped by so many people; it is a little dreadful. In the Quartier Latin students are beginning again to throw away and persecute Jewish students, and they write anti-Semite articles against Jewish teachers, and so on, in some newspapers. It seems it is really fascism threatening. I hope they will not win. A good point is America was not so pleased with de Gaulle. Terrible, in your country too, this loyalty check, and in Hollywood the prosecution of "reds." I should like very much to go to the country and just work, but we have to go on with the "manifesto" about war and Europe, and chiefly with the radio. I am going to work for it now since we do it tomorrow and it has to be good. You cannot hear it, we have not the proper waves for America. As you do not understand French, it does not matter so much.

Good bye, crocodile of my heart. I am happy and proud of our love. I kiss you, darling, and kiss you again. Every day I miss you, Nelson, every day I shall miss you until I see you again.

Your Simone

1) The Leiris.

Monday, 27 Octobre 1947

My beloved crocodile,

First really cold day in Paris. It was freezing in the night. In the morning, people had red noses and wet eyes. They were wearing woollen gloves, scarves, shawls, and winter coats. I am going to take my fur coat from the cleaner where it waits for me. Since three hours I work at the old lady's but she has no coal and the big flat is dreadfully cold;[1] I am afraid my feet have become as hard as ice. We'll go in Sartre's house, from tomorrow. The bad point is he has a mother who is something of a bore, but we'll make her button her lips, as you say, and the little writing room is very warm. My own pink room is just good for sleeping in it with lots of blankets heaped on the bed, but working is impossible. Luckily the Deux Magots are all right. I do not hate this cold, in fact. I think Wabansia must be very cosy with the refrigerator purring, and the oil-burner burning oil, and my crocodile sitting in the arm-chair near the kitchen table. I should like to be sitting in another arm-chair, near the oil-burner, and when we should nevertheless feel a little cold, we would find in the bed a very warm, nice nest. I am just afraid I should very often pretend I feel cold.

We spoke at the radio. There was again a heap of threatening letters waiting for us: the general idea is that we are sold to Stalin and should be whipped or burnt to death. You cannot fancy what things they say, many of them are half crazy. We spoke about communism in a very moderate way, saying why we are not communist, but why we think all the left side now has to coalise against RPF.

Tuesday

The letter came so quickly, once more. I got it yesterday evening, coming back to sleep. And for the first time since leaving you I did not remember your smiles, your kisses, the sound of your voice before falling asleep; I just let the words of the letter fall in my heart. It is such a warm, lively, loving letter that reading it and repeating the words in the dark, I did not even miss you, you were there, the words were yours, they were you. I like your dreams, though people would say they are neurotic dreams, indeed. The second one, about somebody coming and you dreaming you are awake and crushed by a heavy sleep is something I know very well too; it is dreadful. I was in anguish for you. Maybe it was yourself coming to kill yourself, as in the comic strip you sent to me. The smart, daring, talented, conceited local youth came to kill the stupid, shy, off-balanced crocodile.

Nelson, darling, I must confess I do not repent too much for having trapped you. You wanted just a little merriment on a fine spring night, and I wanted just a warm, soothing night after a long, tense, lonely and fever-ish turn in USA, just a warm soothing night in a pleasant man's arms. And you see what happen to us? Both trapped. And we cannot undo what we have done, is not that bad? But it is as unfair for me as for you, so I do not repent. I am even very glad to have been so smart as to trap you. Oh! I shall not let you go, as long as I can help it; I'll keep the trap very tightly closed. I'll have no pity. Now you belong to me as I belong to you.

I quite understand that in America you do not feel compelled to assert yourself as a Jew.[2] But here, I think you would not feel the same way. Anti-Semitism begins again. It is worst and worst every day: articles in some newspapers, and all kinds of injuries. I think, without being a Zionist, a French Jew cannot be indifferent to what the other Jews are suffering, and to what some other ones try to do. Even not being Jews, we try to help them, with money, writing, lecturing and so on. We'll do something at the radio for instance, in two weeks. It has nothing to do with pity, it is only struggle for justice. Then, if there is nothing special to do for Jews, the ver-bal assertion has no meaning, and I am glad you have not this "inverted pride" of which you speak; you would not be yourself. You must just have a nice non-inverted pride to be my local youth.

Thursday

I was a bit sad yesterday. I do not know exactly why. Missing you was not a warm, happy longing, but just sadness. I think the political situation is starting to taste very bad. Communists behave in a crazy, stubborn way; they seem rather at a loss, not knowing any more what to do, and all that helps de Gaulle very much. We hoped we should be able to stand with them for a while, just in order to stop fascism, but it seems impossible, and I am afraid fascism will not be stopped. Then yesterday morning there was in a magazine a huge article about Sartre, with pictures of his childhood, of his grand-parents, and so on; they spoke of me too, saying I was married with Sartre since six months, which is untrue, that I was good-looking and talented but, indeed, in the sense of unkind, hard, without a heart; and on the picture I was not ugly, but very grave, and hard-looking indeed. I thought of this face of me you know and like, always happy and laughing at you, and loving you and missing you. I missed myself too, my Wabansia frog-self such as it awakes every morning in your arms. Then you always feel a sense of guilt, of something dirty about you when you read such articles, though about Sartre they were rather understanding. And Sartre was very angry for the pictures of his childhood being exhibited thus: his mother had given them to the newspaper man, who told her he was sending them to America and many other lies. When she saw what she had done, knowing her son would be very displeased at it, she felt so stupid and heedless (so is she indeed) that the poor woman cried all day long. When we came to work, she was crying her eyes out of her face. We had to confort her, but she had a deep sense of failure and all that was rather depressing in a petty way.

Then I had lunch as each week with my Russian friend who loves me very much by speaking all the time about herself, her lungs which are nearly all right now, her purposes for theater and so on. Then I saw my sister. She came from Belgrade, where she has stayed ten months. What is depressing when I meet her, once or twice a year, is that she pretends to love me so madly (and I hardly care for her), and in fact she rather worships me like a faraway god than really care for me. She knows nothing about me: she never asks anything, never feels anything, but she cries when she sees me coming. I do not like her husband at all; he is a petty little arriviste without heart, neither ideas of his own. She admires him dreadfully. She has to admire people, and as I cannot tell her what I think of him, there are heaps and heaps of lies between us. The whole relationship is a long twenty years deception. Yet I have a kind of feeling for her: I feel her as my sister, with our childhood behind us. I explain too hastily and not very clearly, but maybe you understand what I mean and how this meeting could taste badly too.

Luckily, the evening was better. I went with Sartre to the nice old lady's and we drank champagne with her, her daughter and grand-daughter; we understand very well each other. She has much humour and the sort of non-optimist kindness I like.

Today was good because I saw nobody who was a bore, and I worked very much, morning and afternoon. And I walked in the gardens of Luxembourg. I sat in the sun for it was nearly summer in October here too, with the smell of dying leaves and their wonderful colors. I thought of you, indeed, and felt "good and warm," as you say.

Nelson, my sweet love, I hate to finish a letter; it is like saying good bye, suddenly you feel that you have said nothing of what made your heart so warm. You know, when I speak to you in the streets, when I think about you, I always use English. I speak English very much in this way, all day long, and all the English words I hear by chance in the streets or cafés sound tenderly in my ears. You see how silly I become, and I *was* a clever woman, it was said. So you see how much I must love you to have become so silly.

Goodbye, my own local youth. Words are useless; I want to use my lips, my hands, to kiss you, to hold you, all my body to feel your body, your warmth, your love and to give you mine.

Your Simone

1) Madame Morel, who lived on the Boulevard Raspail. 2) During an interview, Algren referred to himself as a "Swedish Jew"; not seriously, since he considered himself neither Swedish nor Jewish. More than once he emphasized the gap separating him from the Old World, from his paternal as well as his maternal ancestors. He claimed no knowledge of contemporary Jewry in the United States, no Zionist feelings, and scorned colleagues proud of their Jewish identity.

Thursday night, 30 Octobre 1947

Nelson, my love,

As soon as I have mailed a letter, I feel so frustrated that I have to begin another one. I never feel I told you why I wanted to, because love is not something you can *tell*. I went to bed and I hesitated a little while: it would have been nice to put off the lights and just sleepily think of you; writing is a harder job but then writing sounds more true, even if there is some delusion in it. Delusion because you don't care if this letter was written just now, and it seems important for me to tell you *now* what I feel. Now, a strange word when we have not even the same time on our watches; it means so much when our lips encounter, when we say "now, now, I got you." I know you do not care so much for words, and you think I like words too much, always giving hard work to my jaws or my pen. You are right, but I have nothing but words to help me to wait for you.

I was deeply moved when I read in your letter that you loved, as well as my eyes, my ways in love. And I thought I had to tell you these ways were just my loving for you. I had always the same eyes but I never loved anybody in these ways, you have to know, with such pleasure in love and so much love in pleasure, so much fever and peace, in this way which you say you like. I really and wholly felt that I was a woman in a man's arms, and it meant much, so much for me. Nothing better could have been given to me. Good night, honey. It is hard to say it, much harder than before coming back to Wabansia. Just come to me, darling, and take me with your strong, soft, greedy hands. I wait for them, I wait for you.

Saturday

My own Nelson, I was very pleased and excited this afternoon when I read the story of Cerdan's match. It happened in Chicago and you intended to be there, maybe you were? I could know exactly by newspapers the last night you spent. It must have been wonderful, the knocking down in the last round. I should have liked so much to look at it feeling your knees near mine.

I go on working, people go on insulting us, and at night heroic young men go into night-clubs looking for Sartre, to give him at least a good fat eye, but never finding him. Many writers are publishing books about USA this last days, and I was at first a little annoyed for my own one, but then I looked at them and I did not feel so bad; they just try to reduce America into slogans, while I try to say what I felt. How is high-yellow? How is the dealer? I hope you are pleased with your work. Reading your letter once more, I feel a bit sad and guilty when I think there are some satisfactions, even cheap and temporary, which I prevent you to get. I like so much to see you happy; you are so nice when you are happy. In a way, I know I could feel very bitterly sexual jealousy about you, though I disapprove of it. I disapprove of it, but I feel it so deeply; it must mean something genuine. On the other hand, I love you so much. I like so much the idea of your happiness and pleasure that I could help you to get satisfaction from another woman (if it was temporary indeed and not interfering with your love for me). So I do not know what I wish—indeed I know since I am not a saint but just a woman. Anyway I have not to choose, and whatever you do without spoiling our love, I agree with, even if I should suffer of it. Dearest, I don't say all this because it seems careful to say, but just for the pleasure of chattering with you in a very confident way.

Here is the address for getting *Politics*: 45 Astor Place, NY. Editor, Dwight Macdonald. And do not tell me you cannot read it. I worked well though I hate Sunday mornings: too many people in my quiet café coming from mass and liking de Gaulle and preparing to visit grandmother.

I go on seeing my sister from time to time; it is wonderful how little she asks for seeing me, though she pretends to love me so much. It is very convenient for me, but not so pleasant for her. She tells dreadful stories about Yugoslavia; it is not a place to make a crocodile's nest, you must always be with other people, eating, working, walking, singing, thinking or rather not thinking together. We shall not go there. Anyway I should not be allowed to go, since I am friend with Sartre who is looked as the devil. I send you a little cartoon where you can see me, but look! I have kept the face you know, it is not a photography; do not be afraid and say farewell to me!

I must have something to eat or I shall faint. Good bye, honey. I think I am going to spoil you by always telling you that I love you and miss you and think this or that about you, so today I'll be very secret; I'll say nothing. If you want to know what I feel you have to make a guess. Can you guess? Then you must be really smart!

Your own Simone

Wednesday, 5 Novembre 1947

Nelson, my love,

It is wonderful, since you changed yourself into a homing pigeon. The Friday letters all arrive on Monday. They look very young and fresh; it is pleasant. I regret you did not speak about Cerdan; I have to wait for week, but I am pleased you always are the same local youth, guessing so wisely what is going to happen. Your letter was very nice, indeed, but I shall quarrel with you, on two points. First, as a movie critic, I just fire you: I am very desappointed you wrote so badly about *Children of Paradise*. I know it was dreadfully cut and torn; in France it was a three hours feature. It is true the love story is stupid, but did not you like all the part about old Paris, old theaters? Maybe it does not mean much for a Chicago local youth. I think all the pantomimes, the old melodrama, the parody of melodrama was very good. Then I like the way the actors played, chiefly Pierre Brasseur, the one playing Frederic Lemaître, and I am fond of Arletty. Well, maybe you have to be French to really like it. I know nearly nobody in America did. Then, it is very wicked of you to laugh at me because I try honestly not to interfere with your freedom; it's very insulting not to take me more seriously. Well, I will interfere with your freedom: I'll put an electric fence around Wabansia home; I'll poison your skin and lips so that if you touch any woman, she'll fall dead. I must say nevertheless I liked the idea of the Folle (not Fouille, Folle) dancing in the Lapp shoes. Do *you* wear them?

Paris is always very nice. Is our tree losing its leaves? Here, they all do and you can see the leaves floating slowly on the Seine. I took some long walks through Paris these last days. I had a sad, strange feeling which friends tell me they share, now. In old times, we did not think it was possible to live in any other town, and other towns all seemed a little silly and pitiful when compared with Paris. Now, Paris is just a town; it is no longer our flesh and body. I looked at it with foreign eyes and discovered many nice things in it. I saw lot of things I had never seen, but as if I looked to an unknown town. Formerly I should not have been able to write about Paris, it was too near; now, I could. Sunday, on the Grands Boulevards, there was a crowd walking leisurely to kill the afternoon. There were little barracks in the street, selling candies and razor blades, and it all seemed very old and gloomy, as if looked at from another century, next century. It is a dead metropole now, as was Prague or Vienna ten years ago. We do not exist by ourselves anymore. Everything happens in Russia and America, not here.

I met a young newspaper man of *New Masses*,[1] that is, one of your communists. He came back from Greece and Yougoslavia. He sounded personally better than our communists, but about France he said the same things that they do, repeating a parrot lesson. He did not think it was so bad in USA, but then he seemed, though a communist, to have much prejudice for his own country.

We go on speaking at the radio each Monday and we receive all kinds of letters. Sartre got a letter with his own picture soiled with human excrement: it had to happen. The other evening, we went to a bar to drink a little scotch and soda and the people at the next table began to speak about Sartre and existentialism, not knowing he was there. They spoke half an hour, saying for instance that the mere title *Being and Nothingness* was *disgusting*. The same evening we met a man in the street who, passing us, saw who we were and stood following us for five minutes, struggling intensely against himself without deciding to do anything: I don't know if he wanted

94

to say "bravo!" or to insult us. I guess he was rather unfriendly. I don't think I happened to speak about a very good friend of us who is a sculptor, though we see him often and he is maybe the only one we always see with pleasure. I tried to describe him partly in *Le sang des autres*. I admire him as an artist immensely. First because he does the best modern sculpture I know; then because he works with so much purity and patience and strength. He is called Giacometti, and will have a big exhibition of his works in New York next month. Twenty years ago he was very successful and made much money with kind of surrelistic sculpture. Rich snobs payed expensive prices, as for a Picasso. But then he felt he was going nowhere, and wasting something of himself, and he turned his back on snobs; he began to work all alone, nearly not selling anything but just what was wanted to to live. So he lives quite poorly; he is very dirty in his clothes. I must say he seems to like dirt: to have a bath is a problem for him. Yesterday I saw his house, and it is dreadful. In a nice little forgotten garden, he has an atelier full of plaster where he works, and next door is a kind of hangar, big and cold, without furniture nor store, just walls and roof. There are holes in the roof so the rain falls on the floor, and there are lots of pots and pans to receive it, but there are holes in them too! He works 15 hours a day, chiefly at night, and when you see him he has always plaster on his clothes, his hands and his rich dirty hair; he works in cold with hands freezing, he does not care. He lives with a very young girl whom I admire much for accepting this life; she works as a secretary the whole day, and coming back just finds this hopeless room. She has no coat in winter and shoes with holes in them. She left her family and everything to come to Paris and live with him; she is very nice. He cares much for her but he is not of the sweet kind at all, and she has some hard moments to get through. What I like in Giacometti chiefly is how he could one day break into pieces all that he had done during two years: he just broke it and his friends thought it dreadful. He had his idea about sculpture, and for years he just tried and tried, like a maniac, not showing anything, breaking and beginning again and again. And he could easily have got money and praises and a good name. He has very peculiar, interesting ideas about sculpture. Well, I think that now he really achieved something; I was deeply moved by what I saw yesterday.

My sister is always in Paris. I see her as little as I can. Her husband has come. I spent just an hour with him and I was so bored that I think he was too. I hate being bored. The point with him is he struggles so seriously, so hardly for life, and then life means nothing for him: he does not love or think or want really nothing. And then struggling and struggling and boring everybody with talking about this peculiar struggle.

How is your French lazy boy? I love you.

Your Simone

1) An American communist journal.

Nelson, my love,

Nothing happens, always the same love for you, very tedious. Yesterday I went to the theater because it was the last rehearsal of a play by a friend of us, Salacrou, who writes every year a very bad and successful play. This one was very bad and maybe will be successful, but it was pleasant to see the old Dullin, the hunch-backed actor married with the drunken woman, who played very well. The drunken crazy woman was there, all in furs and veils, and looking sober, but in fact as drunk as ever, with dreadful red cheeks and misty eyes. We did not speak to her; we flew away. Many friends gathered with Salacrou and went for a gay supper late in the night, but I care less and less for this kind of things, and I went to bed so I could get up early this morning and work. I had put the mink coat on and everybody said I *was* very elegant; so I must have *looked* elegant indeed. I really deceived myself, looking at me in the mirror.

It is a pity you are so lazy and cannot read French. My last book has just been published and I should like you to read it. It looks very nice with a pale blue cover. It is a little essay[1] about ethics: how can moral and politics be adjusted to each other nowadays, and things of this kind. I'll send one to you when you'll know French. I'll send you little versions to do in order to make sure of your improvements.

Sunday

Tonight I had a very sad evening with my Jewish friend. I am afraid she is becoming really crazy. She was psychoanalysed two years ago and she was cured; she lived rather quietly, with a bad crisis last winter. And since a week she feels very bad again. I told you she was my pupil ten years ago. I had a great influence on her and I feel much responsability about her. She was very disturbed by the war. At twenty she married a boy she did not

96

really love (and who is awful in my idea), because she wanted an Aryan name to escape from prosecutions; then she spent four years hidden in little villages with false papers. She was a very bright student when she was young; when the war was over she had just an exam to pass before becoming a teacher, a rather hard exam, many people trying to be graduated and just ten of them being accepted. But she could really do it if she had worked peacefully. Now the point is her father is dreadfully rich; he is a big business man, selling diamonds. She is nearly a communist and does not want this money; she wants to earn her life. Now the husband tries to pass the same exam; he tried twice and failed. They have no money of their own and have to take it from the rich father; she thinks she can, as long as she works hard, to become independant, chiefly having been handicaped by the war. But it is very sad for her to work still as a student when she is twenty-six and has a little girl. Then, nobody knows why, not even the psychiatrist, sometimes she becomes dreadfully anguished and thinks she just cannot pass this exam; she stays in bed the whole day, crying and quivering and feeling guilty about everything. She never in two years attempted to pass the exam. This year she says she would, and began studying seriously. But a week ago, she began again to feel anguished and she abruptly decided not to make herself sick again about this graduation and asked her father to work in his office. Then she felt worse than ever, because she cannot conciliate this kind of capitalistic business and her communism. So two days ago I found her crying madly, and half crazy. Tonight we spoke for hours about her problem. Her relationship with the unsuccessful husband whom she pretends to love, with her parents whom she needs too much, and chiefly with money, are very important. But it does not explain everything and I felt I was becoming crazy myself, because when I began to see a reason of her crisis and to tell her how to behave about it, she found at once another reason; and everything is true and nothing is. Physically, she is not well at all, but doctors cannot say what is wrong and cannot cure her. She has to try another psychoanalyst, but I am not sure they'll find the truth. When she spoke to me as a very sober and good-willing woman tonight, I thought pooh! It just depends on her; she is free to cure herself. If only she decided, I am not sick, I can go through this exam, she would be cured. But then something distracted showed in her eyes and I thought: Yea! But she is not free to make herself free. It is a very unpleasant feeling not to be able to help at all somebody who needs help so awfully. I did not help, I know, speaking and trying hard for hours. When she is all right, I often feel a bit impatient about her, but when she is sick, she is helpless and touching. She says she has nothing to do but kill herself. I do not think she will, but I hate to think about what is in her heart when she feels so.

Good night, honey. I kiss you as I loved to.

Your own Simone

1) *Pour une morale de l'ambiguité.*

Tuesday, 11th Novembre 1947

Nelson, my beloved faraway husband,

I should like to have strange stories to tell you about strange interesting people, but nothing happened since Sunday. My sister and brother-in-law are maybe strange, but surely not interesting. Sartre is interesting, but not strange, and I saw nobody else. Yes! From time to time, working in the Deux Magots, I see some old man or some young one coming to me in a rather mysterious and promising way. They always propose to me some very good manuscript they have just achieved, or some very appealing idea for the *Temps modernes*, sometimes it is even poetry, and always they seem very sure to give something very precious to me. It is sometimes difficult to be rude, but in two years I learnt to. Something much more funny, working in the Deux Magots every morning, is that I see many little things happening around me. For instance, a week ago a woman came with suitcases and kissed passionately a man I always saw alone; they seemed very happy together (chiefly the woman) and for three days they met every morning. Then one day the woman did not come. And the day after there was another woman kissing the man and looking very happy with him (he did not seem so happy neither). The first woman looks rather like a person with a brain, but too ugly yet. The second one hopes she is pretty, and is not too much in fact. The man, who does not look a man with a brain and is surely not pretty, spent the whole evening, yesterday, all alone, drinking in a bar (I just was in that bar) with the look of a doomed Don Juan. He seemed to suffer so much, and with such pride, to have two women suffering for him! I'll tell you, if I know, if it is the brainy woman or the pretty one who wins the man.

When I think of it, it is a long time I had not been as peaceful and quiet as I am: no fever, no tears, just working and walking in sweet Paris, sleeping well and…waiting for you. I think I am very lucky to have something to long for with all my heart, and I know I'll get it. Good night, honey. It is very sweet tonight to love you.

Thursday

Beloved crocodile, your letter came, at last, yesterday evening. When I have no letter, I feel you could be dead, and it is very sad. When I have a letter, I feel you are so living that I become very impatient; I want to see you. So, I have never peace, but why should I? Love is much better than peace. In fact, I have a deep, genuine and beautiful peace, knowing what I want, knowing I'll get it, knowing I have got it so long as you love me. Then I have a kind of superficial fever — so, as in Villon's ballad, it is peace in unrest and rest in fever, a nice way of loving.

Thanks for the article. It sounds very interesting though there is a very good Chicago writer about whom you say nothing, don't you like him? I mean the one who wrote *Never Come Morning* and whose name is Nelson Algren. A smart local youth, I was told. I have the thing translated and it will soon be published.[1]

I know Bromfield,[2] indeed; he is a great success here too in bourgeois circles. He is a bore and very narrow-minded; I don't like him at all. I should like you to put him K.O. I hate his whole clean morality and fake psychology. I think the best thing to do should be for you to read the translation of Sartre's little book about existentialism; it is published by the Philosophical Library, New York. If you cannot get it, I'll mail it to you. In *Twice a Year*, Dorothy Nordman published a piece of my *Moral of Ambiguity*, and it could help you, too. Then if you are not pleased with these two articles, I'll write something for you about it, but in English it is difficult for me. I hate your not learning French; it is the only thing I hate about you, since you no longer wear suspensers.

We spent a hard day, Sartre and I, trying to explain to our friends they had to give their firm[3] to the manifesto we are producing. These intellectual people (in the narrow meaning of the word) think it is so important to desert themselves that if they disagree about just a word they say "we cannot sign it." You can never have a hundred people agreeing about all the words of a simple page. You have to make a choice about what is important and what is not! It is important now that we try not to become slaves of de Gaulle nor of Stalin. And what else have we to do but to try? The mere attempt is a chance we have not to miss. Really most of these artists and writers care for nothing and nobody but their petty self.

In order to have Bromfield K.O., maybe you could read Sartre's little book about Jewish problem, published by *Partisan Review*. It is not directly about existentialism, but I am sure you would be interested and you could see an existentialist can speak in a very dynamic way about concrete questions; demonstrating thus he is not hopeless and pessimistic—no more than you are. Now I suggest you say to Bromfield: "I know Simone de Beauvoir and when she is in bed with me, she does not look hopeless or nihilist, but with *you*, I don't know what would happen. . . ." I am afraid I should look hopeless.

I love you, Nelson.

Your own Simone

1) It appeared in *Les Temps modernes*, January 1948, number 28, entitled *"Du rire en bocaux, reportage de Chicago."* 2) Louis Bromfield (1896–1956). The American essayist and novelist, author of *The Green Bay Tree* and *La Mousson* (1937). Algren had been asked to participate in a panel with him on the future of the novel. Bromfield had characterized existentialism, about which he admittedly knew little, as "a doctrine of nihilism, fatalism, and despair." 3) "Firme" in French; "signature" in English.

Saturday night, 15 Novembre 1947

Love, and love to my dearest husband.

Last year, in this rainy winter, I had never heard of you, nor you of me. I was waiting impatiently for going to America, feverish as if something were to happen to me, yet not suspecting it would really happen: it would be love and love for you. Darling, if I had my cheek on your shoulder and could whisper softly in your ear, I should dare to ask: Nelson, do you feel more happy than last winter? Do you feel happy to be so stupidly loved by your frog, even if we have to wait some months before kissing again? No, if I should have my cheek on your shoulder, I should not ask anything; I just should wait for your kisses.

I am very pleased because it is decided now: I'll leave Paris the other Thursday, the 28th, for one month with Sartre so I shall achieve my book. I'll be at La Pouèze, at Madame Morel's. I am glad too because I just earn much money with this book, though it is not over yet, and I hope it will be published with good photos; people who read the first part think it is interesting. I should like you so much to discuss it with me. These last days, I have much work because many things have to be done before I can go to the country: first, for the radio we have to prepare *five* features and have them registred. Rousset, who has just come back from Germany where he spent three weeks, will speak for us, then trade unionists, then some Negroes coming back from Africa, and our own gang will go on about socialism, freedom and so on. On the other hand the manifesto has been discussed and discussed for hours, and now it has to be written again, and discussed again; it will be much work too! We hope maybe Wallace will sign it; it has to be done properly and it is difficult to get twenty intellectual people agreeing about anything.

You know, I care about all these things because I think I have to, but I am fed up with it. I loathe politics. I should like a world without politics. I'll be so glad to go away and just try to write a good book, and read nice ones. I'll go to Brentano's[1] and buy those you spoke about.

My Jewish friend is worst and worst: for two hours we nearly spoke three sentences; she would not speak and I did not feel I could neither. She is what we call "psychastenic." No longer anguished now, she just does not care for anything, her husband, her daughter, her friends, nor herself. She can hardly get up in the morning, because everything seems useless and silly. She feels as if she were a ghost and the world a kind of bad dream. Nothing has any meaning; she wants nothing, not even to die. She is dreadfully tired, always sleepy, her head aching, yet, doctors do not find any disease in her. She can hardly stand on her feet for ten minutes. And her face was so terribly sad, I did not know what to say, what to do. She has seen the psychiatrist who once psychoanalysed her. He says she will never become really mad so as to be sent in an asylum, but he seems very worry about her.

I am going to sleep and forget you. As soon as I'll open my eyes, you'll be there and not part from me. Yesterday evening I told to myself the most beautiful story: it was our whole romance, from our first encounter near the little café to our last parting. A fine romance, Nelson, love, and we are lucky to have such memories and such hopes. Good night. I feel so good and warm when I lie in your good warm arms, near your good warm heart. I am your own frog, your true girl and own wife.

Tuesday

My own crocodile, my beloved, I love you so much all along these rainy days. You know how it is when you are far away. Sometimes the one you love fades away, it is just a sweet sad song in you ears, a longing in your heart, a warm smell of life, but you cannot catch it. And then you just meet at the corner of the street *this* man whom you love, with his wisp of hair, his peculiar smile and these shoulders which have the right size for you to put your cheek. So you came to me yesterday morning and took me by the hand and did not let me go. And there was your letter. Darling, I am not such a goose. I knew you were teasing me and I liked the fantasy; don't think I am so bad-tempered and silly. I teased you, too, pretending I felt insulted. In fact, if you would ever hurt me (which could happen since I am so crazy as to love you so much) I should not look cold but very angry, or unhappy, or both. I should not have pride enough to be haughty, cool and aloof. Well, we'll see...maybe we'll never see; all seems so good, so warm and genuine and happy about our love.

Yea, your life sounds a little serious and temperate, though for me, there is so much poetry in your saying "I mopped the floor" because it includes our home and you. But you cannot reasonably enjoy the mere idea of yourself as I do; it would be strange and disturbing. So you may find loneliness and book-revising dull sometimes. Please, work hard, so you can take some holidays in spring, and we'll change this life so much as to make you missing these quiet days and nights. No more peace for you, but always travelling, looking at things and people, drinking, moving your jaws, hearing the sounds I produce by moving mine, and loving me as I love you. Maybe you'll be pleased, when I'll go away. Are you afraid?

No time to be bored here, but time to need and miss and want you. I'll send you the little pale blue book, though you don't deserve it. Sartre's second book, *The Reprieve*, has just been published at Knopf's; tell me what you think about it. I am glad to see we have so many points of disagreement about movies and books. I am just a little sad to like *your* books so much if I have such a bad taste. They must be very cheap and silly. Anyway it will make no difference about my loving you. I am glad of the disagreement because we'll have many things to discuss and subjects of quarrel. We look rather old-fashioned and silly never quarrelling. We have to be a little more challenging, or what about sex struggle, and freedom in love, and love in freedom, and all these fine progressive notions? I am a bit humiliated to feel such a corny kind of wife, never finding fault in you! It is said men despise you if you worship them too much. I am afraid I had the wrong tactic. Well, why is it said you are a big wise crocodile, and I just a little frog? Maybe I am a huge frog, and you a tiny lizard? Let us challenge each other! I'll begin next week; today, I just want you to take me in your arms and tell me, "It will soon be true, I'll hold you in my arms. Go on loving me as a silly frog because I love you too."

Nelson, my love, I write to you by the light of a candlestick, which is very romantic, maybe a little too romantic. The electric lamp has blown up, as it often happens. This hotel is really dreadful. When Sartre lived in it, once his mother came some day because he was sick and she went away crying, because she thought it was such a dreadful place! Since, her husband died and she urged her son to come and live with her, which he did. The walls are so wet; it is so cold when you get up that every winter I feel I *must* go away. But in winter you cannot find any room in Paris, so I have to wait, just for one winter more; and when summer comes, it does not seem so urgent to look for a room. So it goes on, and I live in this inconfortable place. I don't know how to manage my own confort, though I love confort when I find it all done and prepared for me as in Wabansia's home. I liked Southern Confort, too, but best of all Nelson's arms confort; it was so warm and nice. It was so sweet to find the little package yesterday. I did not expect anything—the weekly letter had come—I just began to wait for the next one. And there was the blue and red 1946 greetings—in 1946 you did not know me, sweetheart, and it is 1948 greetings you have to send to me now. Well, it was sweet anyway. I am happy when I can thank you for a sensible reason. You know, Nelson, I should like to be sensible or at least to seem so to you. It would not be sensible to thank you for loving you so much, or for being just who you are, or even for your love for me. You cannot decently thank anybody for such things. But then if you send me a book, I can thank you for the book; all the gratitude and thanksgivings of my heart may find their way. Thank you, darling. Thank you so much. Thank you for the book. Thank you for so much more than a book, even by Edith Wharton.

I shall be very glad to go to the country; this last week is very bad. We spend the days speaking and discussing about radio-features and political manifestoes, every day and evening. Poor Sartre does not like it better than I did; he just thinks he has to do it since he is asked to. I am sure he should like to live freely in blue lagoons with you! But are you sure Chicago and your whole continent would be a very secure place? Maybe you had rather come to Paris, darling? You will surely got an atomic bomb in Chicago. Paris is so little and senseless now, nobody will care to send an atomic bomb on it. Come here, darling, I think night and day of our next Wabansia meeting, but often I think of your coming to Paris, the other year. Oh! I'll make for you a wonderful life! I'll make you as happy as I was in

103

Chicago. I'll show you all the things I love and you'll love them. Yea, it will happen, in spring 1949, not so much to wait for. Work well. Work for us. Work for good work's sake and for my peculiar pride. Work so we may have gay, quiet holidays in sunny New Orleans. And don't bother if your life just now is a little dull. I'll make it disturbing enough for you; you'll get very tired. Enjoy this peaceful, lonely time; it will not last for ever.

Well, one more silly letter with nothing but love in it. Excuse me, darling. I cannot find the way to give you some nice black hate, to make a little change, not even indifference. I am as good-willing as possible, but I just find love. You have to take it, darling. Good night. The bed looks very cold and lonely.

Your Simone

1) One of the largest American bookstores in Paris, on the Rue de Rivoli.

Friday, 21 Novembre 1947

Darling,

It was a lovely day, all mild and blue and golden, so pleasant after this cold, rainy week. Yesterday I just achieved the part of my book I wanted to get through before leaving Paris, so I did today all the little things I had to do and always postponed. I felt like a good business-woman and housewife. I went to see publishers and I got much money from them for my book about USA, and for a little one collecting my last articles in *Temps modernes*.[1] I signed the contracts and was very proud about my shrewdness in money matters. Then I went to the clothes-cleaner, the laundry, I bought little things I needed, I put some order in my room, read manuscripts waiting for it since a long time, wrote a lot of letters to explain why I could not accept them for *T.M.* (very politely), and other letters to people in America to whom I had never answered. Oh! It was a very busy day! I did my duty the whole day and at the end I felt very depressed for having been so efficient and dutiful. I shall not begin again before my going away to USA. To be efficient and dutiful twice a year is really enough, maybe too much. To enjoy myself a little in this virtuous day I went to a big American library, hoping to find some good books, but there was nothing. I had read all the books or did not want to read them. I just bought some mysteries, some short stories by O. Henry, *The Oxbow Incident*,[2] because I liked so much the movie. I'll take with me all the books you sent to me, and French books, too. I enjoy the idea of reading peacefully, as I did in Wabansia.

Yesterday, too, was an efficient dutiful day. The hell with them! The whole afternoon at the radio, because we have to register *four* radio-features before going away. Rousset spoke about Germany; it was interesting, we read the manifesto and gave some commentaries, but nobody felt very gay, because Ramadier had just gone away and we feel more and more probable de Gaulle will be called within two months. My Russian friend is crazy about *God's Angry Man*[3] and tries to translate it for *T.M.*; very difficult to translate. In fact everything is difficult to translate when you try to be really faithful to the author's writing. I read carefully some parts of Sartre's *Reprieve*. It is amazing how the translator never dares what the author has dared to do; he makes everything smooth, mild, easy, conventionnal—he kills the style; it is very bad. But indeed you must be a good writer yourself to translate properly. You cannot understand that, you silly lazy man, since you just know your language, as a very arrogant narrow-minded American man. Yea, you have got dollars and atomic bomb, but French is a good language, too, and you could try to learn it. Do you despise us so much? By the fact, what's new about Malaquais? It becomes more and more difficult to have books translated and published here. There is a crisis about books as about everything. Nobody buys anything if he can help it; money is low. One funny little fact: when we did the radio-feature about de Gaulle, 70% of the bookshops sent back the last Sartre's book they had asked for, most of them are Gaullist and they would not sell this kind of stuff.

I am very bored because tomorrow, too, I must be efficient and dutiful. I had promised to a Swedish magazine an article about American women—five pages. Well, there are eighty millions of them, and all different and I know nothing about any of them, so what may I say, in five pages? Yet I have already got the money and spent it. I walk in Paris with beautiful blue velvet pants and nice red shoes which were paid in Stockholm with this money. So what I have to do but to write about American women tomorrow morning? I'll get up as late as I can. It must be 19*h*. in Chicago. Maybe you are eating tomato soup in the kitchen? Work hard, my love, and enjoy your quiet life. It will not be quiet so long. And we'll have to learn to work together, to live together, Nelson. It will be wonderful not only to love each other in passion and unrest for some fugitive days but to live for weeks and months in our daily works and moods, pleasant and unpleasant moods, together, and every night we'll sleep in each other's arms. I wait for it, my own husband, I wait for you.

I go on to be efficient and rather sad. Yesterday I went and saw an American woman who is a kind of an agent here, Wright's agent and other ones. I asked her to help me to get money in America by writing articles, because we need money to go on the Mississippi; she said she would help. I told her to have your books translated in French too; she'll care about it. My *Sang des autres* is being published at Knopf's, and *The Visitor* afterwards. I am pleased because I think you'll be rather interested in *Sang des autres*. She asked for a picture from me and I sent the one you don't like, my intellectual and American face. I spent a long time with my Russian friend trying to translate *God's Angry Man*, and now it is a hobby. Her husband and Sartre too are interested in the undertaking and we try for hours to get the right French words. It is awfully difficult because of the strange Biblical kind of writing; it is fascinating when you begin to try, as a silly hopeless game may be. The very title is a problem, which is yet unresolved for us.

It went on with socialists and radio. I was very pleased to say good bye to everything and everybody. I had your article translated by a young man who was interested in it, but I have to write a little piece about you: if you can suggest anything? What would you exactly like me to say to French people reading *T.M.*? (Nothing about being such a nice crocodile and a smart local youth, my sweet husband, just about the superficial writing stuff?) Please send another Chicago letter.

Bad things happening there: bad stupid strikes; communists seem at a loss and do everything to have de Gaulle coming to power. Schumann will not last long;[4] it seemed very dark yesterday when Blum failed. I was in a very low mood. You have to know I may be a little neurotic too sometimes, so you are not afraid if it happens to me when we live a long time together. I think it comes from the body; it is chiefly a physical matter, since four days I was very tired, feverish, off-balanced. And then yesterday when I got up I could hardly stand to live the coming day. I have had bad nightmares. You know, I have my problems as everybody has. First I loathe having money when people have not; I am not very rich, but since three years I really make some money and I try to give much of it to mother, friends and so on, but yet I live well. The room is bad but clothes and food are good; I need nothing. Sometimes I feel dreadfully guilty about it, and indeed I am. Most of the time I am superficial about it, but when a little neurotic I can hardly stand it. Then I really care much for writing since I am a child. I gave my life to it, but you never know what you do, and sometimes I am afraid I shall never really do what I want to. Then I try to do something with Sartre in intellectual French life, with the hope it has a real human meaning—and I have not much hope. Sometimes you can work without hope, but when you are weak, it becomes difficult. Then I stay far away from the man I love, from the happiness he gives to me: if I do not believe in my reasons of staying away, everything comes wrong. When I am all right, it is all right to live with this kind of problems; everybody has one's. But yesterday night, I felt I was falling in the bottom of a dark, deadly pit and I struggled for two hours in fever and anguish and a kind of despair. At last I got through and fell asleep, but I had to wear dark glasses the whole day because my eyes were so ugly. Yet this crisis was rather good for me and I feel all right again. It helps, as when you get quite drunk or have a big shock. It seems strange to remember how these same things which I stand coldly now looked so terrible and torturing in these black shadows. In fact they deserve worrying for them, but worrying is useless too and you must not vainly brood and worry when you have chosen to live.

My beloved one, peace and longing of my heart, Nelson, it was sweet to speak to you in this very confident, quiet way; to speak about things I should not tell anybody if I did not feel so mixed with him. I like to tell everything to you, good or bad, and to have you stroking my hair and shoulder and looking at me with understanding, loving eyes. I feel your love so precious. I kiss your sweet, loving beloved lips.

Your own Simone

1) *L'Existentialisme et la sagesse des nations.* 2) By W. Van Tilburg Clark. 3) "Le Prophète de la colère" by Léonard Ehrlich, *Les Temps modernes*, May–June 1948. 4) Robert Schuman, French Prime Minister 1947–1948, Minister of Foreign Affairs until 1952. An MRP member, he founded the European Coal and Steel Community.

Tuesday, 25 Novembre 1947

My own Nelson,

Here is the reward of works and pain: I am in the lonely country house with white roses on my table, a heap of good books around me, and before me a whole month with nothing to do but writing and reading. I feel so good! No Russian, Jewish, or ugly girl-friend to see; no mother, sister, brother-in-law; no authors with bad manuscripts. That is wonderful. I just had a warm bath, and many little glasses of strong apple liquor, and I feel like a queen.

Yesterday was a half-blue, half-rainy Paris day; half-cold and half-mild, and rather nice. I was very excited by the idea of departure. I had a nice ride in a cab to go to an agency and look for some good pictures about America. I should like my book to have twenty or thirty good pictures in it. I went to a big building where there are many magazines and newspapers, and which is very poetical for me, because the last day before German's departure, the first free newspaper began to be secretly printed there. I remember Camus and his young friends, working with guns under their hands, all the iron doors closed, a little scared because at any moment German soldiers could come and it would have been a bad mess. We went through Paris, Sartre and I, to look at things, and we wrote reports about what was happening and brought them to Camus, with a little pleasant sense of danger in the streets where from time to time bullets were fired. And when American soldiers were arrived in Paris, it was such a feast in the offices! The newspapers appearing in light, and everybody drinking and being so happy! In a way, it was the best moment in my life; from an internal, political point of view, it surely was. We had not to care too much for future; it was so wonderful to be liberated from the recent past! I notice, we all remember with a kind of longing this last time of Occupation, the first bewildering joy of Liberation. Well, I remembered all that, coming back to this place yesterday by a blue morning. Then I spent two pleasant hours looking at pictures. But even with this very interesting collection, I did not exactly find what I wanted. Then I went to see the little frog-faced publisher (who went to London with us) who is buying to me a little book made with old articles. He pays much for it and I am pleased with it. We signed the contract with nice smiles. Then, without even eating anything, I went to the radio. We had invited an important syndicalist, belonging to the CGT minority. He was so scared to speak in the mike he could hardly find his words and we had to begin again several times, though we helped him as much as we could. He was as red as a boiled lobster and much more unhappy; yet he speaks well and fluently in daily life, but sitting there, he fidgeted, kicked, coughed, and even swore loudly, so it was necessary to begin again. A hard job! We all became as red as lobsters. Then at 6 I went with Sartre to the very elegant Ritz Hotel and we drank martinis in the bar like elegant people! We were meeting there a dreadfully elegant woman from Buenos Aires, Victoria Ocampo, writer, poetess, and leader of a great Argentine magazine, *Sur*. She is fifty, has been rather beautiful and something of it is left to her, though she is sparkling with too many pearls and diamonds. The point is she is very wealthy and important in her country and could invite us for well paid lectures, so we tried to manage it with her, and it seems in good way. When leaving USA (when leaving you and beginning to wait for your coming to France) I should like to spend summer (that is their mild winter) in South America. It is just a hope, but maybe it will happen, and the expectation was worth drinking a martini in Ritz bar. Then I prepared everything for going away, and I slept some hours: Was not that a busy day? I deserved a reward, and since you are not there to give me the real reward I want, I could not find nothing better than being peacefully here. So, all duties done and maybe overdone, I left Paris. Because of the strikes, we were afraid there would be no train, but there was one.

Wednesday

There is just a bad point in all my happiness: postmen are on strike and there is no mail since two days. The strike is not lasting long, but it will make big delays. I shall not have my Monday letter before long, and I am afraid you will not get this one before long. It is sweet never to be in a hurry, to be able to enjoy all which happens in my heart, remembrances, hopes, and quiet, warm knowledge. I love you.

The village here is ugly, but in a French way — and the ugliest French village is beautiful compared to your villages. I like your big cities, but I loathe your villages! This one has nice grey slated roofs, old little houses, trees and grass, queer little shops, and I like it though it is not really pretty. Anyway it is raining. I did not go out since I arrived. I live in an old peignoir, with slippers on my feet. I have a little room on the first floor, Sartre has a big one in which I work too, and the old lady a very big one where we all meet for meals and tea. So we don't even go downstairs! At the end of a long lobby is the sick neurotic husband. I told you he is neurotic since twenty years and did not leave his bed since seven years. He lives in a dark room with all shutters and curtains closed, other curtains around his bed and just a very little lamp lighted. I never saw him in my life and Sartre not since fifteen years. From time to time we just hear the tiny sound of a bell: he is calling his wife. The old cook and a middle-aged maid live in the bottom of the house, and they bring the dishes during the day. So we really live, the three of us, as on a quiet island. And what is pleasant, everybody does exactly what he likes, and does not speak to the others if he does not choose. The old lady is really the nicest woman in the world; she is ill now and stays in bed nearly all the day, reading and hearing radio. She has big headaches but does not complain; she says she hears in her head the sound of huge waterfalls and hundred cows with bells tied on their necks coming to drink—a very poetical noise to hear in one's head and she feels pleased at it. I slept nine hours, and two more in the middle of the day. I wrote a preface for my little book of articles, re-read all I have written about America, and began to write the last part: I worked about seven hours today. Is not that good? Now I am a little exhausted and I'll lead myself to bed.

Sleep well, honey, and wait for me. I love you.

Your own Simone

Thursday, 27 Novembre 1947

Nelson, my own husband,

No letter from you, but I do not wonder at it. Life is going on very cosily. You see, I never had a home. I never chose to, because it is too much trouble. When I was a girl, my parents were poor and discredited in a bad, mean, petit-bourgeois way. The flat was sad, nearly dirty: I loathed it.[1] I lived with my sister in a very cheap room, very little and unconvenient; two beds could hardly stand in it. When we were up, there was no place to stay, so we had to spend the day in my father's bureau, where everybody gathered; in winter it was the only place where there was a fire. I loathed the people. I hated to read or study in this dull place. I enjoyed it only in the afternoon when nobody was at home, then I could sit in the deep leather armchair and read forbidden books such as Musset, Victor Hugo, and I felt like a queen. But coming back in the evening by the dirty staircase to stand the whole night in the cold grim house with my parents arguing together, no privacy, no peace, I hated it. Maybe it is the reason why I am such a poor house wife, everything concerning the house and a good wife's life, such as my mother's, scared me to death. Afterwards, when I had passed my exams and become a teacher, I chose to live in hotels, and I kept this taste. Now I am a little tired with bad hotels, but I should not make the effort to escape from them; it is such a problem in France. Well, never having had a home of my own, I am very fond of other people's homes, sometimes. I like yours before loving you, you know, but I am not to speak of Wabansia now; it means too much. I just wanted to explain to you why I feel so pleasant to be here, in peignoir and slippers. It smells of burning wood and old times.

I like the food, very fine country food. Every evening, at dinner, I eat soup and pancakes, nice pancakes with fried apples in them, a dish I enjoy eating at every dinner. The days go away very quickly, writing (eight hours today), reading a little, talking a little, hearing a little the radio, drinking strong apple liquor and sleeping much.

I read *Ethan Frome*. I agree with the foreword about the end of the book which I don't find very reliable. But I disagree with what he says about the main central part. I think the love between Ethan and Marjorie is very deeply felt and expressed in a very moving way. I like chiefly the dinner in the quiet home, when the wife is away. E. Wharton succeeded in giving a very rich poetical meaning to this one free evening; it is very daily, very simple; it sounds true and the unspoken quiet wild love sounds true too. I like the idea of a deadly love, such an important, essential love, being lived in half-consciousness, in a daily unimportant way; the contrast between the horrid tearing, the impossibility of departure, and the gentle, ordinary confort in each other seems very true to me. For that, I should forgive the rather conventional and unconvincing end, and the lack of deeper insight in the author. Sometimes it makes me think of Thomas Hardy, but I think Hardy is endowed with much more sympathy for human beings.

Friday evening

No letter. What worries me chiefly is the idea you will have no letter for a long time, and what will you think? I hope you are as confident, as self-conceited as I am, and if you don't receive letters you know it is not my fault, you know it could not mean I love you less even for just a day. I hope, but you can be so unexpectedly modest, so little self-conceited sometimes. I just am not sure.

Nothing happened. I read little novels by Carson Mac Cullers. I like them, though they are a little too womanly, too poetical and quivering and full of secret meaning. Did I tell you the girl is now in the American hospital, half-paralysed because she drinks so much? I heard it just before leaving Paris, and I was displeased at it. I was fond of her when I once saw her, her strange, ugly, sensitive face, her slim elegant figure in grey flannel trousers, her hoarse Southern voice. Maybe she would have written really good books, but there is not much hope about her. Her husband seemed a very decent quiet man, but he drinks nearly as much as she does. Sad.

I ate nice apple pancakes for my dinner and am drinking apple liquor. Now I lie on the bed and read some book, that is the good way to read, as

I did in Wabansia. In Paris I never read because I am always in a hurry and that is unpleasant. But lying for two hours before sleeping, leisurely, that is good. Good bye, love. I wait for your beloved letters, and I never stop to wait for you.

Your own Simone

1) 71, rue de Rennes, Paris, 6th arrondissement.

Monday, 1st Décembre 1947

My own husband,

It is a very long time without any letter from you: two weeks now. It seems a whole century. Nobody receives any letter here. I am afraid you will not get mine for a long time neither; that is what I wired though you do not like very much wires. I hate the idea that you could be impatient, unquiet because of me, not knowing maybe why I do not write. I hate the idea of anything unpleasant coming to you by me when I should like to give you as much happiness as love; you would be too happy maybe for a human being if I could make all my love happiness for you.

You should laugh if you could see how we go on living here: just like regular sick people. We all wear peignoirs and slippers, and lie on beds most of the days and never go as far as downstairs! I was thought a crazy woman because after a whole week confinement, my head aching, I asked for a half-hour walk. The old lady wanted to give me some pills. But I succeeded in persuading Sartre whose head was aching too and we took a little walk on the little roads. Nelson, it was as beautiful as a long faraway trip! The sky was a ball of cotton, thickly white, and all trees and little blades of grass covered with frost, which is nicer than snow because snow weighs too heavily on the little branches and weeds; frost just clothes them tightly; it looks more solid, stony, icy. It was a moon landscape with something human still quivering in it: two peasants in a lonely white meadow moving I don't know what with very old gestures, a wind-mill with big black arms which looked tragic. From time to time a black crow flew away from a white tree. Here and there a very subtle touch of colour: red little fruits in the hedges, or golden leaves, or green grass on the brown earth, veiled with icy white. The country is very plain here, but it was fine to feel the cold air on my cheeks and in my lungs, instead of tobacco smoke. I feel wholly reinvigorated.

I brought many books from Paris, American and French, and I put them in good order on the chimney mantle. I like to look at them. Then from attics to caves the house is full of all kinds of books, chiefly old ones, and it is pleasant to take a basket and to go and pick some of them as you would pick up mushrooms. I read some bad tedious novels: one by Henry James, *What Maisie Knew*, it is a bore, another by Ford Madox Ford, *The Good Soldier*, very boring too, I was not interested at the least. Then I am reading the big book about Negroes, *American Dilemma*,[1] and I am enthusiastic about it. The man is really clever; he knows and understands much. He speaks not only about Negro problem but about many other American problems, and I read it with passion. Would you like that I bring it to you in spring? If you had leisure enough to read it, you would be interested as I am, but it is a big piece. I enjoy touching the big thick book, and thinking I'll read it on for at least two weeks; you feel very intimate with a book when you hold it in your hands for such a long time, but you do not choose to do it with all of them.

Darling, will you send us another Chicago letter? About anything you like. The young translator was very puzzled with the firm: "the crocodile." I had to translate it for him. No letters. We really live as in a lonely island, or rather an asylum. We just hear the radio from time to time, and at times we phone to people in Paris. The strikes were a strong unsuccess and workers are angry; if they could create a genuine working-class party, it would be good; some people are working at it; indeed, it is not easy to do.

Tuesday

Good evening, darling. The little room is as quiet as in my childhood when I enjoyed sitting at a little bureau and writing stories for my dolls. We are very happy to be here. In Paris Metro has stopped. There is very little electricity and people phone that the town is very sad. Here there is no light nor water in the morning, and from time to time lights go away in the evening, but on the whole it is very confortable. Just no letters, no letters from the Nelson I love. Reading the *American Dilemma*, and my own little book about America being nearly over, I begin to think again about the other one, about women situation. I should like to write a book as important as this big one about Negroes. Myrdal points many very interesting analogies between Negroes' and women's status; I felt it already. Can you know, without breaking your back about it, if such a book as Myrdal's *Nation and Family* might be found in USA? I am afraid it is written in Swedish. Thanks

113

if you can inquire about it. I notice I am often asking for little things. Have you never anything to ask me? I am waiting impatiently for your letters. I hope they are not lost; they will come soon. I need them so much: the yellow paper, the typewritten words, the handwritten name of the husband I love; then I should be sure you are not just a smoky dream; you do not fade away, not in the least, but sometimes it becomes hard to believe that you are really flesh and blood; that I did not tell myself a bedtime story. My faraway, dreamy, silent one, I have to believe in you as I had faith in God when I was a little girl; the difference is there is no deception, some day you'll close your arms around me and our lips will encounter.

Let us kiss a very long kiss.

Your own Simone

1) By Gunnar Myrdal.

Saturday, 6th December 1947

Honey,

It is very bad of you not to have changed yourself into a homing-pigeon. You lazy one, now I shall not have anything before Monday. I'll have gone three weeks without hearing of your. For love, I can suppose it is not dead, but can I live without knowing how was the weather on Wabansia Avenue? I feel very faraway and sad. Sometimes I take from my bag old letters you wrote to me, but I know them by heart; it is not enough to know how you *were* and to *suppose* you are still yourself. I have to know all which is happening around you and in your off-balanced head and good warm heart. If I receive nothing next week, I'll wire to you. I become a bit nervous about you. Few things happen, fewer than in your own quiet life, sometimes the electric-current is abruptly cut off; candles make very nice shadows on the walls but it is not very convenient to write. I gave *Ethan Frome* to the old lady who read it with great enthousiasm; myself, I go on learning things about America and American literature. I have to, since my husband is an American local youth. But his wife is a French frog, he does not care to learn about France, which is very bad of him. I read little stories by O. Henry, *The Five Millions*. I like some of them; the humour is sometimes heavy and insistent, but sometimes he tells things in a really funny way, he feels people and streets; he sounds very American to me. Then I re-read

Walden by Thoreau. The man is a little short-sighted and narrow-minded. I do not like him so much; all this stuff about eating vegetables and keeping away from women; it would be so sad if you did! He can be somewhat boring too. But there are things he knows how to speak about, and as I like trees and parks, woods and snow, I enjoy them.

Please, what means the title of the first chapter of *God's Angry Man*: "How Are You on the Goose?" I asked to some American people and was told goose is just the greasy bird I enjoy to eat, or a rather obscene word. Neither meaning fits. My Russian friend and myself are breaking our heads about it. I read a half of the big *American Dilemma*, and it is always very, very interesting. My own book is running on very quickly. Tomorrow I'll begin to speak about Chicago; I'll do my best. Peignoir, slippers, apple pancakes, apple liquor; there is nothing else to say, except the bad news in the newspapers. You know, they were very useful to me, all these papers I read in our nest, lying cosily on the bed while you, most of the time, slept.

What is unpleasant is that *some letters* come, old and new ones, all mixed up. Some mail-boxes were broken by strikers and they threw the mail away into ditches. I hope yours are not lost. I should cry with anger about it.

The new government Schumann fired us from the radio. God gave it to us (under Ramadier's features) and God took it from us, as said old wise Job. It is all right, since we were interested but did not enjoy to do this. I have better be in a quiet room and write for myself.

Tuesday

My own beloved Nelson, I was so happy this morning: at last, darling, at last the old maid brought me a letter from you with my breakfast. I just jumped from the bed to push my shutters open and went back to bed and read first quickly, greedily, then slowly, lovingly, the yellow sheets. It was the letter written on the 29th, so I missed one. I think it is in Paris now. Tomorrow the old lady's son is coming and will bring me all my letters. So I know you have just something wrong in your teeth, but nothing wrong in your heart. Just an hour after, I had a call from my mother: she just received your gift, she says it is so wonderful, so many things in it; she looked crazy with pleasure, in a very childish way. Thanks to you, once more, my love. I can fancy you buying everything carefully and packing and sending them, and I know it must have been much bother, and for all the bother I give you love and love.

So many things to tell you in answer, I don't know how to begin. I shall say things in disorder, just as they occur to me. First for Edith

Wharton, it is true I was a little prejudiced against her. I read once, long ago, a rather tedious book about a son going to the war and his mother mourning for him. But, as I told you, I liked *Ethan Frome* very much. It was nice to intend it for a Christmas gift, darling. There is a very pretty pine-tree on the back of the book, it gives to it a very Christmas gift look. What is not true, dearest husband, though you always say it again, that is my being two women, one is enough to love you in a proper way. Really, the biggest difference between my letters and articles is my writing English or French. You know, if my French was as weak as my English, I should be a very poor writer. But this petty difference must not deceive you: just one woman. Indeed, when I write books or essays, I try to be just as true as when I tell you that I love you; and when I tell you so, I have thought in my heart about the truth of my love as seriously as if I were to write a long essay about it. I am not kidding. I give very long, serious thoughts to our love. I think very steadily about all what you give to me, that is so much, and all I do not give to you. Darling, anyway if you stick to the idea that I am two women, be sure they both love you, and maybe the nicest is the most stupid.

Nelson, honey, I was very much disturbed by your little story about the Jewish girl and the older woman; the whole morning I thought about it, as seriously as about Brasillach[1] death, because the tiniest thing concerning you is important for me. The general idea is *you should feel yourself free*, as long as you don't betray our love, which could be done only if you really intended to. I feel many unpleasant remorses for having deprived you of some pleasant time. I know very well you can sleep with a woman, even a very nice one, and even in Wabansia's nest, without spoiling anything between you and me; if I suggested something else through my letters, I am ashamed of it. There is no reason, I living far away, for you not sleeping with women when you choose. I believe in your love too much to think if would make any difference. Well, indeed, I love you too much, in a physical sexual way too, not to feel any jealousy. I think I should have to be very cold blooded to be able to fancy you kissing a girl, sleeping with her, and not to feel a bad pang in the heart. But this kind of animal instinct does not matter very much. When I began to read the story, I thought you were going to tell me you spent a night with the woman, and the first movement was to be glad for your frankness, for your sincerely telling me; the second was to wait the pang in my heart, with the belief I should go through it. Well, to be quite frank, it was a great relief to find you were so careful of our love, and my heart was suffused with gratitude. But afterwards I felt remorses. Maybe I don't explain things very well. Let us suppose you were very hungry, and were given a wonderful run-cake; instead of eating it, you sent it to me. That is how I feel. It is a *gift*, do you see? A generous and lovely beautiful gift of love. But you *had not* to do it, you could eat the rum-cake. And even I should be remorseful and feel guilty, if you always give me our part of rum-cake. I mean my beloved one, next time when you are tempted by a woman, just do what you please, take her to Wabansia home if you like. I really mean it. You have not to be afraid of hurting me by doing so. I just wish she'll be away when I come, and never too deep in your heart. In this matter, the chief questions is rather: take care the girl will not be unhappy if you drop her afterwards. Just care about it. I think I told you once, as long as you do not spoil our love, it is all right.

You see, it is nearly as long a dissertation as *Eye for Eye!*[2] I sum it: next time, just sleep with the woman if you want to. Nevertheless, I take it as a tender, lovely gift that this time you did not. But a gift is not an alimony; nobody is grateful for an alimony because it is due. You owe me nothing, that is why the gift was precious; don't let us make a system with it. Just one word more about it though I know I have hardly to tell it: tell me always the truth. And one word more: I love you.

I am very glad you get this issue of *Politics* and were interested. Try to find the whole book by Rousset. Did you read the article by Merleau-Ponty? He is a very old friend, the oldest I have. I know him since twenty years. He works hard with us in *T.M.*, and radio and everything. I personally don't like him so much—I'll speak to you about him in spring;[3] but the article is interesting, regarding our attitude towards communism. You made a mistake, or maybe the translator did, about Sartre's article: he was not drunk, and just wrote that people must not make a confusion between d'Holbach[4] and dialectic materialism. Or were you drunk, honey? By the way, you never told me what happened with the strange liquor we bought in order to get a nice flask for me. Did anybody drink it? Did you do?

1) Robert Brasillach, French writer who supported the Vichy regime; he was eventually tried and executed. 2) An article reprinted in *L'Existentialisme et la sagesse des nations*. 3) Especially because she attributed to him a large part of the responsibility for the death of her friend Zaza. See *Memoirs of a Dutiful Daughter*, where he is referred to as "Pradelle"; see also *Zaza: The Letters and Notebooks of Elizabeth Lacoin*, 1914-1929 (Le Seuil). 4) Baron d'Holbach (1723-1789), French atheist philosopher.

Nelson, my own love,

You believed you were in Chicago, this whole day, but it was not true; you stayed in the county house. Le bon pigeon de La Pouéze brought your last letter yesterday, and there was a kind of smoke in it; it became bigger and bigger and at the end it was you and I did not let you go. We just lived again together all we had lived before: going to the little Italy, drinking Chianti, visiting the country jail, looking at the Endor witch, listening to records, eating rum-cake, drinking whisky, wandering in forgotten streets. Once you told me: "I could not have missed you," and once: "Nobody will take you from me," and once: "You made me very happy." If just two letters could do this, making you flesh and blood and true, what will it be when I really see and touch you? I have a very securely locked safe where I keep all these words and looks, smiles and kisses, which stabbed me in the heart. I do not look at them too often, not to spoil them, but today I opened the safe and took all my treasures madly against my heart. It was sweet to keep you so close, all day long, you, my love.

Merry Christmas to you too, darling. I am so glad you told me that you feel really better for our love's sake. Let it be as sound, precious happiness as it is for me. You say it is time now for planning some nice trip. Well, I got a big American map here. These last two days I looked at it very carefully and eagerly. Yea, what I should like better would be to go to Mexico; it is impossible to make very precise plans now. I am nearly sure I'll be in America within March, and quite sure I'll stay five months. But I don't not know about money. I think I'll have to stay at least two weeks in New York to get some, then I have to go to Los Angeles for a month. The other months are yours. According the money we have and your own possibilities, it would be nice to have a beautiful trip together; if not, sleeping in your arms in Wabansia is so nice that nothing else matters so much. And that is all I can say, just now, about our spring life together. Yes, I can say too: I want it so much. Nelson, we have much to share; we were not given our chance yet. We must be husband and wife for a real time. I could faint with joy when I think of it. I'll be nice, darling, you'll see, I'll be really nice. Don't get afraid, you lonely man. I am glad you did well with Bromfield, but what were you speaking about the *four* other times? Why are you bubbling so much if you are not even paid for? Just as I do, by the mere pleasure of moving your jaws? But I like to be so garrulous only when I am with you, and not for silly old ladies. Explain this matter to me.

Strange, you American people think *No Exit* so dull. It was such a success in Paris. I suspect the actors are not very good either; they were wonderful here, and they are very important to give something dynamic to the play.

Schumann, I forgot to tell you, is from Alsace, and communists call him "Le boche," which is very mean. But he is a very conservative, narrow-minded man.

My Californian friend sent me a very funny letter about the Hollywood inquests, funny but awful, the way Gary Cooper and Ginger Rogers and so on acted. She begins to be very scared of America. She was so happy to have married a G.I. and to become an American woman, being nothing (a Russian white refugee with Nansen papers)[1] but now she does not wish to become American any more because she loathes the whole policy, she says it stinks in Hollywood and describes it in an awful way.

Friday 12th

It is a regular Nelson festival this week! Here is the third letter I got from you! Indeed, it is the first one you wrote, the one where were the seven good frog commandements. Yea, I agree with all of them. It was such a lovely letter. I got so feverish about being glad for your love and loving you that I could not sleep last night, neither work today, but just dream, with eyes closed or open, dream of you and you again. I miss you so much, just now.

Yea, I read *Moby Dick*, twice or more. I like it very much. Edith Piaf can be cheap sometimes, but she can be wonderful; she had a hoarse voice which pleases me better that many "nice" ones.

Saturday, 2 A.M.

Good night, love. I never go to bed so late in this quiet country house, but the old lady's son came, with wife and children, from South America, and we all drunk so much! He brought your last letter. We drank fine white and brown, and lightly colored french liquors, very hard ones. I feel so tired and sleepy, nearly sick. But it is not my best sober self who loves you, it is my whole self, as well drunk as sober, sad and happy, sick and healthy. So I could not sleep without drunkly telling you: Nelson, I love you so much. I see nothing wonderful in me, nothing so wonderful in you, but my loving you is more precious to me than anything on earth. I am so lucky to love you and be loved by you. Words make me sad. I'll stop. I need my whole body, all I have, little or much, to tell you I love you; pen and ink look so dry. Let us have some time, three or four months, and I'll show you something of my love.

The drunk frog

1) A substitute passport issued to refugees.

Monday, 15th Décembre 1947

My own Crocodile,

Your life is a kind of orgiastic, thrilling adventure compared to mine, but I am very pleased with this quietness and monotony. The least thing seems so precious when nothing ever happens. Today, I took a walk: it was the third time since I am here, and it was a great event though it did not last an hour. I did not remember how blue the sky may be. There were some roses on the walls of the little houses, though it is December, and some yellow leaves on the trees: yellow is a wonderful color! I was amazed to have got eyes.

Then, the other Saturday the old lady's son came; he is just my age. I knew him when we were both twenty-two — a long time ago! He was Sartre's pupil when Sartre was a student and was giving lessons to earn his life. The old lady was wealthy in this time and could afford private teachers for her son who was very lazy and stupid. That is the way Sartre became acquainted with the old lady, and I knew her through him. We were really friends with the mother, but good comrads with the boy too. And I remember how once I was astonished when, sleeping at the old lady's as I did sometimes when I stayed late, the son came to my room and asked laughingly if he could sleep near me; I was so young and stupid, he was such a comrad I just thought he was kidding and said "why not?," not knowing what to say. Then he brought me a very ugly scarf and said it would be mine if he really slept with me. He was kidding too in some way but he lay near me, and I said it was maybe too narrow for two, and he said it was all right and began to stroke me. I asked if he was crazy! He saw there was nothing to do with me, even by the gift of the scarf, and he went away. As between us there never had been any kind of flirt, I was really puzzled. Now years have gone away; he went to Argentina, where his mother had big properties and he had a rather awful life, alone in a lonely estancia. He married a nice, clever girl who was Jewish and a doctor. They loved each other, but gave each other the hell; she could not live in such a lonely place, she got neurotic. Some day, there were two friends for lunch; she looked a little upset. She went to the bathroom and came back half laughing and said: "I have swallowed all the bottle of strychnine we had to kill rats." He shrugged and said: "That is a silly joke!" She said: "It is not a joke, go and see!" Then she became all distracted, saying: "Help me, I don't want to die!" They called the doctor, and herself, beeing a doctor, told what to do, and drank milk and chloroforme. But at the end of the day she had died in terrible pains. When the policemen came to make a report about suicide, they asked money from the husband not to tell he had killed her; he did not give the money and for some time he was suspected of murder. They had to open the grave and look in the stomach of the dead woman: they found strychnine, the bad cops were put in jail and the man left to himself. Not very happy. Then twelve years ago, he came back to France and half fell in love with another girl, only half of it. He did not wish to take her to Argentina with him. But she rushed to the boat and romantically jumped in when it was going away. He had to wire to his parents for the money to pay the travel. He married her and had two children, but she thought the man very wealthy and wanted his money rather than loving him, so she was very cold and indifferent with him. He spent his days outdoors with his little girl whom he cherishes. He was very kind with her, remembering the tragic death of his first wife, but from kindness he went to hate for her, and just now he wants to leave her and be left alone. So when they came, they hardly spoke a word to each other. The wife is rather pretty, bit in a cold, sad way. It was strange to see him: I remembered a young boy; he was a man, nearly an old one. At first he did not want to speak to anybody; he thinks he must look stupid and wild and faraway. When he saw we were pleased to meet him, he became very gay and asked me if I remembered this night when we did not sleep together. I said it was because the scarf was too ugly, bit I was a little ill at ease about the talking, chiefly in presence of the cold fair wife. Then we planned things for the travel in South America, and he became very funny as he used to be and we drank all of us, until 2 A.M. They went away in the morning, and he came back to America, by airplane, leaving here wife and children. The old lady is very upset by the whole story.

Tuesday

I am glad you did so well with Bromfield and are a local existentialist now; but you were wise not to go and discuss with Jean Wahl.[1] Yes, I know him very well. My last student year he was my teacher, when I was 21, and he was a member of the jury at the last exam—the one I had to pass to become a teacher myself. He is a little Jewish man, with much knowledge but a very dim mind, very abstract too, and not human at all. This kind of monster teachers often are. He was taken by the Germans during the war and sent to Drancy, the place where Jews waited before deporting for Germany; there he was half-crazy, sleeping under a big umbrella. Then, I do not know by what luck, he was released and went away to South America whence he came back to France after the war. He was rather fond of men, on the sexual ground, but he contrived to marry a very young student of him, as tall as he is small, and he had two children with her. (Has he? Anyway she had two children.) They are the funiest pair I ever saw. He knows little about existentialism though he pretends to (little for a teacher, I mean. It would be much for a local youth) and he tried to be rather friendly with Sartre and I, but intellectually we do not think much of him and we kept apart and now we are rather cold with each other. I must say too that nobody understands him, no student ever did, I think he does not understand himself, so it would have been very hard for you to manage any discussion with him.

Darling, I am glad we had just the same idea at the same time: not to go to New Orleans. But don't you think Mexico is better than Central America? I have a friend who just went to Mexico and sent me some pictures and told me how beautiful it was. I am dying with desire of seeing it. Now if you already saw it and don't care to go there again (though it is big, and sure there are a lot of places you did not see), we could make it half and half: we'll go to Guatemala and to Mexico. What do you think? And if you really insist for going only to Central America, I'll do as you please because I love you.

Yea, I love you, my own love. I intended to live until eighty, but since you'll die at seventy-seven,[2] I am willing to die at seventy-eight in your arms. That is two whole years of my life I am giving away for you. Are you grateful? You know, when we'll travel through the big world and when we'll stay in our goat's nest, I'll do two things: I'll teach you French—that is very serious—an hour a day for three months would learn you something, and I'll tell you many stories about myself, girlhood, and everything. I should like you to know me better, but you never ask questions and I am always scared I could bore you. Well, I'll tell something just now: in fact I can cook. When the war began, I was yet a teacher and had little money and my

Californian friend (who was not yet Californian, who was nothing) to support. I hired a room with a kitchen and for three years I did all the cooking for the friend, for Sartre and myself. In a way it was easy because there was really nothing to eat but turnips and cabbages, noodles sometimes and potatoes, but all just boiled in water. Then, the second year, the old lady sent some meat once a week and I even had friends for dinner sometimes in the pink room. In a way it was easy, but in a way more difficult than what you do; for instance the meat always was a little rotten and I had to manage so that nobody tasted the bad stale taste. The noodles, there were often worms in them, and weevils in the beans — it was really some work to take them away. Then, cooking cabbage with water, you must pretend it had been cooked with butter. Then, we had very little gas, and I put the soup and cabbage in my bed when the cooking had began, to achieve it without spending any gas. There were many problems, you see, the first one beeing to find the cabbage, and I am really proud because I never gave much time to it and yet we lived this way, without becoming too lean and weak, for 3 years. The last year I even went with train and bicycle at 80 miles from Paris to buy some meat and mushrooms and bring it back for mother and friends; and once I went with Sartre who was very nice, never complaining about turnips or rotten meat and helping a lot, and in the train, coming back, English or American airplanes shot us with their machine-guns; many people were killed, or badly bleeding; the wagons smelt of stocked meat (all the people having gone to fetch something to eat as I had done) and this mixture of bleeding human bodies and oxen-smell was not nice; it was not nice neither to go on, leaving dead and wounded in the little station where we had stopped, and waiting for a new raid. It was quite in the end, when you tired to stop all trains and kill the machines, as you had to do. Nobody was angry at it, just a bit scared. It was the last time I went to look for meat. Then during a week, while the Liberation, we had no more gas, and we cooked on paper fires. We had to hold newspapers burning under the pan until the noodles boiled, it was long and tedious. Well, I did it for three years and I made a game of it and enjoyed it; but now the game is over, and I loathe cooking a little more than before. But if you become sick in the Guatemala deserts and could not cook any longer, I should be very helpful and I could *cook* again. And you could laugh at me, silly nice man, when you wanted to. You can always laugh at me as long as you love me. I am not so stupid. That is not the way you could hurt me. You would not have hurt me neither by going to the stockyards with the magazine woman. Though I think it is awfully arrogant of her to have given you an appointment in my own Le petit café. Is there nothing sacred on earth?

Good bye, honey, I am deadly tired for writing goes long a letter, after writing seven hours my book. Ah! I forgot to say how glad I am you are working about yours. Yes, it must be readable in spring so that I read it, and so that we can have a true holyday. Nelson, my husband, it is not so faraway: we are about half-way. You are such a nice man, darling, sometimes I just say these words in my heart: such a nice man, my nice, beloved man. I should like you to feel how nice is my heart too. I kiss you, a long, happy, nice kiss.

Your own Simone

1) Jean Wahl, nineteenth-century French metaphysician and historian of philosophy. 2) A German fortune teller had told Algren he would live to age 76, not 77. In fact, he died at age 72.

Thursday, 18 Décembre 1947

My beloved crocodile,

I am going to send you some book reviews, since I do nothing but writing and reading—I eat pancakes too, but what should I say about them? Sometimes I eat them with salt, sometimes with sugar, or I spill burning liquor on them. So, I'll tell you how nicely I go on learning things about my husband's country. No doubt I like so much to read about America because it is a way of getting closer to you. Did you read the letters of Thomas Wolfe which were published in *Atlantic Monthly* this year? They are letters to friends and chiefly to an old teacher, about his books—peculiar books—and the general meaning of writing any book; they are written in a much more simple way that the books themselves and I enjoyed reading them. Now I guess you would be rather angry with the May-June issue of *Politics*: that is about Wallace and very harsh about him. The man, Dwight Macdonald, who publishes the magazine and wrote the paper, is this kind of left wing people who are always a little more on the left than anybody else, and often as the earth is round, running left, and left and left, they find themselves on the right wing. He hates Wallace not to hate communists enough and himself, having been a Stalinist ten years ago, loathe them more than anything. I do not know if what he says is more or less true. Anyway, it was very interesting. I was not pleased, on the other hand, with *Trouble in July* by Caldwell. I read this book already twenty times. I feel, sometimes by Caldwell, sometimes by others. I could write it myself now: a vivid picture of South community from any sociological look. I used to like very much *Tobacco Road* and *God's Little Acre*, but not the last ones. Then I am reading *John Brown's Body*[1] which you sent me (having stolen it somewhere). I like many parts of it. I do not like so much the ida of such an epic poem, so long and about battles. The big book *American Dilemma* is over—a wonderful book; I learnt a lot from it. Shall I bring it to you? I am reading over, by Rousset, *Days of Our Death*. Enough with the books, don't you think I read a lot? And I wrote a lot too. If I went on too long living this way, my brain would burst, but some weeks, it is nice. I like to have much of something at a time rather than a little the whole time: rather ten days of real love than a life of half-indifferent, half-angry phoney love. Don't you think it is better? Yes, it is. But the best is a rich long time of warm Nelson loving.

It is very quiet here. This house was a nice shelter for me in many unpleasant circumstances, that is one of the reasons why it is so dear to me. In September '39 when the war broke onto and all the men went away, I came here for the first time; I felt as sad as sad can be, and the old lady helped very much. The house was very wealthy then and every day she took me to the cave and I chose myself a wonderful bottle of old wine, and wonderful marmalade, and we ate chicken and turkey; I lay in the meadows, picked up fruits, read books, and contrived to find some peace in my heart. Then, in June 1940, when Germans entered Paris, I came here, in a car, when there were not yet too many people on the roads. I was in this very room when I saw the German soldiers for the first time. Since the morning, French soldiers, French officers were flying away through the little village, all the peasants were hidden in woods and meadows, all the people in this house—they were many—were hidden too in the country. But the old sick crazy man had stayed in bed and the old lady stayed near him, and I stayed in the house because you know how I like to see things with my eyes even if they are more unpleasant than a dying hog spilling its blood. The shutters had been closed, but I looked through and I saw very well the deserted, hot, white street. The village was so lonely, so silent. And then something exploded at the corner of the street. The glasses of the next house were blown away. I heard an harsh, hoarse voice just saying: "Ach!" And I saw them, in their green clothes, all tall, fair-haired and pink, looking so strong. I could not help crying. Then they passed and went on walking towards south, hundreds, thousands of them, for three nights and three days. People came back and another life began.

Honey, it is just time to send you my new-year wishes:

First, just stay the man you are because you are just what a man ought to be—they so stubborn are. Just remain my Nelson.

Second, wire a good book, as good as the other were, that means even a little better or at least different.

Fourth, I'll wish you health and some money because it is important enough.

But before, and it will be the third, I'll wish you a nice time with the girl you love and who loves you: I wish nothing spoils your love and it gives you both of you as much happiness as it is worth, and I know it is worth much.

Here are my wishes for my Crocodile.

I had bad news of my Russian friend[2] this morning: she was so happy because her lungs were healed and she thought she could play next winter —she played *The Flies* by Sartre once and was a really good player—but she just learnt she had anew some nasty little beasts in her body. She became all lean and tired and ugly, again, and she will not recover before long, and maybe never, and she knows it. She is awfully sad and though I do not like her as much as before, and anyway, it is sad to say, other's people diseases and worries are always rather easy to stand, I feel a bit sad myself. She was so lively, so greedy for life once, and now I should wish nothing for her but death. It is bad, loving when your life had no more meaning; and she wanted so feverishly to get something from life. I disliked her selfishness, but I liked the fever.

You asked about Edith Piaf the other day. It just happened I receive a letter from a French friend of New York about it. She went to listen to her; she says the singers who sang with her[3] and are not half as talented as she is, had much more success. She explains it in a clever way, I think. She notices that American people when they get something from France, react exactly as we do in France when getting something from America: they like what *looks* very French in them. The singers singing old French songs, they understand and like. But the real French things do not seem so French, they are just new; and in France we like them because they are different

126

from the other French things. In the same way I see very well that I first liked in America what *seemed* to me really American: now, I know a little better and the most important things in America do not seem to me so openly American. You see what I mean? So Edith Piaf in her black dress, with her hoarse voice and very ugly face, does not seem so French, and American people do not know what to find in her—they remain cold. We like her here; we think she is rather wonderful but in this strange way when beauty and ugliness meet. And you told me yourself American people do not like so much this mixture. Then, when she touches her neck, the scope of her neck, in a strange, sensual and distressed gesture, the public does not like it: this is the place where men feel the hang-over at morning, and the place where frustrated women would like to feel a man's lips and don't, so everybody is uneasy. That is the way my friend[4] who likes Edith Piaf, explains the whole thing, and it seems to me it could be true.

Good bye, honey. I love you as much as you know and a little more. I kiss you very hard.

Your own Simone

1) By Stephen Vincent Benét. 2) Olga, who played Electra in 1943. 3) *Les Compagnons de la chanson*, a popular group of nine singers. 4) Jaqueline Breton, remarried to David Hare, and whom Simone de Beauvoir had met in the United States in 1947.

Monday, 22 Décembre 1947

Darling,

Something rather sad is happening to his quiet house: people begin to come here to spend the Christmas week and it is over with our peaceful life. Today arrived an old lady who was formerly a teacher and a clever woman, but who has something wrong since five years, not exactly in the brain but in the surroundings: she can hardly speak, moves very uneasily and when she eats it is dreadful because you always expect she'll be swallowing the wrong way and choke and die. Nobody cares for her; her children and children-in-law are bored by her, and as our old lady is crazily kind to all helpless, hopeless people, they sent the invalid to her. Tomorrow comes our friend's daughter and grand-daughter. The daughter is not at all worth her mother, she is a rather silly, frustrated, unhappy young woman. They were not happy with marriage in this family: the mother married a doctor whom she never loved and who became madly sick; the son, I told you about his unlucky experience; and the daughter found her husband so boring and dull and selfish (he is, indeed) that she went away, without deciding to divorce on account of the little girl. I really think marriage is a rotten institution and when you love a man, don't spoil everything by marrying him. The little girl is fourteen, and rather silly too. I don't enjoy much the coming of both of them. Now we have to dress and wash a little, and we'll go down for lunch and dinner. It is no more a nice crocodile's marsh such as the one we enjoyed: I think mine was even more muddy and lonely than yours. Indeed, you'll not stay long a genuine crocodile if you go on speaking and moving your jaws in bad places where old women meet. You are becoming very smart and I am afraid I'll find you elegant when I'll come to Wabansia and I'll be so scared that I'll fly away. Take care, I do not want any change in my Crocodile, he must stay just such I love him—that is very arrogant self-assertion, it is not?

Well, except for meals, I do not think life will change so much, nevertheless. I have written about Chicago these last days. You would feel it is very poor, knowing better, but I hope it could convey to French people something of what you made me feel and understand. Sartre thought it was maybe the best part of the book and I was glad at it. I thought of you at every word I was writing. I had the sweet feeling I was trying to speak about you and to tell my love for you; it was very exciting but very difficult too.

I took another walk yesterday and it was the most wonderful of all. I remember how I loved country when a child. I told you, in Paris I lived in a mean way. My parents had been upper-middle class indeed, but when I was six, it was the first war; my father who was a lawyer went to the war and lost his clients, the father of my mother had a shoe-factory, he was ruined, and in 1918, we were really poor, nobody knowing how to manage poverty, which was the worst. Then, every summer, we spent two or three months at my father's father's house, in the country, a lovely little house with a big garden and big farms belonging to my grand-father around it.[1] I loved these holidays, I spent the whole days alone in woods and meadows, walking by myself, lying in secret hidden places, reading books, eating unripe apples, dreaming, thinking, feeling happy, feeling life would be wonderful since the world was so beautiful. Sometimes, I romantically forgot dinner-time, looking at the moon above a quiet pool, or looking at a long, lazy sunset. Sunset and moon and wind, trees and water and sky will never be again what they were then; it was as important as God for the pious man, as love for the lover, as you for me now. But I do not forget, and when I find myself again lonely and quiet in a lonely, quiet country, it moves me deeply.

Tuesday

I got your letter with the Christmas stamps, the letter you wrote on a tooth-aching week, on a grey cold day when the oil-stove would not burn. Darling, it made me sad!

The old half-mute lady is rather awful: she is more and more paralysed every year. She can hardly speak, yet she likes to speak and while eating she succeeds in producing some hoarse, mournful moaning which nobody understands; she chokes and coughs, and begins again and you can see she is very near to cry when she does not succeed. Now we take the meals in the regular dining room, at the bottom of the staircase, and we dress in regular clothes, and we fly away as soon as we have eaten; meals are no longer a little feast. But the remaining of the day we do not see the poor invalid; she is very quiet.

Darling, it is cold and grey here too. I need your warmth. A happy new year to my husband and beloved Crocodile! I told you all I whished for you: I wish it very hard. Anyway, there is something I can grant you—that is my love, you have it and will keep it. I have no other Christmas gift for you, but I know you'll be pleased with this one. Lots of fresh new-year kisses, heaps of fresh Christmas love for my local youth!

Your own Simone

1) Mérignac. See *Memoirs of a Dutiful Daughter.*

Christmas night, Mercredi, 24 Décembre 1947

My husband,

It is nearly midnight, the church bells are ringing. Everybody is away, the invalid lady, the cook, the maid, the daughter and grand-daughter have gone to the midnight mass. Sartre is in Paris to see his mother, the sick man is indeed in his bed, and there is just the old lady living in the house, hating churches and preaches, and not caring for mass. But she is very quiet in another room and I feel quite alone here, as I wanted to be, to spend Christmas night with you. I was a bit sad today, as often when I have received your letter the day before and I know I'll not have nay other before one week. And this peculiar tooth-aching letter was a bit thin and let me with an empty stomach. I am so hungry, darling. But now, in the quietness and loneliness of this evening, I feel all right again. It is our first Christmas together, love, and I should like to believe in God to thank him for having given you to me, giving me to you. I have nobody to thank; I'll just tell you you were a more precious gift than any Christmas gift ever was. It is good to feel you just near me while the bells ring rather stupidly.

The daughter and grand-daughter came, rather nice because they are gay, fresh, happy to be there and good-looking, but rather silly too. I read a John Dos Passos yesterday, *Number One*, not as good as the old ones which I used to like very much; there are so many long cold drinks in it, and airplane trips and American summer heat that it made me dizzy with longing for America—not just for you, you over-conceited man, but for your whole big drunken, busy hateful and wonderful country. I drank many glasses of hard apple-liquor to try not to think of scotch and soda, and it gave me wonderful dreams, in South America, with Negroes in silver-golden dresses and beautiful naked women dancing in beautiful gardens and blue pools. But...I woke up with a bad taste in my mouth and a weak sadness in my heart. That is what Dos Passos did to me.

I am sure you would be fond of the old lady. With my Californian friend, she is the only woman I care for; she is the only one I *respect* (I do not respect many people). She is nice even now when she is old. But I saw pictures of her in her early twenties and she was wonderful: *very* small. I look myself like a very tall woman near her; her head hardly reaches my shoulder. She has a round little face with the smallest nose you can fancy, a little round mouth, dark eyes, very human eyes, and beautiful dark hair. All the face was so pretty with something lively and radiant. She spent her girlhood in South America, in a big ranch, without mother, with a very stern but clever father who gave her a very manly education: learning Latin, German, mathematics and riding wild horses through the lonely pampas. She had a sister whom she loved dearly; they came to Paris at twenty, the little Amazones, and they found the French society dreadful: all their family were very well-bred people, with generals, admirals and wifes; no wild horses, no freedom, they hated it. But the sister (I do not know why) married a business-man and the old lady, (who was very young then) wanted to stay with her sister and accepted to marry a cousin of her who was a wealthy well know doctor. What was bad is that the sister soon died, and the other one was stricken nearly to death by this loss. She stayed with her husband she did not love, a big confortable, conceited bourgeois with whiskers and straw hats; I think she hated to sleep with him and she thinks now that sex is just a crazy hobby. She had two children and cared much for them. Then the husband became sick, in a crazy way as I told you, and she began to live by herself. And what I like in her is that devoting her life in a superficial way to husband and children, she really managed to be the best of friends for her own self, which so seldom people are and so seldom women. At forty, she became friends with young men who were her son's teachers, travelled with them,[1] and had a kind of love for one of them,[2] though there was never any sex affair between them. Ten years ago he married and I am sure she suffered much by it, though they remained close friends. Her life is dull, but she is never; she is always thinking things with a good full clever, well-balanced brain, and helping people though not hoping much from them — always gay in sadness, believing in nothing and nobody, yet not cynic, with a warm heart, though never sentimental and even harsh; pleased with flowers, a dog, a cat, a sunshine, a good book, always understanding and sympathetic and warmly interested in everything. She is not old at all in my eyes, and yet there is something secret and deep and very nice in her which makes her different from a young girl. The only woman I know who never *clung* to a man, who did not need a man just to breathe as they all do in France, and in America too I guess. I like a woman who can live, not selfishly, but by herself. Well, I hope I told you enough to make you understand what I feel, beeing alone with her in the house.

Saturday

I spent a quiet Christmas in the quiet house. We had a wonderful goose for lunch, all stuffed with roasted chestnuts, and in the afternoon I worked quietly in my room, and day-dreamt of you. I never write any Christmas letters and I don't receive any. Sartre came back from Paris with fresh American books I was very pleased to get. He brought some cakes and champagne, and in the night when the invalid and the little girl were sleeping we drank and ate. It was pleasant because the old lady became quite drunk and she is very funny when she is so, saying the truth to everybody in a laughing but accurate way.

I'll stay here one week more, then back to Paris, and I hope to spend five days in Berlin. I'll tell you. But I do not enjoy the idea of coming back to Paris; I'll come just because I have to, on account of the *Temps modernes*, the printing of my books and preparing my travel to America, and so on. Sartre told me he found Paris awfully sad, and I know I'll have the same feeling. You know, when my first book was printed,[3] I enjoyed a little becoming acquainted with people and going out from my shell; but now nearly everybody seems boring and the general atmosphere smells bad in France. Better stay in a nice crocodile marsh.

Good bye, honey. Now it is to Paris you must send your letter. Even without letter, I know you have a faithful, warm heart, such as mine. Yet, it is often painful not to hold you, flesh and blood. Nelson, my own husband and lover, I love you.

Your Simone

Honey, why did you not answer about going to Mexico?

1) Guille and Sartre. See *The Prime of Life.* 2) Guille. 3) *The Guest* (1943).

Tuesday, 30 Décembre 1947

Nelson, my beloved husband,

It was nice to get your nice letter yesterday, the one with the little red angel. But you do not seem to respect schedules any more: it was from Monday, you never mailed a letter such a day before! I quite agree with the idea of spending two months in Mexico, and to stay some time in Wabansia. Yes, honey, you seem to me very American with your nice careful way of planning things. You know, on some points I am a careful planner myself: for instance I have very exactly foreseen how I shall kiss you when we'll meet, how my lips will meet yours, and my heart your chest, and many other things I cannot write in long-hand, being a decent woman. I hope you will find my plans convenient. But for travelling through the big world, it does not need so much plans, you know; last year, too, all American people told me I *could not* find a room in any town without reservation, and so on, and with my Californian friend, we never reserved anything, and never planned accurately anything, and everything was all right very easily. You have to feel free and do what you please when you please; you must be able even to change plans, I think. I know for some things some plans are useful, but so many things are beautiful and interesting, well, when you do not do that, you do this. I always travelled this way, and travelled a lot and saw all I wanted to. Yet, I agree we have to get some informations about Mexico. I hope I'll have more than 1000 dollars for just our two months travel, so it could be all right. I cannot say when I exactly arrive, honey; it depends upon many little things. But I should not wait a month and a half to see you, are you crazy? Before California, I'll sure spend at least a week with my husband, to make sure he is flesh and blood and not a dream. I should die with impatience being in American and not seeing you. What do you say, you hard-hearted man? Could you stand to feel me so near you for such a long time without even kissing me? It is a nice idea to have registered your voice for me. When you'll be ill-tempered and not speak to me, I'll put on the little record and I shall not feel so lonely.

Darling, you cannot know how happy you make me when you say this winter is better than last one on account of me. For this new year I wish we never give each other anything but happiness—sure we'll grumble a little and be a little angry, a little ill-tempered, but it will never matter much. I am afraid I am not quite so nice when I travel than when I don't, because I am a little too greedy for things, and too stubborn, and I bet within two months we'll have two quarrels, but very short ones since I love you too much and you are too nice to hate you more than half an hour. I am so glad when I think about it; maybe we'll go unto Guatemala, maybe even Honduras if we choose to do, and when I say "we" I intend *you* have *some* right to express your will.

I have been reading a big book by a bad French writer, André Maurois,[1] about American history. I was proud because on many chapters I knew much better than he does. Then he is so prejudiced I was angry with him all the book long. But then I learnt many things, nevertheless. I'll do a lot of reading about Lincoln, Jackson and other ones, in our Wabansia nest. I read too *Pylon* by Faulkner, which I read once ten years ago; this time it had a new meaning to me since I know America and chiefly New Orleans. I partly like it, partly not. I think Faulkner is too *tragic* about human life: it is tragic, and it is not. In your books one can feel very well this strange two-sided truth, in Faulkner everything is always as pathetic as any other. Sometimes, it makes a sense, as in *Light in August*, but sometimes it is a bit ridiculous, such a tragedy for buying hats or eating a sandwich. Yet there are things he really shows you, you feel them, and in the end you cannot escape from this too tragic world, you believe in it.

The book *American Dilemma* is wonderful, you know. It teaches things not only about Negroes but about the whole America, and about European people too, about every kind of prejudice, bad faith, oppression, and so on.

I read in the newspapers there was an awful snow-storm in New York; they never speak about Chicago; it is not fair. Are you sure you were not frozen, honey? Fifty-five people died in New York.

You know why I seem to write with my toes? It is very sad. It is because the nice red fountain-pen is sick. I hardly can write with him, yet I would not write with anything else since it was one of your honeymoon gifts and so precious for me. I'll try to have it fixed up when I come back to Paris, but if I do not succeed, I'll use it just as it will be. The other gift, the most precious, the silver ring, is all right. I do not put the ring away for one minute. I like this secret sign of my belonging to you. Good night, my love. I am happy by your love. I kiss you as I plan to kiss you in Wabansia.

Your own Simone

1) André Maurois (1855-1967). French biographer, novelist, and essayist.

1948

My own Nelson,

It is very nice of me to write you tonight, for I am dead-tired, having worked and worked the whole day. I am through with my American diary, not quite through. There are little improvements to manage, but I'll do it when the whole thing will be typed; it is such a problem, even for me, to read it over when it is hand-written by my hand. Maybe you'll teach me to type? So I dropped the book, and I came back to my essay about women. I told you, I never felt bad for being a woman, and sometimes I even enjoy it, as you know. Yet when I see other women around me, I think they have very peculiar problems and it would be interesting to look at what is peculiar in them. I have a lot of reading to do: psychoanalysis, social science, law, history, and so on, but I like it. I like the idea of going to public libraries as when a student and reading, learning, and thinking about things I learn. I'll do this in Paris as soon as I'll be back, that is within four days. Just now I read over all that I had written on the subject and I contrived a kind of canvas, the general ideas and the plan of the whole book. I was very excited about it. That is why I worked so hard the whole day.

We had a nice new-year's night. We bought champagne and the old lady and the little grand-daughter were quite drunk; the girl was very pleasant because she danced and did kind of somersaults in a childish, boyish way, and yet she is nearly fifteen and very pretty. It is really funny, such a young girl knowing so many things and not knowing so many other ones. If I were a man, maybe I should be a very wicked one, because I surely should enjoy to make love to young girls and having them love me, and then indeed I should drop them because they are often very silly, too childish and become quickly tedious. When I was a teacher, they often fell in love with me and sometimes I enjoyed it a bit and even three or four times I really cared a little for it, and I happened to behave *very* badly; there were long stories because if pleasant but not important for me, it was important for the girls during at least some time and I had to manage them very carefully. I'll tell you the stories where we'll have long leisurely talks on the blue sea near Mexico. Anyway, now I should not be interested any more in such business. I feel there is both something appealing and something nauseating in very young girls.

I am reading a book I enjoy very much, that is Stevenson's about Southern Seas. We'll go there some year, darling, but I am afraid we shall not find the kind of savages who eat greedily other savages or even white people; I am afraid it became very civilized since Stevenson's travels. But yet it must have remained beautiful and in some places strange. We'll dress with flowers and crown our heads with old men's beards, neatly braided, as they do in this country: we'll eat cocoa-nuts and sleep near the roaring sea. We'll think it over again.

My mother phoned me once more how wonderful was the gift you sent to her. So I'll thank you once more. Every time I think anew what a nice man you are, I feel all warm and good. That was my first idea of you, you remember? A really nice man. Now, well, I think lots of other sweet things, but then, I love you and people say love is blind; a nice man, I am sure you are since I did not love you yet when I thought it.

Saturday

Today is blue and sunny, with mild, soft air, and I took a nice little walk. I am a little sad of going away; here I could work and read and sleep when I wanted to. I spent six weeks here and it went away very quickly. But I have to come back.

Good bye, honey. I'll work a little more. I am your Nelson-loving girl.

Your own Simone

Thursday, 8 Janvier 1948

My own Nelson,

So, here I am now, in Paris. It was a very poetical happy day, as it sometimes happens when you do not expect it. Everything seemed against me: it was raining something which was neither rain nor snow, an icy dark sad water; a strike among sellers closed all shops, cafés, restaurants. It could have been pretty sad, but by some chance, it was not. First thing, I found was your sweet letter, and it made me happy. I spoke with you (in English) all day long. Then I was pleased to see a town again. I love towns. And dark and sad as it was, Paris was a real town. I drank a little whisky (no "scawtch" but bourbon) in some bars, speaking with friends. I went to the *Temps modernes* and found letters, and something which made me very happy: an English translation of *Le sang des autres*, so you'll be able to read it in May. I want so much to make a link between my frog life in Wabansia and my working life. I should like you to read my books, and chiefly this one which is the second novel I wrote and will tell you something about me, I am sure. I want us to know each other better and better. So it was a real happiness for me to find it, though there were some awful mistakes in the translation. It will be published both in London and New York in May, so we'll discuss it through Mexico. Yea, I should stick to Mexico. But I heard by my friend coming back from there that Cuba was wonderful. Maybe we could go to Cuba from New Orleans, then Mexico? Now, I thought you told me West Indies did not appeal to you, you were afraid they were just for tourists? I should be very interested, and we should report Mexico another year. No hurry, you have to think yourself about it. The important thing is travelling two months together: *where* is not so important, is it?

Coming back to Tuesday, on the evening I was alone and walked on the Champs-Elysées to see *Grapes of Wrath*.[1] I was upset to hear American voices once more, and to see just the road I followed with my friend from California to Arizona and New Mexico. I recognized the places, chiefly the bridge on the Colorado. Some plans in the picture I found wonderful: in the bad ranch, when policemen kill the ex-preacher. I never saw such a "tough" picture, in the good meaning of the word. Yesterday went away in doing petty things, lots of petty things, and sleeping. I feel rather tired — maybe I worked too much in the country. Today I read books about women. I am interested, but Paris begins to look sad, as it really is, and I feel a bit sad too. I just wept some little tears because I loved you and missed you so much. I spoke to you a long time in the night. I love you.

Your own Simone

Thanks for the "Chicago letter." Very funny, very interesting. You are talented for writing pamphlets. I like when you become angry and bitter with people, if it is not with me. You can be such a wicked man! But it is difficult to translate; if I do not find a translator within two days, I'll have to do it myself, and it is some work! I'll tell *T.M.* to send the money for both letters to your agent, or what? (It will not be much.) Sartre enjoyed this one very much and laughed as much as he understood.

1) The film by John Ford (1940), inspired by Steinbeck.

Nelson, my beloved husband,

Paris looks sadder and sadder every day: dark, cold, damp, empty. Maybe I should have a real home; I should not feel so chilly. I don't know. Spring seems so far away. I like the pain of wanting you with my body, not this sadness in my longing heart. Well, it is no use to complain. As you told me: people are in hell and wishing a little water and not getting it.

I go to the public library on the morning. I went there when I was twenty and working for my last exam, the most difficult one. I arrived at nine and left at 6 P.M., and I just stopped an hour for lunch. As my parents were not very kind with me and would not understand I really had to work hard and so I should have eaten much, being young, they did not give me money for lunch, saying I had to come back home: but it would have been losing much time and very tiresome, so I did not come back and just ate bread in a garden nearby, and sometimes a little cold sausage with it. And I read and wrote and read again; I could read so much. I had a nice girl-friend then, a Ukranian student[1] who did not work so much but rather flirted with some Hungarian or Rumanian students; sometimes she bought some cakes for me. She was nice, but I wondered at her flirting with men. I never did it; I did not care and they cared little for me. I was so badly dressed, no make-up, the hair badly done and silly round cheeks —just a student studying hard. She was friend with a Spanish painter,[2] and even slept with him, but she dared not tell me so for fear of scaring me, and I was so silly I did not suspect anything though they lived in the same hotel. Later they married and had a child, and he went to the Spanish War—he was Jew and red indeed. Now they lived in New York, and I saw them often last year. He has been arrested last month: they suspected he had politic activities and wanted to send him back to France or put him in jail for being a "red." She works hard in a shoe factory—she is not young now and rather ugly but very sympathetic. Well, I remember all that this morning. When I went out at six P.M. (twenty years ago), I looked at people who seem free in the streets and I thought happiness would be just to have no parents and to come back to one's room without nobody asking anything to you. I longed so much for that freedom! It was so sad the bad, ugly flat with ill-tempered parents and no freedom at all! I could never go out alone after dinner, so I had to read and write and work again; it was the best I could do but my head was tired with it, my body impatient, my heart empty. I liked life *so much*, you know, yet more than now, and you know I like it; so I longed for loneliness and freedom, which I got a year later, when I was gone through my exam. But that year, the evenings were sad, coming back from the public library. Today it was different; I did not feel as young as twenty years before. Do you know? I was forty, today. I feel ashamed of it. I should like to give you a younger girl's love, though I know you love me as I am. I am sad to be far away, to be old, to be able to give you so little of all which I could have given, in another life. Well, you never reproach me anything, and true love, that I give you, I know, but... I don't like to feel old. Last year I did not care; now I do, because of you. I care for many things now. For instance, I am afraid to go to Berlin by airplane, so I'll not go at all, I think; train is too long. Maybe I'll change my decision, maybe I'll go in the end. But I am afraid by the idea of dying now; I really was not before, not in this way. I was always afraid by the general idea of dying some day, but it never prevented me of doing anything: now or later, since it has to be, was not different. Now it is different. I want to kiss you again. I want to have something more with you. I do not want you to be hurt by anything coming from me; I should feel guilty if I should die. Well, I have many silly ideas of this kind. I should hate to die, to be sick, to become old or ugly or invalid, because of you. I should like you to enjoy the love of a living, healthy, nice, fine woman. I'll do my best, darling.

Good night. My heart is heavy, very blue tonight. If I could see you smiling to me! I need your smile. I feel a silly very silly, chilly frog. I should like to curl in the warmth of your crocodile stomach and feel asleep quietly. Good night, my love.

Sunday

Reading over this letter, I find it rather silly. Indeed, I am not the only one here to feel sad; all the friends I met in those two last days were sad too. What can we do, now, in France? The manifesto we worked upon with Camus, Rousset (you remember, I spoke about it for three months) was rather a failure. The left wing of Socialist Party hoped then to contrive something important, really in a revolutionnary mind, really on the left wing, against communism, but now it does not hope much; our paper was published, but in a very bashful way and it went to nothing. We see nothing to do in politics, in fact; but you can write nothing in France now which has not a political meaning, writing becomes a hopeless, stupid job if the world around us seems hopeless. Everybody feels it. That is why everybody is so sad. A young friend of the "young man with the horn," being drunk last week, fell by the window from the 6th floor and killed himself, not willing it. That is what happens to young men in France now: they drink too much, do silly things, not knowing what to do. No, I was not just ill-tempered Friday. Being far from you and from the happiness you give me seems very bad if it has no meaning at all, if there is nothing to do here. You understand what I mean. Don't be too sad for me, neither. I speak to you confidently because you know to what point things are important and are not. Maybe it will be better some day, and anyway, it could be worse.

At the public library they gave me back an old little picture of mine; it was on my student card, just at this time of which I speak to you in the beginning of this letter. I send it to you. I had to live twice as much to know and love you, darling.

I go on reading books about women. I learnt many funny things, very indecent ones! That is strange how people behave, both men and women, and what they have in their heads! Not very easy for most of people to live nicely in this world, and especially not very easy for women to behave properly, both with self-respect and enjoying themselves. Even now when they have many rights, it is not so easy. I'll tell you sad-funny stories stories when I'll have time, along the Mississippi. I wait for this time, honey. I miss you, I need you, I love you.

Your own Simone

1) Stépha. See *Memoirs of a Dutiful Daughter.* 2) Fernand Gérassi.

Tuesday, 13 Janvier 1948

Darling,

Your letter pushed all the sadness away; it was so gay, so warm. I felt your warmth all around me. Shall we have the same berth on the Cincinnati boat, since we are not married people? It would be sad if I had to sleep with old ladies and you with old bearded men. I should be interested to know if you'll contrive to "spoil our love" the way you plan to do; I am not sure you have your chance. Anyway, we have to try. Darling, it seems to be all right about the 15th May Cincinnati boat, but you must understand I live rather far and it is not quite as easy as you think to contrive such a long travel; I cannot grant exactly such or such day. There are a lot of questions. Anyway, it seems pretty sure now I'll arrive in Chicago in the beginning of May, let us say 8th or 10th, and we spend two months together travelling. I'll go to South America for lectures with Camus and Sartre[1] and I'll come back after three months to see you, for a month or more; I do not know. It is not exactly the old plan, I think I'll come directly from Paris to Chicago, dropping California and New York until autumn. Just when you were losing forty bucks,[2] I was winning fifty without doing anything: I'll have them sent to you for the "tire-lire,"[3] but these ones you have no right to gamble. I think I'll have 250 sent to you, too, but no gambling; it is *my* money for *my* travel with *my* husband. Honey, I felt you were a *too* virtuous man now, and I am ashamed. It goes to my heart when you do something for me (I shall never forget your not wearing suspenders and the nice way you told me: "You asked me not to ear them!"). But I am ashamed when I think you do not allow to you any more neither women nor gambling and just live as a monk. Please, don't do it. Really. I mean it. I should not say it if I did not mean it. I thought seriously about it and decided I had to tell you that I know indeed nothing could spoil our love, and you can take to Wabansia as many women as you like, and even not tell me about it if you don't feel like it. For if I tell you: "Do what you please, but tell me," it makes the whole business too important, and maybe you'll not like to tell nor to lie to me by not telling. So just don't think you have to tell; just do what you please when it pleases you. I know you love me. I know you have the true faithfulness. I feel it so deeply, so warmly that I do not care for anything else. I do not think you have to live like a monk, since you are not one, and I am glad of it. Don't make your life too dull, honey. I should not like to deprive you from the least thing. You can indulge gambling and women a little, there is no harm in it. My heart will bless you as well in vice as in virtue, since you'll always be my precious Crocodile. My warm, sunny husband, how much I love you! It will be very hard for you to make me weary and bored with your kisses. I am afraid you will not succeed; the real feat will be to get me out of bed to climb upon the Mexican volcanoes.

My life is a very temperated one now. Every morning I go to the public library for about four hours; then I have lunch with some friend or another; I work in Sartre's bureau in the afternoon; we have a dinner together in some restaurant, and scotch and soda in some bar. I go to sleep at midnight and it begins again.

The friends are not very conforting: my Russian friend is very ill again, with much fever on every evening and knowing she will possibly die within a year; she waits for some remedy from America, which sometimes does miracles, but not often. Then my Jewish friend is as bad as ever. Ten years ago she was deeply in love with me, she was a very young girl, it did not seem to matter so much. But being psychoanalysed, she cames back to the past, and yesterday she told me, quivering in her whole body, that she was afraid she just went on loving me, as deeply as formerly, though having husband and daughter. It was unpleasant, because it was a business I do not like to recall (as the Mary G.'s one for you), and chiefly I do not see what can I do now. I do not even like her very much, and anyway, she has not to cling to me; she must live by herself, but she cannot. People who are being psychoanalysed, really neurotic people spending life to brood upon their problems are awfully depressing.

Well, for a change we had a drunken night with Camus, Koestler and his wife. It began nicely in a little restaurant of Quartier Latin, the owner of which is a very fine colored girl: nice Creole cooking, nice songs, Koestler telling funny stories about blue cinema in Marseille, very gentle with everybody. But then he took us for a drink into one of those silly awful Russian places he is fond of, and we drank glasses and glasses of vodka, hearing very expensive cheap Russian songs, and he became violent as he is when drunk, in a rather womanly, childish way, hurling glasses at Sartre's head and nearly hitting him, and hitting Camus so as to give him a big fat eye; poor Camus went crazy with anger and wanted to knock Koestler down, but we prevented him to do so, and Koestler just vanished in the night while we all came back home. Sartre was dead drunk and a lot of money was stolen from him. Koestler was stolen too; he lost about 200 dollars in traveller's cheques. Camus is really angry with him now, and K. does not remember anything. He phoned to Sartre to ask him to make some reconciliation. But he is a terrible man, any time he has some quarrel with wife or friends. It was not a very funny evening, I do not like this kind of things anymore; I drank a lot but without getting drunk. As you do, I hate to waste time now; my time should be yours and I have no right to keep it from you if I don't do with it something really good, something you would approve of. So the whole thing left me rather a nasty taste in the mouth.

The sun you put in my heart has not faded away, so it is not too bad, in spite of all. You stay near me night and day. I love your love and I love you.

Your Simone

1) This plan never came to pass. 2) Playing poker, he admitted in a letter. 3) "Tirelire" in French; "Kitty" in English.

Sunday, 18 Janvier 1948

My own Nelson,

As it is Sunday I changed a little my schedule, and the public library being closed I am writing to you in the Deux Magots, warm and noisy with the Sunday crowd coming from mass in Saint-Germain-des-Prés church; the man who had a difficult romance with two women two months ago is no longer here. Yesterday I had some nice time: I went with Sartre, Camus and his girl-friend to hear in a little theater Margaret Wood, a very good Negro singer whom I had met once in New York. Do you know her? She is beautiful and I think she sings as well as Marian Anderson; she sang classical music and Negro spirituals — everybody was enthousiastic. Then we had a dinner with the old lady's daughter and grand-daughter (herself being in the country). I told you we do not care very much for the younger ones but we had to do it. We asked Camus to come with us, and it became a very pleasant evening. Every time we see him he is with a new girl (though he has a wife and children). This one is really a pleasant girl, now a singer in little night-club, having worked hard in factories when she was younger. I do not know how she came to be a singer, I know she had very sad experiences with men and thought they all were dirty beasts when she met Camus who was very kind to her. The bad point is, I am afraid he will drop her some day and then she will be more unhappy than ever, for she seems awfully in love with him. Poor Camus was very strange to see; he wore black spectacles on account of the black eye Koestler gave him the other day. The little grand-daughter had her fifteenth birthday on that night. She was very pretty and so pleased to go to some places with grown up people; she seemed a little scared by such a handsome man as Camus, and she behaved womanly, in a childish way. The whole thing was funny. We had a good dinner in a Russian restaurant and some champagne in a nice quiet night-club, with a good show, a real good singer, calling himself "existentialist" singer—what just means now in Paris that he did crazy things. The interesting point is he is really crazy: he made an imitation of Russian singers, screaming and breaking glasses. At the end he broke a chair, was sweating and nearly having a fit. There are many night-clubs where he cannot have any employment because it is known he sometimes breaks the piano or strikes the clients. But he has genuine talent. In the end came a very well known young actor, theatre and movie player,[1] all French little girls and old women are dead nuts on him, and I must say he deserves it; he is very nice. He came to see Sartre and drank champagne with the little girl who was dying with excitement. I think it was the most beautiful birthday a little fifteen years old girl could dream of. We did not drink much; all was very friendly and gay in a quiet way. Now it happens so seldom a really friendly, quiet evening that it was enough to please me very much. Either you have to stay lonely, or you quarrel about politics.

I think I am going to Berlin, in the end, on the 28th for four or five days. I'll tell you exactly next time. I am very much interested, but just now I want to work and work and work again so that I'll feel free in May. When do you send another "Chicago letter"? The second one was very nicely translated but the first one so badly that I have to do it again. You can send a paper about anything, not only literature.

Now it is night. I had a rather sad lunch with my sad sick Russian friend; she is so angry at being sick anew that she does not take care of herself any more and slowly kills herself. Yet she does not want to die. Then I worked the whole day in Sartre's bureau; he worked too, writing a play but not enjoying it because he did it just to be useful to two girls who were not lucky until now and to whom he promised to give a chance.[2] One is my Russian friend's sister. He did it from mere kindness for he is really kind and generous, but the play was not easy to write, and now it is waited by a theater, producers, managers and all; they have to begin the rehearsals and the play is not over! So he has to write as if he were a machine, knowing everybody is waiting and waiting and he *must* succeed. I could not for heaven sake work in this way, and he hardly can, so it is a hard struggle but in some way funny. The bad point is all this theater people are so bad; all their little combinations and petty business are so nasty. I should not like to write another play on account of it.

Good night, honey. I feel peaceful and happy tonight. I know I'll see you not very soon but not very late, for not a very long time but not a very short neither. I have just to wait, and it will happen; for weeks and weeks I'll say with my lips "good night, honey" and the bed will be warm with your warmth and when I'll wake up, you'll be there. It will be very sweet. I feel you near and if not my bed my heart is warm with your warmth.

Your happy, loving frog

Your own Simone

<hr>

1) Gérard Philipe (1922–1959). Internationally acclaimed screen and stage actor. 2) *Dirty Hands*.

<hr>

Tuesday, 20 Janvier 1948

Dearest husband,

It is as cold here as in Chicago; I feel wholly frozen, I had a pleasant morning, though. I had to go to a library to read books of ethnology about women; it was at the Or, very far from Saint-Germain, and I crossed Paris in a cab, through mist and cold, the Tour-Eiffel being all clouded with mist and the sky red; it was fine. Then I read some strange books, these Australian, Indian and African tribes have really funny ways with women. As the library is part of a big National Museum I went to see a very interesting show of pre-Columbian art: beautiful statues, carved stones, blankets, pictures of what we'll see in Mexico. I agree, we'll not go to Cuba nor Guatemala, but try to visit Mexico thoroughly. I am yet hesitating as to my exact coming; it depends upon many things but for us anyway it does not matter so much, anyway. I'll be with you in the beginning of May. Now I am in a little bar of Saint-Germain, drinking a nice hot punch and I feel like a queen.

Thank you for the little lesson about Faulkner and America. I begun to be fairly well acquainted with your country now; I read so much about it in La Pouèze. What you say about Faulkner is very accurate. I read nearly all his books and love chiefly *Light in August*; the short story of which you speak is wonderful, but I still think in *Pylon*, which is not concerned with South in any especial way, the tragic feeling becomes a little stereotyped. For *The Reprieve*, I think the reason of Sartre's skipping is an attempt to gather all events which happened in *one* time in *one* story; he wanted to make simultaneity of the same topic — threatening war — through the whole world something real. And it is true that it asks much from the reader but I felt that it gave much too if you did the effort; as you say, it gathers momentum. The next book, nevertheless, will not be done in this way; it was just an attempt for a very peculiar situation. Now Sartre is writing about his life in the prisoners' camp. It is Mathieu and Brunet's experience, indeed, and it is told in a more direct, simple, classical way. Poor Sartre! He just crossed hastily the bar, going to confort an awful alcoholic painter[1] who is becoming blind from alcohol. He his a Jewish-German painter who was hardly hurt by prosecutions and since some years does nothing from morning to night but to drink. He is talented but never works, just drinks: he is thirty-four and looks ten years older than you. We do not know him in any peculiar way, but he just knows Sartre so as to ask him money from time to time when he wants to drink. And you know, when you begin to help people a little, you find you have got to help them more; they wait it from you. So now as he is really sick; his wife comes every day to Sartre to ask help. The unpleasant thing is he would not be cured in an ordinary hospital, not too expensive; he will go on and become blind within ten days if he is not taken to the American hospital, which is awfully expensive. And he has not a cent, neither has his wife. So they expect Sartre 1) to persuade him to go to the hospital; 2) to pay months of cure at fifteen dollars a day for a man he really does not know at all, just having given him some money formerly. But as the man is nearly crazy with intoxication and nearly blind, which is awful, as he will let himself die if he chooses, what is to be done? Yesterday evening, we were going to have our dinner when the woman appeared from a door-porch; she must have been waiting for us for hours and she seemed in a very bad mood.

Thursday

Well, the painter was persuaded to go to the hospital; he seems to be very sick. Another little story happened: once more we quarelled with Koestler; once more we half made up with him. He is a terrible man! I quarelled with him this time. It was Wednesday, and I had a dinner with the ugly woman, who was very interesting and not too crazy. She told me things about her life and the way she slept with girls when she was a child and so on. As we were speaking and drinking "scawtch" in a quiet bar, Koestler came with a friend of him whom he presented to me. It happened this friend was RPF (de Gaulle's party) and at once he began to say dirty crazy things about Sartre; he pretented that before his talking at the radio Sartre had gone to the RPF to ask money from them and things like that. I was awfully angry; you would not have recognized me as your frog. I quarelled very harshly with the man. I know what they can do with this kind of lies, printing them in newspapers and so on. But Koestler just laughed and said we had to take a bet and the losing one would pay champagne to the other. Well, if a Stalinist had attacked him this way, we should have quarrelled with the man, so I thought Koestler had been really unfriendly and my ugly friend thought the same thing. I even had to prevent her from striking him. I went away insulting the RPF man and a little Koestler too. Next day the RPF man wrote a long letter to apologize, saying he knew now that he had been mistaken and Sartre had never offered to give his soul and body to the RPF. We met Koestler this evening and told him in a half-pleasant, half-unpleasant way very unpleasant things; he looked very childish and treacherous, and in the whole he seems to me a very corrupted man. He comes to USA in the middle of March to give some lectures, maybe you'll meet him in Chicago. I don't think he would seem pleasant to you.

It is very late. I work well, I wait for spring, I think of you first thing in the morning when I open my eyes and last thing at night when closing them. I kiss you as well as I can and as long as you want.

Your own Simone

1) Alfred Otto Schultze, alias Frans Wols, who joined the French surrealists in 1932.

Saturday, 24 Janvier 1948

My own husband,

Yea, you can make me as happy with words as with kisses; you know how much it means. I got your letter and the whole day seemed wonderful. I am very lucky to have met you, darling.

You know, I was not such a sad girl! Well, this peculiar year was not the best of my life, but when I was a child, I had really good time. Until twelve or thirteen I loved my father; he seemed very clever to me. He read books to me, cared much for me, and was proud because I was a good pupil. And I was fond of studying and reading, I had a girl-friend[1] with whom I was deeply in love (not at all in a sensual way, but with all my heart and soul), I believed in God and I felt sure he loved me. I enjoyed the country, studies, books, friends, spring, autumn, sleeping, eating, praying; I enjoyed a nice fire, a nice walk, everything. Then from fourteen to twenty-one it was not so good. I began to despise father and mother (they deserved it); I did not believe any more in any god; I wanted something more than books and apples. I fell deeply in love (not in body neither, but heart and soul) with a young cousin, a boy not older than me, who rather liked me but just did not care for this "poor thing" I was. And I even began to loathe my family, and to feel really unhappy for the cousin, who went away to Africa for his military period. That is when I got this forlorn look. But it was never really bad because I felt young; I expected much of life and knew I should get it. This last year (I mean my last year as a student living in one's family), the year of the sad picture, I worked hard the whole day, and at home in the evening too. But I contrived, I do not remember how, to get a little money (stealing it, I think) and sometimes I got outdoors in evening and went to bad night-clubs and bars, and drunk, pretending I was a whore (nobody believing me). I had some bad affairs with some men—I mean, they could have been bad but with this face of mine I had not much to be scared of, and they never even kissed me. Then I got through the exam very well and decided to live outside my family, by myself, earning my own life, in a little room which I rented. Two bad things happened: the beloved cousin came back from Morocco and told me he was marrying a girl for his money; and my dearest girl-friend died, at 21, in a very tragic pathetic way. It could have been really bad for me, but there I was lucky too; it was just the time when I met Sartre and his friends. They were two or three years older than me and knowing many people, and my whole life became different. And then Sartre and me began to care very much for each other. It was very different from my loving the faraway cousin, it was something real, and my whole life became different. I'll tell you about that another day, and chiefly when we'll go down Mississippi. It was just to explain the forlorn look. I'll try to get pictures from the time when I was a little girl and send them to you.

I go for true to Berlin, by train, Wednesday morning and will come back a week later. I'll write another little letter before going away. Good night, darling. I am afraid I am too happy. I do not see why I was so lucky. Let spring come quickly, that I hold my love in my arms and in my bed. It will happen.

Your own Simone

I asked the little pictures from my mother, send them back to me very carefully because she has no other ones, and I promised her they would come back. I just wanted you to see the chicken in the egg. I am glad you liked *The Reprieve.*

1) Zaza. See *Memoirs of a Dutiful Daughter.*

It is raining a dark, half-melted snow in Paris today, darling, but there is always light and warmth in my heart: it is Mississippi sun and Mexico blue sky. If you have to wait some time before getting the next letter, don't think it is because I am a bad woman who just played with a poor lonely local heart until it went so far as to reserve a cabin on a Mississippi boat, and then dropped it with a dry sarcastic laughter. No. It is just because it must be difficult to send letters from Berlin. I'll write often, but mail when I'll come back to Paris. I go away Wednesday morning and shall arrive Berlin only at 3 P.M. the next day—a long trip. Yesterday I had a nice evening with Richard Wright and wife, Sartre, my Russian friend and her husband who is our best friend.[1] I do not know if Ellen Wright is the one you know; she has just been married seven years. I think she is a really nice woman, one of the best women I know. We went to their home, in a sad wealthy district, at the end of the afternoon, and drank brandy and heard Armstrong's and Bessie Smith's records. The little girl is more and more beautiful, and so lively and eager; I should like to be a fairy and endow her with all possible gifts. We ate couss-couss in a lonely Arabian restaurant: did you eat couss-couss in Marseille? That is wonderful. Next year, darling, *you*'ll fly to me, and I'll have you eating couss-couss in Paris, Marseille, and chiefly Algiers (among many other things I'll manage you to do, willingly or not). Then we went to the College Inn, the nice night-club where we celebrated, on the other week, the little girl's fifteenth birthday. When I was an ugly chicken in love with a silly cousin, I used to go there, so it means much for me; it is a good place with good jazz and nice whisky. Wright spoke much about the African Negro business which I vainly tried to explain to you; he was quite dissatisfied with it, but not too serious and gave a very good imitation of a Negro preacher in a Negro church—he can be really funny. Everybody spoke English. My Russian friend has a beautiful *English* accent, very queer and useless when speaking to coarse American people; she looks too refined. Wright and Ellen hardly say a word in French. I think you American are the most lazy or the most arrogant people in the world, not caring to know any language but your own. There were some pleasant singers, we did not drink too much, nobody quarrelled with anybody, and I went to bed early, so it was a nice evening. I go on working well, not to the library any more. Now, I write about what I have learnt, what I think of it, and I like it better.

The brother-in-law was in Paris yesterday, and I had a lunch with him and my mother: they quarrelled all the time. Both were wrong and very mean. I hate mean people. I could not stand either of them. Sure he is in a bad mess; he has lost his job (because of governmental reduction of state jobs) and has no place to live in Paris. Within a month my sister will arrive from Yugoslavia; they have very few money and do not know what to do. My mother could help them by lending to them her flat, but then he takes for granted that he has *rights* to be helped by everybody, and I hate people who think they have *any* right on *anybody.* So I disapprove my mother, but she is an old woman and leaving her things, going away for months, all alone, would be very hard for her. So I disapprove him too, and I thought the whole business was nasty. And he was angry because in June my sister will have a show, she will exhibit her paintings in an art gallery, and he says I *should* be there. But I shall not, you know why. How could I give her any talent, if she has not? I hate too this idea that talent can be brought by relations, friendship, money, a nice standard of live and so on. She has to paint good paintings, or to stop painting. I cannot persuade people that she is a genius if she is not, even if she is my sister. Ah! I have to stop to take a good fresh breathe, since I wrote all that in a quick fit of anger. Well, you are my husband, you have to know about the whole family though it is not interesting at all.

Midnight

You know, darling, I think you must love me to be able to read these letters, or you must love me very little and not care to read them at all, because I just tried to read it over and I hardly could. How can you? I feel a bit suspicious. Though you answer to them, you seem to make some meaning out of them…I am puzzled. Maybe you really love me, after all. I am happy, Nelson. I am so happy to spend some time with you; it seems incredible to think that a year ago I did not know you, that we did *not* spend, all in all, one month together. Yet you are my husband, I am your wife. No, I don't feel old since you love me this way; I feel all right. I belong to you, soul, heart and flesh, you know. Good night, honey.

Your own Simone

I just found a little American bookshop nearby where I can hire books. There are chiefly classical ones, but some modern ones too: Can you suggest some titles?

1) Jacques-Laurent Bost, who had just published *Le Dernier des métiers.* He met de Beauvoir in 1935. See *The Prime of Life.*

Nelson, my own husband,

This is the first quiet time when I can write to you. I have many things to tell, but the most important one is that from Germany I just love you as I used to do from France and in USA: it looks like an international love. Now, I don't know what could happen in Moscow. How are you, darling? It is a long time without any word from you; the words are waiting for me in Paris, I know.

It was strange: first evening I spent here, there were American people at dinner, one of them called Roditi. First thing he asked was: "Do you know Mary G.?"[1] He explained he had been engaged to her; she lived in Los Angeles, having made up with a wealthy father and she wrote a novel. And then we spoke about USA, and I spoke your name; he seemed displeased. "Did you know Mary after her affair with Nelson Algren?" And he explained with a wrong laughter that she was always in love with some writer or other, but now she'll marry one: himself. It was so funny coming to Berlin to hear about this story of you. The man is of the worst kind, the *Partisan Review* kind, very silly, conceited, decadent and...well, everything bad.

I am seeing lots of bad people, really stupid, conceited, ugly, nasty ones: generals, ambassadors and wifes. I think that it was *you* called being elegant or having a brilliant life; sometimes it makes me so angry I nearly wish I did not came. For instance I am mad with the idea of wearing an evening dress to morrow. I loathe the thing; it somehow humiliates me, you know, making me feel I belong to the women gang and to the bourgeoisie. I have no evening dress, it seemed a shame, and I'll borrow one to a big ugly woman. Indeed, German women have no evening dresses—they have hardly any dress—but then we must all the more show them what it is *not to be* German and be able to wear expensive dresses. Ah! It seems very bad to be French here; very bad to be American too, very bad to be Russian, and it does not seem better to be German, though you rather feel friendly with them because the other ones are stronger. Then maybe you can be British. I do not know, you never see any of them.

I'll try to describe everything good and long, but it is very difficult, chiefly in English. I went away Wednesday morning, and we crossed the ugly country which spread in the East of France; not only ugly but weird too, having a meaning of war. I went there during the war, among soldiers and sad poor civilian people, to see Sartre who was a soldier in Alsace, and I was full of memories of this dim, awful period: always rain, and damp mud and threatening war among these sad plains and hills. I slept and then I felt very angry and hungry because we had thought there would be a dining-car and there was not. I just could buy half a dozen bananas in a station; the wagon was too hot. I read a bad American novel about young students and college girls, called *Folded Leaf*.[2] I was told by many people it is very good, what is not. At 4 P.M. we entered Germany and we saw Sarrebrücks ruins, very impressive ones.[3] Then it begans to be strange and rather unpleasant. In the sad dining-car where we had at last something to eat—not much—there were only French people and chiefly French officers, and in the sleeping-car too. We knew there were Germans in the other wagons, but did not see any of them. Germany was all around us, and we were a moving little French colony; it remembered me of German people in France during the war, I felt we were as hateful as they had been. Nevertheless, I slept soundly. I love to sleep in sleeping-cars, and in boats too, and I thought of our Mississippi berths and the slow gliding of the boat in our sleep. I felt very happy. In morning, Germany looked fine, beautiful forests of pine trees and birches, a wide sad sky, little painted houses. I was excited with arriving to Berlin. Then at 11 A.M., an hour before the station, it began to be dreadful: ruins and rubbishes, rubbishes and ruins, nothing more. I could not have fancied it though I heard so much about it and even when to the movie and saw it. The arrival was unpleasant; it was in the north of Gross Berlin, in the French station. German people had to wait until all French ones were out before being allowed to get away from the train: it reminded me of Occupation too, and you feel worst if you are on the occupating side. Then our going away lasted a long time because of photographs and radio and newspapers men waiting for us. A little man, a French one whose job is to sell French books and culture to the Germans, who thinks himself very clever and witty and humorous, took us in his car to our hotel. The very bad point is this: you cannot go to Berlin if you are not somebody's guest, because you would have no money (they don't give you any marks), no place to sleep, no tickets to eat, no way to live. So, we are this little man's guests, but then we belong to him. (He is paid by the French government to receive people in this way, it is just his job, but nevertheless, he acts as if he was really receiving us by friendship.) And the French section of Berlin is twenty miles far from the center, so we need cars; only he can give them to us. In fact, a car has been lent to us, but he controls everything, you know. Frohnau, the French section, is a very fine residential neighbourhood, with pines and fresh air and nice houses; but I like to feel in the heart of the towns and not twenty miles away. And the little man has organized dinners, lunches, parties, lectures, discussions and so on, and so on, and often with not interesting people. The general idea of the occupation authorities is *to prevent* people coming to Berlin, chiefly writers and newspapers men, from seeing anything genuine, from seeing real German people, real German life. We have to struggle to see something, in spite of them, but much time is lost; I have to go to bad parties, with wrong people. You should wonder how mute your frog has become. I never *un*botten my lips; I just make my head all vacant and say nothing — either I should come angry and say too much.

Well, these are the bad points. But the good one is I see Berlin, and it is wonderfully interesting and pathetic, and it is worth all the little miseries I spoke of. Did you go to Berlin? I remember that you went to Germany and like it much, but Berlin, I do not think so.

Sunday morning

Sartre had a big lecture to deliver about his play *The Flies* in a big theatre, and much discussion to do. As he'll speak German and I should understand nothing. I did not go, though the little French man and his wife were scandalized at it. I just went in the car with them from Frohnau and they dropped me in front of the theatre where there were huge lines of people waiting for the lecture. That is one of the interesting points in Berlin, how passionately they go to theatres and movies, not only to enjoy themselves and forget, but to find an answer to their problems. On Kurfürstendamm among ruins and rubbishes, there are lines of people from morning to evening booking places in the theaters. They were tremendously interested by Sartre's *Flies;* it was written during German occupation and the general meaning was: when you have put yourself in a bad mess, don't have remorses about it, but try to act and make things better. So now, they are applying it to their own situation. Many people are angry at this: all Russian people wanted to forbid the play and many French ones too. Americans on the contrary were pleased with it, because of their politics in Germany. You know, evidently, your American people here are of the worst kind. There were drastic eruptions here, too — all liberal, Roosevelt-loving American men were sent away; it is all a fascist gang working here — and,

153

indeed, French people too are of the nationalistic kind, very bad, though some of them are smiling to powerful Russians and obeying them in a servile way. Well, Germans were so enthousiastic about *Flies* that they gave 500 or 1000 marks for *one* place (300 marks on an average subvey for a month) or even they gave two *geese* for a ticket and you can fancy what means a goose in this country where there is hardly anything to eat. So, this morning I left everybody and walked in Berlin and rode the elevated among ruins and rubbishes, always, always, and came to the Kurfürsten-damm, which remains the most lively place in Berlin. For half an hour I looked for a café, any kind of café, bar, restaurant where I could sit. And after much walking, I just found this café, where they had noting to drink but a kind of broth. You cannot fancy how sad and deserted these places are, how sad and forlorn all the people look here. On Thursday we went to a French hotel in Frohnau and had a lunch at the little man's, in a fine house, very warm. French people have swell houses, and coal, and they contrive to get some good food (all Allied do, indeed). We were thrilling with excitation at the idea of seeing Berlin, and we said good bye. We went to a station whence a train and underground brought us in the middle of Alexander Platz. That was Times Square, you know, a very popular lively place: now, there are walls and walls and nothing behind them. I think I told you that Sartre spent a year in Berlin, and I came and spent a month with him in 1932—that is so long ago! So we were very much impressed in seeing it now. If you have not seen it, you cannot fancy; nothing is alike. What is beautiful, in a weird way, is that it has not at all been erased, as in London or LeHavre; the walls stand up, the bones stand up, but they are hollow, nothing between the walls but plain air. It looks like a lyric night-mare. The district around Alexander Platz was always very poor, but now, among crumbling bricks, hollow houses, torn iron, mud and plaster, it was as terrible as West Madison on a rainy day for the forgotten men without a roof. The faces of people are grey with hunger; many of them are limping, cripple, missing an arm or a foot because of the air raids; they have nearly no coat and they pick up bits of wood in the streets and always are carry-ing things on their backs, in rucksacks, or pushing little chariots, I noticed that during Occupation, in misery and need, people are always bearing sacks and packages. Then we went to Unter der Linden, which was the Chicago avenue of Berlin; all blown up, hardly nobody in the streets. The big park, Tiergarten, has no more trees, people cut all the trees during win-ter to get some warmth and they have now little gardens where they grow turnips and potatoes. They call it no longer Tiergarten but Gemüsegarten.4 People on Kurfürstendamm are wealthier; it did not look quite so hopeless, but as night was coming these endless...

Tuesday

Ink missed suddenly and I stopped writing. Now we'll have a whole nice evening together, honey. It is 7 P.M. I just came back from Berlin by a dark, sad train crowded with overtired people and I sat in my warm cosy room. I asked for bread, jam, and coffee (what a coffee!) and I have nothing to do until tomorrow morning but writing to you, reading, and sleeping. I feel dark, damp winter outside.

I have so many things to tell. I am a bit afraid at the job, but I'll try for the love of you because I know you like being told stories nearly as much as telling them. I'll take it again from the first afternoon, Thursday. So having had a first look at dreary Berlin, we came back to Frohnau by a car which was sent to us and we had a dinner at the little man's house with Roditi, another very bad American politician, bad French diplomats, and a crazy fair-haired beautiful-dressed Hungarian countess who was the most silly woman I ever saw, in a very brilliant way: she hardly stopped speaking. The French ambassador came to greet Sartre, and the point is all this moralistic, nationalistic well-to-do people really hate him, as you can think. Well, it was a bad evening, but I was so interested to be in Berlin that it did not matter so much. Next morning a French commandant took us in his car and gave us a good sight-seeing tour: ruin seeing tour. It was as impressive and interesting as the day before. We visited Hitler's Chancellerie, a real palace all torn and blown up; the underground where he hided in the end and where he probably died; many ancient monuments, streets, parks, all ruins and rubbishes. The commandant did not want to admit that people in the streets are grey-faced and that there are lots of cripples ones. Then, we had a lunch with Russian diplomats and a Catholic German woman writer (the ugliest woman I saw in the world) and her husband. The Russians dislike Sartre, indeed, since he is not communist, but they looked friendly; the German pair was disgusting because they *repented* for the German crimes in front of the Russians whom they dislike, being Catholic, but fear.

The question of repentance is very important for Germans. In all lectures and discussions, and private conversations, they were always speaking about remorse. Once Sartre discussed with them for *3 hours* about it. Indeed all (or nearly) the Germans we have seen are anti-nazis (or supposed to be so); many of them, on the communist side, think Germans must repent and have remorses. The idea of Sartre was they should accept the collective responsability of what they have done, and feel guilty, since in a way everybody is guilty of everything which happens and chiefly in one's country. But this feeling and sense of responsability does not mean shame, humiliation, and remorse; it means concrete will of acting right, now. Many of the German students or writers or intellectuals with whom we spoke were very much interested in that, they argued harshly between themselves too, this questions or "guilt" is the first one they always want to discuss. After the lunch, we had a reception by the Magistrats, that is the kind of congress which takes care of the town under Allied's control. Rather tedious, many speeches made, many words wasted and time. Then we went in a sad, sad café where we drank a nasty kind of beer and looked at the people around. There we felt really in Berlin, it was better. American people had invited us and we hoped we should have a dinner and good drinks since Americans are the wealthiest of all the Allieds. But they had trapped us, really trapped! They had prepared the three hours discussion of which I spoke, and nothing to drink, but at midnight a cup of ersatz coffee! Sad. The discussion was with German people about remorse, hope, freedom, and it was interesting to see their problems. I met there a very, very attractive woman, Anna Seghers.[5] Did you hear of her? She wrote the book *The Seventh Cross*, from which a good movie has been taken; I don't think the book is so good, but the movie was. She is all white-haired, with a most charming face: smile and eyes, chiefly. She is rather communist and attacked Sartre, but in the nicest way. There were Catholics, Protestants, communists, as always. It was so long, and nearly all in German which I don't understand, or nearly not, so I felt very tired.

Saturday morning we went to Berlin, to walk in the streets once more, with French newspapers men we knew already (one an ancient pupil of Sartre). We went again to Kurfürstendamm. People earn from 200 to 300 marks—average working people; they have enough tickets to spend forty marks, no more. That is, if they just buy what they have a right to, they spend forty marks, but then it is hardly enough to live half a month. So they must buy at the black market, but the black market is so expensive they can hardly buy anything. A cigarette package (twenty bad French cigarettes) is thirty marks, a pound of butter is 800 marks, and so on. Same thing for the dresses. Luckily they all had many clothes in past time, more than in America or France, something of it is left. Many women yet wear fur coats, no make up, and most wear pants; many men have some good coats, too, in middle classes. There are tremendous differences, indeed, most of people live in narrow, damp, nasty faraway kinds of slums, but others have beautiful suites in the heart of Berlin. What seems strange is you do not see any shop selling cheap or not too expensive things (hardly any, I mean, dresses, shoes, and so on), but you find many beautiful shops, at the bottom of ruined buildings, selling 2000 marks dresses, jewels, silver, old books, precious china, and so on. That is chiefly because German people have sold all jewels and china to have money to eat. I never saw so much frail china and precious glasses and old books as in this miserable city. There are lots and lots of antiquarians. Something interesting too is the "exchange shop": you can see lots of shoes, shirts, and so on; but you cannot buy them; you must give something which the seller needs in exchange. It is very well organized, now, a regular trade. All the shops, cafés, everything living is in the basement; they have just build it again when it was not entirely blown up, but the top of the houses is just ruin about the clean bottom-place.

I was told the most difficult thing to build up Berlin anew will be first to build it down, since, as I told you, all the walls stand good and strong. Now, there are just some wagonnets carrying bricks and stones away from the middle of the streets, but it is not enough at all, it is just sweeping the dust.

There was a lunch with a Lutherian preacher, a French man who happens to be an existentialist though he is a Christian. I rather liked him, at least he had not the fake moral, the social bias of the general who was there and whom I hated. This preacher sees rather often the seven great nazi criminals who were not punished by death in Nuremberg trial, Hesse and others, and he spoke about them in a very interesting way. After that we had just a little rest, a car took us to Berlin; I do not know why the chauffeur (a French soldier) had the idea of giving us a sight-seeing too, and we rode in interesting suburbs instead of going to the party, just Sartre and myself. We arrived an hour late, which was very bad, but the party was worst: two hundred people, all "important" people, speeches, magnesium pictures being shot from beginning to end; I was given an orchid by the ugly German Catholic woman writer, and she said I looked like an orchid! They are amazed that an existentialist woman is not too ugly. Everywhere they are pretending that we are married, Sartre and I; they know it is not true but they pretend to believe we are because it would be immoral to invite us together if we were not. Oh these people! They stink! I just came back from this nasty stinking party in a fine house of Kurfürstendamm when I wrote to you the beginning of the letter, that is why I felt so angry. I left Sartre in Berlin where he had some friends to see and I spent a quiet evening there.

Sunday I went to another big sad café where people were eating sad grey food (and giving many tickets for it). I drank something filthy and read some O'Hara short stories. At 2 P.M. Sartre arrived with the little man; the whole morning he had been discussing with Marists[6] and Catholics. These Marists, and even Russians, understood, when hearing him, he was not a nihilist, not sold to American capitalism, really a left-wing man, really interested in concrete freedom, in the good of society, and so on: and they became so friendly as to invite us at their club (the Russian club, I mean). But first we had lunch in a British club, a bad lunch, with bad people, and the ugliest woman I ever say (another one: when I saw the first one, I have not yet seen the second one, who is really the ugliest). She is a teacher in philosophy in Berlin University, has a man face covered with pimples and spectacles too, a huge round womanly body dressed up in black silk—wonderful. Awfully servile with us, like a creeping, crawling fat snail, loving France so much and so on. Hateful.

Then we had something better in the afternoon, a meeting with German students, just a dozen girls and boys, and we spoke in a very quiet, friendly way, and so we learnt something. They told us how hard is material life for them: hardly anything to eat, hardly any books, and long, long rides in train and buses, from one to two hours morning and evening, and trains are so crowded and so cold that they cannot even read. They spoke about guilt and hope, once more; they seemed rather hopeless, pathetic, and good-willing, trying to live in spite of all. Indeed, they say themselves all German students are not that sympathetic, many are strongly nationalist, stubborn, and bad-willing yet. But these ones, so badly dressed, grey-faced, deeply moved me, the girls chiefly, with their poor stockings and shoes and sad hair and fine eyes.

Then! Oh, what a terrible thing it was! We went to see *The Flies*. That is when I had to wear the evening dress, but, well, it was a rather nice dress, just a long black skirt with a fine blouse, it fitted well; I did not resent too much the disguise. It was the play which was a shame. The producer purposely did a nihilist play with it; he had cut off whole scenes, and made the actors play in such a way that it meant just the contrary of what Sartre had intended. Then all was so ugly, the faces, gestures, scenery, everything. Nobody can do such ugly things as Germans when they choose to. The actors were always screaming, sweating, and lying on their backs and rolling from the top to the bottom of some staircase: just an asylum of crazy people. All the French people thought it was a shame. But German people applaud for half an hour and it is a regular triumph, that is why Sartre's coming seemed so important to them. Sartre was very nice when they pushed him on the stage and applauded him, because he was so ill at ease, and sad with such a success, when there was such a misunderstanding. Then, at the Russian club, we had a long dinner, with bad food but much vodka. It was very interesting to spoke with Russian and German communists; they were really friendly, made friendly speeches, while French communists, you know, tear us to pieces. So we explained and spoke about many things.

We had told everybody that we went away yesterday, so we could have two days incognito to do what we liked. So yesterday was all right. We went to Berlin by train in morning; we walked in the streets, sat in cafés, and looked around us. We went to many taverns. The only bad thing was we could eat nothing, the whole day (from 10 A.M. til 3 A.M.) because you cannot eat in Berlin when you have no tickets, And what we drank, be it called coffee or beer or punch, was as nasty as nasty can be. We felt in our stomachs what is Germany to Germans. There is *one* big café, with two orchestras, people dancing, other ones drinking, all smoking; it looks a little like old Berlin, but what they drink and eat there is incredible. At seven we went to a show in the best Berlin "Kabaret," a kind of music-hall play, with songs and dances about German life today. Superficially funny, and deeply dim and weird; dark laughter about all the misery of German people, all Allieds offering fine words and ideals: communism and realism, existentialism, hopes and speeches—but no shoes, no bread. I never saw something so good in the kind. Then, meeting with some German intellectuals until 3 A.M., so I slept the whole morning, and there was a last bad lunch with diplomats. You know, these people, they live in Berlin and never see a German person; they were amazed because we often used the underground in Berlin: they never committed themselves to the underground. They live in an awful French way, interested in adultery, petty scandals, petty gossip; no brain, no heart, no blood, no guts, nothing but elegant suites and a chatterbox in the mouth. It was at the French "Ministre," the most important French man in Berlin. Something funny just happened: while I was writing to you this endless letter, a young French man came and said Sartre had gone away with the Ministre's coat and left his own one! I noticed this afternoon that Sartre's coat went nearly to the ground, and I think the other man could not put on Sartre's small coat. He was very distressed, I heard, and even somewhat angry, and I am very pleased at it. He is such a nasty man, too. After the lunch we saw *Murderers Are Among Us*.7 If it is ever produced in Chicago, rush and see it. It is about guilt, indeed, and you can see Berlin in a wonderful way and feel much about German problems.

Then I came back, darling, and here I am. We go away tomorrow at noon, and will arrive Paris on Thursday evening. I'll mail this letter; it is worth two, is it not? I never received such a fat letter from you. I hope you'll be patient enough to read it all over, since I was patient enough to write it. I should have yet much to say. It was so interesting; it gave so much to think, but enough now. You have to love much a man to write such a letter, and in a foreign language too. If you want to know *exactly* how much I love you, you have just to make an exact reckoning of the number of letters I wrote: how many a, how many b, and so on. You take the number, you multiply by 10345, and you have approximately the number of kisses I should like to give you during my life.

Your own Simone

1) A friend of Algren's. 2) By William Maxwell. 3) Sarrebrück, a steel-producing city in Western Germany on the French border, destroyed by Allied bombardments. 4) No longer the "animal park," but rather the "vegetable park." 5) Anna Seghers, a German novelist who chronicled the Resistance. 6) Members of a religious order dedicated to the Virgin Mary. 7) By Staudte (1946). The first German film to be shown in France after the war.

Friday, 6 Février 1948

Nelson, my love,

It is always sweet coming back to Paris and finding a sweet letter of you. In the train I knew I would find it, and I felt a little as if I were coming back to you. No, darling, the old woman has nothing to do with my grandmother; she was a kind of a nurse and I was told (I don't remember) she was very good woman and I was fond of her. I know I am clumsy and plain on the picture when I am grown up, and I even hesitated before sending it with the others, but then I thought you had to know. Yea, I was a very defiant little girl; until ten, I took terrible fits of anger against grown up people; I could scream so much in streets and parks that nice ladies came with sweets and asked from the nurse (another one) if I was a "martyr" and they tried to pet nicely my hair and then I kicked them harshly. I could lie on the ground and just scream and kick for hours; then I became very pious, God-loving and subdued, for just a time. I'll tell you plenty of stories, on the Mississippi. But will *you*? Why don't you send me some old pictures, too? Or new ones? Here are three new ones.[1] The one on the newspaper is shot in the station when we just arrived Berlin; for the others, I explained things on the back. I think you did not know these Simone: I did not, but yet I send them to you since they are supposed to be your wife and you are supposed to love her.

I saw *Mr. Verdoux* on Broadway, the first morning when it was produced there. I was rather disappointed but I must say I expected much, as much as *Golden Rush*. I used to love Charlot and I am afraid he is dead, and Charlie Chaplin is not so good. Some parts are wonderful indeed, but the man has no truth; I don't believe in him as I believed in the old Charlot. I do not feel Chaplin was too bold but on the contrary too shy when plotting the story: he did not really decide who was Mr. Verdoux — and he did not decide if he would do a realistic or a poetical movie, and that is why, as you say, it is not great. Interesting, indeed, but I expected something as great as Chaplin himself. Did I tell you I met him in New York? All a long evening I heard him speaking and I was rather disappointed with him, too, though he was sometimes charming. Once I went to Utrecht, in Netherlands, to a little museum and I saw some paintings by an old painter; he was unskillful and awkward and naïve but he painted very good portraits, there was a soul in it, they were fascinating. Then he went to Italy and admired Titian and Italian painters, skillful ones. When he came back, he never could do anything good, he was through. I am afraid it is a bit the same story with Chaplin. Something is lost since he knows what he wants to do, and yet he does not succeed in doing it. I am reproachful about it because I was so fond of him. And even in *Mr. Verdoux* he is often wonderful. Do you agree with me?

I'll give you a little triumph on me: I am not the challenging kind. I read over *Native Son* and *Black Boy* (in a quick way) and I recognized *Native Son* is much better, you are absolutely right. Communist people begin to attack Wright in the most filthy way, just now, they put him in the same bag with Sartre and spit on them, and say the most evil, meanest things. First, said today a young communist writer, we must no longer now describe the bad ways of living of misused people, of miserable colored men, of miserable poor men, of any miserable men: now we must write about Hope! He accuses Wright first of having been printed in the *Temps modernes*, secondly, to describe Negroes as beastly, cruel, wild men when they are as meek and good as a perfect communists. He said Wright is forging racial discrimination and preventing white and black people from loving each other, which they are so eager to do. Whatever we may think about Wright, and so reluctant as we may be, this piece of communist writing was one of the dirtiest things I ever read. It was written by an ancient student of Sartre,[2] whom Sartre helped very much when he was young and neurotic, who goes on dedicating books to him in a very friendly way, and writes in magazines the dirtiest things about him. I speak of it because I just read the piece today, and all my friends were mad at it; it was a big piece about *good* and *bad* American literature, all communist being good and not communist bad. You would have laughed as much as about Mr. Bromfield, though in the opposite way.

It is 10 P.M. now. I kept a nice evening for you and me. I had a little dinner by myself and I came to the Deux Magots where there is never anybody at such time. It is warn, deserted, peaceful; I drink a cognac; I have your letter on my lap. I see your smile in a three-months haze, coming nearer and nearer every day, and I feel my love for you deeper and deeper every day. you make me very happy.

So I left Berlin Thursday morning. We had a comfortable train, with a sleeping-car, but no dining-car. People gave us sandwiches, but I am just a bit neurotic about butter: I cannot eat butter, yea, I cannot, and please, don't try to reform me when I am nearly old enough to be your grand-mother. So the bread was buttered, indeed, and Sartre was very pleased because he ate all the sandwiches, and from noon to noon I ate nothing at all. But I was stoïc. In Germany it was always the same bad feeling of being on the wrong side, the winning one. At the frontier between Russian and American zones, they stopped the train and all German people had to go down, to wait in the cold open air for hours to show their passports, and so on. They were smiling, but all with rucksacks and bad poor bags: I remembered such long sad waitings in cold and rain, such crowded filthy wagons and Germans in the sleeping-cars. Now it was just the contrary and we felt uneasy, guilty in some way. We had not to go out, not even to wait, our wagons went on quietly. Next morning it was Belgium. It seemed incredible to see the neat, clean little towns without ruins nor rubbishes! I was reading Van Gogh's letters. Oh! It is a pity they are not translated in English. You would love him with real love; there never was a best, warmest, purest man — even you cannot be better.

I'll tell you about Van Gogh on the Mississippi boat, how he cut his ear and brought it wrapped in a fine silk-paper to a whore in a brothel, how he sadly killed himself, how first he worked so hard and never sold more than one painting, and never had more than one article written about him, and did not care but just worked, loving men and art, giving all of himself and never asking anything. And how he had a wonderful brother who gave him money all his life long so he might paint, and who died in six months by mere sadness when his brother had crazily killed himself. It is the most wonderful story I ever heard and I think he is one of the greatest painters too.

Now I'll come home, darling, and read a little and fell asleep in your arms. If you want to be efficient, try to know how we'll go from New Orleans to Vera Cruz. Sure we'll not stay more than three days in Mexico-City since it is an ugly town and the country around is wonderful. Tell me, darling, I though of a kind of bargain since we are both self-assertive and both like to make our own planning: we'll cut the days in two parts, you'll plan the nights (I heard you were not bad at it), and I'll obey your plans in a very submissive way, and I'll plan the days, and you'll follow me the same way. What do you think of it?

Sunday

You'll soon receive 250 dollars from a N.Y. magazine; that is money I earned for us. Please, don't give it to the phoney blonde, don't waste it in poker game, don't eat it in rum-cake shape. Just keep it for our trip, please. I hope I'll soon earn some more. These ones were nicely earned: I gave a chapter of my book about women to a new magazine which was to be issued now, but it is not. So I got 500 dollars (half has been spent last year when I was wasteful, not knowing we should travel together), and the piece is not published. That is very well since the magazine has been said to me to belong to *Time* and *Family Life*, a very bad gang. And then I can sell the thing anew if I find somebody to buy it.

Will you keep the good English book for me? I'll be pleased to read it on the Mississippi boat the days you'll be ill-tempered and not speak to me. I'll rather read a nice book than cry when it will happen. I work hard on the book about women. When it will be written, darling, men will know everything about women and so they will not be interested in them any more. It will do a big change in the world. But for crocodiles and frogs, indeed, it will not make any difference at all.

A very handsome American man with a black velvety beard, and black velvety eyes and hair, just came to speak to me; he is the one who gave me a rose once, months ago, I told you. We never spoke to each other again though we meet nearly every day. Today he came to my table and asked me to go tomorrow to his studio where Ellen Wright is coming too, and see his pictures and read his poems. he is called Puma: does it mean something to you? He told me I speak a beautiful English; I don't understand why you are the only one who always laughs at my English. I fancy you speak it rather coarsely and don't feel what is a really refined English language. Shall I succeed to make you jealous of this Puma? Or are you so conceited as to think a crocodile is so much better than a puma that you have nothing to fear? He is so dark and romanticist, with his little beard, very young you know, and appreciating real good English when he can hear it. Are you a little distressed now? A little unquiet?

No, you are not, you are right. I do not know if crocodiles are better than pumas, but I know a crocodile is my frog's destiny. I wait for you. I miss you and wait for you and I'll go on until I am your wife again.

Your own Simone

1) See photo insert. 2) Jean Kanapa, French communist, intellectual, and Stalinist.

Thursday, 12 Février 1948

Darling,

I work too hard to let anything happen. I am anxious to have this new book written as soon as possible and I spend all my time on it. I did not even go and look at this puma's paintings. Thank you for the titles of books, though I am afraid the little bookshop will keep none of them. Anyway, I don't read just now; but I'll try to buy some of them for the journey, when I'll come "home" again. Tell me, the league of organized crocodiles is very arrogant! Here is what the small frogs' society asked me to answer them: "It is impossible for us to let you know exactly when our most precious frog will be sent to you. It will surely not be before the 1st of April, surely not later than the first days of May. Anyway, you are sure to get such a fine good long meal that you are not to care so much if it is two weeks sooner or later." What is sure is our two months together. I am sending to you within two or three days something which will maybe interest you. I told you once

I had a very good friend who was a sculptor.[1] Now he has a show in New York which is a regular success; Sartre has written an interesting piece about him. Well, I just received a "catalogue" with fine pictures of his works, the piece by Sartre translated in English, and other things. You'll tell me what you do think about it. Maybe you are not interested in sculpture? I am not so much myself, but his sculpture speaks to me very deeply, so I should like to share it with you.

The Russian friend is always in bad moods, she has fever, and so on. I am afraid she will die within one or two years. it is sad now because she looks already half dead. She always was selfish but lively, very warm and sometimes very sweet, and pleasant to see and hear, and you could even laugh heartily with her. Now she looks old, she is ugly, and selfishness became a kind of curse, she can no more love anybody: She is dry, cold, hopeless, and she feels she is so. Her husband, who is as kind with her as kind can be, himself wishes she would die; I am sure that in a way she feels it: she does not decide to stay in bed and really try to recover, and yet she hates the idea of dying. Both guilty and innocent, killing herself and being murdered in spite of herself. It makes me feel very bad every time when I see her.

Sartre is beginning to have his play rehearsed, but he always has the worst difficulties about it. I think I told you he wrote this play to help two girls (one of them my Russian friend's sister) to become regular players. But they are not talented. So it makes things hard when you are to find other actors and producer, and so on. He has to struggle from morning to night, and all these theatre people are horrid, as I knew myself when I had my play acted. Good bye, darling. I am going to write a big part of the book this afternoon. So good bye, good bye.

Saturday

My spring dearest husband, I got a nice letter from you today. Thanks for the little pictures, they are always very fine. I am curious to know where you do get them. Thanks for the titles of books. I read only *Miss Lonely Heart* among them and enjoyed it;[2] I know *Ebony*: tell me if you wrote anything in it. I think I could get it in Paris. darling, you are very sensitive if you resented this Roditi story. Why? It can happen even to a very wise crocodile to sleep with a cheap woman; and then it seems, in spite of her cheapness, she really cared for you. So you could say: "Well, I did not hurt her too much since she was just sleeping with *any* writer" and "Well, she was not so cheap since she cared for *me*;" and so you would be satisfied, without remorse and yet pleasantly proud of yourself. But you are of the sensitive kind, of the not-conceited kind, and you rather think both: "I hurted her" and "she was cheap," you have both remorse and shame. it is too much, darling. in fact, you did not do any harm neither to the girl nor to yourself. I know worse stories, I had some myself. Yet, I was deeply pleased to feel how sensitive you are, because I am rather sensitive myself —not about everything, sometimes I really have a crocodile skin—but for the thinks I care for, if I love a local youth, for instance. So we could think if is very dangerous, and we have to take great care not to hurt each other, being both of such a frail kind. Yet, it is strange. I know we'll have to take no care at all, we'll not seriously succeed to hurt each other, because we are smart enough to feel what love is in each other's heart, are we not? I am beginning to fret about passport, reservations, and money; I begin to realize I'll see you within two months, maybe three months at most—anyway, I'll really see you. It is true! It is no longer a faraway dream. I feel my heart breaking with joy.

I think I told you about his little Jew boy who was a pupil of Sartre some years ago, who worked for Palestinian Jews and kept them in his house.[3] He was put in jail for some months and all burghers and jurys, who were Gaullist and Catholic, all well-thinking people prosecuted him. Well, he was given precarious freedom, and yesterday being the trial, Sartre was asked to come there. It was very short but interesting; he spoke about the boy, about the Jewish problem. And the judge for once was a good man, he spoke friendly too of the Jewish problem, nearly congratulated the boy and just fixed him for 1200Fr—that is about six dollars. We all were very pleased. Then I went with Sartre to a rehearsal of his play. As he wanted a girl called Wanda to play, he had the worst difficulties with everybody because everybody though she could not play; so he got very bad actors, a very bad producer, and so on. Now the strange point is the girl Wanda plays like a wonderful star; suddenly, something appeared in her and everybody has to recognize she is really good. So now, Sartre has to push away the other ones, the bad actors and bad producer—an actual comedy. I am always very interested to see the first beginning of a play, when the players hardly know what they have to say, when nobody knows where they have to stay and slowly, uneasily, the whole thing begins to take a shape. It is always something pathetic, like a poker game, because even when the play is good, nobody knows if it will win or lose, it depends upon too many things. I believe this play is very good, many people think so, but we are all afraid it will be such a scandal (because it is about politics, and as hated upon communists as upon Gaullists, or rather much worst about Gaullists but putting the problems very harshly about communists). We'll see. Anyway, yesterday the question was it was all so badly done that it would surely have been not even a scandal but just a failure. So we had to blow the whole thing up, send the bad people away, find other ones. It was all done in a feverish evening, good actors were found, and a good producer too, by a kin of miracle. Did you ever hear of Jean Cocteau? 4 This very important French poet did many things in theatre and movies. I think *La belle et la bête* is being produced in USA now. He is a pansy, 60 years old now, a very attractive funny man, friend of the poet-burglar Jean Genet. I like him. He knows much about theatre, and he decided to work himself upon Sartre's play, I mean to direct the actors, to find good ones, to care about the way they'll play...I never saw a play-writer care for the success of another play-writer and heartily help him! They are always mean with each other. So I was very moved and happy about this Cocteau being so generous. I like when a man is not mean, it seldom happens. That is why the day was so interesting for me: the way this old pansy writer behaved. I'll speak to you about him once; he lives among beautiful young boys. One was his lover fifteen years ago and he contrived to make him the first French movie player. He really did everything for the handsome boy; they are funny together, so womanlike. I am rather fond of pansies when they are of the right kind — I mean, not too sophisticated, but real human beings as other ones, with just these peculiar ways in love.

Good night, darling, I cannot hold the pen anymore, but I can yet take you in my arms and pretend I am too months older. Darling, we'll get along very well, you'll see. Oh yea! You'll see, and I'll see too. You miss me, darling.5 I want your kisses so much. I am coming to you, my own, Nelson, I am coming, and I'll kiss you as much as I want. Love and love, sweetheart.

Your own Simone

---

1) Giacometti. 2) By Nathaniel West. 3) Misrahi, member of the Stern Group, a Zionist terrorist organization in Palestine. 4) Jean Cocteau (1889–1963). Avant-garde French poet, librettist, novelist, actor, director, and painter. 5) She means "I miss you," but is literally translating literally from the reflexive French construction "tu me manques."

Dearest Nelson, my own husband,

It is a nice cold blue weather all these days and life goes on nicely. Yesterday I had a funny lunch with the poet-burglar Genet and Arletty,[1] the woman who played in *Les enfants du paradis*. I know you did not like the movie, but did not you think the girl was beautiful? She is beginning to get old, 50 by now, but keeps something gay and lively of a young girl. Sad for her, the face is no longer good enough for movies and she even hardly works any more. Then she behaved rather wrongly during the war; in my eyes, it is not important if she slept with a German officer: other ones slept with American officers and were no better for it. Such a love affair in a woman who does not know much about the world, and never cared for politics, does not scandalized me; but yet it seemed very bad to many people and she is lonely now. Yet she remains funny, lively, and witty; she is fond of Genet; they were very gay together. He has found a nice little parachutiste (now all the pansies sleep with parachutistes, as they did with sailors in former times). This boy is Russian and speaks with an accent from Marseille; he has been an S.S. and put in jail. As Genet loves bad boys, murderers, S.S., and so on, he is very pleased. The boy is very handsome indeed. When he is pleased he is gay and funny, and I laughed heartily the whole lunch long with these two people.

I saw the Puma again, just five minutes in the same bar. He gave me a manuscript of poetries which are awful. But I saw pictures of his paintings which look better; I'll go and look at them Thursday. Wright told me the man is rather crazy; he had some articles about him in *Life* and produced a book in New York about modern art, with good paintings. Did you ever heard about him?

I spent a long evening with the ugly woman; it becomes sadder and sadder. She says she is really crazy about sex: she did not sleep with a man since twelve years, and within some years will be fifty, it will be too late and she needs awfully a man to sleep with. She wrote to a man I know, who is rather handsome and kind, and asked to him if he wanted to sleep with her! She *wrote* it, is not that sad? He answered a kind letter, but saying he would rather not. So she was ashamed of it. She told me the story, and cried a little, saying she had offended me; she had to worship me and to care for nobody else. And maybe she will soon kill herself, she says. I heard what she said; it was very difficult to find the right answers. I felt rather sad for her, but the whole thing is hopeless.

For my Jewish friend, she is a little better; not so crazy, not so sad as before; she begins to work again. But even when she is healthy, there is something so dry and dull and gloomy in her that it does not make much difference. When you think my Russian friend is dying with tuberculosis, you'll confess that my girl-friends are really not happy.

Wednesday

I had a lunch with a friend coming back from New York and who has been in Mexico this winter. It seems really wonderful: in Yucatan we'll find tropical forests and heat, on the high plains wind and deserts. We'll go to Yucatan first. I'll get more informations, lots of informations all the month long, but I have enough already to feel excited; the chief one being you'll be near me day and night. I am having a very long, fine fancy gown made, just to stay home with you, instead of wearing the white peignoir; I hope you'll find me really smart when I'll wash the dishes in this silky thing. It is nearly sure I'll arrive New York about 15th of April. What I do not know yet is if I'll go to California. I am afraid it would be too short to be worth it. Anyhow you can think of having your first crocodile meal within two months. Will you not go to some agency and plan something really smart for Mexico? No matter. If you don't, I'll do; I want to see this country for good.

Everything is going on fine, now, with Sartre's rehearsals. Cocteau helps much; he brought very good players. One of the girls was sent away, and she resented it, but Wanda is very nice. I am pleased because poor Sartre had so much trouble in the beginning. Yea, you are right, there are always funny, silly things happening to him: never very important ones. One of the reasons is he never takes anything quite seriously, and chiefly he does not take himself seriously at all, and other people do: so there are strange misunderstandings and people are often scandalized about him. I'll have to speak about him so you know a little what kind of man he is. I guess you would like him very much; he is always laughing, and a good hearty man. You know, I should not go on sharing his life since such a long time if he was just a clever, talented man; I care for him because he is something else, what you and me like people to be. Once you told me you did not like to think I could "spiritually belong" to somebody; that is not a "belonging." But much of what I am now, he helped me to be. And sure I helped him to be what he is too. I hope you'll meet him once.

The book about America is beginning to be printed; the other one I work upon very much. What about *The Dealer and High Yellow*? But chiefly I fret from morning to evening about our trip. I cannot think of anything else.

Good night, honey. I don't know why I feel a bit sad tonight, maybe because I spent the evening with my Russian friend's husband,[2] a very nice boy, fond of writing, movies (he works as a script-writer), travels, and newspapers job. He began his life brightly and now he is really killed by his dying woman; he cannot leave her, yet he cannot live by her. It made me sad because I know him since years and years, he is a kind of young brother for me, and he was so helpless. People are not happy here—no, they are not. And I am longing for happiness, I wait for you so tensely that sometimes I feel tired by such a passionate waiting. Just come and kiss me, darling. That is just what I need: your arms to hold me tight. I love you.

Your Simone

1) Arletty (1898–1992). French actress who rose to international stardom under the direction of Marcel Carnes (*Hotel du Nord*, 1938; *Les Enfants du Paradis*, 1944). She played Ines in Sartre's *No Exit* (*Huis Clos*, 1954). 2) Bost.

Friday, 20 Février 1948

Darling, dearest Mexico husband,

All is going on wonderfully now. I have my reservation on the De Grasse for the 7th April, so I'll arrive New York on the 13th. On the other hand I have to be in Mexico on the 13th July and take the airplane to South America. Then after three months I'll come back and see you a month more. What I don't know exactly is about California. What I should like would be not to go to Los Angeles, just stay ten days in New York and come to you, stay with you the whole time. I have written to my friend in this mood, but I am afraid she will be too disappointed if I see her only in October. So I wait for her answer.

My sister and brother-in-law came from Belgrade. They had a wonderful trip, crossing Italy and France in car; but they are so tedious, unpleasant, selfish, empty people, that is seems always very happy for me when I meet them in Paris. And the ugly woman, the Jewish girl, send always heavy letters to me. They want me to give a meaning to their life, and I cannot. The little Russian sick girl asks nothing, but that is yet sadder.

Well, darling, I was right when I teased you about this Puma. I do not know much more about men than in the time when you say my face could not be used for flirt, but I had felt something and when I went to see his paintings yesterday I was a bit defiant. The paintings are interesting, very interesting really—he has something, and he is nice in his crazy way. But what is this way *you* have in America always pretending to kiss women you don't even know? No French man ever tried to kiss me; there was always first a kind of silent or spoken agreement when I slept with some of them (not many). But nobody *dared* to take his own chance. And this Puma, being American, did it. But *you* know I am not easy to kiss and I did not become more since a Chicago local youth trapped me; so he just caught a piece of my cheek, and we went on looking at the paintings. Then he tried again and I had to push him away, pushing hard on his forehead and feeling rather awkward and silly. Was he not smart? He knew how to bring me home, said very flattering polite words, and then all his smartness was of no use, you see. Well, it pleased me just in a way, because I thought I could be attractive to somebody else than a crazy local crocodile, and so I was not, maybe, abusing this crocodile in letting him love me. Now, you have to know it was not even for your sake I did not let the boy kiss me, but just because I did not care for him at all, though he is really handsome. The point is I don't feel kissing is interesting at all if you don't really give you to it; and then it means much, for me anyway, and it very seldom happens that I wish the meaning to be fulfilled. It happened in Chicago by a strange witchery that I have not yet fully understood. Oh, darling! I love you so gaily today! How I should laugh at you if you were there!

There is snow in Paris, and ice. It is cold and blue weather, but sun on the white ground, and it helps to be happy. Tell me, honey, if I badly drop California, would you be free from 1st May to 13th July for travel and love? Now, you cannot keep me any longer. No, I'll struggle as fiercely as I did with the Puma. I am going to work, and no smile, no kiss can prevent me from doing it. Good bye. I'll see you again some day.

Saturday

I was glad to learn you had fallen in love with me again.[1] It was a sweet letter you sent me, it put tears in my eyes. The idea about Guatemala suits me very much; it seems exciting. I think coming from New Orleans, the most sensible would be to take an airplane to Yucatan, see Yucatan first, then Guatemala, Vera Cruz, then Mexico City. It is all *one* kind of civilization

171

and landscapes. I am more and more tempted to drop California. I wait for a letter from Los Angeles to decide.

A very temperate life today: morning of writing; lunch with mother, sister and sister's husband — very sad people. Writing from three to eight, dinner and a little scotch with Sartre coming back from his rehearsal. Now, I'll go to sleep. I thought so many nice thoughts about you: how you could give so much without ever asking anything, how you understand so wisely all told and untold things, how both greedy and patient you can be. Well, I love you and feel proud of it. I miss you so painfully, darling, but we'll have our reward. People who don't know this sickness don't know neither the happiness we'll know. I am afraid I'll not be kind and good enough to go to Los Angeles: I want too much to stay with you. Well, I cannot say. I'll speak to you about this nice California girl, you'll see why I care about her. She is nearly a daughter for me, and I have a faithful heart.

Nelson, my husband, I belong to you soul and heart and body, I am yours. Just wait a little for me. I kiss the broken nose, the muddy eyes, the elephant ears, the sleeping mouth: I love all of them, all of you. Good night, honey.

Your own Simone

1) Algren had greatly admired a photograph Simone de Beauvoir had sent to him on February 6 of herself in Berlin, explaining that he had fallen in love with her all over again as soon as he saw it, and marveling that she could love a man as unattractive as he was. He then sent her a not-so-flattering picture of himself, which she refers to at the end of this letter.

Monday, 23 Février 1948

My own local pretty man,

It is all snowing in Paris now, yesterday night it was wonderful. Saint-Germain-des-Prés looked like a little village with the white quiet streets and big flakes of snow falling gaily: the yellow lights sent huge shades on the ground. Today it is half melted, black and dirty; it is cold but it is pleasant when you are warmly dressed and the houses warm inside. Nothing to do with the awful winters during the war when I had to sleep in woollen ski-pants, I remember, and all shoes were pierced, and it was dead cold everywhere. Darling, it is 23rd February: a year ago, I was just being acquainted with you. It was snowing in Chicago too. I glided on the iced ground and you hold my arm beneath the El. Do you remember how slyly you tried to keep me out of your life, pretending I had a wrong number?

But then my stubborness served me good. And I felt very cosy and quiet near you, very confident, not suspecting you were just treacherously trapping me, so that I should follow you submissively to faraway Guatemala. I did not suspect anything new could happen in my life; I felt too old. So few things are really worth caring for them, and then you gave me a second youth, such a wonderful local love, that it became an international one. All was so cleverly done, I am yet wondering how you contrived it. It makes me a little afraid of you: if you are so tricky, you could make me very unhappy too. Maybe it would be wiser not to take this chance, not to go to America at all, I am wondering...

Darling, now it is midnight and all I am wondering is: how shall I wait two months more before kissing you? What! I lived thirty-nine years with nights where you did not interfere; it seemed easy. Why is it so difficult? Can you understand it? I cannot. I just know I miss you and missing you so much is hell. No, not exactly hell, since in hell there is no hope, and I don't hope, I know you'll lie near me again. Nelson, I want you so much. I love you, my own husband.

Thursday

I had your letter this morning. Since you seem to want really to know when your frog is going to be delivered to you, I'll tell you it has most chances to be about 25th April. I got a letter from my Californian friend, and it seems she would not be too disappointed if I went to see her only in October, so I'll drop California, just stay ten days in New York to gather some money and come to you. Indeed, I am always afraid something would happen and I don't like to say too precise dates, but it is the way it seems to be taking shape. Next year, you'll see, when you'll come to me and I'll ask when I am to make the reservations for Algiers, you'll look casual and say: "I'll arrive when I can. Just be ready to accept me." Anyway, I had pictures made for passports, and I even ordered dresses to be really smart when we'll meet again. No. For truth, the dresses are mostly for South America. I have a gown made for you and me, that is the one I'll put off when I'll be with you. I love it, not because I'll put it on, but because I'll put it off. I hope you'll find it is really a nice gown for undressing.

Yea, I know *Ebony*. I bought one issue in Harlem with Wright, a year ago, but I had seen it before, in Paris. There was Mezzrow[1] pictured in it, laughing in Harlem streets; I was listening to Don Redman's orchestra, crazy with joy because I was going to America; yea, I did not know what it meant for me, and how many nights of longing and yearning I should go through, for having met you.

I am going Wednesday to see a very learned man in the ethnographic museum. We'll plan something really smart for our Guatemala-Mexico trip.

Not much happened. Always snow and blue sky, always good frog work. I am in the public library today, learning the different ways by which you dirty men oppressed us, poor womanly creatures. So I'll say good bye. Long, loving kisses for you, my beloved husband.

Your Simone

1) Mezz Mezzrow, jazz musician and author of *Really the Blues* (1946).

Saturday, 28 Février 1948

Good night, honey,

I love you so much tonight, among all nights when I so much love you. It is a nice night, nearly mild, and misty (sweet misty nights always make me think of you, I don't know why). Paris was beautiful, in a secret sad way. I had a very good day because I went to a painting exhibition which was wonderful. Did you ever hear of Paul Klee? He was half-German, half-Swiss and died in 1940. He did the most poetical, appealing painting I saw in my whole life. I knew him a little before, but there were never many shows of him because during the war he was forbidden by Germans as decadent and so on. And there were more than hundred pictures today: a whole life, a whole man. It is very fancy painting, sometimes abstract, always irreal. Yet when you go out and look at the real night, you think: yea, it is just like it. The same beauty, the same humour, the same sadness and joy in the red and green lights of the real night and in the irreal paintings with the wonderful colors. So I feel good tonight. I think it is a good criterium for literature or art when it makes you deeply feel good for having tasted of it. Your books have this precious quality, and that is what you ask from man or woman too, is it not? Just to feel: well, the world is worth having been done since this can happen in it: this picture, this book, this love, this smile.

I had a lunch with an American teacher from Columbia and wife. They did not make me feel good, they didn't make the world worth living in. But they were very nice to me in New York, and it was not too unpleasant to see them and to speak about America. They spoke about this Capote

174

about whom you spoke to me too, and give me one of his books. I am curious, though a little defiant. Do you like him?

Now we have wonderful jazz in France, but it is in Nice. I just pick some little bit of it, here and there, through the radio. Next Wednesday we'll meet Armstrong in the afternoon, drink with him and the Negroes about whom you did not understand anything, and on the evening we'll go and hear him "Salle Pleyel," which is our Carnegie Hall. Places are dreadfully expensive and it will be dreadfully smart, but I am a little doubtful. I am afraid it will be a bit phoney, not genuine, I'll tell you. My ancient friend, the young man with the horn,[1] is in Nice as a reporter and seems enthousiastic. It is his own little jazz, the one playing in the caves where I sometimes went (seldom), which has been picked to be the only French jazz in Nice. There was much fears and arguing and anger about it! But professional French jazzs are very bad, and this little amateurish jazz is very good. This young man with the horn, I don't see him any more; it is a pity but he was really spoilt by superficial success. This book he faked was a tremendous boom, and then other ones the same way, with much obscenity in them, pretending they were American. He made lot of money, but doesn't care for anything else: just make money and have one's name in big letters on the first page of newspapers. That is bad the way young men are spoilt now in France, either for caring for politics, either because they don't care for it, as this one did.

One curious thing happened: I told you our political manifesto was a failure, but two days ago another one of the same kind was signed by us; we did not care much for it, it seemed as hopeless as the other one. And then, strange, it is a great success, all newspapers speak about it, socialist and even communist deputies come and sign it, great meetings are preparing, and so on. We'll see how it will go on. It was so unexpected, a pleasant surprise. We saw an old friend, who once was a very close one,[2] and is RPF now (for de Gaulle). It was funny because he himself realized the whole thing was stinking and tried to convince us it did not smell at all, but he knew better. I am pleased with Wallace's little victory. It means something, does not it? Is it because you lectured so well?

Darling, I should like to go on writing many little unimportant things, but here is sleep coming. Sleep is not stronger than love; indeed, it is another way of feeling one's love: curling under the blankets and pretending it is 28th April instead of 28th February. Now, I'll shut my eyes and lie in your arms and fell asleep with my cheek against your shoulder. Nelson,

I love you so much. I am yours, kiss me darling. Well, it is no use *writing* things. You know, Nelson, do you? Just remember.

Monday

It is spring today, the first spring day, mild and gentle with a little sadness in it. But no sadness in my heart. You sometimes said to me that I seemed to expect both sadness and joy at one time: but you have to know that coming to you I don't expect any sadness. I have a brand-new passport with a very ugly little picture, brand-new dresses are been made, just my heart will not be brand-new; I'll keep the old one.

We met Koestler Friday night in the cave-bar where we often go and drink a scotch. He came back from Italy in car, was tired and lonely, with yet all the dark road behind him, but as you told me I had to break a bottle on his head, I was icy cold and he resented it. We spoke hardly half an hour. Then he invited us to drink a bottle of white burgundy yesterday before lunch; he had an awful hangover and was scared to death by what just happened in Czechoslovakia, so scared that he felt sure if there is a war, American people will put him in a concentration camp if first Russians don't shoot him. He is a poor liar, a poor treacherous man, very weak, just a kind of sad rubbish. I felt real disgust for him. He is going to America but not to Chicago, anyway he is not worth seeing. R. Wright met him (I had a nice evening with the Wright family) and felt exactly as I did, he said: "This Koestler has remained a communist; as soon as he sees you, he begins to accuse you." I suspect when Koestler pretends he is so remorseful because he was *once* a communist, it means in fact he is remorseful *not to be* any longer a communist, because now they are going to win and he wishes to be on the winning side.

Many people are scared here. They saw now communists will take all power in Italy, and what about France? People begin to speculate about Russian occupation, saying in that case they will kill women and children, or things like that! I guess people like to be scared, so they have no responsability to take; it is a way of escaping. I am not *very* bold myself and hate the idea of dying. But well, when we'll die, we'll die; I am not to die from fear beforehand.

Yea, the Wrights are nice. Really, he is better than most French intellectuals, much more lively, gay, humorous; the wife is a very nice woman and a wonderful cook! I wish I could cook like her, I would be sure you would love me until we are hundred years old. He spoke to me of a little town near Mexico City whose name means cow-horn and which sounds wonderful. They know this Puma who tried so badly to kiss your own frog, and they say he is just a little arrivist, a silly boy with a black beard. Indeed, now, every time he meets me he asks something: could I help him for a show? For having an article printed, and so on? He comes in the bars even when I am with friends and bores me for whole five minutes.

The Jewish girl told me every week after seeing me, she is unable to work or sleep for days, so it is better not to see each other for a while. I am very pleased with it. But then, you remember when she had seen me the ugly woman used to vomit. I am a little afraid, what is so bad about me? What are you going to do when you see me? cry or vomit? or both? Do you like better if I should not come?

Well, I'll come anyway, I think of it night and day. It will be sweet, a Guatemala spring with you, I wait for it. I wait lovingly and happily. I kiss you very hard.

Your own Simone

1) Boris Vian. 2) Raymond Aron (1905–1983). French sociologist, philosopher, and journalist.

Jeudi, 4th March 1948

My beloved one,

Paris is more beautiful than ever. I sat in the gardens of Luxembourg and I looked a long time to the bare black trees against the pale pink sky. I have a big cold and some fever, and so the whole day long I swallowed hot grogs and kind of pills; that made me a little a stranger to myself. I felt different for once and enjoyed it. Yesterday I had a great time. I went to Armstrong's concert and it was maybe the best thing I heard or saw since years. The Salle Pleyel is as big as Carnegie Hall; it was full of screaming people, chiefly young people mad with enthousiasm. People half killed one another to come in, though indeed all seats were reserved since a long time. There was with Armstrong a wonderful pianist called Hines or something like it, and clarinet, trombone, battery[1] and basse were the best of all USA I heard. There was a big fat Negro woman, Middleton she is called, who sang wonderfully too. Yes, it was a real good jazz evening. In the afternoon there had been a pleasant party at the old Gallimard's (my publisher); he had offered his beautiful rooms to the Negroes of *African*

177

Presence so that they could receive Louis Armstrong. There were all intellectual artist french Negroes of Paris there, and when Armstrong came in, the young Africans did a very good show of tam-tam, a girl had Armstrong dancing with her; it was pleasant. Full of reporters taking pictures, full of American people. This Puma, the black-bearded beau, is hated by everybody now, asking everybody to help him to sell pictures. There were the Wright there and many other American intellectuals; Paris is crowded with them. Next year, there will be one more, a different one: an American crocodile, we miss him very much in Paris.

My own, crocodile, it is Friday now. I was so feverish and tired yesterday night that I could not finish the letter, but just went to bed. For once I did not even want you as my husband, I just wished your shoulder, soft and cool beneath my hot cheek; it would have been sweet. Maybe I'll get a quiet little fever in Guatemala to know in this way the gentle coolness of your shoulder. Next month, darling. I ask myself if you are conceited enough to know how much I love you.

Your own Simone

1) "Batterie" in French; "percussion" in English.

Saturday, 6 Mars 1948

Darling,

I got your last letter and was sorry for your cold. I just have one too and spend my days coughing and blowing my nose. But no more snow here; it is really spring coming, and it is really pleasant. I am afraid you have been scared by my last letters: so many places to see! I'll tell you what I think: first, I want to please you as much as you wish to please me, so we'll not quarrel often. Then if you rather want to stay and I like to move, we'll find an agreement; for instance, we would stay three weeks in Guatemala and three weeks in Mexico, and move from villages to lakes and mountains and ruins for three weeks. Then we'll always be free to do as we'll please, to stay where we had no intended to, to move away quicker than we thought. I'll tell you why I think we should move a little: if we were visiting Europe, I should not insist to go in two months in Paris, Madrid, Rome, and Algiers. I should find it silly, and say as you do: let us see one of them. But I know in Mexico and Guatemala there are no important places where one really enjoys to stay very long. The big cities are rather vulgar, the fine strange places are little villages, little unimportant towns. These ones are very pleasant for just a little while, but not a long stay; it would be tedious. Then the whole bunch of villages, little towns, ruins and landscapes is just one country. It is not running in a silly, hasty way from one thing to another, but rather trying to see and understand and feel a whole: Indian-Spanish old and modern civilization. Well, we'll see, darling. You know I am not of the superficial, hasty hopping kind as you seem to fear. I want you to enjoy the trip as much as I want to enjoy it myself. Generally, we feel the same things about places and people, and we like the same way of living, so we'll have no problem.

Yea, I should like to do the Mississippi journey if it can be done in beginning of May. Do nothing yet, wait for my next letter before changing the reservations. The point is the South American travel depends upon the government and is not exactly settled. So I cannot settle exactly our travel. My Californian friend cannot come to Mexico to see me, because I'll just leave Mexico and you when I have to fly to South America. Just now I am chiefly interested by what I'll do about you: how to spend with you as much time as possible, you wise, frog-trapping crocodile.

Sunday

I feel very happy today. It is a wonderful spring beginning in Paris. The sun came suddenly, so hot that all women were perspiring under their fur coats. Today they are thrown away and new spring suits appear. I have taken the white coat from the cupboard. There are children in gardens, and people bathing their face in the sun at all the café-terraces of Boulevard Saint-Germain. When you walk leisurely you meet lots of friends who are leisurely sitting in the sun and you feel everybody is happy, which is a pleasant feeling. I want you in Paris next spring, honey. With 300 dollars a month you'll live as a king, and with 200 very confortably; 100 would be possible. So we'll manage it, shall we not?

I have a publisher really interested in you.[1] He has read already *Never Come Morning* and is going to ask to Pic and Elris what they are doing. Anyway he took *Somebody in Boots*[2] and *Neon Wilderness*, and he should like to publish the whole lot. He is a nice young man and just beginning to do the publisher job by himself; he should like to do a kind of great boom with you. We'll see. The difficult point is you are hard to read for French people, and so much the more difficult to translate. But he is deeply interested. I am sure he'll manage it.

179

I am more and more interested by the book I am writing. I have achieved a quarter of it now, a really long piece; I begin the second part. I like the work very much and that too makes happy days. Friday was an interesting day. In the afternoon I saw a rehearsal of Sartre's play. It is a bloody, dreary but very ironic, humorous drama about a political murder. I proposed a title that has been accepted: "All is Well that Ends Well." In French it sounds as an old proverb. These rehearsals are always a bit depressing because the actors are not so good. There are two important characters: a young man (the murderer) and an old one (the murdered one). The young one is wonderful, one of the best young French players.[3] He makes you think acting is really an art. But the old one is a very well-known conceited second rate actor, and that is bad because he is too important to accept reproaches and criticisms, and too silly to play really well. He has the part of a communist chief and he looks like a wealthy industrial; poor Cocteau does not know what to do about him. The girl Wanda is really not an actress; she does what she can, but she can very little. I hope it will turn good; it surely will not be fully bad, but it should be very good. Then on the evening, the woman who owns the theatre, an ex-beautiful woman, a dreadful whore having slept with thousands of men, took us to her home for dinner. She is a curious Parisian figure, fifty years old, trying to look thirty, always speaking about obscene things in the coarsest way and showing legs, hips, thighs, all what she may show of her body and even what she might not show. She is a little funny by sheer coarseness. The dinner was strange and wonderful: Arabian dishes, because she was once the mistress of a Morocco sultan. But the interesting point was she had invited with Cocteau, who is a very bright, funny man, the old Colette.[4] I think you heard of Colette: she is the only really great woman writer in France, a really great writer. She was once the most beautiful woman. She danced in music-halls, slept with a lot of men, wrote pornographic novels and then good novels. She loved country, flowers, beasts, and making love, and then she loved too the most sophisticated life; she slept with woman too. She was fond of food and wine — well, she loved all good living things, and she spoke beautifully about them. Now she is seventy-five years old and has still the most fascinating eyes and a nice triangular cat face; she is very fat, impotent, a little deaf, but she can tell stories and smile and laugh in such a way nobody would think of looking at younger, finer women. She spoke the whole evening with Cocteau about the neighbourhood where they live, the Palais-Royal, which is one of the best places in Paris indeed. They described the life of the old whores who live there, the little shops, the little cafés, the people in them with such humanity and such humour that we listened, really fascinated. I hope I shall see her again. I was in love with her, through her books, when I was a girl, so it meant something to me to see her. It is strange an old woman when she has lived so much, so feverishly, so freely, when she knows so much and does not care for anything more because now everything is over for her.

Monday

Darling, I don't care for Mississippi, Guatemala, Yucatan; I care for you. When I already pretend I am with you, Mexico or New Orleans seem important enough, but when I realize you are not yet near me, just one thing I long for: holding you again in my arms, being trapped once more in ours. Now every hour is an hour gliding away towards you, darling. Slowly, slowly but surely time is bringing me to you. Across days and nights, sun and cold, I am coming to end of April and Wabansia nest. Then I'll stop for long, my heart will stop in just one beating. I love you. Longing, waiting, hoping will stop; I'll be where I have my place. I belong to you. Is it your birthday soon? I remember you told me it was in March. Happy birthday, my beloved Nelson! I hope you'll live with my love as long as you did without. Happy birthday! Good bye, honey. I have sunny tropical love in my heart, and it is all for you. We'll be so happy, you'll see. I think of you all day long and as soon as I think of you, I kiss you. I love you.

Your own Simone

1) Paul Morihien. 2) Algren's first novel (1934). 3) François Périer, playing Hugo. 4) Colette (1873-1954). French writer and feminist. Her writer/critic husband, Henri Gauthier-Villars, published her celebrated *Claudine* series under his pen name, Willy.

Sunday, 14 Mars 1948

My own husband,

I had a sweet letter from you yesterday. You seem very busy, talking and talking to old ladies, never giving your jaw a rest! Take care! You'll have to talk to me soon, you must keep some voice. Yea, darling, I should like to take photos with you, to hear jazz and to go to Negro night-clubs. I should like everything you'll plan, and no stockyards. I begin to feel really coming, and all burning with happiness.

Plans seem to have changed once more; it does not depend upon me, you know, and anyway it does not make much difference. I think I shall not go by boat in the beginning of April, but by plane first days of May, and direct to Chicago. I always told you I could not know exactly between April and May. Don't tell me I am whimsical and unfair to the Crocodile League. Anyway, within two months it will be exactly the eve of our departure on the Mississippi boat, we'll be in Wabansia or in Cincinnati, at your time it will be about six or seven o'clock and maybe we'll be drinking some scotch, maybe we'll be loitering in the streets, maybe we'll be kissing each other, or even worse; and sure, sure, we'll be very happy, whatever we are doing.

It is all blue and sunny in Paris now, so warm you don't need a coat even at night. I am always writing, going to Sartre's rehearsals, trying to help with good advices, and discussing with people about the RDR.[1] The meeting last Friday was a success. There were thousand people in a room fit for six hundreds, and newspapers spoke very well about it. But yesterday I had a very nice gay evening, not discussing, just drinking with friends: Sartre, my Russian friend and her husband, my friend who does fine sculptures and his girl-friend, and the movie-player Pagliero whom you saw in *Open City* and who has a nice wife too. We had a good dinner in a little restaurant decorated with good modern paintings, because many good modern painters are customers there and paid with paintings, and we had scotch in a very nice American bar where there are always many drunken American soldiers and a pianist playing bad jazz. Everybody told stories, chiefly obscene coarse stories but very funny ones. I had a new skirt, nearly falling to the ankle and a new bodice all in old white lace and a Yugoslavian necklace. The sculptor told me I was the finest thing he saw in his life since a painting by Bonnard. I was very proud. Yea, after this tiring winter, I begin to have a good face again.

I read the short story by Capote, *The Headless Hawk*, but translated, so I think it had lost something of its American flavour. It is not bad, chiefly for a young man but I am not altogether enthusiastic. It is the kind of stuff young people often write in France too; we have lot of stories about crazy women, madness, and war, the whole poetry of it is a little cheap. Nevertheless, I am going to read his long novel, a Faulknerish marvellous story about South, I heard. Darling, your first "Chicago letter" was published in *Temps modernes* and interested people very much.[2] I am pleased because I am publishing in *T.M.* parts of my own book about America, and people seem to be very interested too. Am I not conceited today, telling you compliments I am gathering from people? It is because I feel so happy, happy because I am going to see you and because you love me.

Honey, now it is Monday 15th, and on 15th we'll arrive on the boat and begin gliding on the Mississippi. I hope you'll be happy waiting for me as I am waiting for you. And then I'll fall into your arms and we'll not need words any more, we'll see our happiness on each other's face. I kiss you happily, my beloved May husband.

Your own Simone

1) *Rassemblement démocratique révolutionnaire* (RDR). Political party founded in February 1948 by Sartre, Rousset, and other leftist intellectuals to unite non-communist socialist forces and build an independent Europe. 2) It appeared in *Les Temps modernes,* January 1948, entitled *"Du rire en bocaux, reportage de Chicago"* translated by Simone de Beauvoir.

Wednesday, 17th Mars 1948

Dearest,

Yea, it is very convenient for you to stay cosily in our Wabansia nest, writing your book and eating rum-cake, and just looking from time to time at the corner of the street to see if the taxi-cab comes. While I spent the whole morning in the American embassy, soiling my fingers with ink in order to have my finger-prints registered and answering lot of intimate questions about father, mother, and what am I going to USA for. I ask you, why am I going, what could I answer? "Lectures," I said. So not to be a liar, I'll have to lecture you. Well, now I have got a big beautiful visa and I may fly away when I want. What is all right too is I managed to get dollars in New York. I hope I shall gather 1000 — it will not be necessary to spend all of them; what we'll have saved you'll take back to Chicago, waiting for the following honeymoon, but so we'll have plenty to do what we'll like, there will be no question at all about it. Then the dentist is working very well on my jaw. I think I'll be able to move it twice as quick as I used to do. I am sure you'll appreciate it. You remember I was sad during winter because I felt old and ugly; spring is working well too. If it does not change, you'll have a good-looking wife. Really, honey, it is very bad: you were fond of me partly because I was a wise woman when you met me. And since I love you I became unwise, as silly as other ones. I did not care for face and look before, and now I should like so much to send to you a fine, healthy, young, fresh, smart girl for our Mississippi journey. You'll take me as I'll be, anyway. Darling, I am just loving you in the most silly way in the world, all these days.

The ugly woman has began to write a new novel. I think it will be good. She'll speak about woman's sexuality in a way no woman ever did, with truth and poetry, and something more. She was pleased because I liked the beginning of the book, and seems a little less unhappy, living all alone, always alone, and just writing. The Russian friend on the contrary is sadder and sadder because she does not feel better. The Jewish friend I don't see any more since she thought it was not good for her. From time to time I see my sister, but her husband whom I dislike is always with her. Today yet, we had a little time alone and we spoke about our childhood. I remembered through her many things I had forgotten.

I have Capote's novel, *Other Voices, Other Rooms* (on the picture he looks very young, fair-haired, and romantic, not unpleasant), but I did not read the book yet.

Here is a little interview a woman wrote about me. You cannot read it, you lazy local youth, but maybe the little drawing will amuse you. I had a busy week too. Thursday evening I went to the theatre. For once, I saw an old vaudeville, fifty years old, played by a modern cast in one of the best theatres of Paris; yesterday, there was the big political meeting in the biggest public room in Paris: 4000 people were there—that was not bad. The first speaker did not speak too good, but Sartre was good and Rousset wonderful. People were enthousiastic, applauded and gave money and their names as members of the party. But then, what now? There is a possibility to do something, indeed, but not great, things go on too quickly.

Yesterday it was all gold and blue. My sister and brother-in-law took me for a ride in their car; we had some nice hours in the forests surrounding Paris (many flowers on the trees, and little green leaves) and we ate a pleasant lunch sitting outdoors. All the ride long, I dreamt of other gold and blue days with the man I love and my heart was thrilling with impatience. I am tired these last days, always sleepy with a light headache. I have worked very much without stopping a single day since I left Wabansia. Maybe that is the reason. Anyway I intend to spend three weeks in the country before taking the plane and coming for my long love-holiday. It seems sure now I'll arrive New York on the 5th May and be in our nest on the 8th or 9th, or 7th, maybe: it will depend upon my New York business, but sure it will not need more than one or two days. So we'll be together for our first love-birthday. Did you think of it? It was about 10th May when you first trapped me so smartly.

I heard Mezz Mezzrow, a wonderful concert, the big hall was full of young people applauding, screaming, kissing with enthousiasm. I enjoyed it deeply. I love good old jazz; it reminds me of many things. I felt near you though we never succeed hearing jazz together. We'll have time to hear some in Chicago. I'll read your book, we'll hear Bessie Smith before going to Cincinnati and on our boat.

Good night, honey. I am tired to death. So you were an Easter gift! The bells coming back from Rome brought you to Detroit for my future happiness! It suits you. Let us have as many years together as you had without me. I have a whole life love to give to you. I kiss your lips.

Your own Simone

Thursday, 25 Mars 1948

My own beloved husband,

It was a surprise to get your letter so soon: yesterday. What a silly man I have chosen to love! You tell my so many things occurred this week that you cannot say *all* of them, and then you say *nothing* at all. I am your wife and I have to know. But I shall not scold you because your letter was so sweet. Yea, darling, our love is growing and growing like weeds and I am afraid it will not stop; it will become a giant love, a real freak. We'll have to do what we can with such a love. Yea, darling, I remember the last minutes, when you showed me the book about the fierce boxer; I cannot speak about them, it is too precious, and too heavy a memory. It seems wonderful now to think of our first minutes, and of all the hours and days and weeks which are to follow. It is quite fixed now: I have asked for my reservation on the 4th May, arriving N. York on the 5th, and Chicago the 8th. Indeed with airplanes, it is always possible there is one or two days delay, but surely no more. I begin to feel nervous; it moves me too deeply the idea of feeling anew your arms around me, of living with you nights and days as we never did. And the mere fact of leaving Paris for such a long time — six months at least — makes me a bit nervous too. It is strange to change one's life so completely. I cannot sleep well, I feel it difficult to work well, I am not restful at all. I was pleased to meet an American friend two days ago, a publisher. *New Directions*, that is his business, do you know it? He is a fairy, and I rather like this kind of men because they often are very friendly with women (and yet there is no questions of being trapped!). This one is nice, though little indifferent to human beings, with a dry, egoistic heart as fairies often are. It is better not to speak about politics with him, he is too complaisant for the State Department, but yet he is not on the reactionary side: he rather does not care. I had a lunch with him, Sartre, Queneau, and speaking about literature and literary people, and gossiping, was pleasant. How much we are involved in politics here! Even if not liking it, as I do. Everything we write or do has a political meaning; friendship always implies political back-ground; it is a bit tiresome.

Within a week, it is Sartre's play being produced; people are already talking about it, and everybody is afraid it will be stopped after a week because sure there will be hard quarrels about it. It makes everybody nervous: so many people are interested in such an undertaking, player, author, producer, and so on! Everybody worked hard and long, so it would be rather terrible if for a reason or another it is a failure. And if the failure happens for political reasons, it is unpleasant; some people say the play is too pro-communist, and others it is too anti-communist, so how can we know? In the last days, it always seem to go along in very bad way; people are feverish. Well, within a week, we'll know how it is.

Good bye, my beloved one. Soon it will be the same joy in our hearts. I wait for it. I wait for you. I do nothing else.

Your own Simone

Friday, 2d Avril 1948

Darling, my dearest next month husband,

When you receive this letter, we'll be less than a month from each other. On the 5th I'll hear your voice by phone from New York, 7th or 8th I'll be in your arms, and a wonderful life will begin. Write to me Hôtel "Bellevue," Ramatuelle, Var, that is the place where I'll spend three quiet weeks before coming to you (from 10th April to 1st May). I hope I'll have your last letter in Paris on the 1st May, manage all that cleverly.

I have a brand-new tooth, all gold and white, and it seems strange in my mouth; it does not really belong to me, not in the way you belong to me, for instance, but everybody tells me I am much nicer to see. Well, I spent five years with a hole in my jaw and I did not care;[1] it seemed too expensive and boring and useless to have such a work done on my tooth. Do you know why I had it done, now? Yea, you know. Though you don't care for a hole or not in my mouth, I want you to have a girl with a whole smile, so I went three mornings a week at the dentist for your sake—a real token of love that I gave you, a much greater proof of love than any kiss I could give you, since I like to kiss you and I dislike going to the dentist.

Much fuss and noise and unrest in the little colony: Sartre's play was produced for the first time yesterday evening. There were only "friends." Tonight there will be newspapers men, critics, and so on, but yesterday there were about 400 people, and all those one calls friends are not, so we were very anxious to know if it would be success—and it was. It seems people agree to think it is the best play Sartre ever wrote, and I agree too. For French people, it means really so much the things he is speaking about that they heard with a kind of passion. It is a story happening in the communist party, in a country of Central Europe during the war; the opposition between a realistic cynic, but generous and humorous old leader of the CP, and a young idealistic boy of the same party who likes purity and ideas more than human beings. He is a young intellectual bourgeois boy, and, you know, it is a great problem here for young intellectuals and bourgeois to decide if they can get along with the CP, so the problems went to the heart of everybody. In the play nobody is wrong, nobody is right, you just understand their difficulties without deciding what would have been done, that is what makes the story true and touching. There was a feverish atmosphere: the last days the play was suddenly changed, a part of it cut away, actors were sent away, others picked up, all the garments and the setting chosen hastily. A friend of Cocteau, called Bérard, came to help about the setting: he is a painter and does the setting in the best Parisian theatres, very talented but horrid. He is a pansy, indeed, as all Cocteau's friends are, and in love with a young dancer who does not love him and takes ether, doping himself to death. Yesterday the dancer was lying half dead somewhere in the theatre and Bérard crying with genuine tears; the whole theatre smelt of ether. Oh, there were lots of very funny little things. I shall tell them to you one day on the boat, when you'll be so tired of speaking that you'll give me a chance. Well, the evening was really good, they play very well. The girl Wanda, for whom Sartre wrote the play, was beautiful and acting well; people were surprised at her and pleased. Sartre is always very nice in these circumstances, because he is so deeply modest and unconcerned, caring for everybody but for himself. He had accepted foolishly a month before to give a lecture at a Jewish association, so he came just at the end, and then we went, only five best friends of Sartre, to drink whisky and white wine until five in the morning: Giacometti, my Russian friend's husband who is a kind of younger brother, Giacometti's girl, nobody more. It was really a nice night. Tonight there will be a formal supper with the actors, Cocteau, Bérard, and so on, and it will not be so pleasant. I have to tell you modestly that I was more stylish than you'll ever see me. I had one of the fine expensive dresses I bought for South America, all wistling silk falling to the ankles, long strange earrings, a beautiful necklace from Yugoslavia, and black lace on the head: nobody had ever seen me in such a disguise. I'll begin again tonight and then I'll wait until Buenos Aires.

Well, honey, I have to mail this letter and go to the theatre where people have yet work to do, and I'll dress and spend the evening behind the curtains, which is a very pleasant way of seeing a play. I'll drink a little but not too much and fall asleep late, but thinking of you. Late or not late, I always do, I'll do until May, and then I'll not have to think any more. Within a month, you'll know how much I love you.

Love, love, and love.

Your own Simone

1) From a bicycle accident. See *The Prime of Life*.

Sunday, 4 Avril 1948

Honey,

For once I dreamt of you, and it was not a success. I met you somewhere in Paris, in a big office, among other important American people; it might have been the UNESCO, for instance. You had not at all your own face; you were very serious, stern, and you reproached me bitterly for having come to see you; you said I always had "compromised" you, given you a bad reputation. I asked and prayed to speak to you in privacy for just a few minutes, but you said coldly that was another of my wicked ways and you would not. I went away crying all my tears out of my body, knowing we should not go to Mexico, I should never see you again. Friends tried to soothe me; they said: "All these American people are of this kind: so puritan, conformist, and respectful of good manners." And I cried more and more, remembering bits of letters, some words you said, your real face, and not understanding what happened. Then still dreaming, I knew and said to my friends: "This is only a dream!" But I felt a little strange in the morning, happily there was your letter. Maybe I had the dram partly because I was disappointed not to find the letter on Friday evening. I do not know why happiness has turned in a kind of anguish when I thought of seeing you; it takes my breathe out of my lungs, my blood out of my heart; it seems to me it will be so much happiness than I can hardly stand it. Yet I know I'll do, you are so warm and soothing that as soon as you first smile at me, there will be no anguish any more, just a wonderful quiet and burning happiness. Maybe the anguish proceeds too of my being very tired. I hardly slept of three nights because of Sartre's play; Thursday I did not go to bed before five or six in the morning, then Friday it was the real dangerous day: reviewers, newspapers men, and so on. We spent the evening half hearing the play from behind the curtain, half in little cafés, drinking brandy, a bit anxiously. Then it was a real triumph, everybody thinks it is the best play Sartre ever wrote, the best play produced in France since a long time. We were all very happy, but after congratulations, there was a great supper, and that was not good at all. Sartre had to give the supper to actors, producers, to Cocteau who helped him as I told you, and so on. But all these theatre people are of the worst kind: there were real elegant women with naked back and breast, and jewels, and long, long silky dresses and phoney hair, big feathers on their heads, and so on. Wealthy unpleasant men, quite snobbish, most of them having been more or less "collabos" during the war, and for de Gaulle now; and then there were all the pansy gang: Cocteau who looked very old, a real old woman, Bérard crying in his dirty beard for the love of a bald Russian dancer who dopes himself with ether, Cocteau's ex-lover, the present lover of Cocteau's ex-lover, and the present Cocteau's lover: silly, hungry young men letting themselves be loved by old men for money. Well, it was a crazy, rather disgusting party. Everybody spoke just of one thing: *oneself*. "How well I acted!" said the actor. "How well my husband acted!" said his wife. "How wonderfully I helped you!" said Cocteau, and so on. Poor Sartre nodded approvingly, and felt as disgusted as I did. They asked him a toast, and he refused. Then they said he had spoken so well at the meeting Salle Wagram, why not tonight? And he said, at the meeting he *spoke the truth*, saying to people what was wrong

189

with them, so it was easy, but now he should have to congratulate them, and that was much more difficult. They had a rather yellow laughter—in fact they hate his ideas, indeed. Well, I enjoyed it a little because I suddenly went away from the central table where the most important people were, and with the little Wanda, we went to a little table with two unimportant nice young boys (Wanda's lover and my Russian friend's husband), we drank and said what we thought about everybody. It lasted a long time, and once more I slept very little. Yesterday we went once more to the theatre, and after the play we met friends and I slept very little. And I had to get up early in the morning because my sister wanted to take me to the country in her little car. All these days I can keep myself awake only by taking benzedrine, a kind of dope to keep pilots awake on airplanes. The whole thing —not sleeping, drinking, taking benzedrine—is exhausting. Well, it is over now. In a week I'll be in the country, working again, sleeping much, enjoying the sun, the landscape, and the happiness of soon, very soon, kissing you. What please me is that really the play was such a success, all the reviews in the newspapers were wonderful, the girl had a personal success too. That is good since the whole thing was done for her.

I love you, my own Nelson.

Your own Simone

Ramatuelle, Thursday, 14 Avril 1948

My beloved husband,

It was sweet to get your letter so soon in this pleasant little hotel! I lay in the verandah on a small sofa, reading some book, when they brought it to me. Yea, we are very near of each other now, within three weeks I'll hear your voice and be only one or two days from you. Sleep well during these last lonely weeks. I sleep so much here that I'll be disgusted with sleep for at least two months; I shall not let you sleep in the night because I'll have to make sure that you really love me, and when can you be really sure, tell me? In the day we'll have lot of volcanoes to climb up, old graves to see, and airplanes to catch. No, we shall not waste time in silly dreams when we'll be together, so sleep well just now if you are a wise crocodile.

I work well too, knowing I shall not work these two months, every morning I work three or four hours in the little sweet-smelling sunny garden. I eat a nice meal and take a nice walk. I went yesterday to a pretty

190

village on the top of a hill, just a twin brother of my own village with its narrow crazy streets, small place and nice petit café. I like the "maquis," the flowers smell of pepper, both day and gentle. I like no country more than this part of France. When I was a very young teacher (twenty-three years old) and left Paris and family and friends and Sartre for the first time in my life, it helped me much to walk in this fine country and to love it. I was a teacher in Marseille, and every Thursday, every Sunday I went away early in the morning, at dawn or even before dawn, riding the earliest bus to some place on the coast or in the hill, and I walked and dreamed the whole day, alone in the sun, and came back at night. I enjoyed it. I have lot of memories in this part of France!

When I came back from my walk I read a little the last book of Koestler, *Thieves in the Night*, about the Jews who try to make their life in Palestine—a very interesting topic, but the book is weak. I heard Koestler is doing a very dirty job in USA, telling people in Carnegie Hall that they ought to fight Russia, explaining USA must begin a kind of crusade against the Soviets, and so on. I loathe him now. He is a traitor, nothing else. I read to the end Capote's novel and don't like it much; a book by Langston Hughes too, *Not Without Laughter*, but it is not worth *Black Boy*; and *Peter Ibbetson*,[1] the old English novel, a strange book, you would like the part about dreams. And some French books too, but nothing worth mentioning. I read until 5 P.M. I work again until dinner and read until sleep, which comes early. Is not that a good girl's life?

I don't like to write to you as I used to, you seem too near now. I always think, "Ah! I had rather tell him." No more paper and ink and "bon avion" between you and me. I am so happy. Every morning when I wake up, the sky is shining blue and my heart at once is beating with happiness and love. Soon when I'll open my eyes, I'll see you, darling: I'll see your beloved crocodile face slyly watching at me. You told once that I was a strange wife, being away so long, giving so little of herself to love. But I think I am a strange wife because I give so much of myself to love, because I live so close to you, so close that you cannot even see me; sometimes you fell me inside yourself, don't you? As I fell you inside me? Well, I'll come *outside* for a change so you can see me, hold me, kiss me. You could not have a more faithful, close and loving wife.

I love you, my husband.

Your own Simone

1) By George du Maurier.

My husband,

I got your letter this afternoon. I did not expect it, they come earlier and earlier each week. It is always sunny here, such a quiet, pleasant life, in such a fine country, waiting for you, coming to you. I never was so happy since I left our home. I am happy when I am awake, happy when I sleep, happy when I walk in the briars, happy when I read American words, when I write my book, when I lie in the sun. I love you.

Before going to bed I'll you the last little events of the week, in fact there was only one: We went for dinner and night at the woman's who is the owner of the theatre where Sartre's play is being performed. (I heard there was an interesting piece about the play in *New York Times*; I don't know the day.) This woman is very funny and interested me. She was really a whore when young; she slept for money with everybody. She was beautiful and contrived wonderful marriages: husbands, lovers, when twenty-five years old she was one of the wealthiest women in Paris. During the war she lost *200 millions* (let us say one million dollars!!), gold and jewels she burried in the earth and never found again; she hardly noticed it. Now she owns a theatre, a wealthy husband, she is fifty years old and rather pathetic. I never heard a woman speak such a crude, coarse language. Sartre cannot hear her without blushing and you know, he is not a bashful maiden. Well, she has a "beautiful" awful house nearby; a beautiful crazy thousand dollars car fetched for us yesterday evening — we rode for thirty miles through this wonderful country. We arrived the house: nine bathrooms, twenty rooms, during the war two hundred German soldiers lived here. It is as ugly as big and rich. She is always dressed in the most expensive and ugliest dresses you can find in Paris: you must pay lots of money to get such ugly hats and dresses. And all the furniture and carpets and so on were as awful as the dresses. She lives here with a forty years old husband and a seventy-five years old lover. The evening was rather tedious: too much wines and business talk. But in the morning it was a little pleasant because we ate the breakfast on the terrace, looking at the sunny sea. Husband and old lover were sleeping and she spoke with Sartre and me, in her wonderful crude, genuine, and awful way: about love and bed and men and money. She asked me such questions I should have blushed to the ear if it had made a sense for me. The point is it is sad a woman who slept with so many men without loving any; she cannot even understand that love makes a difference, in bed. I mean for her physical love has nothing to do with heart and soul and brain, with genuine, full love. She says it so seldom succeeds in giving pleasure to the woman that men and women *hate* each other when sleeping together. I understand what she means. For a woman it must be disgusting to sleep with a man without even friendship, just for money or for "fun." But I should have like to explain her that you can, instead, love the man when sleeping with him, love him in heart because you are so happy to love him with your body, love him with your body so much the more because your body means your heart, too. With you, from pleasure to love I never felt any difference, as I never felt difference between my body and my spirit. I am a whole woman longing for you. I am nothing else now but that burning, proud, impatient, and happy longing for you.

Your own Simone

Ramatuelle, Thursday, 22 Avril 1948

My husband,

Not much to say if I don't speak of my impatience of coming to you, which begins to get tedious, even for me. It is a kind of disease. It is raining since two days, a good heavy rain, but I guess it is nothing compared to our Yucatan rains. So I don't walk, but just write and read. I begin to think about a novel I should like to write and maybe a play, but not just now. I cannot do many things at one time; I have to get through this book about women first. I think I'll stay here until the last day, just coming back Paris the day before riding the airplane; it is so quiet, always empty. A friend came here: my Russian friend's husband, whom I like very much as I told you. He thinks the place is wonderful too when coming from busy, noisy Paris. We went to fetch him two days ago at Saint-Tropez, a pleasant ride through these beautiful wild hills. Loitering in the little town, I bought a nice country dress—blue, white and red—a fine fancy shirt made of old country handkerchiefs, you'll see. I bought them for Guatemala, to be a well-dressed wife. I put on the home-gown for the first time at the wealthy obscene woman's, and she thought it came from a very expensive dress-maker in Paris. I was proud of it. I am happy, Nelson, but I can hardly write, words seem useless and silly now. Within two weeks I'll lie in your arms, I'll speak with you with my true lips, nothing else makes any sense.

I kiss you will all my love, my beloved precious husband.

Your own Simone

Ramatuelle, Saturday, 24 Avril 1948

Nelson, my beloved husband,

Here is the last letter I send to you, that is sweet to think. When you'll get it, there will be no more than one week from you to me. Then I'll wire from Paris on the 4th May to tell if everything is all right, if the plane fly away on the evening or not, and so on; then I'll phone from New York, telling exactly at what time I am due in Chicago. You'll wait for me home, please, as the last time, unless you like better coming to the airport, as you did a year ago, but I think our Wabansia meeting in September was much more of a success than the other one, when you proposed to go to the zoo, don't you think so? You'll tell me by phone, in New York, what you have decided, but I always dreamt of coming up your stairs and falling in your arms without anybody around us, in our place.

I'll bring you a nice gift. The wealthy obscene lady, who is Sartre's producer, came with new husband and old lover in her tremendous huge car, and had a lunch with us here. She was not pleased to come in this small unexpensive hotel; she thought the food was distasteful and so on. But we did choose not to waste time going again to her ugly, over-expensive house, and as *she* wanted to see Sartre about some business (that means she wanted to steal money from him in many crooky ways, which she will surely succeed to do because she loves money so much more than he does, and she knows much more about it), she had to come. Well, it was rather funny, because she really speaks as nobody does! She explains crudely what she has done in the morning with her husband, and what she did years ago with other lovers, and so on. But the point is: she brought to me a fine morning gown and I at once decided you would be so pretty in it! It is a manly dress, being an Arabian dress, in striped white and green velvet. I really think you'll be beautiful in it. You much just take care to tie a little belt around your waist, because it is open on both sides, showing legs and thighs and hips. It would be indecent to show so much flesh on the boat. I hope you'll like it, so I'll have given to you shoes from Iceland and a gown from sunny hot countries.

Good night, honey. I feel in very good temper tonight. I drank lots of brandy glasses to celebrate (to celebrate my coming to you within two weeks). Today rain stopped, and we had a fine ride in a car we hired, in nice little villages, in the hills, places where I went on my own tired feet ten years ago: I could walk about thirty miles a day, you know. So I was pleased to see so easily places and roads again, to remember younger times, and to feel even better than in these times. Younger, because of your love. It is a really beautiful country here: we'll go there together. I'll write a little longer tomorrow, now I just go to bed.

Sunday

Bright sun the whole day. I worked on my book in the lovely garden which smells of orange-blossom, looking at the sea, and in the afternoon I walked in the hills. It is nearly an island here; there is the blue sea all around but on one side. I love the dry wild flowers in the bushes, the woods, the view, the little villages, and everything. I stay here for two or three days, then we'll have a little trip on the coast until the Italian border, and back to Paris, and ...the "bon avion" takes me to you. I hope it will not break. If it does, I'll be a bit angry but I'll die thinking it was worth taking the risk, since it was to come to you. Honey, within two weeks in Wabansia, and within three weeks, at this same hour, we'll can arrive on the desk of our boat and we'll begin to glide on the Mississippi. It seems strange, so far and yet so near. This is the last time for long that I kiss you on the paper, darling.

I love you more than ever and forever.

Your own Simone

1948

Simone de Beauvoir in the United States

✷ *Simone de Beauvoir was to travel for three months with Algren. A few days before her departure, she decided to spend only two months with Algren, waiting to tell him face to face. This time, the flight through Iceland and Labrador was uneventful. In Cincinnati, de Beauvoir and Algren boarded a boat traveling down the Mississippi to New Orleans; from there they went on to the Yucatan and Guatemala, and returned to Mexico.*

"I hadn't yet brought up the question of my departure; I hadn't had the heart to do it since my arrival, and in the weeks that followed I lost my nerve. With each passing day it became more urgent and more difficult. On a long drive between Mexico and Morelia, I rather awkwardly announced to Algren that I had to go back to Paris on July 14th. 'Oh, really,' he said." Several days later, Algren declared that he'd had enough of Mexico, enough of traveling; he was in a bad mood; he pouted. However, they still stopped in several cities on their way back to New York, where they moved into the Brittany. Algren was hostile, morose, disagreeable. "One evening, we ate at an open air tavern in the middle of Central Park, and then went downtown to listen to some jazz at Café Society. He behaved incredibly badly. 'I can leave tomorrow,' I said to him; we had words then, suddenly, he said to me, fervently, 'I'm ready to marry you on the spot.' I understood then that I could never again hold anything against him; any missteps were mine. I left on July 14, not knowing if I would ever see him again." [1]

1) *Force of Circumstance.*

Thursday night, 15 Juillet 1948

So, Nelson,

Once more the cab drove away and I saw your face for the last time; a little later I heard your voice for the last time, and there was grief in my heart, but in my ears I felt love. Oh darling, darling, beloved you, it is hard to write. I did not believe yet, I did not realize that I should not see you before a year — at least, you said — writing makes me know.

Well, Stépha was at Madison Avenue and we spoke quietly. And then I went to the airport and phoned to you, and then we had to wait for two hours. A nice newspaper girl, working at the airport, helped me to wait, but could not prevent some horrid fascist newspaper men to interview me: I was so rude to them they thought I was a communist. The girl and I drank orange juices, and then the airplane took off. The weather was so bad that we had to go by way of the Azores, but it was quick: ten hours to Azores, one hour stop, six hours to Paris. I drank a little scotch and read all the books. The Evelyn Waugh chosen by Stépha, you were right, is just rot; the two mysteries were amusing. I am proud of myself because I did not cry at all during the whole trip, I had cried too much before, I felt empty, and I believed you when you said that I am still your wife, that every good bye means meeting again. It was night nearly all the time, and I remembered. I remembered everything: the blue, the pink, the grey pages, and the purple ones too. And all was good, even the crying nights, because the long, deep happiness and the slight touches of grief and despair, all was love.

Paris was awful. There was a strike of radio and we thought first that we could not land, yet we could. There was a strike at the customs too and it make things easier in a way, but then the airport was altogether empty: not a plane but us on the ground, nobody inside. Just death. And in this holiday — 14th July — Paris seemed entirely dead — poor, dead, brim, sad; it was hard to stand. I went to the hotel; they give me another room, not pink but round; but this hotel seems dingy, filthy. I am fed up with it. I had to meet France again, Sartre, friends, the *Temps modernes*, the newspapers, magazines, and so on. Nelson, I'll have to explain things better one day, but you have to know that it is not for pleasure or glamour or anything of the kind that I say I must stay here. I just *cannot* do anything else — believe me, please, please. I'll explain some of these days but tonight, just believe me. If by any chance I could stay with you, oh, God, I should! Well, in a way I loathe Paris now; I felt just chilly and blank being here. I spent these two days talking, learning all that had happened for two months, and fussing about hair-dresser, dress-maker, and so on. Not believing I really said good bye to you. It was so quick leaving you: eighteen hours. You seem so near, all is near; I don't believe, I cannot believe. Well, when I'll believe it, I'll have a bad time, but I shall not try to escape it; the happiness you gave me may be bought by pain and anguish, it was worth it.

Too Much Salt on the Bretzells is being printed and will soon appear in *T.M.* the people who read it — typewriter, secretary, and Sartre — think it is a first rate story. Sartre apologizes because he kind of stole one of the sentences in the novel he is writing; he thanks for the pipe too. Tomorrow I'll see the publisher about your book.[1] I want it to be published in France; lot of people too love it. I'll not stay here; within a week I'll go to some place in southern France or North Africa, for two months, to work peacefully. I have to help Sartre about a screen adaptation of *Red Gloves* and to write my book about women. I'll write to you my address, go on writing here now.

Nelson, I have too much to say: so much happiness in my heart, so much love. I dare not say it too aloud because I do not want you to feel "tied up," I don't want it and any way, how could I? When you'll stop loving me, you'll stop. There is nothing I could do to it. When you'll choose not to see me any more, I'll have to agree. No, Nelson, I shall never want from you something important that you do not want. Just, I hope you'll still love me for some time, because I love you more than ever, more than I ever loved you.

Oh, Nelson, how much I do love you!

Your own Simone

1) *Never Come Morning.*

✳ *Algren answered tenderly; he was apparently taking their anticipated separation in stride. For two days he busied himself in New York; he went to see some former friends in the Communist Party, saw his agent, played poker with Gerassi, visited publishers. On July 15 he returned home to Chicago, where he began working again, deciding what to cut from his novel,* Never Come Morning.

Saturday, 17 Juillet 1948

Nelson, mon amour,

It is hard to get up in the morning, it is the worst time. Well, I got up at least and had a lunch with Wright and Sartre. We ate a couss-couss. About Mexico, Dick thinks too it is a very dull country; he spent three months in Cuernavaca (you remember, the town where we had a room just on the place, and I could do shopping by the window). Everybody in USA thought he should have liked Mexico since there is no discrimination in this country, but he could not, because of the poor people. He was very happy to have found a flat near Les Deux Magots.

I have some success in Paris with the Mexican blouse and blue-flowered skirt of southern France, but it looks crazy to wear that because it is cold and rainy. I gave the white and all colored jacket to my Russian friend who was delighted, and a piece of material to the nice girl who lives with Giacometti. Poor girl, it was stolen ten minutes afterwards in a post-office, she cried the whole day long. She does not own many things, so I gave her one of my things, and my grey coat too, and she was happy. Paris is sad, awfully sad in cold and rain. The food is good. It is a pleasure to find again French food, but it does not mean much, does it? I think you came back to Wabansia today, honey. Was it nice to find all the gifts you had sent to yourself? The books, the blanket, the napkin, the curtain? I hope you found some memories of your wife, too? You must feel please to be home again. Work well, my love.

I saw the young friendly publisher who likes so much your books. He asked for the book form "Pré aux clercs" (Malaquais' publisher); they answered they have rights on it. Do you remember if any contract was signed between you and "Pré aux clercs"? Cannot your agent take a little care of this business? I am going to see "Pré aux clercs" myself next Monday; look at the contract. We must not let them keep the book and not publish it.

Dick Wright told me he heard much about my *Amérique au jour le jour*; most of people like it very much, but some of these I speak about are angry, Dorothy N., for instance: "Did you read what S. de B. wrote about *us*? I suppose we have to forgive her!" Here is seems to be rather a success. I am pleased. A young Negro writer asks to translate it in English; I'll see him.

Not many changes in Paris. Some new "existentialist" cabarets opened in some old caves. I went to one of them where there is a wonderful show: four young men dressed in 1900 fashion,[1] with long underwears and top hats, singing old silly songs, but they sing and act with much humour—the choice of songs is first rate. Genet is always afraid of being sent to jail. Giacometti works and works; he did new strange, fine little statues. The Russian friend recovers slowly and hopes she will play *The Flies* in the midst of October. My sister paints bad paintings and enjoys it. I did not begin to work still—too many little things to do, people to see, *T.M.* to read, letters to answer. And then it is hard to begin again. I am still very much mixed up; I cannot easily sit in front of white paper and try to concentrate. My mind begins at once to wander far away in Guatemala, or Wabansia, or

New York, I miss you too much. Anyway I go away Friday with Sartre. We'll settle somewhere in North Africa and work hard for two months before coming back to Paris.

It is a silly letter; nothing seems really important, all seems irreal. Reality is behind me, faraway; it is our love, our life. I still fell your chest so warm against my breasts. I can hardly believe I have to write to you again.

Monday

Nelson, mon amour, it was sweet to find your letter. I did not expect it so soon. It made everything real again; it made me feel that now I am beginning to wait for meeting you again. I guess I'll be able to get up in the morning now and to work. Some things please me in the letter, most of them, but I am sad about your Guatemala gifts! Maybe the packages are not quite lost? The one for Stépha was long to arrive and then it did. I do hope so much you'll get blanket and curtain. It is always raining and cold and sad here. Yesterday I had some conference about *Temps modernes*. We are preparing a Spanish issue, by Spanish refugees, and a German issue too, which ought to be very, very interesting. The *God's Angry Man* had been published (parts of it), and I wait for some angry letter from the man. A strange, crazy short story called *Too Much Salt on the Bretzells* will be published in September issue. By the way, Sartre, who loves the story, does not think the title is very good, in the end. Do you think of something else?

I tried to work yesterday. I read again half of what I had written about women. Did I write it? It seemed quite a foreign thing; it had been partly published in *T.M.* already, and thus printed it seemed not to belong to me at all. I have the same feeling of irreality you have. I cannot find my old self again. I know I'll contrive to go on with this book, but I don't know how I'll manage it. Why did you disturb me so much, naughty man?

Good bye, honey. Genet just arrived in the Deux Magots for a lunch with Sartre and me. I have other things to tell you, but it will be tomorrow. Please write next letter Poste restante, Alger. Au revoir, mon amour. Je vous aime.

Your own Simone

1) Les Frères Jacques, the French quartet founded in 1944 who became famous for their humorous performances of Jacques Prévert songs.

Nelson, mon cher amour,

Yea, it was a sweet letter I got this morning, very quiet and loving. "You seem so happy today," many people told me. I was. Now it is midnight. I am not overtired; I have hardly drink a little gin in grapefruit juice (no scotch in Paris) and I'll kiss you good night before sleeping. Honey, the African man who gave me my crocodile bag gave me two big blankets; I'll send one to you since the Guatemala one is lost. It is not as nice as the other one, but fine too. I'll mail it as soon as possible, though I hate mailing packages.

Genet congratulated me about my dress and look, about my last book, and asked for money in the end. He has a new young lover, writes a new play but he goes on being exactly what he is, as most people do. I said good bye to the Russian friend who goes to the country for a rest; a little new tragedy for no change: she has to play *The Flies* within two months and she begins to feel sick again; I guess she will be really sick during the first rehearsals so she will not be able to play. I tried to persuade her to take a year rest before trying anything, but she is too impatient; she wants to know if the worst is going to happen or no, as soon as possible. It is silly, but there is nothing to do against it.

Yesterday I had a dinner with her husband, Bost, the young man who wrote *The Last Profession*. It was in Montmartre, and there was a big carnival on the avenue, in the grey dull evening, all the scenic railways, magic trains, games and shows seemed very sad; it went deep through my heart. Then he is the boy with whom I have slept for many years before knowing you, but I stopped it last year, coming back from New York: you know why. It was no longer a very important thing for me, so the breaking was not very important, that is why I did not even mention it to you. We remained intimate friends, but he is not very happy now in his love-affairs, and then being married to such a wife prevents the love-affairs to be really successful, so there was some sadness in the evening too. And then, when I stopped the things with him, he was not angry. He knew I did not love him, but he did not like it and there remains some uneasiness between us. I tell it to you because you ask me what happens in my crazy head and I like you to know as much as possible about me.

You know, I could give up much more than a nice young man for your sake, I could give up most of things; but I should not be the Simone you like, if I could give up my life with Sartre. I should be a dirty creature, a treacherous and selfish woman. I want you to know that, whatever you decide in the future: it is not by lack of love that I don't stay with you. I am even sure that leaving you is harder for me than for you, that I miss you in a more painful way than you miss me; I could not love you, want you, and miss you more than I do. Maybe you know that. But what you have to know too, though it may seem conceited to say it, is in which way Sartre needs me. In fact, he is very lonely, very tormented inside himself, very restless, and I am his only true friend, the only one who really understands him, helps him, works with him, gives him some peace and poise. For nearly twenty years he did everything for me; he helped me to live, to find myself, he sacrificed lots of things for my sake. Now, since four, five years, it is the time when I can give back what he did for me, help him who helped me so much. I could not desert him. I could leave him for more or less important periods, but not pledge my whole life to anyone else. I hate to speak about it again. I know that I am in danger losing you; I know what losing you would mean for me. But you must understand how it is, Nelson. I must be sure that you understand the truth: I should be happy to spend days and nights with you until my death, in Chicago, Paris, or Chichicastenango; it is not possible to love more than I love you, flesh and heart and soul. But I should rather die than deeply hurting, than making a real harm to somebody who did everything for my happiness. Yet I should not like to die, and losing you, the idea of losing you, seems to me as hard as the idea of death. Well, maybe you think I am making to much fuss, but my life is important to me, our love is important to me: it is worth fussing a little. And you ask me what I think. I feel quite friendly with you, and I like to tell you all what I feel in my heart. Now I'll go to sleep after kissing you a long loving kiss.

Friday

I hope you were not angry at my wire, honey. I'll tell you what happened. If I had to come back to Paris in the middle of July, it was because Sartre needed me for working at a movie script from his last play. I told you I always wanted to help him when he asked, and then that is one of the ways of earning my life; my books would not be enough for me to live on, and things like movies-dialogues and so on help me very much. But then suddenly, Tuesday, the producers changed their mind; there were arguments and quarrels, and the script is not to be done just now. Sartre has to stay here and discuss business before beginning the job, if he ever begins it, so he was terribly remorseful of having asked to me to come back without a real reason; and he proposed to me to fly back to Chicago if I wanted, helping me with the money of the trip. Well, I knew you wanted to work now, you have explained it in N.Y. and I can feel this want too; I guessed you would answer no. But I could not decide not to see you one month more without asking you your own decision. And then I thought: We have not to be shrewd with each other. He has not to be polite, so I have not to be discreet. Was I wrong? I was sleeping this morning when they brought your wire, half-sleeping still I read: "*Not* too much work." And for a small time I fancied it meant come, then I read: "No. Too much work," which was what I expected. Yea, you have to work, darling. I know and I love your work, and I deeply want your book to be achieved and another good book to be written. I just hope we can contrive some day to work near each other so our love does not give you this kind of empty feeling you got in N.Y. in the end. It would be fine to have working days and love nights. I could. Maybe some day you'll find that you can too.[1]

Another thing I thought about you and me: our love began last year like a corny movie story—it was nice. But now it has became a earthly human story; it can be still finer if we care for it in the right way. Don't you think so?

Your Sunday letter, with much joy in my heart, brought some sun in the sky, and Paris looked better. You know, each time it is the same process: Paris seems awful for some days after New York and Chicago, and then, little by little, it takes my heart again. But today is grey and dull once more and the Guatemala shirts look too startling. I had two nice shirts made with the material we bought together. That is something of you on my skin. Go on writing Paris, please. I shall not go North Africa before next month. Have you begun the pictures album? Shall I get some pictures of our honeymoon trip? It was a sweet honeymoon, Nelson.

Work well, mon amour. Send me fat yellow letters. And get as much happiness as you can from the love of

Your own Simone

1) De Beauvoir had suggested to Algren that she return to Chicago but live on her own so as not to disturb his work—an idea he dismissed as ridiculous.

Nelson, mon amour,

No letter. I guess it has taken a little trip to Algiers, but I wrote to the general delivery to send it back. A very close friend asked me to come to Genova for a week with him, for the ONU; but I am so sensible and nice that I refused. I'll stay here and work. I am deeply interested in my work again, which is very healthy for me. I spent the whole day in the public library, reading thick books of biology and physiology and learning when you decided to be a man, when I chose to be a woman: it was just the day when our father's and mother's seeds met each other and contrived a nice little human egg, so we were really young when we took such an important decision. I learnt many other important things and began to dream about them. If I wrote in French I could tell you lot of little things which seem very poetical to me, but in your language it is too difficult.

It is hot since two days, very hot; not quite so hot as in New York, but nicely hot. Evenings and nights are delightful. What is really fine in Paris is this evening life, in the cafés. When you have worked all day long, you just go on the boulevard Saint-Germain, and without any appointment, you are sure to meet some friends with whom you can spend some time before sleeping. You never know exactly which you'll find; it is a little adventure. Yesterday I got Giacometti's girl. We went to a movie together, *Dark Passage*, with H. Bogart and Lauren Bacall; it is not bad. Then she told me the story of her life: I ask stories from all the women I meet, for my book. In the Sunday light, the Guatemala dress was really thrilling; in the Deux Magots people I don't know came to me and ask where it comes from; all the shop-keepers, as well as the friends I meet, are startled. I had a skirt made with the green and violet Chichicastenango material, with the green and violet blouse of Patzcuaro, and on my head I wear the beautiful sash I bought in Taxco, the Negro girl's earings, and the necklace, indeed. I look very strange, but here it is all right to look strange.

Some days ago I met this stupid man who is the official racketer of American literature, translating Mac Coy, Chase et Cain. He spoke to me with enthousiasm of the last Mac Coy. He wanted Sartre and me to go and meet Tennessee Williams; we refused. He came to the bar each half-hour, a little more drunk each time, and then, quite drunk, he said: "After all, Tennessee Williams is of no interest at all...." Indeed, his play was not good, but we saw it together, and now it has a place in my heart. (Women are crazy animals, I'll tell it in my book.)

Young existentialist boys now grow a beard; American intellectual tourists grow beards too. I met Puma once, the conceited black-eyed painter. It was rather chilly; we are no friends any more. All these beards are awfully ugly! But the existentialist caves are a wonderful success. It is funny, just two blocks—that is all Saint-Germain-des-Prés—but within these two blocks you cannot find a place to sit down, neither in the bars, cafés, night-clubs nor even on the pavement. Then all around it is darkness and death.

Tuesday

I was really nice for you today! First, I packed the blanket; it was a lot of trouble! It was too big, not well packed enough; they wanted to know how much it was worth, and if it had been more than three dollars, I should have had to rush to another district far away to get a licence. I hope you'll get it; it is not sure. I spend a whole hour packing it. This afternoon I went to the Pré-aux-Clercs and at last found the man; he has no right at all on the book, so I begin the business all over again with the young publisher. We have a good translator who is ready to begin the work, that is all right. I am just angry a whole year has been wasted because of Malaquais.

It is hotter and hotter, and I am all blue-skinned, as if a Maya priest intended to scratch my heart away: it is the Guatemala shirt which makes all my skin blue! It does not matter since nobody sees me without a dress any longer.

You seem very far, but I love you far or near. I kiss you a sweet kiss, honey.

Your own Simone

Tuesday, 3 Août 1948

My own husband,

Your letter made me feel very good again. Yea, I can wait patiently if I know I am still your wife. We'll be as happy as we were you think as lovingly of me as I think of you. What scares me sometimes is the idea that by distance and waiting we should become faint to each other: just a faint memory, when you were my flesh and blood. Once you wrote to me: Never become faint to me. It went to my heart. I should like never to become faint, but to stand close to you, always, a *real* wife. I know, nothing is quite real for you, and maybe that scares me too.

It has been hot and I worked. Now it is rainy and I go on working. But that is a long book to write; it will need a whole year, at least. I want it to be really good; I want you to be proud of your wife. What pleases me is that I hear several *men* were quite angry with the part of this book published in *Temps modernes*: about the stupid mythical ideas men enjoy about women, and the fake poetry they do about it. So they felt really hit in the weak place. Now that I do is not so amusing; it is rather scientific, but interesting too.

Wright and his wife have got a fine place near Saint-Germain-des-Prés. At dinner there was a fried chicken and Dick ate the bones. Ellen explained that you can eat the bones of an American chicken because they are wholly cooked. So I am a bit disappointed in you, I thought nobody else could do it. I went to this night-club I like; La Rose Rouge it is called. The singers were no longer in; there was a wonderful magician, the best known in Paris, and he gave a good performance using nearly no instrument at all, just his hands, and contriving amazing tricks. I remember the magician in New York with the fleas. I am very glad because it is nearly sure I'll get a nice little nest of my own within two weeks; very cheap, near Saint-Germain-des-Prés, with a view on Notre-Dame and the Seine! A studio, an office, a kitchen, all furnished. It would be wonderful. So when you'll come here, you'll find a nest as nice and cosy as the one I found in Wabansia, and maybe you'll feel so cosy there you'll stay some time. Anyway, I should like to have a place where I can live and work; I am fed up with the hotel.

Yea, honey, maybe I should have spoken clearly before about Sartre. I want you to have clear ideas about me, but I told you, you often make me shy about speaking. And when we are together, so happy to be together, all words seem nearly useless, our understanding seem deeper than all knowledge. Yet, I like so much when you talk to me: once in Casa Contenta,[1] in the bar, you spoke about your youth and women, about Conroy,[2] and once about your writing. These were fine moments for me. And when I talk to you about myself, sometimes I loved it too. We'll have still to discover much about each other; maybe it is not so bad. Anyway, even through letters, I'll try to talk to you more and more. Not now. I worked the whole day; I am tired. I just corrected the proofs of your short story; it will be published next month. I don't know about the title. I'll decide later. I'll just go and mail this letter for a little walk.

Yea, yea, sure, I remember, Nelson. I remember everything. All the nights, and this first Sunday night when our bodies really found each other, and this last night and last morning when they had to say farewell. I remember. When I went away, something broke inside me, and now I feel sexless. But I remember how wonderful it was to be a woman in my husband's arms, in New Orleans and in Merida, in Quetzaltenango, in Mexico.

I hope one thing is really clear about me, it is my love for you.

Your own Simone

1) On Lake Atitlan, Guatemala. 2) Algren's best friend, the writer Jack Conroy, who also lived in Chicago.

Sunday, 8 Août 1948

Bonjour, mon amour,

We opened our eyes just together; you threatened me with your fist, then... well. It seems so cold and lonely when I wake up in the round room!

It is a windy, peaceful Sunday. Sartre has gone away for a week with his mother, and they left to me her nice flat. So I sit here, seeing the church and the Deux Magots through the windows. I'll stay the whole day and work from 10 A.M. (that is now) to 8 P.M. I swallowed a little pill to help. I want this chapter I am working about to be finished at night. I guess you'll be working the whole day too. My last essay, *Ethics of Ambiguity*, is going to be published in America; parts of it have just been published in "Twice a Year." I saw the magician once more and began to understand some of his tricks. I went to another cave which is so crowded with American tourists that I could not stay; it is in the underground of Deux Magots and wonderfully decorated in a crazy pleasant way; there is the best jazz of Paris there, a really fine, little jazz, and some young people dancing in a wonderful way. The "young man with the horn" is the orchestra leader; he just achieved the translation of *The Big Clock* of your friend Kenneth Fearing. Strange, this friend of mine, translating a friend's of yours book—so far away, two worlds, when you and me are so near. I went on working all day and seeing people at night, at the cafés terraces or in the caves with whisky, the same people: Sartre, Bost (the nice young man), Giacometti, Wright—a very steady life. And I went on missing you in a rather dry, hard way. I should rather like to cry a little sometimes, but I guess I cried too much one night, and it left a dry, hard pain in my heart. I can no longer cry easy quiet tears. Yet I nearly cried when I found in my suitcase an handkerchief embroidered with an A, and when I put on the little black sweater you liked so much.

Yesterday I went to the movies. I saw *Ball of Fire* with Gary Cooper and Barbara Stanwick;[1] sometimes funny but in the whole very silly.

In this long, quiet day, I should like to talk with you. As I don't know how to forge nice stories the way you do, I'll tell you real ones. Do you mind? Well, I read your last letter once more and I wanted to say some things about it.

First, it is not because I wanted to boast that I mentioned the nice young man; there can be no "boasting" from me to you, from you to me. If I were proud of anything in my life, it would be of our love. I feel we have to tell to each other as many things as we can, so we are not only lovers, but the closest friends at the same time. Anyway, I have not much to boast about in my life, and I'll tell you today about my love life, as you did in Casa Contenta on a happy loving evening. I told you I belonged to a petit-bourgeois, Catholic old-fashionned family; I was very strictly educated — most books were forbidden. I began to read everything when a student, not believing in God any more, but I remained very "moral." I was very much in love, at seventeen, with a cousin of mine, the same age, who was handsome, clever, attractive and whom I admired for being a man. He liked me, gave me modern books, and helped me to escape from my family intellectually, but he "respected" me as a young bourgeois "respects" a cousin; and as for marriage, he married a rich, silly, ugly girl. Afterwards he wasted his life, drinking and making everybody unhappy. It was a very corny girlish idealistic love; this marriage was rather a shock, but I did not care too much because at the time I had just been acquainted with new friends, students like myself, and among them Sartre.

We soon cared much for each other. I was twenty two and he was twenty five, and I gave enthousiastically my life and myself to him. He was my first lover, nobody had even kissed me before. We spent a long time together and I told you already how I care for him, but it was rather deep friendship than love; love was not very successful. Chiefly because he does not care much for sexual life. He is a warm, lively man everywhere, but not in bed. I soon felt it, though I had no experience; and little by little, it seemed useless, and even indecent, to go on being lovers. We dropped it after about eight or ten years rather unsuccessful in this way. That is when the nice young man, Bost, appeared, ten years ago. He was much younger than I, a former pupil of Sartre who liked him very much. I enjoyed chiefly walking with him in mountains in summer. At this time he had an affair with my Russian friend, but he wanted to drop it; she had been my pupil, and in a way I liked her, but she had behaved unpleasantly with me too: anyway, she is the kind if girl who asks too much from everybody, lying to everybody, so everybody had to lie to her. So, when in a mountain trip, sleeping under the same tent, Bost and I wanted to sleep together, it was not a problem. We never said it to her. He wanted to break with her, but then he just could not. She loved him too deeply already, and he did not want to hurt. Then came the war, and she went sick; he was more and more tied to her and married her, and lives with her, as I told you. Yet we went on being close friends and sleeping together. It was a pleasant relationship, without passion, but without jealousy, without lies, with much friendship and tenderness. So I felt pleased with my life, you know; it seemed enough to have deep friendships in my life, even if it was not love. I thought I was too old for love, now, but I could go until death this way, working and liking people who liked me. Then, you know, it happened. Besides Sartre and Bost I had three times in my life spent just one night with men—men I knew already and liked though there was no possibility of real affair. When I went back to Chicago, I thought it would be something of this kind: I liked you; we could be happy a few days together. And that is why I say you trapped me. I did not expect love; I did not believe in being in love and you made me fall in love with you! And come back to Chicago and love you more and more. So I had to say to Bost, and as I explained, it was a little sad, but we remain very close friends. I see him often, most of time with Sartre, sometimes with his wife, and sometimes alone. It was a long relationship between us. That is why I mentioned it in the other letter. But, as you felt, it was no more really important, as it was in the first years, long ago.

And all that, Nelson, is another way of telling you that I knew real whole love, love when heart, soul, and flesh are just one thing in your arms. There was no nice boy last year; there will be none this year. I guess there will never be another man.

That is the way it was, honey. That is the way it is. You see, for me, now, it is like having a family in Paris. I have known these people so long, so closely, through so many circumstances, for the worst and best, that they are rather a family than just friends. As my real family means nothing for me, I chose another one by myself, I guess. In a way it is lucky to have a family; it helps to live. But in another way it leaves you quite lonely, and chiefly when you love (crazily) somebody, it does not help. Well, I don't know if it makes you see me in a clearer way, but when I write: I saw Bost, Sartre, Olga. I like you to know what I mean. And I'll have to write so many letters, before stopping to use words and melting with you again.

Good bye, Nelson. I felt happy speaking to you. I kiss your lips in dream.

Your own Simone

1) By Howard Hawks, 1941.

Saturday, 14 Août 1948

My own Nelson,

Thanks for the long letter and for having sent the publisher's one. I was much interested but sometimes angry. How silly to reproach the book not to be hopeful enough, to present only characters "who cannot be saved": who can be? They want something heroical and smiling, I see! That is the kind of stuff we find in French papers too, and one of the strongest arguments against existentialism. I hope you will not take any account of that criticism. For the others, it is true the book has to be tightened up, and we must know in the end what happens to Frankie. But I like the kind of game with light and shadow, the way the most important things, as the murder of Louie, are not always said, while you tell a sideway story with many details. I don't think you must sacrifice that in order to be clearer; that is the way Faulkner or the old Meredith tell stories, and it is a good way. Well, you'll know about it. I just wish you don't let yourself be scared by commercial bias in the publishers. Yea, for *Never Come Morning*, I'll wait the copy with the cuttings.

The idea in writing *Blood of Others* this way was this light and shadow idea too. I wanted to convey *one* feeling in the reader, and all was worked out in this design. It is not a general theory; it is just that this peculiar man, Blomart, is the man of *one* problem: as a child, a lover, a man, he always is haunted by this sense of guilt. So I wanted it to be hardly a story going along years and months: for him, it is just *one* fate, a not changing fate. That is why the book begins and ends in the same night, and mixes up past and present. He looks at himself as at a stranger, then he says he, speaking of himself, or he feels the same and he says I. Is it really so difficult to catch? The chapters about Helen are quite clear anyway; she is always spoken of as she. I like shadows in a book, as there is always kind of dimness in life, but maybe I put too much shadow? Let me know if it seemed clearer after.

A month has gone away, honey, since we parted. Well, it went away quickly. Maybe it will not be so long before I kiss you again. And our months are so full and happy and thrilling that they are worth much more than an average month; they are worth waiting for many average months. I'll try to keep my heart patient.

I went with an American girl to the Rose Rouge. No magician this time, but a wonderful mime; he made a very good imitation of Charlie Chaplin, not trying to look like him, no hat, no shoes, nothing, but acting in his way, with his peculiar ways of moving his face and body in the rhythm of old silent movies. He acted, all alone by himself, the story of a man going to a party, drinking, falling in love, and so on, the way Charlot does; it was really fine.

You know, I too deserve some little reward in the evening because it goes on raining and I go on working the whole day, and at night I am tired. When I work on a novel, I cannot work so steadily: it is more distressing, but not so exhausting. On an essay I can concentrate eight hours a day, but then it seems as blowing up, as it is just now. Very bad of you not to be there to give me my reward, the only one I want.

Good bye, dearest dear you. When shall I get the pictures of my honeymoon? I want them, though I remember everything without pictures, and they don't say all. I remember how I loved you, Nelson, and I love you just the same.

Your own Simone

Wednesday, 18 Août 1948

My own Nelson,

I spent some nice days in spite of the awfully sad weather. First, Sunday morning, while I was steadily working in Sartre's house (I told you the mother gave me the keys; there is a mysterious creature sleeping in a back room, I guess she is the old cook's niece, but we never see each other, I just hear sounds from time to time), well, while I was steadily working, the bell rang. It was a very good friend[1] with his girl. I spoke about him: he is in the UNESCO. He told me about the hotel "Cortès," Patzcuaro, and so on. I knew him twenty years ago, even before knowing Sartre: he was a comrade of Sartre and a student at the same time as I was, he worked in the public library where I often worked, and I was very pleased the first time he spoke to me. I could easily have fallen in love with him then, but he was married, though very young, and he did not make love to me; we were just very close friends, and still are. He is married but does not love his wife any more, so he has a girl. I was very pleased to go to the country with them, to the little village where I spent two months last year—you remember? I wrote my first letters to you from this small blue and yellow hotel, and I missed you so much. We had a good lunch in the open air, and took a walk in the meadows. I came back at night, happy not to have worked the whole day. Then Sartre came back, and yesterday night we had a fine time with Wright in a Russian restaurant. Then Ellen, who begins to be very pregnant, went to bed and we rode to Montmartre in Dick's wonderful car. On silly, dingy little places we drank rather much. Dick is really nice because he enjoys so much seeing people in the streets, in the dives; he looks and looks and dreams about them. And I must say there are lots of people really funny to see in Montmartre! So many foreigners now in Paris! One million came this month in a town of three millions. You see nobody but Swedes, Norwegians and indeed Americans. Englishmen too, as they are poor; they travel on ugly black bicycles overcrowded by a lot of luggage.

Friday

My own husband, do you know what I got today? A fine yellow letter from the man I love, a local youth in Chicago, Illinois (not Chicago, Kentucky). So it was a blue day, and now I came to the Deux Magots to drink a brandy and write a bit of a letter before going to bed. I am glad you like the book, in the end; I am surprised you—you American people, I mean—find it so hard to read. In France they never had this feeling; they said the twenty first pages were a little dim, and then it was written too much in an "American technic," but it was not said that hard. I guess you are right when you say there is too much philosophy, but that is my genuine way of feeling; when anything happens to me I am always ratiocinating about it inside myself, it is all mixed: feeling, events and philosophy, it would be rather unnatural for me if I put it away; anyway I am sure there would be a better way of conveying the meaning I want to convey than using so many abstract disgressions. In fact, I should be rather at a loss if I had to write a novel now. I see the mistakes in the old ones, yet I don't want to give up my own way of feeling and I don't know how I could do really well what I want. Next year, when the essay on women will be over, I'll have to find an answer to this problem. In spite of your anger against me, I am very pleased you read the book, it was a way of speaking with you about many past things, of putting something of my life in Paris in common with you. Thank you for loving me well enough to have read it unto the end.

I told you in the time when I read it what I felt about *Wild Palmers*, about the same way as you do. In the beginning, I was very angry with this over-tragic way of telling the most unimportant things, with this lack of humour and emphasis, but then I was trapped. I came to be interested in the people, to believe in their love, and now I see that I remember some parts of the book very deeply — chiefly the erotic scenes. It does not happen often that a writer makes you to believe in physical love, and Faulkner does it with very few words, hardly a touch or two, and you feel the thrilling and the pang in your own body. And since we are book-reviewing together tonight, I'll speak to you about Koestler. Well, indeed, *Darkness at Noon* is a wonderful job. I read it in one time, a whole night without sleeping, so much I was interested. But I am not sure it is really honest; it is really how it could have happen. I guess the mistake is that he gave his hero the feelings of an individualistic newspaper man (of a kind of Koestler) and not those of a real political man. Boukharine[2] was not in opposition to Stalin because he had suddenly discovered the value of the human self, of the individual being, but because he had another view about the general situation. There were people of the same kind struggling for *objective* reasons, not for subjective ones. There was a passionate controversy in France about the book. Merleau-Ponty wrote a long essay to discuss it,[3] and it was said he was a Stalinist (which is not true), he answered to people pretending so, and in the little world of existentialist and communist writers, it was a very big storm. In the issue of *Politics* where you read my piece about Brasillach, there was this Merleau-Ponty essay, I guess. If you have still got it, read it and tell me what you think. Well, you have been reading a lot all this time long!

I am very, very happy the Guatemala things arrived. I had the feeling a little bit of myself had been lost forever. We enjoyed so much buying the beautiful blanket and the curtain together. Now, I'll go to sleep; I begin to be over-tired. I worked a little crazily during these four weeks, nearly eight hours a day; as I am tired on the evening, I drink a little too much, I eat too little, and I don't look so good as when I came back. Maybe I do everything a little too crazily: working, travelling, or loving you. But that is my way. I have rather not do the things at all as doing them mildly. I could not love you mildly, honey, and I can stop travelling or stop working for a while, but I could not stop loving you. So I'll go to bed loving you in my way, and missing you in my way—very, very crazily.

Sunday

I go to bed later and later every night. I drink more and I wake up still more tired, so I take little pills to have strength to work, and I work very well for hours but at night I am overtired, so I have to drink a little, it makes me feel good and not going to bed, and then everything begins again! The last night I stayed a long time with Mouloudji [4] and his pretty wife. I spoke to you often of this boy half from Bretagne and half from Arabia, who plays in movies, and wrote at eighteen a very pleasant book, and now is painting wonderful pictures (you would like them, nothing like Fernand, rather something with Van Gogh); he is really pleasant to see because so happy to do something with himself. The wife plays in movies too; they had a long quarrel about frankness and faithfulness, each saying the other was awfully jealous, each reproaching the other to look too much at boys (or girls) and not to admit it. It was difficult for me because I did not know how to be polite for both. What was amusing was that she was scandalized because he does not speak as if he was interested in the women he meets! In fact he is not; he says men are much more fun, more interesting. That is why he rather speaks about men. But she is much more interested in men than in women; she cares nearly exclusively for men, so she cannot understand this point of view. It is terrible when people who have not much logic and are overpassionate discuss together: they got all mixed up. They cannot find a way out of this tangle, so it lasts and begins again. It is hopeless and tiring but in a way fascinating. So I could listen to them a long time though the point was not interesting by itself. Well, they do love each other, that happens seldom, and that is why they little worry to interest me.

Now I'll work about psychoanalysis.[5] I go on remembering and loving you.

Your own Simone

1) Maheu, called Herbaud in *Memoirs of a Dutiful Daughter.* 2) Nikolay Ivanovich Bukharin, the Soviet economist and director of the communist daily, *Pravda*, in the twenties. A supporter of Lenin even after Lenin's death in 1924. Opposed to Stalin's authoritarianism, Boukharine was tried in 1938 and executed. 3) *Humanism and Terror* (1947). 4) Marcel Mouloudji, a French actor, composer, and singer, famous in the forties and fifties. 5) A reference to *The Second Sex.*

Dearest you,

This is to inform you that I still love you, at least well enough to want the pictures. But as I am leaving next week for Algiers, wait for a wire before sending them. Thank you for the clipping of the *New Yorker*. I am pleased with it;[1] maybe it will help getting somebody publishing it in English so you can read it. I am just a bit astonished the review does not mention my report about "the sexual behavior of the American local male." I had a very interesting experience about it. American local males like to make love (which is strange); they do it every day, sometimes twice a day, sometimes in the day as well as in night; what is stranger is they want the delusion that the girls they are sleeping with like it too: so, if a girl wants to be friendly, she has to pretend she enjoys the disgusting thing. They are really shameless: they walk quite naked in hotel-lobbies, sometimes they pretend to put a kind of towel around their belly, but they manage not to hide what would be hidden; I cannot decently tell you what they do in bed but I can tell you it is not decent at all. I described all that and many other things (their peculiar ways in boat-cabins, the use they do of mirrors, chiefly of round black ones) and it was a very accurate documented report. Maybe the publisher cut it away without telling me. In this case I shall have it published as a special zenzoline booklet.

Honey, I am pleased a play was made from *Never Come Morning*. Is it a good one? May I get it? Maybe it would be possible to do something with it in Paris? They are always looking for good plays. Just now Genet is looking for a play to be acted at the same time as his last one, but I am afraid yours would be too long. Let me know and send me a copy if possible. I hope that working in the strange way you described,[2] you are not going to mix up the little packages of yellow paper. Maybe people will notice no difference if you put the beginning in the end. I'll tell you a *true* little story. A week ago Sartre gave the manuscript of his next novel to a friend, a woman. She read fifty pages and said she felt amazed by this new technic; she did not see exactly the point of it. He was astonished, because it was a very plainly told story. Then he understood: she had read from p. 50 to p. 1 instead of going from the beginning to end! It is the *absolute truth.*

This afternoon I went and saw *Kiss of Death* with Victor Mature, and it seemed to me a regular master-piece, the best Hollywood picture I saw for years. I could hardly breathe from beginning to end. Did you see it? If not, go on your knees, if necessary, and see it. I went to the movie because I was overtired today. As I go on not sleeping, taking pills, sleeping less and less because I took pills (for the last nights I did not go to bed before four in the morning), so today I could do nothing. I'll try to sleep an hour now (it is 5 P.M.) before meeting my sister for dinner. I know it is an unwise way of living, but I'll break it next week. I'll go to Algiers and to some peaceful beach, and work with Sartre about the movie (the work I believed to do a month ago), work about my book more leisurely, and sleep much. Sunday evening I went to a little carnival on the place de la Bastille with Giacometti and his girl, Sartre and Bost; they all went in singing, tossing machines except me because I am afraid of my bad stomach. Giacometti was something to see; he was so scared, and so eager and so pleased. You had to laugh when seeing him coming up and down.

I guess the play you speak about, *The Servants*, is the play by Genet and indeed it is about this old criminal affair; you have a good memory and I am glad to see that you sometimes listen to what I say. How is it you read so many mysteries, suddenly? I am having two beautiful things made with the Guatemala embroidered stuff: just the top of a dress, to wear with a black skirt. I stayed two whole hours standing up with five people around me to fix it nicely. I got mad, but I wanted it to be really pretty and I went to a good dressmaker. They work hard about it! They say it is very difficult to handle, but beautiful. (Remember when you bargained so cleverly the blue thing in Quetzaltenango?) Nelson, it was sweet to get your long nice letter this morning. You are my precious husband, my beloved local youth, my own Nelson. Yea, you are mine because nobody never has and never will love you as deeply and warmly and wholly as I do.

Your own Simone

1) *America Day by Day.* 2) A reference to Algren's method of working on a novel. He could barely find anything among the scraps of paper piling up: additions, corrections, etc.

Sunday, 29th Août 1948

Dearest you, my own Nelson,

I was very tired when I wrote my last letter, so I slept a little. Then I saw a friend (a nice woman whose husband,[1] an ex-communist, died in the war after having dropped the Party because of the German-Sovietic agree-ment; and who was said afterwards to have been a traitor all his life long by communists, his former friends) and drank two bourbons, and then I met my sister and brother-in-law whom I dislike. We went by car to their house in Marly, half an hour from Paris; it was not too unpleasant. We stopped on the bank of the Seine. In the midst of the woods there was a kind of a barge with a bar-restaurant and we had a dry martini. I like boats, drinking on a boat amidst water. I chiefly like to drink scotch on the Mississippi, and I like when you drink with me, but that was better than nothing. In their house, a very old pretty one, nicely furnished, my sister had cooked a good dinner. As I was a little drunk, I spoke all the time so I had not to listen to them. Then there was a hard moment! My sister showed off her paintings. It is really no good; it means nothing she has not in herself what it necessary to do ever good painting, so it is not useful to say these ones are bad; it would hurt without possibility of giving hope. So for years I said nothing and I was not to begin now. Yet one or two lit-tle pictures — flowers, a house, a chair — were a little better than the big pretentious ones. So her husband and myself tried to tell her to work in this way, looking at the world and not just putting colors on a canvas; she was angry and cried a little and it was unpleasant because anyway it is hopeless. Then I came back to Paris, worked the whole day, and for once slept early without any drink.

I saw my new flat; it is nice. Not as nice as Wabansia, indeed, but with proper curtains and blankets and furniture, it could be good enough: a large gay room; a little, very little one; a kitchen which is a washroom too; no bath but a very fine view on Notre-Dame. You know, Nelson, I dedi-cated the place to you in my heart; it will be *our* place. I never lived there before knowing you, and no man will sleep there but you, and you'll do, next year. Some day, you'll come and it will be our view, our kitchen, where *you* will cook meals; it will be *our* bed...

Some day. I wait for this day. Often I fancy how I'll go to the airplane station, take you home in a cab, and at home kiss you and lie in your arms. Some day. And every day I think of this day.

Your own Simone

---

1) Paul Nizan, the French intellectual, essayist and novelist who left the Communist Party protesting the Hitler-Stalin pact.

Nelson, my love,

This is a fine place to write a letter! I am setting on the top of a very high hill, forty miles from Algiers. I see the wild plain, the coast and the sea; there are lots of little villages in the plain and blue cedars from top to bottom of the mountain. The only sad thing is this place is overcrowded by women and children. Men stay in Algiers—they just come for the weekend—and women spend the holidays with the babies. How sad to be a low middle-class French woman! Form morning to night they just scold the children, the children cry, they soil themselves, the mother wash them; when they don't scream about children, they are just knitting, washing, sewing, and while sewing and knitting they just speak about knitting and washing, and the sick children, and the wicked stepmother. God! I did not remember it was so awful. I don't see often this kind of people. And to think that is their holidays! The best time of the year for them! And how stupid to keep children with their mothers; they are awfully bored too, so they cry and make naughty things, and everybody is unhappy.

I spent two days in Algiers, ate couss-couss and lobsters, looking at a wonderful glue, green, and violet sea. You'll not have to eat lobster, but couss-couss. I am sure you'll enjoy it. I am sure you'll love Algiers. I went by a bus to Blida, which is said to be a very nice little town but is not, just at the bottom of the Atlas. From my window I enjoyed the most beautiful sunset on plain and sea, with these red-burned pink colors which you said look like an Arabian smell. Early in morning a cab took us to Chréa, that is this place in the mountains, among wide cedars forests. It was hard to find an hotel. I just found a rather unconfortable one, but there is a kind of garden, a terrace above plain and faraway sea; it is very nice to work there. I go on working from six to eight hours every day; the movie-script and my book go on very nicely. I enjoy writing in the open air, in the sun, with a fine view to look at. The only dreadful thing, as I told you, is these women and children baying around. Go on writing to Algiers, because I'll soon come back there.

Well, honey, you told me once you would not love me if I stopped crying for ever; so at last, after two dry months, I cried a little, one night, in Algiers. I missed you dreadfully, everything was so sweet and beautiful in the night that it broke my heart—such a night to feel happy. I went at midnight through the gardens and the silent lonely avenues and I cried very nicely. I saw Algiers glittering beneath my feet, and the wonderful sky; the smell of flowers and trees went through my heart, and I felt all my love for you. I wanted madly to see you, to tell you how much I loved you. I tell it now, but words cannot do much.

Oh! I forgot to tell you a little story. Some years ago I nearly was raped in Tunisia by an old, ugly Arabian man. Yesterday it was not that bad, but as I sat in a little café in Blida, with Sartre, at 11 P.M. I saw by the open door an Arabian man sitting on the pavement and smiling at me; he had open his pants and he played slowly and quietly with a big pink thing. The street was lightened and people passed by, some stopped and looked at him, but he went on, undisturbed, stubborn. The café was closing and we went away. I don't know what happened to the man. A dangerous country for a woman.

Goodbye, my husband. I think of you so much, so greedily, it makes me happy and unhappy. Maybe it would be nicer not to take the unhappiness, to manage just to get the happiness, but I cannot, I have to take both. I kiss you very hard, through tears and smiles. Why are you so nice?

Your own Simone

Tuesday, 14 Septembre 1948

Dearest husband,

I wanted to write yesterday, but I was suddenly sick in the most unromantic way. I guess it was owing to the Algerian wines, or to my greediness in drinking Algerian wines. No whisky here, so what should I do when the wines are so nice? Anyway the other night I suddenly wake up to find myself sick as a sick dog. Don't feel superior, please; don't say I ate some foolish candies mixed with anchovies and ice-creams. I did not. The food is very sad her; it seems just made for sick stomachs. There is nothing to buy in the woods and on the beach, so the whole affair was really *unfair,* so shut up.

I nevertheless took a cab and had a ride high about the sea, among pine-woods; it lasted three hours. But when I arrived the hotel, I just fell on my bed. I could not eat, nor write, nor walk. I just stayed there very angry at myself, reading a little and sleeping much. This morning I felt wonderful, and so am I now. How are you, my Nelson? No letter last week. Thursday I'll go poste restante in Algiers. It is night, with moon and stars, a high wind blowing in the trees. I can hear the sea; it is peaceful, after the terrible women and children in Chréa. In a deep canyon, there is an hotel where monkeys and other kinds of beasts live quite freely. One came during my breakfast and scared me by robbing so quickly and rudely all the toasted bread. Others came on my shoulders—little ones—tried to scratch my shirt away; they had lots of games among themselves. I went to an old Roman town on the sea-side.[1] On a lonely beach there are little bungalows, so I put my table on the little terrace (the porch, as you say) and I worked all day long, had a nice bath in the sea (no, you told me I should say "I went to swim in the sea"). I remembered how ugly you were in the Pontchartrain Lake,[2] with your wet hair parted in the middle... really ugly! But soon you became quite beautiful again. How is this little naughty, fat belly of yours? Did it come flat again? Are you as hansome as when I first met you?

Life is very quiet: just work and landscapes. I am pleased with both. You'll like Algiers, but you'll loathe Arabians, at least in North Africa. They are much worse than Indians. Poor, sad, sick, ugly, always lying and cheating. Besides Arabians, you find lot of French soldiers and officers; that is not better. You never saw a *colony*. You'll be indignant; colonies are a bad thing. Both are unpleasant here, masters and slaves. But the landscapes are fine, weather is sunny, nobody knows us and we know nobody, so it is a good place to breathe good air and work good work.

I did not cry any more, some tears, but not too much. I try to think of you without feeling sad, and often I succeed. I wait greedily for your letters. I miss them. I miss you, chiefly. I go on loving you in the same crazy, silly way.

Your own Simone

1) Tipaza. 2) Near New Orleans.

✻ *Algren wrote back on Sunday, September 19, but the letter got lost in Tunisia and did not arrive until much later. He confided that having gone all-out to deliver a new draft of his novel to his agent, he had given himself a weekend off: drinking, bar-hopping, even fighting—nothing out of the ordinary for him. But there was something else: he felt extremely lonely, in need of female companionship. He had avoided giving in to temptation, although just barely, ultimately deciding not to spend the night with a female friend. But he knew he still wanted her, and expressed deep dissatisfaction with his empty life. A bout of depression passed quickly, but de Beauvoir was intensely disturbed by this episode. She grilled him anxiously about the depth and meaning of their transatlantic love affair. (See the letters of November 17 and December 3.)*

Lundi, 20 Septembre 1948

Nelson, my love,

It never happened that your letters failed me. That is why I was very much disturbed, not finding anything at the general delivery. All at once, I feel scared that is means you are through with me; then I tell myself it is silly, and anyway you would not act this way. But maybe you are dead, or sick? I try to keep quiet and to think nothing serious happened, but I remained ill at ease all the time; I have no pleasure in writing, not knowing if you should get this letter or what. I guess I was very silly. I know it was not by your mistake, but I spent some unpleasant days with this uncertain fear in my heart.

Still, it would have been fine days. I went back to Algiers—a beautiful drive along the coast. I stayed there two days more. Did I tell you how big are the banknotes here? They look like the magician's big money. You would enjoy them. I don't know why in poor countries banknotes are always so big.

Thursday

Oh Honey! At last your letters and pictures. I am so happy! I had an awful time. Monday I was sure some wire would come and make me quiet. Nothing came, and it seemed impossible that at the same time letters and wire would fail without anything happening to you. I could not sleep, I could not work, I could not eat. I was scared to death for three days. Please, do something for me: give me the name and address of somebody—your mother, or Conroy, or "le gendarme"—and give him my name and address too so I can know if anything happens to you. Will you do that? Maybe you don't know what it is, going twice a day to the general delivery and phoning to the hotel for the wire, and nothing. I guess the big letter with the pictures was too heavy, and there was a strike of airplanes in France, and the mail is not very well done in Algeria. Well, now, I can laugh at it, but it was something of a hell.

I had some other misfortunes, since you seem to enjoy my misfortunes. From Algiers we went to a very fine place in the mountains of Kabylie: I had a nice room with a large red balcony and a view. The last morning, when at 8 A.M. I began to work, I noticed first that I missed my cigarettes. I began to work and suddenly I saw somebody had vomited on the balcony; then I look in my bag: my money was missing (not much), and in the suitcase things were missing too: my blue velvet pants, and two sweaters, among them the little black one you liked. So I was sad and did not know what to do. I should hate to denounce a man to the "gendarmes." I only said somebody had vomited in my room, not telling I had been robbed. It was on the eve of a big market, and the hotel director was worried and said it must have been a butcher from a faraway village; he had slept in two rooms and taken away my key. But they did not find him and so my things are sadly lost. Well, I'll buy another little black sweater.

The market was a wonderful thing. Not as beautiful and strange as in Chichicastenango but it was interesting to see the differences. First, there was not *one* woman. Indian women are as happy as queens, in comparison with these Arabian poor creatures who hardly ever go out from home. Just men in very dirty clothes, white or grey, and red fez on their heads; but then a lot of camels, horses, and these little donkeys you liked. From morning it smelt of dust and donkeys in my room, looking over the road; so you can guess how it smelt in the heart of the market. Some men came from two days walk faraway villages, bringing chiefly wheat and barley. They kill lot of oxen and goats and lambs; the ground was red with blood and scattered with bones. Wheat, meat, fruits and vegetables, and sheep; it was not nice to see as Indian goods, but it was impressive because they are very poor, and meat and food is a question of life and death. When we went away in car in the afternoon, for twenty miles we passed long lines of camels or mules coming back slowly, with empty baskets, to the faraway places where they belonged—wonderful.

Kabylie has 1,500,000 people in a small territory all covered by mountains: people are in the same percentage as in Belgium, which is the most populated European country. At first sight, it looks like a deserted, lonely, poor, inhuman land, and it is poor indeed. But at the top of each mountain there is a village, lot of villages like eagle-nests all around. I went to some of them—they are rather awful. So dirty! With such narrow alleys you can hardly walk in them. No men. Men are away earning money (lot of them in France). You see only dirty children and old women, and behind the doors sometimes a young, very pretty woman looks at you, but she quickly shuts the door again. They have not even the right to go to each other's house; the only good time in the day is when they go and fetch water, half a mile away in the bottom of the valley. French people thought it would be nice to build a fountain inside the village: as soon as it was built, the women angrily broke it, because it should have deprived them of their only pleasure. So you see, making tortillas is not the worst thing for a woman.

Maybe the worst thing is to be crazy enough to love such a naughty man, not even answering wire. Oh God! I should hate you.

From mountains we went down to the coast again, on the east side this time, in Bougie. I'll be very pleased here now I am no longer anxious. I send you *Les Temps modernes* in case they did not do it as I asked, at Gallimard's. The little piece about Bromfield was never published; I am afraid Merleau-Ponty thought Bromfield did not interest French people enough, and it was so badly translated. They are producing *Call North*[1] in Paris now, the movie showing your Polish neighbourhood. I'll rush to see it as soon as I can. Thank you for the pictures. They are very, very fine. How I like the one with you and me! Don't die, honey, please. I have to see you and kiss you again. Thanks for the long letter too, and in the name of all existentialists, thanks for having defended us once more. Write hotel "Saint-Georges," Algiers; I'll write faithfully now I am no longer scared. Don't think I made too much fuss: I was really disturbing by this long silence. I am so glad to be able to think of you with happiness and hope. How nice you look on the picture! Keep yourself alive, and keep a nice little bit of your heart for me: I need it and I deserve it. I love your love and love you, my husband. I kiss you greedily.

Your own Simone

What do you think about the Cerdan-Zale match? I don't see exactly how this new title sounds for American ears,[2] I cannot judge of it. You seem to have a nice life, sleeping and working and playing poker.

1) By Henry Hathaway with Jimmy Stewart, 1948. 2) *Frantic Mc Gantic*, later just *Mac Gantic*, a title Algren ultimately rejected.

Sunday, 26 Septembre 1948

Nelson, my husband,

I like the pictures. We should never have though, the day in New Orleans when we went and looked for the first ones, That you should be so skilful, some day. The Temple of the Warriors is really impressive. And how nicely you smile on our big picture! How I want to feel this smile again through my heart. It is so good not to worry any more about you.

I am in a very fine hotel on the sea side to day. Bost came two days ago to work with Sartre and I about this movie script; it is his job to be a screen-writer, and in France (as in Hollywood, I guess) there are always lot of people working together about a movie. I don't like it very much myself; I like to do what I do alone, with my own responsibility. Well, discussing and working with Sartre and Bost is often funny and always interesting, but it does not seem that anybody really does anything, then, other people will take the thing in hands, lot of people, producers and all, so you feel nothing will be left of what you have yourself contrived. I already told you I do that rather from friendship and for money than by pleasure.

This hotel is pleasant, empty; we are nearly the only customers. I went and swam every day. During my work, for four hours in the morning, I look at the blue water and I think it will be my reward: I am impatient to go and proud to go on working. Did you read the book by Camus which is a best seller now, *The Plague*? I don't exactly understand why it is such a success in USA. I rather like *The Stranger* better, but I should be interested to know what you think when you happen to read it. I am reading now a really wonderful book. God! I hardly dare to write any longer when I find such books, that is Tolstoy's *War and Peace*. When I was a girl I liked it, but did not understand everything then; now it seems to me really wonderful: such an art of telling stories and featuring people, and with such a simplicity. It seems artless, and that is where genuine art begins.

Monday

I had a nice evening. We discovered there was scotch in this hotel. What a rush! I had no scotch since Paris — that is three weeks, nearly four — so we drank the whole evening long. Sartre began to be a little drunk. There was a beautiful moonshine, just half a moon but very bright, so at midnight I went into the sea, all alone, and I felt deeply happy with moon, salted water, and whisky in my blood, and love for you in my heart. This happiness has not gone away. I like to sleep with the sea roaring beneath the windows, to open my eyes and see the blue water glittering and smell the smell of salt all day long. It is a pity we cannot stay longer, but I want to see a little of the desert sands. I saw them three years ago, and since, I long for them. And then I must come back to Paris middle of October. So we'll go back to Algiers within two days. I hope I'll get a fresh letter there.

Good bye. I go to the village and mail this letter. this is love, you know. It would be so comfortable to stay in the porch, looking at the sea. Then I'll work until dinner. Everything I like, I like it with you, through my love for you: you are my sunshine, and moonshine. Good bye, my sweet husband, dearest friend, my beloved Nelson.

Your own Simone

Dearest dear you,

Here I am in Algiers again. From my window I see a big wide garden with palm trees, pink and violet flowers, houses and pines, and boats and a very pale blue sea. A little wind moves gently the palms. I should feel good if I had get these yellow papers of yours; I feel how much I depend upon them now, when they come so irregularly. I'll try not to worry too much, but I am a bit anxious: you did not answer the wire neither by another wire, not by any letter. It really does not look like you. Well, I'll wait a little before getting really scared and boring you with another wire.

Yesterday I saw the most wonderful storm in my life; yea, even more terrific than the Guatemala rain. We came back from the coast by bus; in a quarter of an hour it had rained so hard that the road was a river, all cars and buses and trucks had stopped, trucks had collided. Things don't seem so good in newspapers. You saw how nicely USA "helps" us to get an army so we can struggle against USSR? They help too much. You should say to them, we don't like this kind of help. Indeed, it is really hard to think French people will have to fight in this war; when you don't like Stalin nor Wall Street, you don't know what to do. It really smells bad, don't you think so? I should like to fly to Mexico or even to Chichicastenango; when we should hear an atomic bomb flying above our head, we should just draw the sheet to our nose!

I'll try to work, but I feel like hell today. Sometimes it takes me to the throat, I told you, the world, my whole life; I nearly could jump by the window. Maybe I am a little tired of working so much. I should like to write something else. I begin to think about a novel. It would make me happy to write another novel—ideas begin to gather in my head. But I must finish this first book before; it will still take months.

Work, well, be happy, write to me. This is a silly letter, forgive it. I just tell you how I feel because you are my friend as well as my so much wanted lover. Nelson, dearest you, I love you so much.

Your own Simone

My naughty husband,

Yea, you were silly, as silly as in Santiago of Atitlan, since I was beginning to worry again when I got your letter yesterday. you never know what really is unnecessary; you should know it is always necessary to please me, to do what I tell you to do. If I were near you, I should punish you very hard for having been so silly, heartless, and stupid. But as I have no way of punishing you just now, I can do nothing by forgive you, and pray you not to begin again. Please send next letter "poste restante," Nice; I'll be there until 20th October, and after write 11 Rue de la Bûcherie, Paris. That is my new place. Don't get everything mixed up in this silly head of yours. And tell me if you got *Les Temps modernes* and the blanket. Honey, did you really fall on the head at eight months old? It would explain many things.

Now it is the end of the Algerian trip. Bost has gone away by a boat, Sartre and I shall go away by plane next week. The script is finished at least and I am glad to be through with it. It could be a good movie, but will it ever be a movie? Will it be good? You never know with this damned kind of thing. The point is, anyway, I can care about my own book again and explain day after day what kind of strange creatures women are. Men are no less strange, but I did not choose to write about them. Then I feel more and more the wish of writing a good novel; I have some ideas but it should be such a long, hard job, I feel afraid. It is very cloudy still in my head, I'll tell you later, in some months.

It seems difficult to go to the south. Three years ago I travelled alone through the south of Algeria and Tunisia, and I fell in love with sand and palm-trees; I should have liked to see it again. But it is still very hot, good hotels are still closed, buses very, very slow. So I guess we'll just see one oasis, not too far away, and no more. I don't mind too much because it is wonderfully pleasant here: the view from my window is real happiness every morning, such a silky sea, blue and pink all around me, such Arabian fragrance in the evening, the fragrance of this sunset on the Mississippi, in the blessed time where you made me happy just with one smile. I stay in my room the whole day, working and reading. I take my meals on the terrace, my life has been as peaceful as yours. I long for a peaceful like, you know. I'll try in Paris to see really nobody, and stay in my nest as you stay in yours; when you'll go to play poker, I'll go to drink whisky, when you'll come to me, I'll come to you, and you'll see, honey, next time I'll be really as nice and quiet and obedient as an Arabian wife (but they talk much, you know). I go on reading *The Arabian Nights* and I enjoy it though it is a little too long sometimes. Did you read it? Here it sounds true, these stories of merchants and robbers and travels.

Good bye, honey. I'll take you to the sought in my heart. You'll be loved among camels and palm-trees: few men have been loved in so many places, chiefly for a *local* youth it is luck, is it not? I should like to love you in your arms, Nelson, that is the best place I know, after all. Your lips were so warm and so sweet, mon amour.

Your own Simone

Friday, 8 Octobre 1948

Dearest you,

I am sitting near the window, as always. I see palm-trees and sand; a white plain as wide as the sea, and a hard white town; big camels and smell jack-asses go and drink the filthy water; Arabian women, whom you like, crawl along the walls, all wrapped in white veils, or pale blue, pale pink garments. I see all the town and desert from here, since the houses are so low: being at the second story is as high as the Empire State building top. It is the beginning of Sahara, here. The hotel manager in Algiers asked this hotel manager here (in Bou Saâda) to give us a room though the hotel is still closed. So I feel like a queen. We are the only customers of this very nice building with garden, terraces, little pools near the palm-tree wood. Hardly any French people in this genuine Arabian place, and nights are very fine. The men lie on some kinds of straw carpets and drink black coffee or tea with mint; they play cards and dominos, and Arabian music is going around the streets. As women stay home, you just see little girls in the streets. They are clad like real little women; they walk and speak in such womanly way you would rather think it is a people of midgets; some of them have even make up on their childish cheeks and mouth. Of the other women, you just see tightly wrapped figures, and then in one street, the beautiful Ouled-Naïs. That is something you should enjoy, maybe! I heard the story goes thus: There is one Arabian tribe where the young girls use to earn themselves the money useful for marrying a man, by prostitution. For five years or more they are just regular whores, then they take all

227

the money they have saved, and with that they get a proper husband; for the remaining of their lifes, they live the same way as other Arabian women, staying at home, hardly going in streets all wrapped in veils, seeing no man. When they are young and prostitute, they are beautiful and beautifully clad; they stay on the threshold, all dolled up in silk and silver. They dance too and hear the music coming from these pleasants brothels. French people have to go to a peculiar room to meet them. I should have enjoyed to go with the Arabian crowd, as it is not allowed, I did not go at all. But I like to loiter in the street at night, seeing the eagerness on the faces of men, the smile of the women, hearing the music, smelling the smell of mint and incense and oil, the peculiar Arabian smell. I go on working and working, writing a book and dreaming of another. I like this dreaming, don't you? Later it becomes hard, when you have to proceed from dream to paper, but now it is just a nice game. This afternoon I go away still farther towards south, I'll cross the desert (a part of it) and I enjoy the prospect. You know, if I travel so much, it is because I really don't like Paris any longer, and in a way it makes me sad. I liked it so much, as you like Chicago, but now I like better living far away.

Ah! I forgot to complain: I don't want any more of these ugly stamps for blind people, send nice little pictures or nothing at all, did you think I should not notice this bad trick? Well, I forgive you once more since I cannot help loving you. Here is fresh love from Arabia, honey, heeps of fresh love from

Your own Simone

Friday, 15 Octobre 1948

Dear dearest you,

I though so much of you in Marseille. Oh! That is a wonderful town, I am glad to have fallen in love with it again. That is the place where I should like to spend a long time with you. I left Algiers Wednesday morning by plane, no more than three hours, blue sky and blue sea. I told you Marseille is a place meaning much for me: I spent a year there as a teacher, it was the first time I left Paris, my parents, friends, and Sartre whom I knew only since two years. I was all alone, but I enjoyed the sun, the town, and twice a week I went to the mountains all around and walked crazily for hours. That is the place where I learnt to live by myself, to support myself, not to be dependent of anybody in any way., Then, when Germans were in Paris, it was a big thing to arrive a free town: I remember how I passed "the line," the frontier between free and non-free country; it was a real adventure, sometimes on feet, by night, sometimes on bicycle, being a little scared and proud to do such a dangerous forbidden thing. I always came to Marseille, after some trip or another: there were American movies and French papers, it seemed heaven. The very last time, I remember, I was so poor I could only eat bread and a kind of very bad mustard with garlic in it and some ice-cream without any cream, only colored and iced water. There was nearly nothing else to eat unless you had much money. All shops were empty, no food nowhere. So it was wonderful to see Marseille again with bright markets, wide shops full of all kinds of goods, pleasant restaurants and bars and terraces. A part of the town—the oldest one which I liked the best—has been destroyed by Germans, and indeed it was sad not to find again the little streets with the prostitutes, the narrow market, the clingy dives, the pizzerias, and the neighbourhood I was so fond of. But in the whole, much of Marseille remains. I spent the day walking around, remembering things with a bursting heart. I should have like to stay much more, but Sartre's mother had asked me urgently to come and spend some days in her house in Nice, and I had to. She lives in a silly half-elegant suburb, cosy houses for middle-class people. I hate that. All is quite dead all around. I have a nice ugly room and I work the whole day long. She is kind-hearted, but a terrible bourgeois woman, pretending not to be so. Though I just see her during the meals, I feel it hard to stand.

If you are really a nice man, as you used to be, will you send me a bottle of ink, you know, the one for the Parker 51 pen only?

Monday

I really have the most quiet life you could think of, even quieter then in the Wabansia goat nest. Nothing is more peaceful than this dreary, cosy little house and I should die if staying here a long time. Poor Sartre went sick: just a crisis on liver and kidneys, not dangerous but very painful, so he lied in bed for two days and I stand all alone with the mother, an hour a day, at meals. I spent the whole time in my room, writing, sleeping, reading, and again reading, sleeping, writing. I found by chance on a dusty shelf a little book by Thurber: it seems strange, people here (the owners of the house, I mean) seem to read chiefly books about hens, rabbits, cowliflowers... well, the Thurber was called *Let Your Animal Alone*, and some pieces were very funny, pieces formerly published in the *New Yorker*. I went to Nice three days ago and drank good scotch, and I met the old André Gide at the post office. Do you know him? The old French writer who got the Nobel Prize last year. They have translated his *Diary* in USA, a long tedious book, chiefly for American people who don't know what it is all about: he speaks of many small French people, French things, you would not be interested. But he was the great leader of past times, a very clever man, funny by some ways, struggling for freedom and pederasty. Now he is an old man, with spectacles and a round soft hat and he made me laugh because he was so friendly but so anxious not to see people more than three minutes: he feels tired, being old.

The man who did the movie *Children of Paradise,* which you did not like, the writer who contrived the plot and wrote the script, a very well-known and pleasant poet, always drinking in Café de Flore and Deux Magots, is dying; I learnt from the newspapers. He jumped by a window without choosing to do so,[1] he was just speaking with friends and mimicking somebody, he walked backwards, and the window was open! He tried to catch a big neon-add when falling but the letters fell down with him and he burst his skull. Is not that a sad story? French newspapers told the most stupid stories about Sartre and me travelling in Algiers; they seemed astonished because we rode trolley-bus and street-car, and because I never complained about the food or the bed in the hotels. What do they think writing people are like? I miss you awfully, that is all you have to know. I remember how I heard Jesse James, lying in your arms and crying because I knew that one day I should remember Jesse James in this way, with this crying need. It is not only you, it is me, I guess, whom I miss so sadly; it is us, and Chicago surrounding us, and this happy, unexpected storm in my heart. I feel so blue tonight. Nice is dying and dead, the only town in France where you can find as many houses and flats to rent as you want, and even much more. Old wealthy English people came here, in old times, but they are dead, and living English people are no longer wealthy. So big hotels are closed, little houses decaying, wide avenues empty. I used to walk and even ride my bicycle in these wonderful stony mountains which are Nice background—how I enjoyed it! And I came to the blue elegant town, tired and dirty. But now I feel like an old lady myself, I am fed up with mysteries and tired with my book. Paris will be a change, though I don't like the idea of Paris so much. Things are very bad just now in France. It is hard to say who is right and wrong. It seems everybody is wrong, you cannot help being wrong in this awful world of nowadays. I speak chiefly about the miner's strike; they ought to be better paid, but their strike is political, and drowning the French coal will not help, anyway. I am not for the Marshall Plan, but France cannot live without it.

I hope I'll get my letter in Paris. I'll be there by plane tomorrow night if I don't crash. There was a terrible crash yesterday in Scotland, did you see that? Sometimes I feel you gave me the last happy time in my life, sometimes it seems I have really been too happy with you and I'll never know real happiness again. Maybe I am mistaken, I should like to. You know how much I love you, do you?

Your own Simone

1) Jacques Prévert, who eventually recovered from the accident.

Saturday, 23 Octobre 1948

Darling dearest dear you,

So I did not crash, I arrived Paris yesterday evening after the most beautiful plane trip — from Nice we went right to high mountains and above them for an hour, We could see the snow on the high lonely peaks, not very far beneath; it was a little scaring but wonderful, even more wonderful than the day above the Mexican mountains. Paris is a little sad, it is the fall now but not cold, pleasant. I went to my new nest and found your letter nicely waiting for me. Yea, honey, I *know* what I say: I dwell 11 Rue de La Bûcherie. Do you fancy you know French and can teach me things? It is a very old street of Quartier Latin and has nothing to do with killing innocent beasts, no *butcher* around. Yea, that is my permanent address now. I am glad to have one. That is the place where I'll get your letters, and where, on day, I'll get you. I am going to make a regular settling there, in the afternoon, gathering whatever I own in the world, and putting it there.

Your publisher just passed by the Deux Magots where I am writing to you. He says everything is settled with the translator, but they are waiting for the new reduced copy of the book. So as soon as it is printed (proofs would do), you send a copy to me by air-mail. Don't forget as you forgot to tell me if you received the blanket (well, this time I am kidding; I sure missed one letter).

I always thought this story about sending scotch was just one of your fancy lies! So I was surprised when the letter told me to go to the "Louisiane" and see, yet I did, being as obedient as an Arabian wife. God! How skilful, wonderful, and nice that was, my nice man, my good husband. Thanks for the candies, for the golden corn (I don't know why they don't have it in France), and chiefly thanks for the marvellous scotch— that is a first rate one—and you cannot know what a fine piece of furniture it is, a bottle of scotch on a little table near my bed. yea, now, I feel really at home! And as I intend to take my meals at home now, I'll eat the golden corn tonight. The idea of the flour is really clever, I'll use the flour to make pancakes, and so on. I begin to be in love with my room, I settled yesterday afternoon. I even went to some shops for curtains and shutters, everything I needed. It is very convenient, wide, and gay, and the neighbourhood is as pleasant as possible; I see the Seine and 'les quais" from my windows. Behind the house it is a kind of West Madison place, with forgotten men sitting on the pavement, lot of narrow little streets and little shops. This grey autumn weather reminds me of my young time, when autumn meant coming back to school, seeing the friends and teachers again: I enjoyed it.

It is worse and worse in France. The miners will not go to work again and they are right in most of ways, but the government has decided to be stubborn, and you surely know many people (workers chiefly) have already been wounded and killed in terrible riots. It is awfully sad and silly.

Did you heard about a story that hold me thrilling for five days because I am fond of mountain myself? Two men, professional mountain climbers, tried to climb a most difficult peak (only two other ones had ever achieved the thing). Towards the end of the climbing their rucksacks fell down (I don't know how) with all the ropes, pikes, and things they need to climb up or go down: food and blankets and hot garments were in the sacks too. So they found themselves on a little area of stone, not being able to go up or down, and they had to stay there five days and nights, on that freezing stone. Comrads, as soon as they knew, tried to climb the same way but snow and ice made it suddenly impossible, so they had to climb by another way above them to go down to them. For five days and nights they did not eat nor sleep, yet when they were reached and had eaten a little, they went down by themselves and just lay in an hospital bed when they were in town. They are weak and some parts of

232

them are frozen. You should have died, poor dear you! But you should never have put yourself in such a place, you wise, cunning crocodile!

Monday

Yesterday evening Koestler came into the Pont Royal bar while I was there with Sartre. He stayed six months in Palestine and said little interesting things about it. But we did not want to be friendly at all, so we hardly spoke and hardly let him speak...He had a big dog who vomited on the carpet and then ate back what he had vomited: I nearly vomited myself, being disgusted as much by Koestler as by the dog. We shall not meet again.

My little nest is really fine, the scotch is wonderful. I went to work very well; I feel a good girl and I love you as much as you deserve, maybe a little more. Thanks, my deserving husband, it was the nicest gift. I like the little red song, and I found good sound local love in the box too, that was ever better than scotch. You are my dearest, beloved dear you.

Your own Simone

P.S. Don't choose another title with *never*![1] *Never Come Morning* is all right, but *The Monkey Never Dies* would be too much of it.

1) Algren had sent her a dozen possible titles for his next novel, one of which became *The Man with the Golden Arm*.

Monday, 1st Novembre 1948

Dearest dear you,

It is a kind of holidays since yesterday. I enjoy it because instead of going to the library I stay home, I light up the fire, I make tea, and work and work, and I like my little nest more and more. I have got two fine pictures to fix on the wall, a pleasant armchair, a cupboard. I have people home for lunch and dinner and I cook nice meals: chiefly, already cooked vegetables and cold ham. But I don't know very well how to manage the can-opener, I broke already two of them. It is a hard life for a lonely woman, I should need a nice house-keeper husband to open the cans for me.

I spent an evening with the ugly woman; she was in love with your short story. Many people spoke to me about it with much praise, surely it is the translation which did the trick. The ugly woman was in a terribly bad health; it all comes from the head, she says, but then the head is awfully bad. She cannot swallow anything, sometimes not even the water she has in her mouth, she comes all cold in legs and thighs, she faints and stays unconscious for hours. The doctor says he can do nothing, she should go and see a psychiatrist, but she will not. She spent most of the summer months with her mother; the mother has remained as important for her as in her childhood: she scares her and makes her unhappy and half-mad. The novel she is writing is not very good, and as she has nothing else in life, I don't tell her it is bad. She goes on being in love with me. She is very stubborn! But she does not see me often, maybe that explains the stubborness.

Tuesday

Coming from the hairdresser who nicely piled my hair on the top of my head, I sat in the Flore to write to you. It is a long time since I came here in the afternoon; it wakes up lot of memories. When it was so cold in the town, there was a stove here and everybody wanted to be near it. I always arrived early in the morning and sat at the best place. German soldiers never entered the Flore, I don't know why, and now everybody speaks English. It is a great day in Chicago, you are going to vote for Wallace. Everybody knows Dewey will win; will you be very excited? I'll try to go to Harry's Bar; they have already fixed a lot of panels on the walls with the name of the states and they will write the results of the poll as soon as they will know them. I guess a lot of Americans will be there.

The last important thing in Paris intellectual life is Camus' terrible failure: he wrote a long ambitious play from his book *The Plague* and had it acted in the best French theatre. I did not go to the last rehearsal because all men and women were in tuxedo and evening dress, and Sartre hates it as well as I do; but most of friends went there and they said the same thing as newspapers: it was the most awful failure. God! How hard and wicked people are! All so pleased that Camus did not succeed. And they think Sartre must be pleased. It is strange, writers are not so jealous and hating each others, but when you come to theatre, everybody is everybody's else enemy.

I got your letter a few hours ago. Yea, I feel a rather reproachful frog, but I understand you have to work and make your book as fine as possible. I don't want writing letters would become a kind of a duty. I hate all duties, and love-duties are worse than any others. Do write when you choose, honey, work well, be a nice local youth, don't forget your own little frog.

234

No, the Mississippi was not a foolish time. For me, it was the wisiest thing I did in my whole life, gliding on the waters and making myself happy, making happy the man I love. Nothing else is wise, maybe.

As lovingly as ever

Your own Simone

Honey,

I got your letter this morning. It was a long time without hearing of you, because of the holidays I guess. No, we have not such a pleasant festival here for All Souls Day; it is only the day when old dark women go to the churchyard with sad flowers to put over the graves, nothing nice happens for children nor for anybody. I liked the story when you were a "pretty little girl," you should have get a picture.

So Truman was the winner! Everybody here was very surprised, excited, and pleased. Is it really such a good thing? Liberal American people here seem very happy, what does it mean exactly? It is not so good here; there was a big victory of the RPF, many of them were elected in our Senate, the CP lost nearly all seats it had before—maybe because of the strikes.

The weather was wonderful the whole week, we call it Saint-Martin's summer. But today is cold, damp, nearly snowing, winter has come for good. Not much happened, I work and work like the stubborn ants we saw in Chichen Itza, you remember? Sartre has been cursed by the Holy Church in an official way: no Catholic people are allowed to read his books any more. Newspapers wrote a lot of cracks about it, and were sometimes funny. It does not mean much.

For once, I went to the theatre. I saw some dancers, ballet—I don't know the English word. During a rehearsal of this performance, I enjoyed looking at the work of the dancers (there was a little fifteen years old girl who was wonderful, so young, unspoilt, and beautiful). So it was pleasant, after seeing them in ugly dirty working dresses, doing each gesture over and over, to see the beautiful suits and lights, and the fulfilled performance. It is one of the most costly and elegant performances in Paris now. The girl was really sweet, shy, and simple, and smiling when everybody clapped their hands. But I don't see much meaning in this kind of achievement: I like better plays, or movies, or burlesques. I am sure you should have been bored.

Among lot of tedious or silly books I am reading about women, I read over Lawrence's novels. It is rather tedious: always the same sex-story, the woman being brought to submission by a lover who looks like Lawrence himself, has to kill her own self so they can be both happy. Well, you did not kill my self and we were pretty happy, were we not? Still, sometimes he speaks with real warmth of love life, of such things in love life nobody dares to speak about; it should be more simple, so it could be moving and good. The beginning of *The Plumed Snake* is a story of a bull fight in Mexico, but he doesn't feel it the way I did, nor the way you did neither. Tell me if you think anything about Lawrence.

I guess one copy of your book is enough, but send it quickly. Thanks for the little clippings. I understand very well by myself, thank you!

I waited for your letter before writing, that is how I did not write the whole week; I felt a bit lonely and faraway. I hope I am not fading away in your heart; I don't mind falling asleep a little if you'll wake me up some day, but I should hate to die. You stay so vividly in my own, nearly too much; it is often painful to miss you so much. I love you, Nelson.

Your own Simone

Vendredi, 12 Novembre 1948

Dearest dear you,

It is a strange weather in Paris all these days long, a thick grey fog from morning to night, and at night so deep it is dangerous to ride a cab. It is so thick that it comes inside the houses—the library for instance is all foggy. From time to time sun comes through. When I leave my nest in the morning and walk along the Seine, it is wonderful and makes me happy.

Yesterday it was holiday: twenty years ago, on the 11th November, the war was stopped; we were the winners, so we celebrate it every year. But how bad it was, this year. I happened to be on the Champs Elysées, because of an interview at the wireless station. There was lot of people on both side, nobody on the central pavement except cops, full cars of cops. On one side there were people holding flags and singing "La Marseillaise": left-wing people, soldiers on the last war chiefly, with women and children holding fake doves in their hands. They had been forbidden to walk on the middle of the avenue, they were rather angry at it. But suddenly, when they were near the Triumph Arch, cars of cops rushed to prevent them going on; they were scared, chiefly because of the children, and began to be mad of anger. I saw them kick the wooden fences along the pavement: at the first kick, cops were beating them very hard—many were bruised, and some seriously wounded. God! What a *hate* from cops to people, from people to them! You remember they have gone to the mines to prevent the strikes and they killed one striker, so they are more hated than ever, that is right, but how they do hate people in the street! I went away; later there were more serious fights, and a cop shot a man in the leg, many people were beaten, even newspaper men. So Paris is boiling with anger today. It seems the government was purposely provocative, maybe to prove he is strong and need no de Gaulle to struggle against communists. Anyway, it is really bad.

We hope much from a Truman-Stalin interview; it would mean much for French people because communists would no longer be so harshly against Marshall Plan, and so maybe a league between socialists and communists would be contrived and it would check de Gaulle. We began to work for the RDR again—Rousset, Sartre, myself, and lot of others; it lives in a rather fine way. We have a daily newspaper now, a very important one which was formerly nearly communist, but the communist staff went away for reasons too hard to tell, and the leader is RDR. It is a popular paper, which lot of working men read. Then we hope to contrive a weekly magazine; there is a whole staff of writers ready to manage it, we just lack money. You have not, per chance, 5000 dollars to give us? Or even a little more? It would be a beginning. All that is rather hopeless, the way your speaking for Wallace was, but it has to be done.

Honey, I did not tell you how wonderful the rumsticks were. I had a hard time with it; first, because I could not manage to open the can, then it was so good everybody who tasted it wanted to eat the whole lot—Sartre and my Russian friend had a hard fight about it. Still I managed to eat some of it by myself. For the scotch, I nearly drank the whole bottle by myself, and God, how quickly it was done!

Saturday

There was a strike today to protest against what happened Thursday: no buses, no underground, hardly any cabs. I am so dull, I went to the library without noticing anything. I happened to find a cab at 9 A.M. and worked quietly the whole morning. Then I had an appointment for lunch with Sartre, Rousset, and Indochinese men in an Indochinese restaurant a little far away, and I spent a very unhappy time looking for a cab, looking for

237

buses, and not understanding what happened. In the end, I walked on my feet. We ate very fine Indochinese food and spoke about French colonies, much more dreadful than in the Deep South. I have a friend coming back from Martinique: she says two days after they arrived, when it was known they knew some Negroes and saw them friendly, and rode the Negro street-cars, nobody wanted to meet them any more; the car which had been lent to them (his husband had an official ethnographic mission) was taken away. It often happens you find a dead Negro, an important one, in some bush or some marsh. And did you hear about the dreadful stories in Mada-gascar?[1] They killed 90,000 Negroes against 150 white people who were killed in the rebellion. It is the most shameful thing which happened in France since a long time.

I am always a very nice, faithful wife. I am just living like an old, cold sexless virgin now. It does not suit me too well, but that is the way you trapped me. I should like to get a husband again, but it has to be you. I kiss you with all my old young love, my husband.

Your own Simone

1) The Madagascar Riots of 1947–48, a violent nationalist rebellion suppressed by French authorities.

Wednesday, 17 Novembre 1948

Nelson, my beloved husband,

I just got you letters, the new one and the old lost one, and I feel so dis-turbed I cannot work. It is silly, this Algerian letter went to *Tunis*: The post-man was crazy or naughty, that is why I was so restless about you in Alge-ria! You speak to me in a very close, confident way that goes to my heart, and then I felt you faraway; I was afraid you did not tell everything about your life—now I understand you do. That is always the same old problem: I don't care if you sleep with a girl (indeed, in a way I care but that does not matter), but it is difficult to do so if you are not free, I understand, because of the girl herself. And I take your freedom, or a part of it, without giving you happiness, without being near you; it seems unfair, though I know I am not guilty. I cannot wish you to forget me because I love you too much, but I cannot wish you to feel lonely and sad, because I love you too much. I told you in my last letter, sometimes it seems hard to me too never to sleep with a man, but for a woman it is somewhat different; it seems it is easier to stand than for a man, anyway; and I know no man in Paris I should like to sleep with. I can understand very well your need. Just, tell me always the truth, honey. Let us be friends as well as husband and wife, let us stay friends even if some day you get tired with this faraway love which lets you so lonely. Let us always speak openly and confidently to each other. I am sad I never answered this letter of you. If it is too long before you can come to my nest, I'll come to you again, in June or July maybe? For short or long time, but we have to be happy again in each other's arms as soon as possible. We'll speak about it more precisely a little later. I miss you dreadfully.

I kiss you as hard as I do when after a long tiring trip I find you again. I love you.

Your own Simone

I went to Montmartre with my Russian friend, Olga, and I bought these cards for you.

Monday, 22 Novembre 1948

Poor dear you,

I should have liked to write a nice letter for a change, with a lot of nice little stories, but nothing happens and I don't even remember my dreams. It is cold and grey now in the streets and somewhat so in my soul. I go on working so well that I'll have a first part of the book done in the middle of December. I'll have it published while I go on writing the second book; it will be such a huge thing! An evening newspaper asked me today "What do you think about men?" Indeed, I did not answer. Do I think the same thing about you and Philip Rahv?[1] A "nice man" can be a very nice thing for a woman, but could I explain exactly what I intended by a "a nice man"? So I gave my jaw a rest, as you say. Last Saturday my sister and brother-in-law asked me to show them some Saint-Germain-des-Prés night-clubs; they live ten miles from Paris, and they already seem country people. So I went to some of these places where I never go now, and I felt like a country girl myself. First, they had a dinner in my little home, and they thought I really cooked very well: ham, cold sausage, and a cake from the baker, and full cans of beans and meat. The brother-in-law opened the cans so the dinner was a success. Then we went to some caves: one where they have a very good jazz and nice girls in slacks, young and slim and dancing like the devil itself. In the other cave we drank an awful whisky. It

239

was said to be Irish but was not even French; it was awfully crowded but we had reserved a table.

The RDR is doing fine. There was a silly meeting of the RPF (the Gaullists) with Malraux speaking for intellectual freedom! You can fancy what would be intellectual freedom if de Gaulle was the law! Happily, he will not be, I think. He has made stupid speeches these last times. USA seem very harsh against him, and that is good, because he can do nothing if America does not support him; he is the most silly puppet. We are going to have a big meeting of intellectual RDR members in the middle of December, French and foreign writers and painters, and so on. Wright will speak, and maybe I'll speak but I am not sure, I am afraid I should feel a little scared.

I feel hope again, in spite of all, hope of kissing you some day, of being happy with you anew. You would have a fine time if you ever come here; you would not feel a tourist as in Mexico. I am sure Paris would teach you things, as America did to me. It is strange and interesting to see how American writers or artists feel and behave in Paris; they love it and they are disturbed, it seems to be a real experience. You have to do it some day... Think of it again...

Good bye, honey. As ever, Simone loves Nelson...

Your own Simone

1) A literary critic with a Marxist and sociological bent.

✳ *On November 23 and December 8, Algren elaborated on the painful reflections described in his wayward letter of September 23: unhappy with the existence he was leading, tired of solitude and intellectual isolation, he dreamed of the stability, security, and daily companionship of a marriage. His love for de Beauvoir had not diminished; he realized he had never before experienced a love like hers, and would never experience it again.*

La Force des Choses (Gallimard, 1963, "Folio" edition, pages 232–34) refers to parts of these letters:

Every week I found in my mailbox an envelope with a Chicago postmark; I found out why I had received letters so rarely from Algren while I was in Algeria: he had written to me in Tunis instead of Ténès. The letter was returned to him; he sent it to me again. It was lucky it got lost, because I would have found it painful reading at the time. While speaking at rallies for Wallace, he had fallen in love with a young woman, he wrote; she was being divorced and he had thought of marrying her; she was in analysis and didn't want to get involved in a relationship of that sort until the analysis was finished; by the time the letter finally reached me in December they had almost stopped seeing each other. But he explained what he felt in detail:

I won't have an affair with this girl, she doesn't really mean anything to me. But that doesn't change the fact that I still want what she represented for me for two or three months: a place of my own to live in, with a woman of my own and perhaps a child of my own. There's nothing extraordinary about wanting such things, in fact it's rather common, it's just that I've never felt like it before. Perhaps it's because I'm getting close to forty. It's different for you. You've got Sartre and a settled way of life, people, and a vital interest in ideas. You live in the heart of the world of French culture, and every day you draw satisfaction from your work and your life. Whereas Chicago is almost as far away from everything as Uxmal. I lead a sterile existence centred exclusively on myself: and I'm not at all happy about it. I'm stuck here, as I told you and as you understood, because my job is to write about this city, and I can only do it here. It's pointless to go over all that again. But it leaves me almost no one to talk to. In other words, I'm caught in my own trap. Without consciously wanting to, I've chosen for myself the life best suited to the sort of writing I'm able to do. Politicians and intellectuals bore me, they seem to be unreal; the people I see a lot of these days are the ones who do seem real to me: whores, junkies, etc. However, my personal life was sacrificed in all this. This girl helped me to see the truth about us more clearly; last year I would have been afraid of spoiling something by not being faithful to you. Now I know that was foolish, because no arms are warm when they're on the other side of the ocean; I know that life is too short and too cold for me to reject all warmth for so many months.

In another letter, he returned to the same subject:

> *After that wretched Sunday when I began to spoil every-*
> *thing in that restaurant in Central Park, I had that feel-*
> *ing I told you about in my last letter — of wanting some-*
> *thing of my own. To a great extent it was because of this*
> *woman who seemed so near and dear to me for several*
> *weeks (it's over now; but nothing has changed). If it hadn't*
> *been her it would have been someone else; it didn't mean I*
> *had stopped loving you, but you were so far away, it seemed*
> *so long before I would see you again.... I feel it's a little*
> *silly to talk about things we've gone past. But it's just as*
> *well, since you can't live in exile in Chicago nor I in Paris,*
> *since I'd always have to come back here, to my typewriter*
> *and my loneliness, and feel the need of someone close to me,*
> *because you're so far away....*

There was nothing I could say in reply; he was absolutely right, which didn't make it any easier to bear; I would always have felt a painful regret if our affair had ended then. The happiness of the nights in Chicago, on the Mississippi, in Guatemala, and the sudden botched-up ending would have turned it into no more than a dream. Happily, Algren's letters gradually grew warm again. He told me about his daily life. He sent me newspaper clippings, edifying tracts against alcohol and tobacco, books, chocolate, and two bottles of old whisky concealed in two enormous bags of flour. He also wrote that he would come to Paris in June and was booking his passage on a boat. I grew easy in my mind again, but every now and then I realized with anguish that our relationship was doomed to come to an end, and soon.

Sunday, 28 Novembre 1948

Dearest darling you,

I kept the evening just for you and me. I put your fat letter on the table: that is you and here am I. Outside it is pretty cold, "givre" we call it; the mysterious fog makes me think of Christmas and mountains. But that is behind the windows, they are closed, the fire is purring, I have cigarettes and smoking tea on the table, the bed is waiting for me, white and cosy, and near the bed, some books I should like to read if you don't keep me too long. On the walls I have now a bad painting by my sister—some sad flowers in a sad room. I could not help it; I just don't look at it. But I have a painting by Léger who gave it to me: a very well-known French painter, a little abstract, but the colors are so gay and lively you would like him. And two days ago I bought a good colored print of a very beautiful Van Gogh; it is the little café where he died and the billiard where he was put when he came back from the fields with a bullet in his heart. Reds, greens, yellow—you would love it.

The *New Yorker* was polite about Camus' play, in fact it was worse than that. I read a little bit of it and I saw with my own eyes that it was awfully bad. Camus is so angry that he did not answer a letter Sartre and myself sent him, asking to see him. He never wants to see Sartre when he feels a failure. Still he says and even writes in newspapers that his play is good. I think it is childish. When you fail, you fail and you can admit it. A writer has to try things, he cannot always succeed, he has just to say "I'll do better next time," don't you think so?

I went Friday evening to a great gala—ballets, once more, by Catherine Dunham, an American colored girl, both an anthropologist and a dancer. She took her degrees somewhere in USA, and learnt in Bresil and Cuba everything about primitive Negro dancing; now she has a lot of Negro dancers around her and she dances herself; she tries to give people an idea of Caribbean sea dances. In Chicago, I was said, she performed unsuccessfully. In fact, she is not very good; the whole performance pretends to be wild and is very sweet. I was only half-satisfied. There was let out Paris as they say; I saw Cocteau, the beautiful Josephine Baker in a wonderful bright white gown: maybe that was the best part of the evening. The whole theatre was supposed to be a jungle: high green trees, tigers and snakes in the lobbies, more dangerous than in Chichen Itza woods.

It was a very busy and somehow unpleasant week. First, our publisher, the old Gallimard, told us he did not want to have anything more to do with the *Temps modernes*; he just dismissed us, saying it is too expensive, but in truth it is for political reasons. Malraux,[1] who is a Gaullist, made a heavy pressure on him. We had to find another publisher; happily we found one (a young RDR man). Then Sartre had a rather harder time with his theatrical agent who is a crook: there is a trial and all that, about *Red Gloves*. He had said on the contract it should not be changed at all when performed in USA, and he learnt they did with it a kind of love-melodrama. So he asked many times for the manuscript of the translation, and they

243

never sent it. For some people it sounds quite anti-communist, for others pro-communist, and there is no way of knowing. It was produced in Newhaven, in Baltimore, with big success, but what kind of success?

I had a dinner for the first time at the ugly woman's. Her book has just been published,[2] the one where she says how beautiful and clever and nice I am; you should read it, maybe you'll begin to appreciate me a little. She lives in a rather poor neighbourhood, in a very poor house, but the little home is nice, with plenty of paintings by Van Gogh and pictures of your own frog. We ate chicken and drank champagne. She is always ill and has nearly no money left, so she'll have to go to the country and feed pigs. I can stand speaking with her some time, but what is dreadful is at the end of the evening she comes drunk and then she says childish, silly hysterical things; I hate it and go away as quickly as possible.

I met Truman Capote in Saint-Germain-des-Prés streets; he is as funny as possible, so small! Much smaller than Sartre, and such a pansy! Everybody laughs when hearing him—the way he speaks to a barman! I am going to have a plaster-mask made with my face. I thought it happened to you only when you are dead, but there is a man who lives on such things and he is going to have a show; he wants my head, so he'll have it. The point is he puts plaster on the hair too and you have to go to the hair-dresser for a shampoo when it is over—it is some trouble.

Yea, I heartily agree with what you say about Dostoyevsky; his humour is much deeper and subtle and bitter than Dicken's, and still lighter and easier. Do you like Stendhal? We never spoke about him, it seems to me. I read it over last week and it seemed to me wonderful, but I don't know if you don't have to be French to enjoy it thoroughly, because it implies such a French background.

A little story about Truman Capote: the barman of the Montana, a bar where I go sometimes, was said this young man was called Truman Capote. He could hardly believe it, the name sounds so strange, and he asked: "What? Truman...like Roosevelt? Et Capote...like capote anglaise?" What I like in the story is the question: "Truman...like Roosevelt?" Is not that good?

I too love Lawrence of Arabia and don't like the other one. He tried to speak frankly, genuinely, about sex and sexual love—that was good because nearly anybody ever did it in a convincing way. But in my idea he failed. It is tremendously difficult to do, I guess; words are too coarse or too sweet. Maybe the best thing is to speak of it in an incidental way, as

Faulkner in *Wild Palms*: there you feel physical love; it makes you gasp, yet very little is said.

I too feel people become more stupid each year. I used to be fond of people some years ago, chiefly when Germans were in Paris; it was such a joy to meet friends. Now I just like to be left alone, nearly everybody seems boring to me. Why? Are you really better than the others? Or do I still love you because I don't see you any longer? What do you think?

Now, I go to bed, read a little, and try not to miss you too much. I'll pretend I am just a ten years old little girl who enjoys her lonely bed and knows of nothing else, but, God, I am not. Do come back to me some day, my husband. It was sweet to get such a nice long pleasant letter. You seem to intend seeing me again, after all. If you see me, you'll kiss me a little, I guess...if you kiss me...Nelson, I love you so much. It was sweet to stay near you a long time.

Your own Simone

Thanks for the 5000 dollars. Can you send some 10,000 more? We could use them.[3]

1) André Malraux (1902–1976). French novelist (*La Condition Humaine/Man's Fate*, 1933) and politician, an active supporter of de Gaulle. 2) Violette Leduc; *L'Affamée*. 3) Algren had sent her some fake dollars he'd made, carefully cut out and colored. His letters were often accompanied by drawings.

Friday, 3 Décembre 1948

Dearest darling you,

I am glad I got this September letter and we spoke this thing thoroughly. In a way, I cannot say your last long letter made me happy. Sure, I *knew*, since that night where I cried so much, that our affair should be over in a rather short time, that in a way something already was dead, but it was rather a shock to realize that it could have ended as soon as this fall, that it can end tomorrow. No, it does not make me happy. Yet, I think you are perfectly right, and everything you say is fair. I can very well feel how you need a wife of your own, and you deserve her, and she has not to be careless of her own fate to take you as an husband. You will be a very nice fate for any woman, and I should have chosen that fate for myself heartily if other things had not made it impossible for me. Yea, I understand, Nelson. I should only like you not to be sad about your last year faithfulness; it made a sense. For one year it has meant so much for me to know such a faithful, true, warm love; it went so deep in my heart and I returned it so happily that if you are still a little fond of me, you cannot have regret about it; you cannot reproach yourself to have given so much to me since I was so grateful for it. Life is cold and short, yea, that is why you would not be regardless of real warm and intense feelings. We were no fools to love each other the way we did, to sacrifice other things for it; we have made each other happy for a time, really happy; that is more than many people ever have, that is something I'll ever forget, and I hope you'll sometimes remind it too. Now, honey, all I hope is we'll still have at least one more long time to spend together: you, come to Paris between April and September for instance. And I hope even when you get married we can stay friends and keep in touch.

It is cold and rainy; happily, I stay at home more and more. I really do nearly anything but working from morning to night. Two days ago I went and saw the woman with a pin. I was deeply moved: she is dying; the disease is rather mysterious, doctors don't know how to cure her; it is awful —a kind of blood cancer, all the red lively part of the blood is eaten by nobody knows what. The patient becomes white as snow. She lay on her bed, half dead it seemed, so thin and white, with a twisted long face, something a little idiotic in the look and smile. She does not know she is dying, but Guille, her husband, knows; he should have killed himself, he said, if not for the children (three of them, the older is a seven years old girl). He sees his wife going away slowly and surely, and he cannot help thinking accurately of the burial, the death itself; it is like living with a speaking corpse, and now he only wishes she dies as quick as possible, because it is too hard to stand. I'll go back next week, and when she is dead, I'll see him often, I guess, with Sartre, to help a little.

Good bye, Nelson. It seems incredible my arms are so cold when my heart is so warm. Yet I know it is true: faraway arms are very cold. I hope you'll find them warm again once more (you know they can be). Oh, you should like me, just now! I feel as the day when you killed the egg, a bit topsy-turvy all inside me and not arrogantly happy. But I love you just the same.

Your own Simone

Dearest darling you,

I received the little book with the very lecherous picture on it.[1] Are you not ashamed? It looks like one of these forbidden books people buy secretly

246

on the quays of the Seine, beneath my window. How thin it looks now! It was so big. A long time has already gone away since I first saw the big fat book and read it in the plane, crying at the little poetry you had written in it for me. I'll phone tomorrow to the publisher; he will give it to the best translator I know in Paris, the best indeed, if you don't include myself. I always get many congratulations about this short story, in *T.M.*, and there is no doubt that is my translation which does the trick.

Everybody here gets excited about the Garry Davis affair; you surely heard about the little red-haired man who went to the American embassy and said he wanted to give back his American passport. They said: "But that is the best passport in the world!" And he said: "I want no passport; I want no more separate nations. I am a world citizen!" In the ONU[2] they put him away, so he slept on the stair in front of the building; French people brought him bananas to eat and he stayed there a short time. Then, he went secretly to one of the ONU sessions; people were with him, hiding in the place, and at a time he shouted things about peace, they all shouted together. They were expelled but pictures were made, shouts got printed and everybody was excited; they had a big meeting saying they wanted peace. Sartre did not go, he thought that was not serious; but Camus went and spoke rather well, I heard.

I have read *The Snake-Pit*,[3] it is not very good, but it is impressive. I know this kind of asylums are awful; I saw some French ones and heard lot of horrible stories about it. The book gave me quite the same feeling than a long visit I made to this kind of hospital, near Rouen.[4] Nothing else. Now it is blue and sweet again, and the first part of the book is nearly over.

Tuesday

I was waiting yesterday for the ugly woman and she just came when I was writing. We drank some egg-brandy but she did not like it so much, so we drank grapefruit juice with gin in it, and had a dinner at a restaurant nearly —some duck with orange sauce that was wonderful. I don't enjoy much seeing her twice a month, but I pity her, and she is lonely.

Good bye, honey. I wait for a letter. I wait impatiently as always. And as always I am lovingly

Your own Simone

1) On the paperback edition of *Never Come Morning*. 2) *Organization des Nations Unies* (U.N.). 3) By Mary Jane Ward; made into a movie. 4) In 1936. See *The Prime of Life*.

Honey,

I got no letter this week, but I know now it does not necessarily means that you are frozen to death or burnt alive or anything of the kind, so I do not fret too much, though I liked this time when I had to think you were dead to explain a failing letter. I gave your book to the publisher, he says — and I too — it would be good to keep Wright's foreword; we'll take a piece of the translation for *Les Temps modernes*. What title do you choose for your novel, in the end? I guess you have to decide, by now? The first part of my book is done; the typewriter girl is typing it. I feel much relieved though there is still much work about the second part.

Monday we have a big meeting of all the liberal left wing writers. Every writer who is not a communist nor a Gaullist will be there, some coming from Italy and Germany. Wright will speak and I'll translate. Rousset wanted me to speak but Camus, who is a little narrow-minded sometimes and conceited in a womanly way, was angry, because too many people of Les *Temps modernes* were intended to speak. So I shall not, and chiefly I have nothing to say. Nobody has nothing to say, as you know, or everybody has the same thing to say, so there is no use of anybody speaking rather than any other one. Anyway, I hope the whole thing will be a success. The last Garry Davis' meeting was a real success: 12,000 people came, and in France that is a very big number. People want peace, how much they want peace! God help them to get it!

I hope your letter will come soon. I feel sad when I don't feel in touch with you any more. You never come faint in my heart. Let me kiss you.

Your own Simone

Nelson, my beloved one,

How do you know, you conceited man, that my feelings towards you have not changed? Who told you so? I am afraid they have not changed. I hardly remember such an anguish of love and joy; it was so good to get this letter, Nelson, to know you were coming, to hear you say you still love me. I understand, honey; I remember the other letters too. But it is so good to be sure that whatever happens in next years, you'll keep the memories of Mississippi river just as I do, that our dream was true and will for ever be precious to both of us, and above all, Nelson, that we are going to dream together again! Oh! I feel mad tonight, and here are tears, since you like them, tears of love and joy. Nelson, my beloved lover, I am so stern and dry and old when I no longer dare to enjoy my love for you. Your letter gave me back my own heart and all the sweet memories of this sweet faraway and closest time. I don't know, honey, I don't know exactly what you said and what I understood, but I had a bitter time these two weeks (no letter for two weeks, you know), and then this morning all came true. You speak to me in such a friendly warm way, and you say you still love me (I did not believe it any more, but when you say it, I believe it; I never distrust you) and you say you are coming. It is worth being mad tonight. So within some months—four or five, no more— you'll be lying in this bed from which I write to you, you'll see the Van Gogh on the wall. It seems impossible to stand the idea of you, in flesh and blood, near me, of my flesh and blood melting within your arms.

Let me think wisely. I think the best would be if you came beginning of May for I should like to be through with my book too, and for other reasons (money, for instance) it would be more convenient. Can you? For the coming back Chicago, don't take a reservation; it would be better to keep this money to live in France (I'll get you a plane reservation in July or August). I'll get your French money from *T.M.* for what we published and shall publish (we'll take a piece of *Never Come Morning*) and from your publisher. I'll get money of my own and we'll need nothing. Where do you want to go? Venice, Rome, Napoli, Algiers? Do you want to see something in Paris? Let us plan. Planning is so good when it is to come true.

I'll make you happy, Nelson, as happy as we ever were. You told me once that when I smiled to you, I made you fall in love with me again, so I'll smile to you, honey, you'll have to love me as in the first days. I'll love you as on Mississippi, as I love you tonight. Go and buy your ticket; I can write no more. I'll belong to you again. Nelson, will it be as it has been? As in Casa Contenta? As in Caravenseray? I wait for you, my husband.

Your own Simone

Saturday, 18 Décembre 1948

Nelson, my beloved dearest you,

I feel so good since your last letter! I feel young and happy; I am in love, in love with you. I long for you so greedily. I can do without any man if I have to, but when I come to think of you, I cannot do without you. I sent you a silly letter because I was so happy I could not think of anything else; tonight I feel hardly less silly. There is a fine moon in the sky, not so big as our Mississippi honeymoon, but silvery, glittering above glittering roof of Notre-Dame. But now the window is closed, the fire purring; I drank grapefruit juice with gin and I lie in bed, writing to you: it is nearly as nice as Wabansia nest with you instead of my little fire.

So we had this meeting last Monday; 3000 people in the hall and many of them could not go in because it was overcrowded. The cops were awful; they all stood for de Gaulle. They said everybody in the hall were fairies, pansies sold to Moscow, and they hit badly some of those who wanted to come in. Carlo Levi,[1] had come from Italy, lot of foreigners, Africans and Indochineses too. Camus spoke eagerly and vividly but said rather stupid idealistic things. Sartre said good things but sternly; Rousset screamed too harshly and came all sweaty, speaking too much against Russia and not enough against USA. Since Camus did not want me to speak and I did not care for it, I did not; I only translated Wright's paper, a good paper, striking; my translation was, as always, *wonderful*, so *we* were very much applauded. There was a little drama: because many foreigners spoke in a terribly broken French, and we heard politely no time was left for colonial people speaking, they thought we despised them, having asked them to come and not letting them speak—and it is true. Everybody spoke about colonialism, saying we are all brothers, but the leaders of this meeting, Rousset and his friends, in the bottom of their heart don't think an African Negro or an Indochinese man is as good as a white newspaper man. That was wrong, and too the bias against Russia. Then in the whole everybody said what everybody wanted to here; there was much applause and we had a nice gay supper with "petit chablis," eggs and ham. This morning I had a lunch with Carlo Levi; he is funny! I never saw a man so conceited! Even on Wabansia avenue. I don't hate that, from time to time. He said his book, *The Christ Stopped in Eboli,* is really the Bible for the people of the village he speaks about; he said they contrived a newspaper just in order of discussing the book, and one of them put on this card: "Luigi Origlio, a character of Carlo Levi's novel." Is not that nice? He spoke about Italy in an interesting way. If we go to Italy, we'll see him. He is still proud because the oldest of these Bowery's old singing whores—you remember these fat women?—kissed him on the mouth; he will not admit she kisses twenty men each evening, he believes she *chose* him because he is so beautiful! The old childish singer with the big hat, he told me, is dead now.

Nothing else happened, just working, sleeping, eating, loving you. The ugly woman came one morning and sat crying in the middle of the room; she feels so lost, lonely, hopeless that I should have kindly killed her if it had been possible. I am fond of her but there is nothing to do. She had a kind of a fit when going out; I was rather bewildered and a little upset.

Now I'll dream of you. Thanks for all, thanks for hope. I wait for May. We'll have a nice life, you'll see; it will be good to give you all this love I cannot give on paper. My arms will be warm, Nelson, as yours will be. I love you.

Your own Simone

1) Carlo Levi (1902–1975) Italian writer and painter, convicted of antifascism and sent into exile. His most famous work, *Cristo is é fermato ad Eboli* (1945) was written during and about this period.

Tuesday, 21st December 1948

Nelson honey,

Your letter have strange ways. I just got yesterday the one you sent with the pocket-book, yet it was stamped from the 3rd December, Chicago; it did not stay in your pocket. Something happened with the plane, I guess. That is why I stayed two weeks without any letter! And it was a nice letter; I should not have liked to miss it. Don't care for French money, just care to come to Paris. I'll take care of you nicely, as you did when I came Chicago. I think you have your reservation by now and you already know which day you'll open my door, 11 Rue de la Bûcherie.

I am going away to some nice village in the South within a few hours; I am pleased to go away from Paris. I hope it will be blue and warm near the sea.

Did I tell you the ugly woman came and knocked at my door the other morning? She was all crying and shaking because Jean Genet had been wicked with her the day before. He is sadistic with her—many pansies are sadistic, did you notice?—and as he feels she is weak and ready to suffer, he plays an ugly game with her. He told her she was a pedant woman, non-talented at all, an hysterical comedian; she cried and he was more and more insulting. It happened in a bar where one of two other people were; she was awfully disturbed. And she is dying with fear at the idea of coming back to her mother and living near her; she half fainted when we went into

251

the street. So Sartre decided to give her a little money each month for a year; but as she would not take it from him, he has to pretend it is Gallimard who does that, because he is confident her next book will bring money. It is a shame to help Gallimard look so nice and generous, but that is the way it has to be done. She is really interesting. Her mother gave her the worst inferiority complex I ever saw. Indeed, she is ugly, but chiefly she feels guilty about everything. Her mother used to take her within her hands, when she was seven or eight years old, and shook her to death, saying: "You are bad, you are wicked, you are exactly like your father. Heartless child!" And so on for days and days. So now she had nightmares when she says to herself that she is a failure, she is worth nothing; and the whole day is a long nightmare to her. I feel lucky to have no worse nightmare than you.

I got a copy of *She Went to Stay* in English. I don't know if they will publish it in USA too; anyway, I'll send it to you very soon and you'll see what a good book is. Indeed, it is still better in French, but even in English you can feel it is first rate. Speaking of translation, Sartre got a last a script of his play *Red Gloves* such as it is given in Broadway. A shameful betrayal! There is really *not a single word* left in the way it was; they killed all the humour, all the characters, everything in the least detail. Nothing is left but the most badly written, stupid melodrama. And he has no right to stop the play! He will try anyway, but he was so sad while I translated it to him, every sentence scorched his ears, when he thought it had been given as his own production to Broadway people!

You must read Stendhal's *Red and Black*. I don't know if that is the way they translated it. Don't forget, it is hundred years old and may look a little old-fashioned, but it will learn you something about France, and I believe he is the greatest French novelist we ever had. I take *The Possessed* to the country and shall read it over again. I'll call my book *The Second Sex*. In French it sounds nice. Because they always call pansies the third sex, but they never mention that women came in second, and not just equal to men. Yet, it is always implied. It will be such a big book! I gathered lot of amusing stories to put in it.

Now I'll go and get my train. I'll have your letters sent to me; you just go on writing Rue de La Bûcherie. Tell me what you plan for our love-holidays. I'll just do all what you want, as well day as night. I should like deeply to show you Paris, but that is for your sake, so it is up to you. Your last letters made me very happy, honey. I feel all warm again and I want you and I kiss you.

Your own Simone

Happy Christmas to my beloved local youth!

Happy year to you! I wish the new novel will be a big success, you get glory and money, you are lucky with cards and dices, you stay the wonderful local youth you are, and you come to Paris and let me love you! That is my wish of happy new year. Let us be happy once more as we were, honey; there is nothing I want more. Do you feel, Nelson, that we are much farther than half way now? We are coming towards each other. That makes me so impatient that it is often very hard to find sleep in my lonely bed. I hope I'll get your letter. I sent *three* wires to my housekeeper in order to get it. Oh! you should have been angry at me for wasting so many wires! But I was not guilty. It is pretty difficult now to find any hotel on the Blue Coast, because it is winter and most of them are closed. So I asked a tourist office in Marseille and they mixed up everything, saying this one was open, and then it was not. In the end they sent me in a beautiful place and I hope your letter will reach me.

I left Paris last Tuesday with Sartre, where it was so cold, real winter. in Marseille it smelt of dry trees, the sky was cloudless, sunny and warm in the morning. I spent two days there with a room on the old port and N.-D. de la Garde looking at me. Every time I see Marseille I fall in love with it again, as seventeen years ago. I came back often since this time, but never in winter; it seemed to me I really was seventeen years back — a fresh unspoilt remembrance. Everything was full of all meanings. Now I an in a lonely hotel among the very red rocks of the coast and the blue sea. It is so hot that I worked on the terrace. The whole hotel is made to look like a boat, now it is as empty as empty can be, we are the only customers. Just after lunch, I take some short walk in the beautiful red hills; that is one of the countries where I walked and walked, alone, with a rucksack, when I was younger. So I know every path, every peak, every valley — I enjoy seeing it again!

Good night, honey. I am in bed. The sea is moaning; it beats the rocks savagely, but the rocks don't care. I write with a bad French fountain-pen, waiting for the Parker ink. You'll lie near me once more, you, my own Nelson.

Your Simone

Friday, 31 Décembre 1948

Dearest beloved you,

Thanks for the little Christmas card with the good local love, there is nothing I enjoy more than local love. I did not get any real letter from Wabansia, but I think I'll find one or two when I am back in Paris, within six days. Then I'll know if you have get a reservation, when you arrive in France, where, and so on. I long to know it. I have moved away; the hotel was really crazy, trying to look like a boat. On the wall, the landlord called himself captain, and the customers passengers, the water in the bathroom was nicely pink, and chiefly I got a little tired of the landscape. So we came here which is a wonderful little village,[1] still much finer than the one we stayed last year, on the top of a hill, very old, with narrow vaulted streets. Behind are beautiful mountains and plenty of other old villages around. I have a large room with a balcony where I can work when it is sunny. It is fine to think now when I see something; that within some time I'll be able to show it to you. I am working more and more so that the book is over when you come; I am reading the Kinsey Report,[2] which has just been translated in French: there are some very interesting things in it and other rather funny ones! I should be pleased if the same work was already done for women; it would help me for my book. And reading too a story of the Mormons — that is really fun! This Joseph Smith who enjoyed so much having a whole bunch of wives; he was somebody!

I thought of you this morning when I was awaken by a big red sun rising from the sea and coming into the room. I remember everything since the first kiss in the cab, everything stayed warm and wonderful as it was. And all will be true again. I feel very happy today. I say good bye, because I want to work. Happy year to you, beloved dearest you, my own Nelson.

Your own Simone

1) Cagnes. 2) On male sexuality.

1949

Dearest naughty you,

So, here I am in Paris again. I don't enjoy so much being there, but I have to take care of *T.M.* since Merleau-Ponty is going to New York and Mexico; I sent him to Guatemala, Chichen Itza, and everywhere. If he should go to Chicago, I should send it to you; if I do, be nice to him, he is a little cold and fenced in himself, slow, and not brilliant as they use to be in Wabansia Avenue, but he is clever, he has good brain, and he mans well. I should like him to meet you, would you mind? Anyway it is not sure he'll go to Chicago, but it is sure he leaves Paris, and I have to do some real work so the *T.M.* don't become bad and stale just when a new publisher took it in hands. I an so glad the beginning of the year was gay and lively for you. I hate when you seem in bad moods; you smile so pleasantly. What about the reservation? Why did you not get it by now? Silly man, it was not Marseille, the red rocks, but 100 miles farther. I know *your* Marseille, and even knew a dirtier, crazier one, full of whores and brothels as in puebla, but it had been blown up during the war. It will be wonderful to loiter in Marseille together. Do you know the Gérassi are astonished about you? When I was so much scared in September, getting no letter, no wire, I asked them to phone to you to know if you were really still alive. They phoned and somebody answered you were no longer there; a woman's voice they say. So they think you just vanished away, and not knowing how smart you are, they asked themselves wonderingly how you could manage vanish away. They seemed a little pleased at it in their letter because they always enjoy something unpleasant happening to their friends. They would like me a little better if you had just dropped me without explaining anything.

When I arrived home I found a letter from you, just one but a nice letter; it told me you were really coming. Tell me as soon as you are sure of your reservation. I ask myself if I'll go to Le Havre and take you from the boat (Le Havre has been put to pieces by your American pilots; it is a dreary place for a honey meeting), or shall I wait you at the station, but I could miss you and it is a dreary place too. At home would be nice, but you'll never find my home by yourself: taxi-drivers hardly know the street. You cannot ring at the front-door, you have to get the key, so what? It is worth some months deep thinking about it.

What about this Truman's speech? Does it mean anything? Just a little bit of a thing or nothing at all? I don't know about the titles for your novel; it seems to me other titles we discussed were better ones.

9th January

We had some strange time here. Thursday when I get up at 8 A.M., it was still dark, but I hardly noticed it because I lit up the lights. While I was doing my hair and face, half pink half white, with hairpins in my mouth, the electricity was cut! All light went away and outside it was pitch dark! It was really a problem to do something with my half-red lips, half-done hair, since I had to go to the library. It is only because I am so smart that I could succeed: I used my fingers instead of eyes. Then yesterday it rained the whole day and it was so sad that to make myself gayer I bought a beautiful red waterproof; it was the birthday gift I gave to myself! Since this morning I came older by one year: one year wiser, one year nicer, and loving you just the same, so I did not learn much in one year. I deserved a gift too because the first part of the book,[1] a huge book by itself, is over and I'll bring it tomorrow to Gallimard. But I take no rest because I have to be through with the second one before you come and disturb me. Much is done, but there is much to do, and I worked so savagely today that my back aches. It is not late but I am so tired I have to go to bed. Good night, honey. I feel dead; you should have to be there to wake me up for a little while. But you are not there so I'll go to sleep like a decent old spinster. I'll kiss you to death, Nelson, when I'll see you again; in dream I kiss you to death just now.

Your own Simone

P.S. Please don't stick your letter inside the wrapping paper so I cannot get it out; pieces of it remain stuck inside, and I have to make a puzzle of it to put it into a whole again. It is chiefly hard when I find the letter on morning, going to the library, and have to do the work in the street, in the cold and wind, because I am not patient enough to wait until I am in the café.

1) *Les faits et les mythes*, the first volume of *The Second Sex*.

Dearest darling you,

This last Sunday, for once, you came in one of my dreams, at morning. Oh! It was hard to trap you. I had to go to New York with my sister and brother-in-law, and then by the underground, to Wabansia; then I waited and waited in our nest, and I felt that I should wake up before your coming back. I was angry. But you came in the end and we went to the kitchen and we had a real good kiss. I don't know what should have happened afterwards if my alarm-clock had not rung, because sister and brother-in-law were still in the bed-room...I looked at our little picture once more; you seemed so lively, not a dream, my real Nelson. And you'll find the front door, you say, and the door of my room, and your place within my arms? Will you find it, Nelson?

As for the review about Sartre, it is not silly at all, and that is why it is so sad for poor Sartre, but it is entirely wrong, because it assumes that the play is in fact Sartre's play, when there is nothing left of it. Nobody can fancy what they did, if you have not read the script: they left 10% of Sartre's writing, and what they left, they put it in strange places where it had nothing to do. They took away the whole meaning as well political as psychological. And what is worse, they took away the whole style, the peculiar way of speaking, feeling, being witty or dreary that is the author's. It would make me mad if such a thing happened to me, and chiefly with people going on and saying "in the whole, it is *about* the *same* play!"

The book about the Mormons is a very big one and I need no other one; it tells everything about this wonderful story. I know Graham Greene and don't like him much. He wrote some good mysteries when he did not try to be an important writer, but *Power and Glory*, which is his best book, seems to me to be an ersatz of Faulkner for pious old English ladies. He is a Catholic and loves priests and all kind of things I don't like; he is tedious. I am bored with him—he is very popular in France among good bourgeoisie.

I am not sure you would send anything to my mother, you nice man. If you do, a package like last year one would be better than wool and pins because that we have plenty of it in Paris. I ago on reading more and more dreadful things about women. Yesterday, a terrible story about little girls at the end of last century who used to play with themselves; it did not harm anybody, but unhappily they belonged to a very wealthy family who decided it was not moral. So they began to beat the girls (eight and ten years old, poor ones!) and to tie them up all night, and then even in the day. The girls became quite crazy and could not think of anything else except doing what was forbidden. The doctor who was called to "cure" them deprived them of food and in the end he *burnt* them in the right place with *red iron*—three times for each girl—and Swiss doctors at the time said it was the only thing to do with young girls who "abused" of themselves: just to burn them with red iron. The girls tried to jump by the window. It is the doctor who tells the story in the book where I found it, and he seems proud of scaring the girls to death: they had to blow on the fire to make the iron red. Is not that sadistic? Well, they don't do exactly that now, but every day you find in newspapers some sad story of children beaten or starved to death. French children are not happy; it is really a shame parents can do exactly what they want with helpless creatures.

I read stories and write about them in the grey Paris winter, and not much happens. Yesterday evening I saw the ugly woman. She is another person since she gets "money from Gallimard." She does not need any psychiatrist any more; she works well, and eats and sleeps. So I think the best way of curing people is to give them what they want; but it is not always possible, and then there is no way to cure them. The Russian girl, poor one, has still a hole in her lung; she believed it was all over and she just learnt it was not healed at all, so she went half crazy. She goes to the country and will try to recover. It is sad; she wants so much to be healthy again and to be an actress.

And I want you, honey, and if I don't get what I want, no psychiatrist will cure me. Go, and do what you have to do, but come! If you cannot go to France without digging out the "Queen Mary," you have to go and dig it, you lazy man. Come and find me, and do what you have to do. I love you.

Your own Simone

Tuesday, 25 Janvier 1949

Dearest lazy you,

I got your nice letter this morning. Yea, you are a naughty lazy man not to have written for so long, but I feel too good tonight to scold you. The fire is nicely roaring and I made for myself a kind of dry martini; I ate bread and ham, and life does not seem to bad, in the whole.

I have began to plan things seriously for our next honeymoon. First, I ordered red curtains and red blankets so the room looks a little more cosier, and I am contriving to get some Italian money. You'll enjoy Roma and Napoli. I am trying to have real long time to spend with you, since you are not needed in Chicago till September; I'll manage to be quite free. You are wise when you suggest that I could work on when we are in bed! Indeed, I can abstract myself in the most surprising way, chiefly when I am in bed with you. I can deeply think about most difficult topics, so we'll not waste any time, that is a good idea. But I thought that if we spend three or four months together, we should work even out of bed. I want to speak to you about it a bit seriously: you know, I am *sure* that if we spend four months without working, you'll be tired with me and even a little angry at me, as happened last year. As I am so much wiser, I shall never be tired with you, but I shall not be quite pleased about our life. Is not that true? We cannot spend weeks and weeks only looking at landscapes and each other. You should bring your machine and plan some work to do. We could spend some time doing nothing and travelling — as long as we should like. But when we should be fed up with seeing things, we should settle somewhere, in Marseille, Algiers, or in Morocco, and we should spend quiet days writing and swimming in the sea, maybe, loitering in the streets and enjoying each other. What do you think? Tell me. I want these holidays to be really happy, to be part of our real life. Now I begin to know some little things about you. I know you are lazy but you could not be idle. I don't want to have the unhappy feeling of boring you once more, and you'll be bored if you don't work. Then I know you'll tell me you *cannot* work if you are not in Wabansia, but is that true? Just think of it.

Something else, but that I know is quite useless: you should practise a little your French before coming. You should take a good method, some grammar, a French book and a dictionary, and learn something. I am sure you would enjoy and understand France much more if you knew something of the language. When your book is over, why not spend two hours a day learning French?

I think I'll go and take you at the boat in the end, chiefly if you come by Le Havre. I should like to see how you American people destroyed it. Just tell me exactly the day and hour when the boat is due. It will not be very long now, Nelson. I look at this well-known room, and it seems very strange to fancy you in it; very sweet too. I hope you'll be as happy as I'll be: I know how happy I'll be. The big moon will be nice above Notre-Dame, and we'll see how my cold faraway arms will be warm, honey. I remember how warm yours were, and your lips too.

Your own Simone

P.S. Honey, I told you not to *stick* your letter so I cannot take it out, but I did not tell you not to *close* the letter! This one came in an open enveloppe; it is lucky I ever got it. You have to stick the edges of the enveloppe, but not the paper inside the enveloppe. Is not that easy to do? And, please, don't boil all your skin away; I want a whole nice man with his whole skin.

Saturday, 19 Janvier 1949

Dearest darling you,

It is very cold now in Paris, with a chilly mist the whole day long. But I don't mind too much; I wait for spring and I feel good. I saw Dick Wright two days ago. We ate couss-couss together—he loves couss-couss; he has just got a nice little girl (he says she is nice, I didn't see her) and is very happy with it, but he does not seem to work much. He seems awfully tired by having settled in Paris and get a baby, so he goes to Roma for a month. He spoke about African Negroes, and it is funny the way American and African Negroes dislike one another. You remember Diop, who gave you the blanket, and who had published a magazine about which you pretended not to understand anything. Well, Wright worked with him at a time, and now he hates him. He says this meek-sweet-looking black Negro is worse with his white secretary than any white boss ever was with a black servant. Diop pretended it had been a burglary in his office; it was written in newspaper: if fact, he settled this office in the flat of a woman with a lot of children; she wanted him out, and one night she put all his things away, so he said there had been a burglary for publicity sake. A really black, dark story as you see. Another dark funny story here is the Kravtchenko trial.[1] It is a very important Parisian snobbish business. You know what it is about: *Les Lettres francaises*, a communist magazine, pretended that Kravtchenko had not written *I Choose Freedom*, but indeed an American man. In fact Kravtchenko wrote a bad book which I don't trust at all, since he seems himself a treacherous man: maybe he was helped by some American writer who re-wrote it in an American way, but surely he contrived to it. So the trial is silly, because communists cannot prove Kravtchenko did not write the book, and they will lose. They try to prove K. lied, and often they succeed, but then that is a discussion about Russia, not about K.'s book. And he tells them they are liars and accuse him without proofs: that is true too, though is does not mean his book is reliable. Everybody is lying, everybody is wrong, everybody is angry. Kravtchenko himself acts in a very Russian way: he screams, strikes the table with his fist, has fits of anger, and never answers in a proper way. Communists pretend to trap him by disloyal mean; for instance, they asked him: "What about the end of *Doll's House*?" because he speaks of it in his book; he said: "What house?" and they laughed and said: "He does not know Ibsen, he did not write the book!" But in Russian language, the play is called Nora, so it means nothing. All arguments are of this kind. Do they speak about it in USA?

Our last issue of *T.M.* was really good, better than it ever was before, everybody said so. Gallimard is sorry about the whole thing. My friend's name is Merleau-Ponty; he'll come within a month. I'll tell him to go to Chicago. I saw "the young man with the horn" whom I did not see for a long time. He has two babies now and he spend nights playing horn in Saint-Germain-des-Prés for American tourists. He had wonderful records and at least I heard real be-bop: Gillespie, Charlie Parker—a wonderful thing; I like it as much as I liked old New Orleans jazz when I discovered it twenty years ago. But there is no place to hear some in Paris.

I saw the ugly woman and she gave me flowers because it is just four years since we met each other.

The title of my book is *Never Come Woman*.[2] Is not that clear? What is the title of yours?

Honey, what are you going to do when the book is over? I was fretting about it, all these last days. Will you begin another one? Not just now. Then, what? Gamble, drink, and speak about yourself in bookshop parties, learn French, write to me? You will feel empty and useless, I guess. You know, when you are in France, you can speak to me for hours about yourself and I shall never vomit. I liked when you spoke about yourself; you did it once in the bar in Casa Contenta, about the women you knew in your youth, and another time in a French restaurant in New York, you spoke about your books and why you were writing. Oh! I loved you so much these two nights! I could feel so warm, so rich and happy. Shall I love you as much in future?

Good bye, honey. Now I'll work. I begin to be awfully tired working so much, but I'll manage to be fine again when you come. Anyway, you'll make me fine. I love you as ever; you are my dearest dear you.

Your own Simone

1) Kravchenko, a Soviet engineer, was tried January 24, 1947, in Paris for publicly denouncing the danger of communist dictatorship. His biography, *I Chose Freedom*, was written with the help of Eugene Lyons.   2) A parody of Algren's *Never Come Morning*.

Wednesday, 9 Février 1949

How did I spend such a long time without writing to my darling dear you?

It is a shame. Nothing happened; it is just that time went away so fast. Maybe it is because nothing happened that I did not feel so much like writing what was happening. Winter weather turned a little to spring; my love for you just turned to the same love: Kravtchenko trial went on, these strange Russian people (still stranger than Wabansia ones) went on screaming at each other, lying one after the other and sometimes mysteriously laughing heartily together. Kravtchenko's wife was the most important star. Everybody was anxious to see how she was dressed, this Russian woman! Well, she was dressed like any French or American girl. She said her husband had been bad tempered and did not want children. It seems Kravtchenko lied a lot in his book, but the Russian Stalinists who came to speak against him are lying too; everybody seems very dirty and silly.

The poor woman who swallowed a pin in faraway days died last week without knowing at all she was to die. The poor husband is as sad as sad can be; he had put everything in wife and children, he never wrote (he could have), he just tried to get money to make the family happy, and now he is left a widower with three little children. I did not see him yet, because she was burried in the country, but I am a little afraid of it.

Somebody I saw with much pleasure is the old André Gide, the oldest living French writer, I guess (you know, the one who got the Nobel Prize for having written all his life long that it was fine to be a pansy). He had a wife once, but never slept with her; he slept once with a woman and had a daughter; he contrived a marriage between this mother of his daughter and his dearest love, so the girl slept with two pansies in her life. Now he lives with the nice old lady who is this woman's mother: his daughter's grand-mother. Is not that a pretty family? Anyway, he seems happy with this kind of family; they all love him dearly. He tells lots of stories in the nicest way. He was asked to go to Chicago to get a Goethe prize of 5000 dollars—that is not bad —but he feels too old; he is afraid of USA. It is strange to come so old and well-known at the same time, you really begin to live, you can do and say what you want, everybody is always approving you. Would you not like it?

There are lot of abortion affairs just now in France, and I feel quite indignant about them. They have no kind of birth control here; it is forbidden. So there are every year as many abortions as births, about one million, but abortion is awfully forbidden. They just arrested a doctor I knew very well and to whom I had sent a lot of worried girls; he helped the poor ones as well as wealthy ones. Another surgeon jumped by the window last week, because he had been taken in this kind of bad affair. Still a father who beated his young son nearly to death has only been scolded by the judge: he did not even go to jail. It seems when the child is born, you can kill him if you think it would be fun, and to have been killed in war is just the thing for which he had been made. But when he is in the mother's belly, then it is a murder to do anything against him. I am complaining to you: can you do nothing about this state of things?

What about the reservation? And the book? Tell me, tell me. I had the kitchen stove mended so we can cook here when you come. Everything will be ready for you: you'll bring one nice bottle of scotch, will you? I am sad not to see you packing things to come to France. I love to see you doing practical things, you do them so well! Remember when we bought nice shoes and nice pants for you in New Orleans and a tiger passed by, you would not believe me when I said so?

So, be a nice man as you use to be; begin to be busy about this long trip. Don't forget the paper for the pictures you'll take in France and Italy. Good bye, honey, good bye. See you soon. And don't forget to bring local love to match mine.

Your own Simone

Wednesday, 16 Février 1949

Dearest silent you,

It seems such a long time since I got a letter: more than two weeks, I guess. It makes me rather blue; you seem so far away that I cannot really believe you'll be near my heart in the beginning of May. You will, honey, will you? So I don't feel too much like writing myself. Maybe you are tired with words so much more because we'll soon get something else? Spring is coming slowly, sweetly, through cold days turning to mild ones. My book becomes thicker and thicker as you come nearer and nearer, which is as it should be. Nothing worth telling happens.

The Kravtchenko trial goes on in the same crazy way; it is a pity nobody understands what these strange Russian people say to one another when they scream so hard. We met Koestler yesterday; now he owns a house in Paris surroundings and he asked us to go and spend a week-end: we said we could not. Then he asked to spend an evening in Paris: we said we could not. Then he asked to have a lunch together and then Sartre said he *would* not, and we explained to Koestler that we could have nothing to do with somebody who was Malraux's friend and de Gaulle's supporter. So he was rather angry and looked beaten and I enjoyed it very much.

I had a hard evening, and I am still deeply moved about it, with the poor friend who has just lost his wife and is left a widower with three little children. It was maybe the only married people I know about whom I could say: they really love each other, with the utmost warmth in flesh and heart. He told me all about her death, the burial, and how hard it was to see the children not caring at all bout what happened, how hard to come back home in Paris and find the place empty for ever. He did not complain, was sober and friendly, and that is what made everything worse. I had night-mares the whole night. Do what you want, honey. Be a naughty man, stop loving me if you have to, but don't die, please don't die. I could not stand it. You promise?

You came in my dreams once more, into my bed and something hap-pened. I was a little disappointed; it was not exactly what it used to be, but you cannot expect too much from a dream-man. It was nice anyway to come from so faraway. Did you get the reservation? Is the book over? I wait for your letter. I'll write soon a better one myself. I just wanted to send you some little kisses and remind you there is a Nelson-loving woman in Paris, 11 Rue de la Bûcherie. Don't forget her. Good bye, my lonely one, my beloved one. I keep on being

Your own Simone

Sunday, 20 Février 1949

Dearest beloved you,

I feel much better since I got your rather nice letter. When you are silent, I always fear you have just been married and got five children, and I'll never see you again. I advertise you, honey. You *cannot* do that to *me* just now: now the gas-stove is mended, the red curtains are ordered, the Italian money is being bought. I told everybody I should vanish during summer, and I wait for you from morning to night, and sometimes the night too. So if you cheat me, after having trapped me, I'll just come and shot you (with all the children). I am afraid now I got the letter for another reason: you seem to intend to do nothing but gamble, and drink, and see strange people; you'll be left without money, without garments, without head, and you'll not be able to come, or you'll just bring to me a ruined local man. All of that is very bad. You have to shut yourself in Wabansia nest and learn French and write letters to me — that is enough to make your days joyful and useful. Once a week, you go out and you buy some nice thing to bring to France: a bottle of scotch, some candies, another bottle of scotch, Southern Confort. And then you begin to pack — a hard job; you cannot come Paris without a well-done packing, you must make yourself smart and beautiful. Then you must *plan* carefully our nights and days; there will be many of them, and each of them has to be carefully planned. What do you think of that: Paris-Marseille-Italy-Tunis-Algiers-Morocco-Marseille-Paris? It could be done; look at the map and ponder.

What is the real title of the book? If you don't get the proofs in New York in time, you can have them sent by plane 11 Rue de la Bûcherie. My own book will never be over in May though I am working crazily. Well, it will have to wait, that is all; it does not matter so much.

Did I till you I got a letter from the Gérassi? It seems awful; they have been said two years ago to move to France, and as they did not, they are said now that they will be deported to Spain (as he was a red general in the Spanish War). They have no money at all, she lost her job, he had never any but painting. The boy sells newspapers, but that is not enough to live nor to pay an adviser. I don't know what to do for them.

Now I'll go to work again. I don't write very much all these days because I work too much, but I do love you very well, really well, and I'll make you fell it within some weeks. So there is no use telling it again and again. I wait as impatiently as I did last year, and I'll be as crazy as last year when I'll see this silly face of you. I kiss you, honey.

Your own Simone

Dearest coming you,

Sure, one letter at least was lost. I did not know you had a reservation; it made me very happy. I guess you'll be in Cherbourg 9th or 10th May, is that so? I'll not go to Cherbourg; it is an ugly, sad, destroyed town—you'll sure have a train right on. I'll go to the station in Paris and pick you to Rue de la Bûcherie. I like the title you told me and I heartily congratulate you for having finished the book. I should be pleased to have done the same thing! We go on towards spring, slowly, slowly: my neighbourhood is really poor and dirty but not unpleasant: lot of Arabians chiefly; at night you can hear Arabian music from the little café across the street, and there are Arabian movies; many bums too and forgotten men. Yesterday I saw an old woman with lot of cigarette ends around her and putting the tobacco in a big box: she sells it afterwards on the place Maubert for a quarter of the real price; there are a lot of customers eager to buy any kind of tobacco at a low price. You'll see all these things. I enjoy thinking so!

The Kravtchenko trial is no longer funny; there was an interesting witness, a German communist woman whose husband disagreed with the official CP policy in 1936; *he* was called to Russia to discuss it with the central comity and then sent to a camp in south Russia (a terrible working-place) where he died. *She* was *given* to S.S. who sent her to Ravensbrück. She told the story in a simple dignified way, and even the communists were very much impressed.

I saw the poor widower one evening more. Each time it makes me sick; I have nightmares the whole night long. He goes on reading old letters, not knowing in what time he lives, since past time looks more real than death of the loved woman. And saw Camus too, with Sartre; everybody was nice and friendly, but we found we had nothing more to say to each other. Camus, though he is not for de Gaulle nor for communism, disagrees with us on almost very topic. He took very seriously this Davis affair, which is not serious at all. And I told you, he cannot stand a failure; it is too evident that he resents it.

A young ugly Negro with an awful huge beard had just achieved the translation of *America Day by Day*; he likes it though he says there are some errors. He is looking for a publisher. Can you give me an idea? Who could be interested by such a thing?

Honey, the nearer you come, the less I enjoy writing. I think of you all day long as of a real being, living in Paris with me: you already are no longer in Wabansia. How can I send letters to you? Do you feel how impatiently, lovingly, I wait for you? I never loved you with a warmer love.

Your own Simone

Dearest, sweetest you,

You were really a nice man to send this package to my mother. She was so happy, she asked what kind of people were these Algren folks, and I said the woman chiefly was very kind, and I should thank them in her name, so that is what I do. Thank you, nice local man, thank you very much!

It is winter suddenly. I am afraid spring and summer have already come, you have come and I did not notice it. It is snowing since yesterday, awfully cold, windy, grey, and sad. I don't care too much; I'll soon go to South once more for three weeks or so as I did last year; you'll be near when I come back, you'll bring the sun to me as you said once I brought to you. I have bought lot of nice paintings for our nest: one more Van Gogh, one Toulouse-Lautrec, which you'll like I guess, and one Picasso you'll not like maybe (but then we'll put it away), and I am buying beautiful white-leather armchairs. I hope you'll find my place "really elegant."

I am worried not because I want my book typed before going away. The woman who usually types for me has not time enough to do all of it, and I cannot find in whole Paris another woman able to read my writing. How do you read it so easily? Or maybe you just pretend to? I work more and more feverishly as time goes on.

Yesterday I met for the first time a very good French poet named Char. He is quite a hero of the "maquis"; he told wonderful stories of all kinds; I thought of telling them to you, but I have to keep some for the time you are here. It is nicer to tell them by mouth. You'll say they are lies, but they will not be.

My sister is going away to Morocco and my mother is very happy. She pretends to love her daughters more than anything but she likes anything better than seeing us. The fact which worries me a little is I should like to show you Morocco, but I should not like to meet her. Chiefly, though my sister "loves" me too, there is so little intimacy between us, she cares so little for my life that I should not like to tell her anything about you. That is strange. I could introduce you to Gérassi, and I should to some other friends, but I should feel guilty saying anything about my love life to my sister. We'll see what we'll do.

I saw some American intellectuals. One is a very nice pansy who lived a long time among Indians, wear a ring in his ear and green boots on his feet. There are more American people than ever in Paris now; you could never find a room if I should not shrewdly reserve one for you in some hotel I know. Today I took a walk on the "grands boulevards," the black heart of Paris; it looked very old, very faraway, very moving. I want you to like Paris. I'll show you nice things in a nice way. Come, honey, we'll be happy, you'll see. You are my dearly waited for own Nelson, and I as ever

Your own Simone

Mercredi, 9 Mars 1949

Nelson, my love,

I got an awful cold, a kind of light influenza. I had to take pills and drink hot drinks: the barman gave me a mixture of bourbon, brandy, rum, cognac and boiling water. Not much hot water. I drank glasses and glasses of it, first in order to recover, and second because I was with sister-brother-in-law who are very boring. I am in bed, a little drunk, my eyes crying; it is such an ugly woman who is writing to you! She'll be prettier on the 11th May.

Between Marseille and Algiers, I suggested Italy; I am sure you would like Venice, Roma, Napoli. One month drinking real Chianti, eating spaghetti, seeing Italian towns would be fine, it seems? If you don't want it, I'll sell the money back, though I was very proud to have get it. When we are together *you* may come sullen but never do I. If the book is not done, I'll do it only if it is convenient for *us*. But if not, I'll never be sullen. I looked at our picture; we seem really nice, both of us. I am never so nice when you are not there. Shall I be so nice again? Bring your money; you'll sell it at the black market. It is very easy; you'll get twice what you would get officially. Odessa Hotel is in Montparnasse—my Russian friend lived there once; Lutétia Hotel is much more select—German officers lived there during the war. But I found a smarter place for you, that is the La Bûcherie-Beauvoir Hotel, very select and somewhat peculiar. Anyway, if you like better the other ones, just tell me. I'll get a reservation for you...

Nelson, stupid loved man, how can you think I could have *forgotten* about *Never Come Morning*? The translation is being made, the translator enjoys doing it because he is crazy and enjoys doing the most impossible things. About the publisher, I wanted to be really sure to tell you, one of them said: "They have published too many bad American novels, so we can no longer afford to publish a good one." The fact is he has no money and does not publish anything. Books don't sell now in France.

Nelson, I am dead. I sniffed and coughed and cried all this letter long; now I'll try to sleep.

Saturday

The grogs I drank the other night were not enough to cure me. It is nothing serious but I could hardly work, I stayed in bed, and this morning all my head is sore: eyes, ears, nose, cheeks, and teeth. It will not be a joyful day since I proposed my poor widower friend to go with him in car to see the place his wife is burried. And now the weather is bad, awfully cold, and I am tired.

Why don't you learn French, lazy man?

Next Thursday I leave Paris for three weeks, I go to the same place as last time, in the South. There I'll work quietly and get good health again. I am too tired, good bye, honey. Go on writing a little, even if it seems a bit useless, because it helps to wait, it helps to make you real and enjoy your coming. On this side of the Atlantic Ocean there is much love waiting for you.

Your own Simone

Thursday, 17 Mars 1949

Dearest beloved you,

I am just sending a little kiss before leaving Paris. I am very busy, since I go away within a few hours, but I got your small nice letter and I feel like sending you a nice kiss. It seems spring begins today, even in Paris, and I know I'll find spring in Cagnes, so I feel good and happy with a nice man planning to come and see me somewhere in the world (Wabansia, Chicago, USA). I was rather sick and stupid all these days long. You would have been fond of me as in Mexico, the egg-murder day. Now I am quite bright again and you would not like me so much, I know I scare you a little when I am too healthy. Still, I hope to be as healthy as possible on 11th May.

I told you your novel is being translated; the translator enjoys the job because it is so difficult and he enjoys difficulty. But I think he will be very pleased to have a nice chat with you in May so you can explain him exactly what all this Polish slang means. We'll publish some part of it in *T.M.* It is wonderful how *T.M.* get well since we left the wicked Gallimard: twice as many copies are needed as were beforehand. Gallimard is ashamed; we are awfully pleased. The Indochinese business is as dreadful as any lynching story ever was in USA; it is even worse. At night, yellow people dare not go out in the streets, because if they do, they are beaten to death: that is Paris. In Indochina it is awful as well for your French soldiers as for Indochineses. The French government has just made an agreement with Bao-Daï whom everybody in Indochina hates, who is a traitor to France and Indochina at the same time, and so this war will go on: our Vietnam friends are very sad and even scared.

Good bye, honey. I'll wait for you in Cagnes as I did in Paris. I'll love you the same. A long warm kiss, Nelson.

Your own Simone

Cagnes, Wednesday, 23rd Mars 1949

Dearest darling you,

It is a shame not to have written a whole week, but as I know that you know how I am waiting for you now, how I always faithfully loved you, that seems rather useless to write. As for the pleasant landscape here, what I should like to do is to show it to you. I shall. You ought to bring with you our little diary and the pictures from Guatemala and Mexico. I should like to go through these memories with you near me. I never dare to think of them too much; it is rather painful when you are far away. I got a card from Merleau-Ponty, from Taxco, with the church on it, and I felt a pang in the heart. I was fond of Taxco though you were not. And we had a nice time hearing the radio in the little café in front of the church, at night. Remember?

I left Paris last Thursday, slept in the train, and it was Nice, the Méditerranée, and then this lovely place—the same village where I spent some days in January. I have got a nice room, with a little porch looking towards the sea. What is funny in this old middle-age French village is all the houses now belong to American artists or rather esthets, the kind of old crazy women and pansies and all that you find in Greenwich village, Santa Fe, and in some places in California. They own little peasant houses with small gardens, and in the morning I see the old ladies, wearing velvet pants and pouring water on the flowers. At night they come to the bar in the hotel and they drink. I don't drink. I work feverishly all day long, except after lunch when I take a walk or a ride in a car. The weather was not very fine this first week, but now it is again what it uses to be in the south: blue and sunny. There are lot of little fruit trees all covered with flowers—no leaves, only flowers—the kind Van Gogh painted. I love them. They grow flowers for sale on all the little hills around: carnations, chiefly. They have kind of little houses for the flowers; they put a little roof on them at night and take it away when it is sunny.

I am reading again *The Seven Pillars of Wisdom* and the letters of T. E. Lawrence. What a man he was! A very strange, very appealing one, with a strange sense of humour and yet so hard towards himself, and deeply serious about the things he really meant. He can write too. I don't remember if you read the book. The beginning is tedious, when he describes all the tribes of Arabia, but then it cames fascinating—it would be a good book to read on the boat, if you don't spend your whole time learning French...Had you time enough for gambling and drinking? Well, you have still six weeks left. I forgot to tell you, at the Bûcherie-Beauvoir Hotel you may have for breakfast *everything*. Is not that enough? Will Odessa and Lutétia be better? And at Beauvoir Hotel you get love at every hour, if you care for it, preserved or fresh love, first rate one—in the other hotels it is difficult to get.

I am waiting for a letter myself, and as always waiting for you. I think of you day and night, Nelson. Six weeks. I'll kiss you to death, honey. It will be so sweet to kiss you.

Your own Simone

Cagnes, Wednesday, 30 Mars 1949

Dearest darling you,

Now days are flowing away easily towards 20th May—sunny, quite, and pleasant, just as they were last year at the same time. I spent three weeks in the South too, not very far from here, working at the same endless book, not working so hard because I did not intend to finish it, and waiting for you. It will be pleasant to have you in my country this year. Since you like doing a little travelling-job every day, I'll suggest one: maybe you could ask for an Italian visa? French people need a passport to go to Italy, but no peculiar visa; I guess it is still easier for American people, maybe you could just ask? I have money for a month in Italy, I told you; we'll live like king and queen.

What a strange man this Lawrence (T.E.)! He conquered Arabia, wrote a great book, and then he chose to live for seven years as a mere soldier, with a false name, hating the army, the officers, and the other soldiers. Doing it just because he hated it. Can you understand that you smart man?

Two days ago I hired a cab and I went to see my sick Russian friend. She spent winter in a beautiful village nearby, trying to recover.[1] Her husband was there with her for some time but he has to work in Paris and she remained alone for weeks. She translated bad American books—people make a lot of money publishing bad American thrillers; good novels are more difficult to sell. She walked all around and hoped she was cured. What is sad is I knew from Paris she has still bad germs in her lungs. I had to put her to the train, and before I took a long ride with her. She enjoyed seeing the landscapes, my own beautiful village, and pleasant hotel, and she told me a lot of stories; in this country there are witches and many strange kind of people. I was pleased to see her, to make her a little happy, and I felt fond of her. But then she was afraid to go to Paris and to learn what I knew, and she did not. I felt a pang in the heart when I saw the train moving away towards the awful truth. It must be terrible to hope, despair, hope, despair, months after months, for years.

Honey, I got your nice letter. It was sweet to read it on my little balcony, looking at the blue sea. I always like the stories about Farrell,[2] he seems the worst kind of conceited, dull worth-nothing writer you could find in USA or France!

Now I come back to my book. I don't hope any longer to have it finished when you come, maybe two weeks later, if you sleep enough during the day to let me work a little, what I guess you'll do.

Good bye, Nelson. I feel very happy. I know how good it will be to be near you again! Write to me in Paris, now. Ah! Try to know if you have not a train going straight from the boat to Paris, and at what time it is due. I think it is better to meet you there. It means just two hours difference and I have not to wait during the customs and all that, customs, passports, that is awfully long on boats. I'll go to the station.

Love, love, love, love, love.

Your own Simone

1) Cabris, where Simone de Beauvoir took Algren. 2) James Farrell, an Irish novelist living in Chicago, author of *Studs Lonigan* and *Danny O'Neill*. Like the critic Philip Rahv, he had Marxist leanings.

Dearest beloved soon-coming you,

What a lazy girl you have got! I don't even write more than you now. In fact, I did not get a new letter since a pretty long time, but I guess my Parisian lodger kept it home and I'll find it Monday 11 Rue de la Bûcherie; write there. I left the nice hotel in Cagnes a week ago; they needed my beautiful room and I wanted some change. I came to a big wealthy hotel — not the kind you and me really like, but it is at the end of a cape, directly above the sea, among a big wild wood full of pines and yellow flowers; it is wonderful. The hotel is empty, the room large and full of sun, wind, and roaring sea, so I feel very good. Today I looked at the sea, with the waves coming and coming towards me stubbornly and never going any where, and I thought within a month another sea with other waves will bring you to me. That will make sense. Nelson, honey, I want you so much.

Tell me where you'll stay in New York so I can sent a last letter, or maybe a wire: "Don't come. I just got another man, a black-bearded non-local one." Anyway, tell me everything about your arrival. I am near Menton, here, half a mile from the Italian border. Some days ago I went by bus along the Italian rivieras; I saw it fifteen years ago, it is pretty: old villages with vaulted streets. Maybe we'll go to Italy this way from Marseille: French and Italian rivieras, Genova, Roma. If you are a very nice man, I'll let you gamble in the Monte Carlo big gambling place (Monte Carlo is a kind of Las Vegas or Reno, everything for gamblers and gambling; there are waiters in the garden, waiting to prevent unlucky gamblers to commit suicide). But if you are not really good, I'll just show you the fishes in the aquarium. Walking, working, reading, that is all. I went through the Lawrence's letters: 800 big pages, that is something. What a man! Some people would call him neurotic, some of them did: staying a soldier until he died on a motocycle, twelve years being just a soldier (and not liking war, officers, army) when he was offered a lot of interesting, well-paid jobs — and he was a real celebrity! I am fond of him, though he could be hateful sometimes (so are you, I remember).

Genet came to Menton yesterday with his last dark-haired beautiful lover. They have hired a little flat in the old town and he came to the hotel; we had some scotches together. He was nice. He had written a really first rate book,[1] recently, telling about his prostitute youth in Spain, a hard life.

Hard not the way your can have been, hard because really base, bad, and contemptible—he felt it so; he still feels the guilt of having been a prostitute, fawning people for money, and so on. But he is very depressed because his play was a failure and got bad reviews.

I corrected the whole proofs of my first volume; it will be just published when you come. Let this letter bring you kisses and love as always.

Your own Simone

1) *Journal de voleur,* dedicated to "Sartre and Castor."

Paris, 11th April 1949

Dearest lovely you,

Within just a month, I trap you again, honey, that is a nice thing to think. I got your letters this morning, just arriving from south by night train. Two of them. And nice ones too.

Do you know 375,000 American people are coming this year? You'll hear nothing but American language in Paris and Marseille. Honey, I'll inquire about the boat. I know the station you'll arrive from Le Havre, I'll find the time and come to the station. If I don't find you, I'll come back home. I'll send you my phone number next time (I don't even know it for I never phone to myself). Anyway I know we'll meet.

Put on your bright yellow shirt. Please "just come" and don't care for money. This year I have plenty of it and you can be my guest. Maybe I'll be your guest once more in USA. If not, it does not matter. Don't borrow money, that is *very serious*. The translation is going on and if the money for the book is paid next year and if I need it, you'll repay it to me. It seems money is no question between you and me. Who happens to have some has, and then it becomes ours: or don't we love each other? You need not bring soap! Do you think we never wash in France? We sometimes do. Really, just bring your own clothes and some scotch and, if you can, some love. But since your Marshall Plan we have even American fruit juice and everything here. Don't worry about anything. You'll be my guest and I'll have you feel like the Ali Khan.

I am glad you like Stendhal, he was a nice man. So are you. Come honey and let me love you.

Your own Simone

P.S. I received the cigarettes.

* Algren arrived in Paris by boat at the beginning of May, moving into Simone de Beauvoir's apartment on the Rue de la Bucherie. De Beauvoir introduced him to her friends and to the city. Then they traveled: Rome, Naples, Ischia, Tunisia (Djerba), Algeria, Fez, Marrakesh, Paris via Marseille, a trip to Cabris to stay with Olga and Bost, back to Paris. Algren flew home in September.

Tuesday night, 13 Septembre 1949

Nelson, my only love,

It was the hardest and sweetest parting—the hardest because I never loved you so much, the sweetest because I never felt so much your warm, precious beloved love. We belong to each other; we shall stay together even across the ocean, now I know it for sure. I feel safe in your good warm heart; even if you kiss other girls, you'll never find a heart that loves you so hard, not such a loving mouth as mine.

Honey, the night was so beautiful when I went away, alone in this car where you had been near me. Your seat was there, empty and yet haunted with your faraway presence, and high up in the sky, red lights were silently burning, and other stars moved slowly, carried by planes; there was still a red pathetic sigh in the sky. I came home and cried my eyes out of my head, but it was not the harsh hopeless bitterness of New York tears, when I believed love was dead; it was as crying on your dear patient shoulder, still in my own Shangri-la.

I could not sleep these two nights. I shall not now neither, it seems; it is two in the morning—for you, 8 P.M. I guess you are drinking martini with your agents and telling some lies about camels-dining-cars, or something like that. I am glad to go away; it is impossible for me, just now, to sleep in this home where you are not.

I take waking pills in the day, and I run around a little madly; nothing seems true. My true self, my true life have gone away across the sea. I had a great pleasure yesterday morning, after this first hard night: I found the review in the *Times*, a very good review though not very shrewd, and your picture, not so bad: it seems a good start. Please, will you send me all the reviews, good or bad, about Frankie?[1] The typist is through with all what Guyonnet already translated and I bring it to Cagnes with me and shall work steadily to rewrite it in real good French.

At night Monday, there was your wire; thanks, my love, a stone fell from my heart. Sure, it was nice to dream of you flying high up above white snowy clouds, but it did not seem quite safe. I felt sea-sick the whole day; I began to breathe in a nearly normal way when I got the wire. Honey, I am too tired to go on. I'll write from Cagnes. I just wanted to send my love from Paris. I know you know, as you know that I know. I did not think neither that any-body could be so happy as you made me; I did not think to know again the sweet bitter wonder of love. Nelson, it is so good to love you. I want you to miss me, sweetheart, but I want you to be happy in Wabansia. I should like to have such poise myself. The missing Nelson part is easy to do; the other one not seems so successful just now. Still, meeting you was one of the greatest lucks of my whole life. I know I can begin to wait again for our next embrace. Thank you for all, my love. Tonight I shall not cry; I'll try to fall asleep in your strong warm loving arms.

Your own Simone

P.S. I put your dirty little underwears in a coffin and the good concierge nicely wrapped the package. I am just going to send them before getting into the plane. I send a baby-monster too.[2]

1) Frankie Machine, the hero of *The Man with the Golden Arm.* 2) A reference to a separate package.

Cagnes, Thursday, 15th September 1949

Bonjour, mon amour,

How are you? How is the little pin head, the silly face, the muddy eyes, the strange elephant mouth? How is all my dear nice pack of dirt? I guess you just drink martinis all around New York, telling lies and other lies and other lies all the day long. Here I am, in the nice village where we drank whisky with Bost-Olga, and where you could not live a week, you said, without wanting to kill yourself. Instead, I feel I just begin to come slowly back to life. Since Sunday, I am sick inside, as after some unknown acci-dent. What happen to me, do you know? It seems during my sleep some nasty surgeon came with knife and saw and cut away, what? I still have got two legs and arms, and what I used to use as a head, but inside something is missing, I know; it is all empty and painful. I really spent these three days as a kind of dull dream, with something quietly but stubbornly crying inside me. Well, this morning it begins to heal a little, maybe within two days or three I'll be able to work again.

I already told you I spent these first days wildly running around. Lot of things I delayed when you were there, because I did not want to stop bothering you more than one hour a day, so I had to go to Gallimard, *Temps modernes,* dress-maker, and so on. I saw Mouloudji and read his next novel. It has the same kind of queer quality as this "cyclope" sentence which struck you so funny; I worked a little with him about his manuscript and gave him, I hope, some good advices. The morning following this night when you were so bored for not under standing French, he had to go to work at half past six in the morning. He slept one hour and wake up utterly sick, miserable, and stupid; he had to play the part of a stupid groggy murderer who recognizes his crime by mere drunkness; he acted so good—being stupid and groggy—that everybody congratulated him. Unhappily, the shooting was no good—the pictures were all blurred and he had to begin again in the afternoon. Then he just did the average thing and the sleepless night was of no use in the end.

I have a dinner Monday with Sartre, Bost, and Olga, who came back from Cabris in bus: they say the beginning of the trip, the first day, is wonderful, but the second one rather tedious. Olga wants to play, she did not look too bad. They were very nice and spoke of you with much friendship, though remembering with disgust the way you gulped away the whole bottle of whisky with the singer-woman sitting on your lap.

This old friend, Maheu, who called so urgently the other evening, was in terrible despair, because his young mistress is going to have a child and wants to keep him, and wants him to leave his wife—the wife is old and sick, half crazy with jealousy and sexual frustration. Leaving her would be a murder. A common story for middle-aged husbands but not less terrible for that. He really looked like a lost hopeless man, though he had been a very bright boy, he resents dreadfully the waste of his life without being able to prevent it. He could not let me go, wanting to speak about it, and I dreaded coming back to my lonely bed, so, though tired to death, I stayed at the terrace of the "Lipp" until two after midnight; when I came home, the old woman next flat opened her door, on pretext I had received an important phone call (which in fact was not important) and she begin to tell me about her daughter's suicide, life in concentration camps—a story of utter misery. Then, at last, I could go to my room and I wrote to you a first letter; once more I could not sleep, haunting by this terrible feeling of loss, though I know you are not lost. In morning, Nice, Cagnes; I slept and read stupid books all the afternoon long and at night was eaten by mosquitoes. A strange thing is that I go on speaking to myself in English most of the time. I have lot of books, and letters to answer, work to begin, and I hope I'll soon love you in a less painful way. Though there is much sweetness in this painful way too, for you are still all mixed with me, and I all melted in you, as when our hair was mingled together in the middle of our body.

Your own Simone

Cagnes, Sunday, 18 Septembre 1949

My own Nelson, my faraway love,

Shall I count a week after another for fifty weeks, each of them so long? Yesterday evening I could nearly see you with my inside eyes: you were wearing your best grey suit, a blue shirt and a tie, and sitting in the theater, listening to *Death of a Salesman*;[1] the only bad point was, at 8 P.M. here, it was just the beginning of the afternoon for you, and when you got into the theatre hall, I was asleep. Tell me everything, honey. How you were dressed, what you have just eaten, how many holes adorn your present underwear, where did you put the pots—all these things I cannot live any longer without knowing. I begin to sleep nicely without mosquitoes nor bad dreams, but the mornings are always hard, when I wake up and my legs look for your legs and my cheek for your shoulder. I did not seriously begin to work. I wrote lot of letters, I read and reviewed for *Les Temps modernes* a big book about marriage in primitive societies all around the world;[2] I spent as much time as I could on that job, but now it is over, and I am afraid of tomorrow: I'll have to begin, I can no longer escape.

Honey, why did you give me this book to read, the *Strong Lamb* by some Thorne Smith? The story of an uninteresting man changing himself into a horse, a gull? I knew once a man who was a crocodile and a woman who was a frog, but that was another story...a much better one. I read too a little O'Hara's novel, *Butterfly*, and a good translated book of short stories and essays by Thurber, some were very funny. I have brought *Of Human Bondage*[3] to obey you, but it seems awfully heavy.

Monday

I begin to hope I'll soon get a letter, but I guess you have been terribly busy in New York. I'll send this little scrap of paper without waiting; it means

278

love. Be happy, my love. There is such a nice Nelson in my heart, it would make you happy to think of him. Kiss me good bye, sweetheart.

Your own Simone

1) By Arthur Miller, 1948. 2) *Les Structures élementaires de la parenté* by Claude Levi-Strauss; the review appeared in *Les Temps modernes* in November 1949. 3) By Somerset Maugham, 1915.

Cagnes, Saturday, 24 Septembre 1949

Dearest Division Street Dostoyevsky,

I began to feel a little blue, not getting any news from you. Still, I guessed you really had no time in New York merry go round to write to your poor little gauloise. I kept hoping you nevertheless had preserved some little bit of the old love in some dark, faraway corner of your heart. This morning your big fat letter came, and on my love, it makes you so real once more! You had come back in your blood and flesh reality some days ago, through a letter from Cau to Sartre: he said you came and woke him up, and you took him passionately in your arms, he added modestly that he suspected you were kissing Europe rather than himself; so, maybe it was me you were kissing. If it had been me, some other things would have happened, I am afraid.

Something else stays here with me: I spend these weeks with Bruno Bicek.[1] Every day I work at least one hour by myself on this damned translation, and on hour more with Sartre at evening: he began to enjoy putting Guyonnet's jargon in good French; it is a kind of game, and he manages it wonderfully well, much better than I do. But then he does not do more than five typed pages — that means one printed one! — in a day! So, ten pages in the whole book will be of the most refined, striking style, and then... I don't know. Anyhow I'll try hard to improve what is done. On the whole, you may be confident your book will not be betrayed.

Honey, I am so glad with your success! I was practically sure of it, because I like the new book so much and I trust my own judgment (though you don't always), but I am glad it really happened. These reviews are quite good; send me other ones, the bad ones too. I began working on this novel! I just write everything that comes in my head, not trying to put any order between people and incidents, so it is not too hard. It will be harder when I'll have to make a whole bundle with all these meaningless pages. I live exactly like last year: work from 9 to 13 h., lunch with Sartre on the little terrace you know, and often some drive. Then work from 17 to 20 h., dinner, a little walk in the village and books.

I went back twice to this beach on the sea-side where we swam, Bost, you, and me, but I did not swim, very few people did; the hotels were closing. The second time, the hotels were closed, the sea came dangerous looking and beautiful; there was nobody. Well... there will be another summer, and again your arms around me.

I had a wonderful drive in the mountains too, a long one, among deserted landscapes, on shabby narrow little roads where two small cars could not cross. You should have slept nicely half of the time, I know, but I kept my eyes open and enjoyed it.

Nothing else. I'll be back in La Bûcherie nest on 6th October, then I'll see people again and tell you stories about them. Sartre thanks for the money, the African minister will get it by indirect way; he sends lot of friendful regards, he has been asked for lunch by this cousin Albert Schweitzer but could not accept, not being in Paris, and was glad of it. He works hard on the fourth book of his endless novel. He met a friend in Cannes one afternoon, coming from Paris with Boris in his car,[2] but she is so afraid in it that she just looks at nothing. So Boris spends his days and money mending this car and improving it, but he never uses it for a drive, for they both hate it. Some people make their life really sad.

Nelson, my love, I'll go and see Bruno Bicek for another hour, so I'll feel still near you, yet in a way I never stop feeling near you. We cannot be apart from each other in our heart, no, never. I still hear you calling me "my girl, my real wife," and I am sure no man's girl or wife ever gave him more love than I give to you. It is not even giving: I belong to you. Write to me, sweetheart. Sleep well, Feel warm, Feel loved and precious. Feel my body in your arms, as it has been, as it will be.

Your own Simone

P.S. When do you begin to write again, you man with the golden arm? What happened at the customs? How were the gifts accepted? Did they listen to all your lies? Tell me, tell me, tell me.

1) The hero of *Never Come Morning*. 2) Boris Vian had an old English sports car, a Morgan, always in need of repair.

Dearest man with the golden arm,

How is it when you write such good books you like such bad ones? Maybe you'll answer: how is it when you write such bad books you are so critical about good ones? But it would not be very kind. Don't let us speak about the *Strong Lamb,* which was a dirty joke, but *Of Human Bondage*, really! So solemn, humorless, stuffy, heavy, such a flat unreal realism and pedant talks about art and wisdom! I just spit on this cripple hero; I despise him. Just once I was slightly moved, when the bad woman (how conventionnal she is!) has broken everything in the poor boy's nest; I could not help thinking of Wabansia with the pots broken, the Guatemala blanket torn away, the lap shoes in rags, and it twisted my heart. But, well, if this Maugham can write, then you cannot; he is as bad as Farrell in a different way. The Sherwood Anderson's short stories were pleasant, but nothing wonderful, so I was not lucky with Anglo-Saxon literature. As for Bruno Bicek, I am slightly sick to force him into good French.

Except this deep harsh grudge, I should feel rather happy about you. It is good to have got your letter, to know you have not flown away above the clouds to some nowhere Shangri-la, but have landed at last in Wabansia nest. It makes me cosy to see you there. It seems you are not too unhappy, honey, with good successful books behind you, money at hand, lot of camels to dream about and a good woman's love. I don't know how the woman is worth, but the love anyway is sound and genuine. Your blooming manhood is not too badly disposed of.

We had a wonderful storm here; it thundered and rained the whole night long, and the wind was howling and paddling around like an army of wild beasts; it threw down glasses and plates I had left on my little porch; it seemed in the heart of the night that devils had come to take away my soul. You remember our last year storms? I should have crept into your arms, and you would have asked: "Are you invited?"

I begin to write with some pleasure since two days. The long dreamy hours in Ischia when you pretended I did nothing, and I was deeply *thinking*, were useful in the end. I found lot of people and stories already waiting in a corner of my head, and they want to come to life on the white paper. Honey, I thought this morning I should like to give this new book to you; I man to put your name printed on the first page, to dedicate it to you. It is yours in so many ways, and first because I am yours. Would you accept it? Nelson, my love, it is so sweet to love you and so hard to miss you, tonight. Kiss me, kiss me for good, sweetheart.

Thursday

What did you do about Mrs. Bradley?[1] Tell me about Conroy. I like him. It seems there are still lot of things you did not tell me about your coming back. Use your golden arm to write to me, honey. I got a letter from my sister, telling it was a little sad to think of me in Tunis, so near, and not seeing me — so I was really shrewd to hide so well behind my black glasses.

A last kiss, honey. I love you.

Your own Simone

1) A literary agent.

Cagnes, Friday, 30 Septembre 1949

My own Nelson, my love,

Do you know this nice poem by Verlaine?:

Il pleure dans mon coeur
Comme il pleut sur la ville...,

I just feel like that today. It is raining hard and long on the sad hills, on the roofs, and a bit inside me too. How much I miss your smile, your warmth, your arms, your love, my dearest you.

Days go on slowly and I work much. Yesterday was a little different, because I went with Sartre to see this friend, Guille, one of the few you did not meet, who lost his wife six months ago. With his three children of seven, five, two years old, he spends just now his holidays on the sea-side nearby, in a very big beautiful house belonging to our friend the old lady I spoke often about. That is a place where I spent a month, ten years ago, just before the beginning of the war. It was strange to find myself there once more. I never came to the place again, so it kept all its freshness: the garden with palm-trees, the big terrace above the sea, the beautiful wide sea with white sails and water-skis exactly as in past times. And so many things happened, since: the war, travelling to the States, having my first, and second, and other books published, and meeting you. It seems another world around me, a bit different self inside, and still all was the same. Well, for this man, there are three children and the mother is dead. He had still other children around, nephews and little friends, so it was noisy, laughing, and very gay in the house. I told you—maybe you remember—he had really put his whole self in this marriage; he did not try to write, he dropped travelling, he even denounced some friendships to give everything to wife and children: earning money and staying at home. He said he was wonderfully happy, and when she died, he said he would have killed himself, if not for the children... Well, it was astonishing to see him yesterday! A fine sunny complexion, he seemed younger and much more good-looking than before! He had invited lot of friends and enjoyed them, quite pleased with life. He spoke a little of his wife, very lovingly, but he told us he had already two affairs with women, a sleeping one and a sentimental one. He had been astonished by the hurry of women when he became a widower. They just rushed to him, assaulting him, pretending to be deeply moved by his faithful love towards his dead wife, and for that, wanting him to be unfaithful. He was slightly disgusted at their greediness, but pleased too. The whole thing made me somewhat uneasy: I always feel uneasy when I see how quickly people do without each other, how quickly the deads are forgotten. Sure, I know, if you don't kill yourself, you have to live; if you live, you live. But then, how deeply dead are dead people! God! I don't want to die.

I hated you slightly, coming back here and fancying myself burried and you living on in the very "brave," "strong" way, kissing people living on. Still, I could not stand the idea of you dying first. So what shall I do? Once, you suggested dying at seventy-six years in each other's arms. That would be the nicest, though seventy-six is a little young.

Saturday

I expected a letter this morning; maybe it will come Monday, maybe I'll find it in Paris. I want so much to hear about you. The sky is washed by the night storms but the electricity went out. I had to read by the light of a candle. I am waiting for Guille and his children for lunch and a long drive in the mountains.

I read a life of Oscar Wilde, a new French book—very interesting, but I don't like the man. I go on sweating hard about Bruno Bicek. Sartre took a fancy for the work and some days spend two or three hours on it, but goes so slowly, hardly thirty pages will be done in this way. I must say it is a fascinating game, going from one language to another. I find sweet to do something for you, so little be it, it makes a real living link, this job.

My beloved you, I remember so many things. Sometimes, when you were sleepy, or even a little bit drunk, you began to speak in a dreamy way, in a low quick voice, as for yourself, still you spoke to me. I felt that it was really the same thing, speaking to yourself or to me. I was really dwelling deep inside your heart and for a time you made no difference between your own self and mine. Maybe of all sweet memories that is the sweetest: you lying on your back, at night, or in the car half drowsing and speaking from far away, not making any difference between me and you. So are you too inside me, not distinct from my own self.

I love you so much, my love.

Your own Simone

Monday

Nelson, my love, I got your letter Saturday when coming back from a long drive, and I was much pleased with the clippings you sent. But then, honey, I got a problem. I should write to some woman's magazine: "Dear question-box, I fell in love two years ago with a nice local youth, a poor boy, not very strong in the head. Suddenly he became an international success man, millionaire, and they compare him to Dostoyevsky. What should I do to keep his love? Or must I just forget him? I am a little scared, you see, and your last letter was quite short and busy; maybe soon you'll be too proud to write any longer. Anyway, as long as you are supposed to go on loving me, I am pleased with all that happens to you. It is a real big success, the reviews are wonderful. Oh Nelson, I am so happy when anything good happens to you; you are so nice when you are pleased at something, dearest you. I see a beautiful moon above the sea, slowly coming to you, within five hours it will be in Chicago. How much I should like to travel with her through the silver sky. I feel blue tonight, as sad as a rat. I am afraid of coming back to La Bûcherie; I am afraid your phantom is waiting for me there. I have bad dreams every night. I remember once, in these talks we had sometimes in the dark, in the bed, you were astonished because, I said life was so easy for me. "I believed it was quite easy," you said. And I was astonished myself to hear you saying that. Well, it is not too easy, really I am longing for you day and night; it is not easy to be so far, loving you so much. There is no point in telling you it once more.

Nothing goes on to happen. I got a little letter from Bost. He says Olga has quite recovered now; it seems she is no longer sick at all and will be allowed to play on a stage in the spring: that would be wonderful for her, and for him too. He wants to go to the States, but he says Scipion will not go. His girl-friend wants to keep him: she'll go too (which is impossible) or he'll stay. Bost says Scipion does not know himself how stubborn she is about it, but she is and he will learn...

It was a beautiful Saturday in the high mountains behind the coast; there was much fog on the tops and it blurred the sight, but it was fine to find pine-trees and cold meadows so near the blue sea. Guille was very nice, and I liked his children—he brought two, the older ones, a girl and a boy, very pleasant to see. It is always a problem to me how children can be childish and yet grown up at the same time.

Thursday I come back to Paris by plane. Write to me, you golden arm Division Street Dostoyevsky. I want so much to know everything about you: what with the little Niseï, the Chicago woman, Conroy, the monster's mother, the Gary's friends, the bookseller, all these people who came to be so familiar to me, And what do you do all day long? What happens to my lovely pack of dirt? Don't go way, stay with me, talk to me as you did in the dark, and in the light too. I listen to you so lovingly. I love you so much, so much, my love.

Your own Simone

Cagnes, Thursday, 6 Octobre 1949

Nelson, my love,

It was sweet to get this unexpected letter yesterday, when I had just written the day before, asking a lot of questions and feeling somewhat blue. Here was the answer to everything, and you told me to do and sleep in your good heart, so I nestled there and I shall not go away until I meet you again and you take me in your arms. It is so good to know I stay with you, my love, and you will not try too hard not to love me.

I am glad Mrs. Bradley was disposed of; it is a good idea to have Cau working in the business. I'll give him the letter and your instructions.

The little Lisette Sartre killed[1] was just a nice little whore, working rather in Quarter Latin than in Saint-Germain-des-Prés. Four abortion affairs have just been discovered, about her murder, but still nobody knows why Sartre really used to kill her.

Please send me the *bad* reviews about you too. You know, I cannot be so easily deceived as to believe there are none; I can, but not that!

I'll be in Paris tonight. There is big revolution going on just now in Saint-Germain-des-Prés, I learnt: the owners of the cafés, and chiefly the one of the Flore, are mad at the American pansies. They say: "Well, the old French writers, Gide, Cocteau, it is all right; they are respectable people. But now we have really the scum of the town coming from Montmartre to get money from the Americans. That is too much! The Flore is usually called the Café of the Fairies, and when the manager knew that, he decided to hunt all of them away. He had long conferences with the managers of Lipperie, Montana, and so on. First they asked the most extravagant price for a single beer, but your American pansies did not care; they put some kind of poison in the beer, vainly. They called the police, then, and often cops come and pick up people and take them to the police station. Managers have decided not to accept men without women. The newspapers are filled by pictures of the managers talking together, of the terrace of the Flore, and of lot of good jokes about it, as you can fancy. I heard about Chicago, too. You were the most afraid by the atomic bomb, because you'll be the first bombed, and you had long conferences about the best way of protecting yourselves. It does not seem the little Wabansia nest has much of a chance; you should rather settle in La Bûcherie, nobody will bother to bomb Paris down.

You drive me crazy with your Bicek, or Sartre does — I don't know he other night began working with him at ten, and he did not let me go to sleep before two: his hair dishevelled, red in the face and a crazy look in his eyes, cursing Guyonnet and sometimes you too! He came to the end of the first part. When we met in the morning, he told me he had dreamt of translations the whole night; so did I, and now neither he nor I we can read any news paper without trying at once to translate it in better French. It is an obsession, a disease. The fact is it will stop now; I'll achieve the job by myself; maybe I'll ask Bost's help, because it is better to work with somebody else.

Good bye, my love. It was just a last kiss from the coast. In case I crash, I want you to know that I crashed with love-happiness in the heart. You don't know how happy a letter of you can make me, as happy as your dear smile. Nelson, Nelson, Nelson, it is good to love you.

Your own Simone

1) Algren had sent de Beauvoir a clipping from the *Chicago Tribune*, entitled "The Murder of a Parisian Model Provokes Protests Against the Cult of Existentialism" with variations on the theme, "Does Sartre think he can do absolutely anything?"

Nelson, my love,

I told you I was a bit afraid of coming back here and meeting your ghost, but he was the sweetest ghost, he just took me in his arms, and let me nestle on his shoulder, telling: "We'll see each other again, nothing is surer." So I slept the best sleep I got since you left me, feeling you everywhere around me. This morning, there was letter of you, unexpected since you wrote so much, last week. Thanks, honey, it helps so much. I sat in the small park nearby to read it, smelling of wet earth and dead leaves, this October of Paris I love, and it was the first moment of real full peaceful happiness since your departure. I like the picture on the quays; it seems to me so good I should like to have it enlarged, maybe. I enjoyed the clippings and was not disappointed at your behaviour between the airport and New York; I know your way of saving money, time, and trouble. I was pleased that I bought flowers and put them in the small southern pot, pretending *you* gave them to me. And I wrote the first page of my new novel: "To Nelson." Now it is so brightly began, it will be easy to go on. In fact I did not work since Thursday. The trip was very nice: the air-hostess was an ancient pupil of mine, and the radio-man an ancient pupil of Sartre, so we did not feel lonely! In the end there was much fog above Paris, but I had no time to be afraid. I spent the evening with Bost, who is as penniless as ever. Scipion has a strange time with his girl: they quarrel three times a day in the most awful way, and that makes him very unhappy, but then he lives with her. Bost thinks Scipion will be really unhappy some day. But Scipion's love for you is as deep and bright as ever. Poor Sartre found hard news in Paris.One of the people he helps is a lung-sick boy; he had tuberculosis and could not work, so he got money from Sartre. Then he married, then had a child.Then it seems the money he got was not enough (you see once more how mean Sartre is?), so he stole a million francs worth diamond and sold it to jeweller who was suspicious, because the man was so shabby: he gave only half the money. When the poor thief came and asked the other part, cops were there and put him into jail. Now he pretends he found the diamond in a public lavatory — not a very good defense. So Sartre has to pay for lawyer and to go to the court as a witness, explaining how nice the poor thief was. Coming home I found three letters: a dishevelled love letter from the ugly woman, saying she did not see me for 113 days and cannot stand it any longer, an imperious letter from my Jewish friend saying she wants to see me at once and much, a still more imperious letter from one of these women who use to ask money, telling me to ask Sartre for money and to make haste. That was Paris life beginning again, all right.

In Cagnes, on the little terrace, it happened that a newspaper boy, a caricaturist, had a dinner near Sartre and me, when Guille came with his children. We did notice him and his wife without knowing who they were, one of the children even played with their dog. Well, yesterday there was a whole page in one of these dirty newspapers about the way Sartre eats spaghetti, and I drink pink wine, and everything! They complained we sometimes spoke about food and wine as really anybody, and sometimes we talked in such a way nobody can understand. He was angry when he understood, angry when he did not. He said I have a fine face but his wife did not like the way I was dressed. Here us the cartoon he made about Sartre and me. In the same paper was a story about a singer. A man in a Montmartre night-club makes a parody of her, but he does not only imitate her in mild way, he sings the most dirty obscene sound about her. So she sued him and I think she is right. I send the pictures of her and the man. Bost does not "pick apples" any more with her, and she is very sad of it. He told me that the night we met her Antibes (and you were so drunk) Olga cried the whole night because she felt there was some affair between Bost and the singer. He told her — Olga — during summer he could not sleep with her any more; he felt too much a brother to her. She was rather sad but accepted the idea he could sleep with some foreign whore from time to time; bit she would not stand him to sleep with any girls who knows her; she would feel humiliated.

Well, enough of the Parisian chronicle for today. I put everything in good order: books, papers, dresses, and so on. The little home is all clean and smiles to you. I'll begin to work again on "your" book this afternoon. Work too, my love, since our next meeting depends on your work. You said you had to have the new book started before I come, so start to start it! Oh, Nelson! I should like to fill up this letter with the most precious gifts: pots, chateaubriand béarnaise, red wine, copper trays. There is just my heart, as always, my heart which never stops beating for you.

Your own Simone

Simone de Beauvoir, Berlin, February 1948.

11

Mai 1947

KONINKLIJKE LUCHTVAART
MAATSCHAPPIJ N.V.
K·L·M ROYAL DUTCH AIRLINES

Aan boord vliegtuig
On board aircraft
van   naar
from   to
Datum
Date

When we arrived above New Foundland it was
already the end of the afternoon, though only 75 ...
in N.Y. The island is very beautiful, all dark pine
and red lakes, with a touch of snow here and
there. You would like it, too. We landed and
we are to stay here for two hours. I think of you —
Where are you, just now? maybe in an airplane
yourself. I should like to know. When you'll find
our little home, I'll be there, hidden under the
bed and everywhere. Now I'll always be with you.
In the sad streets of Chicago, under the elevated,
in the lonely room I'll be with you, my beloved
one, as a loving wife with her beloved husband.
We shall never have to wake up because
it was not a dream; it is a wonderful true story

P.P. 619-60 H. B.

Letter, May 1947.

which is only beginning. I feel you with me and where I shall pass you will pass, not the book only but all of you... I love you. There is no more to say; you know. You take me in your arms and bring to you and I kiss you as I kissed you —

Your Simone

Nelson Algren, Chicago, 1949.

Simone de Beauvoir and Nelson Algren at the cottage on Lake Michigan, 1950 or 1951.

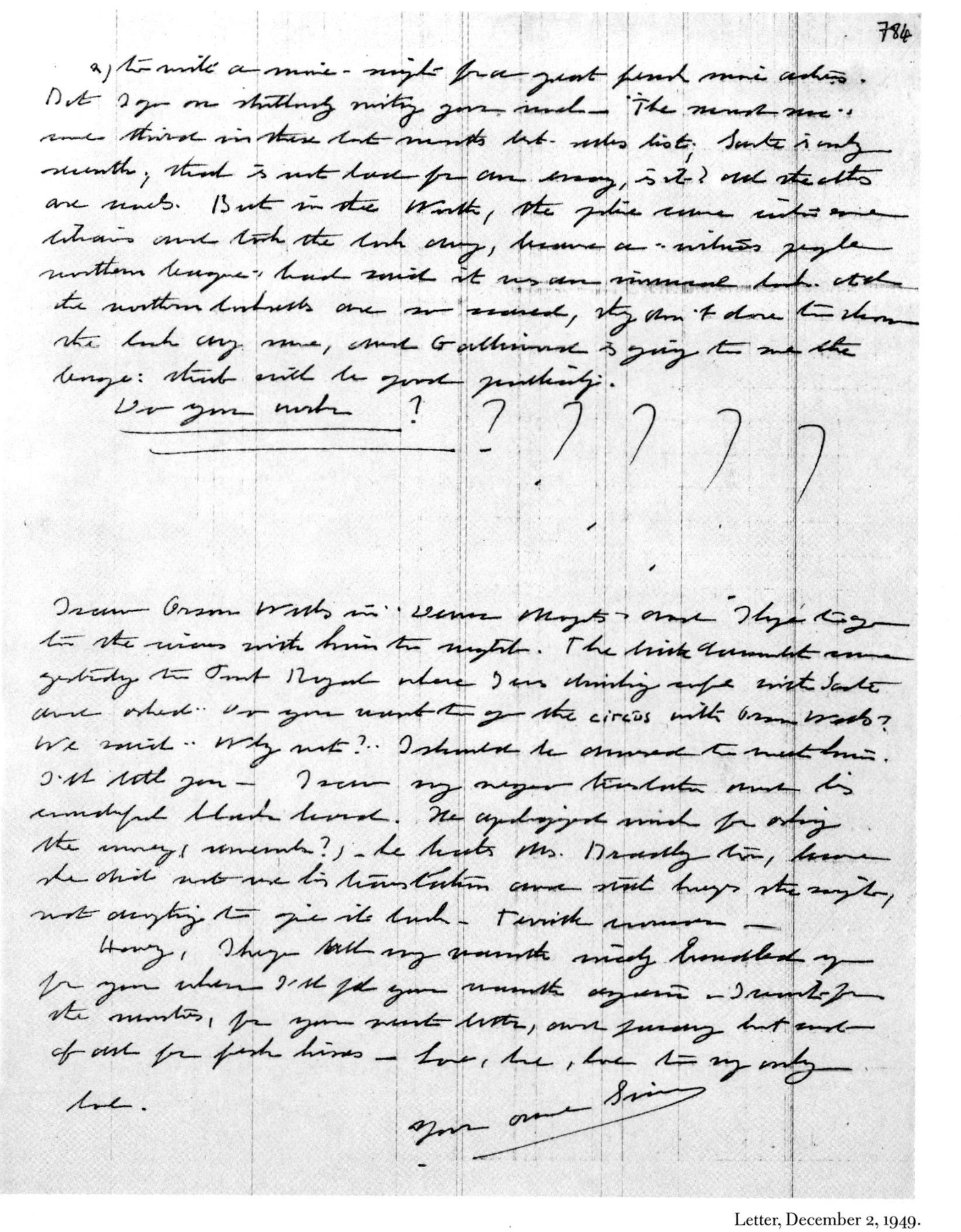

Letter, December 2, 1949.

Hotel Lincoln

"THE HOUSE OF HOSPITALITY"

Thursday evening

JOHN L. HORGAN
GENERAL MGR.

NEIL S. ALLEN
BUSINESS MGR.

44TH TO 45TH STREETS
AT EIGHTH AVENUE

NEW YORK 19, N.Y.

MARIA KRAMER
PRESIDENT

Nelson, my own true love

dead tired, but I cannot go to sleep,
having written to you — it was so hard
half an hour after feeling that you were
for me; it is so bitter to think that I co
managed to stay much longer if I had
could still care for me — I need to yearn
the only kind of peace I can dream of,
I cried the whole trip long in the train dur
during the whole plane flight I spoke to y
you don't like words, but for once, let
you; and don't be too scared of I cry.
In this "introduction" you made me rea
Thomas Mann says that before each fit—I
a few seconds of bliss which were worth t
certainly you have the power to give me
minutes, at times, a kind of fever that s
years health. Maybe as your dirty heart is

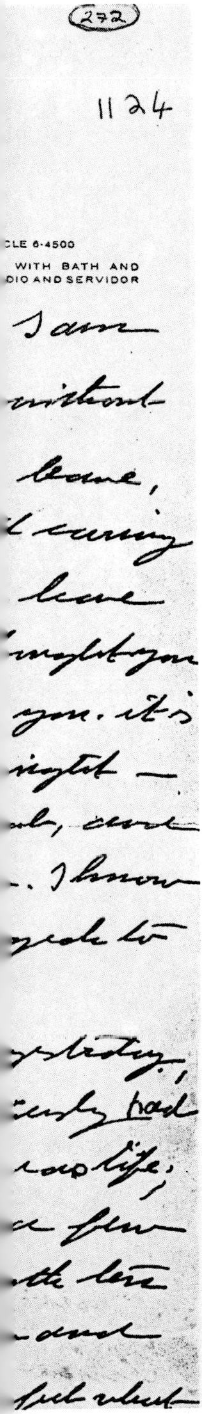

271

272

1124

CLE 6-4500

WITH BATH AND
DIO AND SERVIDOR

(handwritten letter fragments along left margin)

WESTERN UNION

CLASS OF SERVICE

This is a full-rate
Telegram or Cable-
gram unless its de-
ferred character is in-
dicated by a suitable
symbol above or pre-
ceding the address.

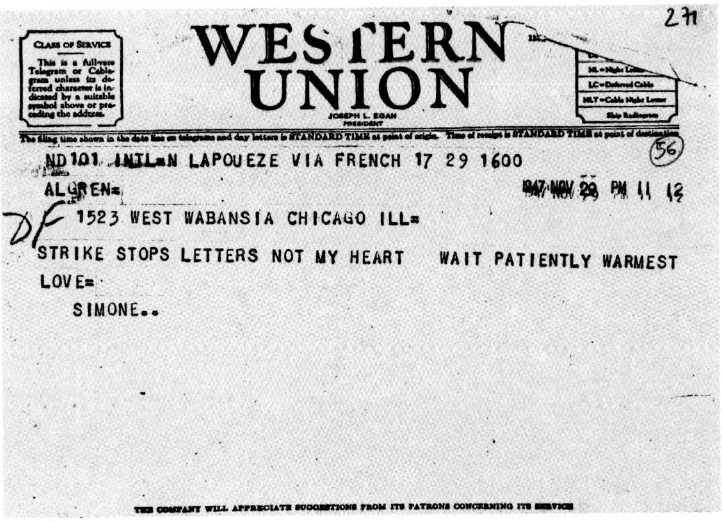

JOSEPH L. EGAN
PRESIDENT

DL = Day Letter
NL = Night Letter
LC = Deferred Cable
NLT = Cable Night Letter
Ship Radiogram

The filing time shown in the date line on telegrams and day letters is STANDARD TIME at point of origin. Time of receipt is STANDARD TIME at point of destination

ND 101 INTL = N LAPOUEZE VIA FRENCH 17 29 1600

ALGREN =   1947 NOV 29 PM 11 12

56

1523 WEST WABANSIA CHICAGO ILL =

STRIKE STOPS LETTERS NOT MY HEART   WAIT PATIENTLY WARMEST
LOVE =

SIMONE . .

THE COMPANY WILL APPRECIATE SUGGESTIONS FROM ITS PATRONS CONCERNING ITS SERVICE

---

left: Letter, October 30, 1951.

above: Telegram, November 29, 1947.

following spread: Nelson Algren and Simone de Beauvoir, Chicago, 1948 (Art Shay).

you just it —

What I did not say enough, yesterday evening, is the sweetness of these days with you. From the beginning you made it so warm and gay than I was happier than I have been for two years — It was good living with you — Good bye, my love — If my plane would crash my last strength would be for thanking you for all I got from you — as it will not, I'll keep on loving you and your very until I land into your arms again —

I kiss you from all my feverish constant heart. I'll keep be in yours —

I love you —

your own Simone

left: Olga Kosakievitch, Nelson Algren and Simone de Beauvoir, Cabris, Summer 1949.
above: Letter, October 31, 1951.

Simone de Beauvoir and Nelson Algren
at the cottage on Lake Michigan, Summer 1950.

SIMONE de BEAUVOIR
11 Rue de la Bucherie
Paris, France

(Sept 13 , 1949)

Tuesday night —

Nelson, my only love — It was
the hardest and sweetest parting,
my love — the hardest because I never
loved you so much — the sweetest
because I never felt so much your
warm precious beloved love — we
belong to each other, now I know it
for sure, I know we shall stay
together even across the ocean — and
I feel safe in your good warm
heart — even if you love other girls,
you'd never find a heart that
loves you so hard, not such a
loving mouth as mine —

Honey, the night was so beautiful
when I went away, alone in this

left: Letter, September 13, 1949.

above: Simone de Beauvoir and Nelson Algren, Chicago, September 1947.

Simone de Beauvoir and Nelson Algren at the cottage on Lake Michigan, Summer 1950.

Saturday, *15 Octobre 1949*

Dearest "modest" you,

You write very nicely. I got a good fat letter yesterday, but let me tell you, you are making fun of me: I cannot believe they all like the book; they are *all* so easily deceived. And this woman who pretends you are a *modest* man! That is really too much! What a lovely, peaceful local youth she describes! But that is not *you*: you travel in faraway countries and love, or pretend so, far fetched woman; you speak for hours without letting your poor baffled gauloise say a single word—no, you really go too far in this trick of deceiving people! I'll tell the truth, some day. The Bûcherie home is getting very nice, I brought the lamps I had ordered long ago from Giacometti: one has a long leg and the other a short one, both are of green bronze of very beautiful color, with green light-shades—green is fine with the red curtains. Unhappily, as the windows could not open when the curtains were put, neither the door open when the carpet was laid; the light went away as soon as the lamps were lit. I had to call the good concierge and now one of the lamps gives some light. I'll call the electrician tomorrow. Do you know what Dick Wright is doing is Chicago? He is shooting *Native Son* with a French director, the one who spoke about shooting *She Went to Stay*; then he will shoot the inside part of the movie in Buenos Aires. And he is acting himself as Big Thomas. I heard it is a great secret, but in the other hand it is written in all French newspapers.

Since I wrote an article saying abortion should be allowed, the poor girl in *Les Temps modernes* office has hard time, because people come and ask to see me, that I help them for abortions. One of them comes every day and says I *must* help him, and she was so bored the other day that she showed him a little black closet and said: "That is place where we *do* it!" Many crazy people come too, and ask with a crazy look to see me at once because I am the only one in the world who can help them. That is the dangerous part of my life, but there is much more flattering one: I got *two* proposals in two days, take care! The first was long poetical letter by a man whom I don't know and who does not know me but he saw my picture in some newspaper—that is just the woman's face he dreamt about his whole life, a wonderful lovely face (that is true, I must admit) and he wants to travel back to his infancy with me...I have to answer before the

22th of October. The other story was much more amusing. You remember this typewriter woman who sent a wire asking for 80,000Fr—she likes women, I told you, though she slept with many men too. Well, some days ago she wrote to thank me for the money and to ask what could I do for you? And then she asked 20,000 more. Sartre had said he should not give her anymore, but he was not that mean after all, and gave me the money for her. I met her; we sat at a terrace and I gave it to her, and she told me how just now she is madly in love with a sixty-three years old woman, white haired and dressed as a man, who is regular Don Juan. This woman taught her what it is to be loved *by a man*, which she never new when she was sleeping with men. "Until now I had a body, but I had no cunt, now I have one!" She had tears in her eyes saying that, because the old woman who gave her this wonderful gift does not love her and is just dropping her. Oh! It would have been a long dreary, sad, tragic story is it had not been so funny! She told me: "My ex-friend is dreadfully sad not to be a man, but I tell her: 'Do you just miss the organ? What is the use? You don't need it, you do everything with your brain—that is much better!'" What do you think making love with our brain, next time, honey? Then when she had explained everything to me—how she writes beautiful lesbian poems, what an exciting body she has got, how passionate she is indeed—she said, blushing a little: "I have been in love with you five or six times…I certainly shall be again." I smiled nicely and asked a question about something else. Each time I give her money, she wants to give me her beautiful body, so I told her in the Sartre gave her the money I cannot afford myself to waste so much. I don't know what will happen.

Sartre's third part of *The Ways of Freedom* seems to be success; everybody says, and I think it is true, it is much better than the other ones. What is funny is that the reviewers recognize it with anger and hate in the heart; they all begin to say that he *should* not write good novels, because of his ideas about literature, but he did, and the book is his masterpiece; but it is *in spite* of him, they say. My translator brought me yesterday reviews in American about *Ethics of Ambiguity*. Most of them say the book is interesting but you cannot really have any ethic creed if you don't believe in God—things like that.

I work steadily and lovingly about your book. I want it to be the best I ever wrote, to be real good one, since it is a gift for you. I live quite peacefully with your ghost now; I hope we'll keep along as nicely until I come back to Wabansia. I already begin to dream about this faraway day, you'll have some kind of strange hat on your head, I'll run away and you'll catch me, and soon after that, you'll hold in your arms your naked moaning wife.

Your own Simone

Tuesday, 18 Octobre 1949

My own beloved you,

It was pretty sad today, to go and meet Guyonnet in the dark bar with the black arm-chairs and bad paintings, the place had a queer empty look. Still Guyonnet was just himself; he gave me the end of the translation, that is the second half, which is just as terrifically bad as the first one. I must say he seems exhausted, bored to death by the book. By the way, he did not get his *Golden Arm*. Sartre did, but Guyonnet did not, and he would like to begin the translation soon. I am going to rewrite the end of Bicek's story with Bost, and sometimes Sartre will supervise. I hope it will be done within a month. Then we'll discuss sharply the contract with Gallimard.

I had dinner with the man who wanted to see nothing in Roma but Etruscan things; he failed many times, and very sharply, then he went to Sicily and saw Sicilian ruins, wasting himself; it seems he should concentrate a little more. I had beautiful dress made with the most beautiful material we bought in some Guatemala market; it still keeps the smell of our first honeymoon and it makes my heart melt.

Wednesday

How nice you are to write so faithfully! I just got your huge letter. Thanks, honey. You cannot know what it means for me to get such rich fat letters and to hear everything about you. I am a little disturbed, because I learnt from the *New York Times* clippings that you don't any longer look nor sound like yourself: please, send me fresh picture, darling. Do you look like Philip Rahv? Or Carlo Levi? I was used to your local face, so it was little shock to hear that. It was a very nice interview your gave there; you certainly look like a modest man. When you speak the way you did, I felt quite in love with you. I showed to Sartre what you said about him; he was very pleased and laughed much, though he was a little disturbed too not to look nor sound like himself. But, heartless you, why did you not speak about me? Why not tell then I don't bring existentialism in bed, and I don't look like a writer at all when you hold me in your arms? I am sure they would have been surprised at that too. Next time, don't forget!

I am very proud about all the good things which happen to you, but chiefly proud of the way you react to them: it seems success does not change you so much, after all; you'll not want a duchess for your wife. I quite agree with you: *don't go to Hollywood!* Please, please! What about writing stupid dialogues for stupid movies when you have your own next good book to write? Sure, they offer a lot of money, that is flattering and pleasant to get the offer, but what do you need this money for? Enough is as good as too much, it seems to me; you cannot eat more than you do, you cannot throw away your lovely, crummy little underwears to put on silk ones, you cannot but love with money since you have got as much as any man can gather in a whole life. So what? Stay in Wabansia nest and write another live-up story, darling you. By the fact, I made a pleasant dream — an open — eyed one: if they made a movie with *Golden Arm*, then you'll go to Hollywood to work about it, sure; it could be nice if it happened at the time when we meet. I could work while you would work and we should bathe on the Malibu beaches, spend week-ends in the beautiful California, I should see Nathalie, she would find a lovely home for you and me. I guess it will never happen, but it could and I should enjoy it. I enjoy the idea of being with you anywhere.

Yesterday evening, with the ugly woman, uglier than ever. We drank champagne, as she always wants to do, and ate chicken. And then I had to spend the night until two reading her manuscript. Parts are really good — sometimes she can write — but it is impossible that her book be openly published. It is a sexual story, a lesbian one, and as crude as Genet in its way. She describes in details how a girl takes off the virginity of another, all what she does with her fingers, what happens in the other's sex, lot of terrible things they do with blood, urine and so forth. I was even slightly disgusted at times, so I don't know how the average reader will react.

I saw my second child[1] for the first time nearly twice as big as the first one, and myself, I like it much better, I think I'll soon begin to be insulted. It goes on with Sartre the way I told you. In a Gaullist magazine a long review was saying, Yea, Sartre is the best: the best in philosophy, in drama, in novel, in essay. His novel is wonderfully good, but when you do so many good things, so easily, so easily, that it is really bad. What do you think of that?

You are very busy, indeed, but when do you work?

How is it I am never in your bed when you are so often in mine? Nelson, my love, your letter made me very happy. I feel in love more than ever, and I know it will be wonderful once more, some of these days. Love, love from your international wife.

Your own Simone

I found out whom you look like from your *New York Times* picture: like Queneau! I sure like Queneau, but I don't enjoy sleeping with him within some months. After all I got along nicely with you.

1) *L'experience vecue*, the second volume of *The Second Sex*. The first volume had already been reprinted in May, and an American publisher wanted to publish the second one immediately.

Sunday, 23 October 1949

Nelson, my love,

I don't know why I love you so much in this grey cold Sunday, but I do. It begins to be really cold and I have to light up the little gas-stove; the only bad point is the gas goes away to my head and I feel giddy after a short time. I go to the public library too, to get better acquainted with all which happened to me during the last six years: how we won this war, what we did afterwards. It seems so far away in the big yellow newspapers of the library, quite a dead past; sometimes they speak about some play by Sartre or some book by me, and that seems the most dead of all. It made me kind of sad, reading about my own story as if I were already in the grave. I don't know if these cold magazines and newspapers will be of any use, but that is my own way of looking around in the dark for a new book.

I heard much about you. First, Cau met a man of a big publishing house who told him: "I am reading a wonderful American book, the best I read since years!" And fancy! That was our Frankie Machine's story! Guy-onnet gave me the whole end of the translation; I spent a first afternoon with Bost correcting it. No kidding, I'll have to spend a whole month, without doing anything else, to get it in the right shape; I feel a bit hopeless. Still, I'll do it. I saw for the first time the *Golden Arm* on Sartre's shelves. What a fine book! I like the printing, the cover, and everything. When you see it, you wish the book to be good.

I saw the old lady from near Angers the other day. She is so much more lively than any young people I know! She found, and her daughter, La Bûcherie home a wonderful place and asked to asked for dinner there. I was very proud. They kidded me about my mysterious disappearance in

293

last May–June, when I was "faraway" and everybody saw me in Paris. I am going to send you my last big child, which you'll not read since it is in French, and Bost's novel, translated in English. But he warns you to take care, it is awfully badly translated. They understood nothing about his slang and killed it; the language was one of the first qualities of the book, the way the soldiers spoke as real French soldiers, so it kills much of the book if it is killed. Still, I send it to you; maybe you'll enjoy it.

I have not the same local youth Wabansia merry go round kind of life as you have, so nothing remains to say. Except what is not possible to say in flat words, but which you know. You know, you do? I know you do. It is always so good to love you my, love.

Your own Simone

Wednesday, 26 Octobre 1949

Do you know why you are so wonderful, honey? It is not because your mother is asked to speak at the radio, nor because you are proposed $600 a week by Hollywood, nor because Cau get $400 advance for you for each book, it is because you write to me so long nice letters. I always get them a little before the day I am waiting for, so they look like the nicest gift.

And do you know why I am wonderful? It is not because I try so hard to write a good book for you, nor because I love you so warmly, it is because I am going to be as flat as a fish when you'll see me again. A woman comes twice a week to massage me, she began this morning. She works hard for half an hour; she bruises my poor body, but you feel quite healthy after that. She says in few weeks I'll have no more belly, no behind, no legs, no neck, nothing; I'll just be a wire. Well if you miss it, I'll keep a little something to hold in your arms but anyway, as I take no exercise at all, and just sit writing or talking all day long, it seems to me it is a very healthy thing to do.

I said Sartre's secretary to write to you because I am tired about speaking business with you; it seems he behaved wonderfully, telling them Faulkner was nothing more now than an old dirty sucker and you were the new star rising in American sky. I guess you have to accept what he got for you; you could not have more. But how are your agents going to manage Mrs. Bradley? They don't seem very shrewd. We had two *long* conferences about you, one Sartre, Bost, and me; the other Cau, Sartre and me. The point is the end of the translation is so bad it has to be *entirely* rewritten. And then Bost read what we did, Sartre and me, and he says we still kept too much of Guyonnet's not readable prose. He is very nicely going to correct all the beginning and half of the end; I'll do the other end. But we need three months; that is sad. But better have the book published three months later and be good. Anyway we have no choice; it is *too* bad. Indeed, there is no longer question of giving the next book to Guyonnet; he has been warned as politely as possible that it was taken away from him. The fact is you are tremendously hard to translate. Sartre gave the book to an American girl he know; she thought it was wonderful, but many words she could not understand. Honey, I should like to drink champagne about your success. I am always kidding you about it, but you know how glad it makes me, do you? It gives sun to my life; it does not make me proud of you, because I could not be more than I already am, but it makes me very happy.

It is cold and very, windy here, chimneys are falling down from the roofs and trees broken down. But it is blue and golden and glorious, Now, I'll work. No, you did not leave me, my love. I crawl in your arms, kiss your lips, I kiss all of you. I never loved you more.

Your own Simone

Sunday, 30 Octobre 1949

Dearest beloved you,

You told me indeed your La Motta was a treacherous man, but I did not think he should ever be mean enough to have forty-eight people burnt away in order not to have to fight Cerdan. It was really a gloomy thing when Friday in Paris we read in the newspaper: "Plane disappeared"; and yesterday every body was disturbed about it—I was too. For Cerdan, for the nice girl who was our best violin player,[1] for the poor young shepherds who came from the mountains and whose first real big adventure it was going to the States. Stupidly, I half fancied you had just narrowly escaped this death: I remembered our parting in the Orly Airport and it seemed to me I had kind of sent you to death. Oh, darling, darling you, never leave me in this horrible way! You'll never fly a plane except with me; I'll not let you burn alone in any plane. Yea, it made a real shadow on this two days. Still, they were good sunny, cold working days for me, full as always of very happy love for you.

I went to Ellen Wright's and met this ridiculous thing which is called Truman Capote. Dressed with a wide white sweater and blue velvet pants, he looked like a white mushroom. He was in Ischia, in Tunis, my love, at the same time as we were; he said he had there a house "confortable enough," but in Fez it was not "really confortable," and he "cannot be confortable" in Paris, so he has to come back to "confortable New York." I don't offer him to go into La Bûcherie Hotel, feeling the service is really not good enough. He complained about Mrs. Bradley and tried to speak about his book, and I tried not to, and I won. Ellen and Capote knew about your big success, and *she* was pleased about it.

Did you get any love-letters, honey? I get lot of them, chiefly from women and pansies. As I never answer them, we shall not go far. Thanks for the advices about the abortion business; it goes on nicely. Bost and Olga go on quarrelling. He says he hates her now because she reproaches him for spending one hour at night with Scipion and Lisa. Bost hates all womankind now and he said to Scipion not to let girls spoil his life. The Vian quarrel in the most awful way, and Queneau banged the door two days ago, shouting to his wife: "I shit on you and shall never be back again." He came back indeed, but are you really so sad about being a bachelor?

The singer owns the most beautiful cat in Paris, a grey Persian one, wild and silly; she is going to win a prize in a cat-show, and has new pictures in the newspapers with the cat in her arms. She is going to have her nose taken away; seeing me, one day, she said: I'll have a nose like that one," and she'll ask to a surgeon the nose God gave me and which you laugh at. She was sure La Motta made the plane crash, this one.

This week I'll speak at the radio about my book, I'll be shot for a movie about Saint-Germain-des-Prés, I'll have a lunch with Maurice Chevalier, and there is my picture in lot of Parisian booksellers, so I am nearly as important as you are, but not so immodest. And quite able to be in love with just a local youth. Do you work? How lazy and vain you seem to have come! How would you deserve a good working woman's love, if you do nothing?

Yesterday I had lunch with the painter[2] who gave me the little water-painting I have home, on the right side of the chimney. He has a big show now in Paris, a very interesting one. He spent four years in the States and was quite in love with Chicago, that seldom happens to French people. So we ate at the Lipperie, speaking about Chicago, and my heart melted.

Did you see in the newspapers how our poor Guatemala Indians were drowned? A thousand of them were killed by the terrible rain. In Paris it is just the icing temperature. How is Chicago weather? Go on telling me everything, you precious you. Go on being happy and, please, loving me.

My wonderful you, I am never tired of remembering our four months with delight. You are my sunshine, my moonlight, and my flying star. You are as beautiful as you are shrewd, and I love you.

Your own Simone

1) Ginette Neveu. 2) Fernand Léger.

Nelson, my love,

You did a treacherous thing, sending me this picture of you in *The Torch*. (What is that *Torch,* by the way?) It is a real lovely one. Until now, I got along fairly well with your La Bûcherie ghost, but now I just long to be with you in the Wabansia nest where you look so nice; the ghost faded away! I send it back to you since you ask for it, but cannot you get one for me to keep? I like the interview too; the man surely got something of you, of your way of speaking and laughing. I could nearly hear your dear voice. Yea, very near, and not here. Where exactly did Hemingway say what he says in the *Torch?* Was it a personnal letter? You are nice to send me all that; I am so interested and pleased. It is a wonderful triumph, my love! Don't forget me from your dizzy merry go round life, Don't become a different man, please!

I come back from lunch at the *Temps modernes* publisher. Oh, God! Oh! poor me! Such ugly elegant middle-aged women, such tedious histrionic men! There was Maurice Chevalier who did not open his mouth, and Sartre did not open his. There was a painter, a music-writer, a politician, a music-hall singer, a publisher, and wifes of all that, nobody had nothing to say to the next one; you feel such a deep misunderstanding from one to others. This one was a collaborationist and so on...you dared not say a single word, you would offence somebody. And such an awfully pretended elegant place, with no elegance at all, just what money can buy. I was sick with disgust for the whole thing. I got a letter from the Gérassi; they are both teachers in a Vermont school; a terrible lot of work to do, but the country is wonderful, and they make some money. They were so penniless in New York, they say, that all their friends avoided them, fearing to have to lend them money. I got a big letter from Nathalie too, and a very sad one. It seems her marriage is a complete failure; he came to hate her; she does not love him any more, they have awful quarrels. She does not know what to do.

I was very proud because the newspaper seller told me with a knowing blink; "Yesterday when you bought the newspapers, I was just speaking with my wife about Simone de Beauvoir!" So I am a kind of local celebrity myself, you see.

I'll try to work a little before going for dinner to Queneau's. So I'll say good bye. Send me back a picture of this Nelson I love so much.

Your own Simone

Sunday, 6 Novembre 1949

Dearest beloved you,

I wrote to you on Wednesday before going for dinner at the Queneau's. It was nice; they did not quarrel. Queneau laughed much, as he usually does. I should have liked you to see more of him. Next morning I was awaken about nine by somebody knocking at the door: "What is it?" "For information." I put on something, opened the door, and saw a scared unwilling young man:" It is for an abortion!" I sent him away, but I felt a little sad, because he was so much disturbed. "Such a conspiracy of silence!" he said, reproachfully. The fact is I know nobody who could help him. I spoke at the radio Friday with an interviewer and two friend who were supposed to discuss *The Second Sex*: four women. A lot of young men came as soon as they heard about it and began to look and laugh from the other side of the glass curtain—very disturbing. A friend told me two young men were speaking in the Deux Magots about *The Second Sex*; they rather liked it but one said: "Well, it is all right, but I shall not let my wife read it; it is too daring."

I had a kind of mild drama with the ugly woman, because I changed the day of the usual dinner, twice a month, on Tuesday. I made this Tuesday a Thursday, so she sent me a letter wet with tears and passion. She had recovered when we spent the evening and she told me how she killed herself with gas once, when she quarrelled with her husband—it seems a mild kind of death. I don't know if plane crashing is a nice death, but there is certainly a lot of that thing! About the Potomac crash, I remembered how you told me small planes used in your crazy country to come out from nowhere and hit big ones. By the way, don't ask me if I remember this or that about this one or that one: I always do. I remember everything you said, honey, everything you did too. I rather remember too much for the peace of my soul.

I got a letter from my Jewish friend: back in Algers with her husband, she says it feels to her like eating back what she vomited—rather horrid, is it not? I must say it seems to me the most horrible thing, living with somebody you really don't like. Olga seems better and better; maybe she will act in *The Flies*, maybe Bost is going to shoot a long movie in Haiti, about Haiti, he is offered money by the UNESCO. Vian has just written a novel where he tells in a poetical fantastic way how his wife and himself make each other unhappy, but what is worst, the novel is no good. Bost sweats on about Bruno, and I perspire a little about him too.

I am always Nelson-loving, hard working, lonely sleeping, and longing for my husband, and knowing I'll get him again and feeling happy for all that, It is very cold now in Paris and I go around in my DDT-smelling fur coat. How is it in Chicago? Nelson, my sweet darling, you, you can get money and fame, but you'll never get such a good love as you have got. I kiss you sweet and hard, my lovely you.

Your own Simone

Wednesday, 9 Novembre 1949

My man with the golden brain,

Thanks for the golden book, written by hand; it is always sweet when I read "love" on the paper or in your eyes, honey. Thanks for the little pictures, too, but they are not so good as the ones I sent back (I don't know how your face turned yellow and red; I did not punch it): on one you look like a laughing monkey; on the other like a stuffy teacher. The old ones with you and me are much better. Reading the paper about forty years man and his dangers, I was scared, but then, I said to myself that you cannot be so dangerous just by letters, and next time I'll see you, you'll be forty-one, which is no longer a dangerous age at all. Your letter was very nicely beneath the door, when I wake up, like your first kiss in the morning. Why do you think the movie would be better if there was a first play, stupid you?[1] I don't think it would help at all. The question would rather be to get a good director and to do most of the screen-script yourself. I understand very well that you don't want to leave Wabansia cosy nest just now and be lost in awful Hollywood, but if it is for your own Frankie, it is not the same thing as just for money. Anyway, you have to do how you feel; it is always better to act according to what you feel, and chiefly when work is concerned.

What I feel is suffering all day long, sitting at my table with white paper waiting. I don't go to the library any longer; I just pinch my brain very hard to get something out of it—a painful job. I am afraid it will be painful all year long.

I went twice to the movie this week, that is much more than I usually do. Once I saw *Louisiana Story*, by Flaherty—slow, nearly tedious at times, but wonderful. My heart beat with joy, seeing all this Spanish moss hanging from the trees; and still better than the landscapes were the parts about the oil well. Truman Capote tells around (it was printed in magazines) that Sartre called him a "fairy existentialist"; he is not existentialist, and not fairy, just a fairy, and Sartre never told such a thing.

I am working at home this afternoon. My nice lamps are lit, the stove roaring, I have beautiful red covers, everything is red; it is pleasant. I enjoy writing to you in this cosy evening; your warmth did not desert me. Yet two months went away since I cried so much in this room, because you had left. I sent today the books and the clippings, Bost's dedication I wrote myself; I wrote mine too. It is grey, cold, rainy. Twice a week the electricity is off for the whole afternoon; I bought nice candles but it reminds us too much of the war-time darkness. Yesterday evening in the Rhumerie martiniquaise, the drunken half-blind, half-lame painter to whom Sartre gives money passed by, really blind, quite drunk and hopeless, terrible to see; he was with a young clean, cosy confortable man who looked much like him, in the way a millionaire can look like an old bum. "How do you do?" said the painter in bubbling voice, and he showed me the clean young man: "This thing which just came out, it is my brother," he said apologizingly and with such contempt! It struck me very nice.

Did I mention I loved you? I do, I do, I do, my love.

Your own Simone

1) Algren had just learned that *The Man with the Golden Arm* would be made into a movie. This didn't happen until 1955, directed by Otto Preminger with Frank Sinatra as Frankie Machine and Kim Novak as Molly.

Sunday, 13 Novembre 1949

Nelson, my dangerous beloved you,

You must be a real good writer, my love, to write letters as sweet as your kisses. I'll tell you what a lovely morning I had yesterday, I was suffering beneath the pinching hand of the massaging woman, early in the morning, when the good concierge knocked at the door: it was your letter. And included in your letter, the first rival you ever had in my heart, this gopher. I don't know if it is narcissism, but I surely fell in love with him at the first sight. I pinned him up on the wall and began to worship him; I am looking at him and my heart is melting. I still don't know who he is; a gopher that means nothing—but I love him. But then, shrewd man, something else happened: there was another knock at my door, and it was a nice copy of *All Men Have to Die*[1] translated in German, with a pretty jacket: a middle-age man looking at a modern one, and I got rather nice letters from Jews, from a well-known actress[2] congratulating me. So I rather felt pleased with my gopher and myself. Then the nasty thing happed: in big yellow envelope, you came in, not a ghost, really you, sitting in the Chicago street among the Chicago dirt. Oh, that is a really awful trick! I pinned you in our little cave (the gopher is in the big room, near the chimney; but what would my mother say about *you*?) and hundred times a day I went and smiled at you; you look ready to get up, to smile back and take me in your arms, but you never do. I know the place, so often we went beneath this iron bridge, coming back to Wabansia nest. I want to be there again, among the old newspapers flying in the wind, near you. Yea, it is a lovely picture, and a lovely letter too.

Thursday I spent the evening lying in my bed and reading *The Skin*, by Malaparte.[3] As soon as it is translated in American, do read it. He is a dirty liar, a disgusting fascist, a son of bitch of nasty Italian, but talented and amusing. Did you hear about *Kaputt*, which was rather wonderful? In *The Skin* he tells about Americans in Napoli, when your great army made Napoli free; you would enjoy it. How all Napolitan girls turned whores, all boys pansies, because of the American purity and money. Knowing Napoli, having been an American soldier, I am sure you would be mad with pleasure and anger. Friday, in the late afternoon, I met an horrible American doctor woman, Mrs. Mead, who wrote a book, *Male and Female*, on the difference of sexes in Samoa, New Guinea, and USA. People had decided we had to meet. I told her: "Sorry, I have not read your book," she said: "We are even, I did not read yours." Then I tried to say how I longed to read her book, but she does not speak French and does not seem to understand my English, so I began to speak to other, more pretty women. The little Wahl was there, the university existentialist teacher whom you challenged in Chicago and nearly met in Cabris. He is sixty, rather a fairy, and has got a twenty-five years old, rather glamorous dark wife who asked me angry questions about women, saying in her country (in North Africa) no woman was ever cold in bed because sleeping with a man was meeting God (she is a Christian). I tried to say I was not *always* cold in bed but it happened other women were. Oh, she got quite angry: "But that must be dreadful! How can they live if they don't enjoy it?" I said: "Well, it is not my fault." "Yea, she said, it is your fault!" How do you like it? She thought speaking about it in a book was making it real. She meant it. Then I spoke about Uxmal with a lot of ethnologues, and everybody agreed Uxmal was the most beautiful place in the world.

Uxmal, or Ischia, or Djerba, you made me aching for you. I contrived to get along in such a sensible way, but your letter, your picture, that was a little too much; I don't feel sensible at all. Tell me we'll see each other. Tell me it will not be within too long a time. I want to look at you again in this way you like. I want to feel you deep in me again and be so happy. I am your faithful La Bûcherie gopher.

Your own Simone

1) *All Men are Mortal.* 2) Gaby Sylvia, French actress in Sartre's *No Exit* (*Huis Clos*, 1954) 3) Curzio Malaparte (1898–1957), a writer expelled from the Fascist Party in the 1940s.

Tuesday, 22 Novembre 1949

Nelson, my beloved loved one,

Do you know why you spent such a long time not getting a letter of poor dear me? It is not because I loved you half of the other weeks, but because my mid-week letter was lost; and not just that! I lost in a taxi-cab my *whole* work of these two months! That was a little shock. I had a big yellow carton with all the papers in it, and some clippings, and the letter for you, and when I came to my room, my hands were empty. It does not seem the cab-driver brought it back to the place he should have. There is another place to go on last hope after three days, and, I'll do there after writing to you, but I am hopeless. By the fact, you know what it is. In two months I had torn away most things I had written and chiefly worked in my head. Then I saw with great pleasure that I remembered really by heart the hundred first pages I had written (I mean hand-written pages, just of this shape) so I began copying then feverishly out of my head. Your book is in no danger in the end, honey; it means just a week work more, which is not much on three four years. What is much worst, that is I am really losing the poor thing I had got for a head. I always behaved in an efficient, sensible way, and now act quite crazily. For instance, the same day when I lost my papers (this awful Friday) Queneau had asked me to let myself be shot in the morning for a movie about Saint-Germain-des-Prés. I said all right;

302

I should go to the Deux Magots for a quarter of an hour after noon. First, I forgot to go, one of the movie-men had to call me. Then I rushed, I saw there was a crowd in Deux Magots, as always about noon, but my real bad luck was the crowd was all students, the worst kind of noisy students. I sat in a dark corner, but indeed as soon as they lit out the big lamps and began to shot me, hundred boys were standing on the tables and screaming at me: "A poil! A poil!", which means off with your clothes! Get away with your clothes! Then they screamed: "She writes too quick; she does not think!" and other jokes. Well, I had nothing to do but pretend I heard nothing, saw nothing, and go on writing until it was over with the shooting. So did I. But for a quarter of an hour, I had a hard time. Then a lot of little things happen: I forgot appointments, I forgot my keys. Yesterday morning I went shopping: at the baker's I gave money for a piece of bread and went away without the bread. Five minutes after I came back, the woman told me: "Which bread do you want? I never saw you!" So I began to think I was getting really mad—in fact, I am sure she was wrong; I had come and given money. Well, that is the way your poor dear to you stands, just now, poor dear you. Here it is rainy, cold, grey, sad, and it makes me very much Nelson sick. I feel my faraway arms must be very cold and grey, too, and it makes them sad. Oh, Nelson! I love you so much, it hurts sometimes.

Bruno Bicek comes to speak French slowly, but we'll win in the end. I just got your letter, my love, with the clipping. I am glad you make the movie, though I am sure you'll have some hard time about it; everybody has with movie people. The point is they should not kill all the truth and humanity of Frankie and his friends by denying them dope, for instance. You'll have to fight your best, and you'll never win the whole thing, just half-win, half-lose, I guess. Anyway, it is worth doing it and struggling about it.

I don't mean Malaparte will make you "mad with pleasure"; it is the mixture of fun and anger that will make you mad, at least it made me. In my lost letter, I told you that the beginning of this week had been very quiet: I had a dinner with Bost, Sartre, and the Queneau, and after dinner they all came home and worshipped the Saint Grévin high priest—they really did! I had hung a bunch of red peppers to the ceiling; it fits nicely, and the Queneau found my place very fine. He was funny and witty the whole night long, and I thought you should have got much bored, understanding nothing, and me telling you "That was witty! Oh, this one was good!...as in the little café, remember? Sartre and Queneau spoke sadly about Vian, who has given them the script of his next book and wanted to know what they thought about it; and they thought it was very bad and did not know how to tell it without making him hopeless, because it is the first book since years which he had written seriously, wanting it to be good and not for money. Next morning, I had lunch with Sartre and Vian, and Vian did not seem too sad about what Sartre told him; he spoke about two other novels he is going to write, but I am afraid they will be bad too. And then Sartre knew that he was very sad and angry after that. He is really a strange secret guy, not very appealing.

Lot of planes go on crashing all around the world. They did a terrible deadly thing here. The girl, Ginette Neveu, who was killed with Cerdan, was to be buried last Wednesday. Everything was ready for a great burial when the brother and brother-in-law said they did not get the right corpse! What difference does it make? They had to look for other bits of bones and flesh, and I am not sure they found the real ones.

Now I'll go on copying my book out of my head. Farewell my beloved you. The gopher misses you, the little Picasso girl[1] misses you, my bed misses you, we all miss you here — chiefly my body and heart miss you. But sun will come back and your smile; I'll be Nelson-happy again. I have to believe it very hard or I should cry again as on parting day. Love and love as ever forever.

Your own Simone

1) A huge reproduction hanging on the wall at Rue de la Bûcherie.

Friday, 25 Novembre 1949

Sweetest beloved you,

Poor dear me did not find back her papers, neither her head. But the heart stays good. Today is rather a sad day; it is a big strike, nearly nobody works, all shops are shut, no newspapers, no cabs, no gas: it was cold for the little gopher, this morning. It is grey and cool, easy to feel a bit sad; chiefly, if you are longing for somebody who is here. Did I tell you about the newspaper-seller near the tobacco you know, rue de la Bûcherie? I guess so. He knows "who I am" and always talks with me. Two days ago, he showed to me a newspaper where they spoke about a kind of evening university in Belleville. "You should do that here", he said. "So many young people want to learn in this district..." I don't know if he spoke about our dear gargoiles,[1] "You should have a place and teach them things, I'll help you. I'll give all my time to that; I'll drop the Sorbonne and everything…" He is fifty, and I seemed a little amazed, so he said: "You know *Martin Eden?* That is me. I learnt everything by myself; it was harder for young boys." So he is contriving to get a room; it seems he'll succeed in getting a neighbourhood theatre; he spoke to Sartre too and some of these days he'll say "everything is ready" and we'll have to go and teach things to the gargoiles. Another day he was excited, saying: "I just spoke in the air for the first time, yesterday." You would like him; he is the kind of some-body you enjoyed finding in Paris and complained not to find in Roma.

About our little family: Scipion is going down to Cannes for two months, working for an American-French (American producer) about an American family settling in France, and his job is to find "French-American gags," which does not seem so easy! Poor Vian is very sad in the end not to have written a good novel; he will be brought to trial in February for his book *I'll Spit on Your Graves*; they are suing lot of people for obscenity right now, and we intend to go all of us and protest. Poor Camus fell sick again; he stays lying in his room the whole day long. Poor Olga is cured but the doctor said it would not be safe to act this year, so she is hopeless. Poor Wanda (her sister) had her dog dying, then dead. She said: "I should have rather liked Camus to die. I know my dog is not as *important* as Camus, socially, and he had hardly the fourth part of Camus' spirit but I liked him so much better!" She really said so. Sartre and everybody who does not much like Camus laugh at that. Poor dear me goes on getting strange letters. An old man congratulated me for two years but then he said: "Why don't you speak about the 100,000 women who were beaten, raped, bruised, half-killed and killed by French young résistants? These girls were right to sleep with Germans; womanhood does not know about flags and frontiers. You should have spoken about they martyrdom. But maybe you were yourself a kind of resistentialist?" Indeed, no 100,00 women were beaten; some had their shaven away and they deserved it, not just for sleeping with Germans, but by betraying French people. That is the kind of letters I happen to get.

I try as well as I can to mend up for what I have lost. I live the most quiet, wise, nice working life, a love life too, though nobody knows. You are the first thought of my heart when I open my eyes at morning; the last one before they close. You never desert me. I remember and I wait.

Your own Simone

1) *A la gargouille*, a bistro on Rue de la Bûcherie, named for its proximity to Notre Dame. De Beauvoir and Algren thus referred to the beggars in the neighborhood as "the gargoiles" (*"les gargouilles"*).

Poor dear me's beloved one,

It is cold, grey, lonely here. I got no letter since an awfully long time: more than a week, I guess. Maybe you are waiting for mine, which was late for some reasons I told. I have your ghost, your picture, and the gopher, but a letter would keep me warmer. Oh, I know it will come soon!

I wrote the whole script again. What do you do, honey? You never say. What will happen with the Hollywood scheme? Not much about me. A girl asked to put *Blood of Others* on the air; she is nice and has got good ideas, all right. The lesbian borrowing typewriter girl is really sick — something bad in the breast, I am afraid; she wants to see me (and borrow money). The sick painter's wife came home and asked for Sartre and me going to see her husband (and borrow money). And the ugly woman wrote a long letter explaining that love which is not physical is nothing, and she lacks money. Everybody is asking for something, complaining about something. I am tired with them. I was asked to go to Mexico in January by the UNESCO; they pay the whole thing, trip and entertainment for the two weeks: there is a kind of existentialist session. I was a little amazed saying "no" so stubbornly, because I remember how I should have been in rapture, four years ago, if I had been offered to go to Mexico, even for an existentialist session. Now I don't care for going alone in any place in the world. All the time I honestly can spare out from my daily life, I want to spare it for you, only for you, as long as you care to get it. For instance, I used to love winter sports, and with the coming snow, the longing awakes in my heart, but I'll not go, because when I don't see you I feel I have to work and stay here. So I can have a good heart, not disapprove myself I mean, when I working and say good bye everybody to see you and make myself happy (and you too, I hope). Anyway, I should not care going again to Mexico.

I'll write a better letter when I get yours and feel a little better too. It is grey, today; I miss you too much. I should like to lie in your arms and cry a little; you are so nice when I cry in your arms, you are always so nice. Yea, it was hard to say good bye; it is hard to have said so. I'll stop, my love, or I should cry and lonely tears are not sweet at all. I never loved you more.

Your own Simone

P.S. I put some order in my cupboard and I found heaps of soap, and among soap mint life-savers;[1] I tried to taste them, but they just tasted of soap so much that I had to spit them away.

1) Mints Algren gave to de Beauvoir for her transatlantic flight, to protect her from airsickness and, more importantly, to prevent a plane crash.

Friday night, 2 Décembre 1949

Nelson my love,

I wrote a short story sad, silly letter last time. This time I'll write a long happy silly one. It is the heart of the night, and I love you so much, Nelson, my love. I am happy, not so much because, in the end, I found back my papers. Yea, I did, there were very honestly left in the "lost things office," which sent me a little letter. I left there some money for the good cab driver; by the way, having no head, I just forgot to ask for my head back. It was a small relief, though I remembered much, I had forgotten some things, too, which I was happy to read again. But, chiefly. I am happy because I got this long letter I longed for; that was food for my heart, sweetheart, not just because it promised of rumsticks, but because it gave me all the love I needed. I am on a diet; I don't take too much food, but I cannot do without your love, be it good or not for my stomach. So this very day when I was sad because I got no letter, I got one in the evening, and the sun shines again in La Bûcherie Hotel.

I have a lot of little things to tell you, don't let me forget them, I am coming from Pont-Royal bar, where I spent the evening with Bost, very proud for your liking Bourret; he asks: did you read the *whole* book? And what do you think? Is it correctly translated? Do you know by chance how many copies were sold? Answer if you can and if you care. In Pont-Royal car was the wonderful, delightful Roosevelt-French contraceptive, I mean Truman Capote. He said "Hello!" with a lovely gesture of his small white pansy hands, and went to another corner, with American men and women. The funny thing was Bost spoke to me the whole dinner long about a book he is going to translate and likes, *The World Next Door* a crazy veterans story by man called Fritz Peters; Bost says it is much better than *Snake-Pit*. Well, he got very much excited because from the jacket picture, it seemed to him the man with darling Capote was Fritz Peters, and so was it! We spoke with him, and he seems a very nice man, though he has got such an ugly woman. So you know this book? He stays in Paris for months and I'll see him sure. Capote flies away in a plane, maybe will crash. He wondered about my round big broach (somebody told me it is worth 300 dollars in the States, so don't despise it so much, thinking it is just twisted fancy). I never saw something as funny as Capote, not even you. He twists his nose when speaking, as I did when fifteen. Really, he is a poor thing.

Nelson, my love, my lover, my only man, I am too tired to go on. The bed looks too nice though lonely. I'll lie in it and dream. Good night, my love.

Saturday

I was pealing potatoes at the window and waiting for calling me from downstairs, when somebody knocked at the door: Alas! It was only the masseuse and I had to wake up far from you! I am glad you are massaged too, honey; maybe we'll not climb volcanoes next time, but you'll sure have to climb up the bed many times, so you have to get a nice young back, not keep this middle-aged worrying one. Your letter made everybody happy, first me, as I said. Then Bost who was very proud to be better than Stendhal. And Scipion was proud to know he was wounded with a contraceptive.[1] I am a little sad, though, you don't think better of Stendhal. Mathilde strikes me much more interesting then Scarlett,[2] and I don't hate the whole romantic stuff; I am interested in Julian, with the good and silly parts there are in himself. Sure it is not a realistic novel, but it has got reality in its own way.

Did you see how nicely the planes crashes go on? Twenty-nine little boys killed in Sweden; in France, a heroic steward preserved thirty-two passengers' life, but anyway five were terribly burnt to death. And our New York-Mexico crashed in Dallas—very hopeful. I liked the story of your bursting stove and the way you so shrewdly escaped.

I was asked 1) to write a play for a great French actress; 2) to write a movie-script for a great French movie actress. But I go on stubbornly writing your novel. *The Second Sex* comes third in these last months best-sellers list; Sartre is the only seventh—that is not bad for essay, is it? All the others are novels. But in the north the police came into some bookshops and took the book away, because a "virtuous people northern league" had said it was an immoral book. All the northern booksellers are so scared they don't dare to show the book any more, and Gallimard is going to sue the league. *Do you work?*

I saw Orson Welles in Deux Magots. I hope to go to the circus with him tonight. Little Cassoulet came yesterday in Pont-Royal where I was drinking coffee with Sartre and asked: "Do you want to go to the circus with Orson Welles?" "Why not?" we said. I should be amused to meet him, I'll tell you. My Negro translator with the wonderful beard apologized much for having asked the money; he hates Mrs. Bradley, too, because she did not use his translation and still keeps the script, not accepting to give it back. Terrible woman.

Honey, I keep all my warmth nicely bundled up for you when I'll feel your warmth again. I wait for the monsters, for your next letter, and faraway but most of all fresh kisses. Love, love, love to my only love.

Your own Simone

1) Algren's joke. He liked to compare the driving habits of American GIs and French soldiers, maintaining that Scipion (in fact, much too young to be drafted) had been decorated with the Croix de Guerre for heroism under fire: while stealing a pack of cigarettes from the pocket of GI, he had been wounded by an exploding condom. 2) Algren disliked *The Red and the Black*, particularly the character of Mathilde, whom he associated unfavorably with Scarlett O'Hara in *Gone with the Wind* and with Amber in *Forever Amber* by Kathleen Winsor.

Wednesday, 7 Décember 1949

Dearest shameless piece of Wabansia pimp,

So that's what you mean when you explain to me that I should not come to Chicago too early, because your *work* needs freedom, real freedom! I see, I see.[1] Well, if you don't marry the girl and get a dozen children before our next meeting, I don't object to your practicing a little your hard manly job, so you have not forgotten everything when I'll kiss your dirty face again. Should I practise a little too, honey? I don't feel so much in the mood, but if you want me to, I can get some nice pimp of my own in La Bûcherie Hotel. For instance Philip Williams (or William Philips) whom I met yesterday in Pont-Royal, you know, this *Partisan Review* leader about whom another stupid man told me: "He is the most clever American man of the whole States."

I had a great good dinner with Olga at L'Escargot, remember? One of these places where I tried to get you used to French food, and not to mix old red wine with Coca-Cola as you always did. Olga was dressed on her best with the Sorrento scarf we gave her, and very nice. After dinner, we drank scotch (not very good one) in Pont-Royal. An American gang came in and I had a strange feeling, looking at one of the men: it felt inside me as if he had been Koestler; still he was more handsome, and it was not him. I looked and looked without succeeding to place him, and he came to me: "Do you remember our big quarrels? "No, where was it?" "In New York?" "Where in New York?" "In my home." Still I could not remember. Then he gave his name; I apologized very much and we got an appointment for Monday. He has an awfully ugly wife, but very wealthy one. This same evening, poor Sartre went and saw Wanda. He wanted to take her to the theatre, to a good funny coarse play I already saw; he had the tickets in his pocket. But Wanda to stay with her new dog, though she hates that dog. I told you that the first one died two weeks ago, then she was given another one, as beautiful and expensive as the first, with a long precious pedigree, but another kind: myself I love this new one; it looks like a little bear, it is nearly as pretty as a gopher. But she hates her (it is a girl dog), because she remembers the other who is dead, and each time she does something for the new one, she bursts into tears, because she did not do so well for the dead one. So poor Sartre spent the evening looking at Wanda who cried, fed the dog, beat her, cried again. I told him your doped girl story; the laughed and laughed, saying that was like *you* to get trapped by this kind of girl; he felt such a silly, soft hearted affair could never have happened to *him*. I don't know how I pick up the men I like or love; they are all of a strange kind, it seems. I'll tell the story to Olga, sure.

Everyone in Paris is waiting for your gifts, impatiently I'll tell you as soon as I get them. You didn't deserve a letter, since you have no time to read them or to answer them in a sensible Try to behave a little, you crummy pimp. Do you think that it is nice for me to think a pimp of mine is getting money from another woman? What a shame!

Still, if you don't get married, maybe I'll forgive you. I kiss you as if you were already forgiven, Nelson, my love.

Your own Simone

1) Algren had taken in a friend who was a prostitute and drug addict, for whom he had to procure, with great difficulty, small amounts of heroin so that she would leave him alone.

Saturday, 10 Décembre 1949

Nelson, my love,

That is just your little week-end kiss so you don't forget I love you. I sent you a Christmas gift. It is not much, because I could not figure what you needed; it seemed you bought everything you wanted in Paris for the little nest and you. But I found a book which I myself enjoy very much. Much better than the Paris pictures book I already gave you: it is Paris suburbs, and though the photographer is not as wonderful as our glorious Wabansia Nelson, it seems to me he did a good job.. The picture twenty look well; it is this Robinson dancing which we saw on the Marne, and sixty-three is one of these dancings, the one where we ate something. Remember the pédalo? A nice day, with the dinner on the little island and you rowing so bravely! A nice day so many nice days, with the nicest of all living dirty pimps. How so business get along, honey? Does *she* work well?

Great literary events in Paris this week. There was the Goncourt prize — that is the most important prize for a novel in the year. The book at once comes a best-seller; it sells 100,000 at least, which in France is much, and the author is covered with fame and money. Ten old men, a kind of "academy," give it, and there is a terrible battle between the publishers; they bribe some of the old men, often. The jury is supposed to choose the best novel, but always chooses the worst. So it was a great amazement this year because they really picked the best, *Week-end in Zuydcoote*,[1] the story of the Dunkerque battle — a book not far from Bost's *Last Profession*, but more wonderful. We published a big part of it in *Temps modernes*. Big triumph for Gallimard, who got smaller prizes, too. A not talented at all woman got one of these smaller prizes; she said in newspapers she had not eaten for thirty-six hours and not slept for three days, because she was so anxious to get *fame*. On pictures, she had a big open mouth and eyes mad with pleasure; everybody laughed at her. The prize winner is an English teacher who spent some time in Cleveland. I gave him Frankie Machine with the hope he could translate it, but he seems to think it was *big*; it comes to be quite a problem.

Wednesday

Dearest most successful pimp, I read a big part of your letter to Bost and Sartre; they were madly jealous; you are quite somebody in Wabansia now.

There is cold white wind here, too, sweetest you, our gargoiles friends are frozen — still I don't forget we panted with heat in hellish Marrakech.

I had a lunch with Ellen Wright Sunday, and I heard Carson McCullers had to be given a strait jacket for trying to kill herself. She got paralysed chiefly because of brandy (her husband and herself drank *three* bottles each day, and then wine, cocktails, scotch — all the regular drinks), but then she was made half-mad by the adaptation of her last novel[2] into a play. She needed money badly, and she thought the adaptation was awful — her friends tried purposely to make the play a failure—she had a stroke, was taken to the hospital, then to New York, with half of herself crushed and dead—it seems she'll stay so until she dies, which is awful. Ellen told me she (herself) had been an actress once, in Shakespearian theatre, when she was young; she would like to begin again and makes some mild work in a an American theatre company. Though she loves Wright really deep, she admitted she was pleased to have him in Buenos Aires for a time and feel herself free. She really seemed to me a very sweet woman. I met awful William Philips who explained to me how great and free your country is: everybody can say what he wants, except if he is a Stalinist; indeed Stalinists should not be free, then most of people who say they are liberal are Stalinist, so they should not be free neither. That is obvious, is not it? Philips is free; he is sure of that. So what? I spoke to him about the terrible situation in Greece. Did you heard about concentration camps? In an island they are keeping 15,000 Greek liberals and communists; it seems like nazi camps. We had dreadful reports about it these last days: the very Greeks who fought against Germans are been starved to death, beaten and tortured by your great American soldiers. Worse than the Spanish situation, which stinks enough. I told that to Philips, he did not deny the facts but said: "Greece does not threaten the world as USSR does." I said: "Well, but that is *American* policy." He said: "It is not proved that America should do that *everywhere*." Is not that great? Don't you like William Philips?

The newspaper-seller really trapped me; he is more and more wonderful discussing Kafka and atomic physics. He hired a theatre-hall, Rue Mouffetard, and the 10th of January we have to go and spoke, Sartre and I. Every Tuesday there will be a lecture; we cannot say no, indeed. Honey, I go for a week with Bost and Sartre at Madame Morel's in the cold country, the 26th, with her daughter and grand-daughter; I'll be back 3rd January. That means send one letter, next I guess, make a good calculation, c/o Mme Morel, La Pouèze, Maine et Loire. I want my new-year letter there. I mailed the book (airmail), which was a little stupid, but I wanted a little gift from me to your heart as quick as possible. Could I, I should have mailed myself by plane, though I dread planes now. I am so lonely, honey. But spring and summer will come true, my Wabansia beam will come true. Each day I love you more than ever, my love.

Votre Simone

---

1) By Robert Merle. 2) *The Member of the Wedding*, entitled *Frankie Addams* in French.

Sweetest darling you,

I had just a lunch with Silone,[1] who was in Paris for a week (without any Darina). He should not do much on Wabansia as a pimp, for he came quite angry when I wanted to pay the bill. "He was an Italian; it was the first time in his life any woman had paid for him." Remember, in Roma they never let me invite them. I succeeded here, in the end, but it was true struggle, quite different from dear Carlo Levi. It seems dear Carlo Levi nearly turned a Stalinist, because he was so proud of a big picture of him printed in *L'Unita*, the CP paper, with some nice words. Silone laughed openly, that time, about Levi's petty vanity. Himself was a little dull, but nice as always, though we spent a very short time together. He contrived to get a big political party, between Moscow and Marshall Plan: 180,000, he said, which is not bad, but he does not believe too much in politics, which I like in him. He had a big quarrel with Philips, the day after I met the man, and I was pleased at it. (Philips told me that my English was really good, that I never did a mistake! What do you think of that?)

We have big troubles here, in our CP, and it pleases me very much. Lot of communist intellectuals feel tired about all these trials, Tito's excommunication, and so on, and they leave the party noisily. Even non-intellectual ones disagree; there are important discrepancies between the different bunches.

Remember this blonde girl I told you so many times, who drinks so much since twenty years? Who thought she was a genius and never wrote nothing and came drunk on the stage? She was a very young love of Sartre, and lived with a great French hunch-backed actor called Dullin. Well, Dullin died this week at the hospital. A weird pitiful story, the kind you would tell wonderfully well, half-laughing, half-crying. She was dangerous for him; she helped him to become quite penniless and poisoned with her delirium tremens the end of his poor old life. Still, it was hard for her, because when Dullin came sick (something very painful in the kidneys; he had one taken away), his friends put him in the hospital and forbade the woman to come. She laid, sick herself, without a penny in her room for eight days, not eating, seeing nobody. An old slave-girl she had had, who is now free and married, helped her a little. Dullin died without seeing her again. Maybe he wanted her, I don't know, but the friends were afraid she would get hysterical. I understand. Then they did not even asked her to the burial (she was not a regular wife); she went by herself, nobody said a word to her, and in the cemetery, she fell in terrible crisis. The slave-girl, called Ziana, phoned to poor Sartre who was no longer a friend since two years, but who wants to help. The blonde, said Zina, had not *one day* stopped being drunk for five years—she has been sent to asylum; it did not help she had no family, not one friend, and not a penny. So Sartre will ask for money to all Dullin's friends and in the end support the girl. That is not the worse, though he really wholly supports too many people now; he is the blonde's only hope; he will have to confort her, tell her to write, prevent her from drinking. I'll have to help too. He is now at her home, very scared because last time he saw her, she fell on his mouth and offered all of her! She is forty-six and looks without any age at all, red and blown up by alcohol, a terrible heavy, shapeless, hopeless thing. What would you so, you smart pimp of Wabansia street?

I begin to feel hopeless about Frankie Machine. The gifted English teacher, a good writer, I thought of for a translation, wrote that "it would ask two years hard work to do the job!" So he doesn't want it. Who will? Who will? Queneau doesn't know, nobody knows.

The New York publisher (Knopf) will give me 750 dollars for *The Second Sex*, but that is two books, more than 1000 pages! I'll get them in New York, which is convenient since you said next time I'II take the plane to Chicago, not you to Paris. I just got my last novel, *All Men Have to Die*, translated in Italian—a very pretty book; I don't send it to a non-Italian knowing lazy pimp. Seriously, honey, what about your next book? Do you think of it? Begin to loiter around? Put it aside for awhile? Merry Christmas, my love. I'll kiss you in my heart at midnight as I do so many times day and night. I'll ask Santa Claus to promise to see you again before too long a time, that will be my most precious present. And I wish you still find me a nice little token for your Christmas shoe.

Your own Simone

1) A friend of Sartre and de Beauvoir, the Italian writer Ignazio Silone (1900–1978) was internationally recognized during World War II for his antifascist fiction. One of the original founders of the Italian Communist Party, he was expelled from it in 1930.

Dearest lazy crazy pimp of mine,

A man just came with a huge package from Robert Fabian; it looked nice but there was a terrible amount of money to pay and I had not it (10,000Fr, 30 dollars). I hope it is worth it. So, I have to go and look for it in some station tomorrow or the day after. French customs are not so stupid as you think, honey. Anyhow, you were sweet to send this big monster; he will not have to wait long before coming home.

Yesterday, it was rather La Bûcherie hospital here, I staid in bed with an horrible cold and could do nothing but sleep and read mysteries, so today I am eager to work again, and I shall not waste much time with a crummy bastard of a local youth who does not even send a letter to me.

The Dullin's girl was no so bad as Sartre expected to find her, after all: she seems rather relieved by the old man's death; she has not drunk since a long time, and as soon as Sartre gave her money, she came very nice with him. She said first she would never sleep with any man again, to be faithful to Dullin's memory (which man would ask her, I don't know). She had decided to give all her platonic love to Sartre; he needs it, she says. She will love him as a dear child, and teach him poetry and mystical life. She knows he doesn't believe in God, but he needs mystical life; she will give it to him. Then she'll write great books an all will be fine. Poor Sartre is much scared. It was the last rehearsal of Camus' play, Saturday evening. All his "friends" were pleased because the play was bad, but then they were disappointed because critics were good. In fact, it is a dead, boring thing,[1] a mixture of Sartre, Malraux, myself, of things said and said again, without any fancy. But I am glad it is said to be good because the poor guy looked so sick; his lungs are bad again and there is not much to do about them but wait, rest, and hope. He looked so tired when we saw him after the play.

I am afraid poor Bost would not find the story so funny. He was a little touchy about his book; he got much appraised in France from writers and critics, but not many readers. So he would be sad not to be translated correctly in the States; I shall not tell it to him.

I am sending you Sartre's *Dirty Hands*, translated by our fried Abel; when you are tired not to know what is literature. you can try to look at it. By the way, Abel was awfully angry at me for not having recognized him at first sight. My God! We didn't see him so often! What so you mean, you liar, when you say you are "taking pictures" with a photographer? *He* takes the pictures and you just loiter around and bother him; don't pretend he lets you handle anything!

Do you feel lonely in your virgin bed, honey? Don't forget to change sheets when I come and sleep there. I'll always remember you so puzzled with the sheets in your arms, when you saw me already lying in the bed, the first, first night. It seems to me I began to really love you this very minute, never to stop.

I'll thank better for the monster I have torn it in pieces and began to swallow it. Tell me exactly what is for whom. You were nice, Nelson, sweetheart, to worry about this hard thing: making and sending a monster. I know what it means and feel sad not to have had at home the money to keep it.

Nelson, Nelson, I don't wish to say goodbye I want you to come in, to hop around the room telling nice lie, then to come and lie in my virgin bed so it is no longer virgin at all. At morning I should put the head on your shoulder, and you'd say: "Are you invited?." Nelson, my love.

Your own Simone

1) *Les Justes.*

Christmas night, 1949

Nelson, my beloved own love,

It was sweet to spend this night with you. I came home at five and never stopped working about Bruno Bicek; and it is now midnight and I am half dead. I did not eat a thing and shall not, just drink tea; it will be a nice reward to write to you. I decided it would be my best Christmas gift to have this translation wholly done for New Year. I shall drop my own silly book; it will be a rest because I am fed up with it, and in the country I shall finish *Never Come Morning*. With eight hours work a day, it will be over in five days. Bost will do his own part at the same time, and we'll spend three days quarrelling about what the other has done and asking Sartre's judgment. So on the first January it will be over. Typed in the end of the month, given to Gallimard beginning of February. And a good translation, I grant it.

Honey, I cannot do less; everybody says you are such a nice man! I went and brought back the dear monster, and took his insides away: the rumsticks are better than ever; thanks for the books and cigarettes! Thanks

316

from me first. Then from Olga, who was greedily delighted; from the singer, who was quite surprised and pleased: "What a nice man!" Thanks from the secretary. I gave everybody the nice cards too. Scipion will get his gift I don't know when, since he is not in Paris. But most of all thank you from Sartre; he was wonderfully happy with the cigars; he says he can no longer smoke French cigars! He smoked two of yours yesterday evening, ashamed of himself but so grateful he wanted to write to you, except he does not write English. I let some money to the concierge, so if brother monster comes when I am out, it will not be sent away wandering in the streets. Yea, it made it a real Christmas, your gifts, but there was some sadness; it was so foggy, dark, and cold. I had a bit of influenza sadness, too. I missed you terribly when everybody in the streets seemed so happy. There is much happiness for me too in this world, but faraway, in a faraway street of a faraway country, and sometimes I want so much to hold it in my hands again, to hold you in my arms which would be so warm. Let this year give us the same happiness as last one, let this year give us to each other. Is it a sound wish, Nelson? I hope it is your wish too. I'll stop because I should cry. It seems strange you are so far, being so near. There is not an inch of me that does not remember you and wait for you.

Tomorrow morning I go to the country, a short four hours trip. I use your brown bag to pack my things; it is on the floor, open, with its blue round piece of paper: "Cunard white star. Tourist class." It speaks of you; it is a little piece of you. All the room remember you; my heart does not remember, it is just with you.

Happy new year, my love! Get all the happiness you deserve, that would be much. Here is a heap of Christmas love, of new-year love, of forever love.

Your own Simone

Wednesday, 28 Décembre 1949

Sweetheart,

You'll get a short letter because I have an appointment with Steffi, the barber, Mama Tomek, and lot of other people, all struggling against each other in very queer French: what a mess! I work more than eight hours a day and so does Bost; it is awfully nice of him because after all he never slept with you and probably never will. That is the kind of work you get angry at, when you care for it; you cannot stop before being through. I am in this ugly little French village of which I often spoke to you. The house is confortable; there is always the old husband, whom I never saw, the old lady so nice daughter and grand-daughter, and an older bearded woman-servant who cannot understand how we do write so much, Sartre, Bost, and myself: "How is it? It all comes out from their head? They do write the way we walk?" she says, quite puzzled. We eat geese, turkeys, pies, and puddings' we talk and translate. I cough, too, as soon, as I stop translating, I cough. How so explain it? Still, I feel better today.

I'll write better when I am through with Bruno. That is a way of telling you my love, you know, breaking my back by bending on this stuff and getting stiff in the hand. I wait for a letter and kiss you with love, and love, and more love.

Your own Simone

Saturday, 31 Décembre 1949

Dearest lazy you,

Maybe that was not a week at all, and sure that was not much of a letter: yet, it was the only letter I got in this very real week I spent about Bicek, and it was a rather poor reward. Naughty you! When I spent ten hours a day translating on and on, I was fed up with it in the end, and so was poor Bosto! Well, yesterday evening each of us was through with his own part, all we have to do is survey each other's part now, and give the last touch — it will be more pleasant. Within three days your book will ready to print, honey — a real masterpiece of translation. Sartre gave a very fine title in the end, *Le matin se fait attendre*; it sounds poetical in French and it is nearly the meaning of *Never Come Morning*. Exactly it means morning is long to come, you have to wait long to get morning, morning is long delayed, you see? The point is it sounds quite like a French title, not a translation. Do you agree? Where did you pick I was going south? Near Angers, I wrote to you. I even said the name of the place so you could write directly, which you did not. Are you sure you read my letters, honey, or do you mix them with Sophie Babet's?[1] Do you enjoy going to Hollywood for the *Golden Arm*? And to get rid of Bradley? Dirty crook, everybody hates her.

Nice life is going on here, though I cough more and more. Each night we go to sleep later, each morning wake up later, so in the end we are going to lose or win a whole day. I don't make up my face, don't do my hair, don't quit my home-gown, hardly wash up; it is very confortable! Sartre is writing a long study about Genet, the fairy burglar, and everybody here reads Genet's books. It is awfully funny to discuss them with the old lady, who is hard-boiled woman in her way, but never read such books when she was young and discover this kind of obscenity with mild amusement. Yesterday, an endless discussion was to decide how dirty or how clean was usually a street boy's ass. Genet tells it is always dirty but Sartre says it is a literary trick, because he wants to impress people with dirty tales. What do you think of such an argument for an old decent lady?

Honey, you deserve more, and then I have nothing more to say. Your book is really a very good one. You know, Bost too likes it very much, though he read it rather topsy-turvy. I like the jail, and the brothel, Steffi and Bruno last meeting. All the end goes very quickly and is impressive. A real good book written by a real good man who can feel and write. I kiss this man, very hard. He is my own Nelson as I am.

Your own Simone

The Dullin's girl wrote an awful letter to Sartre, saying: "Why should I cry for a dead man? I feel free now. Now, it will be my chance. It is hard to live by a too much well known guy." Dullin did everything to give her a chance she never deserved. She will not do more now than before. Then she tells how during the Christmas night she had a whole little theatre with little baby Christ, Holy Virgin, shepherds and so on, and she put Dullin's picture nearby, flowers, candles, and she read to Dullin's picture some pages of Nietzsche! That is how she likes people: dead, and accepting her comedies.

1) The friend of "Gendarme."

1950

Nelson, my love,

So I was not so badly disposed of after all. I got another letter a few days after the first one, with the clipping explaining you should go back to the CP in order to be a real good writer and the one sending you to hell. I came back a few hours ago, by a sad, raining grey day. I am through with Bruno Bicek, now it is the typewriter job to take care of him.

Nelson, now I have a serious letter to write to you. I turned it for days and days in my head because I don't want to bother you, because I am so scared by the idea of your answer which can make me so happy or so sad: Well, it is about our next meeting. You told me: "We'll see each other again, nothing is surer." You told me on the Tunisian roads, when Ameur Djemaïl was driving, that I might go back to Wabansia nest. But I know, you told me, too, it would not be soon. And I have to ask you to let me come as soon as June. It is not whim, you know. Sure, I am impatient of melting in your arms again—I long for you—but if I wished to come soon just from my longing, I should not demand, I should just suggest. I don't like to be demanding, and you know I try not to be much, honey, Now I demand. The point is Sartre *has to* go away this summer for three months, no later than June, and he asks me, very demandingly, to go away when he does—not to wait until he is back; it would seem to him terribly unfriendly to make it a parting time as long as it might be. And sure he has no right at all to ask anything from you, but you see how it is for me: since I decided not to break, even for love sake, the long friendship I have with him (and which he needs very much, as you could feel), it would be stupid and unkind not to act in a real friendly way. Until now, you and me disposed of our meetings without bothering about him; it is the first time he asks me anything about it. *Trust* me, Nelson. If I say it is *important* for him, so it comes to be for me. And he *cannot* go later. I'll tell you once more, honey: really living near me does not mean you cannot work. Remember Ischia. We could both have worked very hard. I'll do all you want; we can try to find a quiet place on the lake or elsewhere, and work. We can stay in Chicago. I can have a room of my own near you and let you alone when you need it, even for a few days, if necessary. I should like to work, too, this year: our love is not just a holiday, it is a real part of our lives; we must be able to live it and go on living our real working life. And then, you know I respect your work, honey; it is the most important thing in you who are so important to me (and the way I spent hours picking up the right words to get for you the best translation possible should be a proof of it among others). But I dare say our love seems to me something very important too; don't make us delay too much living it, enjoying it. Happiness is very important too.

You'll make your own choice: come back here if you feel like it, let us travel around, let us settle in any place, let us stay in Wabansia, but let me come in June instead of waiting until sad autumn or cold winter. I'll have some money anyhow, that is no part of the problem. Answer quickly, please, my love. I shall not sleep much until I'll get your answer. I already got nightmares these nights. Maybe you'll find this letter too solemn and say pleasantly: "Well, sure, come!" Maybe you'll be a bit angry and say: "No. I told you I did not want you so soon." I don't know. Nelson, please, don't say no if you can help it. And anyhow, don't get angry at me. Remember our love, remember me.

Your own Simone

Saturday, 7 Janvier 1950

Darling smart you,

Well, this time you outsmarted us; you can be proud! Thanks, honey, thanks from me and everybody, without forgetting the good concierge. "The thing" happened Wednesday morning; it was a grey cold day and I felt rather bad for having sent you this unpleasant letter. When you ask something important from somebody, it makes him look nearly an enemy, at least it is the way it works for me. So I said, in this moody spirit, "even if the monster came, I should not feel pleased, you must feel good first to be pleased by such things." Then the good concierge brought a letter, a nice fat letter, and I knew you could never be any kind of any enemy. You said nice silly things and my heart became silly and nice too; I was happy again. And then, "rap, rap, rap," it was the monster! Not a penny to give for him, maybe because this time you had pretended to say what stood inside. I took it greedily and opened its belly, proud at your shrewdness. I took away the scotch bottle and began to drink; it is wonderful! Bost is awfully pleased with his pen-set and the book too; Guyonnet with the cigarettes and Sartre with the tobacco. Scipion and Mouloudji did not get their gifts since the one is in the south and I did not see the other. From all your Parisian friends, and from your own gopher, thanks, thanks, endless thanks. The flour is first rate, the concierge says. So, don't be angry at French customs; they don't open all the packages after all.

I spent three days just sleeping on, so tired by this translation hard work. No kidding. It had made me nearly sick; I had no strength left. I had to sleep and sleep night and day. Then I waste a whole day writing a stupid paper for an American magazine and bring you 300 dollars. And I'll resume my own book after two weeks leave. It is not exactly about you, honey, though it is yours. Still, maybe I'll tell something of our Chicago story, I don't know. Anyhow, you'll be well disposed of, be sure of that.

Mary G. went to see some big newspaper man, a big manager, to ask some informations about Marshall Plan. He showed her a young American man standing in his office, and said mysteriously: "Here is one of the Marshall repopulation plan agent." And he explained to her there was a big center where Americans were kept, and their job was to make healthy beautiful children to French women. She was a little taken aback; the man called the embassy and asked his friends not to make dear Mary G. doubtful about the story. So she came back to the States believing it; she is going to write it in newspapers, and if you ever heard about a Marshall fucking plan, you'll know where it comes from.

I saw the drunkard Dullin's widow, Toulouse. She is about fifty by now. Still she came into her living-room dressed in a long pale blue nightgown, with long fair curls and a ribbon on her head, smiling and fidgeting like a little girl. She explained how happy she is since the "fantastic story" is over (meaning the old man's death), and how near to him she feels, and how she *will* work (she always will). She certainly knows a good story and she can tell it. I heard from Nathalie once more. One night she opened her eyes to find her husband and another man in her own bed, playing with each other in the most intimate way; clung "in American way, not in French way," she says, which I don't exactly catch. Often she enjoyed such kind of many people together parties. She is cold and curious, so I am mildly amazed at it, but I wholly dislike it. Maybe I am too much of puritan. In my idea, sleeping with the man you love is wonderful, sleeping with one man you don't love may be all right, chiefly if you like him, but playing sex with a whole gang of people, it seems to me sort of degrading. I don't like to think she did it, do you think I am wrong?

Nelson, I wait for your answer to my demanding letter, so I don't feel too good; I am too anxious. But that is a way of feeling my love, too. I love you as always, my love.

Your own Simone

Despite the courage of bold Bost
The European war was lost.
Russians dropped bombs on Chicago:
Tough Algren had fled long ago.
He heard the noise, though he was far
And whispered: "Poor Polonia Bar!"
Two months after the big attack
Tough Algren boldly dared come back.
No more bars, no more Division.
No more Polacks, no more Mission,
No more Bruno, no more boxing
No more Steffi, no more fucking.
Well, in short, no more Chicago.
"What shall I do? Where shall I go?
I shall miss my wrecked City!"
Tough Algren cried (What a pity!)
But didn't give way to sadness
And straight began to clear that mess.
First he piled the bricks that were left
On his right side. And on his left
He put the iron beams he found.
And then he swiftly swept the ground
With the iron beams he rebuilt the El,
And under it, with the bricks, he built a brothel.

—Jacques Bost

Nelson, my love,

You told me once you loved me, because you made me happy (maybe you don't remember, you say so many silly things). Then you must love me very dearly just now, because you made me still more happy than I had contrived to make myself unhappy about you. Thanks, Nelson, thanks to say yes so kindly. You are very sweet to love. It took a stone from my heart and now I began to travel back to you slowly, but surely. I'll be in your arms in summer. The idea of renting a cottage suits me very well. Will it be possible to get near the beach? Is it a nice beach? Will it be very hot? Tell me about the place since it will be our place for months. Oh, Nelson! I'll be so nice and good, you'll see. I'll wash the floor, I'll cook the whole meals, I'll write your book as well as mine, I'll make love to you ten times a night and as much in the day, even if I feel a bit tired. Yea, it will be smart to live in a little home of our own, writing and swimming and loving each other. Please, make it rather 1st July to 1st October, because I postponed my departure as much as I could, thinking it would suit you better. I'll leave Paris on the 25th June, stop two or three days in New York to get my money, so I'll be in Wabansia last day of June or first of July. Don't bother about cheap flights; I heard about it but it is good only for two months, then I want to go by the best airline, not to begin again this one engine stopping above the ocean.

What a bastard country you have got now! Remember Jean Wahl, the existentialist teacher in Chicago University with whom you nearly discussed *The Ethics of Ambiguity*? He is not at all a communist, but he took part to the big Peace Conference in Paris (which was promoted by communists, that is true, but with a wide audience). Well, he had to go to Mexico for a philosophical UNO conference, and the American embassy did not give him his passport! They said they had a black list of all the Peace Conference members, and had to ask Washington before giving any visa to them. He was so angry he told them not even to ask Washington (they probably would have said no anyway); he will not go. What a son-of-a-bitch of a country!

We spent two afternoons more with Bruno and shall spend two more, but it is pleasant because we drink scotch at the same time; yesterday we did that for four hours and then I went alone to the movies and Paris was wonderfully poetical with sky half-blue — half-pink. I don't know if poetry came from the scotch or from the book. Oh! I forgot! There is a little piece of poetry we translated and had to change a little, Sartre, Bost, and I, now it gives this:

> Brave Algren stood firm until he was shot
> He died without taking away his shoes.

Is that nice? Sure, we'll give the Wright's introduction. And very soon part will be published in *Temps modernes*.

At the movies I saw *The Third Man*. The music, Orson Welles, and the whole end are wonderful. I like the general atmosphere of Vienna. Did you see it?

You care about my business, but didn't seem so good at yours: don't go to Los Angeles without a good contract. I think I'll go away for two months with Sartre in March and April, probably one month in Egypt, travelling, and one in Venice, just staying and working. I'll tell you later. Next time I'll speak to you about Sorokine — well, I'll do now. My idea is, if you don't mind, I should like better you not to see her. I'll explain why. Unless she changed much, the first thing she'll do will be to manage to sleep with you; it is nearly sure. She cannot stand to let me have a man without wanting him. Well, I don't like the idea very much because of the fatality of it. I mean, if she did it by a real feeling for you, it could be different. Or if she let you have a real feeling for her. But she will want you in her bed even before knowing you — against me. Then she'll speak about me in her way. God knows I have nothing secret for you, but I *know* she will speak in a fancy, fake way, complaining more or less about me and all that, and it is not pleasant to think. She'll try to give you a strange idea of me; chiefly, we don't get along very well, just now. I wrote to her too frankly. Then the most dangerous: she has holidays from July to October. I don't intend to see her much. Maybe I'll ask her to stop some days in Chicago; I don't know. But anyhow it will be very little for what she would want. So, I am really afraid if she becomes friendly with you, even not sleeping with you, she will ask very demandingly to spend one month or more with you and me; she sometimes makes uncredible demands. I'll say no, but if she made you say "maybe, I don't know" and so on, she'll really hate me. Do you see what I mean? If she makes friend with you, and she will, she is attractive, lively, and warm in the *beginning* of a relationship, she will want to spend a long time with us, I'll refuse because she would spoil everything, and that will be the last breaking between her and me. Be careful. Maybe if you see her and find her charming, you'll think I am unfair to her, but I have hard memories and I don't want to take any chance.

Nelson, I am sure you never made anybody as happy as you made me. You can be proud of you. You seem so near, if I should turn my head I should see you in the bed, half-sleeping, warm, and confortable; it seems I can any minute go and lie against this warm strong body. I long for him.

We'll be happy in our little cottage, my sweet to love beloved you.

Your own Simone

Wednesday, 18 Janvier 1950

Nelson, my sweet beloved man with the golden heart,

It is a grey, raining, cold, snowy in Paris but now and till summer it will always be the July sun for me, your promised July smile. How can you make me so happy, my love? One man volunteered to translate Frankie Machine; he is French and teaching in Yale. But we have to ask him a sample of what he can do before deciding anything. The typewriter woman is typing Bruno very hard, so anyway this one will soon begin his French life.

Yesterday evening, it was the first lecture organized by the little newspaper-seller. It was narrow escape! He had asked Clouzot, the director of this movie *Manon* which you rather liked and that felt to me anti-Semitic. Clouzot had not answered, but the little man got cards printed and gave them to all his customers. Clouzot phoned to Sartre and said he never intended to go, or only if Sartre went. Sartre had something else to do, but it was impossible to drop the poor little man; so, in the end, he accepted to go with Clouzot. The point is this cautious man was afraid the whole thing would be ridiculous and he liked better Sartre to make a fool of oneself than himself. In fact, nobody was a fool. People were gathered, not many, fifty maybe, in a little room; the newspaper-seller, dressed on his best, spoke to them, very well, and Clouzot spoke about his job, making movies, and answered questions. The little man's wife was on her best too, with fake fur coat, fake jewels, fake red hair, and feathers on her head; she looked very happy, because I guess she been terribly scared it would be an absurd business. So everybody was pleased and they will begin again every Tuesday. Could you guess same success the same way, on Wabansia street?

What with the Hollywood trip, honey? I told you about Egypt with Sartre, but when we asked for papers and said Sartre would go incognito, he wanted to work and rest and see nobody, the people in the consulate explained it was impossible! He could not go without lecturing, meeting people. Egypt is such a fine country, it would be so interesting to meet important people there! So we told them in the end that under such circontances Sartre should not go at all. And he will not. I was mad with anger at these Egyptian people. If you pay your bed and bread with your own money, cannot you travel quietly in a country without *having* to entertain all the Indians we met, explaining them Wabansia high civilization, for instance, would not that have been a bit tiring?

I began to order beach-dresses for the lake side. This year I'll teach you how to swim seriously: are there waves in the lake?

Saturday

Nelson, my beloved poor stupid you, don't let us spend our whole happy time with any other people. If you like these friends and really care to see them, well, we can spend a short time with them, but let us live for good in a little cottage of our own. I want so much to be alone with you. I love nothing so much in the world as living alone with you, on island or mainland, on the sea-side or a lake shore, high up or in plain, in a town or wilderness, among Arabians or gargoiles, but alone with you. Is it very selfish? I already made so many happy plans about our swimming and cooking and working and sleeping in our little Michigan nest! Don't you want it too? Well, sure I like from time to time a good gendarme, a nice punch-drunk girl, or an unhappy thief, but only for a short time. What if they came to be tired of us? Or even just of me? And me of them? No, no, I want my own home with my own only man. Stupid, stupid you! Why do you want me to drink so much scotch with the publisher woman? It is not healthy, you know. Honey, the fact is I cannot just choose a new agent myself; the whole business has already been dealt by Gallimard through his own agents, and there is really nothing I can do about it. Explain it to your own agent. Then, maybe I can get some real money at Knopf anyway. I told you I could not go to Egypt with Sartre. So it seems we'll go to Sahara, deep in Sahara, since it will not be too hot in spring. I should like it; I like Africa and never went far away towards south enough. I'll send you all pictures of camels I can get. I'll think of you every time I'll see a camel, a palm-tree, or an Arabian; it will be much. Remember how you preserved my life in the cab

327

against the mad horse? That was great! You really deserved having Bruno's short life preserved by me. That is through now, after two nice afternoons we spent, Bost and me, drinking prussic acid poison (scotch fini!) and putting the last touch to Bruno's story. How many mistakes this Guyonnet had made — that is not credible! And then he invented French words which never existed. I work very well. I have already covered heaps of papers with silly sentences. One day, it will make a book, it is strange to think.

So, love to Nelson, only to him. I love just him. I want him and nobody else, all to myself to be all his own. Honey, we are nearly middle way now; soon I'll be trembling with joy as I was shaking with sadness in the dark airport. I belong to you, my own beloved. I am your own little love token.

Your own Simone

Tuesday, 24 Janvier 1950

Sweetest darling you,

I have to make haste if I want you to get this last letter in Wabansia nest. Well, it seems you are not local any longer, but always wandering around the world. Do they give you money in the end for your going to Los Angeles? I guess you go by train, the same train I rode when I left Chicago and called you to say "Good bye, good bye! . . ." And all the way long I brooded on *Neon Wilderness*, and wrote to you my first letter on a pink paper. It was in that train, a little later in winter, three ago, the first day is rather plain, but then you get in beautiful countries. In Albuquerque station you'll see Indians selling little tokens: it is a long time you did not see Indians. And you'll wake up among orange groves and palm-trees; it will be Pasadena and Los Angeles. Yea, I can follow you very well during the whole trip. I am nearly sure you'll not like Los Angeles. Tell me *everything* about everything — don't forget, busy man.

If you happen to meet Nathalie in some party, she knows what you are for me, a little; I had to tell her, to explain I'll go to States and not see her more than a few days. She knows I met you in 1947 and the way I did, but I did not mention the trip in '48, Guatemala, Mexico, and all that. I told her the real affair began when you came to Paris this year. Please, be careful to remind that.

I am delighted by the cottage project. It seems your Christine is a very nice woman, from what you told me. I'll surely bring her a print: what kind exactly? Can you suggest something else to bring her? I enjoyed the paper about your "sensitive" self; I learnt you got Mexican pots and Central America pictures: where did you get them? From some woman? But learnt too it was rather disorderly in your home, and your tea-cups were cracked. Are you not ashamed? Take care: *our* cottage will have to be in perfect order and no cracked cups, either you'll be deprived of couss-couss. It seems I got the right man, after all. They all say you are going to be *rich*! Maybe I'll get a mink coat and real pearls, some diamonds and a big Roll-Royce? I am very impatient.

Bost is very pleased with the little poetry. Did I tell you dear Guyonnet calls me twice a week to ask if yes or no the job is done? He waits for the translation to be typed so he can get a little more money from Gallimard and go to northern countries.

I feel exactly what you do about sleeping parties. I'll tell you my own idea of parties: a big bed and one man in it. I am a little peculiar about the man; he must be rather fair haired, with something of a round stomach, about forty one years old, or forty two, and living in Wabansia Avenue, exactly 1523. Nothing in the head but a nice smile, and wearing glass, indeed. Then I can enjoy a little party from time to time.

They say people are quite different after they have gone to Hollywood. Try not to become too much different, honey. I should be shocked if you had suddenly became *too* smart. You are all right just as you are; don't try to get off balanced on two sides of your brain. So a happy trip, a happy stay! Next time I'll send love to Los Angeles. Will the little light stay on in Wabansia when you are away? A little bit of my heart will stay there, too, but most will go with you, as always. I kiss you good luck, my love.

Your own Simone

P.S. I am very sorry you'll miss the brown bag, but then I'll use it very conveniently in Africa, so it is all right, is not it?

Saturday, 28 Janvier 1950

Dearest faraway wandering you,

That is strange to write to you this unknown place where I never kissed you and most probably never shall, and which is called by nearly a French name: Le Moyne! How is it? How is it with the Hollywood bright life? Are you going to sleep with this Sylvia Sydney[1] She must be a bit old now. Are lot of lovely beautiful women courting you? Are lot of directors and producers paying you to let them shoot your strange, seductive smile and your fascinating velvety eyes? Or did a more smart one discover you were a kind of Danny Kaye? Tell me about your movie career, honey; tell me about everything—I am so impatient. I guess it will be hot and sunny when you get this letter, and it is always awfully cold here; it was snowing a bit this morning and La Bûcherie brothel is not very warm; chiefly, how cold you must get in the little chilly cave: still you always smile nicely, you don't seem to care too much, sitting about old papers and dead leaves.

My newspaper-seller who thinks he is Martin Eden and wants to help people to go up, as high as he is, through lectures of any kind, is successful in his way. The second time a painter spoke; there were only twenty five people, but the little man was very proud with the way himself spoke that evening. Lot of most important writers, dancers, actors have said they'll lecture there. I hope they'll get some audience. I'll speak myself next Tuesday, about women I think. He told me: "It's a hard thing to do, but nothing is really hard when you have got Faith!" I went on having dinners with the ugly woman twice a month. She always bring me flowers and pays champagne; then we talk about *her*, I read her manuscript and advise her the best I can, we drink whiskies; at the third whisky she says she loves me and I go away. Always. But she was invited by some fairy to go to the snowy mountains and went away for a month; she is chiefly friend with fairies; she likes to do sewing or knitting with them, while chatting a little. The day before she went away, I saw her from a taxi, without being seen; she stood at the corner of my street and looked at La Bûcherie home with a sad passionate face. I can mean so much for when she means nothing to me. And it seems so obvious I must mean a little, at least be little token, for somebody who means much for me!

Nelson, my best self, now, now it is really half way. We went away from each other as far as we had to, and now we begin to climb up toward Michigan lake, towards each other. Have a good time in between, sweetest you. I hope you enjoy Hollywood. I hope they make a good movie with Frankie Machine, you are busy and pleased. And still find time to enjoy a little the faraway but soon to be near love of

Your own Simone

1) One of the Paramount stars of the thirties.

Dearest faraway glamorous you,

So our child is quite born at last. It was delivered to Guyonnet and he'll give
it to Gallimard tomorrow. A bit amazed when he saw not a single word of
his translation had been left, he suggested I should put my name with his,
but I did not accept this great honour. Maybe he'll get the annual prize for
the best translation in the year? That would be fun. I can tell you it is really
a nice work we did; I'll look at the galleys myself when it is printed. We give
a part of the book in *Temps modernes*, in April or May: I should like the
rape, Sartre likes much the brothel; we'll come soon to an agreement and I'll
tell you. Are you glad to have got a French child?

I got your letter yesterday, a *very* small long one. Yea, honey, I got the
letter sent to La Pouèze, and I thanked you heartily for it: how do you read
my letters, tell me? Once you told me you just put your finger on the words
and the meaning came out. I am not sure it works so well. You should know
that you have been thanked enough for La Pouèze. I'll not thank you very
much for this one: half for Bost (who was very pleased with the poem), and
very little was left for me. I enjoyed immensely the literary luncheon picture: you exactly looked like the man in the starched collar whom I often
meet when I am looking for you in a station. I should have like to know
more about it: what did you say with your golden wise mouth? Did they
clap their hands nicely?

Olga is afraid your poor nice brown trunks are lost, so was my blue
bath-suit. We'll begin a new life, with a new pink trunks and bath-suit. We
are wealthy enough to buy a new fancy clothes, are we not?

Something awfully sad happed to me. Friday night. I was nicely sleeping, having lovely dreams, when I heard a kind of "rap, rap, rap." I sleep
with little waxen-balls in my ears, you know, so it was faint noise and for a
time I mingled it with my dreams; but little by little I became unconfortable. I wake up and put away the waxen-balls. "RAP, RAP, RAP." It was a
real noise and *inside* my room, so what? I lit up the lamp, saw nothing but
the noise was here; it looked like your ghost knocking madly at something.
And then, I *saw:* the rain falling from the ceiling on my white arm-chair! I
pushed away the wet poor thing, and water fell on the carpet. It was 4 A.M.
I went and woke up the poor concierge; She helped me to put lot of buck-
ets, pails, and basins beneath the dropping fountain. A water-pipe had
burst out, she said. The rain fell more and more heavily. It is strange in a

cosy, closed human little room to see this intrusion of outside wild world! It was noisy and unpleasant, and for a long time I could not sleep. At last I did, and when I woke up, it seemed somebody had dumped a whole wagon of mud on my poor carpet! I have to get a fresh one; I'll buy a red small one, as good as possible, and put it on the inky spot and the whole injured place. So it will be still finer than it was, but just now I feel very sad each time I open my door. Your ghost is wickedly pleased, I must say.

Next Saturday there is a kind of festivity about the dead actor, Dullin; all theatre people in Paris—actors, producers, writers, stage directors—will meet in the nice theatre Dullin owned for a long time in Montmartre.[1] He did good work there, as an actor and stage director, he helped young play-writers and tried to serve the old ones. On Saturdays they will play pieces of the plays Dullin staged in past times. He produced Sartre's first play, *The Flies*, during the war, written for Olga, who was a very good Electra. So, Olga will play a scene from *The Flies*. That is a big thing for her, because everybody in Paris has forgotten her; they'll see her again and she wants so much to be an actress again! When she rehearsed her part, she was very good, moving and everything; I have hope for her. But look how terrible she is: I told her she had to go to the best hair-dresser in Paris, to have her hair nicely done in a kind of old Greek way. I gave her money for it, I fixed the appointment, I even went with her and stayed half an hour to advise her. Well, in evening she cried madly on poor Bost's chest: she had half-fainted at the hair-dresser's and missed an important appointment with the theatre new director, the one who organizes the festivity. She said her hair was a mess, everything was lost! She cried the whole day, yesterday, too. Today it seems she feels better, but what a terrible fuss she made! And I guess she fainted by a kind of fear at the idea of meeting Parisian public once more. I hope she'll get a real success. That would be very important for her. Then it would be easy to have her playing *The Flies* for a good next winter.

Lisa came back from the south, all golden and pleasant. She asked urgently for her cartoon, and thanks so much. Scipion had wisely phoned Cannes not to give Lisa his own gift so I did not and wait for him.

Good bye, honey, have a nice time, be wise and busy. Don't get a starched collar man, chiefly always keep nice little holes in your underwear, and in your lovely head too. Always be my own Nelson; there is no better man on earth. I dump a whole pink-wagon of La Bûcherie love on your skull.

Your own Simone

1) L'Atelier.

Dearest faraway you,

I cannot get the feeling that you'll really receive these letters with the strange address. I have to hope — that is all I can do. You are just leaving today; it is 6 A.M. in Chicago, you are getting up hurriedly because you have so many things to fix before going to the station. While my letter will fly over the sea, you'll ride the train through pink wilderness.

I had a terrible evening, some days ago, with Dullin's drunken widow, Toulouse. Sartre already knew by phone-talking with Zina, who is Toulouse's servant and devoted slave, that she had hit the bottle again during the week, and very strongly. When we arrived for dinner, the place was dark; Zina opened the door, crying and smelling of rotten wine. She was nice, thin dark little chickadee in past, past good times when Toulouse was tall handsome thin fair girl. Now Zina is fat, dirty, with hair on her face, awful to see. She said Toulouse had wanted to make a lovely dinner for us, but she drank when preparing the drinks, and she was crying on her bed. Sartre went and spoke to her; I stayed with Zina who complained she would killed herself one of these days; her husband (who is an uncultured simple working man) was fed up with the whole business — for instance Zina sleeps in Toulouse's bed, but Toulouse gets mad at her and sends her to her husband's bed, then she knocks at the door and asks for Zina again. Both cry and scream at each other the whole day long. So, Zina told me all the terrible things Toulouse had told and made, and Toulouse explained to Sartre in a girlish-drunken voice that she wanted to be loved, but she could love no more. No, not even Faulkner or Charlie Chaplin if they gave her their heart; the only she could love would be Sartre, because she knows him since so long, but she is afraid he is too busy and then he is not such an interesting man as he thinks. "I think nothing" said poor Sartre. "Well, *people* think you are so interesting, but that is not true." And she began to explain he was so badly dressed and did not like his mother as much as he should, and Dullin knew how to love somebody. And she cried much. The point is she made him terribly unhappy for the last years when he was so sick. She has some remorses and don't want them; everybody thinks she is guilty, and she knows it is true but will never admit it. Then she sent Sartre away; we stayed alone in a big cold studio, not daring to say a thing, hungry and bored. She came out of her room with the most awful sight: long reddish hair dangling all around a huge red face, so red, a dark, dirty dress falling to her feet, and laughing in an idiot maniac way. We had dinner with Zina still half-crying, the husband who looks like a professional killer and said nothing, and Toulouse whom we must prevent from drinking and who insulted Sartre all the time in a childish but unpleasant way. He thinks it is hard to have to pay every month (she lives exclusively on his money) and to be insulted so hard. She pretended to be nice to me, but it was not better. The whole talk was crazy and we had to play our crazy part too. We went away nearly shaking. And we cannot just dismiss her; she has nobody in the whole world. So what will happen? She was talented once; she could never write but as a director on a stage, everybody said she was very good. Her home is full of the nicest things she made herself: strange pieces by her in lovely garments, and so on. You feel a little like in a Holy Musée Grévin[1] when you are in her place. And something strange too in this evening: how the dead man heavily present. Indeed, it is his place; she kept his chair at the table, she is haunted by him—so is Zina—he was the real suffering heart of the house. We felt him around all the time.

Well, that was long story! I have just time left to send you a little piece of love. Though do you need it, just now, in this glamorous town, among all these glamorous girls? Did they find out you were a glamorous boy? Don't forget your little French gopher, anyway. Remember, I loved you before you were so well-known, so wealthy, so young, so beautiful: A poor little token of a local youth. Good bye, my local love. I miss your arms, your lips, your chest. I miss all of you. But I'll get it, all of you for days and nights. Enjoy your freedom, honey. You'll know to whom you belong on Michigan lake. I love you, Nelson, my beloved lover.

Your own Simone

1) The Paris Wax Museum, founded in 1882.

Wednesday, 8 Février 1950

Dearest you,

While you were picking oranges, it is rainy, snowy here, and for two days we had strikes, so no gas, no fire at all in my poor little brothel. I bought a fine red carpet to hide the muddy spot on the other one, and I was proud, because when I went into the shop and gave my name for the carpet to be delivered home, the man in the blue velvet jacket who kept the shop asked: "Beauvoir, like Simone?" "Yes," I said. "Are you Simone de Beauvoir?" "Yes." I said. Then he dropped the price! He wanted to give me back part of the money! He told me he had written a long nice letter about *The Second Sex*. As I did not accept the money, the next day he sent me a gift, a kind of bowl, very pretty.

Yesterday evening, I went to the lecturing place the newspaper-seller has fixed up, and gave a lecture about women. It is a fine little theatre in Rue Mouffetard, and many people were there, some students but chiefly working people. Bost and Olga came and listened and said I was very bright, though I modestly don't believe them. It was really interesting, because these people discussed passionately, and rather cleverly, chiefly about the social side of the subject. A young Arabian boy, a communist one, was somewhat angry because I had seemed to say women were maybe not in North Africa as free and happy as they could be. He said it was not because of Mahomet but of capitalism, which is only half true. But when he gave quotations of Koran, what could I do?

The ugly woman is in mountains and sends to me a letter *every day*: what do you think of that? Well, I like better not to get a letter from you every day and you are not that ugly. In fact, I don't know much about you since a long time; last week's letter was very short, and this week nothing appeared. I hope everything is the best for you in the big world and in your small head. By the way, what is this stint you get at Chicago University? Scrubbing the floor or lecturing about existentialism?

I'll write a better letter when I get one. Still, here is good first rate love for your unfaithful heart.

Your own Simone

Saturday, 18 Février 1950

My dearest too busy faraway wonderman,

At last, I got a letter! By the noise it made when the good concierge slipped it beneath the door this morning, I knew it was yours and I jumped out of bed. Then I knew it would come since I wired yesterday, the way you know the sun will come when at last you got an umbrella. It seems one letter was lost, the one you wrote on 4th February. I guess you told me about your trip, the Indians Albuquerque, and what a else? It was enough to leave me without any news for more than tow weeks. First I joked with myself, pretending Indians had taken you as a hostage, then I got unconfortable, and then I had nightmares you were dead: I had to wire. I know you hate it, so forgive me, but you have to be forgiven too to have scared me so much. I don't

335

know which of us will have to punish the other. By the way, I did not write since a week, not as a punishment—it could not have been since you rather complain about getting too many letters. But I had heart to write in this loneliness, not even being sure you ever got may letters in that unknown Le Moyne house. No kidding, honey. When you fade away, the sun fades away, and these first days of early spring we had in Paris seemed awfully sad to my poor heart. The only good thing when I have been a afraid to lose you is my happiness when getting you again. I feel happy today; in a way, it is not worth it. For what I have got? A poor little worthless token, but it is my own tiny love token, my own, Nelson, and stupidly it is very precious to me. Is it not strange? Yea, honey, when I had the letter and was sure once more that you were a real living being, I crept into my bed and pretended to sleep in your arms for a short time, with my cheek on your shoulder and your warmth mixed with mine. You were not really there, but I really slept, so it was not all a fancy.

I like San Francisco too, very much, and dislike Los Angeles. But what a stupid thing if the movie is not made! I hope it will be and in a nice way. Tell me a little about Amanda: how does she live now? Was she pleased to see you?[1]

Two nights ago, while I was drinking scotch with Bost and Olga in my own brothel (it is impossible to find some expensive scotch in Paris now), a young flower-selling girl had a quarrel with her lover and jumped into the Seine, near Saint-Michel. The lover looked at her blankly but a young American student jumped into the river to rescue her and both are dead! Everybody was excited in the neighborhood and said the American boy was a fine one. Morality: never try to rescue a drowning woman, except me.

Olga was very fine last Saturday during the festivity about Dullin's death. First, we had to fetch the drunken widow, and drunken she was, with reddish cheeks and reddish hair, and dark dress, hardly able to walk, smelling of wine. The slave Zina was crying; we wanted to leave her but she wanted to come. We put Toulouse in a cab, and then in a dark box near the stage where she was hidden. There was Bost, Zina, Sartre, myself. People came and spoke about what Dullin had been, all important people (writers, stage directors) and not nice to see. Then they played short scenes of bad or good plays which Dullin had staged. Olga looked very beautiful and everybody thought she had been the best of all girls. Except herself. We all had a nice dinner with champagne to make her happy, and she cried with big tears for half an hour, saying she had been awful. Then, she was a little drunk and felt better. The next day newspapers and people told her she had been good and she began to believe it. As for Toulouse, before dinner Sartre. myself, and two young actors took her home. She noisily cried and laughed the whole afternoon long, and when elegant ladies came to congratulate her, she was such a mess, it was not possible to believe! Just like one of our dear La Bûcherie drunken gargoiles. At home she cried and laughed a little more, and then she explained to Sartre and me that Dullin comes and sleeps with her every night, so she has to be faithful to him and cannot sleep with another lover. Still, as he is dead, she wakes up unconfortable with a longing body, so she had this idea: she cannot sleep with a lover as a *woman*; but she could pretend to be *man*; what could Dullin object? She *seriously* asked Sartre to buy for her three of these rubber things which some widows I heard use as a man's penis. She could find rubber penis in Netherlands but the trip would be tiresome, so Sartre who knows many people must find it in Paris: three, of three different size. Then she would ask Genet to come to her home and would sleep with him as a man with another man; she would be the active one. The point is *she was not kidding at all*, she meant it! When Sartre told it to Genet some days ago, he was really bewildered. I must say, since then she phoned and said she was beginning a desintoxication cure, but she'll never be cured, I am sure.

The Bost who worked about *Devil in the Flesh* is our Bost's elder brother, so you hardly lied, after all. I am glad you like this movie, I do. Good bye, my love. I am tired for having slept so badly, so sadly these last nights. I wait for a fine night without any nightmare. Please don't hate me for asking you to wire; it was so hateful for believe you were killed by the Indians. Sometimes I am a little scared when I realize I love you so much. Nelson, Nelson, my own, Nelson, I kiss you happily all over your silly face. Don't die, my love, and keep for me a warm nest in your heart.

Your own Simone

1) Algren's ex-wife, who lived in Hollywood.

Monday, 27 Février 1950

Dearest meanest than ever you,

I am glad you enjoy yourself: if you like the country so much, you may rent a cottage on the Coast instead of Michigan lake; it is up to you.

It is my turn to sue and be sued. I wrote in *The Second Sex* about whores and prostitutes, and among names of elegant whores of 1900, I gave the name of Cléo de Mérode. Last Sunday. Somebody spoke at the radio, pretending to be me. read this part of the book, and insulted Cléo de Mérode. So now I learn in newspapers and a personal letter that she sues me. And I sue the radio for having used my name. I send you a nice picture of the woman and myself. In fact, I though she was dead since long, which would have made things much easier.

Toulouse has got through a desintoxication cure; she is quite different: fair, pink, soft, smiling, dressed in a long white night-gown, looking healthy and sweet. But she spoke for an hour and a half without stopping one second, which means she was not quite normal. She was interesting because she described the way she has been nursed; it seems a terrible thing. It lasted six days. The first they gave her a mild typhoidic fever—a real shock —then every day they doped her in many different ways, pushing long thick needles in her poor flesh and veins, oily things had to go to her brain and give it some grease, for the wine had eaten the grease up, they say. She had to keep a nurse night and day, because she wanted to jump through the window, she had such anguish from lack of wine. Now it seems her brain is little too greasy, that is why she speaks so much.

Yours certainly is not. What a brute, not to send a short wire when I ask to you! I very often wait patiently for letters, but this time a letter was surely lost; you never made me wait for weeks, you used to be kinder than that until now. Shall I think you unkind rather than dead? Yea, now I shall, ugly muddy thing. Don't forget anyway to send next letters to the right places: Algiers, Hotel Saint Georges until 11th or 12th March, Gardhaia, Hotel Transatlantique, until 24th March.

I cannot help loving you in spite of all. Enjoy yourself, when it is still time to, for within a few months. I'll give you a hard life; I'll punish you with all kinds of tricks. And if you are really too bad, I'll send to you Cléo de Mérode. Anyway, today I kiss you with my own mouth.

Your own Simone

P.S. I bought two glass-swords for my home. Very beautiful.

338

Dearest you,

That is the day when I was sued by the old respectful whore; I have a nice lawyer (a woman), so I stayed home. It was big scandal in the radio, because they have no right to use my name when I am not speaking, some people were dismissed on account of their treacherous behaviour: a good lesson for them. I already knew they were hateful people. Lot of people called and came around these last days, but I managed to send them away and not be too much disturbed. I go on working on your book and begin to feel really tired. I enjoy the idea of going faraway into the heart of Sahara.

I met an awful man, a teacher in Notre-Dame University, a small Catholic University near Chicago; he insisted through friends so that I should see him, and then he was rather unpleasant: I had not seen Chicago in the right way, he thought. I did not see it from the Catholic point of view; indeed, I should have gone to Notre-Dame. He mentioned your name, saying you got some success now, but success did not look a very good thing in his mouth. I guess he is the ugliest man I ever saw, do you know that horrid thing?

Another meeting, more interesting, was meeting a cousin of mine who was my first love[1] I really loved him from eight years old to twenty and hoped to marry him; happily, I had no money and he chose a wealthy stupid wife. I guess I told you this faraway story. The point is, this man, who was wealthy, owning a good painted-glass business, lose all his money by lazyness, foolishness, and drunkness; he has five children, but lives far from them, apart from his wife. The wife's father gives money to daughter and grand-children but he hates my drunken foolish cousin who does not get a penny. After twenty years, it was strange to meet him in the street: he is not older than I am, but white-haired, red-faced, all swollen and sick as many drunkards happen to be. I had to give him money at once, and drink with him, then invited him for lunch and gave him more money. And now does not stop phoning to me, asking for a new meeting. Not just for money, but because he has nothing to do in life; he is unable to work in any way and nobody at all caring for him. I don't nei- ther, but I was a little distressed at his distress. There is nothing at all any- body could do for him; it is a hopeless case. I am glad I go away to break up business; but then I'll come back, I am afraid he will beg again for money, time, and friendship.

There is a book by Jean Genet being published by *New Directions*. I should be pleased if you should read it. Though I don't see how they can translate his strange French; and surely they have dropped much of the erotic pages. I long for sun; I'll try to make myself sunny and thin so I can proudly walk naked on Michigan beach. I long for you more than for sun. Keep me in a sunny place in your heart, Nelson.

Your own Simone

1) See *Memoirs of a Dutiful Daughter* for more concerning her cousin Jacques.

Saturday, 4 Mars 1950

Dearest you,

I am fed up with Paris and wonderfully happy to go away. The last days are always very bad, because you get so many things to do and so many people to see. And if you are stubborn enough to go on working, you happen to be awfully tired—so am I. I saw this cousin once more and once more gave him money so he can to the country and sleep and eat a little, instead of drinking all day long. It makes me sad when I see the bright boy I loved who became that poor penniless thing. Then I had a terrible time with the ugly woman. She spent a month at winter-sports (not doing any sport, indeed; she is still more a coward than you are) and during this month I felt really relieved, then I saw her and had to tell her I was going away. As I knew I was hurting her, I spoke more kindly, I looked more friendly than I use to, so she came yesterday with a dead, dumb blind face, she could not speak a word and in the end she explained she had spent a week hoping for impossible things, loving me no longer in a faraway way but in a highly sexual way. I was frozen to death, she cried and said I should be wholly bored, one day; in the cab back she kissed my hand, so at nine this morning she knocked at my door and asked me to forgive her. Sure I forgave her but I am happy not to see her before months.

Do you remember the letters I got from a woman who always asked money from me in a very hasty, haughty way? She is the one who managed this radio-meeting where they pretended I was speaking when I was not. As it became a big Parisian Scandal (I had my picture in newspapers every day for three days), the radio producer came angry and she and others have been dismissed. So she calls and writes and asks my help not to be

340

dismissed. As she is penniless and has got three children, and I am stupid, I do try to help her, but that is quite a mess too.

Well, that is a bad complaining letter. I complain about the weather, which is too cold, too. And days are too short; I don't sleep enough. And ...Oh! After all, everything is not bad. I spent a nice evening in La Bûcherie brothel with Scipion, Lisa, Bost, Sartre, M. et Mme Queneau. Queneau lay on the bed and slept the whole evening long, but the others drank scotch and were fine. Scipion reminded with tears in his velvet eyes how you struggled bravely for my bracelet, in Montagne Sainte Geneviéve dancing. It seems this movie about Paris (when we went in a cab through all suburbs) is going to be done; Scipion and Bost are glad at it. Olga is acting a little part in little play. The author is a nice young friend and I went to a rehearsal; I like it, when things happen half on the stage, half in life, they try to find the accurate light, the right gesture and voice, everybody is feverish and busy, and wanting so much to do a good work. I felt the impulse of writing a play myself, some of these days.

I am a bit anxious, because it will be difficult to get letters quickly in Africa, and I need your letters so much. I need to know you are real, living, still loving me, and we'll kiss for good one day. You don't fade away in my heart, not at all, so I cannot stop missing you painfully. I should like to miss you less, but it is the way it is. You were too nice, my love, and I remember it too well. Don't forget me.

Your own Simone

P.S. Write until 4th April Hotel SATT, Tamanrasset.

Alger, Monday, 13 Mars 1950

Sweetest you,

It was a nice thing to get your stupid insulting letter (but at last a letter) when I arrived Algiers yesterday evening, from Marseille, by plane. It is so sunny here, so gay and bright that I woke up much too early, and I write to you while first birds are singing. You would be afraid if you would see me; My left eye is nearly closed by the sun I caught while walking on the southern sunny hills, my face stripped red and white, my cheeks are swollen, my legs and arms all scratched. I am sure nothing of the kind happened to sweet Mary G. That is because I was walking in the sun with sore feet and empty head that I did not write for a week: writing anything seemed a strange business and so it seems this morning my hand hardly holds the pen.

Monday evening the first rehearsal with Olga was nice, the whole show was fine and she was beautiful in a black tight cow-girl suit, black long pants, bright dark shirt, and a huge sombrero, black too. She was certainly the best of all; this girl can play. The only bad thing was she got a cold in this small tiny, chilly theatre, she caught much and thought she was going to die. We went to a little supper after that, to La Coupole, with brave Scipion, brave Bost, the author, and stage director; they all felt very happy and I staid until two in the morning, which I seldom do; I lived like a nun all this time.

I rode the "blue train" all Tuesday night. Sartre had to go to Cannes to see boring people, and I went my own way, by taxi-cab and feet. The first day I began to walk at 1 P.M. and stopped at 8; I climbed a high mountain and found so much snow on the top that I did not know how to find my way, and for time I thought I was lost and should die in the woods or at least spend the night there. But I contrived to go down in the end, I had dinner and a fat high bed in one of these little villages hotel I like. There, I had a funny dream. I must say first that in the day time, as I needed a knife for cutting bread and sausage in the mountain, I came into a small village shop; there were beautiful knives but nobody to sell them, so I took one and let the money: 250Fr. Then my dream: I was with you in some Arabian-Guatemala town, anyway in souks. You walked a little ahead; I looked at the shops. Something seemed beautiful to me, a kind of brush to scrub the dishes, but in green violet, rich Guatemala colors. I wanted it, still I knew you should be angry if I should but one more token, so I just stole it and went on, holding that in the hand. In face, it became a kind of nice embroidered napkin, but then a girl followed and patted my shoulder, saying: "I am sure it is a mistake, you look like a lady who does not steal, but you have to pay 250Fr." I paid, feeling very bashful. By the time all that happened, you were lost. Impossible to find you in that big town. That was the interesting point in the dream, this terrible feeling of loss, because I did not get letter since long; I was half lost myself in faraway mountains, far from La Bûcherie as you were far from Wabansia. I looked around and called your name. I screamed and was hopeless, and then I fell down on the ground in mere despair. And suddenly it was kind of sandy beach at night, and you appeared, all naked. (Are you not ashamed?) I felt you lying near me and putting your arms around me—at last, I felt the joy of having found you again. But then it stopped...Why does it always stop too early when I dream of you? It seems I cannot be unfaithful to you, even with your ghost. Well, then I spent three other days walking around, but I did not go on high mountains any more, I went in lower lands where almond trees were flowering; it was beautiful and I felt quite happy. Yesterday I met Sartre in Marseille and at night we fled here. Marseille was full of sweet remembrances of you. Algiers is, too. Remember all that, sweetheart?

The Jewish friend who is teacher in Algiers waited for me in the hotel-lobby. I'll spend a long part of the day with her. And tomorrow morning I take a long-way bus to begin to go down toward Sahara. I am very pleased.

I had a *twelve pages* letter from the ugly woman; it would be better to get twelve page letter from you and one page from her. For twelve pages she only says she loves me, knowing I'll never love her, and how sad it is, and what can she do?

Now I'll kiss you goodbye. I am glad to send this letter to Wabansia again. When we are both away from home, it seems we have no love nest any longer. If you come once more in my dreams, naked or not, stay a little longer; we could pick some apples together, I used to like them, and couss-couss too. I am starving, without apples nor couss-couss. And longing for your lips, your smile, my sweet loved you.

Your own Simone

Ghardaïa, Saturday, 18 Mars 1950

Dearest glamorous you,

I am not in a hurry to write, since it is too early you send it to Wabansia and too late for Los Angeles. Yet I have many a thing to tell you! First, it seems it works pretty well when I scold you. I'll begin again: I got a nice letter in Algiers, a nice one here, in Ghardaïa; they came in right time—you managed it wisely. You cannot realize, honey, how this little yellow piece of paper helps me to feel peaceful and happy, to sleep well and wake up smiling. You seem very pleased yourself and that make my heart so warm. I am deeply glad if Frankie Machine comes to life on screen. John Garfield sounds all right. And I am glad to hear you did not forget how to wash up dishes and scrub the floor; it could be useful on Michigan lake if one day I happen to be tired of doing everything myself.

Sweetest you, I saw so many camels I decided not to think of you every time. I even *ate* camel, or rather they tried in the hotel to have me eating camel—bloody liver, strange smelling kind of liver. Then they said it was *veal*, and it was black, hard, and smelt of camel, too. Poor Sartre dared not send back the dish and ate the liver very sadly; but yesterday we both said "no" to the queer veal-steak. All that happens in Ghardaïa. Well, I'll try to tell things in order. I left Algiers Tuesday morning; it was 5 A.M. I felt rather sleepy when the big bus went away. A long but fine trip across mountains until a small town called Djelfa where we ate a terrible lunch. We spent some hours in a dirty little café writing letters and reading. The weather was so blue, and cool, warm and gay, that I already felt very good. Then another bus full of Arabians brought me to Laghouat, a nice town with palm-trees and the real Sahara around. I worked all day long on the hotel terrace, then Gharadaïa: a road all sand and stones, 200 miles of naked desert. In this dry lonely land you happen often to meet some of these black, dry, burnt Arabians whom you liked in Marrakech. They lived anywhere, sleeping on the ground with wife and children, as long as camels and sheep find some dry grass to eat; then they go farther and farther, never stopping, spending their whole life walking along, and proudly never working, though this kind of walking around comes to be a work in the end.

Ghardaïa has the same kind of life as Djerba—the same religion faith; they are peasants, too, not wandering around like the other Arabians but owning a little piece of earth. The country is awfully dry and poor, so many go away to Algiers and sell grocery there, but their wife has to stay here; they are always buried here, so they keep a house in the town. There are five towns and about 40,000 people in kind of hollow large hole surrounded by small mountains, very beautiful towns, somewhat in the way of Fez, with dark narrow mysterious streets. The tower of the Mosquée, on the top of the town, is quite a queer barbarian thing. All around are poor gardens with palm-trees and vegetables, they have wells with a little jackass as in Ischia, but the jackass does not run around the well, he goes straight down a kind of path and back up, the whole day long, and you hear a strange sad metallic whining. The hotel is nice, except for camel at dinner; there is a large terrace, too. But the weather is strange: the sun is hot since morning, but in the shade it is awfully cool; there is a big wind that makes even the sunny places cold. I try to stay in the sun and I am chased away by the cold wind, a real struggle beginning again every day, lost every day.

Now, please write to me Gao, A O F, poste restante. I'll be there on 5th April for some days, and then letters will follow me. I am reading the last book of Miller translated in French, *Sexus*, awfully tedious. Well, when you are in bed with the man you love, it is new each time, and each time it is fine, but when you read about bed-time of the other people, it is not new at all, always the same old game, though Miller tries so hard to make it different. Then he talks and talks a lot of nonsense; he bores me.

No more luck with Hemingway's book about hunting, *Green Hills of Africa*, or something like that. He makes hunting look as tedious as Miller sex. You just wish never to go hunting, never to go to bed, when you read these people. Then Hemingway seems to be a little too much in love with himself; it is certainly the worst of all those he wrote.

Nelson, my love, you never leave me day or night. I have plenty of time for day dreaming and sweet remembrances. I remember all of our happy days so vividly. It is wonderful to think all that will begin again in a few months! Tell my love to Wabansia nest, I'll kiss you so hard in this kitchen, in this room. I wait for this day with a longing heart.

Thursday

Dearest man in the starched collar, I was amazed when I saw the letter came from New York. What kind of man have I got now? You should try to forget you are supposed to be local Wabansia wit, you should write to me as a good middle-aged husband writes to his loving middle-class wife. I mean, *tell* me things instead of just joking about Why did you go in tuxedo to the Waldorf Astoria?[1] Send me a picture of "local youth wearing tuxedo." Did you buy it? Did the starched collar change your heart very much? Is it a strached heart, too now? You wrote nicely. I have to thank and congratulate you for that. Remember it is only because I am in the desert and not because I am lazy or forgetful that my letters will not be so regular now. I visited the five towns in Ghardaïa, the brown, the white ones, the blue one—the blue is lovely in the light. What you would not enjoy is flies: heaps of flies. One day the wind was so cold they died by whole armies, but the day after, there were as many of them as ever. They are eating me, just now, while I try to talk sense to you. There are fleas, too. Then poor Sartre caught another kind of very intimate little beasts, the first day he was here; he was quite ashamed to go to the drug-store and to say that to the chemist, but the man just smiled: "Everybody has got that, here," and he gave to Sartre a big box of DDT powder, and his wife said she put that on her morning and night, chiefly when travelling in bus. So Sartre spilled DDT all around himself and his whole room, and even tried to kill flies with DDT, but did not succeed. I kept this perfume

345

from my own room and self; I hope not to have to use it. They go on trying to make us eat camel in this hotel, but I cheat them by not eating any kind of meat.

Friday

Big market this morning, with camels and all that, the kind we saw in Djerba. I remember how silly you looked in your Arabian dress and I enjoyed looking at these dark her faces which interested you so much. The peasants of the valley are fat and pink; I don't like them, but here come sons of the desert too, and some are beautiful. I read some of the little books you sent to me. Keep me in your heart, my sweetheart.

Your own Simone

1) Returning to France by plane in 1949, Algren learned during a stopover in Gander (Terre Neuve) that he had won the Pulitzer Prize in literature. But the official awarding of the prize did not take place until March 1950 in New York. Algren was honored for his novel *The Man with the Golden Arm* at the Waldorf Astoria gala along with two other winners, William Carlos Williams (poetry) and Ralph Rusk (history). Eleanor Roosevelt gave a speech and received a standing ovation.

Tamanrasset, Thursday, 30 Mars 1950

Dearest you,

Here I am at last, in the mysterious heart of mysterious Hoggar, where mountains are black and men veiled in blue veils, hiding carefully their black mouths. It is really a wonderful country, and the whole trip was wonderful, though somewhat hard. I left Ghardaïa at five in the morning last Saturday: it seems already very far away; I saw rising from the mountains a big red sun, quite like the one rising from the sea near Gabés. In a big unconfortable truck, driven by an Arabian man who prayed God a long time before going away, there were five people: a nun clad in white, Arabians, and us, sitting in the same narrow seat. Crossing this wide Sahara lasted the whole day long, twice a tyre burst off—once it was easily mended, once we had to wait for two hours and a half in hot sun while the Arabians made a little fire and cooked tea. During these fourteen hours, we just met one "bordj," a kind of shabby place you find water and can seat to eat the cold lunch you brought with you. But the ride was never tedious, because the landscapes of the sand, mountains, rocks, are wonderful and forever changing. Then, there is something amusing which lasted four days long; it is the *thing* they call a *road*: it is a wide path, in fact, hardly different from plain, except it is more difficult to drive on it and you have to keep away from it. But the whole French army is working about it, for 800 miles you hear of nothing but this road and meet nobody. Every 100 miles a lonely soldier and ten Negroes work lazily at the *thing*. Then you stop, he asks you for a coffee beneath his tent, and he speaks nervously, as somebody speaking just one time a day, all about the road, the other French soldiers or officers who take care of it. You stop, too, whenever you meet another truck. That is one or at most two times a day, as boats greet each other when they meet on the ocean.

At night suddenly I found myself in the gardens of a wonderful hotel, looking like an Arabian palace, with bright carpets, copper trays, palm-trees and running water: it was El-Goléa, a beautiful oasis. A nice captain's wife who likes Sartre's books and mine invited us for a very good lunch. It was a real rest to eat good food and drink cool water, because really if not chicken you have to eat camel in this country, and if you don't like camel, you starve. Monday morning the ride began at four; it was still deep night. We travelled with a fat Negro woman who looked exactly like your fat New Orleans friend, when she rolled on the chairs after lunch. She laughed with everybody and made water on the edge of the road when she needed it without taking care of hiding herself. It was a big problem for the white nun; the day before, she pretended to go to praying and disappeared behind whatever bunch she could find. This Negro woman was from Ghardaïa, but she married a white man who keeps a lonely bordj; he had asked her to take away the veil, what she did. We came to In-Salah, a town half burried in the sands which the wind brings on and on; it is thought some day the town will die from it. The town is red and people black — these Tovaregs I spoke in the beginning, all clad in deep dark blue, men veiled, women unveiled and covered with jewels, beautiful in the classic way some Negro-girls can be. They work in the oasis, digging the earth, cutting palms, all covered with earings and necklaces, in silver mostly. Sand is a beautiful thing, you know, really high mountains of sand of most purest colors. I enjoyed the sunset there, sitting outside the town in the sand and thinking of you, honey, with a most loving heart. Then two days more through dark Hoggar, a mountain as black as your soul is black, as coal is black; it is strange, sometimes beautiful, often weird. Very hot, hot wind, mist of sand, mirages. We were alone, Sartre and I, in the truck, it was more confortable. I read nearly all the little books you sent me, most of them were good, and slept all the little books you sent me, most of them were good, and slept in a lonely bordj kept by the Negro woman's husband, 250

347

miles from anywhere. Once or twice we met caravanes of camels, thirty of them loaded with wood and lot of things, and rode by some young Toveregs, children among them, clad in blue, walking for 400 miles in the Sahara. Often you see bones along the road, bones of tired camels.

Well, it would be too long a story to write to you everything about Sahara; I'll tell to you about it when we'll lie on Michigan beach. But it is really a great thing to see, a dangerous one, too. I saw a car all burnt up on the road, burnt just because of heat, and it still happens people die with thirst in these lonely plains where life is so hard. Yesterday evening I arrived here, a very small village used by planes as a stop, so there is rather good hotel. I write to you soon enough to catch the morning plane. I spend six days here, resting and working, and then I'll fly to Gao, where you have to go on writing to me. Do you like love from Tamanrasset? Here are heaps of it, a wide Saharian love. I think how nice you would look in a blue dress and veil, with these terrible eyes of yours above the hidden mouth; and I love you a little more.

Love, love, love, love.

Your own Simone

Tamanrasset, 3rd April 1950

Sweetest faraway you,

They say a plane is flying away towards France tomorrow morning, so I hurry to send some love to you. I did not get letters since a long time: the fact is, nearly no letters arrive at all here. Maybe I'll find some in Gao. It was a very nice time I spent in this forlorn, forgotten, faraway little place. Wonderful weather, because it is in the heart of Sahara but high up in the mountains; wonderful landscape all around with black stone and white sand. And then the people here are so amusing! You know, they are just petty, middle-class French people: Officers, teacher, scientist, but being here makes them proud and angry together and the sum pride and anger comes to madness. They hate each other; twenty of them in a wholly artificial village, all made up by French soldiers within last ten years; they are the biggest liars I ever met since I went, on a certain day, to the petit café in Palmer House. Each of them knows the other lie, but how happy they are when they meet new people! When we tell one story we heard thousand miles away; they know the man who told it and laugh! Then they tell another story themselves. You would surely enjoy the scientist forty years old (he is here since twenty years), deaf, he rode about 35,000 miles on camel back (other people checked that), found wonderful 10,000 years old pictures painted or engraved in stones, has got a little museum of his own and knows everything about the country. And it was a country hard to conquer, hard to live in, so most of the true stories are weird and wonderful. Yet, he adds false stories about himself; how many times he nearly died with thirst, and so on. He asked me for a tea with Touareg women, whores (married one live far away beneath tents), beautifully dressed in blue with lot of jewels everywhere. Men are much stranger, because they hide their face, showing only dark eyes. Arabians say they are ugly and that is why they hide their face; the woman teacher who knows them well tried to have one pulling away his veil: he struggled like a raped unwilling woman and kept it. They use to take all sheep, crops, and money from stupid working Arabians, but now, as French government does not allow them to do so, they do nothing at all, really nothing. At least in the upper class, work is a shame, all the work was and is done by black slaves they stole in southern Africa. They court women and sleep. That is all they do! They are graceful, polite, refined; their skin and undergarments come all blue from their blue veils: the bluer they come, the most elegant it is. I guess you could enjoy this life: sleeping and courting women...

Tonight the captain takes us to see the king and queen of Sahara Touaregs, a real king having 10,000 people beneath him. A very harsh, complicated business, because the scientist and a nice lieutenant wanted to take us to the king, then the teacher was jealous of the scientist, and the captain, mad at the lieutenant, forbade us to go (the captain is powerful here; he lets or does not let you in the town, he controls all cars and everything). So, as everybody wanted to take us to this place, in the end we nearly failed to go. Then the captain is to take us himself, in his own car. Oh! There was much fun about it, for two days! All this part of Africa, Sahara, is controlled by officers, because time is still near when they fought and killed all Europeans. They are not unkind to natives, the country is too poor to exact anything. Where I go now, in AOF,[1] it's different and much worse. They have civilian governors and lot of white people try to make money by having poor Negroes working very hard.

I'll tell you more marvels next time, now just the marvel of my stubborn love for you.

Your own Simone

1) *Afrique Occidentale Française*, French West Africa.

Gao, Monday, 10th April 1950

Dearest beloved you,

It is useless to write when no plane is ready to take away the mail, that is why I waited for week before sending you new cans of African love. Very hot love, honey. Even Medenine was hardly hot when you see Gao.

In my last letter I was going to visit the Touareg king. All the "important" people of Tamanrasset went, too: the teacher and wife, the scientist (who divorced two wife and was alone), Sartre and myself. We bought tea and sugar, for the king enjoys little gifts. It was a wonderful moon lit night, and it was really glorious to see the lonely camp in the middle of the desert: no road, the car just goes straight on. The tent is made of fine skin, wide and clean, surrounded by small grass wall; we ate outside, around a fire, and drank tea. A woman played a poor music on a kind of violin-drum with only one string. Then the scientist jumped up, put a kind of big candles in the fire, and in the hands of two big Touaregs, it gave a tremendous light and he began peacefully to shot pictures.

After some more days in pleasant, airy, cool Tamanrasset, something else began. First, the last night, I drank to sickness with two truck-drivers, very nice, who wanted to know about existentialism! I just drank with them in answer, and we joked together late in night. Rather bold jokes, I remember about some pansy they knew who kept a poor hotel in Sahara and wanted all truck-drivers to sleep with him. When I was in bed, beginning to sleep, the door was opened: it was the hotel's owner, certainly much aroused by drink and talk, who said he came so "we could go on talking nicely." I was mad with anger and sent him to devil. On morning he gave me oranges so I should not denounce him to his wife. At 5 A.M. I left Tamanrasset by a little plane. A very beautiful trip above Sahara where little by little some grass began to appear, and some cattle. The arrival above Niger, with cattle, birds, Negroes, pink sand, grey flat water, was wonderful. Water again! But then, after finding the hotel, we learnt sad things: it is too hot to go anywhere from here, except by plane; in winter there is a boat, but now the Niger has no water enough. The market with all the strange mixture of Touaregs, Negroes of different kinds, Negro-girls gorgeously dressed or beautifully naked is very interesting, so are the banks of Niger with little boats, houses, men crossing the river just walking, naked girls and boys bathing, lot of people washing clothes or cooking. But it would have been enough to stay here three days. Alas! The second day

350

poor Sartre caught a terrible fever and lay helplessly on his bed. Everybody eats quinine here, and so we do. I have got a colonial white helmet, and dark glasses. Sartre was so tired next day, he had to stay in bed, and the only weekly plane fled away. We had to wait for next Friday! Another week. Think of that: nine days in a burning Medenine! People sleep outside, on terraces, pleased when the wind gets cool and shakes the bed as if it were a small boat. At five, it is day light, the best time to walk around a little and work. At 9 A.M. you have got to go to your room for shade and little coolness; it comes hotter and hotter, you sleep in beginning of afternoon. Then I try to work again, but it is hard, because it does not get cooler until 9 or 10 P.M. The only good point is the weather is dry; you never get sweating as we were in Marrakech. The hot wind brings sand in the rooms, beds, and cupboards. A hard country. White people hate to be there; they hate the Negroes, and Negroes hate them. The doctor I met in the hotel told me some strange true stories. The wealthy men use to make their wives as fat as possible; he know one whose weight was 250 kilos; she could not move but was always laughing. He husband loved her dearly, slept with her often, helped by four slaves who held the woman in the proper way. How do you like it? Another woman has got elephantiasis, her breasts were breast sixty pounds each — he took them away. And I saw the picture of a young man whose genitals weighed so much he had to carry them in a little carriage he pushed in front of him. It could be cut away, too. The man became quite normal and had lot of children. Stupendous. They have got many specimens of leprosis, too — fifty in the town here, and I don't speak about syphilis! Interesting country. Yea, it is a dry, hard town: houses made of mud, very few dry trees, sandy ground; but the most beautiful smallest birds, green and red living jewels, nice little bengali and pretty yellow birds they call gendarmes. How is the Gendarme? How is Wabansia? How is my Wabansia bean? Has Christine hired a cottage near the lake? Will you accept me even if I come to you with fifty pound breasts and nose taken away by leprosis? I did not get letters since Ghardaïa. Could write now poste restante, Casablanca, Morocco? I'll stop at my sister's. I should like so much to find a letter! Honey, it hurts to think of you so lovingly from so far! But I know it will be paid back within less then three months, by loving you from as near as near can be. Keep me your love. I love you so much.

Your own Simone

Dearest you,

Here it is the kind of land Yucatan was, with big red flamboyants, rich dark green trees, terrible wet heat that makes you sweat all day long. It is a hell of country in many a way, here. I'll just give a little idea of this last week. In Gao it was very hot but dry, not sweating away, so I could feel like working and enjoyed sleeping beneath the cool sky at night. Some people, the last days, offered their car so we could see something of the country, villages made of round straw shacks which people move away when needed; for instance, when the river grows and water overflows the banks. As big as the little huts are the mud-houses built by these awful insects we call termites, those things are real buildings looking like old big cakes, and there are armies of them all along the Niger. The best thing was an evening ride in a little bark-boat, while a big round stormy sun sinking down in a grey flat sky, and Negroes fishing all along the banks.

Then Friday I flied to Bobo-Dioulasso. You could have enjoy seeing me awfully sick; it was a narrow escape if I did give back my coffee. Bobo is the heart of wild country where natives still use to eat each other, where they teach little boys how to kill people with a poisoned thorn, where they cut away part of a woman's genitals when the girls become good for marriage. All women were working naked, the skull shaven, old ones wearing and ivory-jewel inside the skin. Yet the little boys if you give them a chance learn easily lot of things: riding bicycles, driving cars, reading, writing, and politics. In a way they are worse brute than Indians, but in another, much more gifted. Bobo is made of several old villages, dirty, bad-smelling but wonderful to see. You meet everywhere bunch of Negro-girls brightly dressed, jewels and sophisticated hair do, and many colored garments, showing sometimes shoulders, sometimes shoulders, sometimes the whole breasts. There are so many lions all around the town they have to poison them; white important people like to keep home a little lion.

Now I am writing from Bamako, much of a European town, only 200 Europeans but the Negroes have European ways, so not quite so interesting. Yet you meet strange people, yesterday a tall old Negro, adorned with the red ribbon of Légion d'Honneur, which is given only to deserving important people. This man wrote interesting ethnographic reports about the country and was a teacher for forty years. He was just a local boy in a village in the bush: English soldiers came and burnt the village, children and women fled away and French soldiers took away children as hostages. A sergeant taught him French language, this orphan was brought up by his father's and mother's killers, so he is grateful to them, but I suspect the hates them, too. He should rather have stayed in his village, killing wild beasts and knowing nothing. I am angry this morning, because I asked for a taxi and everything was fixed up to a village, but the taxi just did not come. I guess it is hard to live here without being angry at the Negroes, but then a decent white man would not live here. All the white I saw are awful; they keep much of the slave-trader mind; they are afraid by the powerful communist party, Negroes here don't choose to be injured any longer. Politics is very dangerous and passionate game here.[1] Thinking of a night-talk with you on Wabansia porch, I wanted to know more about leprosis; I visited a village for lepers, in fact it is an hospital, the sick people are given little straw shacks where they live with the whole family. The very, very sick ones lie in beds in a big room, but most of them live in a common way with just some kind of curing dope being given to them. The doctor says they begin to cure leprosis fairly well; he showed interesting pictures of sick men before and after nursing; it is really wonderful, though they are never sure the disease is wholly gone away. There are 200,000 lepers in AOF, and thousands of them living quietly in Bamako—not a pleasant idea. He showed me some sick ones. It is really not nice to see. I should rather look at a slaughtered pig.

Something less grim in Bamako was the market, nicer than Indian markets: Negro women are so much more laughing, chattering, so beautifully dressed with little hair-horns and golden jewels. I bought lot of little things for La Bûcherie brothel: big ostrich eggs clad in leather girdles, strange leather bags, and other ones. Another grim thing: prisoners working to build a zoo to keep lions and snakes—strange men, all naked, with hard faces, with many scar on faces and bodies. A few of them were just robbers or burglars or common killers, but most of them were sentenced for religious crimes, religious murders, I mean; they still do that though harshly punished when caught: they give living little boys to crocodiles, poison old people and eat them, and so on. So many villages are lost in a faraway bush where never a white man goes.

Sunday, Dakar

Terrible wild Africa. It was a relief to land in a real town, Dakar, though this one is rather ugly, half-white, half-black, a little of your American segregation, though not so hard as in your South. After Bamako, which was the hell of a steaming sweating place, it is a wonderful thing to see water (it is on the Atlantic coast), to feel a cool wind, to sleep under a blanket! I'll fly to Casablanca within two days. I hope to find some letter of you there; I long for it so much. I hate to know nothing about you, having bad dreams. From Casablanca Sartre will go back to Paris. I'll try to go to Fez alone for a little pilgrimage; I should like to remember you and wait for you there. I wait, honey, I wait for Michigan lake, Wabansia bed, Nelson' arms.

Do you know *Big Cursing*[2] by Alexander Sexton who was a member of CP in Chicago about the same time you were? A fairly good book. I should like to know your idea of it, and to know so many other things about you, my from-everywhere-beloved-you. Sweating or cool, I do love and love and love my own, Nelson.

Your own Simone

1) Encouraged by Leiris (an ethnographer of Africa), Sartre had hoped to meet RDA members, but the Communist Party in Paris made sure that this never happened. Thus they never met a single member.
2) An incorrect translation of *La Grande Malédiction*.

Casablanca, Wednesday, 3rd May 1950

Nelson, my love,

At last, at last I got your 26th April Chicago letter, after over a month silence. Surely of your witty prose is lost in some place of the Sahara; or maybe some Negroes enjoy laughing at it while eating each other. So you are living, as stupid and busy as usual; but I did not learn much about you. Tell me: did you get the April issue of *Temps modernes* with the Nelson Algren's novel wonderfully translated by Bost, Sartre, and Beauvoir under the name of Guyonnet? Did it sound real good French to you? Is our cottage reserved? What did you do in New York with a tuxedo?

Indeed, it was a bad idea to go to Fez in a sentimental journey. If I had got letters, it could have been a sweet pilgrimage; the way it was, it just broke my heart. I walked in all the little streets we liked so much, where we were happy together, and I wanted you so much that I enjoyed nothing and just felt like crying to death. Well, now I feel so much better. Did you know? Pots are dying in Morocco because of your ugly American tin pans. Arabians like better these pans than their pretty pots.

Then I came back to Casablanca to see sister and brother-in-law. It is not funny at all, because business works bad for them. He is really unlucky, all the business he goes in are failures—he is not important enough to make them fail; it just happens. So they are probably coming back to

France, without money, without a job; it makes them very sad. For me, the whole thing is rather boring, I just wish to be back in my La Bûcherie brothel. If you still want it, within two months you'll kiss me for truth, two months will fade away quickly now. So it is a happy love I send you today, lots and lots of it, all to keep for yourself.

Your own Simone

Paris, 8th May 1950

Darling dearest beloved you,

I got one more letter in Casablanca, and two big ones, meaning three, in Paris! Your are a really "nice man," after all. I am proud for Mrs. Roosevelt kissing you in the Waldorf-Astoria, but take care not to wear a tuxedo when I meet you this time I'll fly away for good. Do you know what you look like? Harold Lloyd[1] — it was Sartre's and Bost's and my own feeling when I saw these wonderful pictures of you. I want to meet the man who sat in the little cave with such a faraway, sullen, misty sweet face, just sitting in Chicago fall streets as he sits in my heart. You seem to have a lot of work, honey, that makes a change, does it not? It is just one year ago you arrived Rue de La Bûcherie with your hat on your head.

The end of this family stay better than the beginning: sister and brother-in-law tried to be nice with me; they took me for a motor-trip in Rabat and Marrakech, much more nicer in spring: the mountains in the back-ground were white with snow, the streets and gardens flowering with bushy flowers.

I came back to Paris by plane in night. I don't know why I was suddenly awfully scared, I thought all the time: I don't want to die before kissing Nelson again, I don't. I don't! So, I did not die in the end. Paris is lovely. Why do people lucky enough to live in Paris ever go abroad? What are they at, tell me? Good food, fine weather, nice white civilized people...and no buses, no planes, nothing to do but to work and loiter leisurely. You have to be a fool not to stay here when you can. I met Sartre and Bost, was interviewed and shot as soon as finding myself in Saint-Germain-des-Prés again. Nothing is different; I can fancy I did not go away. And seeing so many Negroes and naked women or veiled ones did not make any change in myself neither; yea, I am always as stupid and silly as before, I love you more than my own life. I seldom felt my love so strongly as these last days, having longed so much for your letters, having be so happy to find them.

Nelson, Nelson, Nelson, Nelson, It is soon, it is really soon. I'll soon sleep in your warm loving arms. I want them, I want your shoulder, your mouth, and everything else. I am in love with you.

Your Simone

1) American actor and director (1893–1971).

10th May 1950

Nelson, my love,

This will be a love letter. You know, I don't send many of them, the way I don't send wires, because I know you don't like it very much. But I remember too how sweet you were last year when I wanted to go to Amalfi: "Let us do it for *my* sake. "Well, then it is all right," you said, with your sweet half-reluctant smile. So I do it for my sake. I love you so much, I cannot help telling it. Why should I forbid myself to be sentimental and silly about the man I love? Maybe because it is 10th May, and spring in Paris, as it was, or the gopher picture, or your letters. I feel a little mad, as I sometimes got in your arms, when weather is stormy and I love you too much, and then you say: "What a mess you are!" Oh, Nelson! Here I am just crying as I did on 10th September when you fled away. I don't know if it is joy or pain, if it is because you come nearer—two months, six weeks—or because you still are faraway. But tonight, it seems wonderfully important to let you know I love you as if I were to die in morning. I feel you can understand that, too, though you pretend never to be mixed up but always to keep a cool clean head and heart. Well, sure I am stupid and silly; you are too nice to find in yourself any reason why I should love you so much, but I do. Remember how amazed you were when I said "I respect you!" Well, it was true, and it is. Suddenly, it came to my heart, tonight, like a wild unwanted tide, the feeling of *who* you were. And don't tell me Mrs. Roosevelt knows, your publisher and your agent know, nobody knows but me. I am the only place in the world where you are truly yourself; even you don't know, honey, or you should get a hateful pride. But I know, for ever. You are sweet to love, Nelson. Let me be silly: I should like to say "Thank you."

Well, I'll stop this nonsense. Crying is no good, so faraway. Please, Nelson, try to feel and know how much I do love you. I should like so much to give you something, anything, to make you feel happy and laughing. I want you, I want you to know it. I want you to know how wonderful and fine you look in my heart, and to enjoy it. You gave me happiness and

356

love, youth and life. I should be happy, loving, lovely, young and living for ten thousand years to thank you enough. I just can cry in my faraway room, my arms will stay cold when I should need so much to give you warmth. I is so long before fainting in your arms. Nobody ever loved you or will as I do, you know. Oh, God! What a mess I made of myself! Forget it if you want, that is the silliest letter I ever wrote to you. But my heart aches tonight, I could not sleep. After all, all that is not insulting, is it?

Nelson, Nelson.

Your own Simone

Friday night, 12 Mai 1950

Dearest darling every-day-nearer-you,

I am as stupid and silly tonight as when I sent you a most stupid letter, stupidly in love with you, but in a laughing mood, not crying one. Honey, it was so fine to get a picture of our home; it made it come so true suddenly. Sure, I should enjoy wonderfully having a little home directly on the beach. The only point is, is one room enough for you and me trying to work for weeks long? La Bûcherie or Wabansia would be a little too small if we had to spend months in them, don't you think? It seems to me we need a kitchen and two rooms. A terrace or a porch is as good as a room if I can put table and a chair. It could be good if one of us could sleep when the other works, or both work in different rooms without hearing your typewriter noise for instance. But anyway, being on the beach is so much better than any walking distance! I should choose the cottage, just hoping we have not to sit all the day long on each other knees.

La Bûcherie brothel becomes lovely. I have fixed up all the little things I brought from Africa: funny pictures (near the pious Napolitan ones), wonderful old leather bags, ostrich eggs nicely clad with leather, children toy, a and so on. It is a really fine home. I hope so much you'll see it next year. Paris is wonderful, too, so sunny and smiling! The only bad point in coming back is all the people you have to see again; and some sad news you always get. Remember the poor lesbian typewriter woman always asking for a little money? She was sick with a pain in one breast when I left Paris: I learn she has go a cancer and will die before a month, leaving a small fatherless girl. I rather liked her; I have to go and see her in hospital, and I hate the idea. The ugly woman half fainted last Saturday, because I promised to see her first Saturday after my coming back; she read in newspapers Sartre was back,

357

and she thought so was I, She went to the usual place at the usual hour, and nobody came. It was awful. I'll see her next Tuesday. Olga made a little trip, acting in little towns and enjoying it. She is happy to be something of actress again! Bost and Scipion are all right. Everybody is excited because the secretary, Cau, just wrote a short essay about "what is literature"; it is very good little satirical novel: the story of a man trying to write really *pure*, meaningless, empty formal literature—sentences, just words; no words, letters; not even letters, in the end he just draws lines ||| like children do. About that he asks silly questions and makes funny jokes. Nobody would have thought Cau could be so funny! Maybe Guyonnet will be, too, some day.

You should rent the house from 15th July: I'll arrive Chicago about 10th, I guess; I want to spend first week in Paris to see the Jewish friend coming from Algiers, and Maybe I'll have to stay two days in New York to get money, and I'll like to spend some short time in Wabansia. So making it 15th, it is a sure thing. Shall we spend all three months in the cottage? Or two months in the cottage, and one in Haiti and Cuba which are not far and wonderfully beautiful? You'll decide. The only thing I really do want is *you*.

Nelson, my heart is full of you, every breath in every minute will be breathed towards you. I have no other aim, no other longing, no other hope or wish but you. Buy a nice swimming suit; I am going to buy one, and we'll lie on the sand as in Ischia, with the sun above our heads and love in our hearts. And will lie at night in our love warmth, without even swimming suits. It seems impossible having been so happy once more; it seems nearly too much for a human life. Still, I know it will be. Nelson, I am going to bed, and I'll fall asleep in your arms.

Your own Simone

I am sending you the issue of *Flair* magazine about Paris. Look at it carefully; you'll find many friends. The stuff I wrote is no good, I just wanted 300 dollars to buy some scotch.

✳ *On the 19th, Algren responded to these letters with nothing but a curt note, bitter ironic in tone. Something had changed.*

Sunday, 21 Mai 1950

Sweetest you,

Another storm day. Women go to and fro wearing white spring dresses and shoes, but rain falls heavily, so I feel much better in doors writing to the man I love. I have nice little thing to tell you. First, the translation of *Never Come Morning* will soon be published. Second, and more important, Queneau at last found a wonder-translator for *Golden Arm*; he is Farrell's translator, which means nothing, but everybody says he is really good. So happy days to him and to Frankie Machine!

Did you hear about this fine business of a young rebellious monk who on Easter day in Notre-Dame, during the most important mass in the year, the cathedral full of bishops and so on, went up into the chair and began to preach loudly against God, saying he does not exist? It was a terrible scandal. The man, Mourre is his name, was tested by a psychiatrist who said the had a kind of "Sartrian disease," and sent him to psychiatric hospital. But the doctor's report was so strange that the preacher was taken out, and many people said the psychiatrist doctor should go in instead. Newspapers were full of the story; most of French writers wrote how shameful or how beautiful the thing was. The young atheist monk publishes the story of his life in a great magazine and makes much money. This one surely knows what is literature.

I saw a little play by Boris Vian about an American disembarkment in Normandy. Satirical, about American, French, and German soldiers, mingling all of them together and kicking all of them savagely. It would have been a mild scandal just at the end of the war, now nobody cares, indeed. It is somewhat funny but not enough, and not a big success. Did I tell you he was sued for immorality and condemned? No jail, money to pay, in name of The Purity.

We have nearly as many American tourists as last year in Paris, but I myself don't see much of them. I was speaking American from morning to night, and even during the night; I cannot now understand why. Were American tourists more interesting last year? I saw most of people: Queneau, Bost, Genet, and others: they live on, work on, just looking like themselves. I don't care much for anybody just now; I am already gone. Truly. My better half is on Michigan lake, and the other impatient to join it. Good bye, my sweet loved one. Which house did you chose? But no matter, since you kept me some room in your good warm heart. I want you greedily. Every night I sleep in your arms.

Your own Simone

Wednesday, 23 Mai 1950

Dearest male-brute,

I am glad we have a home, glad you chose the cottage—I hoped you would. It is all right not to go to Medenine or Guatemala or Cuba; I'll enjoy staying home and swimming and working and, chiefly seeing you working, which was never given to me. Will you really? Are you sure you can? Now, I have a lot of things to ask and, please, for once, do answer.

Now is exactly our home? Can you draw for me a little map of it? How is the country around? How is the beach? Is the water salted? Will many people live and swim around or is it rather a lonely place? Who will do cooking? And how many evening dresses must I bring for the nights when you wear your tuxedo? Shall I buy a diamond or a pearl necklace? Tell me, try to give me a general idea of the life I am going to live for weeks and months with a hateful male-brute. To tell the truth, I thoroughly admit equality is only a myth. I never sincerely thought you were my equal; I just said that to try to be polite. Yet, in away it seems to me all this summer long when I'll be with you, you'll be with be; when you'll feel happy, so shall I; whenever you'll sleep with me, I'll sleep with you. Is not that equality? Or will one of us sleep with the other more often than the other will do?

I spent a nice lunch with Ellen Wright. Dick is still in South America; it soon will be ten months. Nobody ever takes that long to shot a movie, but he says it will be a very good one. I saw some pictures really funny he sent to Ellen; he let his hair grow, came thinner by twelve pounds, his shot half-naked in a cotton field, and really looks wild. She begins to want an extra-man, but she does not dare to get one: ten months loneliness is too long for a woman, she said. Well, *I* can stand it when I know I am going to meet my man.

I saw a very good movie by Pagliero, Lisa's husband, about Saint-Germain-des-Prés. I don't see exactly who can be interested in that, except Saint-Germain-des-Prés people themselves. But you would have been: Queneau did the speaking part, such as you saw it, the "Saint Yves" with the old-fashioned 1900 singings, the crazy man who dresses as if Napoléon was still living, Bors Vian, Scipion, Sartre, myself. It would be nice to keep that for our grand-grand-children. Pagliero made too a pleasant movie about a last night in Roma. We have Queen Juliana[1] in Paris and there is a great fuss about her: Flags everywhere! But Queen Juliana does not matter much. We are really invaded by America: pop-corn and Coca-Cola everywhere. Cannot you keep your dirty drinks home? The shame is Sartre *loves* Coca-Cola and *drinks* it; I have big quarrels with him about that. I gave lot of nice things to be cleaned last week — Guatemala and south of France things, you know them. The cleaner put them behind the window for everybody to see how nicely they were cleaned. A gang of American people came in and wanted to buy them. "It is not for sale," said the cleaner. They wanted my name to offer me a bargain. There was a regular battle; they would never understand something French was not for sale.

Everybody congratulates Guyonnet about this wonderful translation. "Not a word in it is mine," he answers modestly. You know, I feel a little shy when I think this year, you'll get nothing but poor dear me for your holidays: no Indians, no Arabians, no Scipion, no chateaubriand or petit Chablis. You'll just get this small pack of bones you sometimes pretend to love. I am afraid you'll get disappointed. Last year, you told me you had been really happy — I know you were; but how could I make you as happy as Paris, Médénine, camels and souks altogether made you? What could I bring to help a little?

Speaking of equality, do you know this joke by George Orwell, who wrote a bad book against USSR but was some witty? After the Big Revolution, the republic of beasts decide "All animals are equal...but... Some animals are more equal than the others." So, we could agree: *we* are equal but *I* am a little more equal than you.

Nelson, I feel now time is rushing towards you; I am rushing towards you. I just wish you'll be as happy as I shall. It is so good to love you, Nelson, my own one.

Your own Simone

1) Queen of the Netherlands, 1948–1980.

Saturday, 27 Mai 1950

Dearest lovely beloved you,

I spent an evening that could have been pleasant and was a failure. Mouloudji, his pretty wife, and other friends were opening a night-club yesterday in a small street near La Bûcherie; they play and sing in it; the owner is a friend too. So we were all invited, Bost and Olgas, Scipion, Lisa, Pagliero, Sartre, Boris Vian, myself, and lot of others. Everybody knew

361

everybody, we get free real scotch, it seemed very fine; it was the first evening I went to a party since Africa. But the show was awfully bad, just stinking; a Chicago opera and a Mexican joke, silly and tedious, though Mouloudji was lovely in the part of and Italian gangster with a big white hat. Then, he sang in the nicest way. What a talented boy he is, and smiling so pleasantly! But it was the only good thing—everybody was angry; they hardly applauded. Then Olga was quickly drunk and get this weary face, you know; she tried to trap an Italian movie-director who is handsome but never speaks a word, and would not be trapped. Then Scipion and his girl-friend quarrelled; she was worrying everybody and made Scipion so sad he cried and vomited altogether; Bost had to nurse him. I felt all right myself but there was nothing to enjoy and I am afraid Mouloudji will not make much money with that. You have a nice way of getting rid of Negroes now in Chicago barbarian town! Just packing fifty of them in closed street-car and burning them to death! Congratulations! We were a bit scandalized in France, I must tell you.

Sunday

I told you Toulouse got cured from drinking in a harsh way three months ago. The fact is she does not drink any more. Yesterday, she was funny and pleasant as she used to be in a good times, past times, though she always is a monster. She really enjoys the old man death. The whole house is a kind of church, like Chichicastenango Indian church, with flowers, silk, fake jewels, furnitures she got in twenty years in Dullin's theatre—wonderful garments and curtains, masks and lot of beautiful tokens. She has strange but good taste; the place is a real wonder. She was as usual strangely dressed in long black silk and white lace, with velvet and roses in her hair. When Sartre and I were abroad, for two months she lived without seeing anybody at all except her slave Zina and the poor slave's husband. So, it was a big ceremony giving a dinner: the table had been changed into a Saharian oasis with camels all around, sand spread on the wood, and a cake made of a chocolate palm-tree, almond-past Arabians, and imitating a pool of water among the sand! And a nice cake to eat it was.

Now I'll say good bye, sending all the love you deserve and even heap of love you don't deserve.

Your own Simone

Nelson, my love,

It begins to seem useless to write when I think how we shall talk and talk within a month. You'll stay silent for long times in the house, or on the beach, and then you'll begin to talk and talk and never stop. I remember so well all your silly ways. Yet, I don't want you to feel me far from your dear heart during this last month, so I'll try to contrive some letters. It is hot and stormy now in Paris, real summer, and Paris in summer is lovely as you know.

The secretary had a terrific experience: he was invited by little red-haired Cassoulet for a trip in Spain. He went there once and wrote harsh things against Franco, so he would not have been accepted easily but he managed to get false papers and went. Cassoulet travelled with a wealthy woman, friend of her, wife of the man who builds all French airplanes. They ride ten days from Burgos to Sevilla and Barcelona. But the point was the rich woman, young and pretty, is unhappy with her old rich husband, and Cassoulet is always unhappy, so they were hysteric the whole trip long. Chiefly at night, both wanted a man and the only one was Cau. He likes Cassoulet, but should not think of sleeping with her; when she proposed him, he said "no let us be nice friends," and so on. He was not tempted by the other woman neither, but she drove the car, and she got so nervous she began to crash the car against trees and so on, so he thought she would kill all of them if he did not consent a small sacrifice, and he slept with her. Cassoulet got mad and said: "I'll spoil the trip for both of you!" And so she did, crying for the singer, threatening to denounce her friend to the old husband, insulting the secretary. He came back yesterday very pleased with himself and with Spain, but with wide eyes full of awe when he thought of women. He told the whole story to Sartre, who now waits for Cassoulet's story. I'll tell it to you.

Olga acts in a bad play where she holds a stupid part, but I was pleased because she looked young, healthy, and pretty on the stage. I hope she will be a success in the *The Flies*. She begins to long for men, poor girl; some nights ago she and D. kissed greedily, she told me, in the Negro-dancing. He was in love with her since long and she was tempted to sleep with him; she likes him much. But she is afraid and is right, I think, he could love her in a crazy way as he does everything, and she does not really love him so it could be difficult.

The singer and Cassoulet are no longer friends, because the singer had her picture made, naked in the same bath-tub with another beautiful girl, a lesbian one. Cassoulet was jealous. Vian acted the part of cripple man (with a lot of Saint-Germain-des-Prés people) in Orson Welles' movie, in the Buttes Chaumont (near the station de taxis). Oh! I just heard your voice saying: "Où est-elle las station de taxis?" and I had a pang in the heart, my stupid heart. Sweetheart, I am sad the funny bicycle was stolen, but glad the movie is over and will be good. Tell me more accurately what you did. Sad to be still far from you; glad to come soon so near. Sad you are so off-balanced in the head; glad to love you so much.

I am always wise, hard-working, not drinking—a real good girl. If this last sentence is a bit of a lie, the next is not: I never loved you so much.

Your own Simone

Friday, 16 Juin 1950

Dearest nearer and nearer you,

I don't feel neither like writing long letters. Still, I should like to be reminded, sometimes, that I am not crossing the ocean and being scared to death just for fun, and that somebody is waiting for me, in a way. Two planes crashed at the same place, same time exactly, with just two days difference between Saigon and Paris. I felt so sad about it that this morning I asked for a boat at the travel agency, but the trip would last seven days and my stubborn, stupid love makes it too long. I shall not waste on sea seven days I could spend bothering you, so I ordered a plane for 8th July evening; I'll be in New York 9th, stay there on 10th, and be in Wabansia 11th. But I begin to dream of sharks with sharp teeth, and I don't trust my swimming style to escape them. Nathalie cannot see me before middle of August; it is all right. Maybe at that time you'll like a (short) holiday and will enjoy sleeping nights in a bed of your own. She was pleasant and nice in this letter and I'll be pleased to show her to you; we'll decide if she comes or if I go.

Shall I see many pictures of Chicago when I come? It must be a good job. What about the man you are working with? You did not tell much about him.

I have nothing more to say about Paris. I try to go on working but I don't do much; I feel too much nervous. It seems to me when I'll see you, I'll be shaking inside exactly the way I did in the airport, and we shall never have parted. You look so nice, pinned on the wall of the little cave. How I'll like to see you come out of the picture! Will you be hungry enough for a couss-couss, honey? Or some apples? It is so long since I did not pick and apple, no even small unripe or rotten ones. A delicious fruit.

Good bye, my love. You'll see me soon.

Your own Simone

P.S. You should take back Sartre's 200 dollars you put at your agent's. I'll bring 800 more from *Flair* magazine and from New York. Will it be all right? If not, I can try to get a little more through Gallimard. But you are a wealthy man now.

Tuesday, 20 Juin 1950

Sweetest beloved local youth of my heart,

You are lucky if waiting for me is a nice lull for you. I get so nervous I don't know what to do with myself. I cannot sleep without nightmares, I hardly eat, I run to and fro to do all I have to do. It becomes rather difficult to come into your dirty country; they ask all kinds of papers, proving I'll have money, or friends will pay for me in the States, and these friends are reliable. So I have to bother Gallimard and other people to have everything ready in due time.

Speaking of Gallimard, I am pleased to tell you I'll get and correct the gally-proofs of the translation of *Never Come Morning* before going away. It will be published in the fall, I guess. What do want to do with your 400 dollars? Keep them in Paris for next trip? Or have them sent to you in the States? They ask me and I don't know.

Give me the answer 1) for that, 2) your phone number once more, 3) the name of the place where people will have to write to me.

It is a stormy, rainy, hot, mist weather and maybe that does not help to feel all right. I am so happy in the bottom of my heart that it makes me a little mad, too.

I had a sad lunch with Tamy Guld today; it made me really blue, because she is one of the very few women I like: A deep, warm heart she has got, and not just superficial kindness. She always look pleasant and gay when I see her, so it was a shock to find her crying as soon as I spoke about Bob. There is nearly a year her husband is away; she suspects something wrong: he doesn't write to her in a loving way any longer, he did not want

365

her to go and stay with him though they have money for it. Then, as I discussed her fears, trying to confort her, she confessed something hard happened to her in February: Bob sent home a lot of books and papers, and among them, he had not noticed he put a scrap-book with two pages of diary, only two, but two. He said he is madly in love with a woman, she loves him, he bought a car for her, and stays longer than he intended so as to be with her. It must have been awful not to be told but to learn it by chance. She is afraid he will drop the whole family when he comes back, and she does love him so much. Incidently, she explained to me about Bob's marriages: he first lived with her for one or two years; then she went away for 3 weeks and when she came back, he had fallen in love with another girl, a dancer, and married her. After a few months, he came back, divorced the other, married Tamy, and they were happy ten years, without any quarrel. She is not mean or jealous; she can understand anything, but could not bear to be just thrown away from Bob's life. I don't think he will, but it makes me feel bad to think she believes he can; and then she does not dare to day she knows, and I hate lies between people who respect and love each other. It can be so dark in a woman's heart. I guess no man can know how much. It struck me because they were the only married people I thought perfectly happy. It seems to me Bob should be sure he met real love and not just romantic excitement to drop such a woman as Tamy after taking her whole life for ten years.

Well, after all, you'll say it is none of my business, but I am often interested in other people business. Yet, I'll bother you no longer with any kind of business. Within two weeks after you got this letter, I'll be in your arms.

I love you so much, my love.

Your own Simone

Thursday, 22 Juin 1950

Dearest you,

It is so hot and stormy; it seems I am going to melt away So, that is the last letter I got from you: you take an early rest, it seems to me...but then, your jaw will have to work hard and your ears too. I have all papers ready; I think I shall not phone. I hate this faraway voice; it makes me shake too hard inside; I cannot stand this shaking except with your arms around me. I'll wire Sunday or Monday morning, and be in Wabansia Tuesday 11th if I can do everything in one day. You would be helpful, honey, if you asked the agents to send money, because picking it will take time, I know. I bought it from Sartre, because I want to buy some clothes with it—good clothes are less expensive in he States than in Paris. It is not because I fear we'll lack scotch or rum-cakes.

Sartre went to Frankfurt for one day; he met publisher who told him: "I know you translated Algren's wonderful book..." and answered modestly: "No. I only chose the translator." The man is publishing a short story of you (about Polack people in Polish streets) in Hamburg magazine. Did you hear of that? And of this book about Africa, *Sheltering Sky*, by Paul Bowles? I thought this Bowles was terribly bad writer, but everybody here says this peculiar book is good. So, you did nearly as well as we did: Fifty eight students drowned in Michigan lake, not too bad! I'll be scared to meet some corpse when I'll go far away in Michigan waters.

I hope the war will stay local in Korea, I hope my plane will not crash, I hope your heart is nearly as stupid and faithful as mine. I hope I'll find my way to your arms again. I'll write just once more, then wire, then arrive. I feel a bit crazy and kiss you crazily.

Your own Simone

Saturday, 24 Juin 1950

Nelson,

So that is my last letter, the idea makes me sweetly mad. I cannot work any more. I hope when I see you, I find it was not worth so much trouble, and I can do something again.

So, yesterday, I went with a heap of papers to the American embassy where you so proudly fought your glorious fight. The consul asked me why I was going, and I said I was too young to be again a virgin, and the only man with whom I could sleep lived in Chicago, on West Wabansia. He understood I needed an American man for such a purpose, but here were plenty of them at the embassy. I looked at them, and I said "no." Then he made me read a paper about my loyalty duties toward the USA; he ordered me to lift my right hand and swear. So did I. And he decided: "O. K., you go." That is the way I won my own battle at the American embassy.

I just spent an hour with the American pansy Sorokine is in love with. He is a young clever, a little pedant university teacher. He loves her in his pansy way; he thinks she is a terrible woman, so demanding. It amused me, because, with ten years distance, he has exactly the same problems as I had: how to get her out of one's house when you are fed up with her, and so on. Maybe he would be sent away from university, because he did not accept to sign the loyalty statement which was asked from him. Your country becomes a hard place to live in, does not it?

It is a little sad you did not write a bit more, because I feel mild anguishes. Is it you I am going to see, really you? Are you the same, Nelson, my own, Nelson? I believe it, bit I don't feel it, the nearer I get, the more impossible it seems to be that happy again. I am all mixed up and shall stay so until you fix me up right. I am nervous about Corea, too: if they were going to close the borders?

Well, within ten days there will be no more problems. I know it. I'll just lie in your arms. I come to you with more love than I ever had.

Your own Simone

1950

SIMONE DE BEAUVOIR IN THE UNITED STATES

✻ *Simone de Beauvoir stayed at Algren's from July until the end of September. It was a disaster. The Korean War had broken out in June. De Beauvoir left Paris with great anxiety, fearing that if the conflict spread, she might be prevented from returning to France. Although well aware of the change in tone of Algren's letters over the last months, despite their brevity and infrequency, she was nevertheless completely shocked by his greeting: a brutal announcement that he no longer loved her. She spent an unbearable summer on Lake Michigan, in the house Algren rented from Miller. De Beauvoir barely knew how to swim; one day, she nearly drowned. The threat of war devastated her. Nathalie Sorokine came to visit; her presence greatly annoyed Algren, creating another source of tension. It turned out that Algren had seen his ex-wife in Hollywood and planned to remarry her. When de Beauvoir left Chicago, she thought she would never see Algren again.*

Hotel Lincoln, New York 30 Septembre 1950

Nelson, my dearest sweetest one,

You had just left when a man came smiling and gave me this beautiful crazy flower, with the two little birds and the love from Nelson. that nearly spoilt my fine behaviour: it was hard to "weep no more." Yet, I am better at dry sadness than at cold anger, for I remained dry eyed until now, as dry as smoked fish, but my heart is a kind of dirty soft custard inside. I waited for an hour and a half at the airport, because of the weather; the plane from Los Angeles had not been able to land in this fog. It was right that you went away; this last waiting is always too long, but it was good that you had come. Thanks for the flower and for for coming, not to speak of the other things. So I waited with the purple flower on my breast, pretending to read the MacDonald mystery, and then we took off. The trip was very easy — no tossing at all. I did not sleep but pretended to read the mystery to the end, and kept fondling you in my dirty, silly heart.

New York was a beauty: hot, sunny, and grey at the same time. What a glamorous city! I did not want to break my heart by going to the Brittany. I picked the Lincoln where I had landed three years ago, when I knew nobody in this whole continent and did not suspect I should be so strangely trapped in Chicago. I got exactly the same room I had, a little nearer the sky, but identical. How queer to find myself in this faraway past again! As I did three years ago, I went to Lincoln beauty shop: no trouble either, the hotel seems empty, the beauty shop empty. Then I bought the pen for Olga, which was fourteen, so I am glad you gave me so much dollars; I'll just make it. And I walked and walked in the town, along this Third Avenue, which we walked thoroughly down the last night, two years ago, all around the Brittany, too, and once more I found you everywhere and reminded everything. I wandered in Washington park where they have a kind of flea-market and bad painting sale; I went up the Fifth Avenue bus and saw the night come down on New York.

Now it is nine, I just had a little sandwich since the plane, no sleep since Wabansia; I am awfully tired. I came to my room to write to you and drink scotch. But I don't think I can go to bed now. I feel New York around me, behind me our summer. I'll go to bed now. I'll go down and walk and dream around, until I am utterly exhausted.

I am not sad. Rather stunned, very far away from myself, not really believing you are now so far, so far, you so near. I want to tell you only two things before leaving, and then I'll not speak about it any more, I promise. First, I hope so much, I want and need so much to see you again, some day. But, *remember, please*, I shall never more *ask* to see you—not from any pride since I have none with you, as you know, but our meeting will mean something only when you wish it. So, I'll wait. When you'll wish it, just tell. I shall not assume that you love me anew, not even that you have to sleep with me, and we have not to stay together such a long time—just as you feel, and when you feel. But know that I'll always long for your asking me. No, I cannot think that I shall not see you again. I have lost your love and it was (it is) painful, but shall not lose *you*. Anyhow, you gave me so much, Nelson, what you gave me meant so much, that you could never take it back. And then your tenderness and friendship were so precious to me that I can still feel warm and happy and harshly grateful when I look at you inside me. I do hope this tenderness and friendship will never, never desert me. As for me, it is baffling to say so and I feel ashamed, but it is the only true truth: I just love you as much as I did when I landed into your disappointed arms, that means with my whole self and all my dirty heart; I cannot do less. But that will not bother you, honey, and don't make writing letters any kind of a duty, just write when you feel like it, knowing every time it will make me very happy.

Well, all words seem silly. You seem so near, so near, let me come near to you, too. And let me, as in the past times, let me be in my own heart forever.

Your own Simone

Wednesday, 4 Octobre 1950

My dearest Nelson,

It is strange to think that this letter will be brought by the mad mail-man, and will wait in the mail-box which I used to open myself to find my mail. All seems so near, still, though I know it is so far. Not many people went to France; I was alone in the big coach which took me to the faraway sad air-port, and we were hardly ten in the plane. The young American boy, next row of seats, never stopped being sick for sixteen hours. We were given a nice dinner, with champagne. And much tossed when landing in New-foundland. Then it was non-stop to Paris, with a beautiful weather and no night at all. Paris was a little gloomy and grey after glorious New York, but nice enough. It was lunch time when I arrived, but here they pretended it was dinner time: 6 P.M. (11 A.M. for you)—strange. I had not slept at all, but did not feel overtired. Sartre took me to a good French dinner, and we talked late into the night. He was pleased with cigars and red blades, and sends you his most friendly regards. I had a nice surprise home, for the Haitian masks and drums[1] at last have arrived, after more than a year. Our little brothel looks a little too much like a curio's shop now, but it is fine. I spent a poor short sleeping night for as soon as eight my sister phoned, asking me to see me and for a huge amount of money. The good thing is they go to Milan as they hoped, I told you; it is good for them, and they leave for Paris tomorrow, so I'll not have to see them too much in the year. For money I had to phone to the secretary who takes care of things, and he was scolding about it because it seems both Sartre and me are rather pen-niless just now. Sartre has even decided not to give money to some people and to give to others less that he used: how new! Anyhow I'll have lunch with sister and brother-in-law in a few moments and give them the fortune they want. Cau was pleased with the scotch and thanks so much, and so was Bost; they both send their best regards to tough Michigan kid. Everybody seem fine. Bost and Scipion have written during the summer a comic play in four acts, and they pretend it is so funny they cannot read it aloud without roaring madly with laughter; Olga laughed and laughed madly too when she listened to it. So, they hope to make a fortune with it. Cau had his book published successfully; he makes fun of literature, I told you, by writing an abstract book, all made of mere signs like this |||, and he receives congratulation letters just written this way, three pages long:

Dear Mr. Cau,

//// /7/ //// //////7///
/////// /////// ////// // // //.

Yours,

I have *Blood of Others* given in Germany, in a long two hours radio-cast, worked about carefully last year by a nice woman. I am glad it comes to something; they will give records and informations of the time, from old casts, mingled with the story; it could make it quite good. *Useless Mouths* is going to be given on the radio, too. I found a lot of letters, indeed, when coming home.

I would have been the time when I came back to school as a little girl, the air full of dying leaves and pleasant smells. It is a bit strange to find oneself in one's old place, with one's singular identity, when one comes back from your big country. I felt lost and not myself in Chicago and New York. Here, I am just myself again, and it is not much when the world is so big; yet, in a way, it is confortable. People speak about you early; they seem to like you much, here, so maybe I have some excuses to go on feeling as I feel, maybe you are not utterly repellent. Forget and forgive all the tears, sweet you. I realize how tedious and boring they have been for you; but for me they were useful: they washed away all bitterness and sadness, and nothing but sunny tenderness is left in my heart, The beautiful flower died slowly above the ocean, but I keep in my bag the two little birds. Don't forget I am still your Assistant-Inspector and you have to report about birds, squirrels, and the lagoon, the house and the grass. I had a shock when I opened the door of my kitchen: where was my refrigerator and gas-stove and big sink? I could hardly believe my eyes when I saw the poor little things I have got for a kitchen.

It was a fine summer, Nelson. Just now I should like so much to put my cheek against this shoulder which was my Shangri-la! Be happy, dear dearest you.

Your own Simone

1) Sartre bought these for her in Haiti.

My dearest not too repellent you,

It was *very* nice to write so quickly, and stupidly nice too to phone to Wolfe's mother. But silly to feel such a bad pang, nearly as silly as woman's tears. I don't want anything bad to come to you through me, honey. That could make me feel awfully bad, too. Do feel good whenever you think of me. Though, to tell the true, it makes me happy in a way to know that you minded my leaving you, and to go on telling the truly true truth, your dear letter nearly achieved what the flower failed to do: break me into tears once more.

But I did not, though my heart melted and melted. I cling definitely at my dryness. Here is a little story for you: in June, when Tamy Guld cried on my shoulder, I was deeply upset (with a kind of premonition of my own tears, maybe), so upset that I too wept a little about her. So, when Sartre knew I was spending two hours with her in Pont-Royal, he thought I should be upset when he would see me after. He even explained to a friend that something good in me was amazed in the evening, and very disappointed, when he found me just smiling. "Then everything is all right?" said he. I said it was as bad as possible, but it just appeared I was dry-hearted now, and as unable of drawing a tear from me than a drop of water from Sahara sands. Maybe men always feel this way; it is very confortable. But the point is Sartre was so perplexed and kind of reproachful; he did not cry, indeed, but spoke on and on the sad story for a whole evening. For it is really a sad story. Guld just came back after one long year without a look or a kiss for wife or children, trying just to escape for days. Then she got mad and had to tell him she knew. "All right then," and he told her that either he was going back to Haiti for one year, making another movie, and

373

then to Paris with the woman for keeps; or the woman comes to Paris this winter and he lives with her. Anyway he divorces Tamy and marries the other, who has been married twice, has two children, is American, blonde, bohemian, and very beautiful. Now, he'll have two families to support, because she already began to ask for a lot of money. Tamy tried to argue, asking for a year of waiting before he made up his mind. He says he will not even discuss it with her. "It is your life against mine," says he. "I choose mine, and if you love me, you must agree with choice." He says too: "If resent it so much, that means you don't love your children," and "You have not suffered enough in your life, you must learn suffering, it is good for a human being." Yet, he surely feels guilty for he came so nervous as to go to the American hospital for five days because of a breakdown. He pretends — and here is the deception — that he could not work because of wife and children, and his only hope of writing again is to begin a new life. She accepts nearly anything, that he does not love her anymore, that the other comes to Paris and Bob sleeps with her, but she asks for a year to keep him at home. He does not even accept to speak about it. She has lost twenty five pounds, looks like a phantom, is broken into pieces, all shacky and thinking madly of killing herself; he does not even try to help her. I feel sure this new love of him is chiefly an escape of his deeper problems which are about writing and his selfishness, his fake hardness hide an awful weakness. He lies to himself, there is no doubt. At least he should try to make things possible for Tamy, instead of just dismissing the whole problem.

I spent the evening with Olga yesterday, very pleased with the silly little box and the fountain-pen; and, chiefly, so pleased that you kicked Nathalie away. There was always as kind of jealous hatred between them, and she enjoyed the way you ran to the bus to make sure Nathalie went away. She was utterly disgusted with all the pansy and money business. Oh! She laughed and laughed when I said you wanted to put the bed one on top of the other! Well, stupid, when you are alone you don't need two beds, put one of them into pieces again, that is all. You have no shame of playing your crazy game. Olga was good-looking and seemed a little healthier; she spent summer in the little house where we slept some nights;[1] Scipion came and stayed two weeks, writing the comic play with Bost; he was as nice as possible. But his girl-friend came for two days, and it was hell. She is angry and resentful, and very unpleasant with him. Olga said she wanted to beat him, the way you wanted to beat me for being too kind to Nathalie.

I did not weigh myself, honey, but everybody tells me I look awfully well, so I guess you did not mistreat me too badly, as a whole. Yea, and you smile very nicely within my heart. I should like to smile within yours; bad pangs, honey, are utterly forbidden. If you feel anything bad, I'll scream.

Tell me about the Rowland and Amanda and your speech; tell me about everything. I have other little stories to tell to you, but that will be for next time. Lot of dirty kisses from my dirty heart. You are my only piggish pig, and I am not anybody else's piggish pig.

Your own Simone

Ellen Wright says my English has become beautiful: why did not you say so, piggish pig?

The trial about the *The Second Sex* goes on. The lawyer of the old whore has spoken for last Wednesday, mine will speak for me next Wednesday. All newspapers laughed much at her because she pretends to have been such a virtue. I hope I'll win.

1) At Cabris, near Grasse.

Tuesday, 10 Octobre 1950

My own dearest piggish pig,

I caught a dirty coldish cold in this grey townish town, and I write to you from bed. I makes me a little angry, because now I want eagerly to work; I need it. I could not for a week, as Sartre asked that I read his manuscript about Genet,[1] a terrific thing of 850 pages, in handwriting, and it was a week job to read it carefully. It is a real freak, as a book, because he speaks about everything, art, society, and so on, pretending to speak about Genet. It is strange mixture of philosophy and obscenity; for instance, there is an existentialist theory about a man fucking another man, and the difference between shit in Genet's books and in Zola's. As parts of the book were already published in *Temps modernes*, all kind of newspapers attacked Sartre bitterly for his immorality, obscenity, and so on. In fact, the essay is very interesting and very funny. But in a general way the attacks against poor Sartre are worse than ever. Two days ago, in a dirty magazine which everybody reads in Paris, there was a fake long psychoanalysis of him, explaining he saw pa and ma fucking when he was a little boy, and he wanted to sleep with his mother, he is a pansy, and so on. Utterly disgusting and stupid.

I forgot to congratulate you about the number of stamps you put on the big envelope: all of them! I could nor believe it was a letter of you, in the beginning. The poems are interesting. I hope I'll find somebody to translate "Dead in Korea," and maybe the elegy about Madrid, but we have not enough to publish a whole issue about USA now. I asked the secretary of *T.M.* to send to you "The Rape of Steffi," I'll do if she did not. Poor crummy you! Once more the translator of *Golden Arm* collapsed! "Impossible to translate," she said. Ellen Wright who speaks French now told me when speaking about it: "How will anybody be able to translate it!" Yesterday, Sartre told me he should rewrite it with me willingly if the first word-for-word translation was made, but even this first coarse translation is difficult to find for the money Gallimard offers. We'll do our best. My new York publisher was in Paris and mad with anger at me, because she waited for me the Saturday afternoon and I did not appear. Sartre saw her and says she is hysterically anti-communist, and my lawyer (a Jewish woman) told me how she was awful with her when she (the lawyer) was exile in New York during the war. So, I don't mind this dirty womanish woman. Let her plane crash above the ocean!

So, I had a lunch with sister–brother-in-law last Wednesday; they did not leave Paris at once and I had another lunch Saturday. They still did not leave, and I'll have lunch with them tomorrow... You should be indignant, because do you know why they wanted this 1000 dollars which were difficult to find and which they don't intend to ever give back? To buy a beautiful new car! I have no car and had to borrow for them from Sartre, who had no car neither. Why do they buy one if they cannot afford it? They showed it to me proudly and made me angry. Then the man, who is stupid, really, gave me a dirty little piece of an essay for *Temps modernes*. It was nothing and I told him; he was mad at me. He went to see Sartre who told him too that his paper was nothing, and he got mad at him. In the end anyhow, he had to admit it was just dirt. My poor sister had some hard experience, too. Arrived in Paris, she went to three, four painting galleries, showing her own ones: nobody was interested. In the fifth one was a woman who told her kindly: "My poor Madame, your paintings are just worth nothing! Don't try and longer; you'll never be a painter. Look at other people's paintings and see the difference!" And she showed all the pictures in her gallery, comparing with poor sister's ones and saying: "See?

376

That is painting, and *this* is shit!" My sister burst into tears, very much ashamed of it, and the woman went on kindly: "don't cry, just don't try to paint any more." In the end she found a gallery accepting to exhibit her paintings, and the man told her she was talented; it was a great confort. Unhappily, it seems this gallery is going to break down and close before the end of the year. No luck. I wait with impatience for their going away to Milano. The fact, how does it happen that your brother-in-law's wife is not your sister? I did not catch the point.

Do you want to hear about Mouloudji? He was all summer singing on the Blue Coast, in Boris Vian's club. Everybody says he sings beautifully, but he quarrelled with Boris Vian and went away; the singer woman came but people were not pleased with her, and the club closed. Now Mouloudji sings in one of Saint-Germain caves, better than ever, I was said. I'll go hear him as soon as I can leave my beddish bed. As for Toulouse, it seems she had a hard summer. She is desintoxicated but no better for that. She was rather a cold type, but now age makes her sexually mad. When Sartre went and saw her, she had sent away her faithful slave and lived in utter loneliness. She paraded in the room nearly naked and said to him: "Within a few years, I'll be beautiful again and you'll have to love me." A month later, she had an awful black eye. She did not want to say first where and when it happened. In some poor crummy place, she began to try to make a man, a coarse and rough one, a working man of the toughest kind, and, as she did twenty years before with other kind men, she got scared and did not want to go sleep with him. He got so angry he beat her, threw her to the ground, pulled her hair, until cops came and took them to police station. They laughed at Toulouse and let the man go. She was deeply depressed by this affair, and during summer she wrote to Sartre really wonderful letters about herself, letters of twenty pages each, very interesting, because she spoke sincerely, so lost, hopeless, and strange. But then, she sent a essay about Orson Welles for *Temps modernes*, it was nothing, empty and stupid. It is funny how lot of interesting people are able to write remarkable letters, but get scared and lose all qualities when writing to be published. Sartre had to warn her the essay could not be published, and she did not send any more letters. We don't know what happens about her. It is terrible to think of her half mad and so lonely, hustling men in the streets and getting another black eye. That is all the friends you know or heard of. I saw the nice old lady and Giacometti, but there is nothing to say about them. Giacometti works d on; he never stops. There will be another exhibition of his things

New York this winter.

It is a week now I am here I have done all the little tasks: cleaner, laundry, answering letters, and so on, and I have to begin again a real working life. I hope the cold is over tonight and I Begin tomorrow. The gopher stand still near the chimney, and you dream in the little cave. Every morning I miss you, knowing I'll go on missing you for so many days.

Good bye, dear dearest you. I could not love you more than I do, never less.

Your own Simone

1) *Saint Genet, comédien et martyr.*

Sunday, 15 Octobre 1950

My dearest darling you,

Big change in my little brothel. I found that my Deuxiéme Sexe brought me really a lot of money, So I decided to buy a pick-up and I got a big beautiful one, nearly as big as a cupboard. I did not get a radio, because I hate it—the broadcasts are always so bad, and I afraid people would play with it when coming here and bother me. But I'll buy a lot of records, classic ones, chiefly, and I'll hear real good music at home. I am very excited about it. The pick-up is here, near the chimney, and I wait for the pick-up man to come and explain me how I'll manage it, and I'll buy record.

I saw *Henry the Fourth* by Pirandello, and though it is not his best play, it is good enough. Do you like Pirandello? I guess you do. What I saw more interesting this week was an exhibition of madmen's paintings. Organized in the psychiatric hospital by an ex-madman who has been released and taken back three times. In the bar he explained to friends every time he was sane, they put him in and let him go when becoming strange. The paintings were fascinating in many ways; wholly different according to countries: the French ones small, naive, old-fashioned; the Bresilian ones wonderfully lyric and colored; the American one abstract and obviously influenced by cubism and surrealism. In France and England, madmen paint only when they feel like it; in North and South America, painting is therapy; they are taught how to paint. Lot of them contrive to express wonderfully the horror of their inner landscape. There was too a letter 400 feet long, written by a patient to his doctor in past times to explain his story. I

378

should have liked to go again; it was impossible in two hours to see everything. Unhappily, it closes today.

I saw the ugly woman last Tuesday, a little scared because she is always upset the first time; she had decided in her head I had just come back the last Sunday, what I did not. We had to go first to Deux Magots, then in the usual restaurant, and the usual Harry's bar for the usual scotch: the whole thing is a kind of antic holy ceremony of which I an the priest, and a priest must not change anything when he celebrates the mass. Yet, she cried just once. I spoke to her about Nathalie of whom she is awfully jealous, and she was pleased to know I don't like her any longer, but about Nathalie cheating me about money, with this way lot women have to bring all things back to them, she began to cry, saying "she knew *I* and not Gallimard give her monthly money and she will not take it." As she does not try to find any job as to earn her own money, the tears were useless, and even with her heart half stopping, I felt as irritated as you can be when I do the crying job. I had to persuade her, to scold her, and it was all she wanted after all. She gave me, too, a huge manuscript which I have to read—the part of her novel she wrote during the holidays, which she spent in a French village during three months. She told me nice stories about it. It is an average village in the west of France, on the banks of the Loire, one of our big rivers as you maybe know...she was upset to discover that the landlady and her cook were two lesbians. I saw pictures of them: aged, huge, full-breasted, full-buttocked women; strange to think of anything like love between them. The ugly woman spoke with them, and they told there were three couples of peasant women, oldish women all clad in black and church going, who lived the same way. One is married, lot of children, and goes every week to the next town to meet her true love. Then, there is in this village a married father of three children who is the head of the village orchestra and likes just one thing: dressing like a woman. His wife is bold as an egg, wears scarf on her naked skull and dresses in a nondescriptive way. But he takes care of himself lovingly. He has long hair, paints his face and lips, wears a silken open shirt, pants, but high-heeled woman's shoes and silken stockings. They say his buttocks and breast are fake. Yet, they accept him; it is no fault of him, they say, his grand-father was lame, his father had a hunched-back, so it is and hereditary disease. He never sleeps with boys, just dresses like a woman. He is a tailor and sews daintily all day long. Yet this village where they can accept anything from a native, it is forbidden to be a lonely woman walking by herself for miles: everybody laughed at the

woman and she hid far from high roads. Another woman in her cheap
e hotel was a cripple, she tripped: boys threw stones at her. To complete the picture, there is a kind of beach on the river, but the water is dangerous; it gives polyomylite and at least terrible headaches to people who swim in it. And currents and swirls just eat people up. In many places they put signs: "Dangerous! Swimming forbidden!" but French people don't mind them and every week in the local newspaper some drowning-party were told of. I suggested the ugly woman she should write some short paper about this village, but I am afraid if she does, she'll try to make it too good and it will lose the freshness it had when telling it.

Well, no time for Dylan Thomas' story: next letter. Is it still golden, is it all grey on the lagoon? My heart aches for the blue jays, the squirrels, as well as for you. Give my love to all, but keep the best for you.

Your own Simone

Thursday, 19 Octobre 1950

Dearest General Inspector,

I got your long report yesterday, and was pleased to know that your new little nest looks so fine now, but indignant when you spoke of appointing another Assistant Inspector. It seems Amanda[1] did a pretty good job and she deserves some title; but she *does* things, she acts, and, lets us stay the awful word, she *works*. That is not an Inspector's job. You know very well inspecting is inspecting and leaving things as they were before the inspection. So, let her be a fixing-woman or anything else, and keep my title for me.

Two days ago there was in an evening newspaper a huge title: "Rather to die than to work!" It told the story of an old woman and two daughters of forty who until this day had been given some money by the village for sickness or something like that; the money was denied to them, and some neighbours said: Well, let them work!" Then, all the three of them rushed madly into the woods, screaming: "Rather to die than to work!" and they hung themselves.

Thanks for the new poems. When I came back to France, I could think and still can, that I remained in the States. Newspaper and magazines don't speak about anything wise but American policy, American business. Lot of these papers — in fact, all of the ones which are not Stalinist — are sold to the States. That is why, for instance, poor Bost just cannot write in newspaper any longer—even *Combat*[2] speaks of "Liberation of Seoul" by Mac Arthur, things like that. A shame. I heard one of out most black-mailing, disgusting, but most read weekly paper has even been bought by Hearst. I am in a hurry because there is a quarrel at Gallimard's about the title *Never Come Morning*. They pretend, as there is no "s" at "come," that it means a wish: "I wish that never come morning." I know it is wrong and I tell them, but they hardly believe me. I said that I thought it came from a poem, does it? If yes, you could send it so they quote some lines? They asked me a foreword of it. I should have liked to do it, but they just forgot that Wright had written one, which translated indeed and will be used.

You say Amanda too likes tears: does she use as many of them than I do? Can she cry as long? [end of letter missing]

1) Algren's ex-wife, who had come back to live with him, and whom he would later remarry.
2) French Left daily founded in 1941 by Albert Camus and H. Frenay; one of the most politically engaged newspapers of the postwar period.

Thursday, 26 Octobre 1950

Dearest you,

There is a fixing-man in my room, trying to fix the new, beautiful but whimsical pick-up: this little automatic arm of him just does what it wants, stops, begins, begins again when it wants, not when I want, as a disobedient child, so it has to be scolded and tanned. The man works on it with terrific steel tools. I turned my back on it, but I am not quite enough to go on writing the novel, so you'll get this rag.

Who woke me yesterday morning at eight, when I was sound asleep? Darin and Silone. I had a drink with them at Deux Magots. She is not so stout as before, but quite hairy on her face, and she speaks so much that he has hardly a chance of saying a word. I have a lunch with them today, and I hope she'll let him do a little of the talking; he is so much better than she is.

I was sentenced yesterday to pay one franc to Miss Cléo de Mérode; that is the third part of a cent, not much really, but I guess I'll have to pay for the trial expenses and it will get a little higher. Anyway, she does not get all the millions she asked, and it could have been worse for me since after all it seems she was rather a dancer than a whore.

Lunch with Genet, who was very nice. He told how pious he was when a young kid; how he enjoyed praying in the churches, making little

ity scenes with ass, ox, baby, fir-tree; it was so precious for him. He played a strange game with the ugly woman. A friend had camera; they acted in a garden, being shot in kind of movie-picture. Genet took the part of a foundling; he wrapped himself in sheet, white a white bonnet on his head, he screamed and pretended to be a baby. The ugly woman was the mother; she put him in a kind of baby carriage, pushed him around an alley and he whipped her all the time with a whip. If you remember Genet had no mother and resents it, and she hated hers, and enjoyed having *the* mother beaten through her; it makes a kind of psycho-drama they played unconsciously. Now, at last, I have time to tell you the story about Dylan Thomas which Wolfe[1] told me in New York and which I enjoyed so much. Thomas, who is very well-known in New York among teachers, scholars, and all kind of university people (who writes books about him and try hard to understand his poems), was invited by Columbia University to come and give lectures around New York and the States. He was said from pictures of his youth to be handsome, in a byronic way: long blonde hair, thin sensitive face, and so on. Wolfe happened to be invited to the party they gave for him in New York. First, they went to take him at the airport, and instead of a Byronic young poet, they saw a small fat stout man, red and coarse faced, middle-aged, running away madly from the plane, saying: "You have got to arrest all of them! Showing his fellow-passengers. They follow me since I left London, they are Guépéou agents!"[2] He looked really scared. The fact is since fifteen years he never stops drinking, and he drank all the journey long in the airplane. They tried to sober him, and brought him to some elegant room where teachers and wives in elegant dresses were gathered. Dylan Thomas was not sober at all. He just began to jump around, chiefly jumping on the lap of the elderly women and hugging them. Wolfe told me had felt that he (Wolfe) enjoyed the business, so, before jumping he blinked to him nicely and nastily. If he did not sit on the women's lap, he took the top of their blouse and dragged it, and looked inside the woman's boom, asking: "May I blow?" Everybody was horrified. Two men contrived to fix the poet against a wall, nearly holding him so he could not move, and the teachers came and asked questions about Thomas' poems, chiefly about an old one concerning a whale and see-weeds. "I don't understand very well the symbolism," said the respectable scholar. And Thomas, in the most drunken voice: "Oh! It is very easy: the whale, my good man, it is a prick, and the see-weeds, that is a cunt. What they, do? Well, they fuck..." and he went on with anatomical explanations.

Then, he was asked for a dedication. Then he wrote: "To Mrs. Smith," and he drew in the middle of the page a huge penis and beneath: "for she seems to need it very much." Then he sat on the ground and began to write a tremendously obscene poem about the big penis Mrs. Smith needed so badly, and gave it to her. The husband was not pleased at all, and everybody so disgusted they really threw him away. Then, Thomas told me, it was very interesting: the teachers began by saying by he was disgusting, they did not want any longer to write books and thesis about him, they even said: "After all, he is not such a good poet." But the obscenity, the boldness of Thomas had moved them. One of them suggested he would play some records he had hidden (in some record library of the university) and which were intensely obscene; he played them, and said Wolfe, it was as coarse and disgusting as can be: for instance, instead of a base-ball report, a sleeping-party report, imitating base-ball report with noises and all. It was amazing to see teachers and wives, so much scandalized by Thomas's funny and witty obscenity, accepting the most dirty things in a kind of challenge. The end of the story is that Thomas was quite sober when he had to give his lectures, and was a great success. I like the thing because I often dreamt about what would have happed if Joyce or other ones had discovered their real self in front of people pretending to admire them — they never did, in fact. And I am glad for once these "poetry teachers" saw what a real poet sometimes can be.

Well, the fixing-man has fixed the radio; now it works very well. I have already a lot of good records, and I put on the ugly thing (as a piece of furniture, it is ugly) the nice silken material in bold colors I bought with you in Tunis souks. So it is more pretty than it ever was.

Enough "foot-track" for today.

Love and love and love from

Your own Simone

1) Bernie Wolfe, a writer and jazz musician. 2) Soviet security police.

Sunday, 29 Octobre 1950

Dearest nice you,

I got a long fat letter Friday. I am not much wiser than last year, you know, when I begin to hope for our letter. I go up and down the stairs in the cold three times a morning. The fact is (between you and me) I did not try very change my feelings towards you, knowing I should not succeed. So, go on through this new winter with the same old heart, a silly one. You'll get your old Biblical king, honey, and other prints, too. I try to find for you an English translation of Genet, but it is hard to get; I'll so one package with the "Rape of Steffi." Maybe Nathalie is sending you money; you should at least open her letters. Did I tell you she never wrote to me since I left the States, after having written to her myself? Yea, it is Jean Marais[1] you saw in *The Storm Within*, and in the street with me. I like the movie enough myself. I don't know I'll dare give Olga the obscene little token; I was pretty astonished when I found it, not knowing first what it meant. Bost made a copy of the lines of your letter where you say Queneau is a Japanese native, and he'll show it to Queneau—I don't know if he'll like it. Bernard Wolfe saw Jacques Guicharnaud once with Queneau and other people, when Queneau came to New York last year. He asked to Guicharnaud how he lived, and Guicharnaud said proudly every week-end he came to New York.

—And then? what do you do?
—I got a room near Times square.
—And then?
—I walk around Times Square.
—What else?
—Nothing else.

So he does nothing in New York except walking around Times Square, without even getting a woman! He will not be difficult to please if he comes to Chicago! I am glad you got a fine October and rowed by yourself on the lagoonish lagoon. Here winter appears; it is icy cold at night, water freezes, and in day it is not warm neither. In the end I got a coat, a beautiful one, more beautiful than I should have bought one in the States, black with a big white collar and inside, heavier than fur, and so woolly, soft, and warm that I am in love with it. So Nathalie rather helped, after all.[2]

It is strange and sad, everybody everywhere is so hopeless about politics now. I had lunch with Silone last Thursday; he wants to come and live in France, because he is tired of struggling in Italy against church and Stalinism. So, many people ask him help and advice and so on, that he has no time for literary work—he was to the neck in politics at a time—so he will settle in Paris and write books, no more trying to interfere in world nonsense. He was nice as always.

I saw a good painting show by Haitian painters. It's a pity you never wanted to go to Haiti with me. We should have given our souls to some god and goddess, and they would have danced and screamed, laughed, and cried inside us for hours. I should like to possessed by a nice goddess. The Haitian painters contrive to give a fascinating idea of their island; they really invented painting anew. The first one was a priest named Hippolyte who just wanted to make pious holy paintings as a decoration for altars, naive but striking pictures. Lot of others came and imitated him in bright colors, gay and pleasant drawings; you would enjoy it, but there are no reproductions available, no more than the madmen pictures.

My music-box is wonderful now, I bought many records; I get acquainted with modern music, some of which is very, very good. Did you ever hear Béla Bartók, the Hungarish musician? He is wonderful. And the new Viennese one—Schönberg, Alban Berg, Webern? A rather difficult and intellectual music which happens to be a very good, too.3

We had many serious meetings about *Temps modernes*, Merleau-Ponty, Sartre, myself, and we decided to work seriously and meet again, deciding again to work seriously about it. But not much came from so much earnest talking. Our *Temps modernes* publisher, Julliard, who always invite Sartre and me with lot of celebrities—Maurice Chevalier, and so—invited Sartre with the sultan of Morocco who is now in Paris (you saw his palace in Fez), but he did not invite me, because the sultan does not meet any woman. Sartre did not go. Then Julliard invited both of us privately at a dinner with the son of the sultan. and we both said no! He is mad at is; he could never suspect it is just because I hate being bored; he thinks we are the most snobbish people in the world, pretending a sultan is not good enough for us.

I work and work and work.

And I do go on loving and loving my true love.

Your own Simone

1) Jean Marais, 1940s and 50s star of the French screen and stage, a protégé of Jean Cocteau (*Beauty and the Beast*, 1946). 2) By "lending" Simone de Beauvoir the money she herself had saved to go shopping in New York. 3) Alban Berg, Austrian atonal orchestral composer and student of Schöenberg (*Wozzeck*, 1922). Anton von Webern, a student of Bartók.

Thursday, 2 Novembre 1950

Dearest not too repellent you,

It is a grey and sad now in Paris, and since I lost my own inward sun, as you know, it is kind of grey and sad inside me, too. How do the squirrels and blue jays behave in this nearing winter? How so you? Is it warm in the home, and cosy? I sleep in this house every night; it has its own magic, too, as well as Wabansia nest.

Not much happened in these cold days. I go on working and listening to music. I had another dinner with the ugly woman, and she did not cry; I tried to explain to her why what she is writing now is so bad—I am a little afraid because it comes worse and worse, and in the end the book will be a monster. Sartre met once more the drunken woman, Toulouse; she had no black eye, she even looked fine, and Sartre was astonished, because she asked lot of questions about everybody and hardly spoke about herself. She just said she had written two plays during the holidays and would show them to Sartre next time. Then her servant-slave Zina went down with Sartre and told him with real realism the true truth: Toulouse began drinking again and did not write one line, she was wine-mad the whole holidays, and during Sartre's visit, went twice to the kitchen and drank glasses of brandy. She had make herself vomit and taken pills the whole morning so as to look fine and sober in the afternoon. What is really pathetic is she wants so hard not to drink but can no longer help it.

There was a man, I told you, who killed nine men in France last year. Sentenced to death, he moved the heart of everybody by a speech about his unhappy childhood; he explained he was given red wine instead of milk when he was baby. This red-wine business upset Toulouse so much that she struggled for weeks to get a possibility of seeing the man before he has his head cut off; through his lawyer, in the end, she got an appointment with him. But on this very day, when the cab came to take her, she was so drunk that Zina and Zina's husband had to beat her to make her stay in bed. Is not that sad? Another wreck I saw is this cousin of mine of whom I was in love when sixteen; I told you he drank himself so much as to fall from a big fortune and cosy marriage to utter misery. He is real Inspector: he "inspects" the banks of the Seine, getting about 60 dollars a month. Now he is coming blind from tobacco and drink, can hardly speak and hear. He wanted me to see and advice his son, a nineteen years boy who despises his penniless father and wishes nothing but money by the easiest way; as he is good-looking, it must be his curse or his luck. The father tried to get him to speak seriously with me about Latin and Greek; it was awful.

Bost is asked by the *American Mercury*[1] to send every month some "provocative report" about France and will be given 200 dollars and up for that. It makes a lot of French money and he is very pleased. What do you know about this magazine?

What about Truman's killer? Did the democrats want to make a martyr of him, A Lincoln, in view? So that people forget how he apologized to the Marine?

As tenderly as ever.

Your own Simone

1) One of the most important magazines founded in the twenties, with Sinclair Lewis, Theodore Dreiser, and Sherwood Anderson. It launched the revolt against the "tyranny of Main Street" and the parochialism of the middle class. H. L. Mencken served as editor-in-chief, wielding great influence as a critic.

Monday, 6 Novembre 1950

My dearest own you,

You would have laughed with mocking pit if you had been in my little brothel. Saturday morning. I was nicely working when the devilish phonish phone phoned: it was Tamy Guld, sobbing and telling me everythings was so bad and she had to see me. As I am soft to women's tears, knowing how dark they can make a woman's heart, I told her to come in the afternoon, during my working hours. Then I hung down, and the phonish phone phoned again: it was the drunken woman, half-crying, saying it was so bad, I should have written to her during the summer, and she wanted to see me. I said we should soon meet, but I thought I should be paid if I am asked to act as a psychiatrist. Tamy was in an awfully bad shape; some days she is afraid of going mad, it is so black and tight inside her. She cannot drink, because her stomach aches; she wants some dope to help her to go through the next months. I'll send to her a doctor. She tried for three weeks to be just nice, smiling and friendly with Bob, but he is as unfriendly as possible because he feels she does not accept his going away back to Haiti. She was so broken down in the end that, just Saturday morning she acted hysterically, going to her knees to ask him to stay. Indeed, he just wants to rush away when she does that. I told her she had to let him go and hope he will come back to her after one year, or she will have learned to live without him. She can do nothing else, but understand that she hates to do that. She told him the whole business was an escape from his real problem, that he cannot write any longer; he agreed, but that does not change his mind, indeed. "He has suffered long enough, and now she had to." She cannot see—neither can I—why he suffered so much. Even if he does not love her since long, they always get along very well; so, he could miss something, maybe, but not really suffer. he seems to be very deceptive to himself. The

387

most incredible part of the story is he told her she had never been sympathetic (which is lie!) he remembers after seven years a slight criticism she did and reproaches her with it! Is not that wonderful? The poor woman has found nothing to do, except to learn playing piano, so to have "a personal life." I gave your queer little token to Olga and read to her the little bit of the letter about it; she says rather pretty and will hang it on the wall above her bed.

Temps modernes are kind of sick. So, we decided a meeting of three people was not enough, and yesterday we were eleven, drinking French white poison and speaking in quick high voices. Everybody said what everybody else should do, and how everybody else should work for the review, and after that everybody felt much better, and we decided to meet again within two weeks and begin again. The publisher, I heard, is disquieted.

I sent you the Biblical king, and Van Gogh painted by himself, just after he cut his ear in the brothel a "little café in Arles" which I did not know and found stunning, a landscape by Utrillo, and "Thatched Houses" by Vlaminck. I guess you'll get them at the end of the month, and I hope you'll like at least the Van Gogh. I sent much love too in the package—take of it all which you can stand. There is much love in this letter too for the faraway piggish pig of whom I am faithful piggish pig.

Your own Simone

Saturday, 11 Novembre 1950

Nelson, dearest darling you,

I am glad the *Temps modernes* secretary at last sent you "The Rape of Steffi." Is not that a wonderful translation? You said the people who wanted your title to be "Never *comes* morning" spoke American like a native Japanese: that was Queneau and Duhamel.[1] Queneau is a Japanese in this way. Pirandello is a wonderful Italian play-writer who died twenty years ago, who contrived to write lively plays about an abstract topic:" there is no true truth about what one really *is*. He was haunted by the tragedy of madness, having a mad wife. *Henry IV* is about a madman pretending to be King Henry IV, but he recovers and knows he is not; and then seems madder than ever and kills an old enemy; he pretends to be mad to escape punishment. But he seems sane when he chooses to apply the fool, so you never know what the real self is, the sane one or the crazy one? I thought you would like all this game about splitted and ambiguous personality.

Very sad the Farrell's book is not bad, next will be...Today, 11th Novembre, is a great feast: some year, in faraway years, we defeated the Germans,
so there were terrific noisy planes flying in the sky, the shops are closed, all
French people feel proud about being French. What do you do with the
Chicago piece?[2] Why did not *Holiday* accept it as it was? May I have a
copy of the old thing I liked so much? I hope you'll not have to kill the
whole thing to deserve your money. May not I have the picture made by
your photograph-friend, you and me in Wabansia, where I looked like a
bohemian? I liked it. So, sleep well in your ridiculous double bed!

Tuesday

Are you always so warm and sunny? Do you get along, the little house and
you? have you got an TV in the end? Do you miss the gloomy Wabansia
funeral home? Tell me a little about it. And about American election; is
MacArthur going to be president some day? Here, people are rather scared
this Republican success will mean war. I read that Truman revenges himself against the congress by having the law strictly observed, everybody is
closed in Ellis Island now when they come to the States. I hope Koestler
will be, since he once belonged to the CP. Everybody in France is excited
about Thorez, the CP French leader, having fled away to Russia for a cure;
as he was half-paralyzed, Vichinski offered to bring him to Moscow so he
could be taken care of by the best Russian specialists.[3] He fled away two
days ago with his wife. Some people say he will be killed as Dimitriff was,[4]
and others point out that we have good surgeons in France too, and after
all Thorez was a son of France. How did Russians dare to rape him away?
How did French government allow it? Really funny. But except communists, nobody will accept the idea Thorez wanted to recover.

The ugly woman had a hard time last week when she knew that we
had a *T.M.* meeting and she was not invited: she went to her kitchen and
opened all the gas faucets. "But I am not as healthy as I used to be," she
told me. "After ten minutes I had to go away." She did not exactly want to
die: "That was my literary meeting, this opening gas faucets." Later in the
evening, she told me she wanted to read:

—Why now more than before?
—Now I don't cry any longer, so I want to read.

I saw yesterday *City Lights*, really stunning. I remember, years ago, I just
half liked it; we were used to such good movies in that time, but we are no

389

longer and any Charlie Chaplin is a wonder. He was somebody, this man.

We are going to have *Wild Palms* by Faulkner published in *Temps modernes*; it is good since he has the Nobel prize.

Sunday

Did you read the next incidents about Thorez' departure for Russia? How an American plane assaulted the Russian one, and so on; the French newspapers are full of that. Don't be amazed if you get a package sent by some unknown French woman; it is a book by Genet, in English, and I put a fake name, because if the customs officer open it, they will want to sue me. If they bother you, just say you don't know anything about it — it is certainly obscene literature, as obscene as the pictures your doctor Kinsey got from France. All I could get was the galleys, but indeed it kills much of Genet's magic. I am curious to know if you'll enjoy it or not.

Dick Wright never rests, now he organizes all Parisian-American Negroes; they don't get job as much as the white ones. Wright gathered some liberal people; they will have meetings and denounce Mac Arthur, Taft, and so on. It will indeed be of no use at all. But he fixes a big cocktail party next Sunday, and Sartre will be the French guest, so he had to go, so have I, though it seems useless.

Friday

It is a nice evening to write to you, with the fire roaring, fine red carnations on the table, and the music just stopped in the music-box. Bost, Cau, and Guyonnet went to see the killing of Stock by Robinson a few days ago; they enjoyed the way he came to the ring, looking like a black emperor, with four huge Negroes around him and a midget in from of him. While he danced on the ring, Stock knew gloomily he was going to be hurt.

Speaking of victory, what of your son of a bitch of Mac Arthur? He is going to bring a real war on this peaceful earth of Corea, it seems. We were anxious yesterday in Paris, when Truman spoke such nonsense. Today, it seems a little better, but these people are not grown-up enough to be allowed to play with the atomic bomb. The Chinese behave wonderfully, and maybe you were right when you dreamed about a new yellow civilization. But it will be bloody and hard before we came to it, and I am afraid not to see much of it. If there is a war and Russians come here, what then? I hate the idea for a lot of most important reasons. Tell your generals not to behave so silly, will you?

I am going to send you the last Sartre's novel translation, *Troubled Sleep*, with a dedication by him, for your existentialist library. And very soon *your* book in French.

And now some kissish kisses of you piggish pig.

Your own Simone

Do you know about a students' quarterly called *A Civil and Partisan Student*? Published in New York? Against war, against Stalin and American policy in the same time.

1) Marcel Duhamel, editor of the *Série Noir*, Gallimard's famous series of detective novels. 2) *Chicago, City on the Make*, which appeared in 1951. 3) Andrei Vychinsky, a Soviet politician who denounced the Marshall Plan. 4) George Dimitrov (1882–1949), Communist leader and prime minister of Bulgaria.

Friday, 8 Décembre 1950

Nelson, my love

I did not feel like writing all the week long, everything was so bad. Well, in a way I can understand you are kind of pleased with what happens. Maybe the American people will learn something from such a defeat; they surely have much to learn from a war with Chinese beating them to death. But here it becomes a very serious personal matter, since a war means a Russian occupation, and lot of people told me Sartre would surely be killed or sent to Siberia by the CP, and me too. It is really heart-breaking since we never were pro-American, and are less than ever, and should be deeply interested in what Russians will try to do. But there is no question. So we'll have to fly away. Where? Not to US, since we disagree with them. Brazil or Africa? What about Bost and Olga? and other friends? No, it is not pleasant to think, and if it does not happen just now, it is nearly sure to happen within one year, or two, and will be no better. You know, Nelson, for the very first time I was glad that you don't love me any longer because if we never can see each other again, it will not make so much difference now. Yet my heart aches when I think it will probably happen; I'll never see Wabansia, nor Forrest Avenue again, nor see you again. What foolish fools, what piggish pigs you have for a government!

Thanks for the long letter, honey. How did the muskrat contrive to steal the boat? Bost suggests not the muskrat is a liar, but you... The backyard must be nice beneath the snow. Here, no real snow, just white and gloomy all around. Your book is published and looks fine. I am sending with it Sartre's and a magazine where you'll find things about the communist poet writing about pebbles, Ponge. There is a picture and poems by him, though not the one about pebbles. Read the Lautréamont too—a wonderful port of last century—and Apollinaire, on page 136 read about Mourre who preached in Notre-Dame, remember? Denouncing the church and pretended to be mad by a mad doctor. Some people at Gallimard's already think your book is awfully good. A very good review is going to be written soon; I'll tell you.

I try to write the novel—I do—but I don't feel very much like it. Everybody is scared and gloomy in Paris. I hope you'll not be sent into jail. I'll love you everywhere, and I sadly and tenderly kiss you.

Your own Simone

Sunday, 10 Décembre 1950

Dearest nicest you,

I had awfully bad dreams the other night I was looking for you in some forgotten city, and did not remember the street, the number, the place; I remembered nothing, and went up and downstairs, just knowing I longed for something I could not find. Then, it was Morroco. I learned where you lived, but there began an intricate story with the ugly woman, who was Nathalie at the same time, getting killed on a motorcycle. I was involved in that death, and in the end never found you. The pang was in my heart when I woke up, but I just found your letter downstairs and it wiped the dream away. I was so glad to hear about everything. So, the little whore will be the next woman in Miller harem! Will she sleep upstairs, or ask for an ordinary twin bed? My idea is she would sleep in the little boat, so nobody could scare her at night. Is that the way to be invited in Forrest home, honey? Just pretend you are full of dope and bring some phoney white powder? I'll so it if I don't get invited within ten years; it seems a good idea. I don't think Wabansia will easy die, some of the things you try to kill are awfully stubborn and keep on living in their funeral way, you see. Well, I should like the new piece about Chicago, indeed but cannot I have the other one too? I liked it. Congratulations for getting so much money. Send to me some unread good books if you ever meet any.

I went and saw in the hospital the poor ex-dactylo with a cancer in her breast. They had taken away her ovaries and implanted male hormones inside her; it is terrific: she has whiskers, a man's voice, is fat as this eunuch cat we saw once in Paris, remember? I don't like the idea I could be changed in such a strange being, just by some surgeon trick. She suffers a little less, but she will die the same within a few months and I guess she knows it.

Olga had a nervous breakdown when she learned the papers were signed about *The Flies*: she cried, screamed, and behaved as silly as woman can do, but she will feel happy within a few days.

I met the movie-director who made *Manon*[1] which you liked and I despised, newly married with a glamorous woman and coming back from Bahia; brought back some wonderful pictures. Brazil seems much more interesting than Haiti. He spent seven months in Bahia, and two in the place where the initiation ceremonies take place; they drink strange drinks, and chicken fresh blood, they kill goats and pigeons, sing, dance, and come hysterical, and then the Holy Spirit possesses them. He had pictures of black girls (Bahia is all black) with shaved heads covered with blood and feathers glued in this blood, blood on their naked body, and distorted hysterical faces — fascinating. He says it is fascinating and you feel giddy yourself when you live with them a time. For a change he wanted to make a movie with *The Second Sex*, but it seemed a crazy idea and I dropped it. Cocteau, who directed *Inside Storm* (Is that the English name?),[2] Marais' lover, the handsome pansy actor, asked Sartre and me for lunch in this old restaurant where the butler never let you have any wine. For two hours, he did not stop *one* minute talking, always talking about himself. He is writing a life of handsome Marais; he drawed the face of Marais on some scarfs he sells in elegant shops, and so on. Awfully tedious, because he feels nobody is much interested in him now, in France or elsewhere, and he has to pretend they are. It was rather sad. He just told one good story, a cat story. Some stupid movie-director in Paris is directing a play with and old woman and cats; the cats, fifty of them, are dying with hunger, and when the old woman comes in the room without any meat to give them (because she is such a poor woman) all the cats "jump on her like tigers," the script says. So the director required the cats to jump like tigers, but they did not. He doped them, half poisoned them; he put burning poisons on their most delicate pieces of anatomy: the cats did not jump. Some loving-cats people asked him to stop: "the cats could be mad in a meek way," they said, but the director did not listen to them. "That is *written*: they have to jump like tigers!" He put them in close bags, with nothing to eat, after ten days, the bags were open, the cats half dying, covered with shit, not jumping at all. In the end the Beast Protecting Society has been called against the director, but they cannot come inside the studio. And the thing goes on and on, they torture other cats, who neither want to look like tigers. Is not that sad?

I had lunch with Qeuneau, awfully nice, and definitively not looking like a Japanese.

Now good bye, good bye, good bye. With the stubborn funeral not wanting to die love of

Your own Simone

1) Henri-Georges Clouzot. 2) *L'Aigle à deux têtes.*

Thursday, 14 Décembre 1950

Sweetest dearest you,

Yea, it was nice to get such a huge letter. It came very late, indeed, since you are so stubborn about under-stamping your letters, but it came, and as you say, now I have something to read for days. It is all delightful, your stories about Harold and Betty and the little whore, and so busy and useless amidst all them. Thanks for the clippings; I'll certainly be begin to read the Bible one of these days. Sartre enjoyed the ones concerning him. *Iron in the Soul* is the English title for the book I sent you, whose American title is *Troubled Sleep*. Here is a French clipping about you from *Combat*, which was Camus' newspaper and is rather a stinking pro-American paper now, but the reviewer is an honest, not too stupid man; they have a literary page each week and he gave you the leader article. Try to understand, to ask Neal to translate it.

Faulkner certainly belongs to the Confederacy; he gave terrible interviews in the Paris newspapers. I don't like him at all now. He said he was just a farmer, not a writer; he knew nothing about human beings, just about fancy creations in his brain; right-wing newspapers understood that he belongs to them and published with enthusiasm some of the most nasty lines of *Intruder in the Dust*.[1] I got a long, awfully sad letter from Nathalie; it is the first time she writes since I left. She can hardly write, because she came through the worst time in her life (excepting her lover's death time).[2] When coming back to Hollywood she still lived two weeks with her husband, and then it was so bad that she decided to leave. She hired a sad little flat and took the little girls with her, since she got ashamed in the end of the way she behaved towards her. She earns 200 dollars a month, takes from

Ivan what allows him not to pay the income tax—that is 100 dollars—and he gives a little for the girl. She can live. But morally it is awful, because her friend, the pansy, was so scared when she left Ivan, fearing he would have to live with her, that he broke up. She resented it awfully and spent in loneliness two dreadful months. Then his friend came back to her, because he was mad at his little pansy who had sold all his furniture and bought a new one, making 1000 dollars debt when they have not a penny. For two weeks it was paradise; he came every day, slept with her without being obliged to, and even told her "he had hard on for her" while in the office—is not that kind? (she says so in the letter). But the little pansy got so mad at the whole business; he slapped Nathalie and took his friend away with him; since, she is alone again. The husband asked her not to divorce him, because he does not want to marry his mistress. Nathalie hates him now and cries about her pansy-friend; it is rather dirty, nasty story, and it is not the whole true truth since Nathalie is unable to see in other people what does not concern her, and so does not understand much. In a way she deserves it by her selfishness and scold stubbornness, but it is really sad for her. Something will happen, indeed, she said in such circunstances it seemed futile to send me money she promised to send, but she will, some day...

For Tamy Guld, the situation is slowly changing, it seems. Bob is packing in order to leave France as soon as necessary, and he feels responsability towards his family in this emergency. He had not get so much money as he hoped and cannot go giving lot of it to the Haiti woman; but it doesn't give to Tamy the love she needs. She sees Bob with new eyes, discovers he is too selfish and interested in himself. She doesn't love him very much, is interested in a young man and wants much to sleep with him. I told her to try to get this young man, to have an affair with him and let Bob go to the devil.

Now, honey, I'll answer seriously to the serious part of your letter. First, I'll tell you that it was very sweet to hear you intended to make me a miserable woman for long years, if things go on all right. I should like it so much! I don't want you to go out of my life if I can help it; if you keep me a little place in yours, it would make me very happy. Thanks for saying so. I felt a kind of happy quiet tenderness for which I used to feel always in the past times but which had deserted me. It is good to get back in my heart; you are so dear to me, darling.

Then, I'll scold you in my turn! You say am hysterical...but you are certainly too smug. You admitted when I knew you that you made a fake wisdom of this smugness: a crocodile in his mud nest. It is not a reason, because the little house is snowy and cosy, and you enjoy your crazy addict friends, to think in such an optimistic way about the world. I don't say there cannot be peace for some years, but it is not sure. And then it can be peace for you and a Russian occupation for us. The war will possibly not burst even with Russians in Paris, but here, it will not be better. To believe that the CP will at once strike Sartre and his friends is not a vanity delirium; *everybody* we meet in Paris agree — he is terribly hated by communists and certainly, among intellectuals, the No.1 enemy. So it is not hysterical to plan a departure, neither to feel the real horror of exile. You know, honey, I remember in, '39-40, with my Jewish friend, I had the same way of thinking she was little hysterical when she believed in Jewish concentration camps and so on; still, she was right. When you are not interested in a danger in flesh and bones, you feel it far away. She felt lonely and misunderstood among French people, I remember, among non-Jewish French people. So it is very different now for you and me, it is easier for you not to admit that the worse could happen (as you tried first to make it a joke when I was *drowning*.3

Then, about going to USA. The point is not Sartre or I believe we should be sent into jail. But it means, in the eyes of French people, we care for a political choice to go to the States; and it is not our choice. If the war gets to an end and we ever come back, we cannot be the people who fled to Truman and Stalin invaded France. Yea, we have to write, but we have to be trusted by people we write for, and it would be a betrayal to *go* to the States. If you *are* in the States as a native, that is wholly different; you stay, it doesn't imply a choice. *Going* means approval. It is not a question of pride, but of honesty. Understand that all French left wing or even liberal people *hate* American policy now — so do I. We all despise the wealthy capitalists who begin to fly to New York to save their money. To choose US would be to choose capitalism against all we write and said. I agree our choice is not important to the world, but it is important to us. Then there is the money question (intricate with the moral one). To get money in US, what should we do? Broadcast and articles, and so on, or starve? French people in '40-44 had to work in propaganda to make a living (which a native has not to do). It was all right then; we should not accept it now. In Brazil, they have much money, they care for French culture, they could be half neutral, it would be easier.

I should like you to understand, I don't want to feel far from you about important matters. Believe me, we have spoken about it with all friends and thought about it days after days without any hysteria; there is something in the French situation you don't (and maybe cannot) understand from the States, to speak as you do. I should like so much to speak to you about it.

Answer, please and don't begin by be critical and superior before you tried to realize.

Well, my love, that is quite a letter, is not it? You sent to me the nicest Christmas gift by typing such a huge letter. Happy Christmas, happy New Year! Here is all my dirty heart for you.

Your own Simone

1) *L'Intrus.* 2) Bourla, a young Jew deported during the war. See *The Prime of Life.* 3) During the summer of the same year, on the banks of Lake Michigan. See *Letters to Sartre* for more on this period.

Friday, 22 Décembre 1950

Dearest darling you,

You were shrewd not to make me too mad at you during this summer, because I have to be a very good friend for you, to do all I am doing now. First, I had half an hour talk with poor sad Guyonnet. I explained to him all the nice things he should say about you at the radio. Then, the secretary called me: "It is not the newspaper man, it is Algren's agent speaking to you," and he asked me twenty lines about you for *Opéra*. So I spent the afternoon writing about you instead of improving my own dirty book. *Opéra* is a very much read weekly magazine, and next they publish the last chapter of *Never Come*... with this foreword by me. Do you like it? It is just a beginning.

They had Faulkner here at Gallimard's cocktail; everybody was disappointed at him, I heard, but what do they expect a writer to say when he meets hundred of people an hour? Unless he behaves as Dylan Thomas did. I did not go to the cocktail; I stick to *one* American writer, it is quite enough for me. Thanks to my own American writer for the season's greetings. Sartre was pleased with his, too, and thinks seriously of going to church now. I guess it is purposely that you chose *Chinese* engraving, was it?

I just come from visiting my poor typewriting woman with a cancer in the breast; she is really changing into a man — she grows a beard, has man's voice. She screamed with suffering while I was there; she kissed me crying and it was an awful time to go through.

397

Strange time I had last Sunday with Sartre at this crazy R. Wright's meeting. It was supposed to be a French-American liberal meeting to save peace and freedom in the world. Sartre was the chief French guest, and a man called Louis Fischer the American one. Sartre had to speak for five minutes without any political allusions. At seven, we went in a huge hall in some English Embassy, with lot of staircases and glass-lamps hanging from the ceiling, a big empty polished floor; there were about fourty people, Negro men and old ugly women, sitting around small tables. Louis Fisher was once a communist and lived in Russia for fifteen years: he has this haggard, dark deep resentful look of all communist renegades, and never spoke nor smiled until he had to get up and make his speech. He began by attacking USSR for twenty minutes, and said that USA should fail if Europe only helped them to get moral strength, America loved peace and freedom, and the only thing to do now in the world was for everybody to live as Gandhi has lived. Sartre was very angry, because all this was politics after all, so he let in the pocket the soft little speech he had prepared, and spoke harshly, saying that this mutual hating of USA and USSR was the greatest evil, and nowadays nobody is free in no country at all. Fisher was mad at him, and during a terrible dinner he explained how peace-loving America is, so peace-loving, said he, as to throw an atomic bomb rather than have his own soldiers killed. Dick was all right, here; when Fisher said the drama with Russia is you have to lie to survive, he answered: "Everybody has to, everywhere." "Oh!" said Fisher, "who does it?" "I did," said Dick, "I lied during nearly all my life, smiling and saying "yes, sir when I did not want to." But Dick is a big fool to have invited this man. He is about leaving France, too.

Paris is awfully sad, always grey and half snowing, and whenever you meet anybody the question is: do you go away? When? Where? All people with big money begin to go away; they have private planes or they buy boats. Most of non-communist intellectual think they will be asked to go away before. Everybody agrees Sartre would be killed at once and I should be in great danger. So I live now with the idea I'll have to fly away within six months or two years, maybe for ever. A strange feeling.

Honey, I wish to you happy Christmas, happy New Year. I hope you'll begin writing a good book this year; do go on enjoying you little house and be happy. I hope you'll keep a little something for me in your heart and sometimes remember me tenderly. I do kiss you very lovingly from my stubborn faithful heart.

Your own Simone

Sunday, 31 Décembre 1950

Nelson honey,

The piggish pigs in the *Opéra* magazine! I spent the whole afternoon writing about your dirty book, and they did not publish your last chapter, nor my page. Really piggish pigs they are.

We had a nice Christmas night in LaBûcherie brothel. I invited Bost, Olga, Sartre, Scipion, and bought scotch, champagne, foie gras, caviar, pudding, flowers, mistletoe — it was a real ceremony. Everybody drank, ate, was pleased. Bost and Scipion will have their comedy acted in March in some big theatre; Olga is rehearing *The Flies*; it is all right for everyone. So it was a nice evening; Scipion was very funny. The only point is that in the end poor Scipion suddenly went away to "man's room" and never came back. Bost went and looked, fearing he was dead, and found him at the bottom of the staircase, shivering in the cold and Scipion disappeared: he found himself in his hotel-bed next morning,

I offered to myself a very useful gift for Christmas, a big gas-stove, snoring and bright and hot. I was shivering with the poor little half-broken stove you knew; I had an awful cold and spent my nights madly coughing. Now, it is a delight to be home!

I tell you Olga is rehearsing. The play will be presented to the public on the 12th January, that is very soon. The director has the actors working morning and afternoon, a good but hard work. The first days Olga thought she was not good enough, and spent nights crying; she was very unpleasant with the director, who was not pleased with her himself. Everybody was afraid there would be some tragedy, and for once Sartre scolded Olga a little harshly. She behaved better, was better actress; the director was pleased and now it seems it will be all right. Except that it seems to me Olga lost something by being sick: not just youth, but a fire she had, something burning and lively, a little wonderful, which made her nearly a *great* actress. Maybe she will find that again in herself within next weeks, but I am not sure.

We had — Olga, Bost, Sartre, myself — a rather tedious dinner at Wright's. He has brought from US a recorder, and recorded miles of music, bad music. We had to hear it all dinner long. Do you know this terrific gadget? It could be used in a very interesting way, though. Then, all dinner long, we spoke about the topic which is everybody topic in Paris now, at least among non-communist intellectuals: how to get away, where,

399

when? We all agree to go rather to Brazil—well, can't you come, too, instead of waiting for bombish bombs on your headish head? Anyhow, Dick began to organize our colony, everybody living together in a kind of village and trying to feel "deeply responsible." I answered that we should rather live quiet so as not to be over-responsible of anything. But he has found something to live for now and he enjoys.

No, we don't think here war is for tomorrow. But not so far neither. And with this cold, grey, whitish, snowish, weather, I cannot say that Paris is very joyful.

Did I tell you that the beautiful singer is in Brazil, making a huge lot of money? She pretends to be a very serious existentialist, and tries to give lectures! She was so scared that she could no speak, once, and a French consul had to help her by speaking himself. She tries to have people believe she lived with Sartre for a long time as his mistress, and she makes all intellectual Brazilians angry at her by her stupidity. Thinking people had not applauded enough her songs, once she said: "Brazilian people are sons of a bitch." A madman, a real mad one, jumped unto the stage and wanted to eat her hair; she slapped him and was right in this circumstance. Poor little Cassoulet, all alone in Paris, far from her singer-friend, is very sad; she wants to kill any friend, poor thing not knowing what to do of herself. Shall I send her to Forrest avenue and you get some medicine for her?

Good bye, my love. I guess I'll love you this year as much as any other year. I try not to think of past times, neither of future times, but love is here in every present day. I kiss you tenderly in this last 1950 evening.

Your own Simone

1951

Darling you,

Thanks for the nice long letter with the right stamps on the enveloppe. You don't tell me if you got Sartre's and Ponge's books, neither if you read Genet's; did you? [1] It was a very hard week for all of us, because Olga is rehearsing *The Flies*; she hates the director and he hates her, because he would want his girl-friend to play the part of Electra, so he says Olga is wrong—and, indeed, she is so angry that she gets sick and really bad, she cries, and makes poor Bost mad. Sartre tries to help her and gets mad, too, and everybody complains to me about the other ones. I should get mad too if I were not such a wise smart poised woman, as you know. This director behaved very badly. He said to newspaper men Olga is not talented enough, so Sartre threatened him to say *he* is not talented enough—he is not, in fact. She would be much better than others ones if she found some physical strength; it seems she does, these last days; we all wait impatiently the last rehearsal, the reviews, the end of the week...I hope it will not be failure; she waited for so long!

The piggish pigs in *Opéra* published my paper about you, in the end, and all the last chapter of *Never Come*. It was bad for me, because this same day they published a dirty paper about Sartre's next play, which is not written and which they explained from beginning to end, telling it would be a communist play, because he wanted now to be friend with Moscow! When Cau insulted them about it, they said: Well, S. de B. writes in our newspaper; she does not despise it so much! In fact, it doesn't matter at all.

Clouzot thinks very seriously of making a movie with *She Came to Stay*. I should enjoy it very much, indeed. We just had a lunch together in the restaurant where you are not allowed to help yourself with the wine, remember? He will give me an answer very soon, and if it were yes, I should have to work with him very hard on the script.

Next week, I'll go for two weeks to the country, near Angers as usual. I should like it, I need some rest. I did nothing for three months but work real hard; it is very cold and I feel kind of tired. When shall we got the Chicago paper? You don't speak much about working. Did you begin the year nicely? Is there ice on the lagoon? I read about the little Homer Smith[2] is really good. What does Harold[3] exactly do all day long on the roof and in the basement? I cannot figure it at all.

Good bye, honey, I don't wish anything as much as drinking scotch on Forrest Avenue once more. Love and love from

Your own Simone

1) *La Mort dans l'âme*, by Sartre; *Transition 50*, a journal devoted to poetry; *Notre-Dame des Fleurs*, by Genet. 2) When he was denied a place in the dining car of a train, this "unknown" sought revenge by bombarding the railroad company with insulting anonymous letters and by destroying all the printed train schedules in the station. Public opinion was completely with him. 3) One of Algren's strange friends, an alcoholic who did odd jobs for him.

Sunday, 14 Janvier 1951

Honey,

Maybe I was not so stupid after all when I picked you up among all men to give you my dirty heart and my pack of bones; it seems you are really the nicest man in the world and you got two little tears from fried up eyes with your little extra-letter. Keep on your little crock of gold, honey, keep it safely; I do hope I'll not need it before one or two years—things look a little better, don't they? But, yea, if the worst happen I'll ask you 100 or 200 dollars to make a beginning in Mexico or Rio de Janeiro, since French money will be worth nothing. In Brazil, I guess money will be possible to get by giving lessons, lectures, and so on, since Brazilians are so wealthy and many speak French, but the first times would be hard anyway. I told Sartre, and he had no tears in his eyes but was deeply moved, really. He said, too, 100 dollars could be used and you are the kindest friend. Yea, it was nice to think about all that and to offer you little pot of gold. Thanks, sweetheart.

Here is another clipping about *Never Come*, from the chief literary weekly newspaper, a right wing one. Still, they could not help liking your book very much; they just say maybe you are not exactly Dostoyevky. The ugly woman is very clever, you'll learn: she is crazy about your book. To tell the truth, I am not sure it is because of the book; it is rather because I wrote it was so good. It seems treacherous to let her speak so nicely about you, when she would fall dead with anger and jealousy if she knew what happened between you and me, in past-times-happy-times. She was peculiarly in love with the barber, chiefly when in the beginning he goes a little backward to look at the customer's skull: she says such a touch is so "human," it means a great artist—so says she.

I understand very well what you say about Genet, and I think he would like it; it is the right way to react to him. People who say he is obscene are stupid; those who say it is all right are not true. Genet *wants* to do against everything in you, in me, in Sartre, in Bost, and he does. He wants it form his childhood, and jail, and homosexuality; he wants to be admired in spite of us, and he contrives it. That is the wonderful part, that we could hate and enjoy his book in the same minute.

Thanks for the Giacometti picture; I am glad he is a success, but sure, you'll never see him in the States; he is a stubborn thing. Aron, the philosopher, was a great friend of Sartre and myself in past times. We were students together when I was twenty and we enjoyed long abstract talks; he is a Jewish and spent the war in London and I remember how happy I was when I met him in winter, '44: it seemed to mean all the wrong part of life was over, and new era began. We worked together on *Temps modernes* for a year, then we quarrelled to death when Sartre and me spoke against de Gaulle. Since, we never see each other, he turned Gaullist-RPF, and he writes against Sartre as much as he can. Though what he said in the paper you sent to me is true, indeed.

I enjoyed your long letter; it was lovely to get it just after the little one. Poor thing! How nicely you got your radio stolen! I do like this little whore; she tries to teach you something you'll never learn.

It was another hard week, even harder than the one before. I told you Olga hated her director—Hermantier he is called, who is hateful; in fact, does not know his job and wanted to have his mistress playing Olga's part. Well, he did something no director ever did in the world; he spent a night "confiding" to a newspaper man who is friend of him, and this last one wrote a long paper in *Opéra*, and said Hermantier thought Olga was bad, just Sartre made him accept her but she was so sick, could not play, and so on. You guess how pleasant for Olga! Sartre insulted Hermantier to death, had him say at the radio that the newspaper man had lied, but what is printed is printed. In fact, the first public rehearsal was yesterday, and Olga was much better than everybody; she was really good. Tonight, it is the great public rehearsal with all newspaper men and important people. I hope she will be as good. But the performance is a shame! The director

403

uses green and red and yellow light as if it were the Folies Bergére, except it was much uglier, nothing to do with the play. Everything he did, the setting, clothes, were awful. The were of all kind of times in history: Middle Age, Greek Antiquity, nineteenth century, all that among Negro dances and music. Really a shame. I hope he gets the worst reviews and Olga good ones. She was nice, because instead of breaking down when Hermantier was so bad for her, she got excited and decided to act really well, and so she did. But it was a pity in the last act to see her sensitive face going through all the colors of rainbow of the crazy flash lights! Well, she was rather pleased in the whole, because she felt and has been told she was very good. I'll tell you the end of the story next time.

I'll go to the country a week later than I thought, because the old lady is a little sick and my sister coming. Good bye, thanks for all, darling you. I kiss you a long, loving kiss.

Your own Simone

Paris, Saturday 20, Janvier 1951

My own beast,

I got your little blue letter, a nice letter, but I hate this kind of paper: first, it is too small; then when it arrives La Bûcherie brothel, it is open; at last, I loved the yellow thick one: cannot I have it any longer, honey? It is quite true what they say about Genet; he is deeply religious in his way, he says it himself; all he wants is "to be a Saint"; he gets angry if you tell him he will never be one. Yea, Ponge is not exactly, not only a pebble-writer, but did *you* ever write about a pebble? Here are two other little reviews about your novel, one is from a non-communist weekly magazine, the other from a rather right wing one, both are very good; you are a real success, you know. I just send the reviews I happen to find in my way. I am sure that there are a lot of other ones at Gallimard's—a little later I'll have Guyonnet go and look for them. Boris Vian is translating *Golden Arm*, and it seems he enjoys it; he knows some Chicagoans who pretend to help, but it will be a long job.

It was another bad week. I am glad to be leaving Paris next Thursday, at last. First, the rehearsal was awful. Everybody thought this Hermantier killed the play, then the reviewers were mostly bad for Olga. It is strange. All intellectual people like her and say she is the best one; its my idea, too, but the newspapers people, Parisian people, think she is ugly, she has not enough voice, she is a little queer, and don't like her much or even not at all.

And Hermantier did such a dirty job by having printed that Sartre *ordered* him to keep Olga as an actress that many papers were very mischievous and mean. They were good for Sartre who doesn't care about this old play, very harsh against Hermantier, but rather harsh too against Olga, and she is sad, so is Bost, and so am I, because I realize she will never play again, unless I write a play for her: she is too old, and, chiefly, too tired to begin.

Then my sister cane to Paris. She will have a show of her paintings beginning February, and I decided to help her though she is not a very good painter and I don't care much for her. So, I had first to see her, and it is as tedious as seeing poor Christy; then I had to see some "important" people who can help her, and it was tedious, too. Paris was cold, damp, grey, and I go on working well on your book, but I am pretty tired, After two weeks at the old lady's, I plan to go for two other weeks at winter-sport with Sartre and Bost. I hope I shall not break my legs. I am fed up with Paris.

I met O'Brian, a Columbia teacher, yesterday; he came here for three weeks in plane. It seems such an easy trip, but I know trips are never easy for you and you'll not fly Paris even when sun will shine. Well, my own thing, tell every other things around Forrest nest that I love them. I do, and my heart aches. I love you, too.

Your own Simone

La Pouéze, Monday, 29 Janvier 1951

My darling own beast,

So I am far from Paris, at last, and very gladly. I was awfully tired the last days and I did not enjoy seeing anybody I saw. I had lunch with Tamy Guld, and her I guess you will have to laugh — she laughed herself! — about this great love Bob had for an American woman in Haiti! Well, at the same time he had an affair with a French one in Paris, since he is back, and meanwhile he got a report about the Haitian girl: she is sleeping with an Haitian important political leader, and writing to an Argentine landlord who asks her to come and live in his ranch! Bob never said Tamy anything about all that, but she found out. He is mad at the treacherous beloved one, and only half in love with the French girl, and when he left for Italy, he kissed Tamy, saying: "I'll be a good husband when I come back." But she does not know if she still wishes to be a good wife — though I guess that is what she will do. Well, I said good bye to her, to Olga who is rather gloomy: she does not know if she wishes to be an actress any longer. And

I came here by train. The old lady was very sick, everybody in France and England has got a bad kind of influenza. She should stay in bed, having a high fever, but she does not; she is too lively. She was around all day long; at night she cannot sleep and reads lot of books. Then, early in the morning her husband has her awaken by the maid, because "sick people rule," so the rule is to be awaken when she hardly begins to sleep. He cannot stand anybody to be sick in his house; he tried to get as much of a fever as he had but could not. The old, old cook is in bed, too. And Sartre had awful toothache which lasted the whole week and begins only now to weaken. I am all right, though. I live without dressing, doing my hair or making up my face, all day writing or reading, sleeping long nights, enjoying rest and work. I read—or rather tried to read—*Under the Volcano*,[1] which is a most stinking book, pretending to be deep, and only tedious, shallow, and stupid. *The Naked and the Dead*[2] is not so bad but no good either. I read a very terrific book about India, by an Hungarish man writing in English, *India in the Storm* (Tibor Mende). You should read it, since you are so interested by India. But it makes somebody sick to think of the way these people live; it seems hopeless. I began a very interesting one about China of nowadays, but it is by a Frenchman; it is no use for you. I hope the good concierge will send me your letter. I hope she will something to send. The ugly woman, who loves your book so much, says the part about jail is even better than Genet, though she is in love with Genet. She was a terrible thing to see when I said good bye, having thirteen teeth to take away from her mouth, which she let get rotten since the war. A good dentist tried to put one away; he succeeded, but she swooned and was delirious for an hour because of the dope. Still, it is impossible to put her wholly asleep; it would be bad for heart. So the dentist is mad with fear at the idea he has still twelve to pull away for this mad woman. Another terrible sight was my poor cancerous secretary in her hospital bed, with a thick silky beard, whiskers, hair on all her face, this face twice as huge as it used to be, a sick lung, too—she will be dead within six weeks, but does not know it. This hospital was the hell, with old women dying noisily in all the beds around.

Well, it is good to here, far from all that and selfishly quiet. I hope you do begin nicely the year, having just as much rest and trouble as you like. I do kiss you tenderly.

Your own Simone

1) By Malcolm Lowry. 2) By Norman Mailer.

Paris, Saturday, 10 Février 1951

Sweetheart,

I got your big nice fat letter when I came back home, and I felt ashamed for not having written to Forrest Avenue since nearly two weeks. But there was so little to say about life in La Pouéze! Now I have a lot of things to answer back, and I'll do it this very evening, if I don't fall asleep before. It is only half past nine, but I feel awfully tired. I am not sure I got much rest in the country, never breathing a gap of fresh sir, always at home writing hard. Anyway, if I don't get through tonight, I shall tomorrow.

First, I'll answer your questions and you whole letter. Sartre was very pleased with what you tell about him, and with the clippings: thanks for sending them. I wholly agree with all you say about Sartre and Genet. Poor Sartre had a terrible time, no kidding. When he left Paris, he just spent an awful night with the most awful toothache; he went to the dentist who said it would be all right, he could go. Then he suffered hard enough in the country, went to the next town dentist, suffered the hell for some hours, and then felt a little better. We came back yesterday; he went again to the dentist, and at 4 P.M. when I saw him one minute, he sent me away, telling he suffered the hell once more. This morning Cau phoned to me three times, half mad himself, because when coming not work as usual, he found Sartre, who had suffered without a rest since 4 P.M. yesterday to 9 A.M. this morning, had gone to the dentist once more, and then, at 10 A.M. was just mad with pain. "He cannot speak; he suffers so much I guess he is going to *scream.*" The dentist did not understand how this nursed tooth could be so painful—nobody understood nothing; it made everything suspicious. Then, I came to see Sartre in the afternoon; he was still suffering and gloomy, because he waited for going to hell once more. I was anxious myself, and by strength had him go back to the dentist, who looked deadly anxious in the phone: this tooth *could* not be that painful! Then, an hour after, Sartre came back widely smiling: it was *another* tooth, the next one, which was hurting him since two weeks!! Nobody caring for it and only nursing the first recovering one! He could play piano and worked in the end of the afternoon, and from now it will be an average tooth disease.

The most terrible point is he is writing a play which will be performed on the middle of May,[1] very long and difficult to write, and not the half is done, he needs every minute. But I guess he'll do it.

Well, Olga was good, but the whole thing was so bad it is going to stop in a few days. She is rather sad about it. Hermantier could not be used in the Musée Grévin; he would kill the whole magic of it. Mac Coy got a terrible punch in the face from a French writer called Kessel,[2] in a night-club. This Kessel is in fact a Russian and a stinking writer, the kind of Mac Coy, and I thought you would be glad to know it. I am not going to Israel this year. I was invited with Sartre, and he cannot go, because of his play, before June, then it will be too hot. I hope we'll go rather to Brazil where it is cool in June and July. But I don't like planning this year. Betty is really a clever woman. I begin to like her very much. In my idea she knows much better than the ugly woman "what is literature." Do give her *The Blood of Others* and chiefly *Ethics of Ambiguity*.

My sister will have her exhibition within two days; it will be hard for me, because I'll have to see a lot of people I always try not to see. I hope it will a success. Bost is going to Ligne Maginot for *Mercury*, and very angry at it. But the beautiful singer came back for Brazil with three million jewels worth, fur coats, dresses, lot of money, and a lover who owns millions of dollars and wants to marry her. When she "lectured" she said: "You may be an existentialist and wash several times a week." What else? Bost came for a week to La Pouéze, the old lady likes him. We ate foie gras, drank champagne, and old-man-nobody-never-sees got very angry at it.

It is true there was radio-active cloud above Chicago, and snow coming from Nevada experiments about atomic bomb? Are you not going to be sick one day or another? I heard some more Negroes were killed for raping a white woman, you killed a lot of people in a train clash in New York, and a Negro girl died from cold. What a countryish country! I had lot of time in La Pouéze to think to the lagoon, the scotch, the lost key in the sands, and so many things. That is one of the reasons I could not easily write; it made me too blue.

Another sad letter from Nathalie, simple, nice, and sad. Nothing is better for her, poor thing. She will come to Paris this summer. I'll have to be there a little, though she never sent to me the money she had to send.

It was lucky I got your letter. The good concierge sent to me two letters which never arrived. But yours was there, so fat and nice. Do it again. Good bye, my own monster, I remember you loved me.

Your own Simone

1) *Le Diable et le bon Dieu.* 2) Joseph Kessel, a French writer and journalist known for his autobiographical war and adventure stories (*The Lion*, 1958; *The Cavaliers*, 1967.)

Honey,

So I got one of these blue small letter once more, but I did not deserve more since I had not written for long. I noticed it was written with a new typewriter, and I hope to know the story. Poor Betty! Such a clever woman, knowing "what is literature" since she liked *She Came to Stay*; sad she was that sick. You have strange friends, honey, and we have a saying her about people who go together because they do look alike, or in a plain way, "Tell me which friends you have, I'll who *you* are." I can tell. What about your movie? I met Vian some days ago; he has translated thirty pages — ten pages a day, so it will be done in the beginning of April. I hope so.

My sister's exhibition was a great success in a way: thousand people in one evening, in gallery not bigger than Forrest Avenue front room. My woman-lawyer is so devoted to me than she asked all elegant, important people in Paris to come. She is a fifty years old, rather ugly, decent, sad woman, and I feel so old, decent, and sad when I meet her that I cannot understand why she is that fond of me. But, "a fact is a fact," as the mad girl said. When I thanked her for having invited so many people, she looked at me in a stern cold way and said: "Well, you *asked* me to do so, did not you?" Yea. But if I should ask for the moon?" And sternly, coldly, she said: "I should do my best to give it to you." How do you like it? I spent three hours shaking hands with unknown or tedious people. Poor Sartre came for a quarter of an hour; everybody rushed to him and asked: "How are your teeth?" So he was mad at everybody. A photographer made a picture of Sartre, my sister, and, myself looking at a Moroccan landscape, and it was published the day after in the most important evening paper. I was so ugly I did not send it to you, chiefly it seemed by the disgusting way in which I looked to the picture that I was thinking "It stinks." There were some nice papers about my sister, so she left for Milano very pleased. In fact, she did not sell more than one picture, and the whole thing costed very high (200,000fr, which means about 600 dollars), but as it is my money, she did not mind so much. Now, if we come to the heart of the matter: were these paintings good? The answer is "no," but it was much better than two years ago, and good enough for sale, for getting mild reviews, and not worse than lot of well-known paintings of nowadays. So she got many congratulations and was happy with them. Her husband came for the great day, and stayed in Paris half a week, but I only saw him once, and now they went away. Anyway, I go away myself tomorrow, and I am glad at it. It is damned bad weather here, always cold, wet, half raining. I told you I was going to winter-sports with Sartre and Bost; it will be sunny and snowy, high in the mountains. When I'll glide down from the top, I'll think of you tenderly and wish you are here, near me. Please, send your nonsense to Auron, Alpes maritimes, until the end of the month, and after that write to Saint Tropez, Var. Sartre is no longer unhappy with his teeth now, but very unhappy with the play he has promised to deliver on 1st of April. He works madly, Bost works madly about his Spanish book, and so do I about my novel, but not so madly as Sartre. The ugly woman had ten teeth pulled away; there is no other difference in her. Old Gide is mildly dying: Nobel prize, eighty one years old; It is time for him to go, but some people are a little hasty; they have already began asking Sartre for papers about Gide, his life and death! Sartre said no, indeed. *The Flies* go on until 4th of March, and Olga has nothing to do, and it is a pity, because lot of people say she was really good.

What did the birds and squirrels do during winter? Good bye, Nelson, sweetheart. Do tell me about you. You are as dear to me as ever, and as always I am.

Your own Simone

Auron, Monday, 26 Février 1951

Darling you,

I know nothing about you since a long time. I guess the mail has been sent to the Blue Coast where I'll find it within a week. Now I am in the snow, very, very high up among mountains, so high that my fountain-pens spits as if I were in a plane. It is sunny and beautiful. I am sitting on a large terrace on a deck-chair, the sun burning me as in the little garden in July, though I have a little more clothes on. I have no table and feel too lazy to get up, so try to read this shaky sick writing.

Well, it was raining hard, awfully grey, sad, and tiresome when I left Paris Tuesday evening with Sartre, who just wanted a quiet place to work, and Bost, who wished as feverishly as myself to enjoy himself on skis. From Nice, a bus went up to this terrible place in the mountains, a hard job because winter is terrible in France this year: snow falls and falls, avalanches...The road had been covered with rocks, and the bus could not go through them; everybody had to walk for half a mile, with luggage in hand, and through broken stones, up and down, then we found another bus which arrived here at night. How is snow is white and deep! I get up at 8 A.M. and at 9, with my skis on my shoulders, I ride up the mountain in this terrific thing we call a "téléphérique." Then I glide down and begin again; I read stupid books, eat a dinner, go to bed. Sartre works all day long. Bost comes up with me but goes down much quicker. I am scared; I glide slowly, and stop often. In spite of all, I hurt my knee yesterday, and had to stay home a whole day. I'll begin again this crazy, fascinating game tomorrow; I enjoy it. It is different every time, because there are many tracks, the snow is different from day to another, and you are different yourself. You would hate the whole thing, and how afraid you would be on the top of a mountain, poor dear you! I must say many people break their legs, here; it is rather elegant. On Sunday, they come from 200 miles around, from the whole coast, riding the car on snowy roads since 4 A.M., gliding on the snow until sunset and riding back. All the natives—the barber, the merchants, the photographers—are gliding down the whole day long and never working. They are all so gay, pleasant, as southern and mountain French people can be. My knee was nursed by a beautiful young man who did not accept any money. Lot of beautiful you men, here, with copper-colored skin, sunny hair, blue eyes! But I don't even speak with any. My heart and flesh are made of stone now forever, I guess. I dream about you nearly every night, always a nightmare. I don't see you, other people come, strange things happen, but always I have the terrible feeling of an endless, priceless loss, and it comes to an hopeless anguish; when I wake up, I know at once which loss it means.

I hope for letters from you. I do kiss you tenderly, my unforgotten, lost, lost true love.

Your own Simone

Saints-Tropez, Monday, 5 Mars 1951

My own beastish beast,

I had just sent the snowish pictures when I got your letterish letter, a nice one, with interesting clipping. Thanks very much. What did you day with Robert Lowry about *love*? Do you know *anything* about what it means for a humanish human being? Does he know better? It was kind of you to keep a bed in Wabansia in case I should happen to come there once more. Do you think I'll ever shall? It depends upon you as well as upon Truman and Stalin. Old Gide is dead. All newspapers spoke rather nastily about him, though he certainly was somebody. To die at 81, peacefully, among friends, is indeed a clever way of dying. Two Catholic writers hated Gide: Mauriac, a novelist, and Claudel, a poet. Little Cassouolet did a nice joke: she sent a wire to Mauriac the day after Gide's death: "HELL DOES NOT EXIST. MAY ENJOY YOURSELF. TELL CLAUDEL. ANDRE GIDE." Mauriac did not know who sent it and was very angry.

Tomorrow I intend to work again after a two weeks holiday. My knee was cured, Bost hurt his own one but recovered, too, and we glided down and down snowy hills in the most high sun. On Sunday it was a regular brothel, this little resort, hundred of cars and buses arrived from the coast, more than a thousand people rushed up the hill where there were five legs broken and I don't know how many knees and ankles badly hurt in one day. When people have an accident, some special men from the village ride up with a little sleigh and drive the sick one down so quickly you have not time to blink and here they are; but then, in this place, there is no doctor: they have to call one from five miles away. You would be as indignant as on French beaches where they let people be drowned.

Yesterday, with Bost too, we rode to the Blue Coast where it is awfully cool, in a lovely port called Saint-Tropez. I intend to stay one month. The rooms are not very warm, but there is a beautiful view. This place is elegant and snobbish in summer, all Saint-Germain-des-Prés people are here, but now, it's empty and looks like any French southern village.

I read a book about Melville, what a man! I like him. Did you know he stayed in hotel Minerva when he went to Roma, hundred years ago? And an interesting American book about Joyce, too. Did you ever try to have a look at *Finnegan's Wake*? Paris is 2000 years old this year, and there will be great festivities about it; don't you think Chicago is a bit young? The most beautiful house in Saint-Tropez, in the port, belongs to a Mrs. Mac Cormick from old Chicagoan family, they change the whole furniture every year, and always got the most wonderful old pieces: Provençal!

Lot of grand-mothers have been arrested for giving poison cakes to their grand-sons, lot of young men for killing their father; it is the new way of doing things in France. We begin not to believe so much in the war, but Washington tells us such an optimism is a dangerous release and we should fret a little more. But we are tired of getting scared.

Tuesday

No letter. I guess you *over*-stamped it, so it went to Germany, or Italy. It is pity; it's so quiet here that it would have been pleasant to get some mail, chiefly sent-from-Forrest-Avenue-Mail—that is the kind of mail I like the best, though at a time I enjoyed sent-from-Wabansia mail.

Bost went back to Paris. Olga decided not to care for being an actress any more, but she is very sad at it, he writes, and so he is. Scipion and his girl-friend go on quarrelling, breaking, making up, and she drinks more and more. Queneau entered the Goncourt Academy, that is strange and a bit disappointing since it is such a conformist, mild, worth of nothing kind of gang, this thing. Camus, Sartre, and myself always said no when asked to enter it.

Sartre really does not know which tooth does not hurt.

Monday

Not a letter for a week. I waited and waited, but I'll sent this without waiting any more. The weather is more sunny; it is really nice now. I work a lot. This book of yours is a novel about French people from 1945 to 1948; I try to tell the happy revival we felt when the war was over and so many things began again, and the slow disappointment after. It will be a very long book, with lot of people and lot of stories. Among them, I try to tell something of *our* story 1) because it seems to be quite a nowadays kind of story, this love from Paris to Chicago, with airplanes making the towns so near, yet so far, all that, 2) and chiefly because I enjoy remembering things, these things, on the paper. Now I am just writing that part, a rather short part but which I should want to be very good. I work hard on it. And it is not a wise thing to do, because I have too good a memory, and things I remember, seem so real and so near. And I get very blue. So blue it was not easy to write to you. I felt too much useless love. You look so nice, the way I remember you.

I am glad there is forever a dark stain in your poor little virgin heart. They know how to manage a knee and an ankle, but not how to manage a hurt heart; so I guess I'll keep my crippled one and never can use it anew. It is just good enough for you, poor brutish brute; it will remain yours as I remain

Your own Simone

Nelson, dearest you,

It was a long time since I did not get any letter, so I felt relieved and happy yesterday when pictures arrived and some news from, too. You are funny, with your little piggish eyish eyes.

Well, since you suggest so politely, I should come, I feel it not be polite to say no. And then, indeed, I have to see rainbow-colored Wabansia and all-fixed-up-Forrest-Avenue home. The true truth is it was quite a shock to realize I am going to see you again, so soon, and that is the first day I feel happy once more since a rather long time. I'll be a very decent guest this year, I promise. I shall not cry more than twice a day, not scream more than twice a week, not bite more than once in the month.

The only point is: well, if I have to, I'll manage to come in September, but if it happened not to make much difference for Amanda, would she not come in August or beginning of September, so I could come from middle of September to late October? It would be *a lot more convenient* for me. If it is impossible, I'll contrive to come as soon as I can in late August, and stay until Amanda comes. See to that for the best of everybody. Anyhow, it is a great thing for me to think I'll see you again.

The woman with Sartre on the newspaper, I don't know if you remember, I spoke and wrote to you about her a lot: picture she was a great whore, lived in the closed harem of Marrakech sultan (we saw his large palace), was married to a wealthy general, had hundred of lovers, was a movie actress, sang in theatre but get a disease in the throat, slept with German officers, partially had her hair shaved away when they were pushed away, married a Jew who had been actively anti-nazi and was again a respectable woman, with hundred of millions. She owns the theatre where Sartre's plays are performed. I told you how obscene she is—the most obscene woman I ever saw. She said once, in front of Sartre, Bost, myself: "Oh! That was wonderful this morning, my husband fucked my ass. Was not it?" And the husband said: "Yes, but you should not have told the servants: they were amazed." Last week she invited Sartre and myself to her ugly huge house on the coast, but she could not speak, being sick in the throat once more, and silence made her quite mad, which I understand.

Saint-Tropez is full of people, since it is Easter holidays; there was not a table free in any restaurant.

I work on and on and on. Do you? Thanks for the rumsticks, honey, though I have not yet tasted it. I am still a little dazzled by the idea of seeing you again. I am going to learn cooking very seriously, and I'll bring a dozen bottles of brandy for every dish,

Good bye, honey. I kiss you from all my dirty heart.

Your own Simone

Tell Mac Arthur to keep quiet until November.

Saint-Tropez, Wednesday, 11 Avril 1951

Sweetest you,

How nice to have you answered so quickly and to have managed my coming in September. Thanks, honey. Definitively, a day. I'll be as sensible as you are handsome, as wise as you are smart, and you'll never have met such a cook... I have pleasant pang in the heart when I think of the little lagoon, the grey squirrels, and even poor Chris. I guess the garden need a very serious inspection.

Sartre is a little weak in the head just now, because since several months he works ten hours a day on a play which is going to be rehearsed from 15th April. It seems the performance will be eight hours long, and two thirds of the play only are done! Producer, director, actors, everybody gets mad at the idea of beginning to work next Monday, and to present the whole play publicly on 1st June, and it is not written! Only Sartre is very quiet and goes on, making it longer and longer. And suddenly Cocteau, as a real old clown, fancied that he was writing the same play as Sartre, and phoned and wired in a frenzy. Sartre had to go to lunch with, hundred miles from here, and listen to him. Indeed, there was nothing common, except both plays happen in 16th century, but there is as much room in 16th century as in 20th, is not it?

There was another long review about *Never Come* in *Opéra*. The man could not stand the rape of Steffi; it made him sick in the stomach. Then he understood why I liked the book so much: it is a savage illustration of *The Second Sex*. I was amazed at it, as you should be. By the way, it is nice to make a book from your paper about Chicago. I hope we get it for *T.M.*

Oh! I just learn from the radio that Mac Arthur is off. Did you do it? How good! He must be mad with anger, the dirty rat. So maybe we'll not have a war so soon and more sense is left in the poor heads of stupid brutes of Americans. Congratulations!

It was a big game of wind and rain here; in the end, both get tired and we had a real fine warm weather. The Blue Coast is nice without any tourist. If you ever come back to France, I'll buy a car and took you here, a really nice little port. I am very happy since your last letters. And I am envying you when I think with what a nice, pleasant person you'll spend the beginning of fall. This nice person kisses you with love, love, love.

Your own Simone

Paris, Sunday, 15 Avril 1951

Sweetest you, sweetest of all monsters in the world,

How nice it was to get this big package when getting home! It was wonderfully friendly to find all the monsters waiting for me, and pictures of my own monster, looking so nicely monstrous. You look like a real dangerous madman, just out of his cell to be brought to the doctor, when you are sitting on the well where and when and how we got them! Is it possible ever to get the ones Elroy shot in Wabansia and where I am so much better looking than on these ones? The fruit-cake is a beauty and the tea smells so good! Sartre and Bost were very happy with the cigars. As for the rum-sticks, there is no word. It was rather an Easter gift than a Christmas one, honey, but just as good. You'll get your gift in September, too, you'll see: the most lovely monster not only in France but in Eurasia.

So I came back in the night, in a sleeping-car where I slept like an angel. It was a pit, because the last days were so hot and blue! But Paris does not look bad, springs really begins. Everybody here, even the most pro-American Gaullist right-wing newspapers was happy with Mac Arthur dismissal. Maybe we'll not have to die for America, after all—at least not before some years, and it is pleasant thought. The secretary and Bost came to the station to look for Sartre and myself; they are in fine shape, though Bost always has his troubles. Olga knows now she will never act again. She diligently translates English books; she is accepting the situation, but very sad—it is not the same thing at all. And then whenever Bost happens to have a little love affair, half a night off, it is always a very big business—she feels it! Really, she strangely smells the thing every time, and then it is hard time for poor Bost! Though nothing is ever clearly confessed.

Honey, now it is *Wednesday*. Everybody loved the fruit-cake *too much*. And alas! Everybody thinks you are not the best photographer on earth.

They all think you look mad, sitting on the coach. Poor Olga is really worn out, very bitter, and Bost very much bored by her. Scipion and his girl-friend have broken off for the very last, last time. Sartre is terribly busy with his play: thirty actors, sixty parts; it will last more than four hours. While I was having dinner with Bost and Sartre in "Balzar," Wright came, looking like his own ghost, and said quickly: "Ellen is away, looking for a house for our holidays," then suddenly: "I heard Algren is in Paris?" I said. "No." he laughed in a strange way: "I just read *Golden Arm*. That is fantastic!" as if it were too much for him. We said, both Bost and me (Sartre never could read it in English): "It is really good, is it not?" soberly; he laughed again: "It is fantastic!" He spoke in French, a very bad broken French, and I don't know if the word had the same meaning in both languages.

I read a review about Koestler's book,[1] and it seems to me it stinks. He speaks nastily about French writers, explaining they are not enough against communism, because they are coward, lazy, and stupid. Koestler knows better, he says. If you could easily get the book and send it to me, I should enjoy having it, but I can wait.

Paris is blue, sunny, wonderful and La Bûcherie as nice as ever. I feel much more happy than I was for a long time. I only hope they will not forbid me to come to USA, you know, they are awful now. People who are a little bit of Marxists, even if against Stalin, are not allowed to go. If you ever have criticized American policy, you are forbidden to go. I know one anti-Stalinist writer, who has wife and children in the States, and cannot go home because he wrote in left wing spirit a very good book about American working class. In fact, they have nothing against me, I am not really scared.

Good bye, my sweet monster. I'll be the sweetest monster in Indiana and Illinois, you'll see. I kiss you from the unchanged heart of

Your own Simone

1) *The Age of Longing*, 1950, a political tract.

Monday, 23 Avril 1951

My sweetest monster,

I got two letters since I wrote for last time, so it seems you are even sweeter than me. Be sure I am very interested in the peanut-butter business. Sartre's explanation about the octopus and the violin is that an octopus cannot play violin upside up. Just ask the peanut-butter people to produce a Forrest Avenue local youth with any brain in his head: we'll see if they can do that.[1] The Mac Arthur business is puzzling. How is it so many people stand for him and Democrats are against him? There is something I don't understand here. I did not write before, because when the day begins I must first of all write your book, and when the day is over, I just feel sick of any writing. I decided for the middle of day; it was the only way.

Yea, lot of people came into your book. I don't know they managed it. Koestler is in it, and I enjoy hitting him as he tried to hit all French intellectuals. When I don't work I sometimes go and see the rehearsals of Sartre's play. The main actor is Pierre Brasseur who played the part of the wonderful melodrama actor in *Les enfants du paradis*,[2] but I think it was cut in the American production. You would be interested by the man: he was a celebrity at twenty (twenty years ago), a really wild: a terrible addict, he had to be desintoxicated nine times, he raped all women he met, as Harpo Marx, often he was in love too, and most of the time drunk. Now he married a lovely wife—I am quite friendly with her—and he dropped dope, but not drinking. Yet when we had dinner last week he was not at all as drunk as Bost. I'll try to find a little picture on which I hope to be, too. They are the only gay pleasant people I saw since I came back to Paris. The sad ones, I try to keep them away: poor Olga is no more than a shadow of herself; I had an awful dinner with the ugly woman since I had to tell her the book she is writing since two years is just shit; I had to tell, because if she goes on for two other years and everybody laughs at her, what is the use? But she cried and was unhappy. The cancerous woman is dying; she suffers a lot and does not accept any dope, because she wants to keep her head clear: what for? She'll be off within two months. Nathalie pretends her husband is going to kill himself and she'll be sad because of the money; she is in love with her dirty couple of rats again. Maybe she'll be in Paris with them in the beginning of July—I'll not stay long. Maurice Chevalier being banned from the States is a good story! A shame. You know, I nearly put my name on this peace petition, because it was not exactly communist; I did not because I guessed it could prevent me from ever seeing you again. And it happened just this way! I am proud to have been so wise. I hope I'll have no trouble in September. The visa I got last year was meant for two years. I have nothing to ask here, and in Chicago they will not mind me, will they? Unless they remember I cheated eight dollars from them, last year.[3]

We had sun, but now it is rain and cold again; I don't mind, I am happy in my heart. Well, you laughed at me sometimes, because I was so good natured that I could be happy with so little: so am I now. Just happy because I'll see you in September; I ask for nothing else. I don't even care about the way you'll feel: you'll ride the boat, cook steaks for me anyway and with a little scotch that will be happiness.

Sure, the fruit-cake was not stale; it did not even need brandy! The only bad point with it is that it is dead since a long time — "fruit-cake fini!" as the little French boy said. But every morning I have to remember you when I drink my tea — not very discreet of you. Well, you come so often into everything, I don't mind, I begin to get used to it. It is as sweet as ever to keep you in my heart, and I do.

Your own Simone

1) A televised peanut-butter ad called "You Asked For It" promised to broadcast anything the audience wanted to see. They had already featured a man battling a giant squid and a rendition of *La Marseillaise* played on an upside-down Stradivarius. 2) Frédérick Lemaître. 3) De Beauvoir, like Algren, was most likely under CIA surveillance; there were files on both of them.

Tuesday, 15 Mai 1951

Darling beast,

Here is some nice new bunch of lies for you. Thanks for the nice bunch of lies of your own; I hope you did keep a little salted piece of Steve's meat for me, though I don't like children so much, after all I'll have to eat in September. It will be September all right, in the middle, if it fits you, too, but try to keep some sun for me — don't waste all of it in summer.

Well, the fact is Sartre is wrestling an octopus, and most of time the octopus wins; nobody knows how the struggle will end. He told me to tell you never to write a play; it makes you too unhappy. His play will be four hours long, so actors, director, producer are scared to death. They want Sartre to cut off and cut off; they speak about nothing else. Even Cau came the other day and said to Sartre: "I guess you do have to cut." For the very first time of his life, I saw Sartre getting really mad, hitting the table with his fist; the secretary grew white, and I though they were going to strike each other. Cau went away slamming the door and send fare-go-to-hell letter. For two days he was seen in Saint-Germain, white, half drunk, shaking and hopeless. Sartre was all red, deadly sober, but shaking, too, and all the friends, Bost, little Cassoulet, were awfully sad. Then Cau and Sartre met in front of the Deux Magots and fell in each other arms, and in the afternoon Sartre scared all the wicked people in the theatre. He found the right thing to do: no kidding, he just wrote about a quarter of an hour *more* for the actors. I must say the play is much better this way. Nobody dares to say one word, because they are afraid next time Sartre will bring half an hour more. But he feels a stranger to himself; he says for the first time in his life, he cannot say yes any more! Jouvet is directing; he is a bore, but he know much about his job. I learnt Brasseur is not only a dope, but really a sex-maniac. He was seen in dinners looking intensely at a pretty girl, eating with one hand while he played with himself beneath the table with the other. All girls in the theatre are terrified by him; he pinches and assaults any creature with a kind of womanly face. He feels friendly to me because I can drink scotch and he thinks I am funny. So the other day, when his wife was away, be blinked to the secretary and said "I like Castor. I should like very much to fuck her (just like that). Can't you manage it?" The secretary did not dare to tell me; he told Sartre who told me. But I feel highly proud I make him so shy he did not just come and tell me directly: "Fuck, baby?" Now, indeed, I shall not tell you what I answered.

Honey, I want the Chicago piece. We need it for *Temps modernes* — we have nothing to give our readers. Sartre asks for his own collections, and I for my pleasure.

Olga is so bitter about her failure that she hates everybody, and even my patience, which is great, you know, could hardly stand her. I spent a long boring evening, and in the end she said she was bored and she went away, then she wrote to me stupid little letter, beginning by an apology and going on as a accusation act. I look so bored, she says, when having an evening with her that it is no use seeing each other any more. The fact is, I should like much better staying home or going to a movie, but she needs friends. I shall not drop her; I was not even angry at her. But when she always makes her self so boring, how could I help looking bored?

Bost feels bad in his heroic heart, because it seems that after all he will not be asked so soon to be a hero and die for the States. To me, it seems pretty good to feel in peace again. I was sitting in the Lipperie with Bost , and a white-haired American man nearby drank for an hour long a lot of whiskies, looking at me all the time. Then he get up and bowed: "I must tell you how much I liked what you wrote about Chicago in *America Day by Day*. Who was your guide? Was it a man called Asquith?" "No, Algren." "Oh! He wrote some very good books!" Bost was scandalized because he believed that man had said "your guide," then, he began to ask me angrily why you did not come back to Paris, when Paris is so near Chicago, and you have money, you enjoyed France, all you friends wait for you. It was stupid, he said, and went more and more angry...I did not know very well how to plead for you; you seemed rather guilty, I must say.

I saw Dick's movie in a private performance and not being partial for him, as you know, it struck me as a wonderfully good thing. He can act, that man. Slim, looking young, a real man, not a screen puppet. My heart was hit many times with the views of Chicago. The director did a good job, too: you really feel this crummy monster of a town where my heart is rotting, somewhere.

Yea, it was good. Ellen says it is a big success in south in South America and it will be given on Broadway in June.

Very tedious evening with Olga who suddenly pretended that she knew I did not care for her. I thought she was just a child and never told anything intimate. So, I had to tell I cared, scold her, pretend I was angry. A very cold comedy! In fact, all she wants is that I see her twice a week instead of once, but I shall not. In the end, she understood she was wrong, and I liked her better. Poor girl! Not to be able to act at all. That is not so much hysterical to cry about it.

Well, enough lies for today, just a last big one: you are sweetest man in the world; I keep all of you in my heart, and if I don't say love words it is just not to bother you, but I could. I kiss you tenderly.

Your own Simone

Monday, 28 Mai 1951

My own wonderman,

It is a long time I did not hear about you. Here, very few things happen, except poor Sartre's daily struggle about his damned play. Now the players began to act, to learn their part, everybody accepting in silent despair the idea that *The Devil and the Lord* should last for hours. Then the clothes question opened and is not closed. The crazy director woman asked Schiaparelli, who is a very well-known great dress-maker to made them—how stupid! Mrs. Schiaparelli is known for excentricity rather than taste, and she knows nothing about theatre. Sartre's characters are all poor, very poor peasants of 16th century: Mrs. Schiaparelli just dressed them with beautiful materials, bright colors, and all kind of crazy ornaments. Now the idea is to paint in grey and black, to cut into pieces and cover with dust and dirt all her work; but she does not want it, and even so it will not be good. Sartre says nobody would believe a single word coming from man or woman dressed in such irreal suits. Anyhow, the opening is due for the 5th of June, and lot of reservations are already made.

I met Mouloudji, with his face all creamy and painted, going to do his singing work. He sings in a lot of places now an is quite a success in Paris, not as Yves Montand, indeed, but pretty good. But it is a hard job sometimes. On this very day, he had been asked, for money to sing in a communist feast in the suburbs. When he began the usual songs, about love, youth, and blue sky, all that, he felt everybody getting chilly. "Indeed," he said, "all the choirs had songs about Work and Cement and the glory of Iron"; people say he was a bourgeois singer and he understood it was a terrible insult. Just a little misunderstanding. But what he hates is when people begin to make fun of him, chiefly in elegant snobbish places. Once a beautiful girl, beautifully dressed and surrounded by a crowd of admiring males, began to laugh at him and throw balls of paper to him while he sang. He could do nothing, lost in the big stage lights, half blind, perspiring and very unhappy. But on the whole he feels satisfied; he learns a great lot by this kind of experiences.

Some Chicago publisher asked for *America Day by Day*. I don't know which one; I should like it. Mr. Parshley, my translator, is reaching now the middle of the second book (of *Second Sex*) but always wants to cut and condense, he too — I'll let him do. An English publisher bought the thing for England.

Little Cassoulet contrived to get a tiny part in Sartre's play: as there are thirty five players, it was possible to give her two sentences to say. She says them awfully, but it does not matter.

I work really madly because I want to be through with the book before summer and show it to Sartre, who did not see even a line and get the criticism I need. I'll drop it when travelling my holidays. I'll stay in Paris until middle of July. I have to see Jewish friend and Nathalie at least a few days; then I'll go with Sartre in Norway, Iceland, maybe Greenland, and Scotland. In the middle of September I'll personally bring to you an Eskimo equipment, or would you rather have a kilt? If you write nicely, maybe you'll have both. And wear them, too.

I saw a very good exhibition of Toulouse-Lautrec. You would have enjoy it. We all wait impatiently for the Chicago booklet, and I for your next letter. I want so much to see you again, honey. Most tender kisses from

Your own Simone

Sweetest thing,

So I got your letter just as mine was flying away to you. What I should answer to Bost? I don't understand. Why cannot you as well not write a book in Paris as in Chicago? Is Chicago nearer Paris than Paris from Chicago? Since I do write a book and cross the ocean, though? I am disturbed by this problem and find no answer to it. It does not seem very friendly of you not to be in jail when all your friends are. Here since two days it is summer: women go half naked in the street, and you can loiter around with Guatemaltecan or African dresses, if you are me.

Everybody feels a little better in one's heart, and my whole family needed it. Bost, Sartre, and even wise poised well-balanced me began to get mad at these man rehearsals of Sartre's mad play. Brassuer, the bearded actor who has such a good taste about women, said he was not going to play, after all; he would pay the million he owed if not playing, and get ten millions from a movie producer. It was impossible to have it play without him; he is the only one in Paris to be able to give life and truth to the terrific hero. So, it was like death in the theatre. He accepted to stay, but was awfully bad for some evenings. The big rehearsal was supposed to take place today, but Sunday evening the dresses were not ready, neither the setting, and nothing in the performance was real good. So, it was a big fuss, and tears, screams, anger, and it was postponed until next Monday, and suddenly everybody was loving and happy, and said the other ones were genius, and so on. So, let us have hope. We are publishing a very good book in *T.M.*, by an American man (or is he English?) called Stone who absolutely proves there was never a Chinese in Korea, and Mac Arthur never fought any battle. He makes even people doubt there was an American soldier, all was a big Mac Arthur's dream told as a mystery. Wright gives us his long short story, *The Man in the Underground.*

Steffi's story just happened in Paris: a eighteen years old boy invited his eighteen years old friend in a little dancing, he trapped her in a underground where four friends of him, threatening the girl with a knife, raped her in turn. The difference is she complained to the police and all the boys have been arrested.

Wonderful papers of right-wing people about Mac Gee[1] here; they say: "Well, America kills some Negroes, but with shame and self-reproach, that is nothing; whilst Russia proud of her hard-about camps, that is Evil."

What do think of that? As long as you reproach yourself for killing, kill as much as you want. And I don't think the Missouri jury feel ashamed at all. Do they?

Friday

Treacherous thing! That was certainly not very kind of you to come and spend one day in Paris,[2] and not even kiss your poor La Bûcherie gopher, but spend the day in newspapers office, explaining other writer should never write more than one book and pretending to look like a bus driver. Not just me but all your Parisan friends were hurt when we read this lively interview in *Paris-Presse*. Maybe you still are in Paris while I stupidly write to you. What was nicer was to send a long letter with news of the boat and yourself. It certainly seems you had a hard time with the Negro meeting. If you hide Fallon and Du Bois in Wabansia, is some "red conspiration" not going around? Don't be too much of a hero.

Hard time here, too, for your poor gopher. First, the weather is really disgusting, so stormy; it rains heavily, and before and after you can hardly breathe; you feel moist and tired. Terrible thunder and lightnings, as in past times, loving times, when we were in Central America and we had such big storms; these memories rather sadden my heart. Then, after so many working weeks, I had to drink too much and sleep too little. It was the last rehearsals and first performance of *Devil and the Lord*—big excitement for all Sartre's friends, we all drank from midnight to dawn for some days. Olga was awfully tired, but Bost, Scipion, and Cau very happy, and in the end I felt just dead. Well, everybody thinks, and so do I, that Sartre never wrote so good and important a play. It lasts four hours, and people don't seem bored one minute; it was real triumph and, I must say, Brasser was much in it. The critics are either enthusiastic or full of hate anger. What is funny is left-wing people, even communists, approve the play, and so right-wing amoralist or individualist ones; the middle people, mildly religious and decent, are the angry ones. "It is from beginning to end a terrible insult to God. The hero tells Him what kinds of a stinking beast he is, and in the end announces that He does not exist at all." All Catholics are scandalized and want the play to be stopped. It makes fun in a witty way of some religious superstitions. There was a young man on the first rehearsal who came with a whistle and made trouble, but that was all. No scandal in the theatre and wonderful applause. Sartre, Brasseur, everybody was pleased because in the end they were all nervous and scared.

It was not a triumph only for poor little Cassoulet; she looked so red-haired and scared on the stage, you would have laughed. Nobody spoke about her except one critic: "She has nothing to expect from theatre and theatre expects nothing from her." No amusing pictures, only terribly ugly ones and I don't want you to think of me with a fish-face. I put on my nicest gopher-face to smile to you, and I kiss you with all my love.

Your own Simone

1) A black man executed for the rape of a white woman, without concrete evidence. 2) A joke inspired by an interview that appeared unexpectedly in a Paris newspaper.

Dimanche, 23 Juin 1951

Honey,

Thanks for your bitter blue letter; it was certainly better than nothing. You seem to have really many troubles, poor dear you. we are happy people here! Your beautiful, smart, talented sweet-voiced Margaret Truman is in Paris and every day newspaper tell us in what dancing she danced, in what shops she went shopping. Nobody seems to be in love with her beauty or her charm. What a disgraceful thing you have got as a president's daughter!

I did not answer to you a about *Viper in the Fist* by Hervé Bazin. It was rather big success here, because he speaks harshly against family life and chiefly says horrible things about his mother. One pleasant point is that he is a nephew to René Bazin, who wrote for God, country, family, property, and so on, some thirty years ago, so people were amused to see such bitter revolt in a young man of the family. But he is married, had children, began to say his mother was not so bad, after all, and to look a little like his uncle himself. The secretary played a dirty trick on him; he went to interview him; Bazin, wanting to win his heart, invited him home, but Cau told him he did not like his books and would say everything he thought about him. All right, said Bazin, and he confessed among other things he felt a communist "in his heart." Cau printed it and Bazin, who was hoping for the Goncourt prize did not get it. I guess he is not like in US because he speaks against "mother."

If you are interested in Sartre's play, here is a review from *Herald Tribune*. Some people like the play much better, others hate it much more, on the whole it is a big success. But Brasseur, this terrible man, had a crisis two days ago, he nearly died: he drinks so much! The doctor warned him

425

he had to stop at once or he would be a dead man before the end of the year. And he is the only man in Paris who can act this part! So the theatre-director woman nurses him like a baby. She has supper with him, puts him to bed every night, and will spend her holidays with him and his wife in a resort where he will cure his liver. He gets more money every day than Sartre who wrote the play.

Always storms and rather sad weather her; I am impatient to go away. I am speaking about women to an anarchist syndicate tonight. I don't like it. A nice old, old-looking woman writer told me: "You know, when you are sixty five, you begin to a inferiority-complex; you think you are not so beautiful nor so lovely as before, and men don't want you much. You have to fight that feeling." She lived for these lst ten years with a thirty five years younger than her man, and now, having twenty eight, he said: "It is time for me to know other women. You knew a lot of men, I cannot have just you." She cried and said to me: "The only remedy to that is to get another lover: I'll do it!" Gosh! She looks like a grand, grand-mother! Women are wonderful sometimes.

Keep the little boat in nice shape for me. Love and love and love.

Your own Simone

---

2 Juillet 1951

Sweetest thing,

Thanks for the long letter. I like long letters much more than short letters, at least when they come from Forrest Avenue or Wabansia. I am sad you had so much trouble about *Crime et châtiment*;[1] happy I never saw the movie,[2] I like the book so much I feared I should be disappointed anyway by the screen-story, so I have not to tell you now whether you are right or Kreswell. Harry Baur, the French actor you like, was considered a real great actor. He was a Jew, but was not prosecuted during the war, because he died of natural death just in the beginning so his story is not so pathetic as your romantic heart would have liked to pretend, poor dear you.

I have great news for you: Nathalie is in Paris since three days with some students having their life here and travel paid by the university. We made an arrangement: I give her some pocket money (in French money) and she sends you dollars, twenty five dollars each week. Keep them carefully for me and you when I am in Gary in September. By that time, it will be 250 dollars, and I'll bring 100 other ones, so we can drink a little scotch together. The question is... tell me if you really get the money each week, and keep a count of how much, because I don't want to be cheated once more. I have reserved my seat in the airplane of 17th September for New York. I'll be in Chicago 19th, all right?

Yea, the woman who killed Marat was an ugly, fanatic stupid spinster who did all right in having her head off; Marat was a very interesting man, the most progressive of all French revolution people, the only one who wanted to abolish property.

Nathalie is rather nice, always cold, far away, somewhat pedantic, and obsessed by her pansies obsessions. Sartre thought she was very tedious, but I have not seen her too much, and I can enjoy her, sometimes. It seems strange to her to see Paris again after five years; she feels it has changed so much, so much wealthier than it was. It is full of American tourists, as every year in summer. They play an old mystery in front of Notre-Dame, with 10,000 seats, hundreds of players, lot of lights; it is supposed to be tremendous. In the first performance, two days ago, something was wrong with the sound-machinery and nobody heard a word for three hours long... "a real mystery!" the newspaper said. it is supposed to be a Christian challenge to Sartre's *Devil and the Lord* which has been indeed terribly attacked by all Catholic critics — how angry they got!

I give my novel a rest while it is typewritten, and work for a short essay about a strange man, le Marquis de Sade.[3] You certainly heard about him but certainly know little, except he invented sadism. I'll tell you a lot of stories about him in September. Just fancy: from eighteen to thirty six years old, he savagely beated and fucked women, and maybe men and beasts too; he was as wild as wild can be, Then from thirty six to seventy, with only five years of freedom during the French Revolution, he was in jail! In jail, he wrote about all he could not do, and you can guess how many books that was, and the boldest books in the world. It is a pity they are not good on the literary ground — long, tedious, coldly written — but Miller is a baby near to Sade, and Genet a white angel. He hated the idea of God so strongly, and attacked all powerful men. Yea, I'll have to tell you about him.

America Day by Day will be translated in English. I am glad you'll be be able to read it.

Good bye, and long kisses to my own local youth.

Your own Simone

1) *Crime and Punishment.* 2) By Pierre Chenal (1935), with Henry Baur, Pierre Blanchar (Raskolnikov) and Madeleine Ozeray. 3) *Faut-il brûler Sade?*

427

Nelson my love,

I am so upset and sad I could cry once more, if my motto was not now "Weep no more." Your piggish pig of countryish country does not seem to want me to go to the States. They want "information" and I am scared. It happened yesterday. I was very quiet about my visa since I got it last year for twenty four months; I went to the travel agency and they told me since 30th October all visas had to be looked at again. I rushed to the American embassy, feeling sure it was only a matter of ten minutes lost. They were very polite but told me to come back in the afternoon, which made me suspicious. I came back, and an old lady asked to give a solemn oath, with the right hand and all that, telling I never belonged to any communist or fascist party, and so on. I took the oath, put my name on a lot of papers, and then she said: "Well, we have the feeling you belong to the French Women's League (that is a nearly communist league)." It was very coarse I had sworn the contrary! And it was false! I said no. But she knew a little thing which I had wholly forgotten: *three* years ago, I put my name on a kind of petition written by this league, a lot of non-communist women gave their name, and I don't even remember what it was about, but she knew! And I had to write and sign it was the only thing I did according this league. It was really humiliating, though you know I have not so much pride. Having to confess, explain, protest, be meek and apologizing when I should have kicked the whole American embassy. Had it have only been a pleasure trip, I should have enjoyed kicking them and saying farewell to the States for ever. But I want so much to see you. So, in the end, they did not take my word for granted, and asked a week for information. Then they will say yes or no. I never belonged to the League, but if they examine what I wrote in *America Day by Day*, if they get angry about the papers we published in *Temps modernes* against Mac Arthur and American policy? I am scared.

I am so deeply scared, because I can hardly hope, if they forbid me to go, *you* would come. It would be easy for you, you are the kings of the world; no visa, no oath is asked from an American citizen, you just go to the airport, sit in the plane, then in Paris you are. For the money, all what I saved for paying my trip and living with you would be used for paying your trip and for living together in Paris. Yea, it would be easy, but if you don't feel like doing it, there is nothing to say. So, if they say no, and if you don't say yes, it just means I'll never see you again. It is not a new idea, but I had gotten used to our September meeting; it made me so happy that I just feel crushed now. I do love you as much as ever, you know. if you can, you should write for the 21th July in Bergen, Norway, (general delivery) where I'll be back on 1st August; the letter will not be lost. If it is really too short, write to Hotel Borg, Reykjavik, Iceland, for 6th August. Too many people in Paris now, and I waste my time away. The novel is all typewritten. I want to know what Sartre thinks about. It would be a big fat beast 600 pages book. I'll write a nice letter from Norway. I don't feel like telling little things. I am afraid not to know if I am allowed to go or not until September. I'll try to, though.

Good bye, my love. I kiss you tenderly.

Your own Simone

Monday, 23rd July 1951

Beloved you,

Don't be afraid. It is not scotch; it is the moving boat which makes my handwriting so shaking. I hope you can read it anyway. Well, I did not write a very gay letter last week. The fact is I still don't know a thing about the whole devilish business and I don't feel very well neither, but I'll try not to get so blue today. Though it is such a long time since I did not get any letter from, I am not even sure you ever existed: you?

Lasted Sunday, I got into a plane and flied toward north—rain in Copenhagen, but mild enough in Oslo. What is nice in this country, among other things, is they have no night; at midnight it is a strange grey light, you could read the newspapers, and as soon as 3 A.M. it is bright daylight. I must say at noon it is about the same light as at midnight, but you get to like it. Funny to think there are no more inhabitants in this whole wild and beautiful country than your hellish Chicago: three millions people, no more. Sometimes, because of the wooden houses, wooden streets in the towns, it looks little like America, here, but it is awfully poor: nearly not anything to eat, sad clothes. Now I am going north on this boat, unto Russia: I'll see the frontier with my own eyes, nothing else. I read a sad book about Fitzgerald, *The Disenchanted*, not by a first rate writer, but an attaching subject. And a wonderful one about China; it tells much about this country and this extraordinary revolution. We had a rainy 14th July, Scipion, Bost, Olga, Sartre, Sorokine, Oreste, Wanda, and me. People tried to dance in the streets, and we tried, too, until 3 A.M. It was rather gay on place Saint-Germain-des-

Prés, but definitively cold and rainy, and I had to gulp a lot of brandy to warm my poor dirty heart—yet, I was not drunk. Now no scotch, no wine, nothing: it is not allowed. I don't mind too much.

I hope I'll be allowed to kiss you this summer, I hope I shall be. Love and love and love from

Your own Simone

Sweetheart,

Yea, I won the big battle! But don't think I was scared without reason: the secretary had to fight for two weeks after I was gone. He went three times to the American embassy; they were always hesitating and investigating, and it is only three days ago they said yes. The swinish swines! If it was not for being a Nelson-visitor, I should have kicked America farewell for life. So, I'll be in New York on 18th September, and Chicago 19th. You'll not receive money in the end; Nathalie will meet me in New York and give me 300 dollars. Honey, I am so happy! I was terribly anxious since I left Paris, and now I feel like a queen. Hardly a little more than a month, and I'll see the house, the sinking boat, and you, silly little printed head. It seems wonderful.

I got the last letter you sent to Paris only yesterday when arriving here, in Iceland, and the small red one when you wanted to hit somebody, in Norway; it was a long time without any letter and I did not feel like writing neither; Now I'll do. Please, write general delivery London as soon *as you get this letter*; I long for a letter of my own local youth now I know I'll kiss him again.

This trip is rather wonderful, I'll tell you much about it. I spent three days on a boat from which I wrote on the first day. It went along the coast among little island, inside fjords, the landscape was always changing and impressive: huge mountains coming down into the sea, with an admirable light chiefly in the northern north, when the sun never sets and I read books on the deck by midnight. You cannot fancy this kind of light and strange poetry as long as you did not see it. A cab rode us until the Russian frontier-post—it was strange to think we should never see more of Russia. Bergen where we landed back is a very nice old port, and a railway is coming back to Oslo through high mountains: snow, rocks, lakes, no other train in Europe goes up so high. It was beautiful. I only slept in Oslo, and

at eight in the morning, we took a plane for Iceland — a hard day. In Copenhagen, it was raining and stormy, we had to wait in the airport until 5 P.M.,
then we learnt that *we came back to Oslo*! I was mad with anger when thinking how we could have spent a peaceful day in this town. We flew in six
hours, at 22,000 feet high above huge clouds, in plane full of young sport-
ing Icelandish boys. We arrived at two, by a beautiful half sunny night, and
there was no room reserved in the hotel, nobody at the station, no money
in our pockets! Luckily, I met at the airport nice French reporter whom I
had known in Los Angeles and they brought us in their car to the hotel,
and fought with the manager so to get rooms. What a strange, lovable
country! Fancy: all the heating-system is made from natural hot water
which comes from the heart of this volcanic land in high geysers or boiling
rivers. From the springs this water is brought to town by pipes, and so they
need no coal nor wood for the icy winters. It is lucky because there is *not
one* tree on the whole island, and no coal at all. Do you know they had the
first republic, the first parliament in the whole world, as far as 950 after JC?
At dinner I had pleasure in meeting a pleasant, interesting man, who is
famous in France, Paul-Emile Victor. Did you hear of him? He is the leader
of big explorations in North and South Poles, forty two years old now, and
explored Greenland, the icy ocean, and all that, for nearly twenty years. He
lived for three years in an Eskimo village, married with an Eskimo, explor-
ing the unknown country in sleighs drawn by dogs. Now he does something very interesting: he has seventy men in Greenland in different sta-
tions, moving by groups of six or seven in the icy land (a land big as three
times France, wholly covered with ice, 9000 feet high, a kind of high iced
flat plain surrounded with mountains going down straight into the iced sea)
and Victor with a plane goes two or three times a week to send them food
and so on. But he cannot use parachutes; it would break. He has to fly
down a five meters above the ground and have the whole 4000 kilos of
wares dropped in three seconds. He showed us a small movie about it and
I hoped he should ask us to come with him, but he would not take a woman
with him, and then if they had to land for any reason, they could never get
off, and would have to stay until middle of September in the central camp
and come back by jeeps (with caterpillar chains) and boat. I don't want to
take such a risk. There is the risk of getting killed, too, but nobody here
thinks of it, though two young men of one group just were killed three days
ago, falling in a deep crevasse. Victor was very much moved by that. He is
a real pleasant, clever man, as well as daring and adventurous, and he told

the most wonderful stories. He says the most dangerous thing, in this plane business above Greenland, is that the pilot is often drunk: the Iceland people get drunk for anything, at any time; they drink a terrible alcohol made from some wood. But they can make alcohol from shampoo cream, or black cirage, and it often happened to them, finding a bottle in a boat or in packages from France or USA—to taste them without knowing what was inside and to fall dead, because it was sulfuric acid or things like that. The most important work of policemen here is getting drunkard to the police station at night. You cannot find even wine, no alcohol at all in any hotel or restaurant: it is forbidden. But they drink at home, then sing in the streets, usually clad in tuxedo and most elaborated clothes; they love to dress, but they fall down and vomit. The cops wear big leather aprons and leather gloves to handle them. Many American soldiers (because of the Atlantic Pact) are quartered here and not liked; there are many communists here, and when drunk they fought harshly, so the town is out-limits for Americans now. Quite a country to see; I enjoy it. No railway at all, a few bad roads; they go only by planes.

I'll stay a week in this strange paradise, sunny and cool in the same time, where the sun hardly sets at all, then I'll fly to London and I'll write from there. Write to me, keep sun for me. I hope you'll be half as happy to have me coming than I am to come. You are my own nice man and I'll fight no war when being with you and be pleased with everything, even with you. Kisses and love and more kisses and more love from

Your own Simone

London, 24th August 1951

Dearest monster of my own,

It seems to me I wrote very few letters since a time, I don't feel like writing now; I know I'll be speaking to you within a few weeks. But I did not tell you where to write, that is bad. Please do write as soon as possible to Park Lane Hotel, London. Tell me your phone number and the old nest in Wabansia one; I wholly forgot it. I'll come on the 19th in the afternoon, and wire on the 18th exactly the time: shall I wire Wabansia or Forrest Avenue?

I told you Iceland is a wonderful place, no tourist, the most extraordinary landscape of ice and volcanoes, smoking, mingled together. London

432

is gay and wealthy again as it was before the war, when I loved the town very much. It seems strange to hear English language and not be in the States. I saw *Antony and Cleopatra* on the stage, with Laurence Olivier and Viven Leigh—she was not very good, had not such an interesting part, but on the whole it was a good performance. I rushed to the painting galleries, quite a change after so many landscapes. And I loitered in the street. From London we went to Glasgow by train: a dark, sad industrial town, but it had an appeal of his own, then we began to wander in Scotland by steamer and buses, but it is very rainy, misty, gloomy; Scottish people are ugly, thrifty, out of date, the scenery is too sweet—"nice" lakes and tamed mountains. I read some English literature and cannot understand why they made such a great man of Doctor Johnson, though Boswell told his life wonderfully well. You still feel war in this country, and they don't worship America as much as French do. They still don't have butter, chocolate, food and clothes free; they are quite poor, but they live in a much more dignified way. Lot of new houses built in London, on the place of v-1 ruins, but lot of them remain, too; it will need time to rebuild everything.

Nelson, dearest, I am awfully glad to come. Write to me. Most tender kisses of

Your own Simone

1951

✳ *September-October — Simone de Beauvoir returned for the last time to For-*
rest Avenue, to the cottage on the lake. The month passed peacefully, with-
out incident; she finished an essay on Sade. Algren was about to remarry his
ex-wife. But at the last minute, the status of their relationship was once
more thrown open to question by his response when de Beauvoir congratu-
lated herself on keeping his friendship: "It's not friendship. I could never
give you less than love."

Hotel Lincoln, New York
Thursday evening, 30 Octobre 1951

Nelson, my own true love,

I am dead tired, but I cannot go to sleep without having written to you. It
was so hard to leave, half an hour after feeling that you were still caring for
me; it is so bitter to think that I could have managed to stay much longer if
I had though you could still care for me. I need to speak to you; it is only
the kind of peace I can dream of, tonight. I cried the whole trip long in the
train and cab, and during the whole plane flight I spoke to you, and don't
be too scared if I cry.

In this "introduction" you made me read yesterday, Thomas Mann
says that before each fit Dostoyevsky had a few seconds of bliss which were
worth ten years life. Certainly you have the power to give me in a few minutes, at times, a kind of fever that is worth ten years health. Maybe as your
dirty heart is deep and warm but not so feverish as mine, you cannot feel
what a shock it gave me when the gift of your love was once more given to
me a few hours ago. It made me physically sick. Writing to you is a kind of
struggle against this sickness. So, forgive me if this letter looks foolish. I
have to help myself out of that. Then I often wanted to tell you, to tell you
once more, how do I feel about you and me.

I always felt guilty toward you, from the very first day, because I
could give you so little, loving you so much. I know you trust me; I know

434

you understood all I told you. You would never have accepted to come and live in France for keeps, and you had not in USA the tie that above all ties me to Paris. I don't want to excuse myself again on that: I *could* not desert Sartre and writing and France. I admit that you trust me when I say I could not. Yet, I know too that understanding my reasons did not change the fact: I did not give my whole life to you; I gave my heart and all what I could but not my life. I accepted your love, and made it a far-away love — there is not a thing you told yourself which I did not tell me. I felt guilty, always, and it is the bitterest feeling I ever knew when it is toward the very man you love. And as much as I hurt you, deserted you, it hurted me. And always I have been afraid that you could think I took all the pleasant part of our love, and did not mind the bad part I left to you. But that is not true. If I failed to give you the happiness a true love should give, I made myself very unhappy, too; I missed you in every ways, every times, and the idea of my guilt and your possible anger at me made me often utterly miserable.

Because I gave you so little, I found quite fair that you chose to evict me from your heart. But thinking it is fair did nor prevent it to be hard. It was hard the first time in New York — it was very hard last year. And do trust me here, too: if I cried so much and behave a little foolishly, it came from a very deep would which did not heal for the whole year. Yea, it is very bitter to feel unloved when your own love is as strong as ever and the rejection unexpected. Yet, I began to accept the fact when I came to see you this year; I tried to be satisfied with your friendship and my own love. It did not make me very happy, but it seemed I could stand it.

Tonight, I am scared, really, deeply scared, because once more you made all my defenses crumble. You said you do no longer evict me from your heart; so I have not to fight your indifference, I have no arms left of any kind, I feel I can be hurt again and again if you decide again to evict me, and tonight I cannot stand this idea. I am tired to death. I feel utterly in your hands, absolutely defenseless, and for once I shall beg: keep me in your heart or chase me away, but don't let me cling to love to find out suddenly it is there no more. I don't want to go through that once more; I cannot stand the idea. Well, I am not utterly foolish. If you happen to love another woman, there is nothing to do. But I mean: for as much as you choose to evict or not to evict me, think of what it means for me. too. Please don't take your love away from me, just now. Keep me in your heart until we meet again. Let us meet within not too long a time.

And you know as I know that after all it will be as you'll decide, and I shall make no trouble for you. This letter is the most terrible one you'll ever get from me, you know. I just wanted to say that this time I do ask something. I ask you not to try to put me out of your heart, to try to keep me in it. It was so short, knowing you did care for me, so short! I cannot accept that it was just half an hour; it has to last. I want you to kiss me lovingly once more. I love you so much.

I have loved you for the love you gave me, and for the great new sexual longing and happiness you had aroused in me. But even these things gone, or half gone, my love did stubbornly survive; it is because of who you are. Just because you are who you are—whatever you give me or not—I'll have to keep you in my heart for ever. When it seems possible that it should be a happy love once more, it just put me into pieces. I am just a poor heap of crumbling pieces. So, don't be angry at me for writing a foolish letter.

I came back here, hotel Lincoln. I'll try to sleep. I am afraid of the night. I never wanted anything in my whole life as much as seeing you again.

Wednesday morning

Dearest love, I slept a little, but I still have a terrible headache. I just phoned to Air France; they expect me at ten, and once more the dreadful pang is here. I cannot make my mind if I phone to you or not. I guess not. I don't think could stand it, and I don't want to be "crying on long distance" as you put it.

What I did not say enough yesterday evening is the sweetness of these days with you. From the beginning you made it so warm and gay, that I was happier than I have been for two years. It was so good living with you. Good bye, my love.

If my plane would crash, my last thought would be for thanking you for all I got from you. As it will not, I'll keep on loving you all year long until I land into your arms again.

I kiss you from all my feverish constant heart. Keep me in yours. I love you.

Wednesday 31 (Newfoundland)

To "occupant," 6228 Forrest Avenue, Gary, Indiana, usa.

Dear occupant, Newfoundland fishes send tender regards to their brothers in the lagoon. I flied for four hours already. Wonderful lunch with "foie gras" and champagne, but I could not help crying the whole time. It

436

is really bad, because the plane is not anonymous as Gary train; it is full of people who pretend to know me. I hope it will stop now. It seems all the tears I did not shed during the year just had to flow away. I feel as ugly as a woman of eighty, and as foolish as when you reach forty. It is three now in the little home, and cosy there you are.

My love is flying with me.

Your own Simone

Saturday, 3 Novembre 1951

Nelson my love,

It seems I am the wrong kind of international traveller, vomiting the whole London-Paris trip, and crying all along New York-Paris. Well, after Gander, I stopped a little; I was exhausted, and then I had no more water in my whole body—the plane was 18,000 feet high, real high, and I felt utterly dessicated in the dry artificial air of the ship. I had a terrible cold, caught in warm moist New York; I was so feverish in the Lincoln, I had to open the window and sleep without blanket; I felt burning. But I wake up coughing and sneezing, and did not stop until now. The stewardess pitied me and gave me lot of tea. In fact, the plane was a wonder, "The Parisian" she was called—the biggest most luxurious French plane, with seats becoming real berths if you wanted to, delicious food, and champagne. People were babbling and very gay, except me. It was only eight hours from Gander to Paris, and I was not scared at all; I am never scared when I leave you, I notice, because I am too deeply upset to think of anything else. The departure pang is so bad that death seems insignificant nearby. Yet, it looked rather long because I could not sleep. It was grey and raining on the airport, and I had to wait long in an iced cold bus with all doors open in the cold. The custom people and cops looked so French, I could hardly believe there are really like that. All along the side-walks were pots and pots of sad flowers: chrysanthèmes, and people in black for All Saints Day; this suburb is full of cemeteries—really sad. Paris was a little better but very cold. And I not stop feeling tired since I arrived. First, they sleep at strange times here: I have to go to bed just when Kukla and Ollie appear on the screen,[1] and they begin to get up when the last picture fades off the T.V. screen. I cannot get used to these ways. Friday I had to meet Sartre and Bost at 1 P.M. for lunch. I was sleeping when somebody knocked harshly

437

at my door: it was the good concierge telling me my friends were phoning, as it was already 2 P.M. I cannot sleep in their night, and I feel sleepy during their day long. So adding to it my terrible cold, I am rather a wreck. I gave the books and gifts to everybody; they asked all about you and thank you. I showed the Patterson Island pictured and they were all very jealous; it seems so beautiful, nearly tropical, and what a handsome Tarzan you are! And I made them all greedy for T.V. and deep freezer, but sad to know you'll not come to Paris before having done real working—they understand what it means.

Now here are some news of people: Bost and the secretary intend to write in *Temps modernes* a description of Russian occupation in USA: how Josephine Baker will be allowed to eat a steak in the Stork Club (Did you know she could have one?), cossack dances will be danced in Washington, and so on. I hope they will do good. The secretary was in Greece with the rich girl he sleeps with; he is no longer on speaking terms with poor Cassoulet, who is more lonely, poor, and sad than ever. The singer is more and more famous; she sings in the best places, and everywhere in magazines you find adds saying: "Beautiful X., Sartre's existentialist friend, uses O-DO-RO-NO against perspiration smell." Genet has been invited in Sweden by the French ambassador, as being a great French writer, and asked to speak on the radio. He said: "Swedish people are stupid and ugly. This country pretends to be democratic and is not! This puritan Swedish morality just stinks!" and so on. The French ambassador was nearly dead with red anger, the broadcast manager felt mad, but they could not stop him. Olga looks rather fine. She spent all summer in Paris, Rue de la Bûcherie, and made friend with everybody in the house; the good concierge told her all the sad tale on her orphan life, and the big Jewish woman next door— what a bright life she had in Berlin when her husband slept with Marlene Dietrich and Peter Lorre kissed her little girl to bed every night: but she did not let him do that when he had acted the part of a vampire, baby-killer, in the old German movie called *M*.[2] Olga cried when leaving my room for the hotel once more, but when I saw her she was very nice. She does not think of theatre any longer, and dances in Saint-Germain-des-Prés clubs at night, and enjoys it. She lives separately from Bost now, but they see much of each other. Scipion travelled in Lapland with Châtaignier, the crazy communist: they went ten days on a boat hunting whales, and saw four of them captured. That he loved, but now is rather sad, without money or any job. It seems he does not see his girl-friend any longer, Janine Queneau

438

had a little book of poems printed. Bost is working hard on the script *The Respectful Prostitute*; they hope to make something good out of it: he consulted Wright two or three times about it, who was helpful, but is turning really silly in general way. *Native Son* is not at all a success here neither, yet Bost saw it for the second time and says it is good. Ellen Wright has taken a job, it seems, but I don't know more about her.

Oh! I forgot! Everybody enjoyed the story of your lecture at the Jewish association. You should come and lecture in France about the Marshall Plan, they all think.

Sartre met Carlo Levi who never stopped speaking about himself in the most wondering, admirative way, and did not pay *one* drink when they went together for meals or some whisky. He lies as naturally as he breathes, says Sartre, but the told some amusing stories, such as the visit of New York mayor to his native village in Sicily: a wonderful piece of comedy in the best Italian style. Though Italy does not seem amusing with the terrible poverty, which they have no means to check, children being born crazily (400,000 children more than dead people every year), they are more and more numerous and there is less and less to eat. Speaking of children, there was a real nice scandal in a little French town. One day a little twelve years old girl felt sick and said to her mother: I am afraid I am pregnant. She confessed sleeping with some man (did not say who he was) and her school mates did the same. Little school-girls from eight to fourteen confessed having been raped (did not say by whom). They were examined by a doctor, and it was proved six of them had just lied, because they wanted to have been raped, jealous of the three other ones who boasted in school since a year of what was happening to them. For these three girls, nine, eleven and fourteen years old, had been used by men in every ways. What seems strange is that they speak of it in a lewd, crude, nasty way, like regular old whores. And never told who the men were.

Here is a fat letter, fat enough. I'll tell you other nice stories another day, if you behave. Of myself there is little more to say. I put my place in some order, went shopping for winter clothes, saw people, and answered a lot of unanswered letters; tomorrow (it is Sunday now) I'll begin going to the public library to learn something more about French political life in the last thirty years; I need it for my novel. The little paper on Sade had arrived in time and the big one will be printed next month.3

And I wait a letter. I know it will be long, a long silence after your chattering voice in my ears for so many days. And after the letter, I'll wait for another one, and wait and wait for seeing you again, and the idea makes me a little sick. Yea, missing you is a sad sickness, though loving you makes my heart so warm. Nelson, how much I do love you.

Your own Simone

1) A marionette/puppet-show broadcast at 6 P.M. 2) *M. le Maudit*, by Fritz Lang (1931). 3) After reading *Justine* two or three years earlier, de Beauvoir was enthralled with Sade. She finished a first draft of what would become *The Mandarins* and went on to undertake two projects about him: a brief sketch commissioned by Queneau for an anthology on famous writers (*Les Ecrivains célèbres*); and an extensive essay, *"Faut-il brûler Sade?"* for *Les Temps modernes*, which was reprinted in 1995 in *Privilèges*.

Friday, 9 Novembre 1951

Dearest Patterson Island local beast,

Something big is happening to me! A woman cannot live without some passion, and as love is forbidden, I decided to give my dirty heart to something not so piggish as a man: and I gave to myself a nice beautiful black car. I told you I intended to buy one, and Genet helped me to find one, Gallimard helped with the money (he will get it back, indeed), and all was done very quickly. It is brand new, big enough for a French car, really pretty and quick. What is stupid is that I cannot drive. Cau has a driving-license, Bost quickly contrived to get one, and even Sartre found far away in his past a pink paper allowing him to drive (but he will not, everybody decided). But all that seems utterly useless. I have hidden the car in a garage so nobody will put his hand on it, and I began to learn. I had only one lesson, but the feeling I'll learn quickly, and I enjoyed it immensely; so a new life begins for me, and I hope it will be a happy one.

I saw some good movies here, *Miracles in Milano*, the last De Sica, which I like very much in spite of some mistakes. This one you have to see and tell me what you think about it. What a busy man you seem to be! Are all your speeches as wonderful as the one I heard? Did I tell you that I spoke about T.V. such an enthousiastic way that Sartre bought one for his mother? He did not realize French T.V. has nothing to do with American one; it is a mess. Poor secretary tries to fix it every day, never succeeds, and Sartre's mother gets angry at him. Anyway, when it is fixed they just show nothing, really nothing at all; there are hardly two hours show, very bad newsreels and dances, and that is all.

What a lucky woman I am! I just got a call from dearest Darina Silone; she works for UNO in Paris and hopes to see me often. Her husband stayed in Roma. The singer gave an interview yesterday, explaining she became such a success girl owing to Sartre. She nearly said she slept with him and was his dearest girl; little Cassoulett was mad, because she should like so much people to think she slept with Sartre (neither of them did). Sartre is angry; it is not fair, says he: at least, she should have really slept with him is she wanted people to believe she did.

As you wrote to me such a nice pleasant big fat letter, I'll tell you a good story. A true one. It is about an old friend who was a teacher in France, and now is in Madagascar. He has a lovely young wife—twenty two years old; he is forty two—and decided to marry her four years ago, though he had a child. He was a little of a racist when he went away, and when I saw him, he began to explain how white people are scared in Madagascar, because Negroes are so many, so dangerous people, and they poison white ones. Chiefly, colored girls poison their white lovers if they betray them, servants poison their masters if they want to send them away. Himself had an accident in his car; his wife was driving and the car crashed against a tree. He hesitated and said: "She did it purposely, to kill me." I was startled, then he added: "She is mad, a Negro witch has bewitched her. I know you'll not believe it, but it is true." And then came the whole story. They had a colored boy as a servant, a young nice boy. The woman used to pat him and play with him: just an animal for her, and the husband did not care, because *it* was an animal to him, too. She went so far in playing as masturbating him, but not sleeping with this dirty Negro. In the end, she slept anyway. And once the husband found her with a gun trying to kill herself: "Kill me! I deserve it!" She was pregnant. She had certainly been bewitched, because she hated the black monkey, but when she looked at him, she just wanted him to lay her." The husband was mad. He took the gun and threatened the boy, telling he would kill him if he did not say the truth. The Negro said that "Madame" had fondled him and then beaten him until he did what she wanted. The husband told him to lie on the ground and beat him a little with a stick—only five or six strikes on the buttocks, he told me. The woman asked to be beaten the same way, but he had not the heart to do it. Then the boy went away to his native village, and husband and wife came to France where the colored baby will be borned and secretly brought it up: if it was known, he would lose his place as a teacher. He is not angry at his wife (who is dirty bitch in my idea), not even at the Negro; he makes himself believe it is all Negro witchery. Stupendous when you think he was a very rational, positive man. And indeed he is more a racist than ever, though he made his misfortune by being a racist from the beginning, not thinking a Negro could be a man.

I had another lesson this afternoon; it is wonderfully amusing. I am not scared at all, going among all this terrific traffic in Paris. If you ever come to France, within town or twenty years, you'll sleep nicely in *my* car and I'll drive you to the end of the world where you whished to go.

No, honey, it did end badly. Well, no end could be good for me since it was an end, but I am *very* glad to have spent this last month with you. In fact, there was just a slight mistake: the last hour when you said more than you meant and I understood more than you said, maybe, and anyhow took it woo seriously. But honestly I never assumed during the month that you gave me more than a warm friendship, and that is why I began to say when leaving you: "It is good to have you as a friend, anyway," and hoped this friendship would last more than love did. I'll say it again: "It is good to have you as friend." So don't have any pangs about me—it is honest from me to say so, since your pangs seem to have been my best chance of seeing you again, But, truly, I think it could not end better since we have no resentment and memories are not killed; there is no misunderstanding and friendship is possible. Forgive my tears. When I cried, I just could not help it; it was never a weapon, I never purposely plotted or planned anything against you: and for what should I have struggled with tears? I know you don't get love back by crying. So I'll try to give all my love to my nice black car, and be your friend, the best friend you ever had: no other could care for you as much as I do. So in this new mood I'll stay for ever

Your own Simone

Monday, 19 Novembre 1951

Dearest thing,

Something very funny happened today! Maybe you remember when Kreswell gave you some books back, I showed to you a piece in one of the booklets where I was mentioned and strangely compared to Poincaré; it was called "Literature Below the Belt," something like that, and the author was Julien Gracq. In the same piece, Gracq said how disgusting it is to give prizes to authors, and how they degrade themselves by accepting them. Well, it happened this man wrote a book this year, a dull, sophisticated novel,[1] and the Goncourt Academy decided to give him the prize! Indeed, he could not accept after all he had written about it. He gave a lot of interviews saying he would not accept the prize if he got it. But the ten members of the Goncourt Academy, and Queneau among them, said the prize had not to be *accepted* to be *given*; they give it as they choose. And, indeed, today, they gave the prize to Gracq. There is 5000Fr check—that is less than 20 dollars, nothing; he can easily send it back. But the point is the Goncourt prize automatically becomes a best-seller, from 100,000 to 200,000 books are sold at once, that means millions of francs, really a little fortune. And how could he refuse it? So everybody is much amused and waits to know what he will do tomorrow. He is really a man who never tried to get publicity, wrote one, two books which did not intend to sell well. So it is pleasant the way he was tricked.

Tuesday

He returned back the check and decided his publisher not to put around the book the usual yellow wrapping that says it is a "Goncourt prize," but he gave some interviews and said a kind of thank you. He got a lot of publicity and everybody was amused with the story. I found on my table your big nice Wabansia picture waiting for me. There was very nice dedication, and it seemed amazing it had been sent on the 5th November, about the time you wrote the so angry letter, Oh! Don't me scared! I did not take it for more than it meant; but it was nice to think there was a part of you who did not hate me in these angry days. Thanks, honey. I put the picture in the little gallic cave with the other one. I am deeply glad to have it.

My car is in a garage now with it belly full of gas, waiting for me, and I feel silly not be able to do anything with it. I have three lessons a week, it does not go very fast, and I am impatient. Bost's book about Spain has just been published, but it is thin and makes him sad, though it is a very good book.

Did you read *The Watch* by our friend Carlo Levi? Where he says lions are roaring at night in Roma?...Some parts about black market, prostitution, newspaper people just after the war are not bad. But it is too long and when he pretends to *think*, it is awfully bad. We'll give a little part of it in *Temps modernes*.

The dying cancerous woman is still dying in an hospital room where are only dying women: yellow faces, distorted eyes and mouths, a real museum of horrors. I could hardly recognize her, all her face and body are swollen, she suffers so much they have to give her morphine the whole day long. She can die any moment by any accident, yet she can live other months; they nurse them as to keep them alive, which seems the most crazy thing to do. She still hopes, she hopes at the last moment they will find the miraculous remedy.

Thanks once more for the picture. Be good and work well.

I am with all my dirty heart

Your own Simone

1) *Le Ravage Des Syrtes.*

Sunday, 2 Décembre 1951

Nelson, my love,

A very stupid dull week for me. I guess it is a trick, being kind of sick every time I leave you, so I linger a little before beginning to live a serious life again. The fact is I had first a bad cold and then my stomach ached and I staid in be a whole day Friday; I hardly worked. The weather was cold, rainy, disgusting all the time long. Today it is sunny and blue. I feel better; I want to work.

The ugly woman travelled obediently with a ruck-sack in every places I had told her to: she is even more obedient than your Japanese girl. She cried only in the end of the evening and rather behaved. She began her whole novel again, and the new one happens to be very good. I met Genet once, and he told me about his Swedish experience. He managed a long trip through Germany and Sweden very cleverly. First, he saw Gallimard and said: "I am going to Germany and shall write for you *Germany Day by Day*. Give me 300,000Fr (1000 dollars)." Gallimard did it. Then he went to his German publisher in Hamburg: "I am going to write *Germany Day by Day*, give me 10,000 marks." And the publisher did. Then in Sweden he said to his Swedish publisher: "I'll write for you *Sweden Day by Day*, give me 300,000 crowns." And the publisher did. Hamburg is very strange, the whole town having been bombed, but the pleasure district very lively again: dancing, saloons, bars are just wooden barracks so it looks like a western town in American movies. In Sweden he was mad from the first day, because in his hotel restaurant they told him he should have a tie and he could not get his dinner; then in a tea-room, not speaking the language, he pulled the waitress by her arm to show her what cookies he wanted: the manager scolded him and sent him away. So, when he was asked to speak in the radio, he insulted the whole country thoroughly.

It is worse and worse than ever here. A producer asked from some bank money to produce *The Respectful Prostitute*. The bank-manager answered: "Nobody will lend you money for such an un-American movie." But in New York the play had 400 performance!" "American people do what they want to do in America, that is up to them, but here, it is France." How do you like it? A French movie actor called Bourvil asked from a bank some money on a very good check which he could endorse only a month later. I do don't know the technical word for the transaction, but it is a regular thing all banks do with everybody. But they told him "no." "Why?" "Because you are a communist. We have orders from the government never to lend any money to any communist." He protested he was not a communist, and they showed a programme of a popular festivity two years ago: "You sang and acted in a working-people communist feast." He said he had acted and sung in some Gaullist festivity, too, but he could not get the money...

Then in a big painting exhibition where all paintings are carefully chosen by a jury, a very reactionnary one, there happened to be three or four communist paintings about Thorez, war in Korea; the police decided to take them away. They have absolutely no right to interfere with the jury's decision, but they did. A big scandal just now.

Monday

I got your letter. No, it did not hurt much. I wanted to know where I stand with you; it is better to know. But you are not fair. You remember that I did not say a word of love during my whole stay, and *you* upset me terribly, because you said love words, half an hour before I went away. What I felt in New York is that I could not stand this game of taking me back, rejecting me, year after year. Since you had spoken so tenderly and told me *yourself* you did not want to evict me any longer, I asked you to keep to that decision, not to talk me one thing one day and another the following one. Well, that is what you just did, but now it is definite and I'll cling to it. You are not fair when you say I want to keep your life without giving mine. I always accepted the idea (since three years) you would love another woman; and even in Gary[1] the last day I told you I wanted to stay your friend even if you were married. I don't see in which way I "bound you all the year round," since I should not even have asked to come if you had not asked me. I don't see what emotional obligations I put on you this year, since we had a pleasant holiday without any overwhelming emotion appearing until the last day. I know in which way I can feel guilty toward you: the guilt is made by our

445

situation, by my whole previous life, and I told you that I resented it. But I know, too, when I am not guilty. And I really did not try to impose on you anything. Maybe my New York letter was too emotional, that is all, but you made it so in our last moments. It was very important for me to know which was your final decision: to keep on this loving relationship as long as nothing interfered with it, or kill it. What I said in New York is: don't kill it as long as you'll not be in love with another woman, and if you choose the other way, just say it clearly, it will be easier for me.

It is not fair to speak of *one* month meeting when you asked me for no longer this year. If you had wanted it and accepted to come to Paris sometimes, we would have spent three or four months together every year, which is very different.

I think you wrote in a kind of anger. And if I insisted so much on wanting your friendship, it is because I feel I don't deserve this anger. I gave you all my heart and did not ask much since a long time. You could not expect me to react like an obedient machine last year, and not to resent you not-loving me, chiefly when it was such a sudden discovery. And this year I put the things exactly on the level where you put it. No, your anger is not fair at all.

Well, I'll not come if you don't ask. And always be glad to come if you do, even if just as a friend. Anyhow, it was sweet to have a last loving kiss from you whose love has meant so much. I shall not try not to love you, but it will not bother you. I hope you'll stop being angry at me and give me back a friendly tenderness. I'll always be

Your own Simone

1) On the banks of Lake Michigan. Miller and Gary border each other.

Thursday, 6 Décembre 1951

Dearest you,

I saw Queaneau yesterday; he was very nice. He told me Vian had translated about 350 pages of your book and hopes it will be over within two or three months; I was pleased at it. He got the little book about Chicago, but thinks, as I thought, it cannot be used. All your French friends like very much. Queneau wrote a good novel, which we print in *Temps modernes*.[1] It is a pity you cannot read it! He really re-creates French language, the way Joyce did with English, and he is so funny. His wife is awfully proud because she bought a car and learned to drive it; she scares everybody—I was scared myself. Que-neau says he had a hard time during his holidays, because sometimes she just forgot to hold the wheel—she played with the mirror, for instance, and he found himself suddenly in the bottom of a deep ditch. They seemed to get along nicely, though he goes on having an affair with another woman.

I spent and hour with a very nice American pansy whom I had known years ago in Switzerland where he was something like an ambassador; then he was co-editor of *New Directions*, in London. A friend of Nathalie's hus-band and Koestler's wife, he always lived in London or Paris. He hired the most wonderful furnished flat I ever saw, which was inhabited by a French count, a pansy, too, and an antiquarian. I told you once that French elegant antiquarians were all pansies; you would not understand it, that is another example. The man has decorated his place in the most crazy way, with a lot of deep red velvet curtains, large strangely-shaped couches, extravagant things; but chiefly there is a room which is the inside of a hearse! All black. Black material covering the ceiling, black and silver walls, black ground and furniture, and silver crucifix on the walls. The poor American says it gives him the creeps and sometimes he gets claustrophobic and has to rush out. He is translating for Knopf the last Camus' book *Revolted Man.*[2] Don't ever read it. All right wing people love it, because it explains that you are romantic revolted man just by staying in your armchair and getting money. The translator himself was sad at it and awfully bored.

There was a big party given some days ago for *The Devil and the Lord* 100th performance. The theatre director invited everybody to Paris; she had thirty boys from Marrakech, the sultan musicians, coming by airplane; they never had been as far as Casablanaca and were startled. A very bad music, said Scipion and the secretary, because the nice thing was Sartre sent some guests to look at the feast but did not go, and Bost, Olga, myself did not. We did not want to meet the dirty people meant by the word "every-body in Paris." And we were right, because the secretary and Scipion said it was boring: people sitting in a big hotel hall and eating cold food, because when there was music or dance they did not give food at all but waited; it lasted like that four hours. We all went together in a little joint, and our spies —Scipion, the secretary—came there too after an hour of elegant Parisian festivity. A nice night. Scipion was gay and bright as usual; he told us about hunting the whales in northern seas. He told to some consul in Norway he was a penniless newspaper man wanting to report about Norway in French newspapers, and given free trips in all trains and airplanes. "Sometimes we

had not a penny for eating, and so we to get a plane just for the meal..."
Don't you like the idea of a guy having to fly a plane every time he wants to
eat? Chiefly, if he is air-sick and scared in airplanes!

I have made a big change in my life: I don't drink at all! It is better for
the health, I decided. And I want to work seriously and be through with
this book. I do work now, six or seven hours a day.

It is rather cold and rainy here. Rather cold inside me, too. You
insisted on the things my love deprived you of: other love-affairs, chiefly.
But I did not win much, you know! Though I never wanted to speak about
it, I can tell you this affair did not improve my relationship with Sartre. As
soon as I knew you, I have broken a sentimental sexual relationship with
Bost, which was easy and pleasant, and indeed I never looked at any man
for these years and don't wish to look at any any more. So, my love life is
closed for ever, and it is not very pleasant to think when you have kept a
warm heart and living body. I don't complain. I just want you to have a
glimpse to my side of this story, too. I don't complain, because even if the
world is forever cold now, it was worth it.

Good bye, honey I'll get a letter soon. Good bye.

Your own Simone

The American pansy told me Koestler kept his ways of getting drunk and
hitting people. In the States, he invited people to come to his island for
week-ends, then he gets drunk and hit them. Indeed, he has not a friend left
in the States, no more than in any other countries. When he had nobody else
to beat, he beats his wife. He always used to sleep with other women, but
recently he used to bring them home, and often they were of the worst kind.
Yet, my former said it is him who sent his wife away, a nice English girl, but
her tragedy is she could love nobody except an intellectual. And the pansy
said uglily, in England it will be difficult for her find anything of the kind...
Graham Greene, Maybe? Poor woman, she certainly had a hard time.

1) *Le Dimanche de la vie.* 2) *The Rebel.*

Saturday, 15 Décembre 1951

Dearest nice you,

We have no indian summer here, but a very pleasant cold pink winter, the
sky is slightly misty and gloriously pink when evening comes. That was the

good thing this week. The bad one was my sister came, with the purpose to see me, and since yesterday my brother-in-law is here too—but they will go away next Tuesday. I am glad you are no more jealous than you are about my new love, but it is manish stupid pride to call "her" a "him": she is a "she," and I love her more for that. You say you can climb my stair and she cannot, but as you never climb my stairs and don't intend to, I don't see it gives you a great superiority. To tell the truth, if it is a happy love— she never makes me cry—it is a rather dangerous one. Last Sunday I went in the country around Paris with Bost and my sister and I kind of nearly killed all of us. But only once. And I had not driven more than three hours all in all, including the lessons, so they agreed I did not behave too bad for being a beginner. It is wonderfully amusing, that is.

You'll certainly be very sad to know what happened to poor dear Darina Silone. No kidding, I respect her for that. She left Silone and came to Paris to get money by herself, for her self. What I understand from what Sartre saw in Roma, is that Silone more or less fell in love with another Irish woman, so Darina did not want to depend on him any longer, not being loved. I guess she is slow to understand a thing, but when she does, she acts in the right way. She contrived to find some hard work in UNO, making something like eighty dollars a month, no more, working the all day long; she sleeps in a friend's dining room and has hardly money enough to eat. She was used to quite another life. I proposed to lend her some money, but she did not want it. The letter you sent back to me was from Sartre, and 16th October! He made the mistake to ask an Italian boy in the hotel to post it, and boy indeed kept the money for the stamps, though he was kind enough not to keep the letter. Is my writing so bad since I quitted drinking? I really did. I hardly drink one scotch every other day, and no wine, nothing else. I feel very good for it.

Boris Vian translated *Golden Arm*, which we are eager to publish in *Temps modernes*. The ugly woman travelled with a ruck-sack around France, during summer: I had told her to, and to write a diary about it. Now she wants to be published in *T.M.* and by Gallimard, but it is so bad I am quite at a loss. I am afraid to despair her by telling the truth. Yet, it is a curious example of a writer being killed by his moral failure. I mean what is so bad in her writing is the deep insincerity of her heart. She says she loves poverty, for instance, but she has to prove that poverty is more glamorous than pearl and diamond, and she keeps the cheapest feeling about "glamour." she says she would die for me, but she never learnt one thing about me, never cares in what mood I can be, nothing. And all that makes even her way of writing insufferable.

You wrote a big fat nice letter, honey, and it made me very happy. If you don't write long fat letters, then I'll contrive to give you bad pangs. I'll mail them by special mail and make them terrible; they will creep in the whole house and you'll never get rid of them. But if you do write such nice letters, I'll send you pretty little dingy voices whispering through the whole house: what a nice, smart, pretty, sweet, lovely, talented man this man is! And you'll smile at yourself in the most complacent way. Yea, everything is nicely clear now in my head and heart. And make it clear to yourself, too, that you'll never have a better more loving friend than I am.

Your own Simone

Christmas 1951

Darling you,

I hope you had a nice Christmas, a got a lot of cards with the Christmas wishes. I did not think that you would not get mine in time if I send them this very day. But you'll get happy new-year whishes on the right date, with old Christmas ones mingled with them: do write another good book, making half of the people happy and other half very angry. Be happy and keep a small place for me in the basement of your heart.

On Christmas night I had a little supper home with Bost, Scipion, Sartre, Olga, Wanda; we ate "foie gras," caviar, French pastries, with champagne and scotch. Nobody was drunk, and we played an amusing game. Sartre happens to have a recording machine (made in Chicago). Bost, Sartre, and me, we have hidden it carefully in my room; the other people did not know it was there. Poor Scipion, chiefly, answered innocently to all my questions, tricky questions, making him talk about women and everything. In fact, he talked very pleasantly as always, but it is terrific thing when you hear your own voice. Everybody was ashamed as well as amused when the reading was given back and we heard the silly things we had said. I did not drink much, not sleep much either, and spent the whole day working hard today.

It was terribly misty the whole week, such a deep mist that from my window I cannot see Notre-Dame. So it was hard to drive; all the cars had yellow lights on. But I drive every Sunday, bravely, so bravely that Bost was scared to death. I drove so quickly on slipping roads, and after all I don't know how to drive; I have not got my licence, but I do love the game. I drove about eighty miles the first Sunday, and 100 the second one. Olga came with Bost and me; it is strange because with this weather you see nothing at all, or if you see anything, the landscape is as dreary as dreary can be. The surroundings of Paris are not very interesting. But she has so little to do with herself that she is happy to come and kill time, poor girl. I guess next time, when I'll be a little more confident without knowing anything more, I'll be really dangerous. Yet, I am scared by accident. I saw a wonderful crash just two days ago; I'll not drive in Paris before long.

It seems *The Respectful Prostitute* will give a movie. They chose a pretty nice girl, a young not much known one; they tried her with a well-known actress and the girl was much better.

Scipion has bought a Middle-aged (or do you say medieval?) castle in the sea-side—only ruins, he says, but kind of ruins you can live in in summer, and he intends to spend all the warm months there and really work to write a book about all his travel. Boris Vian is divorcing. Olga thinks vaguely of singing in some night-club; she has a good voice but neither the health nor the will to begin something new just now. Sartre and Bost are all right. So am I, as far as it goes. I had a bad time with the ugly woman the last time. I am so patient with her, and so indifferent, too, and every evening we have (two every month) is so exactly the same as any other one that it makes her mad in the end, and she tries to open some drama, but I make it impossible, so she becomes sadder and sadder, but it does not succeed. Then she writes foolish letters, much more foolish than I ever did, and I don't answer.

So happy New Year to you, my nice sweet you. Tell happy New Year to Christie, to our little friends Kukla and Ollie, to all of them. I think of them often, as of every other things. I kiss you happy New Year very tenderly.

Your own Simone

1952

My nice faraway wrapped in the blizzard you,

It was a long time without seeing my faraway blinking local star in my poor lonely sky. Now I know you were a miserable miser once more, and to *try* to spare fifteen cents (not even to spare them really), you kept me without this big fat letter so long. What a shame! Here we had no snow, not at all, but much mist that we could compete with London, no airplane could land, cars crashed against each other. Yesterday, I wanted to go for a ride with Bost; as soon as we left the suburbs and enjoyed the idea of being in the country, the mist came so thick we had to turn back; it was useless and dangerous to go on blindly, through darkness and no fun at all. The car is always my big affair, but not such an easy affair as though in beginning. The teacher says I drive all right, but it is only a theoretical knowledge; when I find myself on real roads, with real trucks to pass by, real spinning curves, and children and bicycles trying to frighten me until I kill one of them, then it is different and I am scared. I dream much more about this car than I ever dreamt about you. The other night, I was on a road and drove pretty well and killed two men on motorcycles; the second one was just put into nothing, they only found a button left of his coat. I was very much upset at that, but the teacher told me: "Well! Only two motorcyclists! For a first real ride, that is not too bad!" Is not this dream nice? And the other Sunday, I nearly began to kill a little child, but Bost on one hand and the mother on the other hand, did not let me do it. As a lesson for me, a twenty eight years old girl, daughter of a great French actress, not having her driving-licence, tried one night to drive a friend's car: it was near this canal Saint-Martin where you complain they put nothing to prevent children from falling in the water. Well, she was on the pier, she did something to go forward, and she went backward. Then she pretended to stop the car, but once more she made a mistake: she accelerated. The car quickly went backward into the water, and she was drowned. That is nice, is it not?

I don't understand how you can read my letters. I am afraid you just put them into the waste basket, because I just tried to read over what I wrote this morning and I hardly could. What a pity I cannot write such nice poems as you do! Then I should buy a typewriting machine, red ribbon, and learn how to type. Really, I love this poem about the poor little boat, "the little dead boat that depended on you," or was it a gopher?

No, Poirier-Gracq is not such a likable man; first, he sold 82,000 copies, so we have not to mourn about him, and then, I was told by Queneau that if he had really not wanted the prize, he should have said it privately, and he would not have get it, but he said it publicly in such a way they had to give it to him. He is a very tedious writer and, in my idea, uninteresting. I don't think you could stand him for two pages.

I heard Sophie Tucker on record very often. She was a great love of me when I was young; a wonderful voice she had and I cried about "The Man I Love" and "Some of These Days," when I was twenty. We had a nice affair in France this week in the jail of Amiens, a small town eighty miles from Paris. Two men sentenced to death, with chains on feet and wrists, were waiting for guillotine; the warders used to play cards with them—it is usual in France, cops and sentenced to death criminals play card together—so these last ones "keep high spirits." Well, they were playing card when one of the criminals took a gun out of his pocket and threatened the warders *who had no guns* (they are not allowed to). So the scared cops gave the keys, the criminals put their chains off, the cops into the cell and went away after having put all the warders into jail. The most clever of them wrote a long letter, explaining he was sorry to escape with the other who was just a bloody brute, himself not being guilty. They went away on bicycles, and were taken back two days after. They said that a warder was a accomplice, he had given them the gun, because the clever one told them he could make him wealthy and powerful when he was out, and he believed it. It was a big scandal in France, chiefly the idea of cops and murderers nicely playing cards together. But if the men are really put to death after such an escape, I say it is a shame, is it not?

I am one year older today. it is better to feel old sometimes. Really. Two years ago I hated the idea; now it is rather conforting. Why should I be young now? You remember the story I told you of the old French woman (more than eighty) deaf and blind, and Horace Walpole came through the Channel to see her every year?[1] So, maybe you'll cross the ocean when I am

453

eighty, and every year I get makes you nearer, crazy beast.

A nice birthday kiss from your orphaned gopher. Good night, my sunny beast.

10th

The cancerous woman died this morning. I just got a call phone from her sister. She first asked me to come and see her this afternoon before she dies, telling she looked like an eighty years old woman now, and she suffered in the most horrible way. I felt a real coward: I did not want to go at all, and now she phoned once more and said it was all over. What a horrible death after such a sad wasted life. Death always seems to me the more stupid when the life of the person has been stupid. It is nothing into nothingness.

Darina Silone is getting a divorce. Ellen Wright tries to be a literary agent for French-American books, and she takes it so seriously she waked me up a 8 A.M. to ask informations. She will try to have my paper about Sade published in your dirty country. I should be pleased, because you could read it then. Half published here last month, the second half this month, and people seem to think it is good.

Bost has quite an affair on his arms! A certain woman-writer called Meg, thirty six years old, half-white, half-Indochinese, not pretty, but pleasant, was a communist but was expelled last year, and her husband, too, so now they see non-communist, left wing people, and are friends with Queneau, Merleau-Ponty, Bost, and Olga. On Christmas night, Bost and Olga, after leaving my own brothel, went to their place and found everybody drunk. Meg jumped on Bost, fixed him on a couch and never left his mouth for hours; the husband was red with anger, and Olga much unpleased but Bost very pleased. I saw Olga two days after. She cried with anger and hate the whole evening long, cursing Bost; I guess she will never really forgive him, though they pretended to make up. Then, another night, Bost went to another party (without Olga) and this Meg began again, the husband was mad again at him, and there is an ex-husband, too, who has married again but yet remained very jealous. Both of them explained for hours to Meg that Bost really not worth much: he was not even a communist! He was not even expelled! She answers nothing, pretends to knit and listen, but wants to sleep with Bost, even if he never was a communist. So she met him in a café two days after, and said in a very business way: "Well, now we for to the hotel and fuck: I have exactly one hour." Bost argued: for the first time he would be better to do that when they had a little more time. She said: "I want it to be done so I am through with you; anyhow, I'll never spend more than an hour with you. I don't want to fall in love and my husband doesn't let me go more than that." They argued in such a way they had only half an hour left, and she still wanted to get rid of this obsession, but Bost did not want so much to have her rid of it, and did not give her his beautiful body for that time. She explained, too, he had to talk with the husband, a very nice boy who is good friend of Bost. So Bost doesn't know what to do. He wants the girl, but should like to have more than one hour a week to sleep and talk with her; he is scared to make Olga mad, scared of the husband, though Meg told him: "It is rather my ex-husband who would kill you." Everybody waits impatiently to know what will happen.

On this Christmas night, Scipion tried to sleep with Wanda, Queneau and his eighteen years old son tried to sleep with the same ex-communist woman, and Janine Queneau told everybody how she slept with a move director who has a terribly ugly wife: "He likes ugly women," she said pleadingly.

Except me, who slept in my virgin bed, dreaming of my only love, my nice shining car, and sometimes looking in the faraway basement of my heart to catch a glimpse of somebody else. Gosh! I am tired to write. Give my love to the little white boat. Keep just as much as you wish for dirty you.

Your own Simone

1) Madame du Deffand (1697–1780), whose famous salon was frequented by writers and philosophers. She was blind, but not deaf.

Un Jeudi, fin Janvier–début Février 1952

Darling disgustingly greedy you,

You do deserve a long letter and you'll get it, poor thing, since yours was so fat and full of nice clippings. What I like the best is the *New Yorker* paper, about the way you ate all the bones of the chicken. How ugly you look, honey, in this blue shirt, on the picture!

Well, you have to send me congratulations, because in the end we were married, my true love and me, two days ago, at 8 A.M., on a dark and cold morning. It was not an easy affair! First, they decided not to give licenses so easily any longer, and I had to wait for weeks; then, on the appointment day, I was in bed with the flu: nothing important, but a high fever during two days. In the end, on Tuesday morning, I got my license.

Though I drove as bad as I can do: my motor stopped, which was a terrible thing, and I nearly got upon the side-walk. But it is really a mock-licence they give: the test doesn't last ten minutes; they have no time to see what you know or don't know. Anyway, it was a success. And then the secretary told me he could have got the licence for me by some friend, without any test! So much emotion for nothing! After that I went away with Bost for the whole day, though the roads were covered with snow and rather dangerous. We hardly stopped for lunch; I wanted to drive on and on. And did it pretty well. We saw the north of France, which has been wildly destroyed; they began to rebuild it now, but it is so ugly what they build, it is terrific! These dead, growing again towns in snow and mud, on Sunday chiefly, I saw real pretty forests and little old towns in the surrounding of Paris. I enjoy this weekly drive—a nice holiday after the week long work.

I do like very much the wonderful New York party. If Bost had spoken in such a manly, elegant way to the woman who wanted to make him at the Christmas party, things would be easier for him now. But he did not. And it is a terrific mess. The girl lives since eight years with her husband, has a son, they slept a little with other people but not much (before she says she had at least 300 lovers). And now she is very fond of Bost and wants stubbornly to sleep with him—though he says she does it with such an indifferent quickness he doesn't understand why she cared so much for it. Anyhow, she sees him about for times a week, one hour in the afternoon; he thinks it is a little in a hurry, but on the whole, as he doesn't want a serious affair, he should be rather pleased with the business. But the husband, a handsome boy, rather clever, is not pleased at all. She half lies to him, half not, because it seems she enjoys making him unhappy; he suffers so much that first he could no longer sleep with her, and now he never stops, and when he does not, he broods sadly. In the end, he wrote to Bost he wanted this affair to be over. She said she would go away, she could not stand this comedy; nobody knows what will happen. Bost is chiefly scared at the idea Olga could learn something. I'll tell you if the husband killed Bost or what.

Yes, I saw *Los Olvidados*.[1] I don't know if I like it or not. There are some wonderful things, indeed—chiefly the story with the legless man. Yes, it is a very good strange movie, but not likable in a way, not as *Sciuscia*,[2] for instance. It is just Mexico is so harsh, so dry, hard to love, though so attractive in many ways. It was a great pleasure to see something of Mexico City again; it really gives much of the town.

Olga is going away for a month, invited to Germany by little Cassoulet who had friends there. She "wanted" to go, but it is a terrible business to have her doing anything, even things she "wants" to do. Bost had to take care of papers and tickets, I had to take care of clothes for her, and Sartre gave money; she is not actually gone, but I suppose she will in the end. Where did Scipion find money for his castle? Indeed, in Sartre's pocket! what do you think?

We had some beautiful days but now it is cold, misty, snowy, disgusting. The poor cancerous woman's death struck me so much that for a week I fancied I had cancer myself. I went and saw a doctor who said I was all right, which I suspected, in fact, and yet I was scared when I waited in his room.

The more I work, the more I have work to do; it seems I shall never get out of this damned book. I am tired of working so much. When Olga is away, I intend to go with Sartre and Bost for a little trip to Mont Saint-Michel, or something like that.

Brassuer has got sick with hemorrhoids and suffered terribly; it is forbidden for him to drink, that makes him mad. He comes mad, too, because he believed the play (*Devil and the Lord*) was a mere nothing and people came only to see and hear *him*. But when he is away, another bad actor playing his part, people came all the same. So, he had pictures shot, lying in his bed, hoping when people really know he does not play, nobody would come: the pictures were published in newspaper, and people came as before...He was so mad he wrote to Sartre, who had done nothing at all, the maddest letter in the world, written in a mad writing, all in curves, and saying: "*Devil and the Lord* fuck you, and so you know what hemorrhoids are...I am mad at the idea of shitting blood because of you..." like that for two pages. A real nice man, is not he?

Well, that is something for you to read! Write another red big letter. I try to keep you in the basement of my heart, but you always jump up and down and everywhere; I cannot prevent you. Well, I don't mind too much; it is nice to have you everywhere.

Good bye, honey.

Your own Simone

1) By Luis Buñuel, 1950. 2) By Vittorio De Sica, 1946.

Darling you,

For once I agree with nearly everything you say in your letter; it doesn't always happen that you have so much taste and sense. Yea, T. S. Eliott is a dull, falsely wise and deeply reactionary ham. And when I saw Dos Passos in New York, four years ago, he still had two eyes, but very little brain; he did not believe in a world war, only in local war, in China, for instance. China is local, said he; and he seemed really pleased with the idea of a war in Korea. Yea, it is sad, but Dostoyevsky was not a very pleasant man, though he could write such wonderful books. He understood evil, but there was much evil in him, too. Your blonde Barbara looks like a Fitzgerald woman; I like her: why don't you come to Paris with her in "Tourist airplane"? I just read millions of Americans will come at low price this year by the new "tourist plane." She should fly in the Montagne Sainte-Geneviève little bar, and shake foot with Scipion while you would take care of Lisa, Olga, and little Cassoulet. Well, little Cassoulet has found a beautiful German boy to sleep with her; anyway she invited Olga to come with her in Germany, and they both send crazy letters and pictures of themselves in the German carnival, with fancy paper hats on their heads. They both seem to worship this German handsome boy (an anti-nazi happily, but I guess all are, now); the boy chose Cassoulet, who is very happy with it. Olga is not too sad about it, chiefly because Bost decided to drop the affair with the passionate drunk woman writer. This last one went away to Italy with her "sick" husband, and the whole Gallimard family is still gossiping about this terrible sickness, and very angry to give him a month holiday.

When you speak of infatuation (about my car), you are wrong; it is real deep love, which comes deeper and deeper. We see each other only once a week. Maybe that is why we never get tired of each other. But then it is for a long time. Two weeks ago, I rode all along the French coast from Le Havre to Dunkerque; I saw towns ruined by the war and the wide, impressive Dunkerque beach where so many English and French soldiers were killed, while American lazy cowards stayed cosily home. With Bost I looked for all the places where he had been a soldier; we spent an hour in dirty little snowy roads, searching for the very hole where he had been wounded: he never found it. But he found in a deserted ruined village a monument to the brave regiment who defended this part of the country, and it was *his* regiment! He was awfully proud. I drive quickly now and enjoy it more and more; in the little towns there are always wonderful restaurants with wonderful old wines; it is a nice way of spending a holiday at the end of a week work.

Sartre works hard about your book.[1] What is difficult is to find words not too coarse and not too dignified to translate your words: French slang is usually very coarse, and the usual language not familiar enough. Bost helps, and so do I; it is very amusing a work, more amusing than cross-words.

We have a friend, a reporter, coming back from the States where he has a wife, and he loved to live some years ago, he is just horrified now; he says people don't ever dare to speak about politics when they are six friends together, fearing one of them will denounce them to the FBI. We gave Fitzgerald *Crack-up*,[2] translated indeed, in *T.M.*; it was a great success, so was *The Mint*, by Lawrence.[3] It is a pity it is only allowed to publish eight little chapters of this astonishing book; what a man he was! I don't think it is available in America neither, or I should command you to read it.

We had the first spring day, very moving after such a long grey, dull, cold, misty winter. Blue sky, warm air, and something light and gay everywhere; the whole life seemed different.

Well, I cannot write such nice letters as you do; first, because I don't use typewriter, my ink is not red, and I don't know this language I am trying to write. And nothing happens here. I just hope you'll not be disgusted of sending such nice fat letters; I like them so much. Have a good time in the "Tip Top Tap" and elsewhere, and when you take me to the lake, don't drop me behind a dune. Good bye, dear thing.

Your own Simone

There is a wonderful trial these days: a provincial woman accused of poisoning eleven people so as she got the whole money of the family.[4] But when they analysed the corpses to find arsenic in them, they just mixed up the old aunt's eyes with the grand-father's stomach and the husband's bones, so nobody could know to whom anything belonged, and who had arsenic in his body, if anybody had! The woman will be released, though she certainly did the killing, because the experts proved quite inexpert, and there is no real proof against her.

1) *Chicago, City on the Make.* 2) *La Fêlure.* 3) *La Matrice.* 4) The Marie Besnard affair.

My dearest violet pumpkin,[1]

I just got your letter when coming back home; it was nice. I'll tell you today why I wrote such poor letters these last times: I was rather in low spirits, not because of my Tip-top-tap stupid friend, not because of my brand-new motored love, but because of my poor own self... I'll tell you the whole story, now I am happily out of it, though you will not think I am so wise, after all.

I told you, these last years long, the story of the poor cancerous woman who died in twenty months in the most horrible way by a cancer in the breast. Every time a woman has a friend dying by a cancer in the breast, she begins to be scared about her own breasts, and though I have not much of them, I was not an exception. I began to feel little pains in my right breast, and sometimes last year, I alluded laughingly to my own cancer, though not believing in it. The point is, when I came back from Chicago this year, and the cancerous woman died, I had a real pain and there was something swollen in this breast, I was sure. Yet, I felt silly and did not dare to take it seriously. In the end, Sartre saw I began to be a bit amazed about it, inquired about a good doctor, and I went to, half sweating with fear, I must say, because cancer is no joke. He looked and felt and said: "There is something," and reasoningly he explained that very probably it was a non-important small thing, but if it got bigger, it would have to be taken away; they would then look at it with a microscope to see if it was a cancer or not. The fact it was painful was a good thing, because cancer is not painful; and my wholly good health was a good thing, too. So, I had seen the doctor in January, I spent six weeks rather peaceful, but he had said to come back and see him after six weeks; and I could not hide to myself that the little swollen point in my breast was getting bigger. I felt very scared these last times. Ten days ago, I went and saw the doctor, and he said: "It is bigger, it had to be taken away. The chances are it is nearly nothing, a little accident lot of women have when getting middle-aged, and in four days you'll be yourself again. But it is possible it is cancerous: then we take away the whole breast, you stay in bed two weeks, and then it is all right, *but* you have to take some cares so it does not come back, and so on." Well, I know they cure cancer now when it is taken in the very beginning, but it is rather a gloomy idea to think you can have one, is it not? So, on last Thursday morning, I had my blood taken and analysed: I was all right and fit for an operation. I spent two days driving with Bost, trying not to think, one very blue Sunday in Paris with Sartre, trying to face the worst, and one night, I entered a very good clinique where I was given a big nice room. I felt accepting anything at that time, only eager to know. They helped me to sleep with pills, and on morning they took me to the anaesthetizing room. I was peaceful. But you see the situation: the surgeon operates, takes away the sick part of the breast (a very small piece of flesh), then a scientist nearby makes a microscopic study of the cells; if there is nothing cancerous in them, all right, the surgeon sews the wound back; it is nearly nothing. If there are cancerous cells, the surgeon takes away the whole breast. So when anaesthetized, you don't know how you'll wake up: cancerous or sane — that is the nightmare touch in this affair. Well, they put you to sleep in a wonderful way now, with Pentothal, just one sting in a vein; the doctor told me: you'll taste garlic in your mouth and you'll sleep. I think after that they give you other anaesthetics, but I know nothing more. I hardly opened my eyes. I heard a voice saying: "You are absolutely all right, no cancer at all!" It was like an angel voice.

So after that, there was no story. I spent three days in bed in that place, reading books, with Sartre and Bost coming and speaking with me. It was Monday I was operated; I had never been in my life. Yesterday, Olga, just coming back from the trip in Germany, took me home with Bost in my own car. In the restaurant I drank two scotches, I got your letter, and this morning I begin my usual life again. I am so happy to feel healthy again, no more scared, having kept what I have for breast, after all: not much, but mine.

Somehow, this whole little story made quite an ending to this ended affair with you. It meant that even if you had not ended it, it had naturally to come to an ending, because of my age. It makes me confortable to think that my love life has ended when it decently had to end. Because I hate the idea of aging women with aged bodies clinging to love. I am glad that the end of my love life was its climax, too. Glad you are such a nice friend as to send such nice letters. I only do regret you are so far, because even friendship needs some presence from time to time. I do hope you'll go on writing to me very long and some day I'll see you again.

Did you see how the nice plane we went into from Nice to Paris crashed in Nice with thirty-three people burnt to death without any possible reason? There were nine young actresses coming back from the carnival. Olga coming back from Germany trip with Cassoulet says that you are right: this girl knows nothing at all. The young Prussian boy was first interested in Olga because he has seen her playing Electra and admired her. But Olga saw Cassoulet was deeply interested and gave him up to her. Cassoulet seduced him by pretending she would help him to make money in Paris, because she knew Sartre and everybody. He was seduced and asked to marry her. She said no, and did not even managed to sleep with him! She fell madly in love with another German boy who is the grand grand-son of the King Louis II de Bavière, prince named Constantin. He was interested in Cassoulet, but she became so senti-mental he was scared and dropped the affair without sleeping with her neither! So in Milano (where they came and saw my sister) Cassoulet had a nervous breakdown; she screamed and cried and Olga had to solace her, as well as she could, with hot beverages and good words. She (Olga) felt very pleased with herself, very superior to Cassoulet. They both say that around Munich the old nazism is not dead at all; by the name of neo-nazism it is even very strong and American occupants do support it, who are all smiles for ancient nazis, saying after all they wanted to fight Rus-sians and were right to do so. Yet, it is forbidden to any German people to go alone to Hitler's eagle nest in Berchtesgaden; they must go with a French or English or American escort, or not at all. There would be an endless pilgrimage if it were otherwise. They went to a strange and amus-ing dancing party: a woman exclusive party. Peasant and town women meet in a dancing room, in the afternoon, with men disguised as women playing music, and they eat and drink and dance by themselves the whole day long. In the evening, husbands and brothers are admitted, and it is a nice family orgiastic feast. Olga was so happy to have been out of France for once, poor girl.

I am leaving Paris next week. I'll go to Saint-Tropez as last year. I'll enjoy getting some sun. But do write in Paris as usual, because I'll not stay long. You are older by one year, one of these days, so happy birthday to you, honey! Try to be rather a violet chrysanthemum than a square pump-kin. Anyhow, I'll keep you in my heart.

Your own Simone

---

1) Algren claimed that in the United States, "progress" was such that square pumpkins and violet-scented chrysanthemums were bred.

Darling you,

I hope you got my little birthday present; when I discovered the most elegant men in Paris were wearing this kind of scarf, it was sold in the smartest shops, I decided you *must* have one. How do you like it? If you don't use it yourself, you can give it to Barbara, if she deserves it. You seem to have a really hard life, poor thing! Why not give the little whore to Neal for a change? And have Christie killed by the Ohio husband, if he really has to kill somebody? I don't see why you are so proud about the way you behave with the poor girl. She was nicely satisfied with a little white powder, here and there; it did not hurt nobody. And now you made a sexual fiend out of her! That seem to me a real sin. As to your sins towards me, honey, I don't find many of them, except making me starve once or twice and not taking me to the Tip-top-tap often enough. But, really, you are white as snow in my heart, and even if I had been killed in an air-crash, it would not make you black. I am glad because Ellen Wright has sold for 130 dollars my piece about Sade to Grove Press in New York. So you'll learn what is a real black man.

I had a nice trip from Paris to Saint-Tropez. We decided to go away early in the morning, Sartre, Bost, and me. I waited and waited until half past nine and then got a call from Sartre: Bost did not wake up in time! And Sartre had to go hastily to the dentist, because his tooth ached! We started at 11 A.M.; but then it was raining, the luggage on the top of the car were drowning, we had to buy a tarpaulin, it was a long job to fasten it, and in the end we left Paris at noon! But we drove quickly, had plenty of time to eat in good restaurants, see some beautiful towns and wonderful landscapes: we did not follow the classic high road but small twisted country roads of my own choice. We saw some thing astonishing on the second day, the Ideal Palace—here is a picture of it and of the man who made it, a postman.[1] At forty he decided "to make his dream reality," and for thirty-one years without stopping to be a postman, he gathered stones, pebbles, and shells in the country around, carried them in his "brouette"[2] (which you see with him), and alone, pebble by pebble, stone by stone, he built this strange thing—Half Arabian mosque, half Angkor temple. There are three giants on the left side (look with a magnifying glass, it is worth it).

For ten days I lived here, the same hotel as last year. Bost stayed a few days; we went for long drives in this beautiful country. Much work and a little drinking. Why don't you marry a nice *clean* American girl, who could make you a real American man? Good bye, honey. You should not have been scared about me, but it was nice to be so. I kiss you very tenderly.

Your own Simone

1) Cheval (1836–1924), a mailman, created this remarkable building in Hauterives (Drôme) between 1879–1912. 2) Wheelbarrow.

Paris, 4th May 1952

Darling poor old ugly rejected you,

I am sad you did not get the scarf; it was something really special. I'll try to find another one of the same kind. I am not so sad you were rejected by the Fitzgerald girl, because I know you did make her reject you. But very sad for the poor little whore living in a whorehouse, because of the tender love she had for you in her poor little virgin heart. What a piggish pig you are!

There is a story in France nowadays, looking exactly like a Nathanael West[1] story. Did you hear about it? A young lovely girl, seven years ago, walking with dear mother in her pretty little garden, heard a big crash and screams. She rushed out and found an American truck which had collapsed, burning, with an American corporal burning inside; she did what dear mother had taught her a nice girl would do: she took the poor man off. He was lucky, indeed: no wound at all. But *she* was terribly burnt by fire and kind of acids: she lose one hand, had the other paralysed. A year later, the nice corporal said "thank you" and went away. And then they had to cut her leg; she became ugly, sad, and poor because of all the money she had to pay to survive. Now she is dying with burnt lungs. The story was told to Truman, who thought it was a very nice one. Do you? We had another heroine. In Menton, a lovely little town on the Blue Coast, it rained so hard that a stream became huge, the mountain crumbled down, and people died beneath their collapsed houses. A young girl saw two children nearly drowned in this stream. She rushed to them and took them in her house, but then the stream got her, and lot of people, a good gendarme tried to rescue her and could not. She went down beneath a long tunnel into the sea where an American boat fished her out. But she had so much sand and mud in her lungs that she died. So, you have to understand (if you want to live a long and happy life) never to take anybody out of fire or water. I understand very well.

464

I do like *African Queen*² very much, maybe because it is a middle-aged peo-ple love story. In my idea their first kiss is very moving, much more sexual than sentimental, but with feeling coming out from sex. K. Hepburn is won-derful, and though he is good, too, she deserved the reward more than him. I saw an old Hitchcock, *Vanishing Lady*, and a good French movie, *Casque d'or*.³ And a rather strange Japanese one, *Rashomon*,⁴ which I feel you would like. I saw some movies because Bost and Olga were having a trip in my car these two last weeks; it gave me some free evenings which I enjoyed. Paris is warm and romantic now. In a way it is stupid to go away again.

I should tell you a little more clearly about my going around. I had a very good time in Saint-Tropez, working hard as always and climbing up mountains with my new love, which is not so brand-new now: rather dusty and a little hurt, because I don't know very well how to ride backward and, bang, I crash into a tree or a wall . . . very delicately. Anyhow, we had a good time together in this beautiful country with all flowering almond-trees. I came back to Paris partly alone, partly with Bost who came by train to meet me. I was happy he did, because the roads were crowded with cars, it was Easter eve, Easter day, and insurance companies had foreseen sixty people were going to die on the roads—I did not want to be among them. In fact, there were only fifty-eight people killed—a general disappoint-ment. Well, I spent three weeks in Paris, and tomorrow morning I go away again—first with Bost alone, then Bost and Olga, then Sartre—all around France and Italy. I hope I'll work a little, but chiefly I enjoy the idea of dri-ving around and seeing things.

Ellen Wright really got money for me with this Sade business. It hap-pened we talked about you; it always happen with her because *she* talks about you. No kidding, I think she got a romantic womanly feeling for you; she speaks in a dreamy, regretful way of what a great writer and a nice man you are; she asks reproachfully why you don't come here. Dick is working hard now, somewhere in a small house in London suburbs; he never lets alone for one minute his book-script—when he goes down to phone, he takes it with him, when he goes to London for a lunch, he takes it beneath his arm, and during the lunch if he goes to the man's room, he takes it with him too. It seemed very funny to her; so it does to me. The more and more I live on, the more it seems to me there is only one sane person on earth: meaning me.

Is the last Mary Mac Carthy's novel, *The Groves of Academe*, any good? I heard it was, but I doubt it. And everybody says Ralph Ellison's book⁵ is

the best one ever written by a colored man, is it true? Sartre goes on translating the Chicago book. I did not hear about *Golden Arm*; you should ask
through your agent once more. What happens with the scenical adaptation, will you get money? Will it be good? How are things about it?

Yesterday I saw a preview of *The Respectful Prostitute*—more than
half is done. It will be a rather good movie after all, looking very American, strangely. The girl is lovely. I doubt you'll see it in the States. It is a
pity. I should have liked to know what you thought. There was a question
that Orson Welles would get the part of the senator, but he said he would
do it only if there was a new scene inserted: a speech of the state governor
(Georgia or South Carolina) explaining how Negroes were respected and
liked in America, and if ever one of them was lynched, all the mob was put
into jail and harshly punished. He wanted too a little speech in the beginning saying the story did not happen in any peculiar country! So there
was no question having Orson Welles in the movie. What a stupid conceited pig he is!

So the little house is peaceful again? It must be nice now spring has
come and all the birds have meetings again on the grass, I guess. Give them
my best regards, but keep for yourself the love of

Your own Simone

1) Author of *Miss Lonelyhearts* and *Day of the Locust*. 2) By John Huston (1952), with Humphrey
Bogart and Katherine Hepburn. 3) By Jacques Becker (1952). 4) By Akira Kurosawa (1950). 5) *The
Invisible Man.*

Paris, 2nd July 1952

Darling you,

It is too hot to write, much too hot. I can hardly keep the fountain-pen in
my sweating hand, and I have nothing but hot bubbles in my head. That is
my punishment for not having written when days were nice and cool, I
have to write to you now. Yet I have. First, because I want your next letter;
then, because I got this morning a nice card from Japan,[1] where you seem
to have a wonderful trip; and because you sent a very interesting heap of
jail letters.[2] And chiefly because such a nice man deserves here and there
a little Parisian letter. But what can I write when I am half dead!

Well, it seems I was lazy about writing for no peculiar reason. I had
some nice days in Italy, saw my sister in Milano, and came back here three

weeks ago. I gave my car to a big garage, so they wash and cure her; she began feeling sick — her tyres were utterly dead, one of them just burst out. So I had an entirely loveless life, being far away from the only car I love. And began to work and work again about this endless book. At least one year more is needed to achieve it, and what a huge monster it will be!

I saw few people. Darina Silone is going first to Williamsburg, poor woman, and then to Columbia University, New York; if she has a chance to go to Chicago, she certainly will go and kiss you. She had been so scared by the American consulate in Paris, it reminded her so much of fascistic Italy, I had to tell her all Americans in the States were not FBI agents or State Department employees, but I am not sure she did believe me. Ellen Wright doesn't think Dick's new book [3] is good at all; he wrote it in three months, and from she says, seem rather pretentious and over-intellectual. She goes on working earnestly as an agent. It is Grove Press that will publish my booklet about Sade; I don't know when, though I already got the money. I began reading Ellison's *Invisible Man*. I don't like it and I don't think you would. To please you, I rejected a short story by Paul Bowles [4] who wanted to have it published in *Temps modernes*; incidently, it was very bad.

A lot of important things happened in Paris, just when I was coming back. I guess you heard about them. I suppose they are pleased in the *Chicago Tribune* about Duclos being put in jail and the working people not going on strike about that. [5] It does not mean they are less communist than they were, but they are fed up with useless strikes, and they did not love Duclos as they loved Thorez. The whole thing was not cleverly done by the CP. All the right-wing people were pleased; they are more disgusting than ever, so that we — in *Temps modernes* — are coming closer to the communists than we ever did, not liking them, indeed, but believing we must be with them against the others.

The thrilling little "respectueuse" story is really thrilling: I am curious to know what happened next. In my idea, the brave, deep-hearted hero should marry the heroine; they would get a lot of little whorish girls and little pimped boys; the hero would have much money and honour in his old days, surrounded by lovely whorish whores and pimpish pimps who would call him "Daddy!" Tell her if she is interested in hair do that I changed mine. I put my poor hair on the back of my head and no longer on the top; everybody says it is much better. I don't think it makes any difference.

Yea, I really enjoyed your Florida friend letters — an interesting man. Bost and Olga are translated him. What about money? I guess he needs it, but it makes a few dollars. Shall I give the whole payment to Olga and Bost? Or send half to your friend? Tell me. Anyhow, he will be very carefully translated. He knows how to write and he knows something about books, though he sometimes overestimates people. What does he think you are? Have you some picture of him? In fact these letters made you strangely present, more than your own letters, lively as they are. It seemed to me I was reading them in the Patterson Island house and we were about to discuss them together, drinking scotch in the living-room; it gave me a little pang in the heart. I had rather forgotten this kind of pangs, though I'll never forget you. Rather, I *remember* you now — I mean, you begin to belong to remembered life rather than to living life. Maybe it is why I don't feel so much like writing: you don't write to a memory. Yet, I'll write again and again because I like so much to get your letters.

Tell me about your speech in Missouri: did they wish to lynch you as in Chicago, that day? I heard it is terribly hot in Chicago, too. Did you swim? Did you sleep in the deep freezer?

It seems to me I put my love for you in a deep, deep freezer, and it will never get out of it, but never get rotten or dead, neither. And I'll live with this useless deep frozen love, which is no trouble at all anyhow.

Good bye, my deep frozen old love. Don't get killed by heat or anything.

Your own Simone

1) As a joke, Algren sent a postcard of a Japanese temple from Missouri. 2) A reference to letters from Jim Blake, being held in a forced labor camp in Florida. 3) *The Outsider.* 4) Author of *The Sheltering Sky.* 5) Jacques Duclos, head of the French Communist Party during the Occupation.

Italie, 3rd August 1952

Darling you,

Thanks for sending the Missouri lecture. I guess people half liked it, the way things are now in the States, but it is a really good, bold thing you did, speaking as you spoke. I should like very much to have it in *Temps modernes* — the only point is that, as usual, nobody seem to be able to translate it. I asked Scipion, I asked other people, and all what they answer is: "Oh! Algren! That is impossible!" Thanks too for all the interesting things you say about Blake. He sent me a nice letter, and I'll answer through you, one of these days. I manage to have forty or fifty dollars sent to him; it will not be very easy but I want him to get them since he needs and deserves them. Yes, Olga kept carefully the original letters. I'll send them back as soon as I come back to Paris; I rather do it myself than let her do it; it is much safer.[1]

So, no more little whore, no Japanese girl, no Barbara! You have to find an utterly new stock of women, it seems to me. I am writing from a little Italian town. I left Paris some days ago, a bit scared because I left alone in my car, with a real long way to ride. Sartre was going by train and meeting me in Milano. I left in the late afternoon, Wednesday, and drove the whole day after, and Friday morning. Happily, I had picked in Switzerland two English girls, lesbian I guess, travelling together by hitch-hiking from London to Yugoslavia; I drove them unto Milano. I nearly killed all of us on a rainy slipping road near a big lake. I said to one of the girls: "I must be slow, it is a dangerous road." And two minutes later, the car just slided away, utterly out of control, and crashed against a milestone which was taken out from the ground, and then against a wall. The stone saved our lives, the crash was not harsh, the car not even damaged. I felt proud having my first accident, and no danger of any kind. Yet, when I met Sartre in Milano, I was a little out of control myself. The idea is going from north to south of Italia, and in Sicily, for two months, seeing little towns and nice landscapes, and working on about *your* book, so it is done within six months or something like it. It begins to take shape, and even to get near the end, you know. But when will you read it? Since it will have to be translated, and all that.

Well, Nelson, you know the most incredible things happen: so, it happened to me that somebody wants to love me. It makes me half happy, half sad — happy because it is hard to be unloved, and sad because I did not want to be loved by anybody else. He is a young, twenty-seven years old, Jewish boy with black hair and blue eyes, whom I saw in *T.M.* working-meetings and liked; I knew he considered stupidly I was "beautiful," the secretary told me that in the beginning of the year, and I thought they were kidding, but noticed the boy always looked at me in a very nice way. I was fond of him, though we never talked a single personal word. A week ago, Bost and Cau were flying away to Brazil, to write a guide book; they are paid for it and wonderfully pleased with the trip. We had a little farewell party at Olga's place, with good scotch, and I asked for this young man to be invited. He was a little drunk. I spoke nicely to him, but as I spoke to Scipion, for instance. He looked at me the whole evening, and next morning he phoned: "Can I take you to a movie?" It meant plainly:

"Can I sleep with you?" I said I was going away, had no time, but he seemed so disappointed, I said I should have a drink with him. Strange thing: when I came back to my room, after answering his call, I just burst out crying, as I did not cry since leaving you. I cried because somebody wanted to love me and he was not you. If I accepted, it meant another farewell to you, and yet it seemed sweet to be loved again, even not by you. Well, we talked on whole afternoon, and then another one, and then he came home and spent the night there, and came another time, the day I was leaving for Italy. I am fond of him; we are going to have a real affair in October, and it seems strange, because utterly and sincerely I had accepted now to live an old woman loveless life. He believes I am still young and he loves me. It seems strange, too, to write that to you. I write as I should to a friend, since friendship is all which you accept from me. But you never have been nor will be exactly a friend for me: I loved you too much. Nobody will ever be what you have been for me, but nobody can help that past is past, and if you are a living being, in spite of all, you cannot stay in the past. So, nothing is changed in the past, but I shall not cling to the past as stubbornly as I did.

Good bye, honey. It seems to me I cannot pretend to be your own any longer, though I keep the same tenderness for you in my heart. Do write poste restante Bari, Italy.

I kiss you lovingly. Simone

1) Blake's letters appeared in the August 1952 issue of *Les Temps modernes* as "Letters from an American Prisoner."

Sur deux cartes postales du Cimetière des Capucins
Rome, Août 1952

Darling you,

Is not that nice? We did not see it when we were in Roma and it is a pity. It is *real human bones*, you know, some monks made up the whole crazy thing, two centuries ago. The nice designs in the ceiling are bones, too; they made a *clock* with bones and a lot of other things you cannot see on the pictures: five chapels like this. Do you like it?

I am in the hotel Minerva. How should not I think of you? You did not like Roma very much, but you were not cross more than one time, and all the time very sweet. Yes, now, it is done; I *remember* you, and you are a most precious memory. You remember the big storm? We were in a cab and the town was deserted, the rain pouring in the streets. I walk in Roma tonight, lonely, the heart full of this past.

Remember you are bones and will be bones again; try to live for a decent death.

I do kiss tenderly your living face.

Simone

3rd October 1952

Dearest you,

I was very disappointed when I only got once more Blake's letters and not a word from you. I guess some letter has been lost; the fact is I did not hear from you since I left Paris, more than two months ago. I don't know what you think about the way I deserted my poor she-car for a young blue eyed, dark haired boy, neither what you thought about the monks' bones; nothing about you, the lake, the house, the birds, anything. I hope you'll write very soon. I wait for a letter before sending a real long one.

Here I am, back in La Bûcherie brothel. I drove from Napoli to Roma, from Roma to Milano, and saw interesting things on the way, especially Etruscan graves, six centuries before J.C., with very crude paintings in gay colors, showing a man sleeping with another. I said in a silly way (it was pretty dark): "What is that? Man and woman?" and the guide sternly: "No, madame, two men." Genet would have enjoyed it.

In Milano I stayed four days with my sister and her husband, very tedious. I was car-lazy and I came back by train last night; the brother-in-law will drive the car back. In Paris I found a lot of amusing letters. Bost and Cau had hard time in Brazil, chiefly Cau, utterly terrified by Brazilian airplanes — not being quite a hero as somebody I know. So terrified he *pretended* a burglar had stolen his plane tickets and his money; he played very well a real burglar's act, Bost says, but it was obvious there was no other burglar except him. So he stayed in Rio, and Bost went alone in north and south of Brazil. The funny thing is Cau did not dare to say he was that afraid; he had to build all this complicated story.

Is it true Hemingway's last book is that good? From what I hear it seems so, but you never can tell until Nelson Algren has told the true truth.

Blake's letters interested everybody. I'll manage to have money sent to him, though he lets Olga and Bost have it; he needs it more than they do.

The new ones are not so much interesting, because the circumstances are not so thrilling. I don't think we'll use them. If you wrote some letter which was lost, tell again the most important things.

I dreamt of you one of these last nights. I told you I should be burried with your ring at my finger, which I intend to do. Your ring at my finger and your face in my heart as long as I live.

Simone

Monday, 13th Octobre 1952

Dearest sitting and brooding local beast,[1]

I got *The Nation*, the new letters from Blake, this pleasant interview and nice pictures of lovely you, and a real letter, at last! You answered all my questions, even some I did not asked. You ask about "your" book, honey: It comes to an end, at last; it is a very thick novel and there is only a part of it about lovely you. I already told you what it is all about: the hopes and disappointments, friendship, love and quarrels among some French writers from 1944 to 1948, their relationship with politics in general, and the c p. peculiarly, their nowadays problem about writing. I put a lot of things in it, travels, drunken evenings, young and mature people, some of Koestler, Camus and Sartre, and myself, indeed. Only Sartre read it; he says now it is all right, it is the best I did — I hope so. Maybe within three months I give it to Gallimard. But when will the beasty beast Knopf have it translated?

Did I tell you Bost and Cau were nearly killed? Two motors stopped when they left Lisboa; luckily, they were already high in the sky, yet not too far from the airport! But they were delayed for two days. Olga was mad with fear the first night, and this girl is that crazy: she did not think of phoning to the airport; I had to do it for her when I knew she was mad with fear. Bost and the secretary are utterly disgusted with Brazil, though they enjoyed themselves immensely. They hope to go to India now.

The Respectful Prostitute got a prize for music in Venice. American people were mad at it and did not shake hand with the director neither the actors.Now it is a big success in Paris. It rings much truer that the play, but I don't think you'll ever see it in the States. Communist people gave very good reports about the movie; in general way they are in a good relationship with Sartre, now. After the disgusting affair of 28th May, when Duclos was arrested, Sartre spoke for the CP in *Temps modernes*, that is why mister Mauriac called him a "rat visqueux." Communists invite him in meetings, the idea is to work together, but when he sees communists people, he does not feel so happy neither. It is better not to see them if you have to speak for them.

Did you hear about the big affair of Marty and Tillon being excluded from the Party? A very dark story, nobody knows exactly why it happened, but anti-communist people are very happy about it, indeed. And many communists, too, because Marty was crazy. He is the one Hemingway described under the name of Massart in *For Whom the Bell Tolls*.

How is the stupid newspaper man says you are *not impressive*, and the little home is *nearly plain*? He does not know nothing, this guy. You tried to look impressive on one of the pictures, not on the other, indeed.

It seems a good idea to marry Amanda again since you get along nicely; it is a bit lonely this Patterson Island nest. In past times, you said you wanted children; I guess you would be a moody father sometimes, but a very nice one on the whole.

You know what is really sad, Nelson, and why it always is a narrow escape if I don't cry when you come real as your letter made you? It is not that love is more or less dead in the end, it is that, keeping in our hearts so much tenderness for each other, we cannot have a happy daily friendship. We are living so far from each other that maybe I'll never see you again. You are very stubborn with not coming to France, I have no reason at all for coming to the States. That does not seems fair for us, because when love dies in this tender friendly way, so much is left which should be enjoyed. Yea, that is what I cannot stand without tears when I think of it: we are almost lost for each other, being so far away. But I told you last week, I'll be burried with your ring on my finger, and as long as I live, I'll never be utterly lost for you, you'll be evicted form my heart, never. Yea, I remember when I left, and when I came, and everything we lived. It was a nice indian summer, last year. I kiss you lovingly.

Your never quite lost Simone

1) A reference to the title of a long article on Algren he'd sent to de Beauvoir: "The Writer Nelson Algren: Sitting and Chewing His Cud."

Dearest you,

It would be nice to see you one of these mornings grinning in the middle of place Saint-Germain-des-Prés. Why don't you come to Paris with Amanda as a honeymoon trip? I am sure she would enjoy it and we should get along nicely together, I feel. Think of it.

I sent back Blake's letters and managed so that he'll get forty dollars through you; it will need some time, because sending money to USA is always a job, but I'll get it. Tell me if he does not. I enclose the speech.[1] The problem with you is that you are nearly impossible to translate in French: *Chicago* will be ready "very soon," but when we asked Boris how it is with *Golden Arm*, he answers always, this year as last year, he translated 150 pages, no more, no less. So, we just wait. He is divorced, by the way. How with my *The Second Sex* translation? You sent a clipping which tried to say how good it is, but was the book published? I knew that Edmund Wilson was supposed to be a clever critic, but I did not know that he really was. Now I am sure since he says my paper about Sade is the best he knew. Do you like Sade, honey? You were amused, in good past times, when I told you Albert Schweitzer and Sartre were very near cousins; so you would have enjoyed the idea of them having a lunch together, at Sartre's, with Mrs. Sartre mother. All the newspaper people were quite excited about it,[2] they knocked at the door during the lunch a lot of times, asking for pictures and the "menu." Schweitzer kept on calling Sartre "dear cousin," he was friendly. Sartre liked him. In the end, the old man said in a rather unexpected way: "After all, we are looking exactly for the same things, through different paths…" I saw a nice movie, something I guess you'll really like: *Jeux interdits;*[3] Bost's brother wrote the dialogue. About French peasants in 1940; it gives a good idea of their way of living, and there is the most wonderful little girl you, or anybody, ever saw—not an actress, a real little girl who cries and laughs just as in real life; I was told she did not make exactly the difference. I am not crazy about children but you have to see the movie, for her sake if for nothing else. My sister and brother-in-law came here tonight. She painted pictures for *She Came to Stay*, had an exhibition of them, but quite unsuccessful. In fact, what she does seem worse and worse every year, and there is no way of stopping this going down; it is really wrong now and she never was very high.

Sartre met Janet Flanner some days ago. She was nice but very much disturbed about USA and all this business of "un-American activities." A woman has been accused and they kept against her the fact that she slept with her husband before marrying him; she was never heard giving any anti-communist speech. Flanner was a witness for her, and for an another woman in Germany, who was reproached for having said in 1943: "So, now we are allied to USSR." "Why did you say so?" "Well, we *were* allied to USSR, were we not?" "Yes, but why did you *say* so, what did you mean?" "Just what I said." Then the man, in a threatening voice turned to the secretary: "Write that, she meant *just* what she said." Does not it seem crazy?

Did I thank you for *The Nation*? Very interesting. Guyonnet makes a summary of it for the next issue of *Temps modernes*. When you see interesting stuff for us, do send it, please. And go on telling me anything about the house and you. I shall not worry any more, since it is forbidden and I never do forbidden things, even going to the Tip-top-tap...Very tenderly,

Simone

Everybody here is anxious to know who is the winner of your elections. We are dying with fear it is the general.[4]

1) A speech in which Stevenson announced his candidacy for the presidency. 2) Albert Schweitzer received the Nobel Peace Prize that year. 3) By René Clément (1951), with Brigitte Fossey. 4) Eisenhower.

9th December 1952

Nelson, darling,

I got the long letter, and then the small one, with the little token of the far-away beach and good past times love—thanks, honey. I send you a kind of token, too, though not small as you'll see in a few days (I guess it will come after this letter).[1] It seems a sweet idea, coming to Paris this summer! Does Amanda agree?

It is a terrible winter, It already was, while you were telling me about the sunny beach in the warm indian summer. The whole month was awfully cold; we got snow, and now something of the awful fog covering London; it's misty and dark, and rather sad in Paris.

I saw *Los Olvidados* long ago and spoke to you about it, it seems to me. I liked the picture, hard as Mexico itself, and I remembered now we loitered around in the slum district. I should like to see it again. Yes, it hits. What did you think about *Limelight*?[2] First, did you see it? There were big quarrels here; we divided in two sects, for and against *Limelight*, and there was a hard hatred from one side to the other. I was for, Sartre against, Cau for, Bost against. Yes, it is too sweet, Calvero too good and speaking too much, but this man has a wonderful face and he gives a lot of non-conventional meaning to things which look conventional. And the girl is lovely...well, what do you think? A "big" thing happened, though I had no part in it: the secretary played a funny little trick to Sartre, pretending Charlie Chaplin had invited him, and saying to Chaplin that Sartre invited him, and in the end they had dinner with the secretary, Guyonnet, Bost, Olga, and Picasso. Everybody was delighted with Chaplin. He explained he would not come back to the States, since Eisenhower had been elected; He told a lot of stories, was so good-natured and friendly and pleasant that even Sartre, who is hard to make, was fond of him. Picasso was angry the whole time, because he is used to be the first one everywhere he goes, and he was nothing at all this time, everybody interested only in Chaplin. They all drunk much. Oona, Chaplin's wife, did not speak a word; it seems she never does. If Chaplin lives in London and comes often to Paris, we'll surely see him again and show him something of Paris. I should enjoy it, because when I saw him in New York, the party was rather formal and it was not so pleasant. I did not go to this dinner because my new friend was just coming back from Israel this very evening, a month ago, and we had much to say to each other. I only had seen him alone three times before summer, and then we spent three months far away. We get along very well, though he is so much younger than me. He is one of these Jewish Jews for whom it means something to be Jewish; I mean, he feels really apart from the others, and the whole family, though not religious at all, feels apart too. Chiefly, coming back from Israel, he resented deeply the anti-Semitic jokes people do here more and more. He tells a lot of interesting stories: in Israel there is a racial discrimination among "black" and "white" Jews, the "black" ones being the North African ones, those we saw in Medenine for instance, and the "white" being the German, Polish, Russian Jews. These last ones are wealthy and honoured, the first ones are poor and despised. Well, it is a long and complex story; he'll write a book about it. If you do come to Paris, I'll have you meet him, and I am sure you'll be much interested.

I was deeply interested by what you said about the elections. No, I did not know Stevenson was that good; the sentences about God and all that

476

in the speech sounded silly, but I guess it was only what you call "lip-service," and what he really meant was different. Yes, it made everybody who likes something of America sad, here. And since you wrote, now things do go on! The fantastic story about FBI working in the ONU, the UNESCO accepting Franco, ridiculous movies like the *The Spy*[3] with Ray Milland, and the terrible Rosenberg affair.[4] How sad this last thing! Sartre and a lot of others had a meeting for them, sent letters to Truman, and so on; all left wing French papers are full of that, but it is useless, it seem. The situation in the Party is not very happy neither, here. These ejections, these trials makes it difficult to be heartly with them. Yet, Sartre thinks that now we all must try to work hand in hand; he is going to Vienna for the Peace Congress. He asked me to invite you, but I knew it was too far for you to go, too difficult and maybe impossible. No American left wing man will go, because they cannot, and not many no communist French people, neither. So it will remain a communist meeting instead of what it should be: a big meeting of all people who want peace and real freedom. Sartre works alot in politics; he does not like it, but his reward is that he wrote about "Communists and Peace," one of the best things he ever wrote in his life. He was asked by *Look* to give a declaration about his actual political standing. He said yes and only asked a written promise they would print exactly what he would say, and they could not make an insulting paper about him as an introduction: such conditions were not possible, they said, so he did not give them the interview.

I did not write for a long time, because my life was a little difficult to settle with this new boy in it, your book to achieve, the old friends to keep, and I had to time for sleeping or eating or anything. I was a little dizzy the whole month, and even my poor car did not see me more than twice. But it will be different now, I hope. As soon as you write, I answer. You have surely lot of things to tell me, since my silence made you silent too for long.

The little token was a "little" token, but I kept preciously this dust from a faraway beach which will never be stolen from my heart. Bring me some others in your own hands. I do hope so much to see you again. Nelson, whom I loved so much. Tell me about you. Good bye, honey, and lovingly.

Simone

1) The American edition of *The Second Sex*. 2) Charlie Chaplin. 3) By Russel Rouse (1952). 4) Julius and Ethel Rosenberg, accused of leaking atomic weapons information to the Soviet Union, were sentenced to death in 1951. Despite an international campaign to save them, they were executed in 1953.

1953

✻ *On January 4, pleased at Simone de Beauvoir's invitation and thrilled at*
the prospect of seeing friends from 1949 again, Algren decided to go back to
France with Amanda. They had tickets for the March 24 sailing of the Liberty *and planned to stay in Europe for six months. Algren waited impa-*
tiently for his passport. February came and went. Then a profound, bitter
disappointment: on March 10, the State Department rejected his request "in
light of his former connection to the Communist Party." During the Spanish
Civil War, he had worked for the Lincoln Brigade, and since then had
worked with a dozen publications linked with the Communist Party. The
Liberty *left without him. It would be another seven years—and he had no*
idea, in 1953, that it would be this long—before he returned to France.

In March, he remarried Amanda. This triggered a long period of
depression. The preceding October, two days after his engagement to
Amanda, he had fallen passionately in love with a young woman; she
wanted to marry him, but it was too late, as he had just gotten engaged.
They continued to write each other, until she announced she was marrying
a wealthy Arizonan. Algren insisted that he could not live without her. In
May and June, trying to get over his depression, he wrote long letters to de
Beauvoir: had he been right to sacrifice everything for his writing? He tor-
tured himself with memories of the lost magic of Wabansia, of rue de la
Bûcherie, of their not-so-distant past, assuring her that his feelings for her
were still unique and everlasting.

Saint-Tropez, Avril 1953

Nelson, dearest,

Your letters made me very sad. The first one because you don't think
you'll be able to come to Paris, even later on. The second one because of
the terrible pangs you get. I wish so deeply to see you, speak with you,
give you all that is and always will be in my heart for you! How sad you
could not come. I am sure the warm friendship of your friends, and mine
—which is more than that—would have helped. You know what I hope,

honey, from my selfish point of view? Maybe with this big political change in Soviet politics,[1] a change will come in USA politics, too, and that Iron Curtain will be lifted. Don't you think it is possible? I do. So maybe within a year you'll see your French friends again. I don't expect to come to New York—no, I should not have any visa now, for sure, and I don't feel like asking for it. Anyhow, lot of things make it difficult; it would be so much better if you would come.

Your second letter leaves me rather speechless. I am deeply grateful you sent it. I don't especially like collecting pangs, but *your* pangs are very important to me, and it means much to me that you chose to report them to me. I know you had some about me, and I some about you, too, which I'll never forget. And any pang of yours gives me as an echo a slight pang, too, because you'll always stay so near my heart. I should like to be your pang-collector all out life long. But it does not help you, I cannot help you, nobody can. It is a sad story. I am sure you were wrong by acting as you did; I feel rather you were right, but I understand the suffering you speak about, I understand very well. Well, as you can do nothing about it now, please, try not to make other people suffer by it: it would make the whole story too stupid. As I know you, I am afraid you'll make it bad for everybody: tell me you did not. Now you have began to report, honey, you have to go on. Tell me even about the whole affair if you feel like it. I am so much concerned by all what happens to you. But, indeed, if you don't feel it, don't say a thing. Thanks for the picture, you look like yourself, thanks for Blake's letters, and "la folle's" and crazy people's. Thanks for the clippings, for *The Nation*. What a nice man you are! You should be happy, surely you will.

Reading again your first letter: I don't think Wright's book is good. They like it because it is against communism, and everything. Being against everything is helping the right side, is it not? I am afraid it tries to be thoughtful and fails to be good. I get several letters from USA about my *Second Sex*, most of them were nice. But on Chicago man sent me at the Deux Magots a little parcel, a very little one. I opened it: paper, paper, and paper. And in the bottom, some "laxative pills to help evacuation of bile" or something like that. How witty! Certainly not Wabansia wit, maybe Michigan Avenue wit? Did I tell you a Hollywood guy wanted to have a movie made from the book? It sounds slightly crazy, even if you did not read the book, no?

I am on the Blue Coast. I'll be back Paris within ten days (write here); the Blue Coast was not so blue, rather windy and rainy through pretty country roads. Sartre and I often speak friendly about you, and sadly because you don't come, but saddest of all, Olga keeps saying you are the most poetical man she ever met. She stayed in Paris, and Bost in their little house in Cabris (you remember?) began writing a novel he deeply wanted to do. Then he was asked to come back to work on a movie script—a stupid thing but he was offered a lot of money and had to say yes. But at once he got sick, a real liver sickness which prevented him from working for three weeks; he knew it was a psychic trick, a sickness forged from anger, but he could not recover before a long time. Now he is right again and sadly make money.

There is a movie festival in Cannes. I saw Orson Welles and E. G. Robinson in saint-Tropez today, lot of beautiful girls and strange men. I guess you are right about Chaplin, though I am sentimental about him. Sartre and all sensible people feel the way you feel. I suppose was not sensible the day I saw the movie.

Work and work. A long, hard book, but it comes to an end. Knopf asked it, so you'll have to read it within one or two years. I should like you to like it since it is "your" book.

Honey, do speak to me about you. I have no pangs in my own life now, things are very smooth, so it gives me a guilty feeling when you have pangs; and that gives me pangs. But do speak to me. I want to sleep in tomb with you, and let us hope we'll soon drink scotch together! My heart is full of you, Nelson. I have a good memory, you know, and a faithful heart.

Your Simone

1) Stalin died in March.

May 2, 3, 4, 5, 6, 7, 8, 9, 10, 11, 12, 13, 14, 15, 16...1953

Dearest Nelson,

I am glad the sky is back in place after all. Since I am your pang collector, I have thought much about this affair of yours, and I am really convinced you did not lose. Well, the best thing indeed would have been to live the story unto its natural end, I mean the end of your own feelings, because I feel sure they would have came to an end within a year, maybe, or two, since the girl was not exactly who you thought she was. It would have been the best thing if you had been allowed to say good bye when love was over. But what if you have been tied with wife, children, duties? And probably without the friendship and esteem you have for Amanda. Seeing things from far away, it seems clear you made the good choice. The pangs and feeling of loss don't mean so much; they only mean you had to cut in unnatural way the feelings because they were not dead inside yourself. And now it will be difficult for them to die, since they will stay a thing of the past, a thing that has not been lived to the end. I guess you'll keep the idea of a loss, and a longing for the past for a long time — maybe a longer time than love would have stayed in your heart if it had accomplished itself. Try to think it in that view, too; it is true though maybe not kind. Proust whom you don't like said wonderful things about this dependence on somebody who is not here, when you are no longer dependent when she is here. So instead of saying " I did not know that I had become dependant upon her until she was not there," maybe you should say "I should never have become dependent upon her if she had stayed there." Things don't seem that senseless in this view. Anyhow, darling you, I am sure you'll not going to have colorless, loveless life, you'll have "things that come for a moment and go," you'll have them, it is in you to get them. Don't believe everything is over; it cannot be so.

Do go and see *Le Salaire de la peur*. There are hateful, ridiculous thing in it, and bad taste and bad psychology, but the travel of the trucks with the nitro on the terrible roads is something to see. It seems to be a little better for the Rosenberg, is it not? Maybe they will not be killed after all. What do you think? I still do hope things will get better, and we'll drink scotch in Paris next winter or spring, before twelve years...[1]

I got a lot of nice letters for American women and men, too, sometimes about the *The Second Sex*. One of them told me there was a discussion about it on the T.V.: did you see it, lazy man who did not even read it? I feel you'll never be sure I really did write it. Well, I am sending you my essay about Sade, which was written in Forrest Avenue nest,[2] for a big part; there are excerpts of Sade himself and the book is nice to see.

Bost was very proud yesterday, because he fought with a man who was not a cripple. I promised to him I would report that to you immediately. He was in some of these crazy places, in Saint-Germain-des-Prés, drinking scotch at 2 A.M. with Cau and Olga, when two middle-aged men stopped in front of the table and sneered at Olga for too long time. Then Bost just sent his scotch to the face of them. One of them hit Bost in answer; Bost's nose began to bleed on his brand-new suit, He jumped across the table and tried to hit back the man, and Cau jumped, came behind the man, held him tightly, and said to Bost: "Hit him!" But Bost could not hit a paralysed guy, so he waited until he was loose again, and then there was a regular fight. People came to prevent Bost from fighting, and five of them sent him to the ground and kicked him. Olga jumped and kicked them, and pulled away a big lock of hair from one of them. And it ended, indeed, because it had to end, but Bost doesn't feel he hit back enough; he hopes to make up for it another day.

Paris is warm and sunny; within two weeks I'll go for a long trip in my car, in Switzerland and north of Italy. But do write Rue de la Bûcherie; the good concierge will take care. There are always terrible fights in this street; the other day it was like in your short story "Too much salt in the pretzels," they began to fight, nearly to death—one was on the ground and the other kicked him terribly: people around just looking and the café owner closing when everything was over.

Send me your new writing when it is finished.3 Maybe it will not be too difficult to translate and we can have it in *Temps modernes*. If you write back within ten days, I should get it before going away. Sartre sends best regards, and so do Olga and Bost. I kiss you from my faithful heart.

Simone

1) With an odd prescience, Algren had predicted that after the Korean War (1950-1953), he would sink into a depression lasting ten or twelve years, at which time another war would break out. And it did: the Vietnam War, 1962-1975. 2) During her stay in 1951. See *Letters to Sartre* (September and October 1951). 3) An anti-McCarthy essay.

Hotel Luna, Venezia, 21 June 1953

Dearest Nelson,

It is a long time I did not write, because since three weeks I am wandering through Switzerland and Italy, and always so busy or so tired I cannot write anything, even a letter. Well, in Venezia I take some rest, the first thing I do write to you. I came here with my young friend, and met Sartre who is on a tour, too. We spent some days together, all deeply moved by the Rosenberg affair. I kept thinking of you more and more than ever, knowing you belonged to the committee and were surely upset, though I wonder if you ever hoped anything, knowing how things are now in this country. We hoped, the last day, when Douglas had the killing postponed, and it seemed possible the Supreme Court could be ashamed. The next morning at paintings, or anything. We read the paper, and Sartre wrote a very good article for a Parisian daily. In Paris it made a tremendous noise, this killing, people threatened the American embassy and shouted in the streets; in many Italian towns, it was very noisy, too. Here in Venezia, it seems a little dead; we felt impatient reading papers and being able to do nothing. In France and Italy, even right wing people agree on one point: this is the biggest mistake made by USA in the Cold War. Nobody could have done such a propaganda against them as they did themselves, all pro-American French people are terribly embarrassed with this scandal. Gallimard published Rosenberg written in jail letters, and will give the money to the children. Some are moving, chiefly the woman's. Tell me some more about them, if you know some, and about the way they reacted in the States. As I left Paris since so long, I did not get *The Nation*, and your last letter was of middle of May. Do they publish you book about Mac Carthy, after all? Could we have something of it for *Temps modernes*?

I am glad you read *The Second Sex* with such perseverence. My poor translator is dead, do you know that? Dead from a heart attack. I guess he could not stand living when not translating *The Second Sex* any longer, life had lost all meaning for him, so he died.

I did not work since I began wandering on all Swiss and Italian roads, trying to go up, up, up in my little car, sometimes much afraid to go down, down, down. It is impossible to work and travel together, really. But I read a very interesting book you had in Forrest Avenue nest, I don't know if you read it: *The Wall*, by John Hersey. Not utterly good; in my idea, he could have told the story in a more direct way. It lacks some violence, people one by one are not quite convincing, but the whole ghetto crushed and killed little by little. *Murder Incorporated*, which I began, about the racket-killing in USA, seems amusing.

Well, Venezia is a beautiful city. *When* you'll come to Europe, you must go to Venezia; you'll find some magic here. Honey, I am sure you'll find some new magic in your life, one day or another; you don't have to but it form this little man you speak about. I like the story of the senator who spoke for twenty four hours. I like all the things you tell me, tell me more. I have no stories at all, except mountain, landscapes, and that cannot be sent in a letter. Yesterday, I walked on the Lido beach; there were a lot of little shells, and I reminded acutely Michigan beach. I don't need any shell to remind lot of other things. I miss you, too, Nelson. I want deeply to see you again, as soon as possible. Do try something.

As always, from my tender faithful heart.

Your Simone

Nelson, dearest,

I was wandering through Italy, Switzerland, and Yugoslavia—that is why I did not answer your business, your friendly letters, any of your letters which kept waiting for me in the lopsided room and I just found yesterday evening when coming back (my she-car is not brand-new at all after tasting Yugoslavian road). First of all, thanks, thanks for the heap of little tokens, for the book about Dickens which looks interesting, for your paper[1] which I began tomorrow to act like the little picture by Grandma Moses, and the ones with your mother. I cannot say you are really pretty, neither you do look like a first rate brain, but there is something in this man . . .

Friday

Honey, I got your new letter this morning. Well, you know, I don't miss you *too much*, but I do miss you all right. I'll tell you a little secret, just between you and me: when I found your letters Monday, specially the one you say sometimes at morning you feel a kind of death setting in you—death between you and me, far being too far, for too long—it gave me a real pang, not a mere whine, a real pangish pang. And then Olga and Bost were flying away to Roma the next morning, so we went and drank this last Bost night in Paris, and I drank much too much, and suddenly at 2 A.M. the jazz played some American tune we heard together; it gave me such a pang in the heart that I just fainted away for the first time in my life. So, you see, though I fight pangs my helicopter-heart is still deeply bound to you. Nelson, do make money and come to Paris. I cannot think of not seeing you once more. But since you want come, I know you will. I keep waiting for you, and shall wait until you come and drink scotch with me. We have to. I fight the pangs, but I shall no fight joy and happiness when you'll land here. It is a sweet idea, writing some day some book for me.[2] You should do it. I go on writing "yours"; it comes to its end, though it was an hard book to write, the hardest I ever wrote.

Yea, I should like the book of Geismar, and probably use it. I want *Temps Modernes* to make people know here what is or was good in your country. I enjoyed his review about you; he certainly knows something about what is literature. And I enjoyed what you say about Mickey Spillane; I read some books by him, since I like this kind of non-literature, but never should have expected he was a religious man! I liked very much *Somebody in Boots*[3] in spite of its faults. It seems a good idea to remake it now you really know how to write. And I hope you'll get money.

I was much interested by what you say about the Rosenberg. I remember the first time I read about then, in the *Guardian*, sitting in the couch, and you told me things about them. I guess you are all right, yea; it is difficult to confide much in Russia. The Beria business is quite strange.[4] We should like to hope in America, but when I spoke of it you sounded rather hopeless.

The Yugoslavia trip was a very exciting—terribly poor country, but what a difference with South Italy, which I saw last year awfully poor, too! In South Italy nobody has work, all the land belongs to rich faraway owners; you feel disgust and pity in your heart for the hateful way things are. In Yugoslavia nobody is rich, everybody works and hope, they have big schools where all children have to go until sixteen; you feel the struggle of good-willing men against a harsh earth. A difficult struggle, because these peasants, nearly as primitive and ignorant as the indian peasants, have to become industrial workers and mechanics. They have already succeeded in building towns, roads, bridges: the least road, every bridge, is moving, because it is a hard conquest. How far from wealthy Switzerland or even wealthy north Italy! We had to bring oil for the car; they have none, they have nothing to mend a car and nearly anything to eat—that made the trip a little hard, chiefly when it was very hot. That is why I did not stay more than ten days. Beautiful landscapes, some towns, chiefly a Musll one, with mosques and veiled women in large Turkish pants, very interesting, people really lovable. We could speak with them in German, though they hate Germans and so like France.

Now I stay in Paris for a while. The weather is mild, lot of people away. I hope I'll work steadily. I got a letter from Nathalie who seems a little better and wants to become a child psychoanalyst! Strange idea since she understands nobody and cares only for herself.

Honey, be sure everybody here misses you at least twice a year, and I never spend one day without loving thoughts for you. I have kept all our memories and never lose them, never lose you in my heart. There will be no death between you and me.

Your Simone with a faithful heart

Nelson, dearest,

It is a long time since I did not get a letter from Patterson Island, because of this French strike. And I could not write neither these last ten days, but now I left Paris for two months trip with Sartre. I happened to be in Holland, so I can mail a letter to the States. You can answer at once, if you feel like it (I should very much feel like getting news from you), to Trier (poste restante) for 28th August, then to Zurich, about 9th September. The idea is to go down the Rhine, through the German Black Forest, and through Switzerland unto Austria. It is a peaceful trip, not too hot, with much time for working. I have to work, because "your" damned book is not achieved; it still needs three or four months polishing it. But in my case, the polishing makes it bigger and bigger.

Holland looks like a nice American house-wife's dream; it reminds me often of your residential districts. There are wonderful paintings in the museums; two days ago I saw a Van Gogh's exhibition. The last he painted in his life were desperate, landscapes of very simple horror, by a man who is going to commit suicide. A lot of self-portraits, too, very strange the way he saw himself! It tells a lot about the man. Another wonder is Rembrandt, not only a genius as a painter, but you feel the man in his self-portraits, in his last paintings. Some despair, too, though not mad as Van Gogh. Rather a deep, quiet sadness about what the best of men can achieve and cannot, and the drama of old age, threatening death, and nothingness. Well, there are not only paintings here, but many lovable little town and villages, large plains with channels (or canals, I forgot the English name), a pleasant mixture of water and earth, boats in the middle of the fields and houses built on the water. Above all that, pretty wind-mills and delightful sky. Everything is a little too clean, too dainty, too nice. I came with my faithful car; she begins to be a little old, bit like you I am fond of old things. I am fond of this car as you were of old trousers, old shirts with holes, you could not throw any; I had to drown them in the Mississippi in spite of you, remember? So I'll be sad when I'll see this old car to get a new one.

I just finished reading a wonderful book; if translated do read it, though it is so big: a German book, very unpleasant in many ways, but telling a lot about Germany before and during the war. The end of the war, the American occupation, all that, are told in the most interesting way. It is not a novel, but a true report of what happened to a curious, interesting man, Ernst von Salomon, who in past times took part in the murdering of Rathenau.[1] He took a list of questions which every German citizen had to answer by order of the American police: there are 131 of them! So he answered all of them, exhaustively, and managed by this way to tell his while story. The book is called in German *Der Fragebogen*.[2] Look for it.

Well, I have not much to say, I chiefly write to tell you where to write to me,. Though these strikes are not convenient, we are pleased with them; it means stupid reactionary people cannot do exactly what they please in France and the working ones are still able to struggle. No doubt they will win something, and maybe we'll soon have a left wing government, something as the "Front populaire" we had in '36. We do hope.

About *A Walk on the Wild Side* (I like that title, better than the other), I enjoyed much the beginning, and much a lot of things in it. But it seems to me a little—how do you say?—unorganized, made of pieces which do not exactly clutch together. It lacks unity, I think; it goes one way, then another, and sometimes you don't know exactly where you go. It is so *allusive*, too, that it makes it somewhat difficult for French people—to get a quite impartial idea. I am a bit puzzled. Maybe it is too much poetry for this kind of essay? Well, this time, that is all. Tell me everything, as always; it will go deep in my heart, as always. Me, too, I have a lot and a lot of memories; they come back often, at any times, and they are very, dear, important, and sweet.

Good bye, darling, dear you, from my tenderly faithful hart.

Your Simone

1) The German minister of foreign fffairs, assassinated in 1922. 2) Ernst von Salomon, *Le Questionnaire*, Gallimard (1951).

---

31 December 1953

Dearest Nelson,

My last letter has just crossed your last one. You seemed a little angry at me, and, indeed, I feel guilty when you say I am becoming a kind of ghost, but I explained why I don't like so much to write letters now, and it does not mean I have a ghost heart, not at all. I asked a lot of times about Blake being repaid; money had even been sent twice through the exchange office, but twice the exchange office sent it back to Gallimard: it seems difficult to get money out of France as an honest American man out of the

States. I did not read the books you sent, for lack of time. I wait until my damned dirty novel is over, that means two months more.

We have mildest winter ever known in France: Christmas was blue and sunny. We had a little party with Sartre, Olga, Wanda, my friend, and me, indeed. No Bost. Bost is in a strange, faraway African country where Negroes rule everything, owning land, money, and paying the highest prices to get white cooks or servants: it is Liberia. Did you hear about? Men in upper classes live in dark suits and top hats the whole day long though it is as hot as it was Uxmal and even more. In the low classes they live naked, indeed, with the most horrible diseases spoiling their bodies. Lot of German Nazis, S.S., and men like that came to Liberia because they are accepted without papers. They make a living there and get Liberian papers, and then they may go to the States and become honest citizens. Bost and a producer called Ciampi wanted to make a movie about that, so they flied to Liberia in and extra-quick airplane, a Comet. And two weeks went away since then; we got only a wire from Bost saying he is stunned with surprise. He had been said no letters come neither go from and to this country. So we drank champagne and scotch without him, played record, and so on.

I saw some movies. Yesterday, *Little Fugitive* — a very good one, deeply moving, with a wonderful child, not sweet or cute, nothing of the kind, but lovable and true. And you see Coney island at every hour of the day and night, as if you were there. I remembered this hot day when we were there, not a very happy day but so lovely and rich. Go and see it. Scipion makes money, Cau is becoming stupid, little Cassoulet has got a boy-friend — they hardly can sleep together, because they don't like it, and can hardly speak, they are silent people, so they don't know what to do with each other. The singer is married with a young actor and going to be a mother; she makes a lot of money. So does Mouloudji. He owns a wonderful American car and his wife dresses at Dior. But we heard him singing at Bobino the most stupid, unpleasant corny things, he is not half as good as he was. It gave me a real big pang in the heart when seeing New York so well in this movie. I don't want to think I'll never see again New York and Chicago.[1] But it does not seem possible to go, not before years. For your coming, I asked to somebody who knows American important people here, but nobody can do nothing. Honey, you put a question which I ask myself sometimes with a little fear: what when we'll see each other again? It will be strange, certainly. I figure that friendship is not so easy when people loved each other as we did. You live with somebody, and so do I, and I am sure we'll both find that strange. Yet, I am confident it will not be a failure. I'll be too deeply happy to see and hear you again. Anyhow, let us try it as soon as possible; we have little to lose for even a failure would not spoil nothing in our past and between us, and we have much to win. So, please, dearest you, don't be angry at me any longer. be sure I am not a ghost. Do write again. I love letters. I wish you all the happiness you deserve, from a very deep in my heart, I hate when you don't feel happy.[2]

With all my best new-year kisses, honey.

I am your faithful ghost.

Your Simone

1) She visited New York again in 1970 and in 1983, but never went back to Chicago. 2) In his 1953 Christmas letter, Algren had expressed his great dissatisfaction with his life. He was depressed, never satisfied, and felt trapped. In fact, he often signed his letters "the American Prisoner."

1954

17th January, 1954

My poor dearest American dilemma,

Since my last, I got a bright Christmas card, a small letter and a long one, and Sartre a lot red blades. Everybody had a thought for you in one's heart in this beginning year, and first of all, me. What a nice man you are! "Did you get *America Day by Day*?[1] It got a rather funny though unfair review in *Time*. Did you see it? If so, don't believe the ugly picture they give of me. I did not become that ugly since you saw me. I'll send another one, not very good, but nicer, which is to be on the jacket of *She Came to Stay* (going to be published in March). Vian swears half the of *Golden Arm* is already done; he will achieve it within the year. He promised it to Queneau, who is willing to keep the book. I can do nothing about it, you know. I should like so much the book to be published in *T.M.*, but I have no time to translate it myself, so I wait and hope. Yea, let us hope about everything. I hope, and hope, and hope next year will be better year for local youths, for my own local youth. I hope he will get out of his life as much as he wishes, as much as he deserves. And I hope we'll drink some day unprocurable whisky, honey. Be sure, even if I don't write very well, that it will be a great day for me when we drink together again unprocurable whisky.

I agree, as far as I know, with what you say about American literature. The short stories by Truman Capote are skilful, but nothing more. How is it your review about Farrell was so kind? You did not use to like him. Was this book really better, or what? We are going to publish a long paper about Mac Carthy in *Temps modernes*; our *T.M.* go on nicely, though there is so scarcely good French books to take. Sartre's mother had a big T.V. now and though the programmes are so bad, I often have a look at it, and remember. What happened to our little friend, the snake and the witch, and all that? Did they disappear? And the funny woman of Saturday show?

Stepha and Fernand Gerassi's daughter-in-law has just come to Paris: she is nineteen and Tito she married last year is twenty two. I was pleased to see her. She is an American girl, though French by her mother;

490

he goes on having no nationality at all, and it is very hard for him. Stepha is teaching in this liberal school in Putney, Fernand painting, Tito wants to write a thesis about existentialism and plays poker. We spoke about New York, and I felt a sickness for this country of you. that too, I hope: coming again, some day.

Well, the atmosphere is not too bad in Paris. Nobody thinks any longer of an imminent war, people relax; communists are more open-minded and friendship with them comes possible. Sartre is very pleased: he is invited to go to Moscow for a month in May, as a personal guest of Ehrenbourg — funny when you remember how it was between them some four to five years ago. Poor American dilemma! It is unkind to speak to you about other peoples's travel. Why so you say anyway you could not come this year? Even with a passport? Is it a question of money, or what? Tell me, too, what about the book you are rewriting. Are you pleased with the way it turns out?[2]

Good bye, honey. Your last letters made me sad, because you looked so sad your self. But I reproached myself for fearing the sadness I got when I write to you. I do want deeply and strongly you letters, even if they give me pangs in the heart. I want to be forever your pangs-keeper and to take my part of them with you. So do write, please, do write as much as you can. I'll try to help you to hope, and hope for everything. And I'll hope and hope for our meeting again. I kiss you with all my heart.

Your Simone

---

1) The American version. 2) Algren responded bitterly to these questions. He felt he was caught in a double trap: money and marriage. Even if he escaped the first, the second wouldn't disappear on its own. There was little chance of obtaining a passport at this point. Since 1949, he had suffered a serious financial setback every year. He had accepted advances from his publisher for books which had either not been published or, like *Chicago*, had taken a loss. Four years of literary failure had sunk him severely into debt. He could afford to write nothing less than a bestseller. Rewriting *Somebody in Boots* weighed on him; it was a constant burden. He had lost a great deal of money playing poker the summer before. All of this left him with an inevitable sense of his own downfall. Not long before, bright Hollywood promises of financial success had blown up with the Rosenberg trial; aligning himself with them had cost him dearly. His marriage was a total failure. But Amanda clung to him because she was tired of living alone. Algren dreamed of escaping the dull routine of married life, and fleeing to Paris with nothing but his typewriter.

15th February 1954

Dearest Nelson,

You are as you always were: a really nice man. It is really nice to send such long letters when I keep silent. this time I had sensible reasons to do so.

First, I travelled, and as soon as I came back, a week ago, intending to write to you, first thing of all, I was stupidly ill. Nothing important, a kind of flu which kept me in bed with an empty head. Today I feel a little better, I got your third letter, so I decided to write anyhow. swallowed one benzedrine to give me some strength and go up, sat at my table, and I begin this letter even if I don't achieve it today.

Thanks, honey. Thanks from the deepest bottom of my heart for speaking to me so confidently, I mean so intimately. Well, what you tell is what I guessed; it is a bit sad. I am afraid you make it harsh for Amanda, too; frankly, I don't like the going away to Chicago and not telling good bye, not writing. I don't see what you'll gain by this kind of behaviour. It is surely not the way to unlock anything. The best way, indeed, is to work, get money so you can once more write the book you want to write, and get happiness from your work. That could be an important thing, it seems to me, if you were no longer trapped in your work, but pleased with it. Then coming to Paris and living there, when you can, seems a good thing, too. But fake escapes are useless—am I too much moralizing? You ask me if there is still "magic" in my life. I never spoke about my life since a long time, because, as you say, it is always do difficult to tell the truth. Yes, we should need long walks along the Seine and new rivers to tell everything in the right way. But I'll try to as you tried. Well, "magic" is certainly gone, It has been and will never be again. First, or second maybe, it does not matter, because I get older, and the world around me is more and more present to me, and there is not much magic in it. Then, and chiefly, in fact, because I'll certainly could not and don't love again as I have loved you. Something is over, for ever. I told you that once: Van Gogh could live without an ear, but he lived as a man with only one ear. So, I live a magicless life. In spite of that, I must say too that I am happy. Quietly, but positively. This young guy I live with now (so much younger than I am) is for me rather a kind of incestuous son than a lover. he loves me this way, he asks for a motherly tenderness rather than something else. And maybe that is why a relationship was possible between him and me: because it was different from any other relationship I had and did not lead to any comparison. The fact is he won my heart by his own stubborn love and faithfulness, and the way he gave himself entirely to me—as a child could do—though he is not childish. You see, it is difficult to explain in letter. But guess you'll understand how this kind of love he gives me and this fondness I have for him can give me happiness though no magic. I must add that I believe it will be a long life affair. It seems a little crazy to say so, with this difference of ages, but indeed, he is a little crazy himself, as all the people I ever cared for. As long as he loves me as he does, I could never in my life be non-responding.

Then you know how Paris is pleasanter to live than Chicago. Work is a little hard, sometimes, because I tried something really difficult and am not quite sure I succeeded. But there are friends to help me, give courage, and chiefly Sartre who is as important and helpful than ever. So, yes, now it is all right with me. It would be entirely all right if you were *positively* happy, too, not just "not unhappy," and if we could have a living flesh and blood friendship, instead of this paper and ink relationship.

Well, now, about this last month: my friend had a winter holiday and wished to do something with it, and I needed a little change, too, having worked very hard for three months. So we decided abruptly to go away for a short trip with the new car, indeed. We rode Paris-Marseille in one day, put the car on a Bost, and wake up in Algiers, rainy and sad: too many beggars, too much poverty. We rode towards south, unto the edge of Sahara, west to east toward Tunisia. It was sometimes epic, because the roads are terrible, stones and sands; you don't even see a track. We were stopped by the sands a lot of times, but happily, always somebody passed by in time to rescue us. Honey, I saw again Medenine, and Djerba. Yes, they still live one, the Jews and Arabians in Medenine and Djerba, as strange as it used to be. Just the magic was gone, really it was. For instance, in the dark funny vaulted café in Djerba, nobody smoked kif, the man did not jump in the water to make beer fresh, he did not even speak to me. No Ameur Hassine, no narguile; landscapes, indeed, and camel driving cars, but no little elephants in the night, no magic. They hate French people more than ever now, and it is sensible of them, but not pleasant for French tourists. Beggars, paupers, dirt, and hunger are too obvious; you can hardly feel well in your heart when you see all that around you. I came back by plane, sending the car by boat to Marseille where it waits. I did not work, did not write during this trip, but I read a lot, and first of all, Van Gogh's letters. You must read them if they are ever translated. When he is becoming *mad*, and knowing it, living it in hope and despair together, it is great thing. What an artist and what a man! I should like to write about him one day. Then, at last, I read *Barren Ground* you sent me,[1] a very good book, a little slow as most of these old books, but going deep. I believed in it and lived the story from the heart. *Absalom Absalom*! by Faulkner, irritated me though it is technically often a masterpiece. How he can tell a story, that man! But most of

493

them don't interest me any longer. This one does not. Geismer's piece about Faulkner tasted very good to me, and I was interested, too, in his Hemingway and Dos Passos studies — sure he is and excellent critic. He wrote to me a nice letter about *America Day by Day*, and I am glad he'll review *She Came to Stay*. Well, honey, they published the novel in England only, not in the States, and now they give it in the States.

Yes, *La vie commence demain*,[2] is an interesting movie. We were just disappointed when it was done, because we knew (Bost knew, and Sartre) it could easily have been still much better. Everybody says *Moulin rouge*[3] is not good, but I'll see it... Sartre goes on jumping with joy every time I give him little red blades, that is very often.

Well, honey, I am tired to death. If I forgot to answer things or tell other ones, I'll make up for it in my next letter, but tonight, I have to stop. I don't know if all I told you make sense, and what sense it makes. After all, you are a smart man, if not the cleverest. Good bye, smart man, magic man. I remember the magic, I'll never forget it.

Your Simone

1) Ellen Glasgow (1925). 1) A film by Nicole Védrès, in collaboration with Bost. 3) John Huston (1953).

24th March 1954

Nelson, darling,

I too waited and waited for a letter which did not come. I got a small one saying: " I just mailed a big one," and day after day went away, and the big one never appeared. The, suddenly it was there. Foolish you! You forgot to send it airmail, it came the slow way, by boat. Along nice letter full of nice stories, and you looked happier; it made me happier, too. Though just last night I had a terrible dream about you! In the evening I had seen a good movie, a rather old one, *The Champion*, from a Ring Lardner story, with Kirk Douglas and a not so much known actor, but very good, called Arthur Kennedy. Well, it is a terrible story of a boxer who gets first very bad and then killed on the ring in a most savage way. So I dreamed about a long cruel, bloody business, half a fight and half not, in which you were concerned. Suddenly, I knew you were *there* (not knowing where was this *there*); I got upstairs and stairs with a pounding heart and found you in a kind of closet; you turned a harsh face to me, first it was just hard and hateful, and then bloody — you were dying. I jumped from the top of the stairs

494

unto the floor of a big hall to kill myself in despair. The dream stopped before I was dead but I wake up in anguish.

No, I don't feel guilty for returning to Medenine. I could even return to Uxmal;[1] there is nothing I can do that will ever be a betrayal of the past.

Let us speak business! Thank for the Potter's book, or whatever the name is—a fairly good book, and we'll get part of it in *Temps modernes*. I gave Vian your letter, but as he is the one responsible for translation and the printing delayed, he cannot go away from Gallimard. He promised to translate quicker the end of the novel, that's all. His translation is pretty good, not very good, but that is impossible, I think, to translate such a peculiar writing as yours.

Dick's *Outsider*? He can tell a story, but what a meaningless, crazy, stupid story that is—don't you think so? Ellen is awfully nice with me and get me money from the States. It seems *She Came to Stay* is well reviewed —did you read the *Time* one? I hope not because of the awful picture. Other photographs came, and do you know whey I let them shoot me? Because I hope one will be good to send to you. But they are all awful. The best pictures I ever got were made in Chicago and Patterson Island.

Everybody in Paris tells *Moulin rouge* is not good, honey, except Suzanne Flon, who is wonderful. I am afraid it seems so good to you because you are not in Paris and long to be there, so it gives you something of France, at least. But sure the same kind of movie about Chicago should please me; I should cry on it, But Paris, I don't care to go see it on a screen. Yea, I saw *Hamlet* with Laurence Olivier and I agree with all you say; it is very good and deep thing, it gives new meaning to the old play, a meaning which is inside it for sure. Oreste wrote Nathalie has not been well at all last year, but is a little better now. I am ashamed I did not answer since June. But even writing to you is not easy when I work as much as I actually do, so she will wait. In the March issue of *Temps modernes* is a paper interesting for you: the diary of an addict pansy writer telling minutely how he tried to "take the monkey off his shoulders." He chiefly tells wonderfully how bitter-sweet was the monkey.

We had some nice days of spring in the beginning of March. Now it is rain and rain, but not *inside* my room any longer, only outside; it is a lot better. Work, work, work again. Sartre is very pleased with new book now. When I'll write again it will have been delivered to Gallimard, I hope. I'll feel better then! Though, indeed, I'll be in working on something else; it is an habit you cannot get ridden of so easily! Honey, a promise is a promise.

Now I *know* you'll come to Paris, and it is good to know that. I'll not have too many white hairs when it happens. Anyhow, I'll always have health enough for endless talking and warm happiness. Write soon and airmail your letter, foolish you! Be well, my magic man.

Your Simone

1) She went back in 1970.

30th April 1954

Dearest you,

I got the pretty postcard yesterday, and I felt ashamed to have been silent so long. Well, I have two reasons to hope for forgiveness: one is I saw *Moulin rouge*, the other, the last word of the novel is at last written.

I saw *Moulin rouge*. the story is poor when you know who really was Toulouse-Lautrec, how he lived night and day in brothels, how he died saying to his father: "Vieux con!" But you were right about the colors, they are wonderful. Colette Marchand wonderful too; Suzanne Flon very good. The actor cannot have the peculiar sharp face of the real Toulouse-Lautrec; he does what he can do. Olga and Bost feel the same as I do. The opening of the movie is stupendous. So, stop being angry at me about that, at least.

I finished the book. 1200 typewritten pages, meaning about 800 printed, lot of people and things happening. Sartre, Bost, Olga, and my friend all say it is the best novel I wrote, much better that the others, and the best part is the American story. Man and woman, they say, are both sympathic and moving. I really hope I did something good with it, though it's just a small part of the book, but very important by the way it comes in the whole story and the meaning it has. How sad you'll not be able to read it before it is translated in American! I am afraid it will not be done before long, and maybe never, because it's a very anti-American book, on a political ground. Though I speak lovingly about Chicago and some peculiar American people. Now, I'll spend about two weeks cutting and fixing some little things here and there, and I'll give the monster to Gallimard. No title yet, not even an idea for a title—some day somebody has to find one, so I don't bother.

I sent back the letter and clippings you asked for. And thanks for the little pictures, I should like to get a good one for you, but they are all awfully bad. We'll take more of Potter's book than the part marked off. For French people is portrait of nowadays Babbitt,[1] is interesting—that is what the book is, isn't it? Tell him we'll send him the *T.M.* issue, with a Guyonnet's translation.[2]

I live nearly the same way you do; except the old friends you know, I see nobody. too much work. Not enough interest for strangers. Well, I have a right to speak about movies again, since I saw *Moulin rouge*, I'll ask: did you like *From Here to Eternity*?[3] I did, chiefly Sinatra and the very end, when the Japaneses attack Pearl Harbour and nobody understands it is the true war beginning. Sartre did not like it very much, and, indeed, it is not a revolutionary movie as *The Potemkine*; it is not great, but in my idea very well done and thrilling—I just don't like the love stories. Then, *The Wild One*?[4] Intellectual people do like it, and I don't. I must say there are very obvious cuttings that kill the story; there is something in it, about ten minutes really hot, but you feel all the time it could be so much better. Now, at any cost, if you did not see the English movie *The Cruel Sea*,[5] go and see it. The best thing I saw since years—true, moving, nothing fake as in Hollywood stuff. I did cry when seeing it. In a general way I don't like war movies, but this one is different. You really live on the boat, on the sea haunted by death. We translate for *T.M.* the big paper by Faulkner in *Holidays* about Mississippi; he was in Paris—maybe he still is here. I saw him in a restaurant with people I know very well, but I did not care to speak with him; I should have, some years ago, but I don't like him so much now. He looked very white and old, he drinks in a terrible way, his friends say.

Sartre goes on fussing about politics. I must say he did a good job; nobody thinks he has become a communist. He stays as free and independent as he wanted, still the communists look at him as a friend now. In a general way, since Beria's death, it is very different in France: communist are no longer sectarian as they were; all left wing people begin to work hand in hand. The result is Sartre invited in Moscow and Leningrad in the end of May; he is very happy at it. It was an amusing thing, the French players of Comédie Francaise going to Moscow and discovering Russian people don't eat little girls and can understand Molière. The government has forbidden public meetings and défilés in the street tomorrow (1st May). Everybody is waiting: what will happen? Will people obey or not?

You see, time went for me in a peaceful way. I'll write better, now the book is done; as soon as I got a new letter from the American prisoner, I'll write. Good bye, darling you. Tell about your own work. With the old endless tenderness,

Your Simone

P.S. Sartre goes on slowly with your *Chicago*, which we hope to publish before August.

We are passionate about the Schine-Mac Carthy affair,[6] and chiefly about Oppenheimer. He seems somebody, this man.

1) The hero by the same name as Sinclair Lewis' novel (1922). 2) *La Pesante Journée* by Jack Potter appeared in *Les Temps modernes* in July–October 1954. 3) By Fred Zinnemann (1953), with Burt Lancaster, Deborah Kerr, Montgomery Clift, and Frank Sinatra. 4) By Laszlo Benedek (1953) with Marlon Brando (1953). 5) By Charles Frend (1953). 6) A military scandal in the U.S. Army administration, linked to the Rosenberg trial.

10th May 1954

Dearest you,

You see what a difference it makes when my book is over: I answer as soon as I get your letter! The fact is too it gave me my own pang in the heart when you tell me: "the weeks between letters are long," and at times you feel something could be lost. No, Nelson, what is between you and me cannot and will never be lost. I cling to it and shall always do as hard as you do.

I said the hero in Potter's book looks for me like a modern Babbitt—I mean a nowadays Babbitt, very different of the old one. And, yes, I read about the two-headed baby; they spoke about him even in France. Terrible thing to think of. I am glad "it" is dead.

What you seem to have a little lost is you magic power of reading my handwritting. Well, Lautrec died saying to his father: "Vieuz con!" which means "Old Cunt!" (But I don't know if you use the word "cunt" as an insult, meaning stupid, beastly man). I meant the letters Van Gogh sent to his brother; most of them had never been translated nor published in France, which is a real shame. What a man this man was! Thanks for the little picture, one of the best you sent. I'll keep it on my heart. No, I don't care too much for a title. Anyhow, the book will not be published before October, and I'll have surely found a title at the time.

Our friends are angry today, because they have denied the Soviet dancers the right to dance in opera. They were to give a month performances; it was to begin today, and people had paid the highest prices at the black market to see them. Suddenly, because the French government is angry with the defeat in Dien-Bien-Phu,[1] they decided it could be a scandal to have Russian dancers dancing in Paris. They seem to believe the Russian dancers are the ones who took Dien-Bien-Phu! We do hope this disgusting Laniel will break down this afternoon in the Chambre. I am sad Blake could not have his book published. The same kind of trouble is happening to me with the ugly woman.She worked for five years on this book she just achieved.[2] I helped her to cut off the worst things, and on the whole it is an interesting book. But so long, so dull, all the time so over-written and strange that I understand Queneau is hesitating. He wants 300 pages in the beginning to be cut off, and he is right, but I am afraid that even so, they will be reluctant publishing it. I am afraid, too, the ugly woman will be mad with sadness and despair, and maybe she will jump beneath the subway, too. What can I do?

Speaking of Blake, one of these days I'll send you the huge amount of papers exchanged by *Temps modernes* and the banks in order to send him forty dollars! You cannot imagine what it is! In the end, we have to be authorized by the first minister! I don't know what it means. I'll ask Ellen Wright how it is usually managed when you have an American writer to be paid from France. We certainly made it the wrong way.

13th May

Honey, I got three issues of *The Nation*, and the blades inside. Sartre is always jumping with happiness when he gets them; he thanks you. You can thank him, too (in your heart); he did a beautiful job translating *Chicago*; it will appear in June issue under a supposed translator name. In fact, it's Sartre, on a word for translation, who put it in French. It was not easy; he had to recreate entirely the language, and he did it. A beautiful text, your book and the translation. They had to cut off some things, to have all of it in one issue. I'll send it to you, though you'll not be able to see through this French.

Suddenly came a stormy summer, hot and heavy. As soon as Sartre goes away to Moscow, I'll go to some green country and I'll work again there, something short. I am glad of it. The *Temps modernes* October issue will be on "Left wing: what it means today to be a left wing man, and all that I have to study, as a conterpoint, what is "right wing" way of thinking and feeling things: Koestler, Camus, Malraux, anti-Marxist philosophers, and all that. I have to read a lot of stupid books, but the stupidity is interesting in this kind of approach. After that, I don't know what I'll do. I'll dream about it during the holidays.

My sister is in Paris; she is going to show her paintings, alas! I hope she will get some success, though her pictures have no meaning at all. They are skilful now, but no meaning.

Good bye, honey. Write soon. We'll make weeks short between our letters. I'll keep the little picture on my heart, and you in my thoughts, as always.

Your Simone

1) May 17, 1954. 2) *Ravages*, an edited version of which appeared in *Les Temps modernes* in 1955.

Londres, Juin 1954

Dearest you,

This time my helicopter was not speedy, but it does not mean I went away from you. I can never do that. I tell you again, since you live in my heart, and I take my heart with me wherever I go. Well, it happens just now I am in London. Now my book is done and Sartre far away in Tachkent, I no reason to stay in Paris, and I wander around a little. I spent a week in the French country with my car, and flied to London: just an hour and a quarter, how quick! The only sad thing is it keeps raining in Paris and country, in France and England, a rotten summer. Monday I'll be home again in La Bûcherie brothel.

Sartre seems to enjoy immensely his trip. Letters are very slow, ten days to get one, but all papers tell very day what is happening to him: he is Leningrad, he flied to Tachkent, he spoke in Radio Moscow. He says he can go wherever he wants, discuss freely with students, with teachers, with writers, and everywhere it is easy to feel a big relax since Stalin is dead. He saw on million people walking through Red Place with flowers in their hand: A Macbeth flowery forest—impressive. All his friends wait impatiently for his return; for sure he will have a lot of stories to tell.

Few things happened. My sister was disappointed, because lot of people came for her picture show, said it was wonderful, but when it came to write it in the newspaper, critics were quite indifferent; it was just another woman-painter among so many others. So she said they lacked "courage"! She did not sell one thing, indeed, but she will not stop; on the contrary, she'll paint more and more, to have them drowned with paintings in her next show. Well, she left Paris at last, and will not bother me before long.

I try to get the ugly woman published by another publisher, but it seems hard. The minister said we could send the money to Blake in the end, so we did: did you get it? And what about your own money? I asked the *T.M.* secretary to send you two copies of the *Chicago* issue. Everybody,

500

knowing you or not, though this text was beautiful and you are a great poet. Really. The ugly woman is crazy about it; it's awfully good, and beautifully translated.

It seems they are very pleased with my book—*your* book—at Gallimard's. Queneau said it is the best and most moving love story he ever read. Blanch Knopf tries to see me about it, but Ellen Wright sold the option to another publisher; I am glad she did, so I hide from Knopf. Go and see *The Knave of Hearts* (*Monsieur Ripois*),[1] with Gérard Philipe, if they give it in Chicago. Most of people dislike it, but I do love it; a strange, clever, and subtle thing it is, this movie, in my idea. Honey, tell me some about you. I hope to get a nice summer on the little lagoon and the big lake. I'll write again soon. I kiss you lovingly.

Your Simone

1) By René Clément (1953).

Barcelona, 12th July (1954)

Nelson, dearest,

Last time I wrote from London, now, it is Barcelona: travelling again as you see. Well, I did not stay long in London, only four days. I like the town, though not pleasant to live in, within everything closed, everybody asleep at 11 P.M., and 10 on Sundays. Sartre was supposed to come back to Paris, too, but on Saturday I met who looked gloomy: "Somebody phoned from Moscow to a communist paper, they phoned to the secretary, who phoned to me, telling Sartre is sick and stays in Moscow hospital." I was terribly afraid, thinking he had over-tired himself and got some brain-attack as happened to Thorez. We tried to get in touch with Moscow through communist newspaper, through the Soviet embassy, and they told us: "Just phone to Moscow!" It looked impossible, and yet, nothing easier. I called Sartre's hotel, and in five minutes they answered, gave us informations, and I called the hospital. Sartre answered. I said: "How are you?" "All right," "Not all right since you are in a hospital!" He was taken aback and asked: "How do you know?" "Well, I know," I said. So he told the truth: they made him drink so much vodka, Georgian wines, they took him in the train, in plane, in car in so many places, and let him take so little sleep that he collapsed, with a heart beating twice as quick it should have and what we call "hypertension." So they put him to rest: sleep and rest for a week. He came to Paris by plane five days later, still very tired but very pleased: *to have been* in Russia and *to be* back in Paris. We went to the country for some days, and now he is all right. He says he could not do less, chiefly he could not eat and drink less than he did, because in the beginning Russians were a little diffident about him. Then, during a dinner, one of them said: "Since the beginning of the dinner, I watch this man: and now I know he is good man, because he eats and drinks *sincerely*." So he had to go on eating and drinking *sincerely* to make them sure he was a good man. Then they were so nice, so eager to show him everything, to please him, that he had to look at everything to please them. On the whole, he was pleased with his trip. they surely and deeply want peace; they did a lot for people — get a better life for them year after year — and there is some freedom since Stalin is dead. Indeed, everything is not all right. On the intellectual and literary ground, it is rather poor; they know it themselves. It is poor, strangely, because writers are overpaid and write anything to keep their standing, on book a year, good or bad — bad, in fact. Then each writer is supervised by other writers, who want him to do the same kind of stuff as they do; there is no real creativity. Painting is bad, but Sartre brought back very good music: Uzbekhistan and Russian choirs. A symphony by Chostakovitch too — not the one you got. Well, he talked and talked for days and days about his trip, but I cannot report all that. I am nearly sure to go to China with him next year: that would be great!

I began to correct the first galleys of my book; it is called *Les Mandarins*. I don't know how you call in English this Chinese intellectuals among whom some revolutionary leaders were picked, but who looked a little out of date, first: Mandarines? It makes a nice title in French. The book will be printed in the beginning of October. I am anxious to know how it will be accepted.

We had no real summer in Paris. It was rainy and cold, so I am happy to go to Spain, hoping for sun. I just arrived two days ago with the car and my friend. Barcelona is not different from what it was twenty years ago, when I came with Sartre — what a lively, pleasant place! How nice, gay, human, and sympathetic the people are! I mean, people in the streets, for "bourgeois" and priests and all that are more disgusting than in any other place. They live on late in the night; at 2 A.M. all cafés and lot of shops are still open, people go up and down the Ramblas, talking and talking. There is a wonderful district here called the Barrio Chino, awfully poor and dirty; it is the pleasure district: lot of brothels, cafés with women, and so on. In every street you have little shops selling preservatives[1] as other shops sell candies, wrapped in bright colored papers, in silver paper, closed in nice little boxes. On big cartons above the preservatives you read "blennorrhagia-Syphilis": a man in white clothes is waiting in front of the door. And I don't know how many "Curing-home for venereal diseases." I thought of you, how you would have been amused, you would have looked at the huge monsters of women waiting for customers. Maybe you will, some day. I know you would love Barcelona.

But come to Paris first, honey. Ellen keeps your money there: come and spend it. You can write Madrid, poste restante. I'll have your letter sooner. Love from

Your Simone

1) "Preservatifs" in French; "condoms" in English.

Dearest Nelson,

It sure was a shock to get the Mexican postcards, so full of wonderful false colours. Well, you nearly did something forbidden yourself. Chichen Itza is forbidden, if not Uxmal. You were not sick in New Orleans when you were poor and confortless, and now with money in your pocket, nothing hard to do, you just collapsed! How well I remember the burning heat in Houston airport! For me, too, some days, there is something in the air—fragrance, heat, a quality in the light, something—which makes you so near I could scream. When will you come near? Yea, Americans come to France by planes, boats, but not so many as they used to be. Though, I was sitting with Sartre on the Champs-Elysées some days ago, and a big fat man with round head, round face, said pleasantly: "Hello! Don't you remember seeing me in Chicago?" He looked somewhat familiar but I could not place him. I had an unhappy feeling, getting a little thing connected with you forgotten.

In spite of Franco and everything, these Spanish people are so lively so human, you have to love them; the more you love them, the more you feel sorry for them: poverty, no freedom, nothing. It is a sad country but beautiful, lovable. The big ones are more hateful than in any place, fat, arrogant; but the little ones, the people, are thin and nice. Such a difference! As in a child's book.

I went nearly everywhere with my good little car: coast and mountains, towns and villages, lost colleges, wide plains, Grenade, Séville, Madrid, and

503

so on. I contrived to speak a little: nearly as much as you did in Mexico. I saw bull fights, but did not enjoy it as much as in Mexico City. The bulls were young and small, not these wonderful beasts of Mexico; yet, terribly dangerous.

Well, often, swimming, climbing mountains, riding the roads, looking at pictures and at bull fights, I came back to Paris. Sartre had enjoyed some rest in Capri, but he has too many political friends in Italy—he had a dinner with Togliatti[1]—and is still rather tired. I am going away with him for a serious holiday, in Austria, where we'll stay in some quiet place without fooling around too much. A month in Salzburg, and then Wien and Praga, where we are invited, coming back in October, and then I'll begin to ask myself: what am I going to write now? I really don't know at all.

I got some nice pictures from Nathalie (there was a year since we write each other), from her little girl who looks lovely, and a pleasant looking man, the chemist she was in love with and from little paintings of her. She says in two sentences things are better for her and she'll send a real letter. I must write to her.

The ugly woman will have her novel printed by Gallimard in the end; she had to cut off the part she liked the best—a very dull, crude lesbian story,[2] and other obscene scenes—so she is not too happy. But she thinks it is better than not being published at all. Bost is working on a script with a very pleasant Hollywood man who says he knows you, a Hungarish Jew, friend of John Garfield, called Berry. He was accused of being a communist and left three years ago with wife and children. Do you know him?[3]

Sartre enjoyed very much the poem about him and Mr. Gillette. I did not get the indian Don Quixote. I hope I shall. Jack Conroy's one is really a tragic story.[4] I guess you had not a very happy time in his home. By the way, I found the script of *The Disinherited*; I remember he wished me to send it back to him, but he forgot about it, though, let it be forgotten. Did the trip help in the end?[5] How is this work going? Tell me.

Good bye, honey. Travelling so much, it seems impossible we don't meet some day, under some cloudy sky. I wait for you with all my loving heart.

Your Simone

1) Palmiro Togliatti (1893–1964). Leader of the Italian Communist Party for almost forty years. 2) *Thérèse et Isabelle*, published in 1966. 3) The actor John Garfield was shooting *Menaces dans la nuit* with John Berry in 1951, a film noir classic. Garfield himself had been accused that year of subversive leanings, during the famous witch-hunt that shook Hollywood. He died soon after of a heart attack. 4) His son had just killed himself. 5) To New Orleans, for his book.

Nelson, dearest,

I was told from Paris that a strange wooden man with a thin face came to visit me; I am eager to get acquainted with him, since it seems "he came to stay." I am sure I'll be fond of him, since he comes from Mexico and from you. Thanks, honey. Try to send me some day a Chicago man in blood and flesh, called Nelson. I got the Salzburg letter.

My own book will be fully printed next week, I guess. I'll send you one at once, though you'll not understand a word, but you'll see your name printed on the first page, and know all what it means to me. Gallimard makes quite a fuss about this book; it is good as long as it will get money for me. But what is bad is he makes believe the novel had "keys" — such a hero would be Camus, another Sartre, and so on. It is altogether false! The general idea is to describe the state of mind and experience of French writers after the war. But I invented the peculiar people I speak about, and it is unpleasant to think that readers will look at the book as to a cross-word puzzle, or something like that.

I got a long letter from Nathalie, at last. She seems very happy now because the chemist she was in love with, after trying to fly away, was persuaded to stay; he'll marry her as soon as she gets her divorce. He has plenty of money; they live together in a big house, with a garden and a washing-machine — her love seems based essentially on the washing and cooking machines. She intends to have children with him, writes little baby stores, over-feminine and meaningless, though nicely told. She will not some to France before three years; she seems to be scared by France.

And I got many letters from American women about *The Second Sex*. One of them spoke about me with a teacher in English at Bedford, Virginia, who had met me somewhere in the past with Nelson Algren: do you remember anything of the kind? We did not meet so many people together. How is it they come out of nowhere and tell me: "I met you with Nelson Algren"? Did you get a copy of me and go around with her ? I am in Italy now, and had a nice surprise when I arrived Verona. I bought an Italian magazine and suddenly, in the first pages I saw you! I was you, indeed, with a big add about *Golden Arm*. I kept it in the car and will send it to you. And in the book-shops, among Mondadori books, with a nice green cover, I saw your book: how strange... How stupid it is not yet done in France! What is Boris Vian doing with it?

Let me tell you a little about my last travels. I went away Sartre for two months; we wanted to see each other better than we can do in Paris, with so many things to do and so many people around us. It was necessary for Sartre to get some long holiday, because he was a little better than when coming from Moscow, but not really well. In fact, he was even very tired. We drove to Strasbourg, in Alsace, then to Munich—still half in ruins but very lively all the same; people look wealthy and rather happy. The beer-houses and beer-garden in Munich! Dark and light beer in glasses, pots, jugs, cans bottles, and thousands of people with little green felt hats on their heads drinking greedily. Then, we went to Salzburg, Innsbrück, old towns, old streets and memories. Vienna rather sad, half lively, half dead, not knowing what to do with itself. But the best part was the trip to Czechoslovakia, where Sartre and me had been invited: it was the first time I crossed myself the "Iron Curtain." It was very easy to have the visas in Vienna. We could go by car. The frontier was lonely, with, between two little houses, a real iron curtain—a kind of door made of wires and watched by a young soldier, from a mirador. An old man came—as in a child tale—asking for our passports through the bars; the soldier sent down a key, the old one opened the door, and we could go on the little Czechoslovak roads; nearly no car, only bicycles and motorcycles, and not many. In Praga nobody was exactly expecting us, so we went to a hotel and walked through the town by ourselves: it looked like any occidental town, with shops and cafés and restaurants. Sartre says Moscow is not at all like that. The people Sartre knew—writers, most of them—were awfully nice. I was afraid they would show us manufactures, farms, schools…not at all! They showed the beautiful old town, good paintings, churches, a romantic old Jewish cemetery, a synagogue, and on the evening we went to the opera. What was still better was some movies they do with puppets, a wonderful thing, much better than any cartoon I ever saw. *The Emperor and the Nightingale*, from Andersen, became a real masterpiece; you would enjoy it. Czechoslovaks want intellectual and artistic freedom, and yet have real problems about it. They gave us lot of presents: books, Bohemian glass, laces, records, and brandy. Alas! Two days ago, the car spent the night outside, as every night, but it was in Italy, and we should have taken everything out…the presents were nearly all stolen! These Italian devils contrived to open the carefully closed doors! Well, it was beginning to rain in Austria, so we went to Italy, Verona, Bologna, Firenza, a beautiful autumn, golden and blue here, not very warm but sunny. We lived a quite life, Sartre is very healthy now and works again;

he started a book trying to explain who he is, beginning by when he was a child — the first chapters are very good and amusing. I am through with the article for *T.M.* and don't know at all What I shall do after.

Roman Holidays is a very nice movie, I think. It is indian summer just now on the lake? I see in my heart a the beautiful red and golden leaves, the birds, the water, the night sky above the bridge and the lagoon, I see everything so well. Three years went away since we said farewell. I'll never see the lagoon again, but I'll see you, you promised. I know it will happen. I wait for it. Good bye, honey. I kiss you tenderly.

Your Simone

(Fin Octobre 1954)

Nelson, darling,

Coming back Paris, I found you did not get any letter from me since a long time. I wrote from Italy and told you about Vienna and Czechoslovakia, a lot of things. I hope it did not get lost. Tell me quickly, I should not like you to think I can be lazy when it comes to write to you. The long thin wooden man waited for me on the chimney; he looks like a friendly don Quichotte. Thanks for this silent messenger.

Does Mac Carran[1] death means I can hope to have you some day at the corner of the chimney?

I arrived here two days ago. My novel had just been published: I am pleased because it looks like a real success. The first reviews are very good and, what is strange, the book is liked by the right wing people as well as by the left wing ones, and the communists themselves. The first ones say it is the story of a defeat, the defeat of left wing French intellectuals; the last ones say it is the story of apprenticeship, of a conversion, the French intellectuals coming to the discovery of the truth: they must rally the communist party. Neither interpretation is good, indeed, but I guess that is the reason why the novel is better than my others: you can find in it very different things, the meaning is not over-obvious. They all say that the "American romance" is very moving — I wrote it with all my heart. It makes me sad you are not able to read it, lazy man who never could learn French. I mail one all the same; you'll find your name printed on the first page: it is *your* book. Let us hope somebody in the States or in England will translate it for you.

There is a "Panorama of American Literature" which had just been published in France, written in French by an American teacher, John Brown — not interesting at all, very conventional. But here is a nice picture of you, the one I have in my room, when you are sitting beneath the iron bridge in Chicago. He speaks well of you, but not well enough in my idea.

I enjoyed very much all the little stories you told me, about you being called a "lousy Frenchman." Yes, I saw Mozart's house in Salzburg; it is just a house. I don't think the explanation about Touaregs[2] is good. This way of veiling the men is religious, not meaning at all they ever thought themselves as women.

It is not sure people here would be interested by the Pachuco story, nobody knowing who you are and who were the Pachucos. But if you happen to go to the anti-communist meeting, that could be a great thing to publish in *Temps modernes*.

The end of the trip in Italy was very nice. Do you know I am a very good driver? Very quick, the little car flies on the roads and lets all the other cars behind, but I am very careful, too, and never come near any accident. What I like best is going up, up, up hills and mountains along little narrow winding roads. So we saw lot of towns, landscapes, and paintings, not working much, sleeping a lot and eating spaghetti. All that was very good since two years, lively and gay and all right again.

I saw *The Modern Times* of Chaplin, which I did not see since fifteen years. What a movie! He was great in that time. I felt deeply enthousiastic. You surely love this movie, don't you? Speaking of less important things, I saw a nice movie with Mitchum and Marilyn Monroe, *River Without Return*,[3] just classic Hollywood, but she is really a nice girl; she was a kind of Tza Tza Gabor, but she is a good actress and a pleasant woman. I'll go and see *Living Desert* as soon as I find time.

How with your work? Let me read the proofs or the script. I am curious about it. It was good, as a young man's book, if you re-write it now in you mature way; I am sure it is a new, very good book. Honey, I am going to the post-office to mail the book and this letter. Do write soon, and this time, staying peacefully, I'll answer quickly. Whether I am lazy or not, you always remain in my heart.

Your Simone

1) A senator and Franco supporter, in charge of immigration and emigration restrictions. 2) Nomadic Muslims living in southern Algeria, northern Mali, and Niger. 3) By Otto Preminger (1954).

Nelson, darling,

I am glad you can read French so well now, or must I understand you only read American French? Well. I'll go on writing my letters in English; it seems a little safer, is it not?

Well, I'll speak to you about *your* book, *Les Mandarins.*I'll say modestly that it is a big, big success: the biggest I ever had. All the critics say it is my best novel, and Gallimard sells a lot of it, more than he did for any book since a long time, says he. Within a week they are going to give the yearly reward we call Goncourt Prize, a kind of Pulitzer Prize. Nobody knows if I'll get it or no; all the members of the jury say it is indeed the best year novel, but I already too much known since *The Second Sex.* So we wait impatiently: everybody would like the money, Sartre, Olga, Bost, as they hope they would get some of it. But anyhow the book sells well, and I shall not mind very much if I don't get the prize.

Gérassi's son came to Paris last week with his wife. You remember the poker game at Gérassi's? The son is twenty three, looks very much like his father, and is a really nice boy; you would enjoy him. He deeply loves America but feel about American policy exactly as you and me, with juvenile enthousiasm, which is very pleasant. He told the same kind of stories you told in your last letter. Once, being a student, he had an argument about China with fellow-student: "Well, we all agree that Mao China must not be accepted in the ONU; but let us *suppose* I say it must, just for the sake of arguing..." and he talked pro-China. When it was over, his best friend told him: "You *supposed* too hard; you were too convincing: I should inform about you." "What? Inform about me?" "Well, you know we get money from FBI for informing. I shall not do it this time, because you are a friend, but take care!" And they are proud to get money from the FBI. We all contrived to show him Paris nicely, and I had a lot of pangs in the heart: first, because he made the States so near by speaking about them; and because I was showing Paris to somebody from the States. He is not American; he will be after two years in the army. He feels it is better to stay there; now he has no country, he can become French or American. He wants to try to do something rather than to go away. Maybe he is a little idealistic, but there is some truth in it.

Oh! I forgot to tell you: they are publishing very soon *All Men are Mortal* in New York, with a beautiful red jacket. You'll be able to read this one, at least. I enjoyed the UNIVAC brain story.[1] But how sad if the little lagoon was to disappear, and the little home to become just one city house like the others! Don't let them do that! Sartre is trying to write a play,[2] that is, he promised to a theatre director to write one and already got money for it. But he does not find any intrigue, and since a month he thinks and thinks and thinks without finding any. So he is a little sad, though not too much, because he still hopes.

Yes, I read Memoires of Hadrian.[3] She had a very ridiculous play about Electra just showed now in Paris, but the book about Hadrian was good.

We had a beautiful November in Paris; people were still sitting at the terraces yesterday. Today it begins to smell like winter. What shall I do during winter if I don't find an idea for a new book? Indeed, I think of a lot of things, but I did not decide for any. Surely it will be an essay, though I should like to write short stories, too. I never did. Anyway, I could not begin another novel before a long time. I put too much in this one; I have nothing left for another one.

I lived an interesting small experience last week. I received months ago a letter from a man in Switzerland asking me to come and give lectures; I said no, but I noticed his name was a young student's name I had nearly been in love with when I was eighteen. He had been very friendly for some months, and then had gone away to Australia; I never heard about him. Well, I asked if he was him, he said yes, but was perplexed, because he liked my books so much that he kept a photography of me in his room since four years, but reminded nothing about me as a student; he was in love at that time with a girl he married and cared for nobody else. Well, I saw him in Paris: thirty years after; it never happened to me to confront with anybody at such a distance. It seemed strange, because he looked very much like himself and was not himself at all: not a romantic fine young boy with communist ideas and juvenile hopes, but a middle-aged father of big girls, with moderate, rather stupid ideas. He did not recognize my old me, though very much interested in my new being—exactly the contrary of what I felt. How these thirty years of distance were both so real and irreal! How I felt so exactly the same and so far away! But I am afraid I did not make you feel the point. It does not matter.

We shall not spend thirty years without seeing each other again, shall we? No. We shall not. Love from

Your Simone

1) A kind of computer used to tabulate election results. 2) *Nekrassov.* 3) Marguerite Yourcenar (1953).

1955

Honey,

I answer at once, because I want this letter to bring you my New Year whishes before it is really too late. Go to the end of the old book, have money with it, do begin a new one you'll enjoy writing, and be happy with your work. Don't waster too much money in poker game, win sometimes. Keep yourself in good health, stay the nice man you are. Keep in your heart a stubborn will of coming to Paris: it never will be too late to drink to the *Mandarins'* health with your French friends who all miss you. The last wish will be: do come to Paris this year. Maybe it will happen, after all. Have nice dreams, honey, when you sleep, and find happiness when you are awake. Well, these are my deepest whishes for the year to come.

Did I tell you *The Temps modernes* are publishing a strange novel by a strange writer, *The Man with a Golden Arm*? We cannot publish everything, but we gave large excepts in two issues (December and January) and the end of March. It's not very well translated. Always the same old story: Vian is not paid enough to do a really good job. It's a long, hard job translating you, and in fact it does not pay at all. So Vian wrote the thing too quickly. I corrected it a little, but not enough; it would eat too much time. Anyhow, I hope the whole book will be published at Gallimard's this year at last!

I am sending you by airmail, as a small New Year gift, *All Men Must Die*, my last translated novel, and some pictures of me. There is one I really like, shot some days ago. The big one, on cardboard, is two years old and not so good, but a little amusing.

9th January

I let time pass once more. I begin writing again on my birthday: Forty seven years old today, dear you; we are really middle-aged people now. I got your small letter, with the foreteller woman's prophecy. I don't believe in these things. Are you sure she did not know about you—for instance, about your marriage? Anyhow, she told you would live old, that is a good thing.

Now, I'll tell you some small stories about the Goncourt prize. It is the use, here, when you got the prize, to go to the Goncourt lunch and thank the jury, then the publisher has a big cocktail where all newspapers men gathered, ask questions, take pictures—you had that with the Pulitzer, I guess. But in the States it is really compulsory; here, after all, if you don't want to do it, you can manage your way. By the fact, writers always want because they like being public: I did not want. Chiefly, because newspapers here are dirt, always writing dirty things about Sartre and myself. And I was already well-known in France, since *The Second Sex*. And...well, I did not like the idea of being a kind of gorilla in a zoo, and everybody looking at me. So I begin a nice little game of hide and seek with the newspaper people. Two days before the prize, they settled in the little bar you know, on the other side of the street, in front of my own brothel, and watched the door. But I found a backward door, and slipped away on the Sunday evening. I went to a quiet flat nearby which a friend had found for me; it belonged to a nasty general who was killing people in Algeria, but it was a good retreat. I could on in and out and in without anybody suspecting anything. So on the great day, we had a nice drinking party with Sartre, Olga, Bost, and another party in another private place. All the time, there were journalists sitting on the stairs inside the Bûcherie house; they spent the all day there, eating sandwiches, listening every noise, sure I was there and should appear. One of them phoned to the good concierge: "I am Sartre. Please you must let the young man who will come within five minutes enter Miss de Beauvoir's room." But the concierge knew better: "I'll open the room if Miss de Beauvoir herself tells me to do it." "She just left our, but she wants the door open." "She must tell it herself." So she won. They took lot of pictures of her, all the papers spoke about her in the week, she was very proud. They spoke about the laundry woman, too (the one who put S.B. on your underwears)! "When does Miss de Beauvoir go out for lunch?" "Miss de Beauvoir never eats lunch." That is true, I usually work until 3 or 4 in the afternoon and then eat very lightly, and have a dinner later. That made them hopeless.

The big bosses, I mean newspaper editors, were angry, because the whole thing meant I did not think them so powerful after all; I could do without them. One of them was so angry that in his magazine, he published a fake picture of me; he took a nice one and had it deliberately spoilt with shades beneath the eyes and all that. I was so old and ugly that all the people knowing me could not understand what happened. Happily, I had a lot of other nice pictures and nice papers. I must say nearly all the reviews were very good and the book sells, even more than usual Goncourt. I get lot and lot of letters. It is nice, because people long-forgotten come to life for some minutes just saying "Hello!" Old, old friends of the time I was a little girl, or a student, ancient pupils of the time I was a teacher. The paper by Genet was nice; thank for sending it.[1] I should like to know how the book will be reviewed in the States. Knopf wrote to me an angry letter, because I promised the novel to another publisher: but she did not want it before the Goncourt, and he did. I should like very much to know what you'll think. Everybody, praises the "American love story." In fact, it is not our real story; it could not be. But I tried to put something of it, to describe a real love between a man looking a little like you, and a woman looking a little like me. I tried to make both of them very nice people, and most of readers here say I succeeded in that. But I should like your feeling.

Well, I have an important work to do: to choose the excepts from *Golden Arm* for the March issue, so I'll say good bye. Do write soon, even if you have to go ghost fishing in faraway places.

You'll never be a ghost to me.

Your Simone

1) About a New York critic.

Marseille, 5th February 1955

Dearest you

Thanks for the good book[1] and the wishes on it. I like it very much and don't understand why we didn't hear about it in France; it should have been translated. I was a nice gift. Did it sell well in the States? Did your appreciation help? Thanks for the picture, too—yes, a good picture; you look like Frankie Machine himself, a real tough poker-player. Let this be a lesson to you not to speak so much! Oh! How so I remember L'Aiglon, the dead-pan comedian, and the whole evening as well. Did not I tell you some man hoped to make a movie with *Never Come Morning*? He is this Berry whom Amanda knows, this Hollywood director considered as a "red" who is now friend with Bost. He is interested in *Golden Arm*, too, but nothing sure, just an idea going on in his head. Maybe there will be more serious propositions; I should like it. All the *Temps modernes* readers I saw think *Golden Arm* is a wonderful book. Did you get the issues? I hope Vian makes the translation a little better before it is published at Gallimard's, because it ought to be a success.

I write to you from Marseille. After this prize, I was really sick with the phone-callings, letters, and so on. In a way it is pleasant to feel you have interested people, but it is a burden, too, and even if you say "no" nine times or ten, there is one you have to say "yes," and that is too much! So I went to Marseille for three weeks. It was a strange ride from Paris to Marseille, because in the heart of a huge flood, all the Rhône plain was just water, with lonely houses lost in the big water. In Paris, the Seine was impressive, too; there was water in the cellars of Rue de la Bûcherie, and the good concierge was very afraid. Thousands of Parisians came along the river and on the bridges, on Sunday afternoon, and at night, elegant people in cars, women in furs, after theatre; it was like a big picnic. Marseille is as beautiful as ever, except they built ugly houses on one side of Old Port: so sunny, lively, it smells so good pine and sea! I work, and then go around with the car through the country and along the sea. Yesterday, there was a terrible wind, much worse than the day when we were nearly drowned coming back from Château d'If. To cross the Corniche I had to wait five minutes, clinging to a pole, because the wind blowed so hard I was afraid it would blow me down, other people were clinging too, looking stupid and hopeless. Two people were drowned, two months ago, near Château d'If, in a little yacht; they were told not to go, and they went, the boat turned upside down and dead they were. A dangerous sea. I am reading Kafka's *Diary*— a real nice interesting man. Nobody is sympathetic to me, I mean seems to me so perfectly likable, except Van Gogh. I don't remember if you are interested or not in Kafka. But you cannot understand him if you have not felt in the *Diary* how the Jewish community he belonged to, and his own father terribly crushed him, and how he struggled not to be crushed.

I hope to go to China with Sartre in September. I should be very happy at it. Good bye, honey. Let us have an appointment for 9th January next year. So try to come. Make money and don't waste it in poker or in income-tax. Manage to get a passport and come! I give you a year, more if you need it. I'll never stop waiting to see you again.

Love, Your Simone

1) A Sardinian novel, *Perdu*, by Paride Rombi.

❋ *Summoned by Otto Preminger, who wanted to turn* The Man With the Golden Arm *into a movie, Algren went to Hollywood in February. Political suspicion ruled. The film was one of the first to portray the hellish world of drug addiction. While the film seems innocuous by today's standards, Pre-*

514

minger was forced to wage a war on censorship, against those whose solution to social problems was to look the other way.

The project was an enormous disaster for Algren, who felt he had been exploited. Opening in 1955, the film brought in a million dollars, but not a cent for Algren. He projected all his hopes for deliverance onto his new book: it would allow him to wipe out his debt to his publishing company, dig himself out of the legal mess created by the film, and escape the farce of his marriage. As Amanda intended to remain married, there was only one legal justification for divorce: abandonment. Despite his great attachment to the cottage on the lake, he moved out. At the end of March, he moved into a dark, depressing, furnished apartment in Chicago, paying the rent by playing poker on weekends. Tormented, with no plans for the future, Algren dreamed of one day starting from scratch in Havana.

1st September 1955

Dearest you,

I did not answer because I was wandering on Spanish roads. When I came back two weeks ago, I undertook to move off Rue de la Bûcherie, and, poor dear me, it is a terrible business to settle in a new house, even when it is not so big as Forrest Avenue. Tomorrow morning I am flying away to China, so this will not be long letter, but I wanted to say good bye before going so far.

Well, I read in the newspaper that they will give visas to local youths now, even to those who are no longer very young. Maybe you'll be in Paris for my next birthday, or in 1957? Maybe even before that? Honey, all your friends will acclaim you, and cheer you again, shower gifts upon you, so you'll not mind being as old as I am. Everybody here hopes you'll come, and I deeply do. Past times are past times, but new times my be good in their own way. It would be better to live in Paris than in Havana. Your bad dream must have an end and will have: don't let time frighten you. You'll surely be the strongest in the end. This death you speak of not being yours, you'll soon find yourself living again—in Paris. Finish your book, get a plane ticket, and we'll find a little Parisian student to walk hand in hand with you in Parisian streets.

I got your New York letter too. How I do remember our walking in New York. Yeh! Maybe I'll come back to New York some day; now the world is a little changing.

My Spain trip began in the wrong way: my car whirled upside down when I was inside, on a wet sliding road, but I drove slowly and was not hurt at all, only the car was badly hurt. After some fixing, it could move again, and on the roads I went everywhere. I saw lots of bull-fights: fifty six bulls were killed under my eyes, and some of these corrida were very good. While fixing my home, some days ago, I found again the bull-fight pictures of Mexico, they are very good.

I write from my new place. It is large and sunny, with a little staircase inside and a porch with two windows, which is lovely. I have a real kitchen, a bath-room, and nobody on the other side of the street except dead people: a big cemetery. So all the sky some in through the window. It is in Montparnasse, near the boulevard, and all the people who see it say it is one of the nicest home you can find in Paris. In November I shall finish to settle it, and when you come, I'll have a refrigerator, with ice and good old whisky, and we'll drink it to your new life.

Honey, I have too many things to do: within twelve hours I take off via Pékin, and I want to sleep between. I am too much excited with China to enjoy writing about Spain, Paris, Bost, or Scipion. I *promise* to write more often and less flatly next year. I hope to find a letter when I come back, and I'll answer at once.

Struggle hard, keep hope, remember your friends in Paris wait for you, and more than all of them put together, I do.

Your Simone

3rd November 1955

Dearest you,

I got your business letter yesterday, coming back from China. You seem not to be sure about my trip in China: didn't you get the letter I sent you just before leaving Paris, that is two months ago? You said from Forrest it would follow you. I should have liked to know about you more than what you tell in the business letter. Mine was not a very interesting one, but I told you how you would be welcome in Paris, in spite of your gray hair, and I don't like to think you could have fancied I just disregarded you last letters. Tell me quickly how it is.

About your short stories, I have enjoyed them very much: in my idea it is as good as anything you ever wrote, and sure the whole book will be a fine success. But can we use then for *T.M.*? Anyway, a bit scandalous for a magazine; it's not the kind of things we publish now, but I say the true, true truth: I like them deeply.

Well, it would be a long job to write a seriously about China. I am going to write a whole book about it, but I'll have to work for more than six months; it will not be published before next October, and anyway in French … It was a two months trip, and I spent about 124 hours in planes or airports, and 130 in Chinese trains — is not that something? It was not always amusing: as we don't speak Chinese, and they were anxious not to let us get lost and to show us things; they were always near us, following us everywhere, and sometimes we just get fed up with them, though they are so kind and nice. We seldom could loiter leisurely in the streets, as we like to do. But, though you should have often lost your temper, as Sartre did and myself, and dear Carlo Levi, whom we met in Moscow (always so pleased with himself, so sunny and funny), on the whole we see more of a country travelling this way than just left by ourselves. So, first I saw Moscow, where I stayed a week, part on the going trip, part of the coming back. Russians are so deep in the "coexistence plan" that they will not publish excerpts of *America Day by Day* as they intended to, because it is not mild enough about USA! Think of that! But China was yet more interesting. After the long airplane trip above Russia, Siberia, above Mongolia and Gobi Desert, we stayed a month in Péking, a big quiet peasant town. Wonderful celebration of 1st October: half a million people with flowers and flags in their hands, acclaimed Mao Tsé Toung. The most cynical ones just remained speechless. Then we went to the industrial part of China, in Moukden, near Korea — interesting, but stern. And the south: Shangai, Canton, that was passionately interesting and wonderful. The greatest wonder is how poor these people are and how they conquered through poverty a more decent and dignified life, working hard to get wealth in years to come. I remember how indignant you were seeing poor Indians carrying heavy burdens on their backs, seeming utterly acceptant of their dirty, beasty life. Chinese peasants, too, carry everything on their backs, work with their naked hands, but they don't *accept* anything, and their life, though hard, is no longer beastly; they work to get houses and tractors in a near future — it makes all the difference in the world. For instance, they killed flies, mosquitoes, and lice which brought cholera and other infection diseases. They teach each other how to read and write and understand the world. How patient and stubborn they are! They know it will be at least thirty years before they became a big industrial country, but they will do it; they will har-

517

ness the Yellow River; they will make tractors and plough the whole land. It is an astonishing sight when you travel by train, those miles and miles and hundred of miles from the earth by their only strength, without even an ass or a camel, working and working nearly with any tool, and how they *build*! Houses, dams, everything without trucks, without anything but their hands; yet, so quickly. Working just the way the poor old Maya did when they built these Uxmal temples, but working for themselves, not for priests and gods.

Well, I'll have to wait my birthday or yours to tell you more about China. Please, tell me about yourself. Do you really think of coming? I am not in La Bûcherie any longer; my new place is much bigger, cleaner, and it does not rain inside. Tomorrow I'll begin to work about China. Good bye, Nelson dearest, and may next year bring you to Paris!

Your Simone

P.S. When I get a sure address I'll send you my last book, a little books of essays which were published in *T.M.*[1] One is the piece about Sade you already know. And I'll send a very good book by a 1937 Chinese writer, Lu-Hsun; it is translated in English and I feel nearly sure you'll like it. And some stupid Chinese tokens for you. My new address is 11 Bis Rue Schoelcher, Paris, 14e.

✱ *In November, Algren finished his book. But his publishing company in New York, having paid him an advance of $8000 over two years, rejected the manuscript. Not only was there no question of a new contract, but they wanted him to repay the advance. In the face of such adversity, Algren traveled around with friends and ended up in Florida, where he rented a house; he planned to stay until spring, writing.*

1) *Priviléges*, which contains *"Faut-il brûler Sade?"* as well as *"La pensée de droite, aujourd'hui"* and *"Merleau-Ponty et le pseudo-sartrisme."*

15th December 1955

Dearest you,

You seemed to live a strange life, lying in Florida sun when it is snowing in Chicago. I cannot understand this story about the publisher not publishing the book: he asked for it, did not he? I am sure it is a good book, you could not write a bad one; even if not as good as *Golden Arm*, since it is a remake, it is surely worth reading and publishing. Tell me better what happened, what is happening just now. By the way, I should like to read all of it. Cannot you send a typewritten script? I should enjoy that better than Robinson Jeffers;[1] I heard about him, but no more. I send you the Chinese books, *Privileges*, and some stupid Chinese tokens. I hope you'll get them for Christmas, with my loving whishes: a whish that will maybe come true, of your coming to Paris at last. Olga and Bost were excited about it; Bost planned a whole life of poker-playing with Scipion and himself, and drinking your health and everything. There will be much to say about China. I shall not have forgotten, since I am writing about it, and for months will go on forging nice lies about what I did not see. A long job and not so easy, because I did not see much, and I knew little about what China was like before. So I have to learn things at the same time I am writing. I did not know much about America neither when I wrote *America Day by Day*, but I met a nice man who happened to be a local American youth, and taught me much. Then I could speak and at least read the language. Now, I cannot read Chinese, and I don't know any nice local Chinese youth. So I don't know what *China Day by Day*[2] will be worth. All know is that I work hard about it, and am very interested in all what I learn.

Life is very quiet here, with so much work. Sartre works hard, too; he made an adaptation of Arthur Miller's *Salem Witches*[3] for a movie — much better, in my idea, than the play itself. If the director is good,[4] it could even be a great movie. He met Huston yesterday about playing in New York *Le diable et le bon dieu*. John Huston is living in Ireland with a French actress and seems a nice man; Sartre hopes to work well with him. Speaking of movie, did you see *The Seven Samourai?*[5] It is really good. Thanks for the paper about the *Golden Arm* movie; I like Sinatra since I saw him in *From Here to Eternity*. It seems that censorship will lose and the movie will be seen in the States, and I hope in France. I guess you'll not get a penny from it, is that true? Is the movie good? *The Mandarins* will not be translated in American before July 1956. I hope at last they'll make a good job. I doubt it will be a success in the States; they like it too much in the other side: USSR, Bulgaria, and so on. We'll see.

After ten months silence, I had a letter of Nathalie, the poor girl was really unlucky: she had a bad fall, her bones became weak, she spent months in plaster after very painful work being done in the legs; she narrowly escaped remaining a cripple for life. Now she is in good health again and married the chemist with whom she lived since about two years; she had somebody to give her real money at last, and for her that is happiness.

The ugly woman becomes really mad; her book[6] was a sad failure. Though rather good reviews, though it was rather obscene and scandalous and would have somehow hit people, she did not sell more than 500. That was such a shock! She began to feel people creeping in her house and stealing her thoughts, and a lot of strange things happened around her. Happily, she does not include me in the system, and I try to help her; to begin with, I sent her to a psychiatrist.

What else? Scipion is in love and will soon get married. The secretary wrote a not too good play about Don Juan, and weeps for a Mexican love affair. Olga is all right. Wand everybody wait for you. I more than anybody else. Have a good time in Florida, honey, and in nice French spring, do come! I wait tenderly for you.

Your Simone

1) A Californian poet, author of Tamar (1925), a poem about incest. 2) *La Longue Marche.* 3) *The Crucible.* 4) Raymond Rouleau; the film would come out in 1956. 5) By Akira Kurosawa (1954). 6) *Ravages.*

1956

✴ *At the end of February, Algren sent his book, entirely rewritten, to another publisher. He continued to drift between Florida, Gary, New York, and Chicago since he couldn't go home if he wanted the divorce to go through. The book was scheduled to appear in May, the same time as the American edition of* The Mandarins. *Algren lost all interest in* The Man with the Golden Arm, *refusing even to see the film version when it came out. He reapplied for a passport. In July, he responded to de Beauvoir, embarrassed for several reasons. When the passport division had demanded a sworn statement as to whether he had ever been a Communist, he had perjured himself by answering no. He feared that this discrepancy might hurt him in his suit against the producer who had "stolen" his novel. He knew he had sunk to a new low, and considered the whole period a disaster: he had made one mistake after another, wasted his own time, cut himself off from his work.*

Algren had succeeded in divorcing Amanda, but was still not free from her; she expected alimony from him. He was still embroiled in a financial disaster; he was penniless. And then the worst of all: when The Mandarins *came out, he made nasty statements about Simone de Beauvoir to the press—for the first, but not the last time. He went back and forth, admitting he had been quick to attack and done little to deserve her dedication of the book to him. According to him, the journalists ignored all the positive things he said; he claimed to have expressed his great admiration for her and for the book, but the press cast him as an ogre. On July 1, he called to try to explain and excuse himself. This was the first sign of an unpleasant Herbert Hoover–like alter ego: a rigid, cold-hearted man in a starched shirt. He seemed struck by an impression Simone de Beauvoir had shared with him a long time ago; once, waiting in an airport for her beloved Nelson Algren, this other, frightening man had appeared instead.*

In December he hit rock bottom, having lost himself in the draining battles against his marriage, his publishers, his agents, his lawyers, and his poverty. He felt he had lost his driving force, the spark fueling his writing and his entire being. He realized that he was losing Simone de Beauvoir forever, and in this dire mood was not afraid to admit that he missed her terribly. The best days of his life were spent with her. Why had he let her drift so far away?

18th March 1956

Dearest you,

You are such a grasshopper that I never know where to write to you. I know very well this little place where you lived in New York:[1] there is a kind of square, and a big clock lighted at night, is it not? I begin to be craving for seeing America again. Some American people here told me about the El in New York being down: I remembered our last walk along the Third Avenue, with something like death in my heart—and it made me feel a little dead once more. I am angry about Third Avenue not being itself any longer, and yet I should forgive New York and come back, if it were possible. Maybe it will. But first I wait for your coming next October. All your friends here feel they have been waiting really long, now you *must* come, they say.

I read a lot of papers about *Golden Arm*. I understand that now it is Sophie who is the murderer, because she was caught faking her infirmity! How bad! What was so good in the novel, among so many good things, was that nobody knew, not even herself, how much she believed in her sickness, how much sick she is really. Yet, I should like to see the movie.

I wait for your proofs too, I got a nice advertisment about it with a good picture of you against a back-ground of old torn ads on a wooden wall. My American publisher was sorry not to publish it himself; he says there was some misunderstanding among agents. I don't know exactly what. Sorokine wrote she enjoyed *Golden Arm* so much that she wants to write and tell you what a great artist and poet you are, in case you would not know. She seems happy because she has a man and money, but finds life awfully tiresome.

I am working about China very hard, lot of people here write about China, and I have to achieve the book soon, or it will not be up to date: before July since last summer I always go wandering around the world and cannot work. I spend hours just reading and writing; stopped for two weeks because I began to feel a bit tired, and chiefly fed up — "China-happy" as you would say. I went away in Switzerland, up, up, up, by trains and teleferic,[2] and coming down in skis. how frightened you would have been! If you have been siting, as I was, in a small bench hanging from a big wire, floating in the air hundred feet above the ground! It was cold, deep, deep beneath the freezing point. I did not ski since five years, and it was a real pleasure to glide again happily along snowy slopes. In Paris it was terrificly cold; there never was such a cold winter since hundred years. I guess you saw pictures of the Seine looking the North Pole. I found my beautiful new home all spoilt: the American old lady, on the flat above, had let open the water, which flooded everywhere — my walls were all wet. I sued her and should have get money to pay all the works made, but so you know what the old witch did? Suddenly, opening the concierge door, she fell down and died! She managed that on purpose. Now I don't know if the heirs will repay me. I don't care too much. I just tell the story to show you how wicked people can be.

I am invited to go with the French government to Moscow one week in May. Maybe I'll go. What is happening in North Africa is very sad. You remember Algiers, honey? Well, the Arabs don't want us and we should go away; we did nothing for them, far from it, and they are right to hate us. But the government does not dare to drop Algeria, and even communists had a vote to support him. So they are going to begin a war as bloody as in Indochina, and they will lose. When a whole country is against you, you do lose. But before they acknowledge it, blood must be shed, much blood. We try to struggle against it—meetings and all that—but we cannot do much. What do you think about what is happening in Russia? Interesting, isn't it?

I saw Ellen and Dick Wright with my American publisher. Dick seems a little lost; he does not know what to do about politics, becomes quite quietist, hoping only Asia and Africa will change the world. But you cannot leave America and Europe out of the game.

I read a pleasant interview you gave to *Paris Review* I'll read Blake's letters when they are published, too. Tell me if you like Lu Hsun. What are going to do now the book is done? Have you a new, really new novel in the head? People in Paris should like to see with their own eyes what a good American is; they don't believe such a thing exists, but I assure them it does. So do come! It will be strange to see each other in such different circumstances, but no matter, we'll manage it, we have to. I do wait you.

Tenderly,

Your Simone

1) Gramercy Park. 2) "téléférique" in French, "cable-car" in English.

---

12 *July 1956*

Dearest Nelson of my own,

I did not write for such a long time, because I had too many things to say. I always waited for a long, peaceful afternoon when I could leisurely chatter with you... it never happened. It does not happen yet. I leave Paris within two days for months and am killed with things to do. But I decided anyway you'll get a long letter, even if I write it by little bits, stealing minutes from sleep and work. I did not bother about not writing, because I knew you would understand: you know what real work is and what a real letter likes to be. You understand all, always. So do I, honey. I was not disturbed at all when I read your statement about "not digging one's private garden" and saw this monkey-like picture of you, I "put it in my head" exactly as you said it, and I knew why. I understood *that* was the reason why you called from New York, and I understood too why after all you did not call: I should not have liked it; I am too emotional. I could hardly stand your voice without seeing your face, not after all this time gone.

Well, you say *it* was hard to die; it was hard for me too and in a way, it will never fade away. Now I have made a new life, in a definite way. But my

523

love for you is more than a memory; I'll always care for you deeply, with a warm, living, wonderfully important feeling, and understand you as I know you understand me. It always seemed strange to me how *near* we were—nobody was ever so near my heart—though in many ways so far away. I though intensely to the past times these last weeks, with all these clippings coming from America about you and me, and it made my heart ache for the lagoon and Wabansia which will never be again in my life. You *are* in it, and I have to hope you will come to Paris. In fact, in *The Mandarins*, the love story is very different from the true truth; I just tried to convey something of it. Nobody understood that when the man and woman leave each other for ever, they still are in love and maybe this love will never die. But it just could not go on. When I think of the past with a clear head, I see again I could never have lived in the States, and I don't believe you could live for keeps in Paris, and this coming and going affair could not make us happy neither. Yes, I can tell you again, quite privately, it was hard for me too.

Honey, in what a maze you put yourself? How is it you always take the wrong way after having very wisely meditated about what you should do? Tell me, as quickly as possible, how the thing will develop. Maybe nobody knows nothing about the past and nothing will happen. Will you get your passport, anyway? And do you still plan to come? I saw *Golden Arm*. Yes, it is a shame! But all the same, some parts are good; I was deeply moved to see Machine on the screen. I remember the yellow type-written paper, when I read the script for the first time on the Mexican blanket. I liked Sinatra in Machine, though he is too sweet. I love his friend with the stolen dogs, and the part about playing poker seemed to me good. It is the drug story that stinks. Then I read the book.[1] I liked all the first part very much; I like Dove who always hurts those who are dearest to him. You never wrote a more poetical and strong and moving language. Then the second part is too much of the same stuff as your other books, too much a remake. I don't feel any longer Dove as a living boy, but just a puppet with things happening around him; he is no longer convincing. you must write once more what you call "a book for yourself," I hope you can. I read a lot of critics about you. Some wonderful put you as the greatest American writer, other hated the whole idea. Do you make money?

Well, I have no more time for a real letter. The book about China will not be done before fall; I'll work on it during these holidays. Just now, I am writing the end of a long paper for *Temps modernes*,[2] and the commentary of a very good movie about China, giving a good idea of the country as it is nowadays. But I begin "China-happy"! Work was the chief thing, all these months. We had rotten spring, nobody even knew it was there — maybe it was not. Summer is kind of rotten, too, so I did not leave Paris and just worked like a beast.

When I spoke about Russia, I meant the XXth Congress and Khuschev's report: is not that something happening in the world? Dreadfully important, I think. French communists don't know how to manage this affair; they make a mess of it, they are worse than ever.

I am going away for a rest trip to Greece and Istanbul through Yugoslavia. After six foolish weeks in my car on dreadful roads, I'll take a working-rest, which will be a real rest, in Italy with Sartre. Write, please, this time I'll answer quicker.

Try to be wise, honey. I kiss you dearly. You know how I feel.

Your Simone

1) *A Walk on the Wild Side.* 2) "Eyewitness" on China, *Les Temps modernes*, September–October 1956.

Novembre 1956

Dearest you,

I wrote a long letter some months ago and got no answer. I should like very much to know what is happening to you. Are you coming to Paris this year or not? All your friends are patiently and impatiently waiting for you. Do you work? On what book? Where? How?

I am afraid you did not get my letter after all, and you believe I am angry for you having been angry at me. Or are you angry, really? You should not.

Tell me. It gives me bad pangs not to know, and I don't like pangs neither.

I travelled in Greece for two months, by boat and car; it was beautiful, though people are so poor, so sad. Then I stayed six weeks in Roma with Sartre and we worked ten hours a day. My book about China is nearly done, not a very good one, because it is too difficult, but it may teach you something if you read it. Now I am home again, just arrived yesterday, and hoped a word from you. I am going to stay here, and work along. The world is awfully sad, nowadays, is it not?

Do write, please. You stay in my heart for ever.

Your Simone

1957

1st January 1957

Dearest you,

I told no man in the world that you were not nice with me. I never though so; I never said so. But I am glad the liar, since it was the reason you wrote to me. I was waiting for Christmas, telling myself: "If he does not write now, if he does not send at least a Christmas card, that means he feels hard against me." It would have made me very sad. But you sent a card, and even a letter. They made me sad, though, in another way: because you seem to feel so hard against yourself! I know you are mistaken: the little light inside you could not die, it never will; from here, I see it with my own eyes, through earth and sea, so faraway. You are not the man with the hard collar, I can see that too. You just struggled a little too hard during these last years, so you don't feel the light inside you, but there it is. Some day, when things are settled, when the struggle is not so hard, you'll find yourself again. Some day, you'll write anew because you have things to say and want to say them, you'll write then a very good book and feel pleased again. I don't say that just to confort you, but because, indeed, I am sure of it. sure your friends in Paris would find you the same and be happy to see you. I should. I still hope we'll meet again. I changed myself. I was a young-looking middle-aged woman, and I am nearly old, not young-looking at all. You'll be a little sadly surprised when you see me. Honey, it is nearly *ten* years since we met for the first time in Chicago. A long, long time. Still it will never be far from my heart.

I have finished my book about China; it is not too good. Anyhow, I did not put much in it. I am beginning something quite different: memoirs of childhood and youth, trying not only to tell a tale but to explain who I was, how it came to make me who I am, in connection with the way the whole world in which I lived was and is. It is interesting to try this job, even if I don't contrive to achieve it.[1]

We were all much upset by what happened in Russia and Hungaria. I hope to go to Poland, but that is another story, and a long one.

526

Do write sometimes. Olga, Bost, Sartre send from the deepest of their hearts best wishes to the "good American." You know what I wish for you: be happy again. I kiss you "happy new year" with all my tenderness.

Your Simone

1) A reference to *Memoirs of a Dutiful Daughter,* published in 1958.

✴ *Algren wrote only once in 1957, in December, still despondent and nostalgic for the old Wabansia magic, for their life and travels together.*

1958

Janvier 1958

Dearest you,

All the Paris friends send their loving wishes to you and hope you will come here some day. Will you? I had just got your nice Christmas card when a friend arrived from New York: he learnt by the newspapers that, last winter, you fell through the ice in a deep hole and nearly died. It is so much like you, honey, to fall in a hole! But take care not to die. I had a pang in the heart when I heard it.

I remember, too. I remember everything. I am happy, in a peaceful way. But for me, too, the time of miracles is over. As you say, *one* miracle in a life is much. I should like to know a little more about you. Do you still live in Gary? With your wife? What do you write? What do you do? You could send a letter from time to time, could you not? As soon as my book about China is translated in American, I send it to you. Now I write an autobiography: only childhood and youth. Sartre and Bost think it is amusing.

We are much disgusted about this Algerian war. It is a shame!

Will you come? It seems impossible not to see you again when you are so deep in my heart. Nelson, Nelson, darling, you'll stay there for ever. I kiss you, honey.

Your Simone

1959

2d January 1959

My own Nelson,

Thanks for the picture—the big one's really good, and the little ones remind me of so many things! Thanks for the book. Sartre thanks too, very pleased to see his name on the English edition of *Never Come Morning*.[1] Your letter was not a very happy one; mine will not be neither. It was a hard time, since May 1958: we saw the country going down to fascism, we struggled against as much as we could, and were defeated. Now, we don't feel we belong to this new kind of France; we are strangers in our own country. When I say "we," I mean myself, Sartre, all our friends. Now, we'll go on torturing Arabian people; we'll have to pay for that, and starve. It is stupid, it is hateful, it is disgusting.

Sartre worried so much and worked so much that he nearly had an attack: it could have happened to his heart, or his brain; he had some very bad days. Now, he is out of that; he wholly recovered and will take care of himself. My own health is all right. My last book (the story of my childhood and youth) sells very well and has the best critics. I'll send it to you when it is translated. Lot of forgotten people, and unforgotten ones too, wrote to me about it; it was often interesting or amusing, I enjoyed the thing. I enjoyed having written this book more than any other one, but now I am hesitating: I don't know exactly what to do. You don't feel like writing in this kind of France. Then feel I get old...and sometimes I have a pang in the heart when I think I could never see you again. I am sure I could have a visa for the States; I don't feel like going there. I hoped you would come to Paris, someday, and your letter saying you could not made me sad. I sad too for the Wabansia nest. Yes, you were a nice man. I have only nice memories of you. I always kept your ring; it shows on the picture, if you look well.

Love from all you friends here. And loving kisses from

Your own Simone

1) Sartre chose the French title, *Le matin se fait attendre.*

✳ *Algren was finally granted his passport in July. His letters brightened considerably. Elated, he planned a trip to Europe.*

Juillet 1959

Forever dearest you,

I got the books, which seem very interesting. I'll read them during the holidays. I got the paper about "Simone, a new kind of nun"—are you sure I *was* a nun? But it is a nice paper, thank you. There is not much to say, about what is going on here: the power people pretend every day that next day something really big is going to happen, and not the least thing happens ever. It is like that since more than a year; people who said "Yes"[1] should not do so now, yet they don't want strongly enough to say "No." So, we just wait. And work. I worked much, about a second to Roma with Sartre. I'll spend a month there and ride a little in Italy, then come back here. I am dreaming about going to the States next summer, but I am not sure it could be done. Yet I have to see you, you have to see me, before we die. I'll never stop remembering, and remembering.

What about you? Do tell me something. I grab all I can hear about you (from Ellen Wright, for instance), but it is not much.

With the old, forever living love.

Your own Simone

1) In May 1958, during the Algerian crisis, President Rene Coty gave de Gaulle "complete authority" to set up a new constitution, thereby inaugurating the Fifth Republic.

Septembre 1959

Dearest always-the-same-kind-of-you,

How is it I send this letter to Gary? I believed the little house and the garden with mosquitoes and the lagoon did not belong to you any longer?

Well, indeed, come to Paris in spring to fill the magic-bag! I don't know if we shall travel far, but it is not my newly-built life that will prevent us to do so, because now I am un-building it. I felt the need of living like a bachelor again, and that is the way I live now. So you could even be my guest, since my place is wide enough and you could have a little room of your own. Well, we'll see. What is really important is your coming. How many stories, true and false, I'll tell you and you'll tell me! Do come, honey. You don't need much money if you live in my place and travel in my car (will you be much afraid?) and eat my cooking (that, I know, scares you). Do come, and in our oldish way, we'll be wonderfully happy together.

I wait for you.

Your own Simone

Sartre, Bost, everybody wants so much to see you before you get dressed in a shroud!

20th December 1959

Dearest you,

Have you become a millionaire? You sent a wonderful pack of books! And my own was the most beautiful one! We should travel very much to see all the "thrones of earth and heaven"[1] we have not seen: Egypt, Syria, Greek islands…I began to read Mark Twain's autobiography, though it is not mine, I keep it sometime. And Sartre's gift, too, which tells the true truth about America. Everybody thank very much and waits impatiently for you.

I am busy, busy, busy, not tearing off or building up my life—it takes care of itself—but building up a stupid script for a movie—I did it for money. Yesterday, it came to an end, so I write to you. Now I am waiting for the director and people around him to build down to nothing my script, but I don't care; I got the money. I come back to my real work again.

Paris is sad, France lousy, but I am happy, and so is Sartre and Bost; Olga is as well as ever. I have a lot of long stories to tell you, but I like better to tell them with my tongue. You'll wait until May. Incidentally, I have to learn how to speak American, as I really cannot any longer. I forgot nearly all. So first, I'll have to listen to you, and I should talk twice as much after.

Happy Christmas, happy New Year. You know what I wish the most: that this year *really* brings you to Paris.

With love from

Your own Simone

I have more than a sink in my house: a full bath-room.

1) The title of a photography book Algren sent to de Beauvoir.

1960

ALGREN IN FRANCE

✱ *Algren traveled for six months in Europe. From mid-February to March 20, de Beauvoir and Sartre traveled to Cuba for the first time. Algren, coming from Dublin, arrived in Paris before them and installed himself in de Beauvoir's apartment on rue Schoelcher. They rediscovered each other, taking long walks in Paris, going out, playing at being tourists. Then they traveled to places Algren had always wanted to visit: Spain, Marseille, Istanbul, mainland Greece, Crete. In August, de Beauvoir took a long trip to Brazil with Sartre. Algren stayed in France until September. He and de Beauvoir would never see each other again.*

Rio, Friday, 26th Août 1960

Dearest wonderful thing, beautiful flower of the rue Daguerre,

I am proud of the way you made money in Deauville at the horse-track, Calairefontaine was a nice horse, but I don't quite understand why people screamed so much you bet on it. I am glad you improved the kitchen: please, don't grow too many flowers on the window-sill; it would make the other people ashamed of themselves.

Well, in its way, Brazil is all right, too. Since yesterday I am, and so is Sartre, a citizen of Rio de Janeiro: they gave us solemnly the title, and that makes a lot of rights. Is not that nice? Yes, it is nice, because it is an insult to the French government. I learnt this dirty government tried very hard to prevent Brazil to invite us; they were afraid Sartre should speak about the Algerian business, and he spoke: he said how Algerian people are tortured and all that. Brazilian people don't like colonialism, because they feel they are a United States' kind of colony, and they were very pleased with Sartre's speech. We do a lot an anti-de Gaulle propaganda, and so they made us citizen of Rio.

I am very fond of Bahia, the black city where nearly everybody believes in black gods; even white intellectuals go to the strange ceremonies where the gods take the bodies of flesh and blood women. The "mother of all saints" (that means the highest priestress) discovered Sartre is the more powerful god's son, and I am the loveliest godess' daughter—everybody told us if she said so, it is the true, indefeasible truth. They don't have real "fights" in Bahia; they *dance* a kind of fight with hands and feet, like the one which was practiced in France before English boxing: they dance it, and the point is *not* to hurt the partner, going as near as possible of hurting him; it is very clever and skilful. Now, at night, in lonely streets they often do the same fight, a knife in hand, they try to hurt, and succeed, and kill.

We saw cocoa, tobacco fields, and the terrible way poor, overpoor peasants live and work like no-human brutes; only in big oil-fields workers begin to live like human beings. In huge cattle markets kind of very poor cowboys come from far away, and sweating Negro-girls, with magic beads around their necks, are stamping the tobacco leaves hard and hard, with their naked feet: a sad, fascinating world of work and utter poverty. That was the worst of the country, the most ancient and blackest part; they complain they are a colony of the South States, a little in the way the South States of USA were a kind of colony of the wealthy industrial North.

We are in Rio now—a big, terrible, ugly, and beautiful city, really full of the utmost contrast. The sea, the bay, the beach, the mountains which come deep inside the town, all that is wonderful beauty; the long and narrow streets in the heart of the town are a little alike down-town Chicago: high and heavy buildings without any charm but powerful. It is pleasant, in spite of all, because so lively. Then, on all the mountains around and in the city, there are the "favellas," 750,000 people (out of four millions) living in slums. Each favella is a big village, from 6000 to 80,000 inhabitants, living in wooden barracks they built with planks on belonging to the city, the state, to private owners; they have no right to settle there, they are squatters. But the police can put down the barrack only during two days after it has been built by poor emigrant people coming from the inside desert where nothing grows. They travel for days and days in trucks, hoping to live better in the city, and they cannot find any place to sleep, unless they make it themselves on stolen ground. No electricity, no sewers, no water, no water: women have often to go up and down 600 feet, to find and bring back a little water. So...at night, they dance wild dances, asking the gods to help them...so night and day they smoke drugs which help them to forget everything. These miserable districts are all and everywhere mixed with the most elegant and wealthy ones in Rio. I live in Copacabana; with the silver beach beneath my window and the wide blue-green ocean roaring; from morning to night, people are swimming and getting sun, children flying kites. I should like to lie on the sand myself, but there are too many things to do: lectures, meetings people, lunching, dinning, and trying to see something.

Next letter, I send to Chicago. Go on writing here unto 15th September; it will follow me. From 1st to 10th October, I'll be in Havana, then Paris. Thanks for the letters and for the poem: I love him. And I love you, more than ever and forever.

Your own Simone

Brazilia, 23rd Septembre 1960

Subversive beast of my heart, my faraway love,

Now I guess you are in Chicago. For a long time, I did not know if you were rue Shoelcher, on a boat, in New York, or at home; that is one of the reasons why I did not write before. Another is I have the feeling letters don't arrive from Brazil to anywhere, for they don't arrive to Brazil from anywhere: after your three first small letters in Rio,I got nothing for weeks. Then I had so many things to do that, when I had nothing, I did not feel like doing anything, even writing a letter. Some things are interesting, other just mildly so, other really tedious. There were lectures to give, newspaper people to speak to, official people to smile to: I hardly smiled. There were too big towns to see, real people and strange ways of life and beautiful landscapes. Now I am in Brazilia, the most crazy thing a human brain ever forged, Kubitschek's brain, and I met the man this morning. He had excellent architects working for him, and some make first rate work: bold, unusual, and handsome buildings. But it is crazy to build such an artificial city in the heart of a desert! We crossed by car about 800 miles of dreary desert to come here. One thing is wonderful: the working people who came to build the city first built their own town, some miles away, only wooden barracks, small shops; no roads, no street, no stone. It grew and grew, as the big stone city grew, and now, it holds 50,000 people, a lot of restaurants, bars, shops, all in small wooden dirty houses; it looks like an old western, with jeeps instead of horses. It's full of red dust and life; I enjoy walking there and drinking in the "little cafés." But I'll leave Brazilia willingly; this town will never have soul nor heart, nor flesh and blood.

You'll be proud of Sartre. He decided it was not enough to have one dark Algerian girl, one fair-haired Russian, and two fake blondes. What was he lacking? A red-headed one! He found her and began an affair with her: she is twenty five and a virgin (as her thirty and twenty three years old sisters are). In the north of Brazil, well-bred girls don't sleep with men. I like her very much, but I am scared of what is going to happen again to crazy Sartre if he succeeds. He doesn't know himself what he exactly wants, but he going to meet her again in Amazonia, and if the affair comes to be serious, so what? I thought you would enjoy learning these news.

Well, I shall not try to tell you what I like in Brazil and what I don't; it will be a tale for a long summer evenings, on 1958 W. Evergreen. I'll just tell you I remember Heraklion, the chich-kebab, the king Minos; I remember Almería and Goytisolo; I remember rue Shoelcher and pineapple juice and you. I want, I order long yellow letters in my home when I'll be back (10 October). I shall not write much until I am back, it's nearly impossible, and except from Rio, mail doesn't arrive. But from Paris I'll be your writing Simone once more.

And Paris or Brazil, I am as ever, for ever, your loving-Simone. I remember a lot of new dreams which were true, magic dreams you made me dream, as good as the old ones. I kiss you, my own magician, with all the love of

Your own Simone

Dearest beast of my heart, my own Nelson,

Lot of things happened since I tried to reach you from Bélem. (Did I succeed?) We went by plane to Manaüs, on the Amazon River. Strange town.
Having been wonderfully wealthy for two or three years when they began to
grow rubber-tree and sell rubber all around the world, they built the most
extravagant theatre, and a lot of extravagant and ugly houses; then, all of a
sudden, English people stole the rubber-tree seeds and began to make rubber in India: In six months Manaüs was ruined for ever; the houses decayed,
and now it is a poor dreary town, with the equatorial forest all around in
which you cannot put one foot, and big water rolling on another side. It is a
hell of damp heat. Amazon! Mississippi is a small trickle of water compared
with Amazon. Suddenly I felt feverish; I did not want to be sick in Manaüs,
so we immediately took a plane at four in the morning, going to Recife in fifteen hours! I felt nearly dead when we landed. Recife was another kind of
hell—not so hot, with a nice wind. But my fever grew; I had to see a doctor.
He said "typhoid fever," which certainly was wrong since I recovered
quickly enough. Anyhow, he sent me to an hospital, they gave me a lot of
antibiotics, which killed the fever, but I was very tired. I stayed a week in the
hospital. I had a room of my own, but it was hell all the same: noise! No way
of sleeping, nearly nothing to eat, and it was so boring. Then Sartre went
mad. We had gone to Recife partly because from there we should take off for
France, partly because there lives the red-headed girl he had begin to care
for. As I stayed in bed, he went around with her the whole day long. Nobody
can fancy what is a Brazilian town in the north, what Recife is! All girls are
virgin and could not marry if not. If they go around with a man, it has to be
in view of marriage or they are lost. The girl was very much interested in
Sartre, she has will and personality, and she saw him a lot; but she resented
being blamed by her family, her friends, and the whole town. Then she
believes in God, and when she understood Sartre should not have hated to
sleep with her, she though he was the Devil himself. They quarrelled. Sartre
had a hell of a life in this dreary hostile town with me in the hospital and the
half friendly, half scared red-headed girl; he drunk a little heavily and at
night, to sleep, he swallowed heavy doses of gardenal. The result was that
when he get up at morning, he could not stand on his legs; he went banging
against the walls and walked in zig-zag all long. When coming to the hospi-

tal he looked groggy—that enraged me but I could do nothing. The girl drank too, when I had recovered we spent a crazy night, she broke glasses in her naked hands and bled abundantly, saying she should kill herself, because she loved and hated Sartre and we were going away the next day. I slept in her bed, holding her wrist to prevent her to jump by the window, after giving her a heavy does of gardenal, too. She is a nice, attractive girl, I must say, she will come to Paris and Sartre says maybe he will marry her! What of the Algerian one then? Well, that is the future. Let us speak of present time. So I was sick he was mad, and we got phone-calls from Paris and wires, telling us not to come back before receiving a long letter from our friends—it was a life and death matter. We vaguely knew things were wrong and dangerous for us in Paris, so we waited for the letter sent through somebody in New York and never coming. We were stuck in Recife. I had the feeling I should never escape from this hellish town. In the end the letter arrived; it told us things you have probably read in the papers: Sartre sent a very bold, provocative letter at the "Jeanson trial," he promoted a subversive declaration telling young men not to accept to be sent in Algeria. So the government wants to put Sartre in jail (in fact, he will not dare just now), and French fascists want very seriously to kill him, so he will have to hide more or less. Our friends told us not to come back to Paris by plane: policemen and OAS[1] fascists would wait for us at the airport; we'll stop in Spain and they will pick up us with a car and take us to Paris without noise. It was decided. But before, the Cuban people kidnapped us…It is so difficult to get in touch, in Brazil, by phone or wire, that the Cuban consul came by plane from Rio to Recife (2000km.) to beg us to go to Havana: we said yes! But we had to fly south to Rio in order to fly north to Bélem, Caracas, and Havana! What a trip! In Caracas they pretended to detain us. Well, we spent a week in the same hotel as in March, but Cuba is not quite the same; they are scared by the prospect of an American aggression, everybody is tense, ready to fight but bitter, which I understand. It was a busy week. Today we take off and I must stop, because we have to visit a big plant, lunch with the workers, then we see Fidel, then we pack. We fly to Barcelona where Bost and friends will pick us. Next time I'll write from Paris and I hope to find there a lot Nelsonish letters. Do write, beast of my heart. I am afraid rue Schoelcher is to be very lonely without you.

I kiss you long and hard as I should like so much to do.

Your Simone

1) *Organization Armée Secrète*. A right-wing extremist movement constituted by French military forces who waged a campaign of terror, 1961–1962, to prevent Algeria from gaining independence from France.

Flower of the rue Shoelcher,
Giacometti de la camera,
Silent beast of nowhere.

I was awfully disappointed when I came home: I expected a heap of letters telling all about you, and nothing! There was a beautiful book, magazines, wonderful pictures of Istanbul, and a nutty bar, but not *one* letter! Did you get all my Brazilian letters or none of them? In any case, why don't you write? I had news of you through Serge: you were dead drunk, they had to carry you to your room. Is that nice? No, it is not; you should be ashamed! He will tell more, but anyhow I miss the yellow letters.

Cuba was not so happy as in March. They do a lot of good work, life is better for the peasants and working people, for everybody, but they are afraid of fake Cubans (in fact, American veterans mascarading as anti-Castro Cuban) disembarking on their shore, and they are very tense. Castro took us to the airport, as lively and wonderful as ever and very pleased with his adventures in Harlem. The trip to Spain was so quick that I still believed we were landing in the Açores when I discovered Madrid; from there, without waiting, we flied to Barcelona. Bost and two friends came to meet us and tell exactly what happened in France. We spent two happy days in Barcelona (but I did not find the place where they sell coffee without milk), and came back slowly to Paris. We have not much to fear from the government. We are 121 people having signed the manifesto they incriminate; they cannot put everybody in jail. The cops asked very politely some questions, we'll see the judge who will inculpate us, but there will certainly be no jail and no trial. The only danger is ultra-rightwing people should like to kill Sartre or at least to beat him to death, they are over-excited and really dangerous, so he takes care not to show himself in public places, and he doesn't sleep in his own home.

The Shoelcher home is clean and very empty, something missing or somebody maybe? I'll write to you about everybody when you'll deserve it: when I know something about you. This letter is long enough for a non-writing beast. I kiss you in the dark, nevertheless, lovingly.

Your own Simone

Subversive beast of nowhere,

You don't deserve a long letter, because I wrote at lest six ones and got a
short one, where you did not say much. I saw one of your letters to Olga:
how witty you can contrive to be when you really try! So don't bother
being witty with me, tell me the plain un-witty true truth. I'll be much
more happier because — fancy that — I am interested in you. I promise
myself to be as un-witty as I can (it will be hard), so there is no challenge
between us; if I happen to be over-witty in spite of myself, don't try to
catch up — understand?

   Next time, tell me about you life, your friends, and my pretty enemy:
did she like the red shirt and the scarf? How is Studs and everybody? I forgot to thank you for the poem I found on my desk; I love it, really. You
should publish your poems; they are among the best things you write —
this is no wit, it is true truth. And thanks for the pictures. You really are the
Giacometti of the camera — this is half wit, half truth, because some of the
pictures are good.

   I am having a strange life. All our friends decided it was dangerous for
Sartre to live in his place, not because of the government, but because of
over-excited ultras who could beat him to death, and for me, too, to stay
rue Shoelcher. So somebody we don't know was told to go away from his
home (where is he? I don't know), a big flat in an elegant district; each of
us has a big room, in fact a living-room for several people. We stay here
nearly all day long. It is forbidden to Sartre to go to restaurants and cafés,
so *I cook* for him: ham, sausages, a lot of cans. That is what he eats except
when Bost or other friends come and cook a dinner. I go shopping except
when Bost...I listen music at the radio, and I ask myself: what kind of
book am I going to write? Well, it will be the last part of my life, that is
what I planned when you were here, when I went to the national library
and worked home; but since I came back, I hesitated, I thought of writing
a novel. Now I am decided: it will be the third and last part of my memoirs. The second had just been published; it is called *La force de l'âge*, and
I am pleased about it. Gallimard sold 45,000 copies before it was in the
bookshops, and the first week after he sold 25,000 more; the critics are
really good, so I hope to sell 200,000 — that means money for years; when
I am in Chicago I can lose money at race-track...Serge loved race-tracks

with you! He told all about it: how you won fifty dollars, and nicely lost all of them in the next race. Listening about you I felt a huge longing for going to Chicago. It was a nice dinner at Monique's home, with Goytisolo and Sartre, we ate paella, and spoke about Spain, Barcelone, and political life... We should have been inculpated (guilty of endangered the state safety), but the day when he had to listen to Sartre, the judge decided he was sick; maybe he is and will stay so for two weeks. Anyhow, we are not declared guilty, and everybody in the newspapers laugh at it. We are supposed to ask imperiously to the judge to declare us guilty and even to arrest us, and he cried and says he has wife and children—we cannot ask him such a thing. A nice little comedy. We wait to see what is coming next in Algiers and even Paris.

The red-haired Brazilian girl wrote nice letters, but Sartre doesn't think he will marry her after all. All his women seem to have new lovers, so that makes things easier for him—not too easy anyhow. Olga has no lover, and things are not easier for Bost. Did I tell you about Nathalie? It is really a bad life this girl made for her. She had another baby, but he died when she gave birth to him, because of a convulsion of the mother, so she feel guilty of his death. After that she had a bad infection disease in the bladder, and stays dangerously ill. I had these news by a letter from Oreste. Yes, I get every week Mr. Stone magazine, and your *Nation*, which I decided not to send back to you. You beast, that is a real letter full of real news; do write soon and long, please. Don't forget, I love you as ever and, it seems, for ever. Amour, amour, amour, amour, amour, amour de

Your own Simone

Décembre 1960

Dearest beast of Almeria, beautiful flower of Istanbul,

I live rue Shoelcher again and I remember with emotion what a nice landlady I was. How happy was an occupant to have such a nice landlady! Paris is awfully cold, but not pleasant, and I feel in high-spirits because my books sells very, very well (130,000 in a month) and I am making lot of money.

Everybody is the same as ever. Bost quarrels with Olga who quarrel with Bost (he even left home forever, slamming the door, yesterday, But I guess he will come back soon.) Geneviéve does not quarrel with her dentist; it is though they will marry. Odette quarrels with her son who goes away in the streets for days, nobody knowing what he does. Wanda quarrels with herself; that is the worst of quarrels: she bled nearly to death, some days ago, because she had stabbed my book with a big knife (I don't know whey she suddenly hates me) and, by accident or more or less willingly, she had stabbed her hands and wrists too. I'll have all this quarrelling people to drink and eat on Christmas eve in this place where you were such a sloppy occupant.

You certainly know that Richard Wright is dead. It was quite unexpected. His elder daughter, who is lovely eighteen years old girl, is terrificly stunned by his death; Ellen did not resent it so much. She was moved but, on the whole, she feels she will be much happier now: she will be able to live in Paris and have a life by herself. By the way, we had a nice chat about you; it made me a little awkward, because evidently she did not know about out actual relationship, and she spoke in a very free and intimate way of your meeting in London. Why did not your tell me about it? That is the trouble with these witty letters of you, they hardly tell anything.

You suggest we should leave Algerians to themselves; we found a better way of ending this mess: it is killing all of them. We began last Sunday, and now we have to go on, because if some survive, I don't think they will love us. What can we do with these dirty beasts who don't love the nice French people? Kill them?

Did I say that Sartre thanks for the book about Cuba? It is pretty good.

Have a good Christmas, honey. Keep me some warm place in your heart; you are very warm inside mine, and it is a good thing, because outside it is so cold.

Your own Simone

1961

Dearest nutty king of nothing,

I hope Christmas and New Year were not too bleak. Here it was very pleasant, having at supper all these quarrelling people who did not quarrel so much, because I gave them whisky and akvavit, cuban rum, red wine, and a lot of things to eat. Sartre was nicely drunk and entertained everybody. Geneviéve hold the dentist's hand and Monique Goytisolo's floor. There was much talk about you, but it is kinder not to report it.

Your book was sent to Sartre "from Nelson Algren," not by Brennan, I forgot the name. I heard much about Wright Mills by our Cuban friends who like him very much.[1] I hope we'll meet him. Thanks for *Contact*; it is an interesting magazine. Send me your dirty papers about Istanbul and Heraklion.

We are preparing dutily to answer de Gaulle question next Sunday; most of people will say "yes" once more, but we hope there will be a good number to say "no." Yesterday evening I talked in a big student's meeting to tell them to answer "no"; they applauded very much because they intended to do so anyhow. That is a good way of being successful. I read, by German or Swiss writer, a report of the horrid way you behaved in Hiroshima—real hateful people you were there, not only when dropping the bomb, but the way you behaved after. Are you not ashamed? A striking book. And I read the first good, very good Russian novel published since years: by a woman, about an engineer and a big plant, work, love, and real people.[2] And Schwartz-Bart, *The Last Just* (is it the American title?), a bestseller in Chicago. What do you think of it?

I work, work, work, and nothing really happens, but I enjoy not being in jail, not being in an hospital, not being in Brazil, but an occupant in my own place. I still think of going to Chicago if nobody else seems to want to go, but when the weather will be nicer and if there are not too many green cats.

Love,

Your own Simone

1) C. Wright Mills (1916–1962). the American sociologist associated with Marxism and with the theories of Max Weber. 2) *L'Ingénieur Bakhirev*, by Galina Nicolaïeva.

Dearest crazy you,

Thanks for the pocket book,[1] though it is not so good as could be hoped from Wright Mills, whom everybody in Cuba worships and who wrote really good books. But you don't say much about yourself. I guess you work, work, work... that is what I do. Yet, I gave myself a short three days holiday; I went to Belgium where I had promised to go, months ago. It happened to be very interesting because the big strikes had just come to an end, and I saw workmen and extreme-left leaders, real good and strong men; then I met deputies, senators who call themselves "socialists," but are hated by workers: they have sold their souls to the "bourgeoisie." They were so naively disgusting when they spoke with me that it was a real comedy: you would have enjoyed it. I asked them what, in their idea, the working people thought of them, and they said: "Oh! They just loathe us!" At last it was frank! I spoke about Algeria, Cuba; the young people and the left ones like it but a lot of bourgeois did not, which pleased me very much. Next time you come to Europe, if it ever happens again, we have to see something of these northern countries, the coal mines and factories, and the cosy little towns. I spoke in a lot of places in Paris to tell people to answer "no" to de Gaulle, but they did not obey, most of them said "yes" or nothing at all. He is the dirtiest freak in the world; the war goes on and on and on, everybody waits for him to do something, which he does not, so nothing is done. It is disgusting. You saw what happened in the C P? All the communists who whished to work hand in hand with the non-communist left, and peculiarly with Sartre, got a serious blame and now they are asked to repent! It is hopeless! Thorez' successor is worse than he was, everybody says. De Gaulle would be nothing if Thorez had been another man.

Tell me more truth about you.

Love,

Your own Simone

---

1) *Listen Yankee!* 2) "Pocket book" a literal translation of *livre de poche* or "paperback."

5th March 1961

Dearest flower of Istanbul,

Well, I got two letters! That is wonderful! An old yellow one, and fresh white one. Which do I like the best? Both of them.

You will be pleased to know that Bost used the key you gave him to come and fuck the lady of his dreams; then he found the money you had been careful not to spend, and he took it. He told me that in November, adding he would give it back to me, some day. I shall not remind him; I have money this year.

It has been spring with blossoming trees, during the whole February and now, in March, it seems summer begins. Paris is awfully nice, I must say, with everybody sitting outside the cafies.

I got the *Nation* with the paper about Wright; I felt you wrote it because you had to, not from the deepest depth of your heart, but I guess nobody will feel it. I can send nothing to *Contact,* though it is a good magazine, because I don't care neither you get rich or not: anyhow, if you want to get rich, why don't you cook and sell pancakes? Then you'll get rich!

I hope very much de Gaulle will have trouble, but he does not seem to do. Nothing happens in France, really nothing. The only pleasant affair was these six girls escaping from jail with a rope (La Roquette). Do you remember the movie together, *Le trou?*[1] It is nice when such a story comes true. The girls are not caught back; thinking girls have no boldness, no strength, nothing, they were hardly looked after; they could speak quite freely with the visitors and get from them what they wanted, it was a well planned, well done job, and everybody on our side enjoyed it immensely. Did they gave details bout this escape in your American papers? It is the only fun we had for weeks. We wait for a meeting between de Gaulle and Ferhat Abba,[2] for a peace which is hardly nearer than it was last year.

I have not much to say about myself neither; I earn my morning fruit juice and my nutbars. You really were not too bad an occupant. I should find a lot of things to tell, if you were here, or I were there, but through paper, you seem very far away. So I just say good bye, and wait until we meet again.

Love from

Your own Simone

1) A film by Jacques Becker (1959). 2) Ferhat Abbas (1899–1985), the leader of the Algerian national independence movement.

543

Dearest beast,

Everybody was pleased, getting such nice pictures of himself: why did I not? Well, I had a literary picture made by Mary Mac Carthy in *L' Express*. She said I was an "athletic nun"; she does not believe in my frankness, because I don't spell correctly American names; she thinks my "happiness" is sadness and I irritate her terribly. The interviewer, a girl, was mad at her and says in the end she is just a fake; but there is somebody in the world who doesn't love me: this dear Mac Carthy girl. How can you believe it?

Sartre went to Milano, where Italians gave him one million francs for having spoken so well about the Algerian war; he gave it back to Algerian prisoners, so he did not make a penny from this war: stupid man! But he got two letters this morning, warning him he will soon get a "killing package"; you know, you just pull the string and off you go! So he will carefully let his mother, the Algerian girl, the secretary, or Bost or anyone open the packages for him. I shall not. While he was covered of laurels and gold in Italy, I went to the country, not far from Paris, in a kind of Shangri-la, a little castle in a big wide park—and I was alone. I read, played records, worked, lay in the sun, with big white airplanes roaring above my head. In the night, the nightingales sand and I realized I had never heard a nightingale—in fact, I thought Shakespeare had invented them. But they do exist, and it is wonderful when they sing.

In Paris it is better and better; We do torture and kill Algerians in the heart of the town; we found a clean, nice way of doing it: we get some poor treacherous Algerians, we pay them well and made cops of them. When an Algerian is taken by French policemen, they give him to "harkis,"[1] who "work" him in some underground until they murder him, or he kills himself or gets mad. But the French cops say honestly: "We don't torture anybody." Is is not shrewd?

It seems your dirty Kennedy is going to make serious troubles for Castro. I hate this grinning boy and his grinning wife.

If we travel together once more, some day instead of Istanbul, what would you say about a trip in the moon? It seems so easy to go around the earth; it will soon be easy to go farther. It is funny to think within fifty years, maybe twenty, Gagarine will seem a nice faraway ancestor, something like Blériot or Lindberg, who were "the first" to cross the Manche or the ocean!

He will stay for ever the first, the ancestor, and young boys who will go easily to Venus will remember him with a smiling and superior tenderness. How did Americans like this new Russian triumph?

Now I go with Sartre on the Blue Coast, at Antibes, near Nice, the place where with Bost we heard the singer sing, where you got drunk and danced with a chair. I hope I'll get sun, silence, time, and I'll work and work.

I like very much the story of the Playboy club. Sartre got last month a copy of their magazine which looked like mere pornography. Honey, I cannot much help you: read what I say about Montherlant in *The Second Sex*; he is one of these men, but I don't know much about Don Juan. Do you know anything about Casanova? This man could fuck, at least he says so in his *Memoirs,* but he did not despise women so much. Send me a copy of your paper when it is done; I should be very interested. I saw Olga yesterday evening, she was pleased with your letter. Well, good bye, honey, I have to pack. Love from

Your own Simone

Second anonymous letter telling to Sartre he is going to die. It does not seem serious, but it means some people really don't like him.

1) Algerian soldiers who fought for the French during the war for independence.

10th June 1961

Dearest thing,

Thanks for the letters, the clippings, and everything. I am glad to have the pictures: old dreams dreamed with my old bony bird. I was busy having tea with Queen Fabiola and Mrs. Kennedy, that is why I did not write before. I must say Mrs. Kennedy is more pleasant to look at than Fabiola. I should like to think she is a really nice woman. If your country is desintegreating, I don't know what is happening to mine. German killers struggle for the truly true France, right wing people are killed by ultras who say they are left wing, left wing ones are put in jail by right wing ones. One of my friends just spent two days in a cage: there was nothing against him, except the fact he writes in *Temps modernes*. In a way there were worst times, when nothing at all happened, except silent tortures in Algerian and Parisian caves. Maybe this war is coming to his end. We'll have to obey de Gaulle until he dies, then, it is not pleasant but better than these daily horrors.

I spent nearly a month with Sartre in Antibes. It was sunny. I worked hard, but took some nice rides in my white car which you never saw. One day in Marseille: I remembered last year. I remember much, but I don't know how much you do. I don't know if you should be really pleased if I came Chicago? It is not easy for me, because I want to go to the end of this book, and I don't like the idea of asking a visa for the States now. If you think it is as well if I wait until next year, I would rather wait. If not, I could come for three weeks in September. Tell me how you feel. It is difficult to get any idea about it from your letters. My plans for this summer are anyhow to work; I guess I'll go to Roma with Sartre, stay here and work. It is hard to do, what I am doing, more than anything I did. Olga and Bost and everybody speaks about you praisely, but it is too long to write. If some day you ever come back here, you'll surely be welcome. You are a nice old bony bird and I kiss you tenderly.

Your own Simone

Août 1961

Dearest you,

Yes, I got the nice "Tiquetonne poem" in a strange magazine showing what a vicious man you are: I had to hide the pictures from the nice people coming to my nice place—are you not ashamed? I got, too, the piece you wrote for the re-publishing of *Chicago*; it is harsh, sharp, and really good. I met Wright Mills and an American friend of him; they will live in London for some years, for there is no way for people like them to live in their own country; they like better being an exile outside than inside, but it is not pleasant neither, they say. The youngest one has no right to come back to the States, because he has spent five months in Cuba just when it was forbidden; and his wife has no passport to leave USA, because she has been to China in past times. So they just can meet in Mexico or Montréal. As they have two kids, they don't enjoy the situation. They were very interesting and really good people.

Not pleasant to be American now, and still worse to be French. I come back from Fresnes jail where are kept a lot of Algerians; it was managed I could see some of them. I saw one who has been so much tortured, beaten and starved (a very important leader) two years ago that he looks more than fifty, and he is thirty. He will die before two years. They say

546

they like Sartre and myself, but in spite of that, I don't feel proud when I speak with these men. We killed *more than one million* of Algerians (women, children, and so on).

I am going away for two months to Roma. I hope to go to Tunis and meet Algerian leaders and even fighters (with Sartre, indeed), so I shall not see your place in Chicago this year. I felt you did not wish my coming now—that is the main reason why I did not think enthusiasticly of coming. Yet, we were happy together last year. Maybe it will happen once more, some day.

Funny, Sartre is just writing obituaries too: he writes about Merleau-Ponty and doesn't like it. He says too many people die in the profession: Hemingway, Céline, Merleau-Ponty. He should rather write about you than Merleau-Ponty; by any chance, what is exactly your birthday?

Good bye, honey. I hope it is not a farewell we said to each other. My heart has not changed.

Your own Simone

Décembre 1961

Dearest beast,

Are you still breathing? Or dead, or what? I read a nice piece on Barcelona which reminded me of something and somebody. A fierce piece in the *Nation*: everybody laughed about Cau when reading it, and some in Paris did. But then, what? Did you marry Mary G., not daring to tell me?

Here it is cold and sad; now we kill Algerians in Paris. So we go in the streets shouting: "Peace in Algeria!" I narrowly escaped a cop's bludgeon.

Anyhow, happy Christmas! Anyhow, whatever happens to you, you should remember some people here care for you, I do, and you should write. Love from

Your own Simone

1962

Février 1962

My own old owl,

I did not write since a long time. Well, this country is not only mad, which would not be too bad, it is smug too in its own foolish way, and wholly disgusting. Three officers were convicted to have tortured to death a Moslem woman, they even confessed, but the court declared it was all right and relaxed them without even a day of jail. One was a school teacher; his superior thought it was not well to keep him at his place and sent him away: all the village went into a rage, saying he was such a nice man, they wanted him as a school teacher, if the woman died, so what? And I say, too, so what?

I thought and wanted you to be forever my last occupant, but now I have a dozen occupants bathing in your bathroom, cooking in your oven, sleeping in your couch. Somebody phoned to the concierge I was going to blow up, so I found a lot of students, most of them communists boys, who keep watch over the house to try to catch the enemy. I have not yet blown up, when so many people have, owing to them. But I have to live elsewhere, with poor Sartre whom nobody accepts as a lodger;[1] we hide under a false name in a big stupid furnished place, in an ugly wealthy district, but with the Seine beneath the windows, and that is a beauty.

So many things happening, I have no time to tell everything. The killing of 8th February was an hideous thing; the cops strangled with their hands a young boy, among other niceties. Happy I did not go; all the friends who went there had some broken or black eye, and were lucky not to get more. The funerals were a very moving wonder, really all the Parisian people in the streets, peaceful, dignified, angry, friendly; it gave hope, hope something could yet happen here, but it was a frail hope, even if the day was great.

Well, the peace is done now. We waited so much for it, yet it gives no joy. Too many were killed among Algerians during these years (two millions, they said; the concentration camps were nearly as deadly as the nazi ones). The GPRA had to concede much; it is not a frank defeat for colonialism.

We don't know what is to happen in Algeria with the army, neither in France. So we keep joy for another day.

It seems better on your side, on the contrary. What do you think of Kennedy? It seems, after all, he really tries something for peace. Cau has become a complete hyena; he writes against the French left wing, pretending he loves it so much that he has to scold it. Bost answers to him a very hard paper in next *T.M.* issue. Cau is a regular fascist now; he doesn't blow up houses, but he admires those who do so. Cassoulet's husband does it; he works with the OAS. Olga met her, with the singer (who sleeps, too, with a regular OAS killer): "Olga!" cried Cassoulet, "why don't you see me any longer?" "Because of Marc." "Well, but soon it will be over, Marc will be in jail. Will you see me then?" He has blood on his hands, this guy . . .

Well, that is how we live here, day after day, peacefully. I work and work, living more than ever like an owl, because I don't accept the faces of people in cafés and restaurants. If you should write sometimes before Christmas, it would not be a bad idea. When all that is over, maybe I'll go, maybe you'll come, maybe we'll see each other again. I should like to say "farewell Chicago" before dying. I kiss you as tenderly as ever.

Your own Simone

1) After his apartment on the rue Bonaparte was bombed.

Avril 1962

Dearest you,

Bost and Olga spoke to Bluestone,[1] who spoke to them about you; it made you nearest. He likes your endless book very much, and from what I read I like it too—when shall I get the whole thing?[2] They are giving a movie in Paris, *A Walk on the Wild Side*,[3] you never told me about it. When did they buy it from you? Does it keep something from your book? If you say yes, I'll go and see it. Just now, I don't feel like seeing bad movies.

It has been a very long winter in Paris; suddenly, it is nearly summer. I could come back rue Shoelcher but the young people who kept it from bombs and plastic took a liking to the place; they don't seem willing to leave. I shall have to use strength and they are many of them; so what? I should need a brave American to frighten them and free the room for me. So I still live near the Seine. Little boats pass by, the brothers of the one on which we had a dinner. So you will be cruising on the Pacific? What is exactly the idea? Writing a book about it or just being on the sea, doing nothing? I'll go to Moscow in June with Sartre for a month, then a week maybe in Warsaw, then it will be Roma and hard work to get to the end of my own endless book.

In the end, something like peace has been won: something very unlike peace, indeed, since they kill at least twenty Arabians a day in Algiers and Oran. Nobody is really glad about it, though it is better than this everlasting war. But it means de Gaulle until he dies and we don't like it. You know, the French madness is very dull, too.

I should like to see Chicago again, sad as it is. It is difficult to make plans now, but you'll have to invite me, once. I don't invite you; you are always invited. Have an happy time on the ocean. Send some postcards and work well.

Love from

Your own Simone

1) A critic and friend of Algren's. 2) *Who Lost an American?* appeared in 1963, dedicated to Simone de Beauvoir. 3) Produced by Edward Dmytyrk (1962), with Laurence Harvey, Capucine, Jane Fonda, Anne Baxter, and Barbara Stanwyck. Algren's name did not appear in the credits.

Automne 1962

Dearest you,

You wrote from such strange cities that I did not know how answer.[1] Just now I learn from Studs[2] that at last you are back home, and you look delighted by your trip. Well, you are surely a hard-hearted man to enjoy seeing poor Olga with leper and Bost starving, so that you wished to bomb off the whole planet! I hope I'll hear more about all that.

I am back to the lion of Belfort and very happy to occupy my own place. It has been all washed and painted anew; it is as fresh and clean as it was before you came. It is good too not to have this dirty war going on any longer! Even if we are not in love with Ben Bella, now what happens is their own business. There were men much more clever and progressive than him who could have been at the head of Algeria; he is for all the old traditions, religion, veiled women, against the Jews and not really for an agrarian reform, but well, things will happen in their time, at least I hope. How long are you going on pretending to invade poor little Cuba? I am very angry at you.

I work on the last book of my memoirs; it will be *much longer* than the other ones, so don't even try to read it. And working on it now, I made it still longer and longer.

Did I tell you about my trip in Russia and Poland? It was very interesting. Poets, painters, writers are slowly conquering freedom, everybody speaks openly, there are some very nice people. The nicest was a writer who looked much like you: Sartre noticed it, too. Then I spent two months in awfully hot Roma. I am glad to know where you are, at last. Love from

Your Simone

1) From a cargo boat in the Pacific Ocean, and then from Calcutta. 2) Studs Terkel.

1963

Avril 1963

Dearest you,

It was nice to hear about you before you die. It was a long cold winter here, too, and I did not feel like writing a letter neither, as long as you did not. Then I worked hard; I went to the end of this endless book,[1] I cut a lot of things after all, though you will think once more that it is much too long. I got a picture of you, in colors, from a magazine, a very good one in front of a Chicago wall; you look rather sad and the day seems cold. Yes, I read *Lie Down in Darkness*;[2] it is striking, powerful, and sometimes really good; you believe in it and not forget it afterwards for days and days. Much better a book than his most recent one, *La proie des flammes* — once more a Faulknerian story of rape and murder in the South. I am not really interested in it.

I went to Moscow and Leningrad with Sartre at the end of December. Moscow under the snow and a blue sky was a real marvel: like a long and beautiful childish Christmas; Leningrad was strange: a long dawn, then evening came, without an afternoon. We met most of the young (or less young) writers who are being attacked now and were in really friendly terms with some of them. They are much talented; one of them, Soljenytsine, wrote against Stalinian camps and is a first-rate writer. There is a great hope they will win in this stupid battle the old academic people and Khruschev began against them. You should read *Voices in the Snow* by Olga Carlisle; it gives a good idea of intellectual Moscow nowadays and it is a pleasant book by a talented woman (half Russian, half American).

It would be nice to see you. I am fifty-five, which is just a little worse than fifty-four. Do you plan coming to Paris one of these days? Or should I try to come to Chicago for a month? I guess I could get my visa. I still don't know what I'll do exactly in summer.

Yes, go and see Castro you'll like him.

Love from

Your own Simone

1) *Force of Circumstance.* 2) By William Styron.

Juin 1963

Dear ape-man,

Thanks for dedicating me this book, a delightful book;[1] Bost, Olga, and myself enjoyed it, and even Sartre when I read some parts of it to him (what he looks like in your eyes). Though, once more, it will be the hell to translate; we should like to publish in *Temps modernes* Chicago I (your childhood) and Chicago IV (about the Playboy bunny club). Olga showed to me another review, as bad as bad can be; you made them really angry and it is a very good point for you. Dearest man with brass lungs and tin ear, I don't understand exactly what you are doing in New York, but I hope you enjoy it. I have put the last word to that long, long new book of memoirs, and brought it to Gallimard. It covers 1944–62, and though I *don't* try to tell *everything*, it will do 750 or 800 printed pages. It will be born in September they say, but I doubt it; I'll not have time to correct the galleys in such a short time!

I am spending about two months in USSR with Sartre, and go south; it pleases me very much now we know very interesting people among the writers and painters whom Khruschev attacked. And they wish to see us. I heard Georgia and Crimea are beautiful places, so that will be a beautiful summer.

Everybody is all right here, except Olga *knows* Bost loves another woman, and does not like it. Except several others who said to Sartre they wanted to marry him, and he did not accept. Except Wanda who is more and more crazy. So poor Sartre...but he is happy with his writings.

Do write again. When do you come back to France? Not before '66? It seems kind of far away. Love to the bearing ape-man from the *dean* of existentialism.

Your own Simone

1) *Who Lost an American?*, unfavorably received by the press, was considered a great fiasco by Algren. Ostensibly in New York to promote the book on television and radio, he spent most of his time at the racetrack, at the theater, and playing poker.

Juillet 1963

Dearest you,

I got a letter, Olga got one, so I know some little things about you. She worries, because it seems you did not get the long letter she sent to you, telling how much she liked *The Lost American*; she was delighted with it, and she swears she sent it to Chicago, so she feels rather insulted when you let her know you did not receive anything. I am very proud because, three days ago, I had an interview with the American T.V. A man called Webster made me speak about "modern woman"; I began in French and little by little they had me speak English, and said I spoke fluently. In the end, the whole thing is in English. And in colours! One of the first pieces of coloured T.V. It will be shown in September or October, and I should be pleased if you see it, though I say nothing interesting.

Now I enjoy being in Provence, near Avignon. I love this part of the country. I read, I work, I drive on little roads, I enjoy myself. I am passing every other cars, driving really quick and being very proud of it. It is funny you feel I cannot drive. I am reading *The Gothic Tales*[1] which you ordered me to read long ago; I enjoy it. In August I'll go to Russia with Sartre for six weeks, then back to France and Italy. Scipion wanted to fly to USA: he was not given a visa, because he wrote in a communist magazine in 1945! The movie you have to see is *Les Abysses*,[2] really, do see it.

As ever, love from

Your own Simone

1) By Karen Blixen. 2) By Nico Papatakis (1962).

Rome, Octobre 1963

Dearest you,

So many things happened since my last letter! Six weeks in USSR with Sartre, first of all. There was a big literary meeting in Leningrad between East and West European writers, and nothing pertinent was said, but private encounters were meaningful. And an amusing party; being invited at Khruschev's place, on the Black Sea—himself friendly, a wonderful dinner, caviar and vodka. Though I don't like him much and I don't think Chinese are definitively wrong in their quarrel with Moscow. We travelled with a nice woman, our interpreter, really a friend, and saw the south of Russia, Georgia and astonishing Armenian, with a lot of natives coming from Chicago or Paris or Calcutta, and the mount Ararat where Noë waited in his arch: They even showed to us a real piece of the real holy Arch, hardly a little rotten by the long raining and passing of centuries.

After that, back to Paris, then Roma for one month, at the Minerva. Sartre's *Saint Genet* has been published in USA; you should read it if patient enough, because it's rather thick. My *Force des choses* will be published within two or three weeks. It is very harsh against nearly everybody and will be hated by most people, I guess, like *The Los American*: "It had no right to be written." I hope you'll not be unpleased by what I tell about you, because it was written with all my heart.

Last news of Olga and Bost were bad; they had quarrelled in a horrible way, and he had gone away from her.

. . .

I don't know where to send this letter, since you breathlessly wander from New York to San Francisco, talking and clowning everywhere. Let us try Chicago. Thanks for the letter, the clippings, the story of "the underworld man"; Sartre enjoyed it, too.

I just spent three delightful weeks in Roma; it was blue, a little misty, mellow and tender. Too many people because we have more friends here than in Paris, but it was often amusing. Carlo Levi is more and more like himself: he wrote a long letter to Khruschev to explain how he must behave, and is to the utmost surprised he did not get any answer! Darina Silone fell in my arms and kissed me, she said she would phone and did not; Silone has certainly forbidden her to, for he hates Sartre and myself now.

Tomorrow we go back to Paris by plane. Olga is angry at me, because she knows I knew, and did lie to her: I'll try to persuade her I did right. She spends much time with Bost; he gives her much money she will survive the parting. He seems very happy. I'll tell you more next time.

So life in Chicago does not seem very pleasant? I wish you find some other place. Do write again. Love from

Your own Simone

Dearest Nelson,

Thanks for the good affectionate letters; thanks for the "audiotope," I heard part of your babbling with Olga and we enjoyed it very much. Then I heard, alone, the whole thing. I was amused and moved hearing your voice.

Novembre was a long sad month for, indeed, my mother was dying, and at last, she died. But, as you say, how these old women cling to life! My mother fell down and broke a bone in the hip; she was taken to a clinique, and there, was discovered having a cancer; she would die within a few months, or days. We did not tell her, indeed. They operated her, and then she felt much better; she was sure she would soon recover. She had two very happy weeks, everybody taking care of her, my sister and myself spending our days and nights in her room. Not from love, in my case, but from a deep and bitter compassion—she wanted so much to live! She began to feel very tired, pains began, too, and we *ordered* the doctors to give her a lot of morphine, and in fact to kill her slowly. They were obedient: no hope, anyway. The last three days she felt good, and slept nearly all the time. All right, but she said reproachfully to my sister, one evening: "Today, I have not *lived*." The day before her death, when I told her it was good for her to sleep much, she said: "Well, I am wasting days." What did she called "life"? Interesting thing was that she never wanted to see any priest, none of her old pious friends: she wanted young faces and smiles around her. During this month she was nearest my heart than she had ever been since my early childhood. And I had an irrational guilty feeling of cheating her, promising she would see spring and summer and long years, and knowing she would not.

. . .

I was surprised by your friendship with this hideous little Dutchman; he was stupid and unpleasant. He looked around my beautiful palace and said

555

depreciatively: "I am astonished! I thought you lived in a better place than *that*!" He fancied I owned a kind of a castle in the country near Paris, and kept asking me why not.

Serge Lafaurie has wonderfully well translated the piece about your childhood, and all the French friends enjoyed it. They all think it is one of the best things you wrote. It is a shame they did not appreciate your book in the States.

My book gets very bad, hateful reviews, but it sells very well and I get a lot of nice, kind letters. It is strange this discrepancy between what they print in the newspapers and the commercial success. In fact, all right wing people hate the book and try to kill it. In one of their dirty papers, they translated parts of *Who Lost an American?* with skilful cuts so it seemed you were contemptuous about Sartre and me, taking away all the humorous sentences, all the little friendly words. It does not matter, really, but it enraged me a little: these dirty people know nothing about nothing, chiefly when it comes to friendship and love.

I don't work just now. After six weeks of incapacity, I had a heap of letters to answer, people to see, scripts to read, and so on. Now I have to think about writing again, but I have not the faintest idea what it will be.

Somebody wants to write a script from *The Mandarins* for the screen, but from the synopsis it seems to be pompous and stupid; I don't accept it.

Next time no mother will die and I'll not wait so long before answering you. So do write again. With my most loving love...

Your own Simone

1964

Dearest Nelson,

I am really a disgusting beast not having written to you for months. I was madly busy writing the story of my mother's death; I explained to you why it upset me and I had to tell it. It never happened I felt so much compelled to do a thing. Now it is achieved. Sartre likes it very much. It has about seventy-five printed pages and will appear in *Temps modernes* in May. Then I'll see what Gallimard decide; it is so short...[1]

I got a heap of letters about my last book and answered most of them. It was a very good trimester in a way for Sartre and me, because his book,[2] too, was a best-seller, and much praised by critics. But that was saddened by the awful story of Olga. She thinks of killing herself and Bost; she will not kill Bost but suicide is possible. And if not, what?

How strange Nathalie Sarraute wanted to meet you! She hates me, a fascinated hate; she painted me as a ridiculous, untalented writer in *The Planetarium*. Did she let this hate appear? I am curious to know how things went between you.

Sartre and me are planning a trip to USA in 1965. He is invited in an university near New York; he would stay there about a week, which I could spend in Chicago. He would come and see Chicago with you, and we could come back to New York some time? I should like very much to see something of nowadays USA, not speaking of my wish of seeing you again.

Winter was not cold but grey. Bost is unhappy for making Olga unhappy. My ex-friend rather pleased with his wife. Sartre very interested with his new place, a 10th floor, which is very high for Paris. He sees the whole town from his window. He had first decided he would make the place as ugly as possible, but somebody gave him a beautiful table and now he decided everything should be beautiful: he does not succeed, anyhow.

Dearest beast, tell me about you and you'll get a little more gossip about Paris. With love from

Your own Simone

1) *Une mort très douce.* 2) *The Words.*

My own rat,

This is a great national day, when we took the Bastille. But there is not much celebration: all Parisian people seem to be out of town. I am the only living soul in the whole house, the whole street, and perhaps the whole Paris. It is silent, pleasant, summer-smelling; I like it. They have painted our Belfort Lion in a chocolate colour, so hideous that newspapers protested, but what is done is done. *I* cannot paint it green anew.

Well, I hope you'll not be on sea in May '65. If you are in any other place in the States, I can fly there as well as to Chicago; I don't mind Chicago. I should like to see you again before *you* die.

The trip in U S S R was very pleasant; we have good friends there now, of the "left wing," indeed, because there is an everlasting struggle between progressive and reactionary people as well in U S S R as in any place. Writers are slowly, very slowly but surely gaining freedom. They translate Kafka now, and some of their writers are really good. Did you read Soljenytsine (*Ivan Denissovitch*, or *Matriona*)? I don't remember if I asked it to you. White nights in Leningrad and in northern towns are something wonderful. But in Moscow, evenings are pretty dull. To drink vodka you *have* to eat a whole meal, to eat a dinner, you *have* to listen to a terrible orchestra and look at people dancing in a terribly bad way!

My dearest own rat, I hope to see you some not too remote day.
Tenderly,

Your own Simone

Do you know Sartre really turns out a ballet?

Novembre 1964

Dearest you,

It is a long time since I did not send nor get a letter. But I heard a little about you: a very good paper in the *Nation* about the author of *Dr. Strangelove* (I forgot his name).[1] An amusing interview on women in I don't remember which magazine, on women, love, marriage, and so on. I heard, too, from Alain, or Serge, that you were wonderfully well-dressed: is it you?

I just spent two months in Roma and Sardinia: a sad, poor, beautiful island you would like. Doing nothing but looking at things, reading mysteries. I just don't know what I am going to write, which makes me a little unconfortable, because I feel like writing.

The Heller's book, *Catch 22*, seems to be a great success here, and is nicely translated. Violette Leduc's last one, *La Bâtarde*, will win a prize and be a best-seller. Knopf and Braziler offer lots of dollars to get it; I am really happy about it. The book is written in a magnificent French, an excellent book. She is so pleased, too!

Sartre is very well, and thin (he has purposely lost kilos). I have not yet seen Olga; I saw Bost. Things are no better. She raves, rages, and sometimes bites. She is terribly unhappy, but not quite unguilty for it.

I'll certainly go to the States in May and I'll find you, wherever you hide. In the end, Bill Targ got me; I'll be published in spring.[2] Tell me something about you, dear old beast. Or are you too busy dressing well?

As ever, with much love,

Your own Simone

1) Terry Southern, who co-wrote the screenplay for the Stanley Kubrick film (1963). 2) The American edition of *Force of Circumstance*. This book led to the ultimate break-up of Algren and de Beauvoir. Its publication provoked a violent reaction from Algren. This rift notwithstanding, de Beauvoir's 1965 trip to the United States with Sartre was canceled because of the Vietnam War. They became actively involved in the Russell trial intended to denounce war crimes committed by Americans.